# BASEBALL'S PENNANT RACES:

# A GRAPHIC VIEW

# *BASEBALL'S PENNANT RACES:*

## *A GRAPHIC VIEW*

JOHN WARNER DAVENPORT

*First Impressions*

*Madison, Wisconsin, U.S.A.*

*1981*

*To*

*Arlene and Leslie*

First Edition



Library of Congress Catalog Card Number: **81-67611**

ISBN: 0-934794-02-2 (paperback), 0-934794-03-0 (hardcover)

Published by:

First Impressions
P.O. Box 9073
Madison, Wisconsin 53715

Printed by:

Straus Printing Company
1028 E. Washington Ave.
Madison, Wisconsin 53701

Printed in the United States of America

# Preface

One day in the summer of 1955, as a student in Iowa City, I became quite excited over the progress suddenly being made by the beloved team of my Massachusetts boyhood, the Boston Red Sox—so much so that I was moved to plot a graph of the American League pennant race, in order to project the date on which the Sox would grab the league lead away from the New York Yankees. They never did, of course, but the graph got to be so fascinating that I wondered what all the other pennant races look like in that form for 25 years.

When I wrote and self-published my *Baseball Graphics* book two years ago, I got acquainted with about twenty more pennant-race graphs. But when some readers responded to the book by saying "Give us more pennant races!" I groaned, because of the unpleasant labor involved in getting the numbers to plot. Unlike batting and pitching graphs, and most other kinds of baseball graph for which you can get the data from the daily paper, the *Official Baseball Guide,* or an encyclopedia, you have to go to newspapers on microfilm at the library to get the weekly standings of the major league clubs for plotting a pennant race. At many public libraries, the microfilm may be scratched beyond legibility and the archaic technology of the usual microfilm readers and printers is a continual frustration; with luck, you might get one year of pennant-race data in a day's grimy work, whether you use the printer or copy the numbers by hand.

Last summer, however, I was elated to discover two libraries on Cape Cod that had the last 80 years of *The New York Times* on microfilm in remarkably unscathed condition, and more importantly, had just installed the marvelous new Minolta RP 405 microform reader-printers. With these speedy and clear-printing devices, I was able to collect the weekly or biweekly standings of all the major league races since 1900 at a reasonable cost and expenditure of time. So quickly, in fact, that I had 80% of my time left for plotting the graphs, which is always a joy to do during the daily Red Sox game—with TV announcers as good as Ned Martin and Hawk Harrelson, a visual task that interferes with watching the TV screen is no problem.

In doing the plots, I used every trick I could think of to cut down the inevitable errors; plotting a single team at a time through a season, for example, rather than a given day's set of standings across teams, enables you to spot errors in the plotting more readily and errors in the newspaper as well. Suspected errors of the latter kind were checked against *The Sporting News* and its various statistical publications, other newspapers besides the *Times* and, of course, the major baseball encyclopedias—Grosset and Dunlap's *The Sports Encyclopedia: Baseball,* by Neft, Cohen, and Deutsch, and MacMillan's *The Baseball Encyclopedia,* edited by Joseph Reichler.

After I finished the rough pencil plots of the 186 title races, it was an easy matter to pick out the closest and most dramatic races, which numbered about fifty, and go back to the Minoltas for day-by-day scores and details of the contending teams in the last few weeks of a race. These minutiae soon took the form of 52 more "closeup" graphs. Not having a computer handy, I had to accomplish the conversion of the whole-season and closeup plots to camera-ready drafts by dry-transfer lettering in light-table tracings and using plastic drafting tapes of the Chartpak, Formaline, Letraset, etc. types. After these drafts were done and shrunk down to a convenient size, they were sorted and traced (or placed) for the multi-panel summary graphs at the end of the book.

Then came the hard part—the writing—and the best part—the page-by-page pasteup of the book. (I suspect every self-publisher finds that the pure fun of the pasteup makes any of the tedious work leading up to that stage worth it; it's also fun because you can have the music blasting away without that impeding the process—my award this time goes to Joni Mitchell, Jaco Pastorius, and Pat Metheny for that magical "Shadows and Light" album.) I wasn't far into the writing when I realized that it would be foolish to make this an analytical work; there is enough to do and enough space taken up in just presenting and describing the pennant races and their surroundings. I hope it will be understood, then, that the factual material in the text is intended more for background, context, or atmosphere than for explanation, and that where there seems to be an explanation for the twists and turns of the curves, it is just a suggestion on my part and then only a guess.

Once again I've had the good fortune to work with Dan Duerst of the Straus Printing Company in the overall production of the book and thereby also to gain access to Chris Keller's talents again in the cover design. Two of the greatest clutch hitters in the typography-graphics business, Donna Kruse and Nora Cusack of Madison's KC Graphics, again set the type. Jim Johnson and his "shrinkers" at Master Blue Print, also of Madison, did the photographic reductions of the graphs again, and some miscellaneous photography and typesetting was done by Total Type of Madison.

I am also grateful to the library staff at the Falmouth (Massachusetts) Public Library and the Cape Cod Community College, in particular to Adrienne Latimer for her assistance with the Minolta machine at CCCC. I would also like to thank my mother-in-law, Mrs. Helen Halfacre Rudman, for letting me convert her normally-tidy home on the Cape into a graph-manufacturing plant last summer, and her sister, Doris Halfacre of Williamstown, Mass., for her moral support of these strange endeavors.

Madison, Wisconsin
June 4, 1981

# Contents

# BOSTON "ROOTERS" IN TO

## Well Prepared to Encourage Capt. Collins and Team On to Victory.

The Boston baseball team, accompanied by about 200 "rooters," arrived in this city and registered at the Hotel Marlborough. The New Englanders wore big red badges with the words "World's Champions" on their coats, and all were enthusiastic over the prospects of their favorites beating the Greater New Yorks to-day in the closest and most interesting contest for the championship in baseball history. Quite a number of the visitors carried the suit cases and satchels which they took with them to Pittsburg last Fall "just for luck," they said, while others were well supplied with megaphones, tin horns, and other things to give encouragement to their team.

It was the opinion last night that Gibson and Dineen will be used by the champions in the two games. The Boston men think that Chesbro has been worked hard, and that the drubbing he ... Saturday marked the beginning ... downfall. The "rooters" ... American Lea... They will ...

# Pennant Races in Graphs

In the so-called modern era of major league baseball, we have had 146 pennant races in the National and American leagues prior to divisional play (1901-1968) and 48 divisional title races since the leagues formed East and West divisions in 1969. Adding the two seasons of the short-lived Federal League in 1914 and 1915, we have a total of 186 major league pennant or title races in the 1901-1980 period. This book presents all 186 of these competitions in full-season graphs and 52 of these in more detailed "closeup" graphs.

### "Games over or under .500"

The measure of a team's performance used throughout this book is "games over or under .500." This measure tells at a glance where a team stands in relation to the break-even point—a .500 won-lost percentage—as well as in relation to other teams. It is easily calculated by subtracting a team's losses from its wins at any stage of the season. A team with 60 wins and 45 losses, for example, is 15 games over .500 (that is, 15 wins better than a 45-45 record), and a performance of 20 wins and 30 losses is ten games under .500 (ten wins short of a 30-30 record). A pennant winner is often around 30 games over .500 at the close of the season (that would be a 96-66 record in a 162-game season), but the measure can go much higher—the 1906 Chicago Cubs finished the year with 116 wins and 36 losses, 80 games over .500! At the other extreme, the 1916 Philadelphia Athletics won only 36 games while losing 117—that's 81 games *below* .500!

Compared to other measures we might plot for pennant-race graphs, this index has distinct advantages. See for yourself in the three-panel graph below. In these panels we have the 1938 National League season plotted in terms of the familiar "won-lost percentage" and "games behind" of the daily standings compared with our "games over or under .500" ("games re .500" for short).

The '38 NL season had some standout features—a sudden rush by the Cubs in September to snatch the pennant away from the Pittsburgh Pirates, a sad showing by the Philadelphia Phillies, and a strong start by the New York Giants in the spring—but overall, this race was not a freakish one. After studying how our preferred measure portrays the season in the left panel of the graph, notice how the won-lost percentages in the middle panel magnify the small differences between teams way out of proportion in the early part of the season. Note also that the Giants show a declining won-lost percentage through the month of May even though they consistently won more games than they lost that month; the Phillies show the reverse of this pattern. But what happens late in the season is even worse—it takes a good-sized winning or losing streak to make a noticeable difference in a team's won-lost percentage in September, and some small but important changes hardly show up at all in the middle panel. A further disadvantage of this index: after the first few games in April, it's hard to calculate the percentages in your head.

With "games behind" as the measure, scales and calculations are more convenient, but interpretations are often more difficult than with the won-lost percentage. If you had just the right-hand panel of the graph to go by, could you tell whether the big story of 1938 was a collapse by the Pirates or a grand rush by the Cubs over the month of September? The mere fact that the Cubs reduced their "games behind" doesn't really tell

***One Pennant Race --Three Ways***

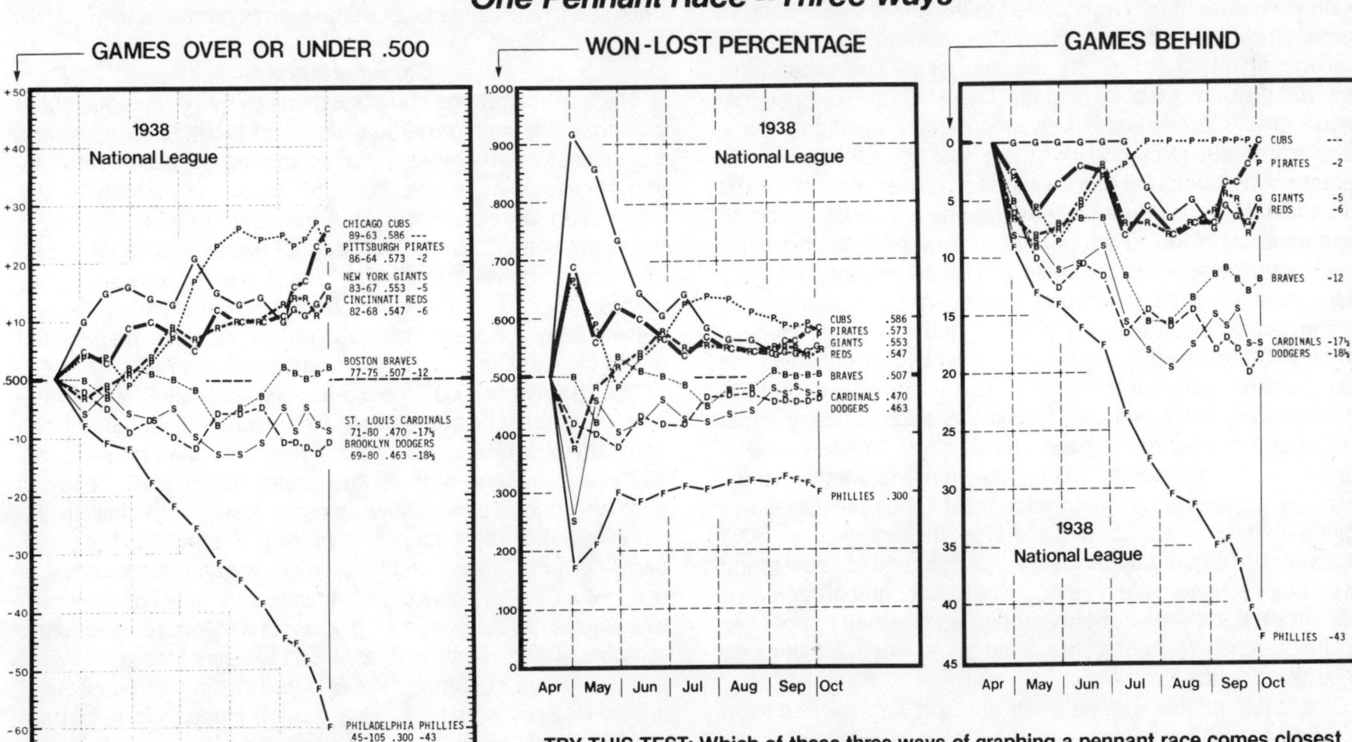


**TRY THIS TEST: Which of these three ways of graphing a pennant race comes closest to the way you picture one in your mind?**

you; if anything, the Cubs' pulling away from the Giants and Reds is a better clue as to what went on that month. The left panel, on the other hand, makes it clear that the Pirates did not collapse in the first three weeks of September, but that their lead was shrinking mostly because the Cubs were winning nearly every day and kept that red-hot pace going into the last week, when Pittsburgh finally did falter.

Besides being more informative, the "games re .500" measure gives us a pennant-race graph that is psychologically natural, that is, more in line with the way most of us visualize title races in April, July, or September. This comes from the fact that the one-game unit stays the same all season long—a team's curve goes up from a victory or down from a defeat the same distance on the graph in April as in September. So in the spring weeks we find all the teams fairly close to each other, as they have to be, since they simply haven't played enough games by then to be very far apart. The more games they play, the further apart they *can* be, and usually turn out to be, but if it's a close race a two-game lead won't look any bigger on the graph in September than it does in mid-May.

Furthermore, if "games behind" is what you want, you can get it directly from "games re .500." To convert a team's "games over or under .500" to "games behind" (the leading team), just figure the difference between the two teams and divide by two. If the leader is 28 games over .500 and your team is four games over .500, the difference between them is 24 games re .500 and half this difference is 12, so your team is 12 games behind the leader. Or take the case of the miserable Phillies, who finished their 1938 season 60 games below .500 as opposed to the Cubs' 26 games above .500. The two clubs thus finished 86 games apart on the "games re .500" scale, as the left panel of the graph shows, and dividing by two we get 43 games behind for the Phils, as the right panel shows.

### Full-Season Graphs

For easy comparisons, all 186 full-season graphs in this book were drafted and reproduced to the same scale. Each of these shows the positions of all the teams in a league or division at all stages of the season. With few exceptions, the full-season graphs present biweekly standings from around May 1st to Labor Day and weekly positions thereafter to the season's end; for most years the plotted points represent positions on Monday mornings. Hashmarks on the left and right vertical axes of these graphs enable the reader to determine (with the aid of a ruler or straight-edge) precisely how many games over or under .500 a team stands at any weekly or fortnightly point where a team symbol is located.

The teams' positions are given by letter symbols, for example, "C" for the Chicago Cubs. Except for a period in the 1960s when there were ten-team races, the size (vertical height) of the letters used as team symbols is approximately equal to the unit of one game over or under .500. This provides a further aid in reading off precise positions: two letters separated by a gap that is about letter-height thus represent two teams that are two games apart on the "games re .500" scale and one game apart on the "games behind" scale, and two letters touching each other in vertical alignment represent the smallest difference between two teams that is possible on the "games re .500" scale—one game—and a half-game separation on the "games behind" scale.

The latter of these rules does not apply to the ten-team graphs of the 1960s, when smaller letters were used for the sake of clarity. For all years, however, whatever the letter size, two or more letters touching in *horizontal* alignment represent teams that are tied in "games re .500" and "games behind," but not necessarily tied in won-lost percentage.

The letter symbols representing the teams are used consistently over the 80 years of full-season graphs for all National League teams and most American League teams, regardless of changes in team nicknames or franchise locations. Thus, for example, "R" represents the Boston Red Sox and the earlier Boston Somersets or Pilgrims as well, and "D" represents the Dodgers (or Superbas, or Robins), whether they were in Brooklyn or Los Angeles. The symbols are identified in each graph, but those readers wishing to trace a single team's history over many seasons should be forewarned of some minor inconsistencies in the use of American League team symbols in the past two decades, namely, that the Los Angeles Angels' "L" was changed to "C" when they moved to Anaheim and became the California Angels around Labor Day, 1965, and to make way for this symbol change, the usual "C" for the Cleveland Indians was temporarily changed to "I" in the 1961-1968 period.

The lines connecting the symbols in full-season graphs are not associated with particular teams as are the letter symbols themselves, but instead are determined by team performances. Medium solid lines (C—C) are usually used for the first- and last-place teams. For visual distinctiveness, medium dashed lines (D·····D) usually connect the letters of runnerup teams. Most races have an Interesting Nonwinner who shows, for example, a surprising downfall or upsurge from the previous year, or a striking midseason turnaround; these are highlighted by heavy solid lines (H▬H). And when there is a second also-ran of special interest, that team is distinguished by heavy dashed lines (C▬▬C). Occasionally the heavy solid line is used for spectacular or unusually significant winners or last-place finishers. Other connecting lines are used for third- to next-to-last-place teams, and the choice among them was governed by the need for visual clarity rather than by any intention to indicate a facet of the team's performance.

### Closeup Graphs

The closeup graphs show the game-by-game changes of the contending teams in the final weeks of those seasons having the closest or otherwise most interesting pennant races. Unlike the seasonal graphs, these 52 graphs vary widely in size as reduced for final printing, but they were originally drawn to the same scale. This means they all have the same 1:2 ratio of units on the vertical and horizontal axes—a change of five games over .500 on the vertical takes the same distance as ten calendar days on the horizontal. Vertical grid lines are provided on the closeups to indicate which days are Sundays.

The "games re .500" measure works especially well in the closeup graphs, because every win by a team is a gain of one game (over or under .500) on the vertical scale and every defeat is a one-game drop on the scale. This makes it easy to spot and count consecutive wins or losses (streaks). In addition to indicating a team's victories ( ↗B ) and defeats ( ↘B ), game by game, these graphs also show games that ended in ties ( —B ). The letter symbols for teams in closeups generally follow those of the seasonal graphs; in a few cases geometric symbols, clearly identified, are used instead of letters. When teams are tied in games over .500 (but again, not necessarily in won-lost percentage), circles around the symbols (Ⓟⓔ) are used for highlighting.

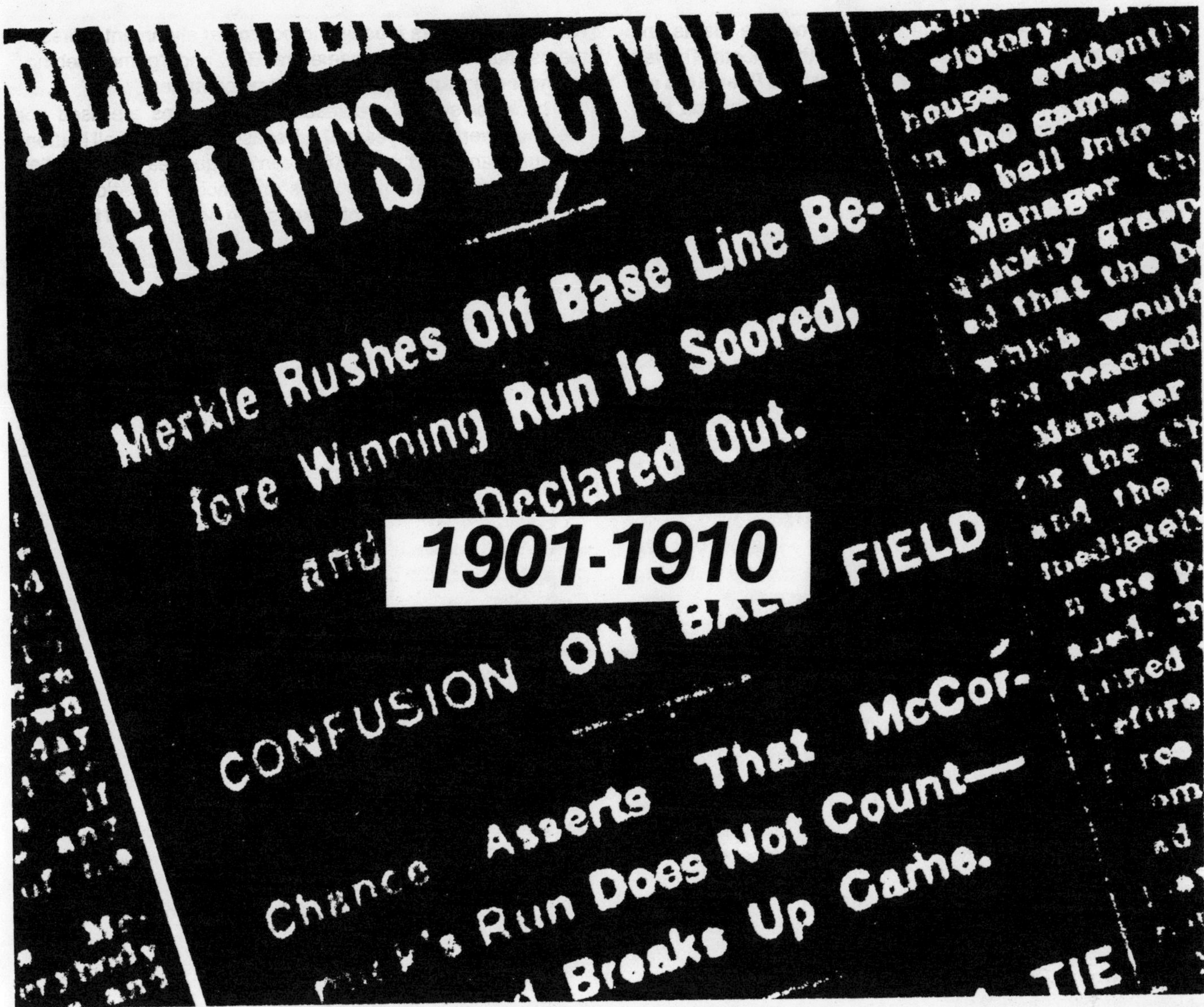

BLUNDER

GIANTS VICTORY

Merkle Rushes Off Base Line Before Winning Run Is Soored,
and Declared Out.

CONFUSION ON BA[LL] FIELD

Chance Asserts That McCor-
[mick]'s Run Does Not Count—
[an]d Breaks Up Game.

TIE

# 1901-1910

In terms of heated pennant races at least, the modern era of major league baseball took a few years to warm up. But there were other sources of heat—by no means did the brand-new American League come into existence in 1901 through a series of smooth and amicable procedures like today's expansion draft. Many of the players in the new league's first season, in fact, had been rather rudely wrenched from their National League owners, whose resulting attitude toward the AL's organizer, President Ban Johnson, and his collection of new owners could best be described as livid. Indeed, the raids on the NL rosters by Johnson's group—netting such stars as Cy Young, Nap Lajoie, Clark Griffith, Joe McGinnity, and Jimmy Collins—were successful enough to put the two leagues into a position of near-parity as well as a condition of war.

## 1901

Against this background, the 1901 American League race was almost a pastoral scene. Sometimes a major league baseball season will seem to decide by mid-July which position each team will occupy on the closing day, and the teams will devote the remainder of the schedule to spacing themselves in the standings as evenly as they can, instead of contending for first place or any other place. The AL's first season had this appearance; with two exceptions, the eight new clubs behaved in August and September as if they had recognized and accepted their October destinies by the middle of the season.

One exception was the Baltimore Orioles, who fell from an apparently secure third to a disappointing fifth place in September, despite having the league's best team batting average (.294), getting 26 pitching victories from Iron Man McGinnity, and being managed by a .352-hitting third baseman named John McGraw; lack of pitching depth accounted for much of the Oriole collapse.

A more important exception was the Philadelphia Athletics, managed by Connie Mack, who was already 38 years old and five years past his playing days. Mack had a .400 hitter, Lajoie (who won the Triple Crown with a .422 batting average, 14 home runs, and 125 runs batted in), three .300 hitters named Lave Cross, Socks Seybold, and Harry Davis, and a pitching staff that found winning consistency in the last half of the season. From a dozen games below .500 in sixth place around the Fourth of July, the Athletics climbed to a final fourth place 12 games over .500, and were clearly on their way to a 1902 pennant.

But the 1901 pennant belonged to the Chicago White Sox, who moved out to an eight-game lead in early September after

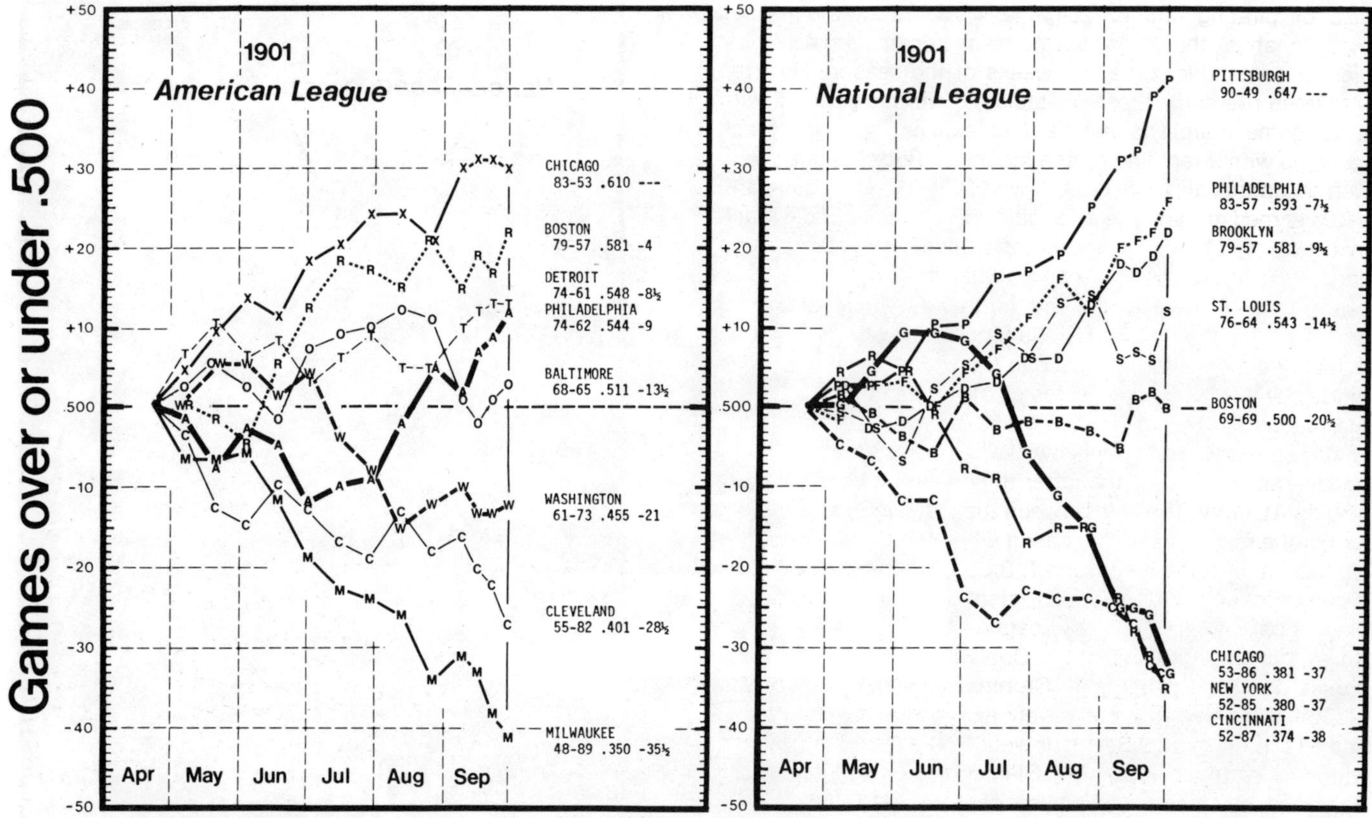


an August slump had briefly dropped them to the level of the Boston Somersets, and coasted to the title. The Chicago club got triple duty out of Griffith, who not only managed the team while pitching 24 victories but also batted .303 in 35 games. Fielder Jones, a good-hitting outfielder formerly with the Brooklyn club, led the Chicago batters with .311, but (starting a famous White Sox tradition) their overall team batting was only fifth-best in the league. They made up for this, however, by stealing 280 bases that season, which was 73 ahead of the #2 team in thievery.

The American League's raiding, which totaled 38 players, hurt some NL clubs a good deal more than others. The Brooklyn Superbas, the 1900 champions, couldn't make up for the loss of McGinnity, Jones, and Cross even though they held onto Willie Keeler, whose nine-year career BA was .384 going into the '01 season, and they came up with another pitching ace in Wild Bill Donovan (25-5 in 1901). Similarly, the Phillies found Nap Lajoie irreplaceable, but remained strong with the hard-hitting trio of outfielders Ed Delahanty, Elmer Flick, and Roy Thomas.

At Pittsburgh, on the other hand, a bunch of relative youngsters were just coming into their prime years—pitchers Jack Chesbro, Deacon Phillipee, and Jesse Tannehill, infielders Honus Wagner, Tommy Leach, and Claude Ritchey, and outfielders Fred Clarke, Ginger Beaumont, and Lefty Davis—and with no successful pirating of the Pirates by the AL owners, they won the pennant fairly easily. Chesbro, Phillippe, and Tannehill put together 61 of the team's 90 wins, and Wagner led a strong offense with a .353 average.

The Interesting Nonwinner in the 1901 NL race was the New York Giants, who took a spectacular dive from first place in early June to a near-tie for last at the season's end. In falling from nine games over .500 to 33 under, the Giants were second only to the 1914 Cincinnati Reds in the depth of a midseason tailspin. This the Giants achieved with all-time ace Christy Mathewson winning 20 games in his first full season, and with shortstop-manager George Davis hitting .309 and 35-year-old George Van Haltren batting .342. But the New York team had little else for talent, and the Advent of John McGraw was still in its future.

## 1902

The outcomes of the 1902 races matched expectations formed by most observers the previous September—the Athletics and Pirates were the class teams of their leagues—except that the Pirates overdid things a bit, and the A's had some tough hurdles to clear before pulling away in the last month.

One of Philadelphia's problems between seasons was losing Nap Lajoie, at first to a Pennsylvania court decision that he be returned to the Phillies, but later, through some clever finagling by AL President Johnson, to the new league's Cleveland team. Connie Mack also lost a 1901 20-game winner, Chick Fraser, and a 17-game winner, Bill Bernhard, in the interleague squabbling.

In addition to these difficulties, the White Sox were naturally reluctant to hand over the AL crown to anyone, and served notice to that effect by jumping to a commanding lead in early July. Surprisingly, however, Chicago developed pitching problems in midseason, and faded to a fourth-place finish. Still, the Athletics had to beat out a solid Boston team, led by the legendary Cy Young (winner of 33 games in '01 and 32 in '02), and a strong new St. Louis club which had replaced Milwaukee's short-lived and unsuccessful entry in the 1901 AL membership. By luring better than half of the Cardinals' 1901 starting lineup across town, including a .382 hitter (Jesse Burkett) and two good pitching Jacks (Harper and Powell), and also by pirating another 20-game winner from the Phillies (Red Donahue), the St. Louis Americans became the Athletics' closest contender in the last weeks of the season. How the Mackmen overcame these obstacles to win the pennant with a five-game margin is not hard to explain, however: Mack came up with a real find on the mound in Rube Waddell, who won an unofficial "triple crown" with 24-7, 210 strikeouts, and a 2.05 earned run average. In addition, sophomore Eddie Plank matured into a 20-game winner, and the Philadelphia batting lineup featured six .300 hitters even with Lajoie gone.

The 1902 season saw the end, for half a century, of a great major league franchise, the Baltimore Orioles, which had dominated the National League in the previous decade. In its heyday of 1894 to 1898, the roster of the Old Orioles carried the names of Hall of Famers Willie Keeler, Dan Brouthers, Hugh Jennings, John McGraw, Wilbert Robinson, and Joe Kelley, but by '02 only the latter three were still on the club, now an AL entry. The war between the leagues took a radical turn in the midst of the '02 season when the Chairman of the NL Executive Committee, John T. Brush, bought the Baltimore organization with the nefarious intention of bringing its best players back to the National League—not only McGraw and Kelley, but some talented newer Orioles, including Roger Bresnahan, Joe McGinnity, Jack Cronin, Cy Seymour, and Dan McGann. Brush released all seven men to sign new contracts, and all but Kelley and Seymour went to the New York Giants, with McGraw becoming the Giants' manager. The gutted Baltimore roster had to get players contributed by other American League clubs in order to field a team, and struggled to the end of the season, finishing last, with Robinson as manager in place of the pilfered McGraw. When peace broke out in the interleague agreements of January 1903, the Giants grudgingly accepted the American League plan to move the Baltimore franchise to the big New York market under new ownership. Thus did the course of history twist sharply in both leagues, creating the rise of the Giants in the NL and the birth of the New York American League Baseball Club, better known later as the Yankees.

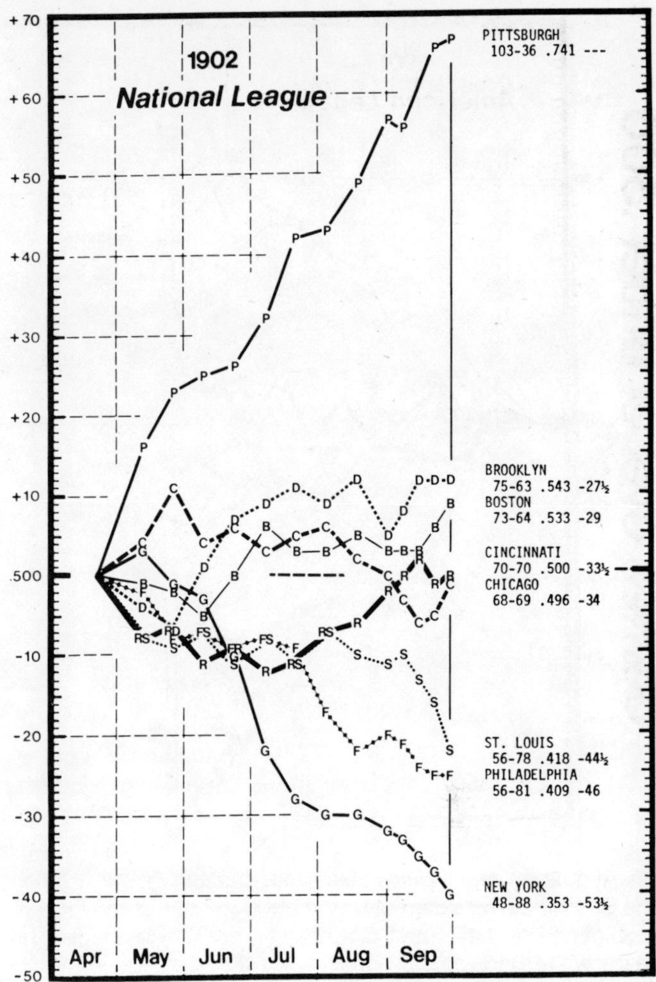


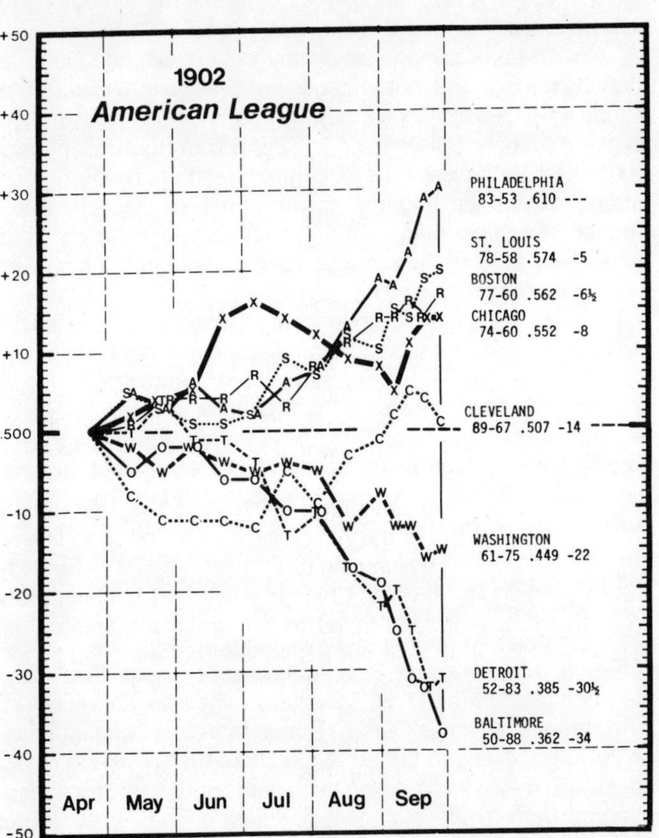


A final note on the AL's 1902 season: Cleveland showed a striking midseason transition from last-place incompetence to fourth-place respectability. There was no great mystery in this change, because the court decision that gave them Lajoie that spring also brought them Bill Bernhard, and during the season they acquired .300 hitters Elmer Flick and Piano Legs Hickman, plus a leading basestealer, Harry Bay. Later seasons proved that Cleveland's upturn was a valid indication of contender status.

The National League's 1902 race was over in May, for the simple reason that the Pirates got stronger, again losing no players to AL raiding, while their competition got weaker. The result was the major league all-time record for the size of a winner's margin—27½ games over second-place Brooklyn. Chesbro, Phillippe, and Tannehill were all 20-game winners, and this time they were joined by two 16-game winners, Ed Doheny and Sam Leever to form the league's finest mound staff (team ERA: 2.30). The Bucs also led the league in hits of all kinds and stolen bases. Individually, Ginger Beaumont's .357 average and Honus Wagner's 43 base thefts and 91 RBIs were league-leading performances. Even allowing for the weakened condition of other teams in the league from AL piracy, this 1902 Pittsburgh team can be rated one of the ten

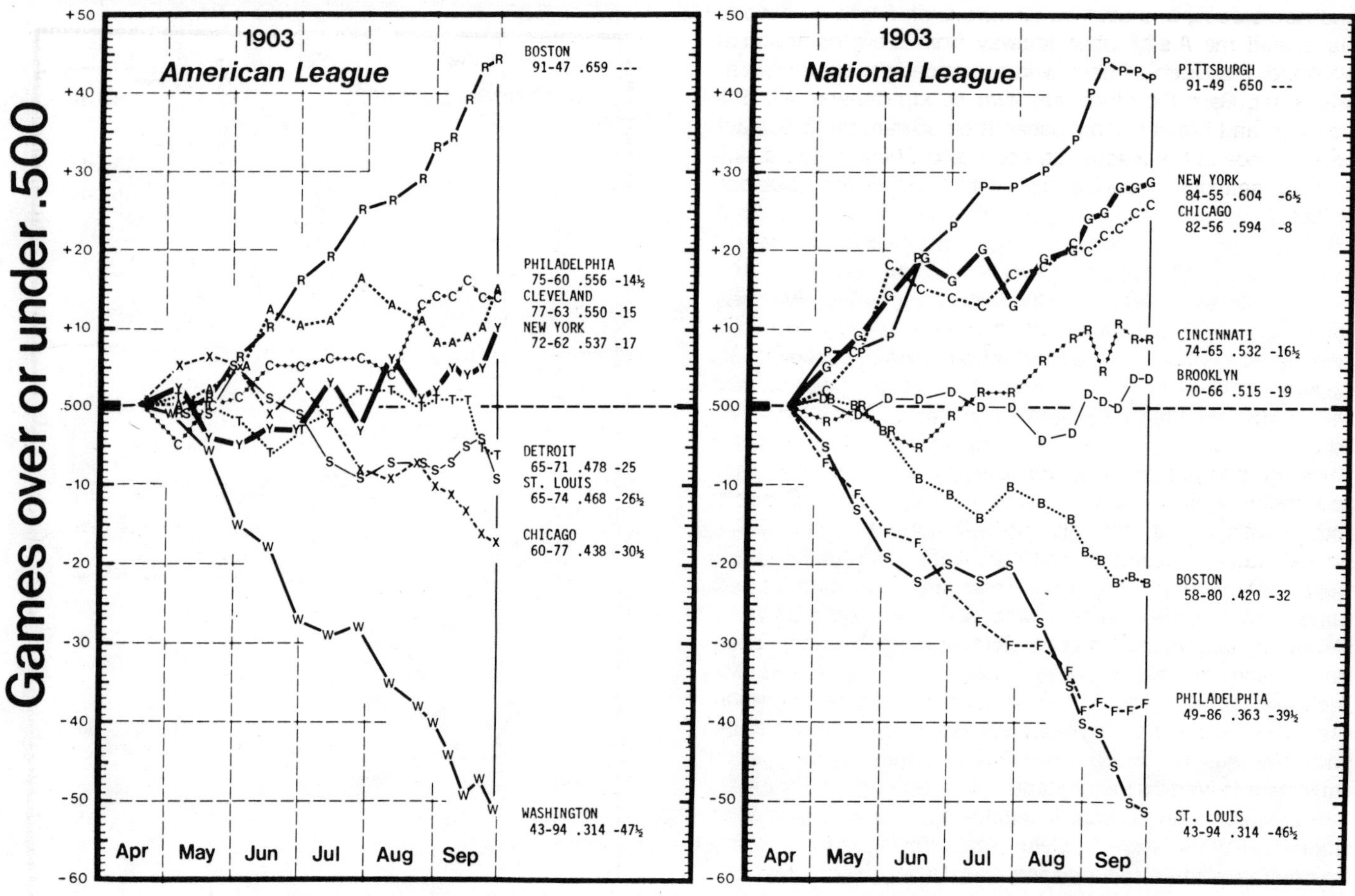


greatest of the 1901-1980 period.

Actually, not all of the other NL teams were depleted of talent that year, especially after Brush's counterraid brought five of the Baltimore Seven to the Giants and the other two, Seymour and Kelley, to the Reds. Combined with Jake Beckley's .331, Sam Crawford's .333, and Noodles Hahn's 23-12 full-season performances, the Seymour and Kelley acquisitions help account for the upturn in Cincinnati's curve in the latter part of the 1902 NL graph.

The Giants, on the other hand, didn't achieve a turnaround from the influx of Orioles, but they did slow their rate of descent into last place, dropping by only ten games re .500 in the last two months as opposed to their 30-game plunge up to August. Aside from Mathewson, the New York team was essentially talentless in the first half of the season.

## 1903

In 1903 the Pirates won easily in the NL despite losing two mound aces, Jack Chesbro and Jesse Tannehill, whereas the Athletics couldn't repeat as AL winners even with the same lineup. When October and the first World Series came, it was the Boston Pilgrims who represented the junior league and made history somewhat the way that Joe Namath and New York Jets did in a well-known football game on January 12, 1969.

With Chief Bender's 17 victories added to Plank's 23 and Waddell's 22, Connie Mack's problem at Philadelphia was not so much pitching as a sharp dropoff in hitting—from .287 the previous year to .264 in team BA and from six .300 hitters to only one. But his biggest problem was that there was a better team in the league. The Pilgrims had a smooth blend of age and youth, and a nice balance of offensive and defensive strengths, leading the AL in team BA and ERA. Cy Young, now 36, won 28 games, manager Jimmy Collins, 33, hit .296 as a third baseman, and outfielder Buck Freeman, 31, was the league's RBI leader. These three veterans combined with two 20-game winners, Bill Dinneen and Long Tom Hughes, and two .300 hitters, outfielder Patsy Dougherty and shortstop Freddy Parent, to put the Pilgrims securely in first place by early August. Their final margin of 14½ games was a far cry from the Pirates' 27½ of the previous year, but still in the top 20 of all winning margins in the modern era.

The new American League club in New York started in Steinbrenner style by acquiring three superstars from the National League—Chesbro, Tannehill, and Keeler—and another from the White Sox, Clark Griffith, who continued in his pitcher-manager role. With these names the Highlanders quickly grabbed their share of the NYC area market, putting their young league on even more solid footing. The fourth-place finish by the Highlanders seems remarkable, considering that Tannehill was off his 1901-02 form with the Pirates, Griffith was well past his prime, and the only batters who hit over .280 were Keeler and Kid Elberfeld.

As for other AL teams, the Washington Senators, already suffering a desolate season in last place, lost their only star, lifetime .346 hitter Ed Delahanty, when he was killed in a mysterious fall (push? jump?) from a train over Niagara Falls on July 2nd. Going in the other direction, the Cleveland Naps (for Lajoie, they weren't called the Indians until 1915) got added strength from the development of young pitchers Earl Moore and Addie Joss, and seemed to have a firm hold on second place until the A's grabbed it away from them on the final weekend. The Detroit Tigers, who had raided the NL for a first-rate hitter, Sam Crawford, and two good pitchers, Will Bill Donovan and Frank Kitson, began their upward climb to later preeminence in the league. St. Louis and Chicago had disappointing seasons, dropping from their contending positions of 1902.

Besides the Pirates' third straight win, the big news in the older league was the rise of the Giants and Cubs. And this set a pattern: 1903, it turned out, was only the first year of a ten-year span in which these Pittsburgh, New York, and Chicago clubs would be the top three contenders, except for two minor, late-season incursions by the Reds in 1904 and Phillies in 1907.

The Pirates had Sam Leever (25-7, best ERA of 2.06) and Ed Doheny (16-8) to thank for filling the gaps left by Chesbro and Tannehill, and they also had Deacon Phillippe (24-9), Honus Wagner (batting titleist with .355), and Ginger Beaumont (.341) to thank as usual. Their strongest competition came from McGraw's Giants, who got 30-win seasons from McGinnity and Mathewson, a .350 year from Roger Bresnahan, and excellent run production from two new acquisitions, George Browne and Sam Mertes. The New Yorkers' jump from their woeful 1902 finish (48-88, .353) to second place (84-55, .604) is the modern record for season-to-season improvement in won-lost percentage.

The Chicago Cubs had six regulars who batted over .290, among them the fabled infield combination of Joe Tinker, Johnny Evers, and Frank Chance, assembled for the first time on a full-season basis. They also had three pitchers who contributed 20 victories apiece—Jack Taylor, Jake Weimer, and Bob Wicker—but unlike the young infielders, none of these hurlers figured importantly in the Cubs' later triumphs as a pennant winner.

To the total delight of fans all over, the presidents of the Pilgrim and Pirate organizations agreed to a best-five-out-of-nine World Series which began on October 1, 1903. It was only Year III of the new American League, and the Pilgrims won in an upset, five games to three, establishing the AL's claim of parity between the leagues very much as the New York Jets' defeat of the Baltimore Colts in Superbowl III argued for the Americans catching up to the Nationals in pro-football 66 years later. The analogy is not perfect, however, and the parity claim in 1903 was denied by many National Leaguers, because of the Pirates' loss of Doheny to mental illness on the eve of the Series and the impairment of Leever's pitching in the Series by an arm injury.

## 1904

When the modern baseball era produced its first exciting pennant race, the contenders were, lo and behold, the Red Sox and Yankees. Except that in 1904 the Boston and New York Americans were still called the Pilgrims and Highlanders.

Up to mid-July, the Pilgrims had been cruising smoothly toward a repetition of their 1903 triumph, but the Highlanders and White Sox caught them coasting in August. By the first week of September, the latter had slumped badly enough to reduce it to a two-team contest, but a late spurt by the Chicago Americans put them only two games behind Boston and New York on September 30th. The Pilgrims, however, made this only

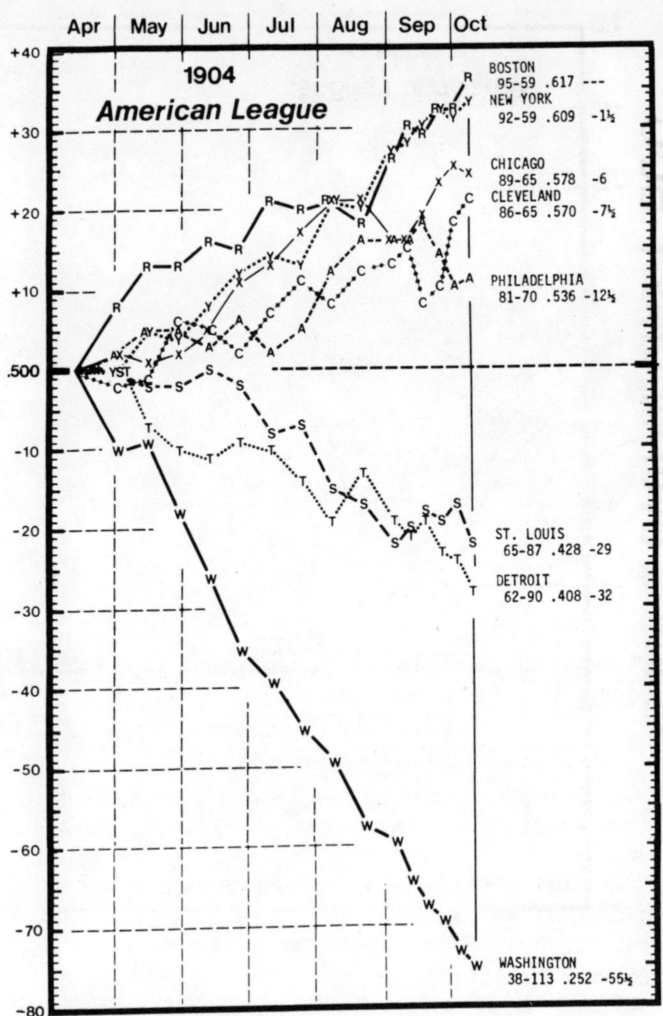


a temporary return to the race by sweeping the White Sox on October 3-5. Meanwhile, the Highlanders had stuck to the Pilgrims like flypaper over the last seven weeks, grabbing the lead from the champions seven times.

What made the Highlanders so competitive was the truly great pitching of Happy Jack Chesbro. Most pitchers are satisfied to win 20 games in a season, but Chesbro didn't rest even after he had done this *twice* in a season. His final total of 41 victories on the mound still stands as one of baseball's hardest-to-match records, considering that only one man (Denny McLain in 1968) has won as many as 30 games in the past 46 years, although Chesbro's mark was approached by Ed Walsh's 40 and Mathewson's 37 wins in 1908.

The first crucial series between the Pilgrims and Highlanders, three consecutive doubleheaders on September 14-16 at Boston's Huntington Avenue grounds, ended in a draw—two wins, two losses, and two ties for each team—leaving New York only half a game in the lead. Three more weeks, also inconclusive, followed, and the agitation of the fans all over the Northeast grew daily in anticipation of the real showdown between the teams, luckily scheduled as their last five games of the season. Going into this final series, Boston led New York by only a half-game.

This was reversed in the first game on Friday, October 7th. Before a packed house in New York, Chesbro pitched the Highlanders to a 3-2 victory, his 41st. When the teams met again in Boston the next day, however, the Pilgrims swept a

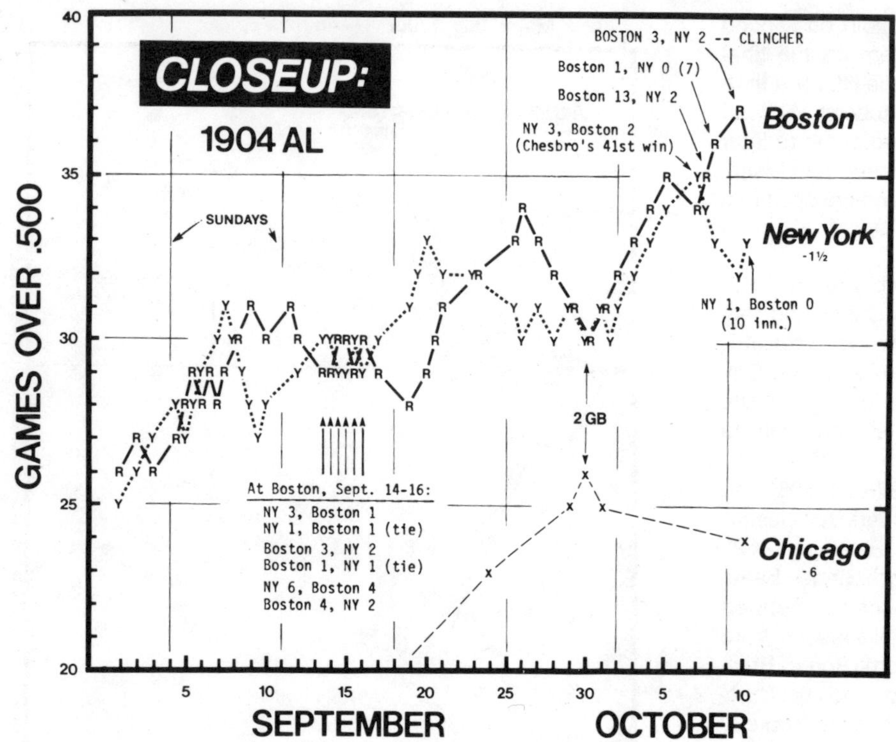


**BIRTH OF A RIVALRY.** The first thrilling pennant race of the modern era was the 1904 struggle between the New York and Boston AL clubs, before the nicknames Yankees and Red Sox or the parks, Yankee Stadium and Fenway, existed. The Chicago White Sox joined the contest briefly around September 30th. The Boston-New York battle was not decided until the closing day, Monday, October 10th, when Jack Chesbro's wild pitch gave the Pilgrims a 3-2 victory over the Highlanders in the first game of a doubleheader.

doubleheader, 13-2 and 1-0, giving them a 1½-game lead. Now Boston needed to win only one of the final two games to clinch the pennant.

Somehow, 28,540 fans managed to squeeze into Highlander Park, which seated only 12,000, for the closing-day doubleheader on Monday, October 10th. It was up to Chesbro, against Boston's Bill Dinneen (23-14 that year), to keep the home team's pennant chances alive in the first game. He was well on his way toward doing that with a 2-0 lead in the seventh inning, when his second baseman, Jimmy Williams, threw wildly to first on a grounder, letting Candy LaChance and Hobe Ferris score after they had reached base on scratch hits. With the score still 2-2, Lou Criger opened Boston's ninth inning by beating out an infield bleeder, and advanced to third on Dinneen's sacrifice and Kip Selbach's right-side grounder. Needing only to retire Freddy Parent to get out of the inning, Chesbro unleashed a pitch that soared past both Parent and Red Kleinow, the New York catcher, and Criger was easily home with what proved to be the pennant-winning run.

When Dinneen set down the future Yankees quickly in the bottom of the ninth and the Highlanders won the nightcap of the twin bill, it became clear to a very unHappy Jack that not only had the ball sailed to the backstop but the game and the whole season along with it. Later he insisted that Kleinow "should have caught it," and after his death his widow spent many years trying to get the wild pitch changed to a passed ball in the official scoring, but Chesbro's own shortstop, Kid Elberfeld, testified that "that ball rode so far over Kleinow's head he couldn't have caught it standing on a stepladder."

By 1904 John McGraw had built his New York Giants into a team that led the National League in runs, hits, home runs, doubles, RBIs, walks, stolen bases, batting and slugging averages, earned run average, strikeouts, shutouts, saves, double plays, and fielding average. And one other category—games won (106)—for a pennant that was in little doubt before the Fourth of July. Joe McGinnity had his best year, with 35

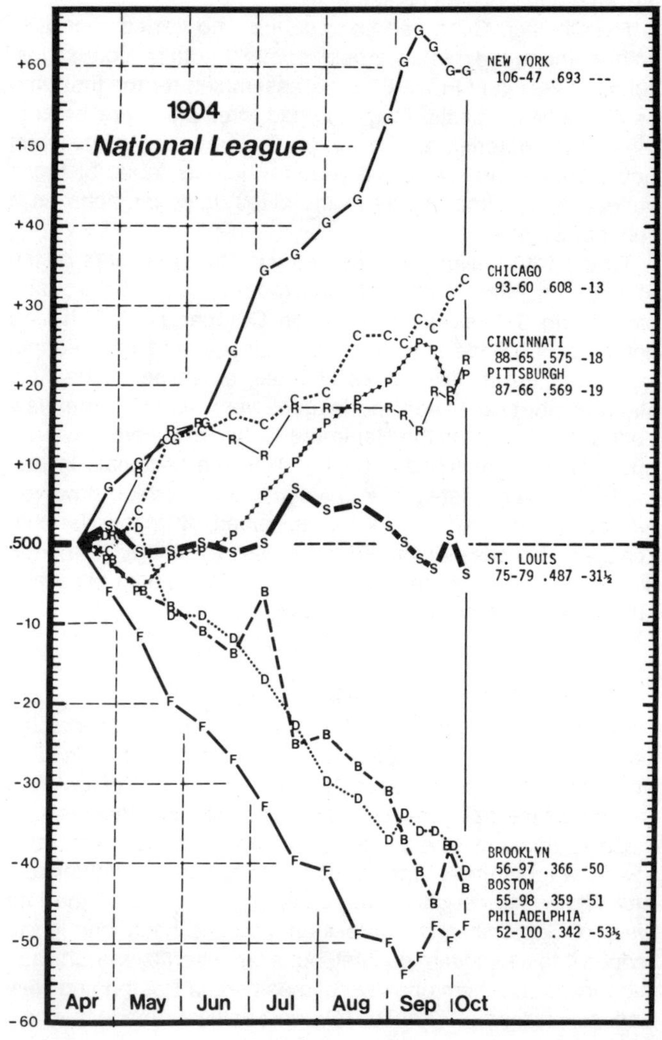

wins, nine shutouts, and 1.61 ERA, Christy Mathewson (33-12, 2.03) was nearly as superb on the mound, and solid contributions were made by Dummy Taylor (21-15) and Hooks Wiltse (13-3). McGraw's strong infield now consisted of Dan McGann, Billy Gilbert, Bill Dahlen, and Art Devlin, and in the green pastures he still had George Browne, Roger Bresnahan, and Sam Mertes. Oddly, not a single Giant regular batted .300, or even .290, but in that dead-ball period their .262 team batting average still exceeded Pittsburgh's despite .300-plus years again by Wagner, Clarke, and Beaumont. With iron discipline, McGraw got the most out of every man in the lineup.

The Pirates' try for a fourth pennant in a row was foiled not only by the Giants' continued strengthening but by their own pitching problems. Ed Doheny never returned to baseball from his psychotic breakdown of the previous October, and illness reduced Deacon Phillippe's output to only ten wins in 1904. This time, although Sam Leever and Patsy Flaherty had good years, the necessary replacements did not materialize.

The St. Louis Cardinals surprised everyone by playing above .500 over much of the season. Two aging stars from the 1890s had a lot to do with this jump from the cellar: 36-year-old Jake Beckley, who batted .325, and 34-year-old Kid Nichols, who won 21 games with a 2.02 ERA. Jack Taylor, obtained from the Cubs between seasons, also won 21 games for the Cards.

Still annoyed by the AL invasion of the New York market, and perhaps more because of old enmities between McGraw and Ban Johnson from the Baltimore days, the Giants refused to meet Boston in a World Series: "We don't play minor leaguers." Since this put the Giants in the role of defaulter and the Pilgrims already held the world championship trophy, they simply kept it and proclaimed themselves champions again.

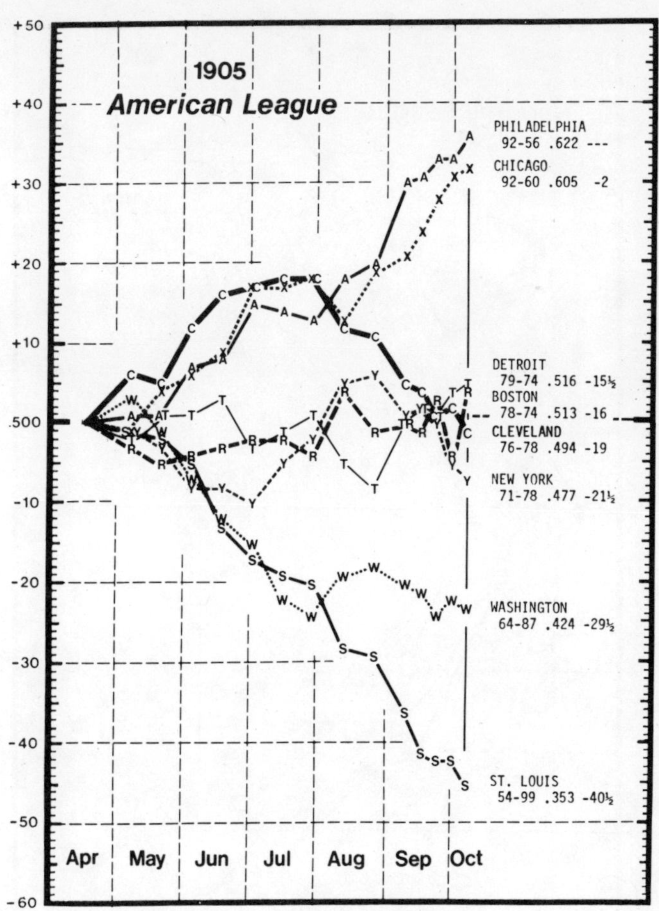


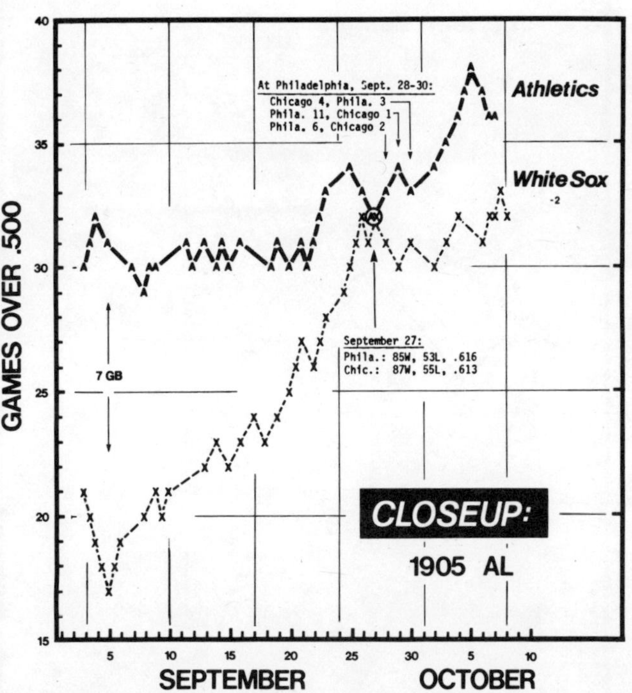


**BRIEF ENCOUNTER. It took only three weeks for the Chicago White Sox to abolish the Philadelphia Athletics' seven-game lead in September of 1905. When the two teams met face-to-face in Philadelphia at the end of the month, however, the Mackmen destroyed Chicago's momentum with 6-2 and 11-1 trouncings and regained their firm grasp on the pennant.**

## 1905

Up to August, 1905 looked like the year for Cleveland's arrival, but instead it was time for the Athletics' revival. The Mackmen's return from a two-year exile was based mainly on a strong mound staff again headed by Rube Waddell (26-11) and Eddie Plank (25-12), after whom the gaps were filled by a pair of 22-year-olds, Andy Coakley (20-7) and Chief Bender (16-11). Philadelphia and Cleveland shared team batting honors at the meagre level of .255, lowest leading team BA in the American League until the 1960s. The Naps faded badly in August and September, in part because they were Napless—Lajoie was out with a case of blood poisoning; beyond Addie Joss (20-11), their pitching was thin as well.

The White Sox matched the A's in getting 80 wins from four pitchers, Frank Owen, Nick Altrock, Frank Smith, and Doc White, plus eight more from a promising sophomore named Ed Walsh, and held their opponents to fewer than two earned runs per game (team ERA: 1.99). Even with only a .237 team batting average, this league-leading pitching prowess was enough to give the Athletics a good scare in the last fortnight of the season. In fact, as the closeup graph shows but the full-season plot does not, Chicago charged up to tie the A's in games over .500 on Wednesday, September 27th.

Again the schedule maker showed his prescient flair for drama, because the two confronted each other in Philadelphia on September 28-30. The season was essentially decided when the White Elephants took the first two games on Thursday and Friday, and after a White Sox win on Saturday, Mack's club went on to the actual clinching by sweeping three games from the Browns at home and a doubleheader from the Sen-

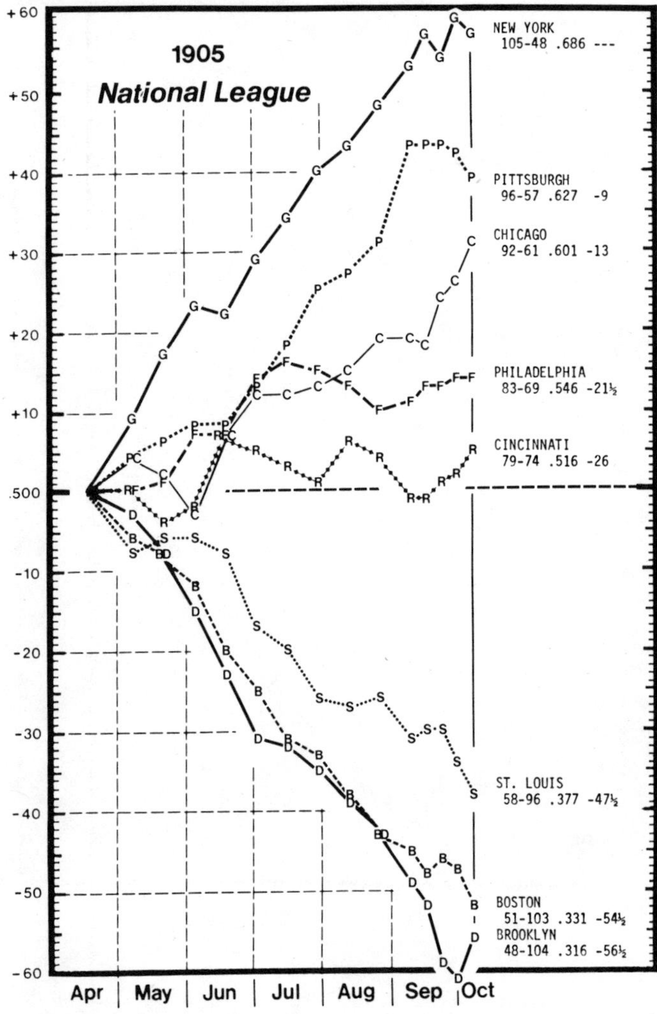


ators at Washington.

Among six other clubs not in the running were the Boston Pilgrims, who played unlike champions all season long. Despite an ERA of 1.82 over 321 innings, Cy Young lost 19 games as the Boston bats remained silent from April to October. Their 1904 rivals, the Highlanders, were again near-equals, finishing in sixth place.

The 1905 Giants differed little from the '04 club, except that their hitting improved with Mike Donlin's full-season performance at .356 and Bresnahan's at .302, and again they won the NL title easily. Pittsburgh had Phillippe back in good form (22-13), and they reduced the New York margin of victory from 13 to nine games. The Cubs hardly contended until September, when they showed the league's steepest (upward) curve—a sneak preview of their 1906 show. The Phillies' acquisition of Togie Pittinger (23-15) from the Boston Braves and a rise in the Phils' batting averages pulled them up to a surprising fourth place from a basement finish in 1904.

Unquestionably, 1905's most memorable feat came in the World Series, when the Marvelous Mathewson followed up his 32-8 season by shutting out the Athletics in the first, third, and decisive fifth games.

## 1906

On Sunday evening, July 29, 1906, the Chicago Cubs were perched at the top of the National League standings with 61 wins and 26 losses, more than five games ahead of the Pirates and world champion Giants. The Cubs will never be accused of complacency in that year, because they then proceeded to win 55 of their remaining 65 games (.846). By the end of the season Frank Chance's charges had set the modern major league records for wins, 116, and won-lost percentage, .763. This amazing performance left them with a 20-game edge over a runnerup team that had won 96 games, a margin (tied by the 1975 Cincinnati Reds) exceeded only by the Pirates' in 1902.

The Cubs' winning binge was mainly due to their pitching. Only three times in the NL's modern period has a team ERA dropped below 2.00, and the Cubs have monopolized this feat—1.76 in 1906, 1.73 (the modern record) in 1907, and 1.75 in 1909. Their #1 stopper in 1906 was Mordecai (Three Finger) Brown (26-6, 9 shutouts, 1.04); they also had 12-to-20-game-winners Jack Pfeister (1.56), Ed Reulbach (1.65), Carl Lundgren (2.21), Orvie Overall (1.88), and Jack Taylor (back from the Cards, 1.84) that year. The Cub offense also improved over 1905's, particularly with the addition of third baseman Harry Steinfeldt (.327, league leader in RBIs) to the Tinker-to-Evers-to-Chance combo, and a 94-point increase in catcher Johnny Kling's batting average (to .312). Chance himself was in top form, leading the league in stolen bases again with 57 and hitting .319. Eighty more stolen bases were contributed by the Cub outfielders, Wildfire Schulte, Jimmy Slagle, and Jimmy Sheckard.

Across town, the White Sox combined the American League's weakest offense (team BA only .230) with pitching that was nearly as good as the Cubs', classy fielding, and lots of base stealing, and won the pennant, for which they were

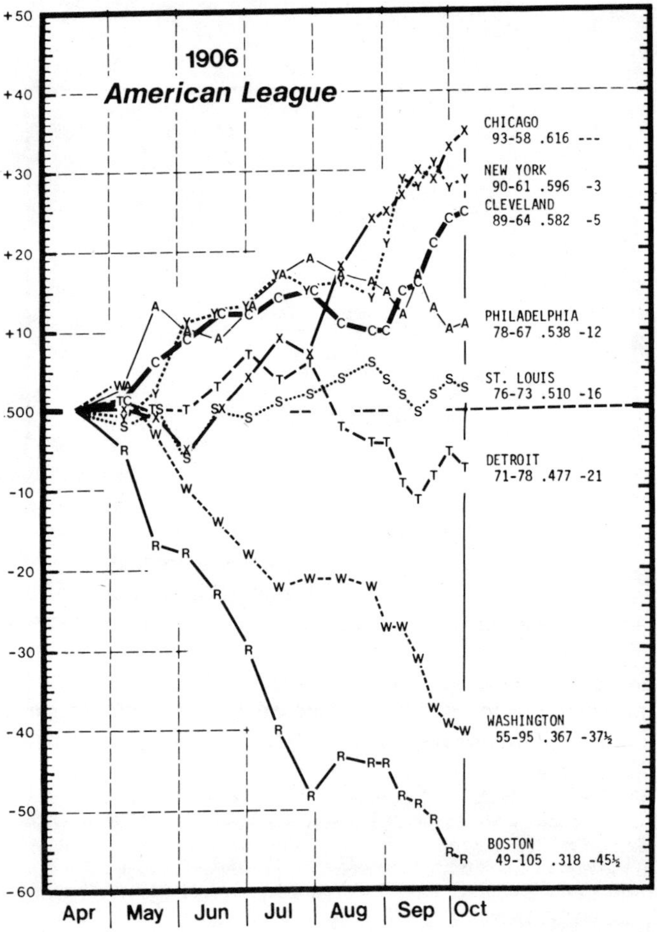

MAJOR LEAGUE RECORDS were set by the 1906 Chicago Cubs for wins (116), won-lost percentage (.763), and games over .500 (80). Their amazing performance also produced the modern era's largest spread from top to bottom, with the Boston Braves finishing 66¼ games behind the Cubs. Note that the New York Giants won 96 games (out of 152 played) and still finished 20 games behind Chicago.

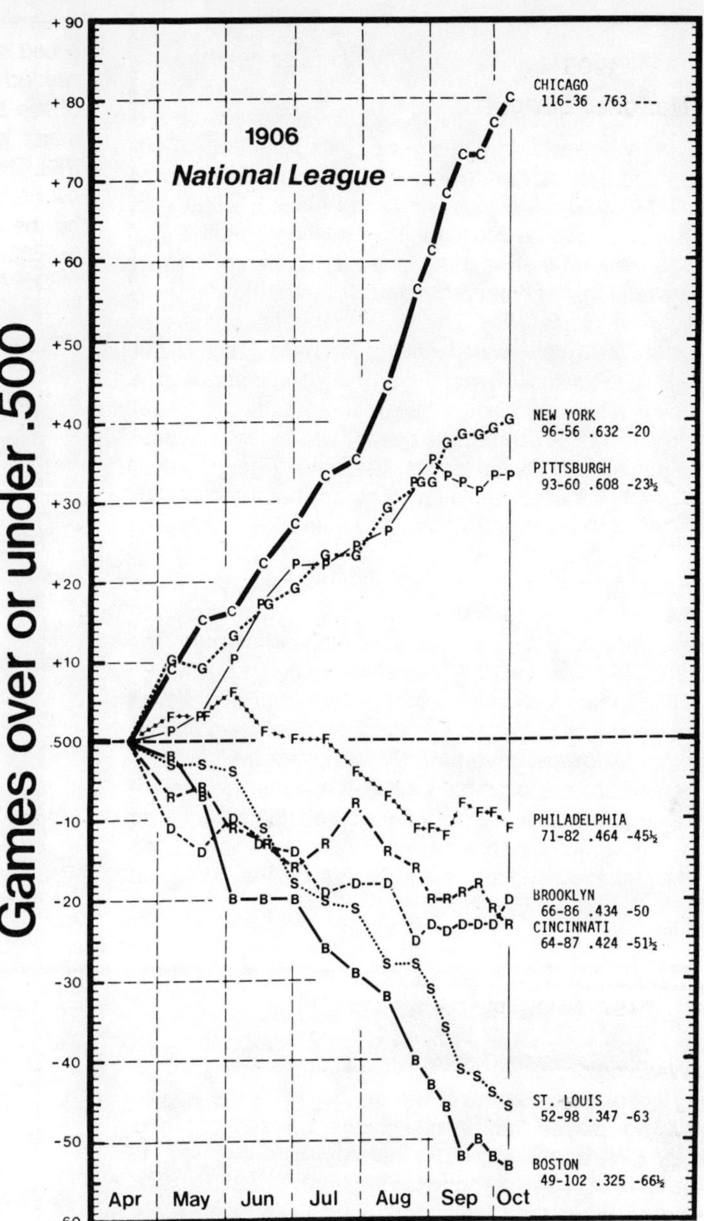


aptly branded the Hitless Wonders. Not only was their pennant victory wondrous, but also how they bested Nap Lajoie's team at Cleveland, which led the AL in hitting and pitching (Addie Joss, Bob Rhoades, and Otto Hess were all 20-game-winners with ERAs below 2.00). And yet it was the revived New York Highlanders, not the Naps or the deposed Athletics, who hung close to the Chicagoans in the season's final weeks. After the latter had leaped into first place with a 19-game winning streak in August, the New York team, still managed by Clark Griffith and led by Chesbro's mound work, took the top spot away from the White Sox in the first and third weeks of September. Eventually the Owen-Walsh-Altrock-White combination pulled the Chisox through in the last week, to a three-game winning margin.

Wonders did not cease when the first, last, and only all-Chicago World Series took place that October—the White Sox beat the winningest team ever, four games to two. And in typical fashion, Fielder Jones's men batted only .198 as a team, holding the Cubs to .196.

The exact mirror-image of Chicago's euphoria could be found at the other end of the circuits, where the two Boston teams were the big losers of 1906. The Braves lost over 100 games again, and accomplished this via four 20-game-losing pitchers—Gus Dorner (9-26), Vive Lindaman (12-23), Big Jeff Pfeffer (13-22), and Irv Young (16-25). The Boston AL team (briefly known as the Plymouth Rocks, and probably called some worse names that year) dropped from a break-even '05 season to nearly 50 games below .500 by the end of August, 1906. The ravages of age, illness, and injury appeared up and down their lineup, with 39-year-old Cy Young losing 21 games and most of the other former Pilgrim stars slipping badly. The funereal atmosphere in Boston became a literal reality with the suicide of playing-manager Chick Stahl during the following spring training period; the source of Stahl's despondency was never revealed, but considering it was March of 1907, we can rule out the radio talk shows.

## 1907

Enter Ty Cobb, and presto—three straight pennants for the Detroit Tigers!

It was not that simple, of course, but when you search the records for the key ingredients of the Tigers' 1907-08-09 triumphs, you don't find any other players to account for their ascendancy to the throne from sixth place in 1906, and since the AL had close races in all three of those years, Cobb was probably the difference that made a big difference. Playing a full season for the first time at age 20, he led the league in hits, RBIs, stolen bases, and BA (.350). He and young reliable Sam Crawford (.323) constituted most of the Bengal attack, but with Wild Bill Donovan (25-4) and Ed Killian (25-13) returning to form after off-years and George Mullin contributing his usual 20 wins, more did not seem to be needed. All of which would convince some veteran observers that the Tigers' rookie manager in 1907, Hughie Jennings, had as much to do with their pennant victories as the blossoming of the Georgia Peach did.

In July the Tigers made their break with the past and turned toward the top of the standings, which they reached in early August, in a crowd that also contained world champion Chicago, Connie Mack's A's, and the ever-contending but never-winning Cleveland club. The race drew tighter until, on the first Sunday of September, the four teams stood within two games of each other. A few days later the Athletics took the lead and by mid-September the Mackmen were threatening to run off with the flag just as the Tigers were completing their home schedule. But Jennings' crew rallied, at the expense of the White Sox and Highlanders, to tie the A's on the 20th, and

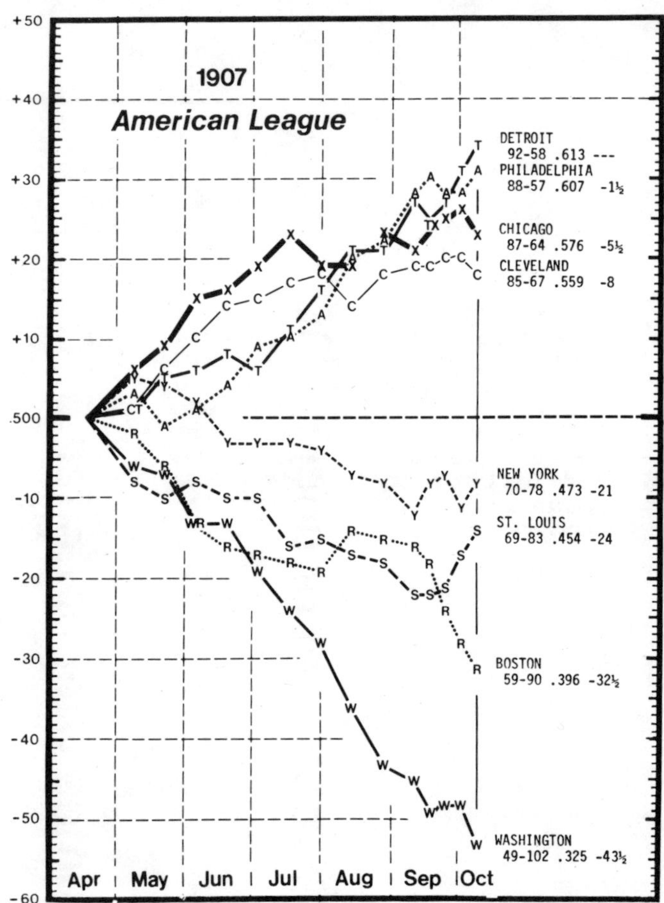


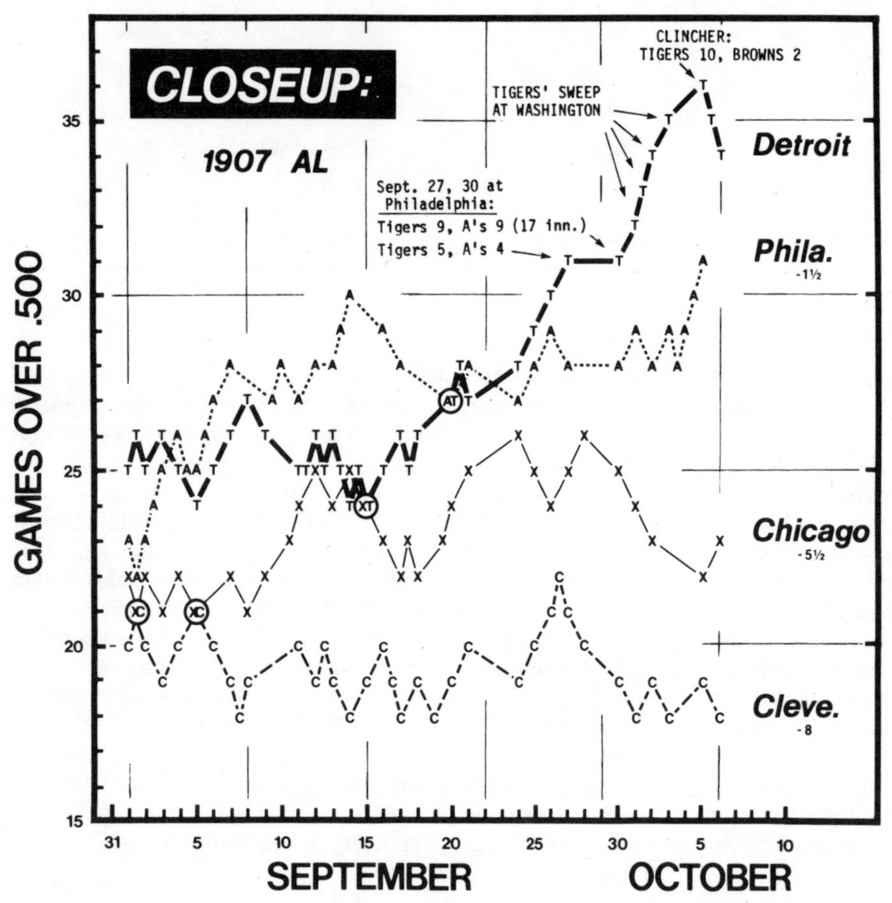


**TYGER! TYGER! BURNING BRIGHT, thanks to the "immortal hand or eye" and feet of the Georgia Peach, Ty Cobb.**

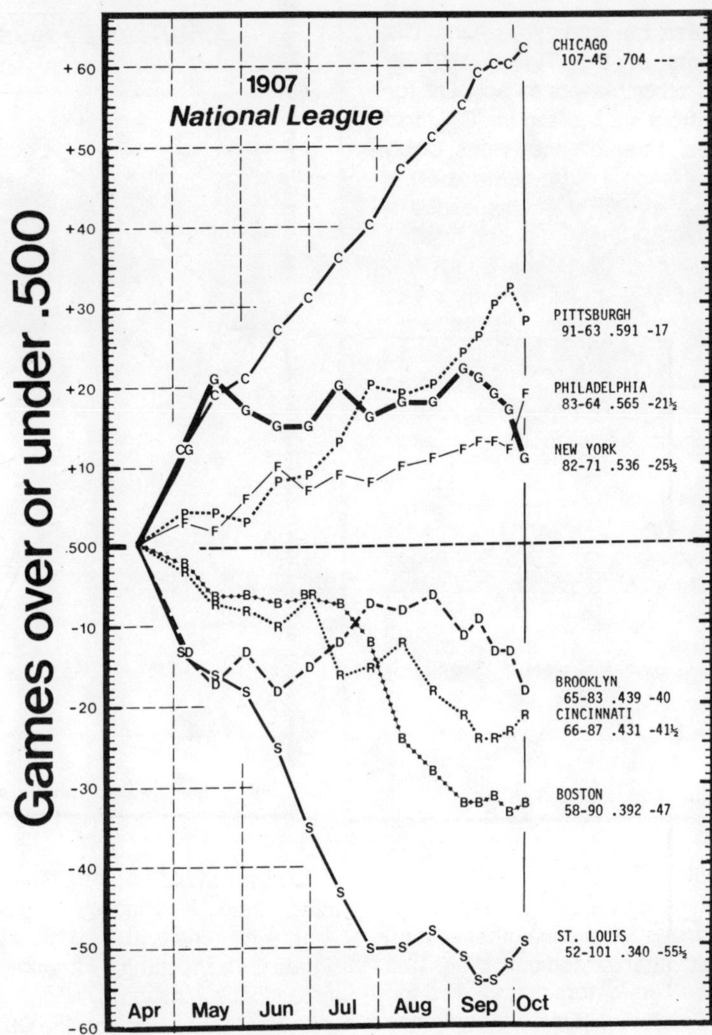


moved slightly ahead with a three-game sweep at Boston. On the eve of a crucial series at Philadelphia starting on the 27th, Detroit led the A's by a half-game, the White Sox by three, and the Naps by 4½.

The Tigers expanded their lead with a 5-4 win over the A's on Friday, the 27th. After a rainout on Saturday and the usual Sunday blue-law observance, the two teams wrestled to a 9-9 draw in 17 innings on the 30th. One of the few pivotal tie games in baseball history, this prevented the Mackmen from getting any closer than a game and a half, as Detroit went on to sweep four games at Washington and clinch the pennant with a 10-2 victory at St. Louis on the next-to-last day of the season. In summary: one of the better road trips a major league team has had.

The outcome might have been different if the other contenders had not developed some gaping holes in the late stages. The Athletics were hurt by arm ailments suffered by Chief Bender and the promising young Jack Coombs and a sudden unreliability of Rube Waddell. Chicago never quite made up for Nick Altrock's (8-12) and Frank Owen's (2-3) off-years, and were generally about as hitless as in 1906. Cleveland now had the superb Addie Joss in his prime (27-11, 1.83), but not enough help from the rest of the hurlers, and their batting, even Lajoie's (.299) was well below normal. As the full-season graph shows, the hot pennant race took its toll on the second-division tams (especially the Senators, who were just breaking in a 19-year-old pitcher named Walter Johnson), and put a large space between the four haves and the four have-nots.

In the National League, the Giants tried to preempt a repeat by the Cubs by leaping off to a 24-and-3 mark on May 19th, but the Chicagoans reached 23-and-4 the same day, and roared past McGraw's men to uncatchable levels of 56-20 in mid-July, 82-31 in late August, and the nice round numbers of 100 and 40 with two weeks left in September. They finished 62 games over .500 and 34 games higher than the second-place Pirates on that same scale, in another breeze.

The Cubs had no .300 hitters in 1907, but with five pitchers having ERAs under 1.70, they didn't need any. Four of these moundsmen—Overall, Reulbach, Pfeister, and Brown—mowed down the Tigers in four straight (after a 12-inning tie in the first game) in the World Series.

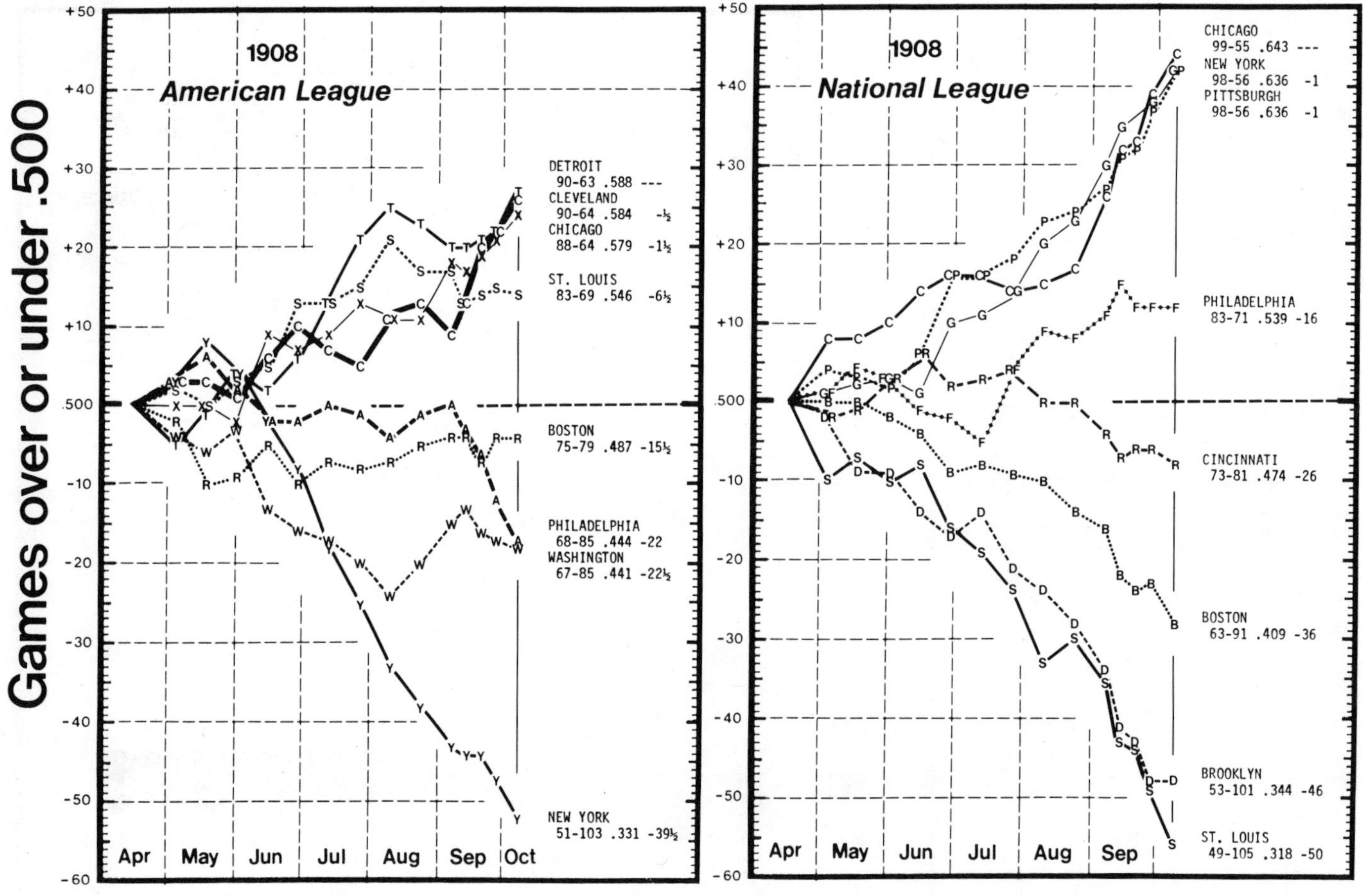


## 1908

In 1908 both major leagues had thrilling pennant races that were not decided until the closing day. Only one other season of this century (1949) can make that statement. When the smoke cleared, the Chicago Cubs were victors over the tied-for-second New York Giants and Pittsburgh Pirates by only one game in the NL, and the Tigers won the AL flag by only a half-game over the Cleveland Naps and a game and a half over the Chicago White Sox.

While there was tingling excitement in both leagues, the older circuit staged its drama in bolder outlines. The Cubs were just enough reduced in strength for the inevitable three-way clash among the National League's perennial contenders to occur. By the end of June, with Chicago and Pittsburgh tied and the New Yorkers moving up rapidly, it was clear that the three were headed for a beautiful brawl. As the summer wore on, they pulled closer together, to only a one-game spread on September 3rd and only a half-game difference on several days in the final two weeks. The one-game separation at the end represented the closest three-team race of the modern era other than those ending in ties and playoffs.

Three Finger Brown (29-9, 1.47 for the season), Ed Reulbach (24-7), and Johnny Evers (.300) were leading the Cubs, while Christy Mathewson (37-11, 1.43), Hooks Wiltse (23-14), Mike Donlin (.334), and Larry Doyle (.308) held up the Giants. With Fred Clarke starting to show his 35 years with a .265 BA, the Pirates were down to only one true offensive star, Honus Wagner, who won his sixth batting title with .354 and his fifth base-stealing title with 53 at age 34, but their pitching staff, now led by 21-year-old Nick Maddox (23-8) and the veteran Vic Willis (23-11), kept the Bucs in the thick of the fray.

On the 8th of September the Giants started an 11-game winning streak, feasting on the pathetic Brooklyn and St. Louis teams for nine and then sweeping a doubleheader from the Pirates. The resulting 4½-game lead on September 18th vanished quickly, however, when the Bucs took the two remaining games of the series and the Cubs followed them into the Polo Grounds on the 22nd. That day, it was the Giants who lost a twin bill, 4-3 and 3-1, leaving both the Cubs and Giants at 37 games over .500 with the latter ahead in percentage by .006. The next game made every baseball history book.

Wednesday, September 23, 1908, two outs in the bottom of the ninth, score tied at 1-1: Jack "The Giant Killer" Pfeister, on the mound for the Cubs, was showing signs of weakening. A 19-year-old sub for ailing Fred Tenney named Fred Merkle had just singled, advancing his teammate Moose McCormick to third. The next batter, Al Bridwell, drilled a sharp single to center, McCormick easily scored the apparent winning run, and the 25,000 Giant fans broke out of the stands in pandemonium. But Merkle, instead of advancing to second on Bridwell's hit, turned from the basepath as soon as he saw McCormick cross the plate and ran for the Giant dugout, joining in the celebration himself. The alert second baseman for the Cubs, Johnny Evers, yelled to Solly Hofman in center field for the ball, to make the forceout on Merkle and nullify the winning run.

Depending on which of many accounts one chooses to believe, the ball—or some ball—made its way back to Evers at second through the huge crowd that had poured onto the field and already blocked Hofman's view of Evers by the time of the latter's frantic call. By one account, the actual ball hit by Bridwell went from Hofman to shortstop Joe Tinker to Joe

THE MERKLE GIANTS. Baseball's most famous mental error and most historic tie game occurred right in the midst of the most exciting pennant race of the century's early decades. Fred Merkle's fateful dash to the dugout when he should have run to second base converted Al Bridwell's game-winning hit for the Giants to a forceout and a Giant victory to a 1-1 tie with the Cubs on September 23, 1908, at the Polo Grounds. Two weeks later the regular schedule ended with the Giants and Cubs again tied and the Pirates only a half-game behind. When the September 23 game was replayed on October 8th, Three Finger Brown outpitched Christy Mathewson at the Polo Grounds to give the Cubs their third straight pennant.

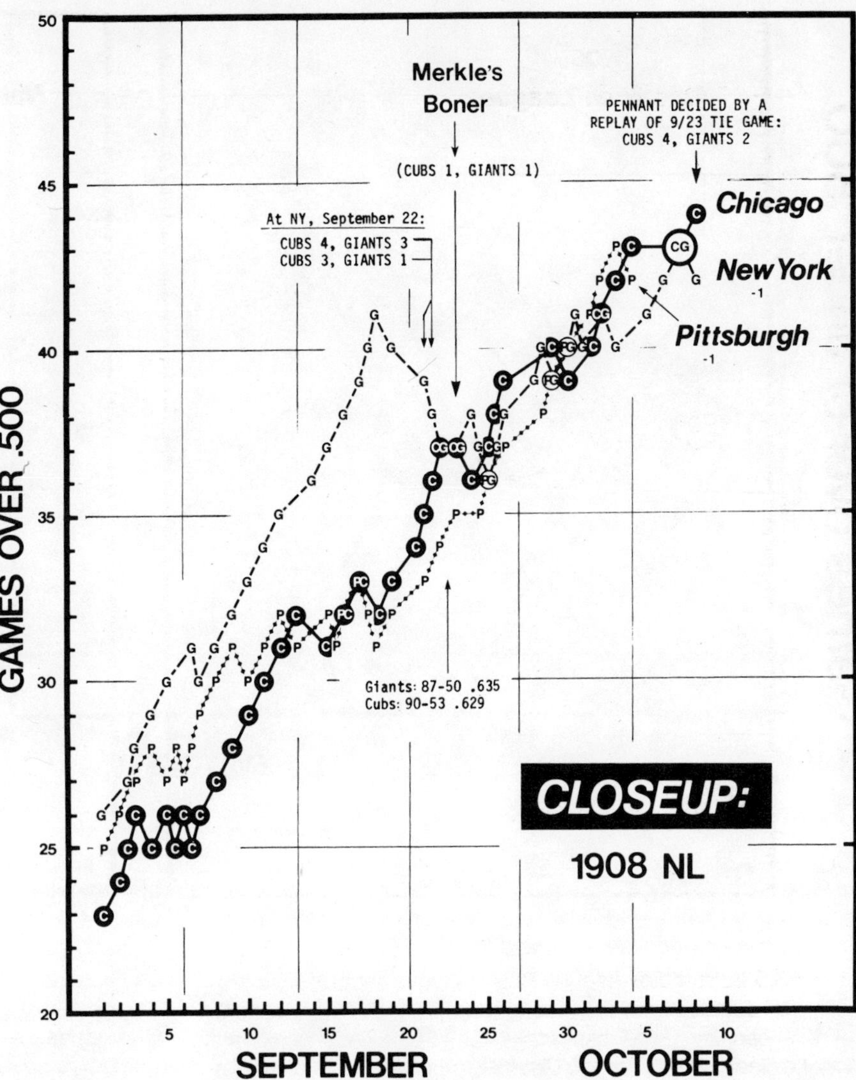


McGinnity, the Giants' first base coach (in a brute-force interception), thence to a fan, and to an obscure Cub pitcher named Rube Kroh who wasn't even in the game (and who had to commit assault and battery to get the ball from the fan), and finally to Evers. By another account, McGinnity heaved the ball into the stands as soon as he had wrestled it away from Tinker, and another ball somehow got to Evers for the touch at second base. Whatever the route, Umpire Hank O'Day sided with Evers, calling Merkle out and negating the run, and declared the game a tie because of the impending darkness and the mob on the field.

A huge row ensued, and two weeks of legalistic jousting before the NL president and board of directors. Merkle, the Giants contended, did not commit a mental error in failing to go all the way to second—he was merely following the common practice of those days on a game-winning hit by the home team in the last inning, and umpires did not enforce the rule saying that a runner on first who is forced by the hit to second must touch second base for the game-winning run to count. But just 19 days earlier, the rule *had* been enforced, again at Johnny Evers' insistence and by the same Umpire O'Day, in a game between the Cubs and Pirates. On October 5th, the league officials upheld O'Day, denying the Giants their 2-1 victory.

In the meantime, the pennant race got even hotter. The Pirates won 12 and tied one of their last 14 games, and briefly took the lead just before completing their schedule on October 4th. After the drama of September 23rd and a loss to the Giants the next day, the Cubs resumed their torrid pace, losing only one more game; on October 4th their defeat of the Pirates at Chicago proved to be the fatal blow for Pittsburgh. The Giants, on the other hand, lost five more games—a doubleheader to the Reds on September 25th and the other three to the Phillies. In all three losses to the Phils, the winning pitcher was a brand-new rookie named Harry Coveleski whose whole 1908 record was 4-and-1; he was aptly christened another Giant Killer.

By sweeping a three-game set at the Polo Grounds from the Braves, McGraw's club pulled up to a tie with the Cubs at 98-55 at the end of the regular schedule on October 7th (the Pirates already had finished at 98-56). So the much-argued tie game of September 23 had to be replayed to determine the pennant winner. In front of a record 35,000 disheartened fans at the Polo Grounds on October 8th, the mighty Matty allowed the Cubs four runs (and Frank Chance three hits) while Pfeister and Brown held the Giants to two tallies, in the deciding match that "might not have been necessary if Merkle had touched second two weeks earlier." That is what was said, and repeated a million times in later years—hardly fair to Merkle himself, whose sprint to the dugout had been the accepted practice and who was in no way to blame for the six subsequent

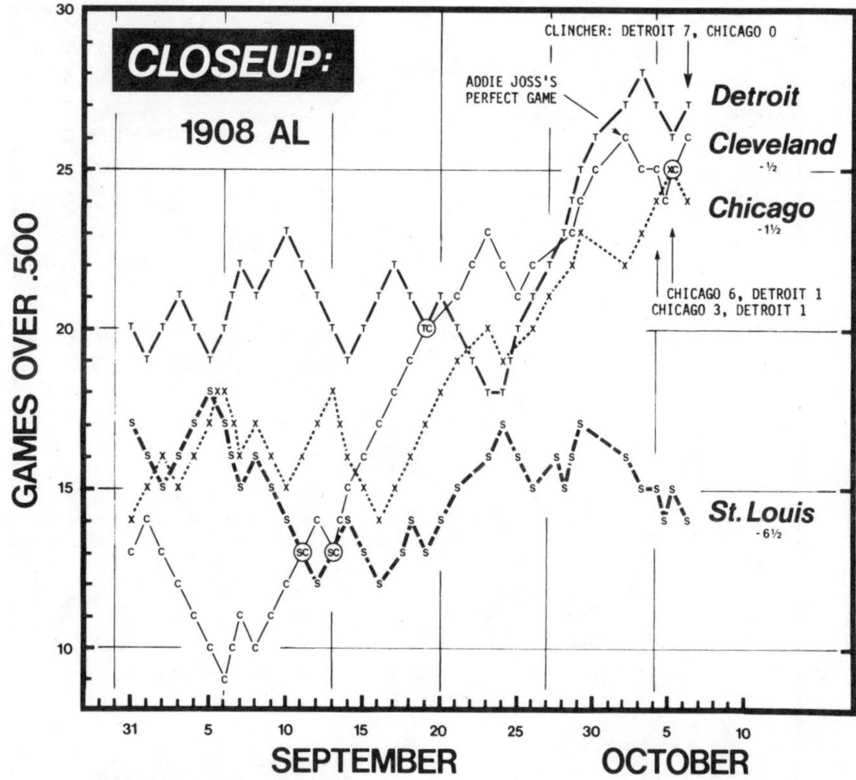


**THE RAZOR'S EDGE.** When the Detroit Tigers won the second of their three straight AL pennants in 1908, it was by the tiny margin of half a game, over Cleveland. The only other time a title race in the AL or NL was decided by a half-game edge was in 1972, when the Boston Red Sox were nosed out for the AL East divisional title by—once again—the Tigers. In 1908, Cleveland yelled "We wuz robbed!" because a rained-out game that Detroit never made up might have been lost by the Tigers if they had, producing a tie with Cleveland and forcing a playoff. The "1908 rule," requiring teams to make up rainouts or ties affecting the outcome of a pennant race, was adopted by both leagues as a result of this squabble.

defeats suffered by the Giants. Justice would have been far better served had the 1908 NL season been remembered more for Evers' mental agility than Merkle's Boner.

The 1908 American League race also had three teams in a free-for-all in its final week, but it should be classed as a four-team affair. The Sunday-to-Sunday standings of the whole-season graph show the St. Louis Browns faced with a pretty hopeless task in mid-September, only 14 games over .500 with three teams to overtake, but the closeup reveals only a 2½-game spread of the four teams on September 24-25, so the Brownies should not be counted out. Among the four-team races of the past 80 years, this one was in the top three in how closely the contestants were bunched at the finish.

At times during that summer, the Tigers had looked like certain repeaters, with some needed bolstering of their pitching staff coming from 23-year-old Ed Summers, who eventually won 24 games, and with Cobb and Crawford banging the ball as usual. But the surprising Browns kept challenging, even taking the lead briefly around the Fourth of July; having acquired Rube Waddell from the A's during the offseason, and Bill Dinneen from Boston the year before, they had five starters in the ERA range of 1.99 to 2.11. The White Sox were also in the race, with one fairly strong hitter, Patsy Dougherty, and one sensational pitcher, Ed Walsh. In 42 starts and 24 relief stints, Walsh won 40 games and earned seven saves. The Sox also had an apparent genius in manager Fielder Jones.

The Cleveland Blues (which they were also called during the Lajoie regime) threatened to become hitless wonders also, as their batting decline continued from the previous year. But with 24-game-winner Joss leading the way, they snapped out of an early-September slumber with a 16-out-of-18 spurt, as if they had peeked ahead in baseball history and seen that this would be their last chance for many years to come. In a series at home against the Senators on September 24-26, however, they faltered, letting the Tigers and White Sox move up to a near-three-way tie. Then the Tigers, who were in the midst of a ten-game winning streak, took the lead by sweeping four from the Senators while the Naps swept only three from the A's. For Cleveland, a reasonable chance of wresting the pennant from the Tigers now depended on a victory over Chicago, and when the White Sox came to town on Friday, October 2nd, Cleveland fans were treated to one of the greatest pitching matchups of all time—Ed Walsh vs. Addie Joss. Walsh struck out 15 and allowed the Naps only one run, but Joss didn't let a single Sox batter reach first base!

That didn't finish the Sox, however. They recoiled with a 3-2 win over Cleveland on Saturday and two more victories over the Tigers at Chicago on the next two days. In character all the way, the Naps muffed their chance to overtake Detroit when they were held to an 11-inning tie by the now-kayoed Browns on Saturday and only split a twin bill in St. Louis on Monday. So on that evening, October 5, with only the final day remaining, Detroit still held a half-game edge over Chicago and Cleveland.

The veteran Wild Bill Donovan settled matters on Tuesday by pitching the Tigers to a 7-0 win over the White Sox. Cleveland won over the Browns, but that was only good for second place, still half a game back, and now the season was over with the Detroit and Cleveland records differing by only one game in the lost column. Rightfully, the Naps squawked loudly about getting gyped out of a possible tie for the pennant—if the Tigers had lost a rained-out game of some weeks back which they never made up, the two teams would have finished with identical, 90-64 records. Cleveland's strident demands that the Tigers be forced to play that game were not met, but did lead to the adoption of a rule by both leagues that all rained-out games affecting the outcome of contention for first place must be made up.

Had this "1908 rule" been in force in earlier years, some other teams might have profited from it. The 1904 Highlanders finished 1½ games behind Boston with three games unplayed or undecided, which if played and won would have given the New Yorkers a tie for the pennant. The White Sox finished in that same position in 1908. And in 1906 these two teams both had three games to make up when they finished three games apart—again the Highlanders were "robbed." Still another case occurred in 1905, when the Athletics, six games short of a full schedule, finished two games ahead of the White Sox, two games short.

The 1908 World Series, won by the Cubs in five games, showed that the year's two pennant races were tough acts to follow.

## 1909

After all the commotion of 1908, the two leagues settled into a seven-year period in which there was little contention after Labor Day. But the twists and turns of seasonal curves continued in fascinating ways.

As in the previous two seasons, Cobb and Crawford were the Tigers' only .300 hitters in 1909, but with superior mound work by veteran George Mullin (29-9) and the younger Ed Willett (22-9), they cruised to their third straight pennant. Their final margin of 3½ games was slim, but they led the league almost every week of the season. Philadelphia was the only real challenger—Connie Mack was remodeling his sixth-place 1908 team into a winner again.

When the A's grabbed a brief lead in August, the Tigers suddenly found themselves caught in a pincers movement between Mack's club and the surprising Red Sox. The latter had retired or traded the last of the old Pilgrims, including Cy Young (who had moved to Cleveland after winning 21 games at age 41 in 1908), and Boston's youth movement had already brought the Red Sox back to second place in team batting. One of the new faces in the 1909 Boston lineup was 21-year-old Tris Speaker, who batted .309 in his first full season.

The Cleveland Naps got good years from Lajoie (.324) and Young (19 wins at age 42!), but with few other players contributing, they drifted off to sixth by season's end. The Washington Senators had another disastrous season, with Walter Johnson losing 25 games despite a 2.21 ERA, but this would be their last year in the cellar for a long time primarily because of him.

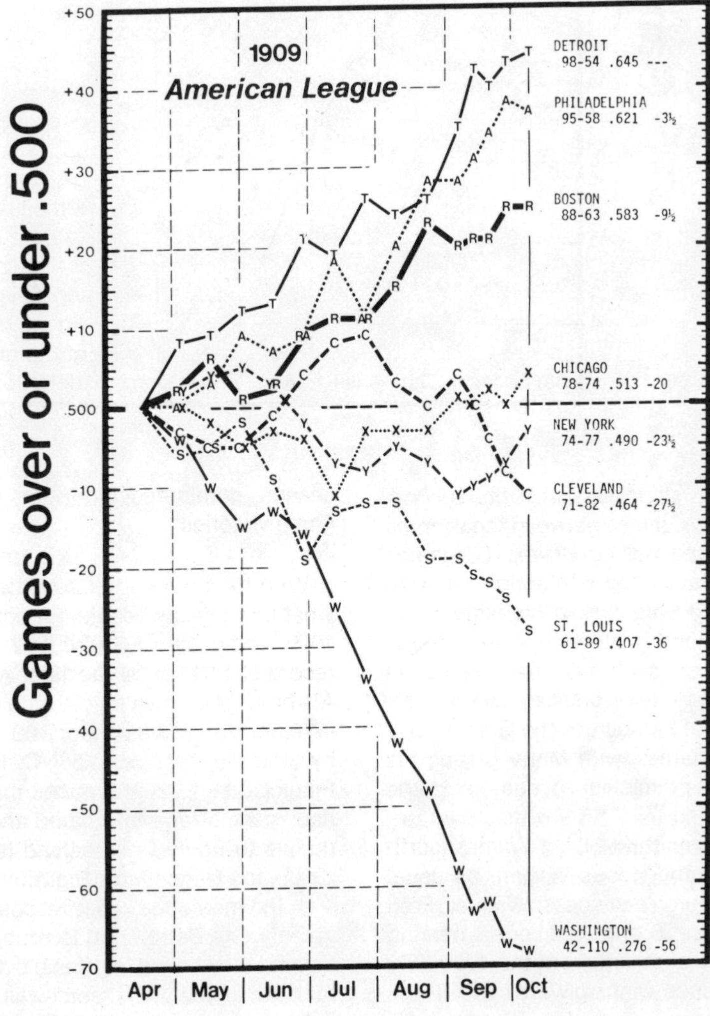

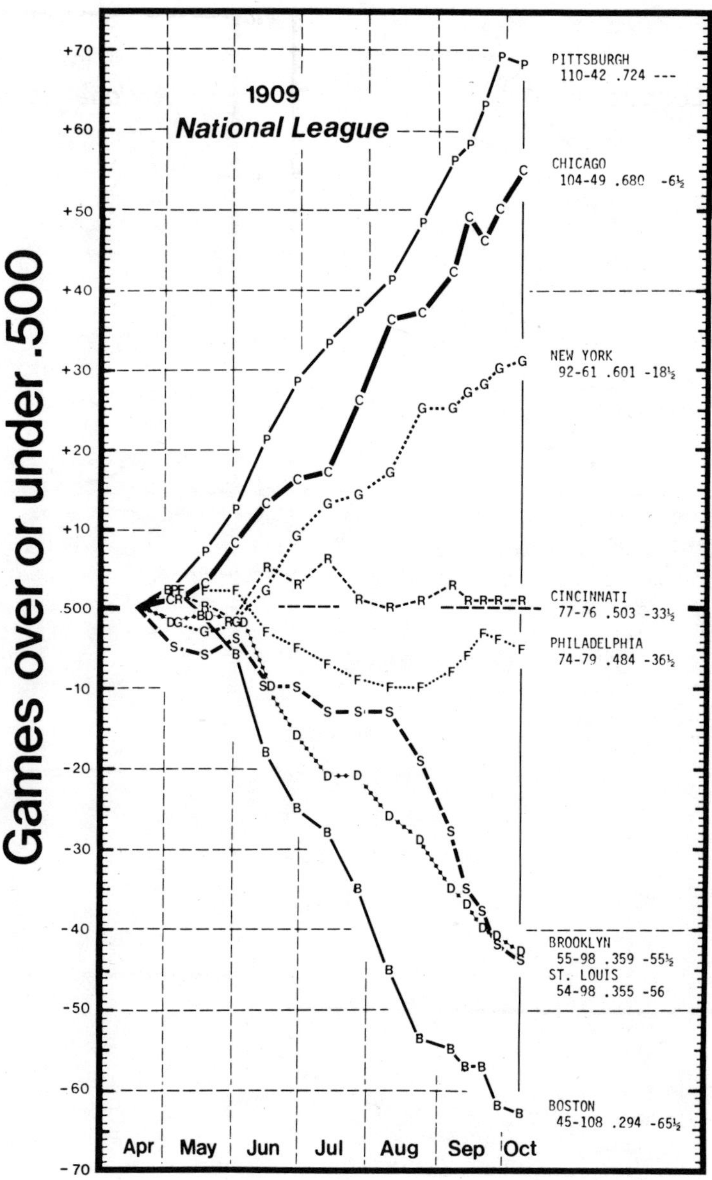


The National League in 1909 stretched out to its second-largest range—a distance of 65½ games between the winning Pirates (68 games over .500) and trailing Braves (63 games below .500). Except for some unspirited contention for sixth place between the Dodgers and Cardinals in September, the eight teams pulled away from each other in a remarkably spaced-out manner. The Cubs had much the same roster as in 1908 and won ever more games—104—but had to settle for second place, 6½ games back of Pittsburgh. The Giants, 18½ behind in third place, won 92 games, with Matty getting his usual 25 victories and several promising youngsters in the lineup.

The blossoming of Howie Camnitz (25-6), Vic Willis's fourth consecutive 22-victory season, and Honus Wagner as usual (.339) were key factors in Pittsburgh's success. Wagner, Fred Clarke, still player-manager at age 36, and Sam Leever, nearing retirement at 37, were the only ones left from the 1901-1903 flag-winning Pirate roster. The Bucs' winning ways of 1909 continued through the World Series, as rookie pitcher Babe Adams, who was 12-3 with a sizzling 1.11 ERA in the regular season, dominated the Tigers in 4-1, 4-0, and 8-0 complete-game victories.

### 1910

With the maturing of Jack Coombs, the Athletics improved what had already been the American League's best pitching in 1909. Their team ERA of 1.92 in '09 had broken the league record of 1.99 set by the 1905 White Sox, and now in 1910 the A's broke their own record with 1.78, the last time a team ERA in either league was under 2.00. Coombs (31-9, 1.30) was joined by Chief Bender (23-5, 1.58), Cy Morgan (18-12, 1.30), and Eddie Plank (16-11, 2.02) in turning in a good year's work. These men had more offensive support than in the previous year also, thanks to Eddie Collins (.322, 81 stolen bases), Rube Olbring (.308), and Danny Murphy (.300).

In the meantime, while Cobb and Speaker slammed the ball aplenty, the Detroit and Boston clubs were too weak in pitching and too lacking in offensive depth to pose much of a threat to the Mackmen. The result was an easy pennant for the Philadelphians, who won by a 14½-game edge. They also created, in collusion with the hapless Browns, a 59-game spread from

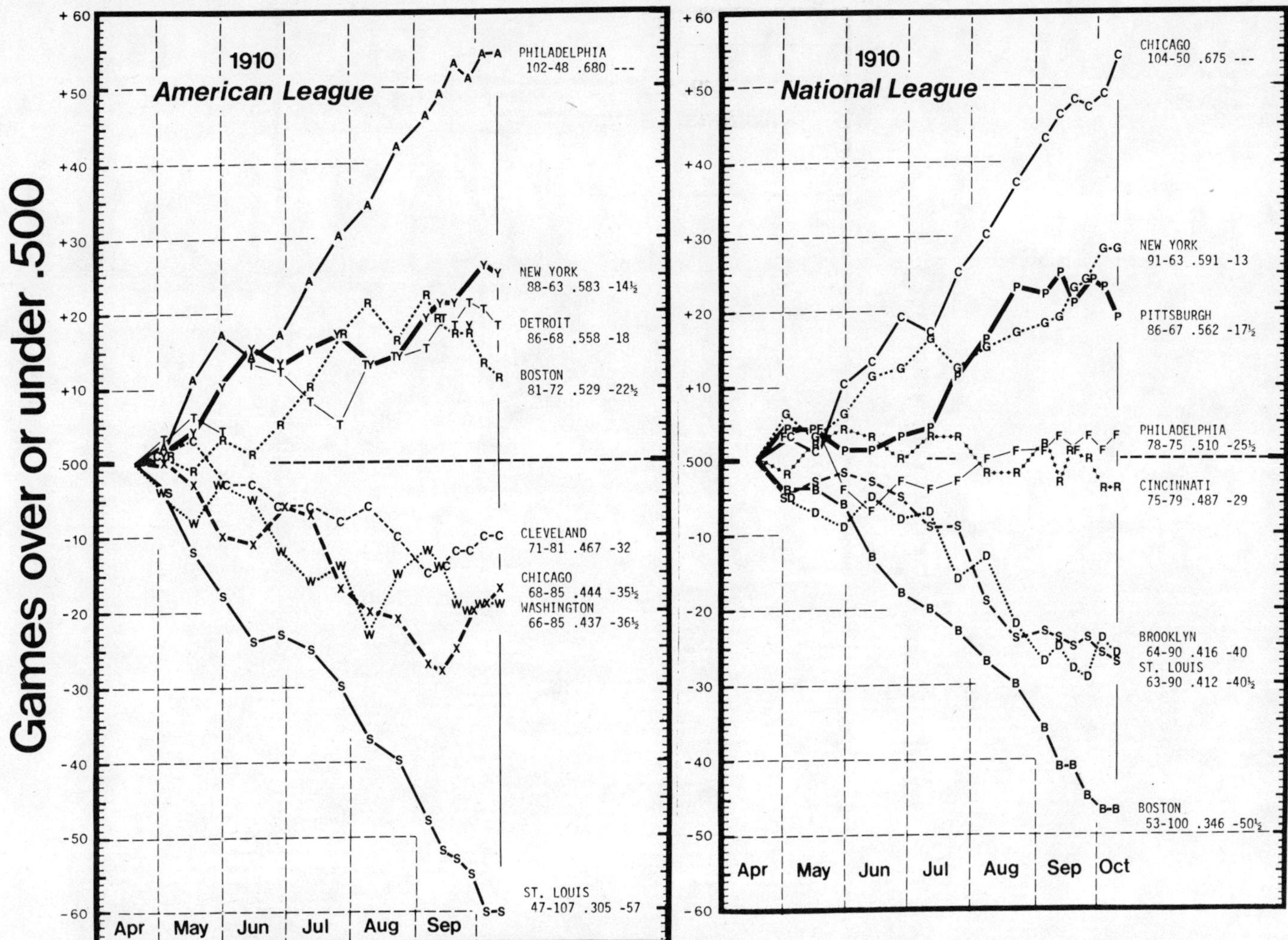


the top to the bottom of the league.

The runnerup at the end was neither Detroit nor Boston but, in a big surprise all season long, New York. The Yankees (now called that as often as Highlanders) got sterling hurling from rookie Russ Ford (26-6, 1.65) and stole many more bases (288) than any other team. Washington began an upward move from the basement with an equally-brilliant display by Walter Johnson (25-17, 1.35, 313 strikeouts). The White Sox became Hitless Losers (their highest BA was Patsy Dougherty's .248), and were so unsupportive of Ed Walsh that he lost 20 games with a league-leading ERA of 1.27. Cleveland got a .383, 227-hit season from Lap Lajoie, beating Cobb's .382 for the batting title (according to new research reported in the April 18, 1981 issue of *The Sporting News*), but the Naps lost the services of sore-armed Addie Joss during the season. The following April, all of baseball suffered a far more tragic loss when Joss died of meningitis two days after his 31st birthday, perhaps nearer the midpoint of his superb career than Lou Gehrig was in the comparable tragedy of the late 1930s. Over his half-career of nine years, Joss's 1.88 ERA is second only to Walsh's 1.82 in major league baseball history.

The Chicago Cubs returned to the top in the 1910 NL competition, of which there was little after July. The Cub roster still had Tinker-to-Evers-to-Chance, Steinfeld, Schulte, Sheckard, Kling, Brown, Reulbach, and Overall from the triple-flag years. Filling gaps handsomely were Solly Hofman (.325) in the outfield, and a dazzling rookie on the mound, King Cole (20-4, 1.80). Despite the usual productivity of Three Finger Brown (25-13) and their league-leading team ERA, Chance's crew was no match for Connie Mack's in the World Series, won in five games by the A's when Coombs pitched three complete-game victories.

The Giants and Pirates were the equals of the Cubs in hitting but far behind in pitching, even with another 27-win season by Mathewson for New York. They fought it out for second place, while the Phillies and Reds battled each other for fourth place. Following their rehearsal of the previous year, Brooklyn and St. Louis staged the closest contest for sixth place in the modern era—they couldn't get untangled from each other all year. The poor Braves didn't contend for any place.

The Wisconsin State Journal

VOL. 124 NO. 9 MADISON, WIS., SATURDAY AFTERNOON, OCTOBER 10, 1914 PRICE TWO CENTS

BRAVES 1, ATHLETICS 0

EXTRA!

JAMES BESTS PLANK IN A GREAT BATTLE OF PITCHERS TODAY

ACQUIT TWO IN RIOT CASE; ONE FOUND GUILTY

PROGRESSIVES IN WISCONSIN ARE FAR FROM DEAD

—GILSON GARDNER

BELGIAN CITY FINALLY FORCED TO HOIST WHITE FLAG; THOUSANDS FLEE

Noted City Badly Damaged by Assault of Germans; Cathedral of Notre Dame Also Injured

KING ALBERT WITHDRAWS TROOPS

HOW TO VOTE FOR U. S. SENATOR IS COURT QUESTION

# 1911-1920

## 1911

The Detroit Tigers were up around 21 games over .500 on Memorial Day of 1911, nearly ten games ahead of the Athletics, but when the latter jelled into an even stronger team than their 1910 world champion edition, there was no stopping them. They caught the Bengals in early August and won by 13½ games.

Batting averages were running about 30 points higher than usual that year because of the introduction of a somewhat livelier ball. Ty Cobb hit .420, Sam Crawford .378, and infielder Jim Delahanty .339 for the Tigers, but with George Mullins ill and a dire shortage of other pitching skill, Detroit could only manage a .500 pace after the Fourth of July. Connie Mack had six .300 hitters and his club batted .296 as a whole, in addition to good seasons on the hill again by Coombs, Plank, Bender, and Morgan. His famed "$100,000 infield" was fully functional for the first time, with Stuffy McInnis (.321) at first, Eddie Collins (.365) at second, Jack Barry (.265) at short, and Frank Baker (.334) at third.

The livelier ball gave the American League a second .400 hitter that year—Joe Jackson, who hit .408 in his first full season with Cleveland. The Red Sox came up with an all-.300 hitting outfield of Harry Hooper, Tris Speaker, and Duffy Lewis which would go on to greater fame. The Yankees got some strong hitting from their first baseman-manager Hal Chase (.315) and outfielders Birdie Cree (.348) and Harry Wolter (.304), as did the Senators from first baseman Germany Schaefer (.324) and outfielder Clyde Milan (.315), and even the White Sox had a pair of .300 batters, third baseman Harry Lord and outfielder Matty McIntyre.

But all of these middling teams had the one-good-pitcher syndrome—Vean Gregg (23-7 and leading 1.81 ERA for Cleveland), Smokey Joe Wood (23-17) for Boston, Russ Ford (22-11 for New York), Walter Johnson (25 wins again for Washington), and Ed Walsh (27-18 for Chicago). Or to put it another way, not enough pitching depth to contend for the title. Things were even worse at St. Louis—the Browns had just one good hitter, second baseman Frank LaPorte (.314) and no pitcher who won more than ten games.

The now-traditional contenders of the National League had a good pennant race going until the middle of August, when the Pirates abruptly faded and the Giants just as abruptly spurted to a final 7½-game lead over the Cubs. John McGraw accomplished this pennant victory with a few holdovers from his '04 and '05 teams (Mathewson, Wiltse, Ames, and Devlin) and some very capable younger men, including catcher Chief Meyers, infielders Larry Doyle, Fred Merkle, and Buck Herzog, outfielders Fred Snodgrass and Red Murray, and 24-game-winning pitching Rube Marquard.

The Philadelphia Phillies unveiled a rookie pitcher named Grover Cleveland Alexander (but usually called Pete), who won 28 games and led his team to a 20-and-6 record in May. With good hitting as well, from Fred Luderus, Hans Lobert, John Titus, Red Dooin, and the 1910 NL batting champ, Sheree Magee, the Phils stayed in the thick of the competition until August. But injuries to the latter three brought them to a #4 finish that was only a game better than the previous year's. The St. Louis Cardinals, under Roger Bresnahan's managership for the third season, were another surprise team in 1911, and had less on paper to account for their temporary improvement than did the Phillies.

In contrast, the Boston Braves suffered through their third straight season of losing 100 or more games, and there was no mystery here even though the Braves had four .300 hitters for all or part of the year. Their most-winning pitcher was Buster Brown with only eight victories, and their best pitcher was probably the 44-year-old Cy Young, who won the last four of his 511 career victories (and absorbed the last five of his 313

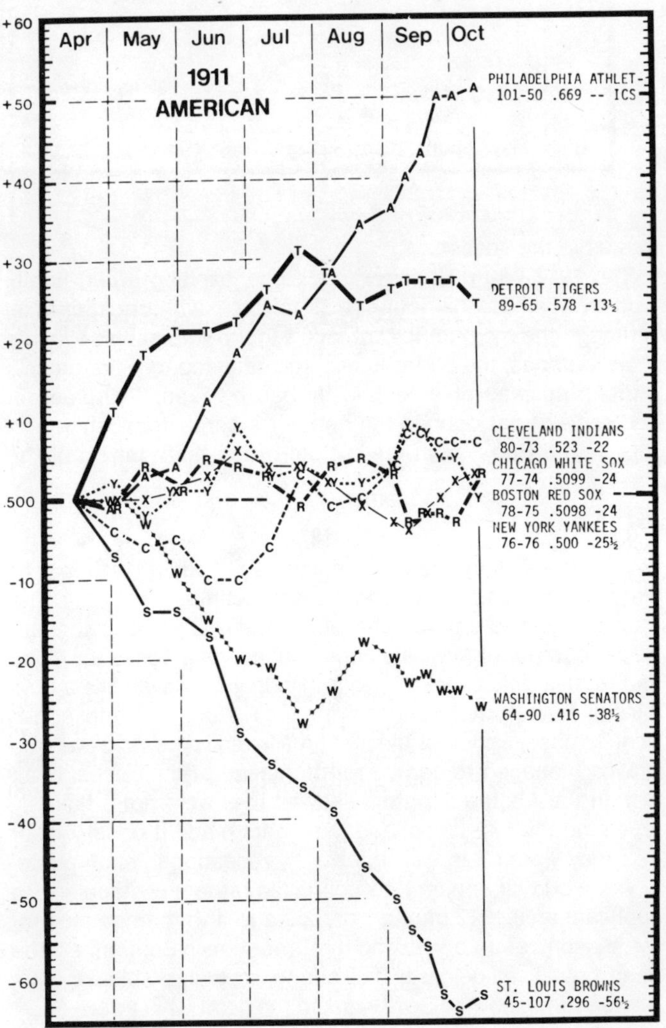


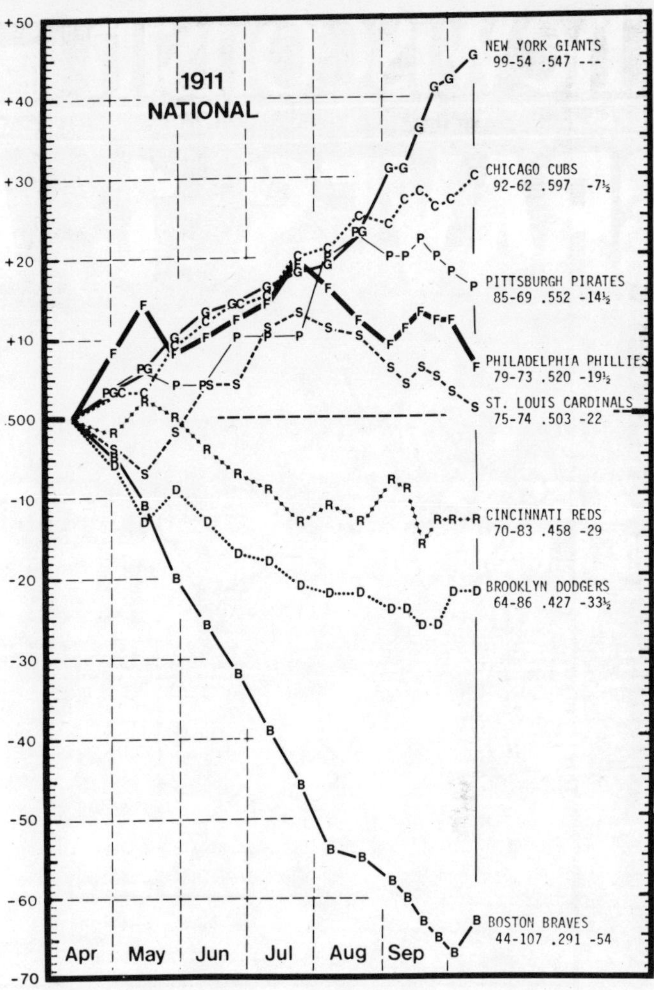


losses) after moving back to the Hub from Cleveland during the year.

In the 1911 World Series, the A's beat the Giants in six games with Bender, Coombs, and Plank doing all the Philadelphia pitching. Frank Baker became forever known as Home Run Baker with game-tieing and game-winning homers in the October classic, following his league-leading 11 clouts in the regular season.

## 1912

With a new ballyard named Fenway Park and a new manager named Jake Stahl, the 1912 Boston Red Sox soared to their third AL pennant. The Bosox won a league-record 105 games, finishing 14 games ahead of the runnerup Senators and 55 games ahead of the New York Yankees. Boston's big hero was Smokey Joe Wood, who won 34 games and lost only five, hurled ten shutouts, and had a 1.91 ERA. Others pitching in were Buck O'Brien, who won 19 games, and Hugh Bedient, whose won-lost record was 20-9, 18-9, or 20-10, depending on which encyclopedia you consult. Strongly supporting the mound staff were Speaker's .383, third baseman Larry Gardner's .315, and Stahl's .301 performances at the plate, and the fielding finesse of the Hooper-Speaker-Lewis combination.

The Senators enjoyed their first finish above sixth place, and it was not just Walter Johnson's doing. He won 32, but they also got 24 wins from Bob Groom and .300 seasons from Clyde Milan (who led the AL in stolen bases with 88 as well) and Chick Gandil. The Tigers continued their decline, mainly due to poor pitching but perhaps hastened by an uproar in May when

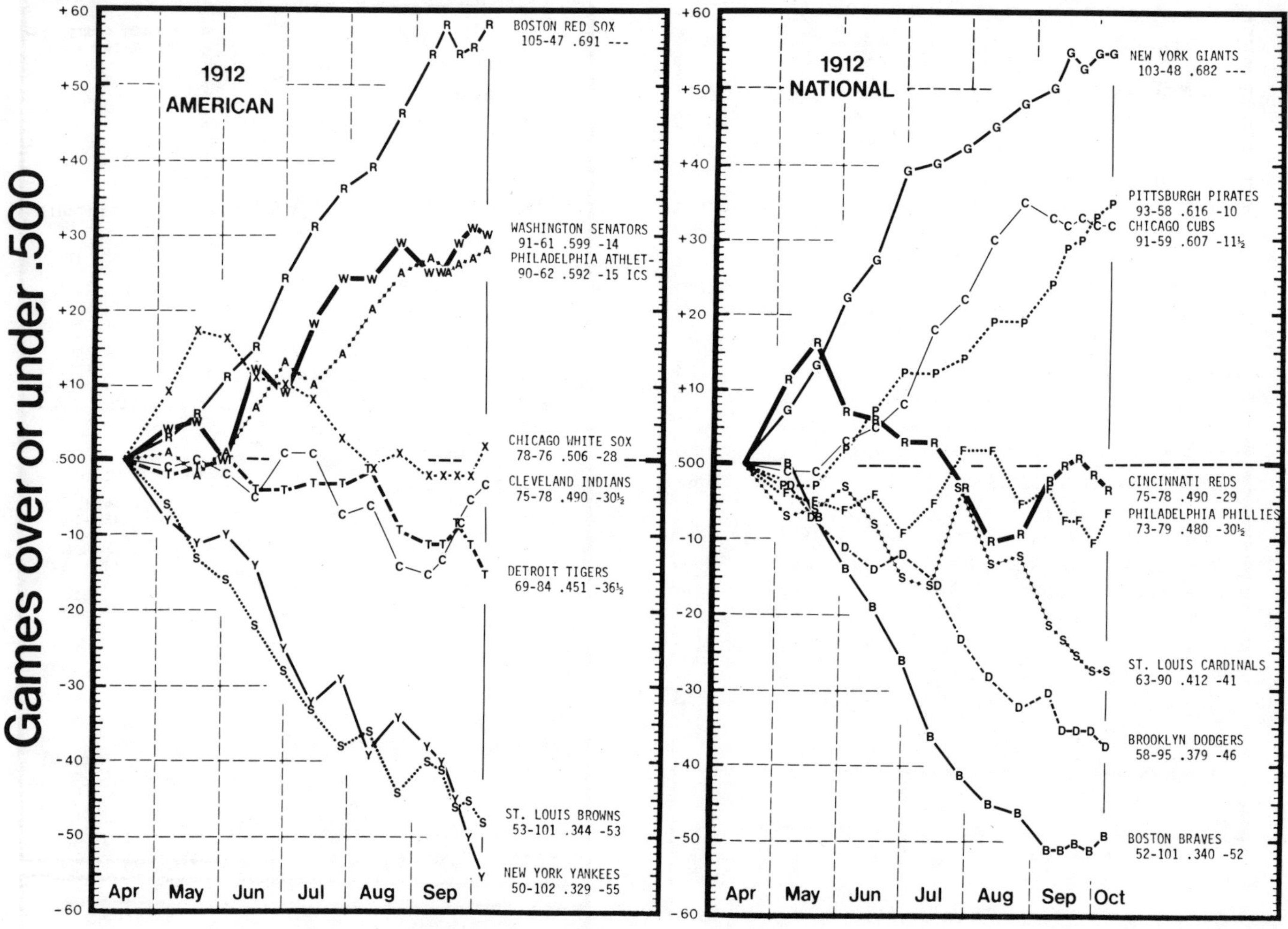


the whole Detroit team went on strike in response to President Ban Johnson's suspension of Ty Cobb for assaulting a heckler in the grandstand.

There may have been some extracurricular factors in the Yankees' descent, too. Several baseball historians have noted a suspicious pattern of fielding errors by Hal Chase, still regular first baseman but no longer manager of the Yanks, against noncontending teams such as the Browns, coupled with an unusual degree of interest paid to such noncrucial games by New York gamblers. With this information, and the knowledge that eight years later Chase was finally brought to justice for moral transgressions along these lines, the curves for the Yankees and Browns in the 1912 graph—which seem at times to be interacting—take on a new and darker meaning. In any event, the Yankees were decimated by injuries to Cree and Wolter and bereft of any strong pitching in 1912.

In the National League, almost nothing new happened. The Giants won again, the Braves lost over a hundred games again, and there was only a slight reordering of the teams in between. McGraw's forces were nearly 40 games over .500 by Independence Day, in part because Rube Marquard won 19 games in a row from April 11th to July 3rd. Only one or two teams in the modern period have gotten off to a better first half, and it's doubtful if any other pitcher ever has. Through May 19, however, the Cincinnati Reds were 22-and-6, starting even faster than the Giants, but they soon fizzled, winning only 53 more games in the season.

The 1912 World Series was a close, exciting affair, finally won by the Red Sox, four games to three, with one tie game. Although the most important factor in the verdict was Wood's three victories, the Series is best remembered for Snodgrass's Muff, a misplay of a routine fly ball by Fred Snodgrass in center field that opened the gate for a come-from-behind victory by the Red Sox in the bottom of the tenth inning of the final game.

### 1913

With the Giants and A's winning easily again, 1913 looked like a replay of 1911, but change was definitely in the air. The Phillies signaled a power shakeup in the NL by occupying first place for most of May and June and finishing above the Cubs and Pirates. The Brooklyn Trolley Dodgers behaved like a first-division team through June, giving the Flatbush Faithful something to cheer about for the first time in ten years. And even the Braves managed to come in fifth instead of their usual dead last. In the AL, the Senators showed they were not a fluke by repeating their #2 finish, and the Tigers made it equally clear that they were no longer a power by repeating in sixth place.

The world champion Red Sox failed rather spectacularly to duplicate their 1912 triumph, dropping to fifth through most of the season before overtaking the Other Sox in September. The Bosox wallowed below .500 all spring, severely displeasing the Boston fans and Red Sox brass, to the point where Jake Stahl

1913
AMERICAN
PHILADELPHIA ATHLETICS
96-57 .627 ---
WASHINGTON SENATORS
90-64 .584 -6½
CLEVELAND INDIANS
86-66 .566 -9½
BOSTON RED SOX
79-71 .527 -15½
CHICAGO WHITE SOX
78-74 .513 -17½
DETROIT TIGERS
66-87 .431 -30
NEW YORK YANKEES
57-94 .377 -38
ST. LOUIS BROWNS
57-96 .373 -39
+50
+40
+30
+20
+10
.500
-10
-20
-30
-40
-50
-60
Apr
May
Jun
Jul
Aug
Sep
Oct

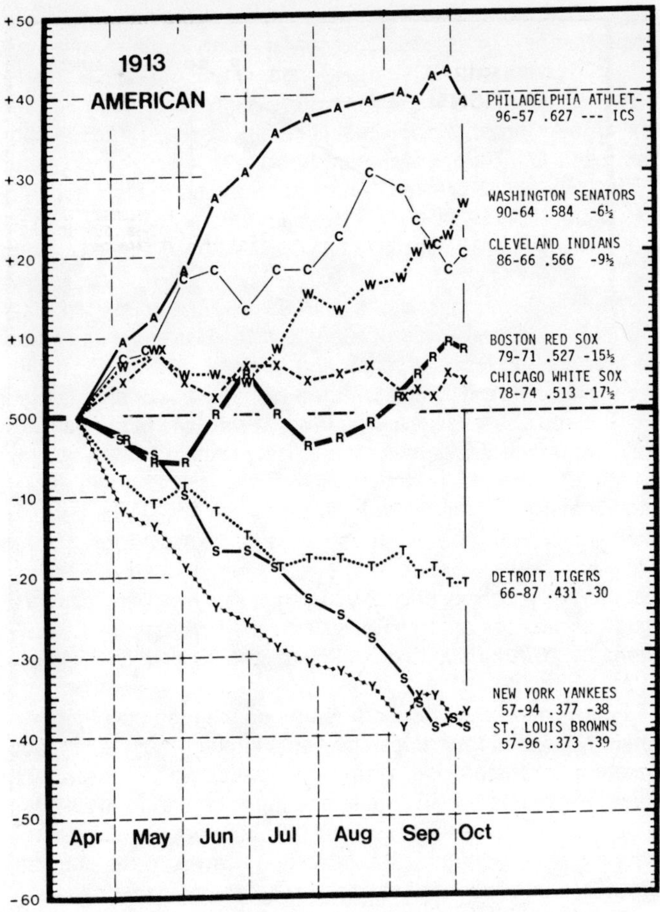

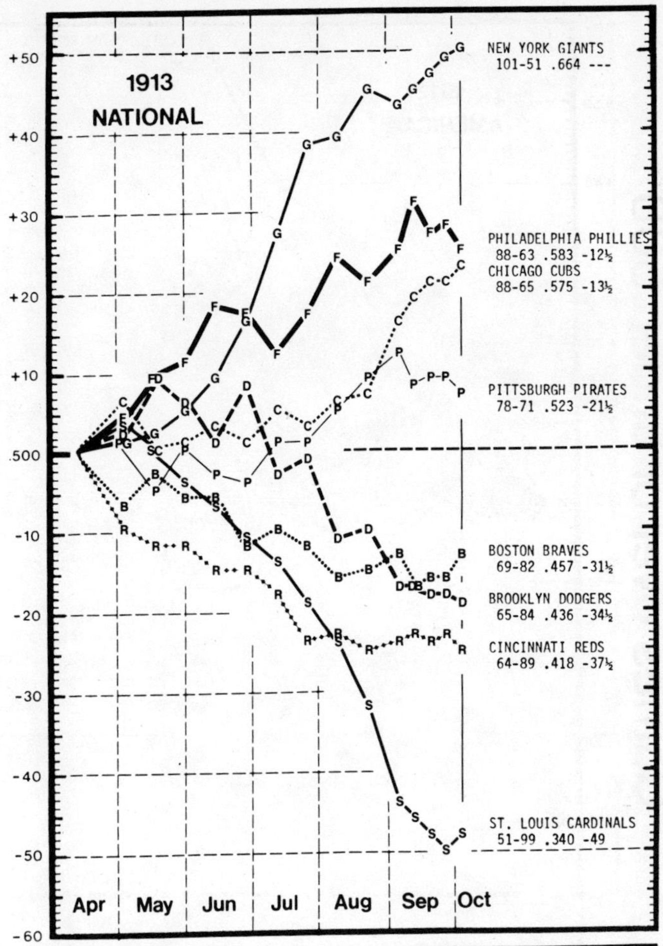

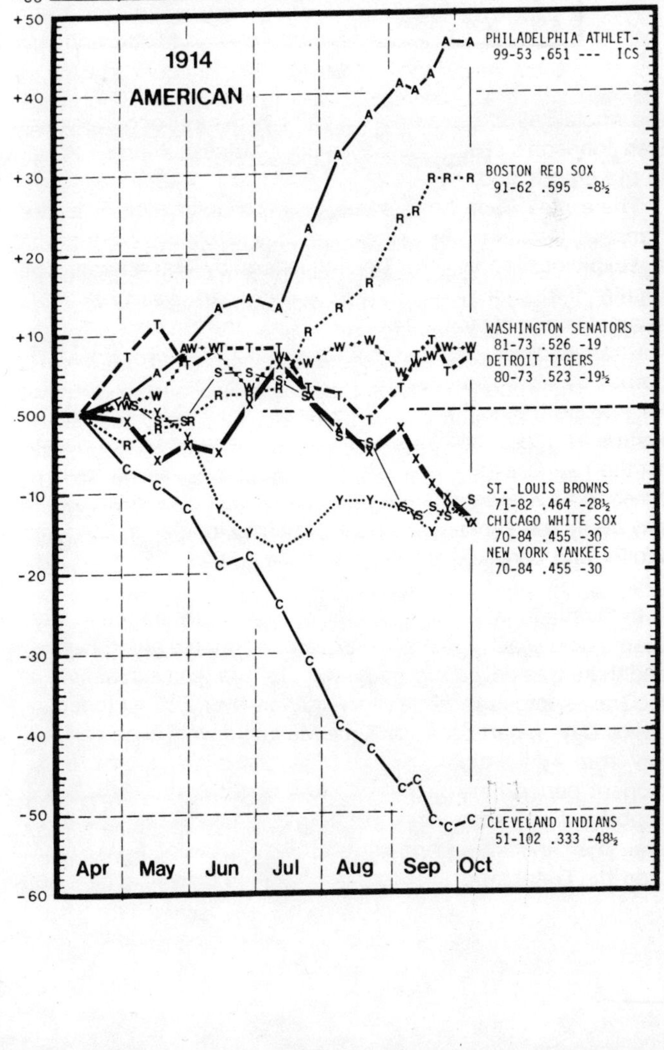

1913
NATIONAL
NEW YORK GIANTS
101-51 .664 ---
PHILADELPHIA PHILLIES
88-63 .583 -12½
CHICAGO CUBS
88-65 .575 -13½
PITTSBURGH PIRATES
78-71 .523 -21½
BOSTON BRAVES
69-82 .457 -31½
BROOKLYN DODGERS
65-84 .436 -34½
CINCINNATI REDS
64-89 .418 -37½
ST. LOUIS CARDINALS
51-99 .340 -49
+50
+40
+30
+20
+10
.500
-10
-20
-30
-40
-50
-60
Apr
May
Jun
Jul
Aug
Sep
Oct

was replaced as manager by 29-year-old catcher Bill Carrigan in July (this would not be the last time a Red Sox manager was fired less than ten months after leading his team to a pennant). They also lost their ace pitcher, Wood, who broke his hand in midseason (also paralleled in more recent years), and except for Speaker's fine output (.365), a team slump in hitting prevailed through the summer.

Cy Falkenburg won 23 games, and Vean Gregg another 20, for Cleveland. With Nap Lajoie still stinging the ball (.335) at age 37 and even more run production from Joe Jackson (.373), the Naps were unexpectedly in second place until the middle of September.

After overtaking the upstart Phillies at the end of June, the Giants breezed to their third straight pennant. This time they had a 22-win contribution by young Jeff Tesreau, who had compiled a 17-7 record as a rookie the year before, and another good-looking freshman, Al Demaree (13-4), to complement the usual skills of Mathewson (25-11) and Marquard (23-10). McGraw's infield looked as strong as Mack's in the other league, and in Chief Meyers he had the best-hitting catcher in the majors by far in those years (.332, .358, and .312 in 1911-13). But when the New York and Philadelphia dynasties clashed in the 1913 World Series, McGraw's mound staff was not the equal of Bender, Plank, and Bullet Joe Bush, and in only five games the Giants lost their third consecutive Series.

The Phillies' Gavvy Cravath was the NL's answer to Home Run Baker (who in turn might be considered the AL's answer to Wildfire Schulte's 21 homers for the Cubs in 1911). Cravath hit 19 home runs in 1913, 10 in 1914, and 24 in 1915. He and

1914
AMERICAN
PHILADELPHIA ATHLETICS
99-53 .651 ---
BOSTON RED SOX
91-62 .595 -8½
WASHINGTON SENATORS
81-73 .526 -19
DETROIT TIGERS
80-73 .523 -19½
ST. LOUIS BROWNS
71-82 .464 -28½
CHICAGO WHITE SOX
70-84 .455 -30
NEW YORK YANKEES
70-84 .455 -30
CLEVELAND INDIANS
51-102 .333 -48½
+50
+40
+30
+20
+10
.500
-10
-20
-30
-40
-50
-60
Apr
May
Jun
Jul
Aug
Sep
Oct

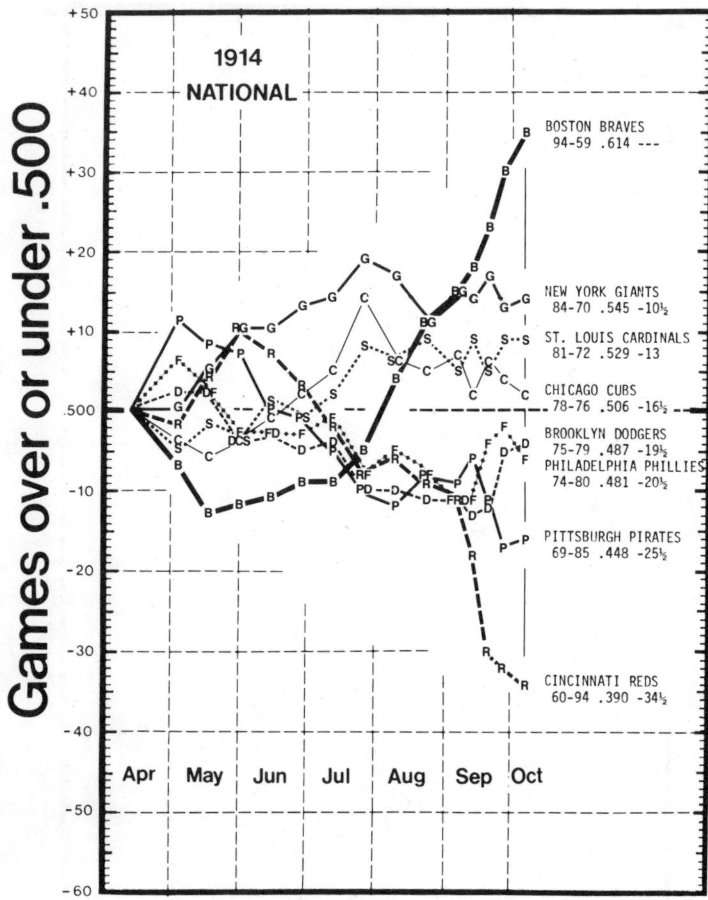


23-year-old Tom Seaton (27-12) were the new ingredients in the Phils' surge to a #2 placing in 1913. With Pete Alexander, a trusty double play combination in Otto Knabe and Mickey Doolan, and the perennial power from Magee, Lobert, and Luderus, 1914 was shaping up an all-Philly World Series year. Except that the Giants were still so strong . . .

### 1914

Well, neither the Giants nor the Phillies won the NL flag in 1914, of course. Who did, and how, became one of baseball's all-time dramatic peaks. And a wonderful piece of Americana that transcended the National Game.

Imagine what was on George Stallings' mind on July 16, 1914, a day when the Boston Braves and Reds were rained out at Cincinnati. Stallings was the man who had steered the 1909-10 Yankees from the AL's bottom rung to second place, and hoped to match that feat now as manager of the Braves. Fifth place in 1913 after their four wretched years as doormats was a good start, but here they were, back in last place again. Pretty discouraging, he must have thought, but then again there was hope—they were only three games behind Brooklyn, only five behind the fourth-place Reds, and for that matter, even the Giants were looking a little soft this year. And his young pitchers were looking better every week—Dick Rudolph was up to 10-9, Bill James 8-6, and Lefty Tyler showing good signs even though he was 6-8. The Braves still might amount to something this year . . .

The next day, James shut out the Reds, and two days later the Braves completed a three-game sweep at Cincinnati. Then they took two more at Pittsburgh, Tyler and Rudolph pitching shutouts, and within five days they had passed Brooklyn, Pittsburgh, Cincinnati, and Philadelphia in the standings. Two more shutouts, by James and Tyler, made fourth place secure, and now the target was St. Louis, six games further head. Home to Boston, and (after a loss by Otto Hess) nine more victories over the Cubs, Cards, and Pirates: Rudolph-James-Tyler, Rudolph-James-Tyler, Rudolph-James-Strand. By now, the baseball world was abuzz, the fans and writers gaped in disbelief, and the daily BRAVES WIN AGAIN headline grew in size—as did other headlines, ENGLAND AND GERMANY AT WAR! (August 4).

When Bill James beat the Reds at Boston on Monday, August 10th, the Braves passed both the Cardinals and Cubs to take second place by a percentage point. After a 0-0 tie with Rudolph going all 13 innings the next day, it was time for the Braves and Giants to meet head-on at the Polo Grounds, with the Giants still 5½ games ahead. The invading Braves quickly slashed that to 2½ on the 13th, 14th, and 15th, Rudolph beating Demaree, James beating Marquard, and Tyler beating Tesreau. That sweep presumably made a believer out of John McGraw, and perhaps even undermined the New Yorkers' belief in themselves, because by the end of another week they had lost nine out of ten games. Their third straight loss at Cincinnati on August 23rd triggered the headline BRAVES, GIANTS TIED!

Two more weeks with both teams on the road saw them exchange the lead four times and come into another face-to-face meeting at Boston tied again, at 67 wins and 52 losses. The newspapers and public had reached the stage of frenzy by this time, and in the great American tradition, people all over the country were rooting for the underdog Braves. In the process, some of these new Braves fans even became baseball fans!

On Monday, September 7th, Rudolph bested Mathewson in the first of two, but the Giants restored the deadlock by shelling Tyler in the nightcap, Tesreau hurling a 4-hitter. Tuesday, James put the Braves into first place for keeps, with Marquard the loser, 8-3. In case there were any doubts left about the eventual outcome, the Beantowners came up with another sensation on Wednesday: while the Dodgers were beating the Giants, a 24-year-old Yankee castoff named George Davis pitched a no-hitter for the Braves over the Phillies.

Thereafter, McGraw's men could do no better than break even, while the Braves continued their upward flight amidst further exclamations of amazement and joy. By the time the two teams had their final meeting at the end of September, the race was over (October 1: BRAVES CLINCH PENNANT!), and the Braves were already resting their frontline pitchers for the World Series. They deserved the rest: in the miraculous rise since July 16, James had won 18 games and lost only one, Rudolph had won 17 and lost only one, and Tyler had won ten while losing six. The three finished the season with 26-7, 27-10, and 16-14 records.

The Athletics, who had easily won the AL pennant for the fourth time in five years, were heavily favored to beat the Braves in the Series. Philadelphia's hitting was still the league's best, they now had Bob Shawkey and Herb Pennock in addition to Bender, Plank, and Bush on their mound staff, and the A's were veterans in World Series play. But they didn't have Rudolph, James, and Tyler, who held the Mackmen to only six runs and 22 hits over four games, or catcher Hank Gowdy, the Series batting hero who hit .545, or that magical force so prized in the sports world, momentum. After the Series finale at Fenway Park (borrowed from the Red Sox for the occasion), the miraculous epilogue, BRAVES SWEEP SERIES!

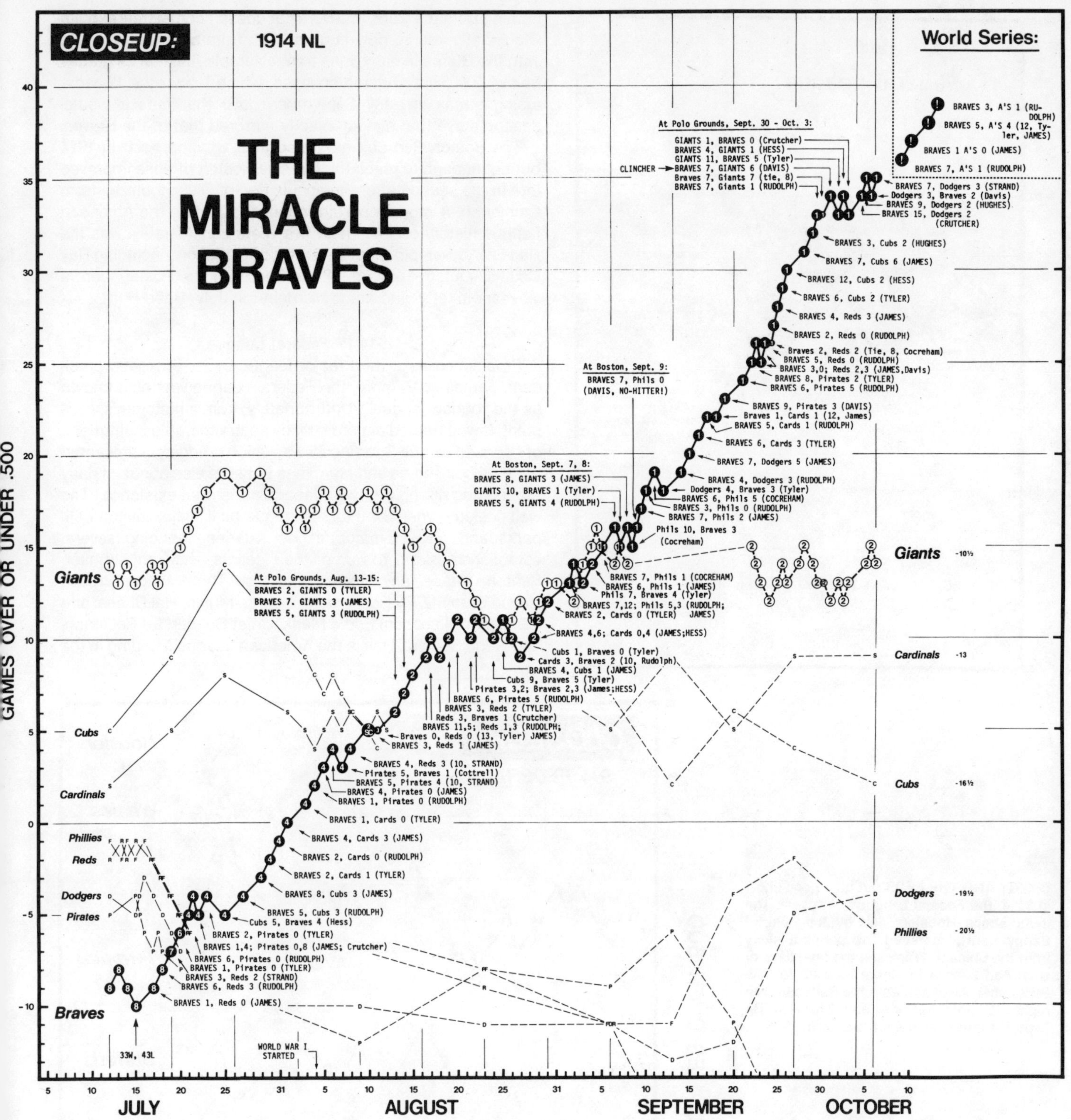


**RUDOLPH AND JAMES—AND TYLER TOO! Those were the young men who pitched the 1914 "Miracle Braves" from last place to first in 37 days, and thereafter, ever onward upward. Not counting the World Series sweep, the Braves won 61 of their 77 games after July 15th, a .792 pace.**

was shouted in four-inch letters around the nation. And the dapper mastermind, Stallings, who had been juggling and platooning his pathwork lineup behind the Triumphant Trio to the very end, was aptly christened The Miracle Man.

The Phillies' progress toward the NL flag was interrupted not only by the Braves' takeover, but also by the new Federal League's raiding of their roster—they lost their 27-game-winner, Seaton, and their keystone combination, Knabe and Doolan. The Reds were also hurt, by the Feds' capture of Joe Tinker, who had hit .317 for them as shortstop-manager after

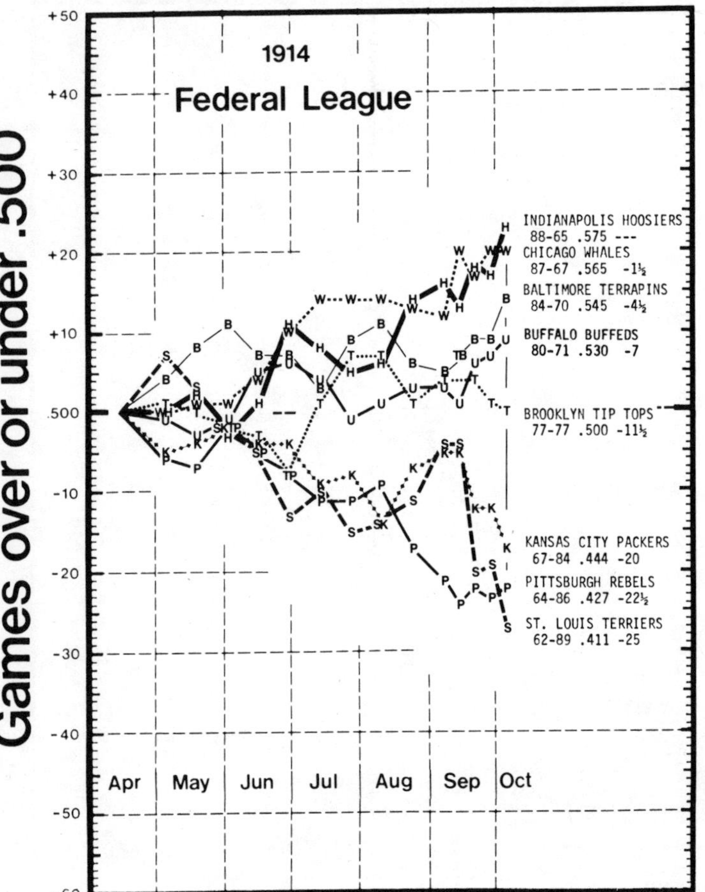


coming from the Cubs in 1913. That doesn't completely explain Cincinnati's record downturn in 1914, from being tied for first with the Giants in early June to a miserable finish at 34 games below .500. This 44-game collapse, which featured a 19-game losing streak in early September, gave the Reds a whole-season curve that almost exactly mirrored that of the Braves.

The Boston Red Sox recovered their winning habit in 1914 but not enough to reach the A's. The Boston offense improved late in the season after the acquisition of Dick Hoblitzell from Cincinnati. A more important change, affecting the American League history over the next five years considerably, was the Red Sox' development of several young pitchers, including Ray Collins, Dutch Leonard, Ernie Shore, Rube Foster, and a 19-year-old lefty who made his debut in July, Babe Ruth.

### 1914-15 Federal League

Proclaimed as a third major league by its energetic president, James A. Gilmore, the Federal League was also known as the "outlaw league." (Unfortunately, from a historian's viewpoint, it was treated accordingly by such venerable institutions of baseball as *The Sporting News,* which grudgingly presented the FL's box scores and standings but little else about its daily functioning during the two seasons of its brief existence.) The well-heeled owners of the new league built major league ballparks and offered major league salaries, inducing several established stars to jump their teams—not only Tinker, Seaton, Knabe, and Doolan, but also Three Finger Brown, Howie Camnitz, Cy Falkenburg, George Mullin, Hal Chase, and (after the '14 season) Eddie Plank, Chief Bender, Ed Reulbach, and Hugh Bedient. Unlike the American League's raiding in the

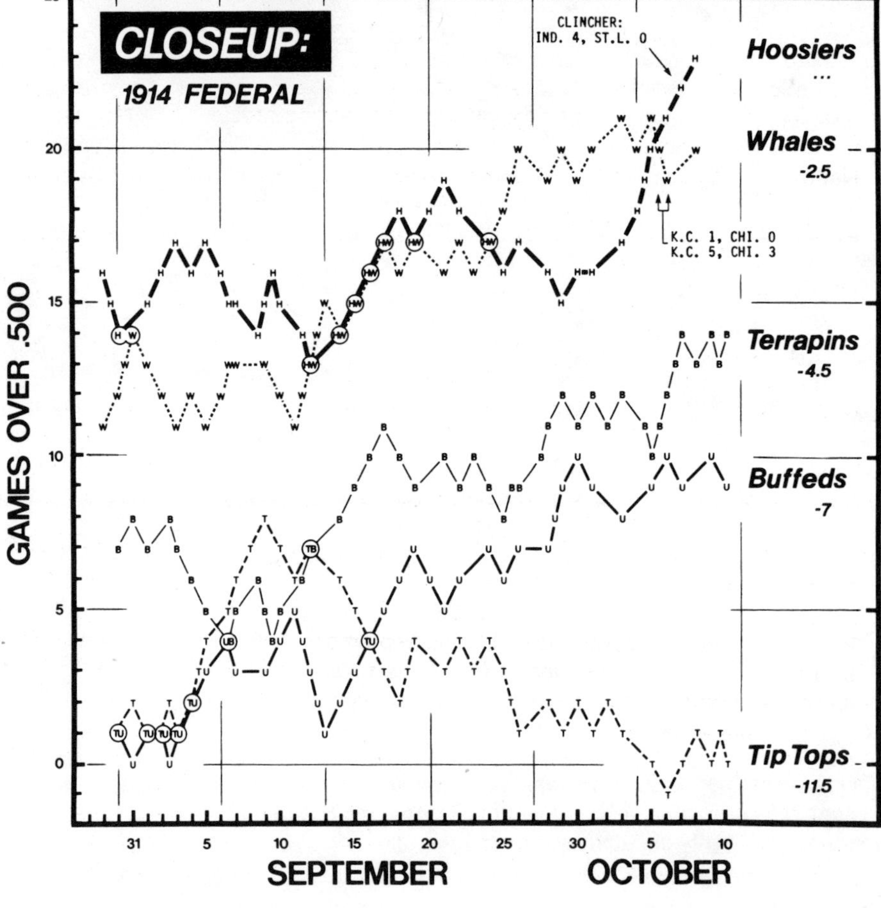


**BENNY AND THE FEDS put on a good show in 1914, the Federal League's first year. The Indianapolis Hoosiers, led by the colorful Benny Kauff, snatched the pennant away from the Chicago Whales in the final days of what had been a five-team race up to mid-September. Also-rans were the Baltimore Terrapins, Buffalo Buffeds, and Brooklyn Tip Tops, the latter being Kauff's team in 1915.**

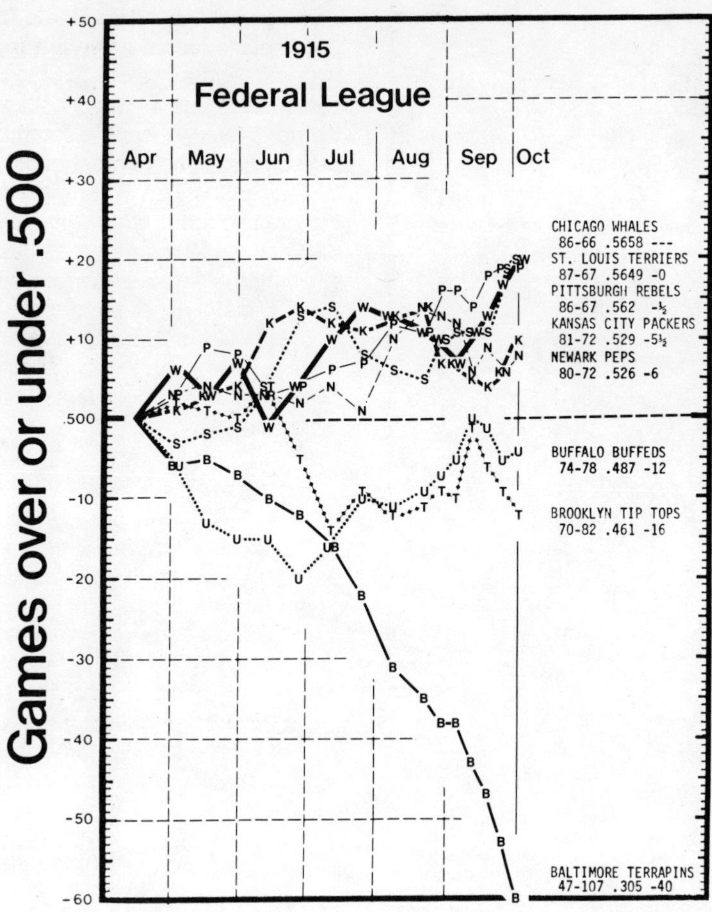


1901-02 baseball war, however, many of these players were well into their declining years, and the filling of the Federal League rosters did not come right after the disbanding of four major league teams, as had been the case when the old National League dropped from twelve to eight clubs in 1900. Gilmore's new league, then, was like a collection of eight expansion teams, on the order of the 1977 Toronto and Seattle clubs, except even closer to what today would be called triple-A level because of the number of minor league players needed to complete the rosters in 1914.

Nevertheless, the Federal League left some thousands of fans limp from suspense and last-minute dramatics in both its 1914 and 1915 pennant races. The '14 race was won by the Indianapolis Hoosiers, by only a 1½-game margin over the Chicago Whales, and not far behind were the Baltimore, Buffalo, and Brooklyn teams. At one stage (September 11-12), all five were within five games of each other, and as late as September 30th, with ten days to go, the top four were within a range of 4½ games.

But the real contest was between the Hoosiers and Whales, who were tied on seven days in mid-September. Matters seemed to be getting resolved in Chicago's favor nearer the end of the month, when the Whales pulled away to a two-game lead. By that time, however, the Hoosiers were unknowingly past their last defeat of the season and into a terminal eight-game winning streak. The Whales still led until Tuesday, October 6th, when they amazed everyone by dropping a doubleheader to the sixth-place Kansas City Packers. That handed the pennant on a silver platter to Indianapolis, who clinched the flag the next day with a shutout over the St. Louis Terriers with only one more game left in the schedule.

The Hoosiers' victory owed much to Cy Falkenburg's 25 wins and strong batwork by Frank LaPorte (.311) and ex-Braves Vin Campbell (.306) and Bill McKechnie (.305). But the shiniest star of the Hoosiers and the whole Federal League was the flamboyant Benny Kauff, who led the league in both batting average (.370) and base-stealing (75) in 1914 and duplicated this stunt (with .342, 55) in 1915. Kauff's only previous major league experience was a brief tryout with the Yankees in 1912; the Brooklyn Tip Tops of the Federal League acquired him in 1915, and he finished his career with a lifetime .311 average after six years with the New York Giants.

The 1915 FL race ended in the closest finish of all time, and was never properly resolved, by the standards of the American and National leagues adopted after the 1908 season. The contenders were the Chicago Whales again, the Pittsburgh Rebels (up from seventh place in 1914), the St. Louis Terriers, the Kansas City Packers, and the Hoosiers again, who between seasons had moved east to become the Newark Peps in a dubious try for the north-Jersey share of the New York metropolitan area customers.

These five teams came into August already in a dogfight, with first the Packers leading, then the Whales, then the Peps, and later still (August 24th), the Rebels. The Pittsburgh club, led by ex-Cardinal and Pirate Ed Konetchy (.310 that year) and a young lefty named Frank Allen (23-13), put a little breathing room between themselves and the other four in early Septem-

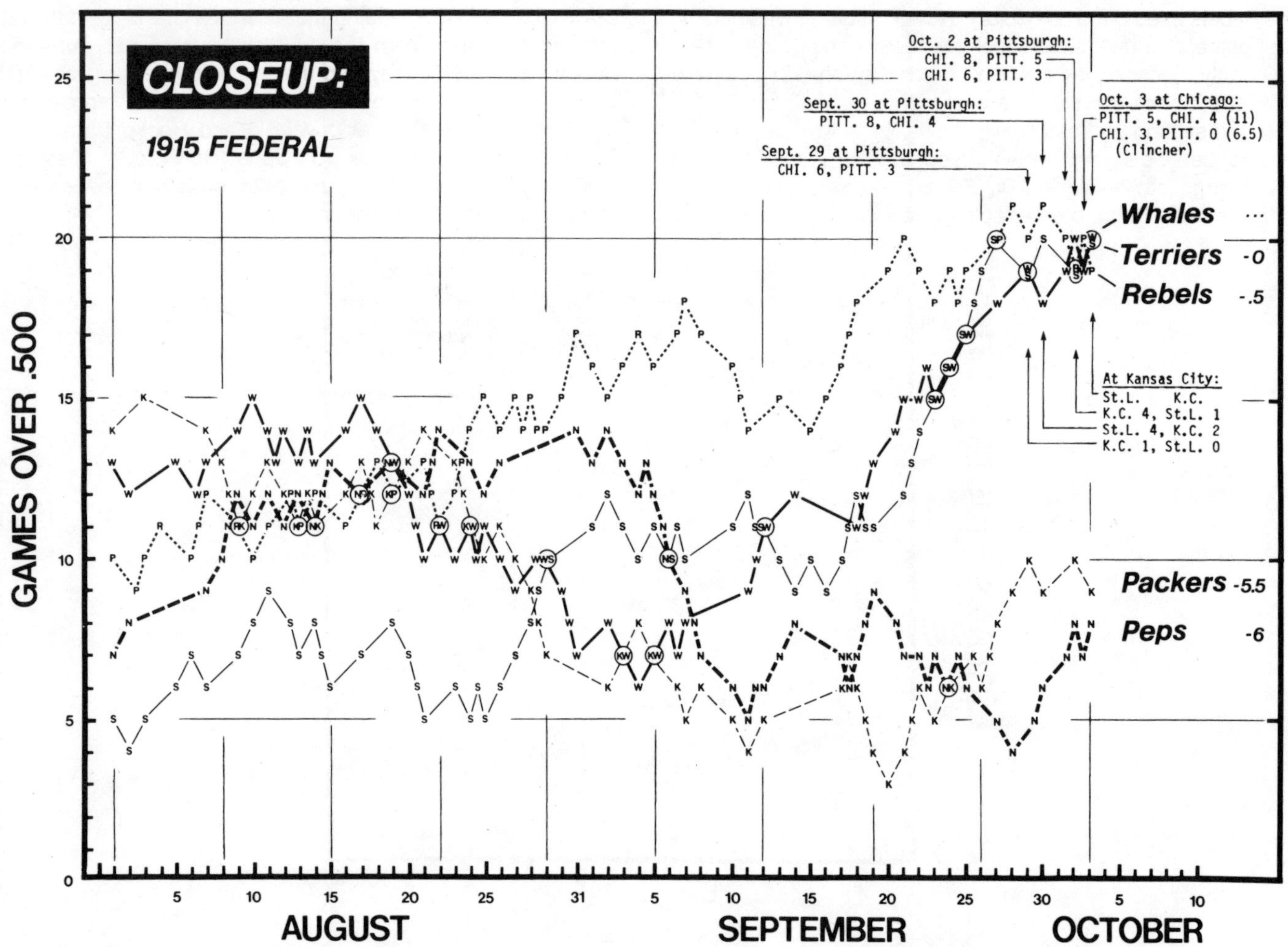


**TWILIGHT ZONE. There wasn't much daylight left in Chicago when the wierd 1915 Federal League race was decided (?) by a 6½-inning game on October 3rd. A 20-game loser named Bill Bailey pitched seven shutout innings for the Chicago Whales against the Pittsburgh Rebels, giving the Whales the pennant. The St. Louis Terriers finished second even though they won one more game than the Whales (and Rebels).**

ber, but by the middle of the month the five clubs were still in a 4½-game range. To many, Chicago still looked like the team to beat, because the Whales had a new mound ace, George McConnell (25-10), and an old one, Three Finger Brown (17-8), in addition to holdover stars from 1914, outfielders Max Flack and Dutch Zwilling and 29-game-winner Claude Hendrix.

Graphically, the race assumed the shape of a Chinatown-parade dragon the next week, when the Whales, Terriers, and Rebels pulled away from the Packers and Peps. Hottest were the Terriers, paced by 23-year-old Dave Davenport (22-18), 39-year-old Eddie Plank (21-11), ex-Giant Doc Crandall (21-15), and ex-Miracle Brave Charlie Deal (.323). Winning nine in a row, St. Louis passed the Whales and joined the Rebels at 20 games over .500 on September 27th.

Only a few degrees cooler, the Whales won nine out of ten, so on Wednesday of the final week, when St. Louis's streak was snapped by the Packers, a mere half-game separated the Whales and Terriers from the still-leading Rebels. The spread was widened to 1½ games by Pittsburgh's defeat of Chicago on Thursday while the Terriers were beating Kansas City. After everyone was rained out on Friday, the Whales stunned the Rebels on Saturday by beating them twice at Pittsburgh, Brown and young Mike Prendergast pitching the clutch victories. That put Chicago into the lead for the first time since August 19th.

The Terriers lost their Saturday game at Kansas City, not only muffing the chance to take the lead and clinch the pennant on Sunday, but finding to their horror that they were mathematically eliminated from the race! This oddity—no chance to win with one game left to play and (like Pittsburgh) trailing by a half-game—came from the fact that the Whales and Rebels had two games left against each other and both would be finishing the season with fewer than the full 154 games played, whereas the Terriers' single game on the final Sunday would be their 154th. If either of their rivals swept their final-day doubleheader and the Terriers won their game, they would still finish a half-game behind (Pittsburgh) or a full game behind (Chicago). If the Rebels and Whales split the doubleheader, St. Louis would still lose the pennant to Chicago by about .001 (.5658 to .5649) because of playing two more games than the Whales.

The deciding twin bill between the two survivors took place that Sunday at Chicago's new northside park that later became the Cubs' Wrigley Field. To win the pennant, the Rebels had to win both, the Whales only to split. The first game was a drawn-out affair, not resolved until the 11th inning, when the Rebels eked out a 5-4 victory. Now Pittsburgh was back in first place, and things were looking dark for the Chicago fans—literally, because there wasn't much daylight left (and that park didn't have lights *before* it was Wrigley Field, either).

In the second contest, chronologically the last game in the Federal League's history, the Whales failed to score in the first 5½ innings, but 26-year-old Bill Bailey, who had lost 19 games with the futile Baltimore Terrapins that season before coming to the Whales the previous month, was holding the Rebels in check. Finally, the Whales drove three runs across in the bottom of the sixth, and with just a few minutes of twilight left, the umpires gave the Rebels one more half-inning to alter the 3-0 score against them. Bailey set them down again, and the pennant was Chicago's.

The Rebels dropped to a third-place finish, a half-game and .004 behind the Whales, because St. Louis won its final game, putting the Terriers in a tie with the Whales at 20 games over .500 but losing the pennant by .0009 even though they had won one more game than Chicago. It's doubtful that they were consoled by their #2 finish—if anything, they had more of a right to yell "we wuz robbed" than Cleveland did in 1908. There was no hope of getting Chicago to play its rained-out games, especially as the Federal League was in a hurry to disband and make peace with the other leagues. With the war on the other side of the Atlantic growing in size and intensity, the FL venture had proved to be a case of bad timing, along with other difficulties or mistakes (such as moving east to Newark and Brooklyn instead of south and west); had "Gilmore's Glory" been attempted, say, ten years later, the Federal League would probably still be the third major league today, especially if it had begun with pennant races as exciting as those in the FL's 1914 and 1915 seasons.

### 1915 AL and NL

Back in the "real" major leagues, the 1915 season saw the Phillies win their first modern-era pennant in the National League and the Red Sox their fourth in the American League. But what happened at the bottom of the standings in each league was more remarkable.

Connie Mack had to break up his Athletics. Already plagued by financial problems, he found that he could not meet the higher salary demands created by the Federal League's competition for star players. Gambling on his untested youngsters, he sold, traded, or released his veterans after losing Bender and Plank to the Feds, and the list of ex-A's grew to include Eddie Collins, Eddie Murphy, Jack Coombs, Frank Baker (who was a holdout all year and became a Yankee in 1916), Bob Shawkey, Herb Pennock, and Jack Barry. The result: a calamitous plunge from a first-place 46 games over .500 in 1914 to a last-place 66 games below .500 in 1915. This is by far the largest season-to-season drop on the scale (or in won-lost percentage), and still the only first-to-last-place drop, of the century.

Boston and Detroit rushed into the vacuum at the top, overtaking the Chicago White Sox just after midseason. Bill Carrigan's 1915 club bore little resemblance to the Red Sox of recent decades, batting only .260 as a team with mostly left-handers in the lineup; Tris Speaker was the only .300 hitter. They won 101 games with five good pitchers, headed by Rube Foster (20-8, 2.12), Ernie Shore (19-8, 1.64), and still-rookie Babe Ruth (18-6).

The revived Tigers still had their one-two punch, Cobb and Crawford, the former leading the AL with a .369 BA and the latter with 112 RBIs. With the addition of freshman outfielder Bobby Veach (.313), they had the league's strongest offense, and for a change they came up with pitching, well represented by 23-game-winners Harry Coveleski and Hooks Dauss. The Tigers chased the Red Sox from June 1 to October 1, seldom trailing by more than three games, but finished as the league's first 100-game-winning losers.

The White Sox were building a winning combination with hitting as well as pitching. They not only got Collins and Murphy in their prime years from the Athletics, but Joe Jackson and Nemo Leibold from the Cleveland Indians as well, and developed two young pitchers, Red Faber and Jim Scott, into 24-game-winners.

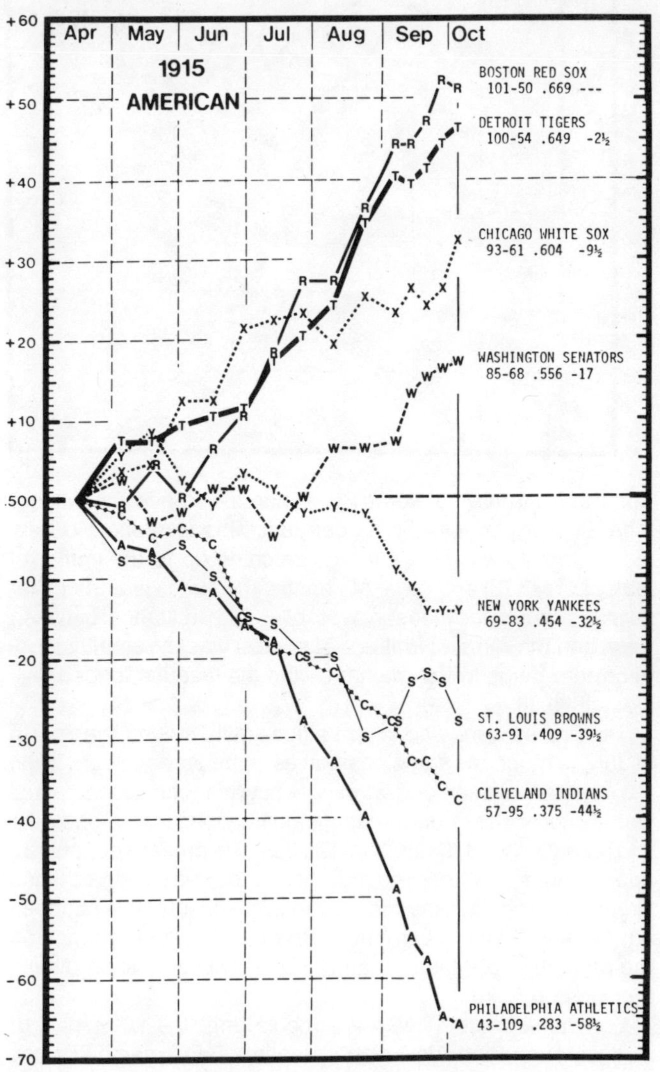


In the National League, it was if the grand sweep of the Miracle Braves had leveled the rest of the league like a tornado. With the additional damage done by the Federal League raids, the 1915 NL teams seemed headed for an eight-way tie at midseason—at one point in July the top and bottom clubs were separated by only nine games.

The power structure was so altered that the once-mighty Giants were in last place nearly all spring, and in the last six weeks of the season, five teams—including the ex-champion

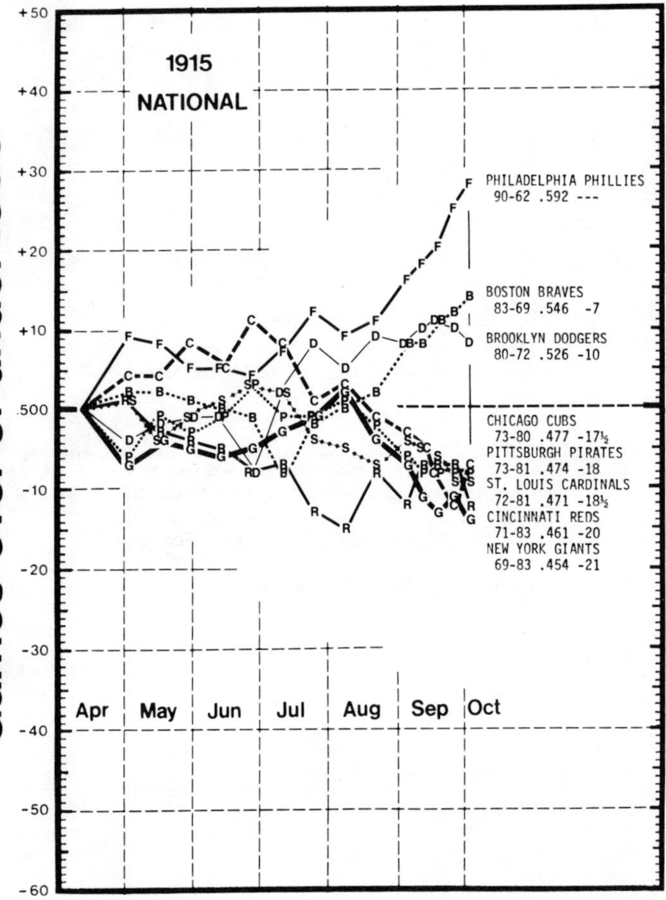


Cubs and Pirates as well as the Giants—staged the wildest race for last place in the modern era. This was one McGraw didn't want to win, but with age catching up to the immortal Matty (8-14, 3.73) and other old hands, the Jints were the cellar dwellers when the season was over. The distance between them and the winning Phillies, 21 games, was the smallest top-to-bottom range in the majors before the leagues formed divisions in 1969.

The Braves were also in last place again, around the Fourth of July, in much the same position as in the previous July. Then they started winning and winning—but this time second place was the best they could manage, mainly because a shoulder injury sadly ended the brilliant Bill James's career after only 13 appearances on the mound. The Brooklyn Dodgers also slumped to the bottom rung near midseason, but then snapped out of their 12-year hibernation, amazing everyone by reaching the runnerup spot faster than the Braves. Events soon proved this was no fluke.

For the winners, it was a struggle until the latter part of August. Then Pete Alexander's Ragtime Band marched away from the rest of the parade. Backed by Gavvy Cravath's record 24 homers, a new defensive gem at shortstop named Dave (but called "Beauty") Bancroft, and Fred Luderus's .315 pace at the plate, Alexander compiled the glittering figures of 31 wins, 12 shutouts, and a 1.22 ERA for the season. In further support of the victorious cause, righthander Erskine Mayer repeated his 21-win contribution of the previous year.

Alexander beat Shore in the opening game of the World Series, but the Red Sox swept the next three games with consecutive 2-1 victories by Foster, Leonard, and Shore. Boston made it four straight the next day in a 5-4 win by Foster, with two homers by Hooper and one by Speaker. Babe Ruth, never used on the mound by the Red Sox, sat on the bench watching baseball's greatest home run hitter, Cravath, as he was held to a double and single over the five games.

## 1916

Few major league seasons have been as bizarre as the 1916 one. In the American League, the bottom—meaning the Athletics—dropped out. The A's fell into last place early, and by mid-July had lost three times as many games as they had won. Then they had a 20-game losing streak, which left them at 19 wins and 80 losses (.192) in early August, and by season's end Mack's bludgeoned crew was 40 games behind seventh place. This distance between last and next-to-last teams gave the A's the all-time major league record for "furthest behind all other teams," approached only by the 35-game gap between the trailing Cleveland (20-132, .130) and Washington clubs in the 1899 NL season.

About the same time as Philadelphia's 20-game downer, the St. Louis Browns had a 14-game upward streak. That produced an anomaly in which seven AL teams were above .500, and with all seven picking on the A's mercilessly, they stayed in approximately that position for the rest of the season.

The Washington Senators also had a streak, 16 straight road victories in May, which put them in first place temporarily, but they quickly faded, and then the Yankees got hot. In July the Yanks seemed to be on the way toward their first pennant, but they too collapsed in a losing streak. Finally, a replay of 1915 developed in which Boston again outplayed Detroit and Chicago. This time, however, it was a more exciting fracas.

The three teams were in a virtual tie in the middle of September, with the Tigers and White Sox having home stands and the Red Sox on the road. Babe Ruth led the latter, compiling the best pitching record in the league that year with 23-12 and 1.75-ERA marks. Boston invaded Chicago on September 16th,

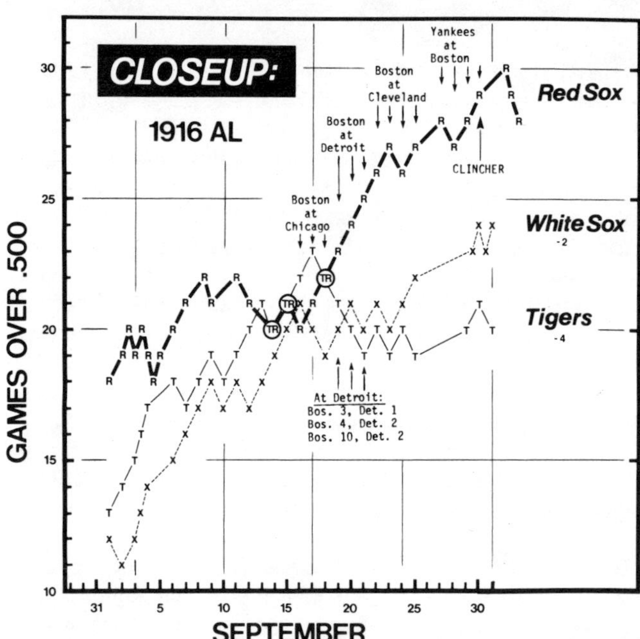


**CARRIGAN'S ROAD SHOW. With the American League's best pitcher of 1916, Babe Ruth, leading their mound staff, the Boston Red Sox invaded the west in a virtual three-way tie with the White Sox and Tigers. Manager Bill Carrigan's club won seven in a row at Chicago, Detroit, and Cleveland, and came back to Fenway with the pennant all but clinched.**

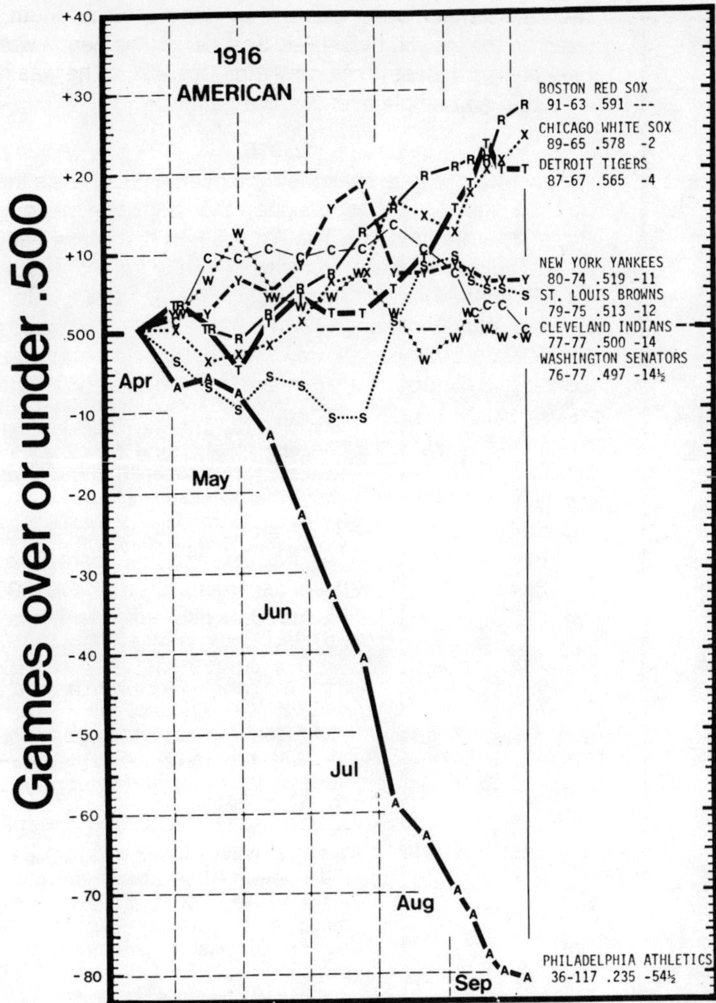


**THE WORST SEASON a 20th-century major league team has had was this disaster suffered by the Athletics in 1916. The Mackmen's terrible plunge to record lows of .235 and 81 games below .500 included a 20-game losing streak starting in July. All of the other AL teams feasted on the A's like vultures, producing a freak situation in which all seven had winning records on several days in August and September. (For an interesting comparison, see the 1969 NL West and 1979 AL East graphs.)**

and after being dumped to third place by a loss in the opener, took the remaining two games of the set; that put the Red Sox back into a tie with the Tigers as they traveled to Detroit. There, on September 19-21, they swept three games from the Bengals, sending them to third place for good, and followed this by taking three out of four at Cleveland. That put Boston too far ahead for Chicago to catch, and they clinched the pennant back at Fenway against the Yankees on the 30th. The Red Sox ended the season on October 3rd in Boston by losing a doubleheader to—of all teams—the Athletics.

After 13 years of domination by the Giants, Cubs, and Pirates through 1913, the National League was in a different pattern, getting a new winner every year. In 1916 it was the Brooklyn Dodgers, now more often called the Robins, because of their popular manager Wilbert Robinson. Brooklyn had a collection of able pitchers headed by Jeff Pfeffer (25-11, 2.12) and including Rube Marquard and Jack Coombs. They had also rather quickly developed into the league best-hitting team with stars Jake Daubert (.316) and Zack Wheat (.312).

The Robins' victory was not an easy one, as the Phillies remained strong with Pete Alexander (33-12) and the developing Eppa Rixey (22-10), and the Braves still had Dick Rudolph, Lefty Tyler, and a fair replacement for James in Tom Hughes (16-3, 2.35). Brooklyn led the league nearly all season, but (as only the closeup graph shows) the three fell into a tie at 23 games over

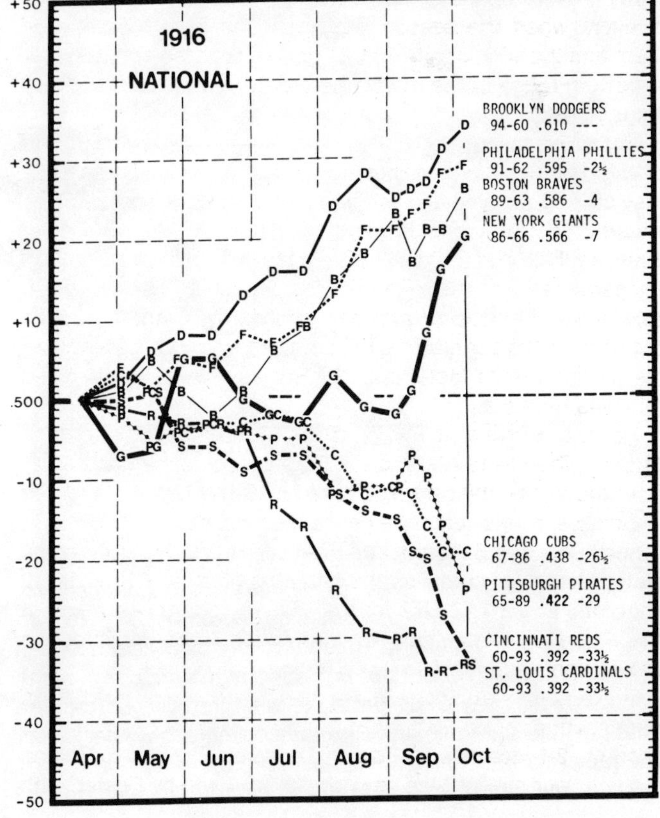

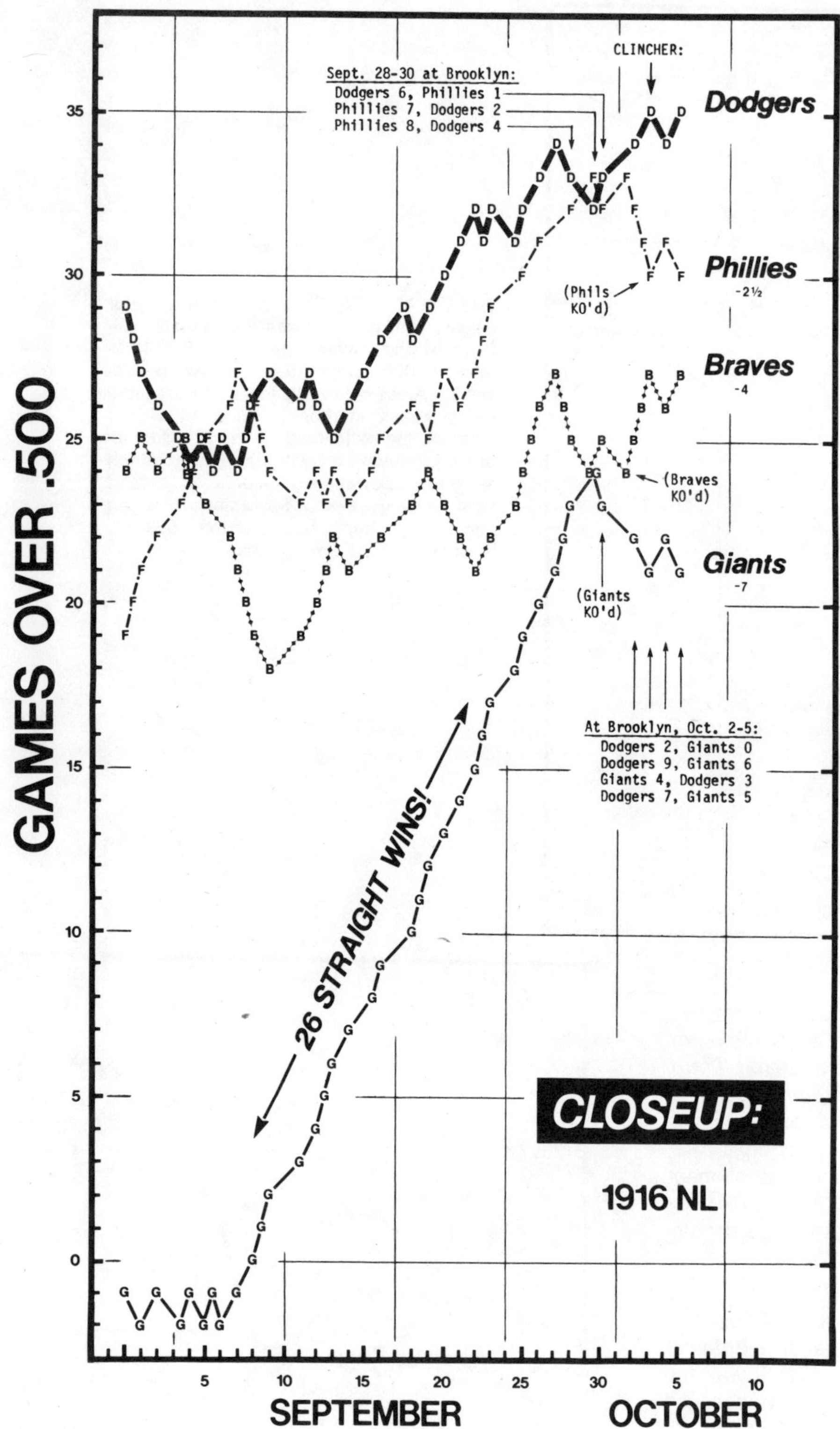


**TWENTY-SIX GIANT STEPS only brought John McGraw's club from fourth place to fourth place, but the Giants did join the Dodgers, Phillies, and Braves in the close 1916 NL pennant race. It is fun to speculate about the possible outcomes if the Giants had won 31 straight (after all, what's five more when you're already up to 26?). That would have produced a tie between the Giants and Dodgers at 28 games over .500, because it would have meant the Dodgers had lost their final last four games—to the Giants. Most likely, it would also have given the pennant to the Phils (who actually finished at 29 games over .500), except that "1908 rule" would have demanded that the Giants make up their two rainouts, and the Phils their one, making it possible for the Giants, Phils, or Dodgers to win, tie, or lose the pennant. And if the Braves had won just one game in their last six against the Phils, even after losing on the Giants' 27th straight instead of breaking their streak, they could have joined in a four-way tie for the pennant, and so forth, and so on. . .**

.500 (Braves ahead by .002) when the Phillies swept the Robins in a Labor Day doubleheader. The Phils even took the lead for two days later that week and again on September 30th, for two hours, after a first-game win in another doubleheader between the two at Brooklyn. But the Robins took the important nightcap game that day, and went on to win three of four from the Giants while the Phils and Braves knocked each other out of the race in a final six-game series at Philly.

Until their actual clinching of the flag on October 3rd, the Robins had most of the headlines in September grabbed away from them by the Giants, who turned out to be the most amazing fourth-place team in baseball history. The Giants had won the bidding for Benny Kauff in the disbanding of the Federal League, but were developing soft spots elsewhere in their lineup. The New Yorkers began the season miserably, losing 13 of their first 15 games, but then won 17 in a row on the road. That streak was followed by another slump, so extended that John McGraw had to revamp his roster, bringing in third baseman Heinie Zimmerman from the Cubs, player-manager Buck Herzog from the Reds, and pitcher Slim Sallee from the Cards while sending away Fred Merkle, Larry Doyle, Bill McKechnie, Edd Roush, and Christy Mathewson (the latter became the Reds' manager).

The new combination jelled, and beginning on September 7th the Giants won 26 straight games, establishing the modern record for consecutive wins by a team. Except for four games at Philadelphia early in the string, the victories were at the Polo Grounds. It was primarily a pitching streak—only three times did the Giant pitchers (Sallee, Tesreau, Pol Perritt, Ferdie Schupp, and Rube Benton) allow more than two runs, and ten of the 26 wins were shutouts. Since they were 13½ games behind when the streak began, the Giants had little hope of winning the pennant, but mathematically it was not completely hopeless (see closeup). Near the end of the string, McGraw proclaimed his new lineup as the best he had ever had.

The Robins became the latest victim of the Red Sox in the World Series, four games to two. This time, Ruth got to pitch—for 14 innings all in one game, which he won, 2-1, over Brooklyn's Sherry Smith. Shore and Leonard took care of the other games for Boston.

## 1917

Unlike the Red Sox, who had even sold Tris Speaker to Cleveland before the 1916 season, the White Sox were steadily gaining in offensive strength—they weren't interested in becoming Hitless Wonders again. After getting Collins, Murphy, Jackson, and Leibold, they added some other solid players who became valuable regulars in the batting order, including Chick Gandil, Happy Felsch, Swede Risberg, and Buck Weaver. And by 1917, Lefty Williams had developed into a sturdy moundsman along with Eddie Cicotte, the latter a late bloomer who had had many mediocre years after his first full season with the Red Sox in 1908.

This array of talent was more than enough to overtake the Red Sox, who stuck with their '16 lineup virtually intact and won only one less game than in the previous year. The Battle of the Soxes was close from mid-May to late August, after which Chicago leaped to a nine-game edge.

The Indians looked like near-future champions in the latter part of the season. Jim Bagby and Harry Coveleski's younger brother, Stan, were maturing into top-flight pitchers, and Tris Speaker's usual .350-level batting was accompanied by Ray Chapman's .302 and Joe Harris's .304 outputs.

Nobody was surprised by the Giants' return to the top in the National League after their astonishing feat of the previous September, but the collapse of the Robins to seventh place was totally unanticipated. Brooklyn's pitching was far below its sharpness of 1916, and an off-year by Jake Daubert featured an overall dropoff in their hitting as well.

The St. Louis Cardinals jumped from a last-place tie to a very respectable third place in 1917, their first good season of the century. Since the Cards' pitching was still weak, the upswing largely reflected the rapid development of 21-year-old Rogers Hornsby, who hit .327 in his second full year.

The Giants had breezed to their sixth pennant, carried offensively by the strong outfield of Benny Kauff, George Burns, and Dave Robertson and defensively by a stingy group of hurlers led by Ferdie Schupp (21-7). So it was a rude collision for them when they lost to the White Sox, four games to two, in the 1917 World Series.

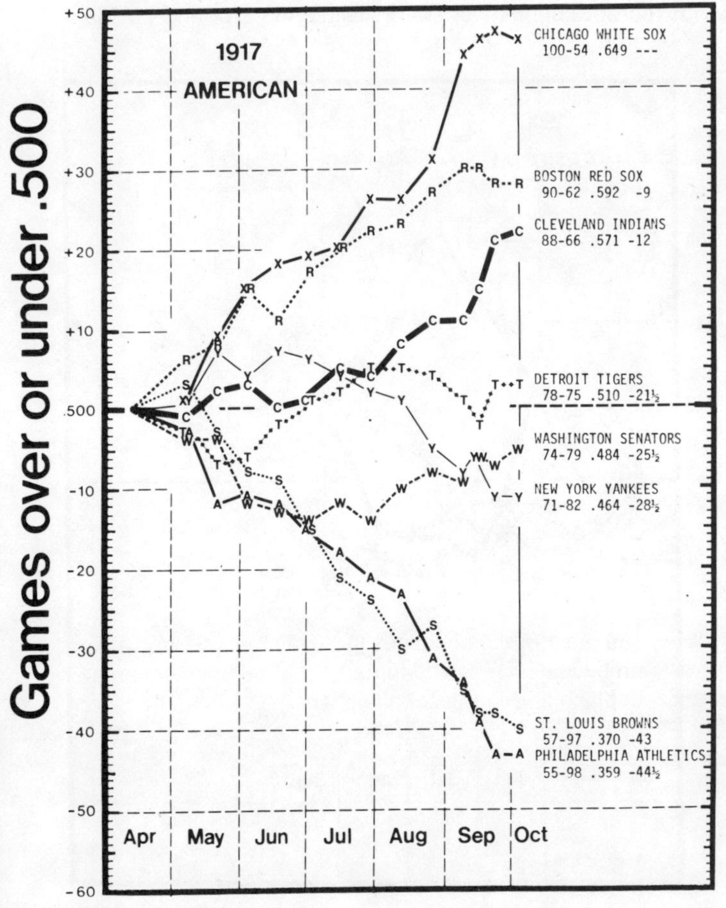


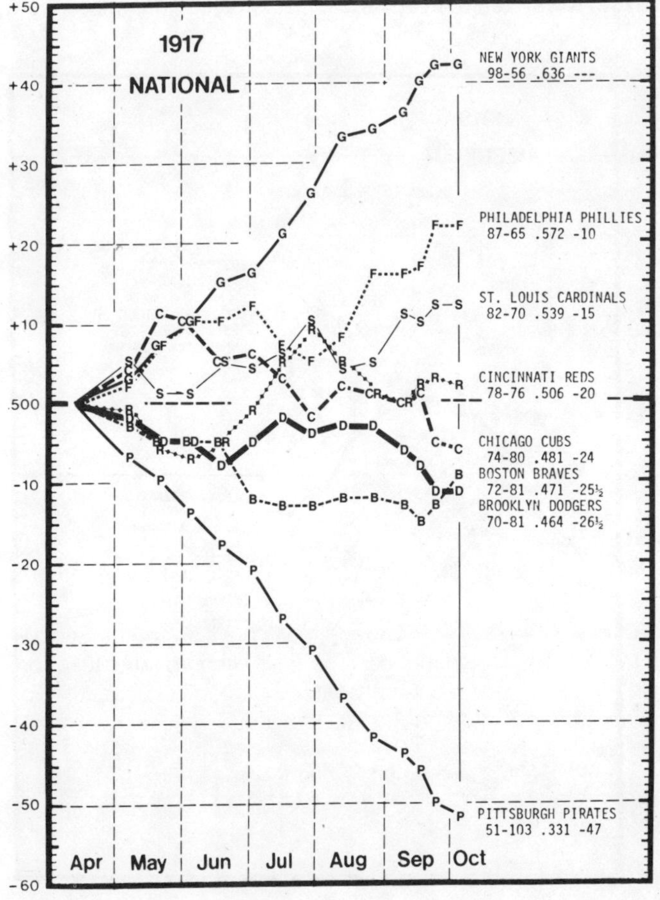

## 1918

World War I had barely touched the major leagues by the end of the 1917 season, but in 1918 baseball was not only war-torn by players going *en masse* to the military or to war industries, but also had its schedule shortened by a month by a government decree defining the game as "nonessential." Hardest hit were 1917's winners. The White Sox roster was so decimated by the war that Chicago could finish no better than sixth. The Red Sox, after filling gaps by acquiring Stuffy McInnis, Amos Strunk, Wally Schang, and Bullet Joe Bush from the Athletics, capitalized on Chicago's demise more than the other patched-up teams did, and won their sixth AL pennant.

Carl Mays led Boston's pitching with a 21-13 record. The Red Sox had a new outfielder who hit .300 and tied Philadelphia's Tilly Walker for the home run leadership with 11, and this same man, Babe Ruth, displayed his usual skill on the mound (13-7, 2.22). For the third time in four years, the Red Sox pitchers squelched the NL opposition in the World Series; Ruth set a Series pitching record for consecutive scoreless innings, 29⅔, which stood for 43 years.

The Giants had a sparkling rookie outfielder named Ross Youngs and got off to a good start in the spring, but lost Benny Kauff, Jeff Tesreau, and Rube Benton (among others) to the war and Ferdie Schupp to an arm injury. The Cubs had purchased Pete Alexander from the Phillies before the season but lost him to the draft in late April. They nevertheless came up with the league's best pitching, from Hippo Vaughn (22-10), Claude Hendrix (20-7), and ex-Brave Lefty Tyler (19-8), and won the pennant easily.

The Cincinnati Reds had the league's best hitting but its next-to-worst team ERA. These facts, plus the midseason suspension of Hal Chase, may be part of the explanation for their strange curve in the 1918 NL graph—the wierdest in the early decades of the century. The highlighted curve in the year's AL graph calls attention to the Yankees' fifth consecutive season of fading after a promising start; one can easily imagine the pressures building in Gotham to eradicate that pattern.

## 1919

The Chicago White Sox got their 1917 world champion team back from the war, and with it, the 1919 AL pennant. They probably could have gotten the world championship back, too, but by World Series time half of the team wasn't playing the game of baseball by the rules—or the Game of Life, either.

Those ugly facts did not come out until much later, of course. In the meantime, the 1919 season itself unfolded, presumably, in all honesty by all teams, with the White Sox staving off challenges by Cleveland and Detroit after a June slump. Eddie Cicotte (29-7) and Lefty Williams (23-11) were in fine shape on the hill, Joe Jackson hit his usual .351, and the team had a league-leading BA at .287 in what was still the dead-ball era.

At Cleveland, the Indians continued their progress and showed a strong finish, thanks to Stan Coveleski (24-12) and the infield trio of Ray Chapman, Larry Gardner, and Doc Johnston, who outhit Tris Speaker (.296). The Yankees seemed to be following their annual custom, taking the lead briefly in June and then flopping, only this time they surged again in September, nosing out the Tigers for third place. The late upswing reflected, in part, New York's acquisition of Carl Mays, who won nine games for them after jumping the Boston club in the midst of the season. Detroit had regained contender status with the development of Harry Heilmann (.320) and Ira Flag-

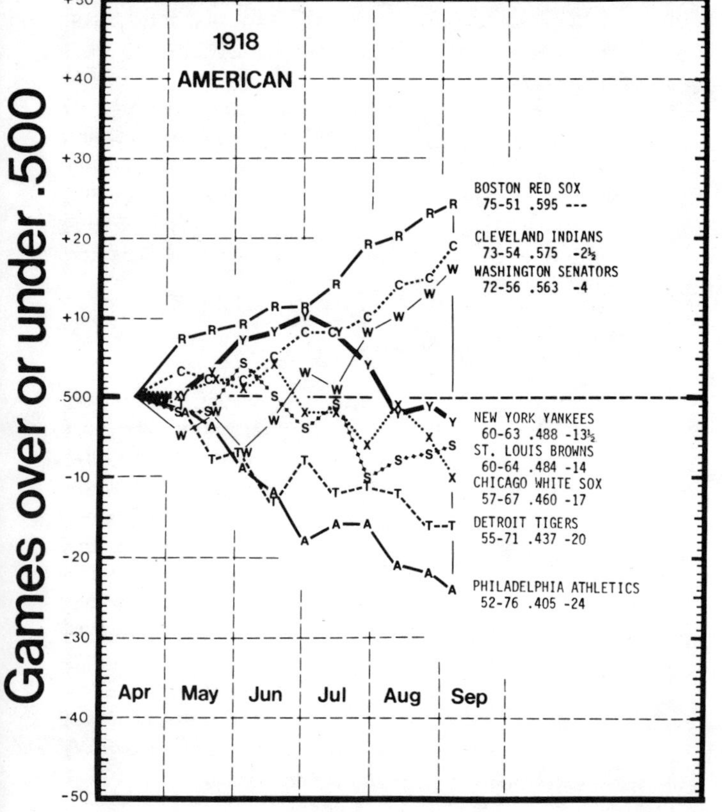


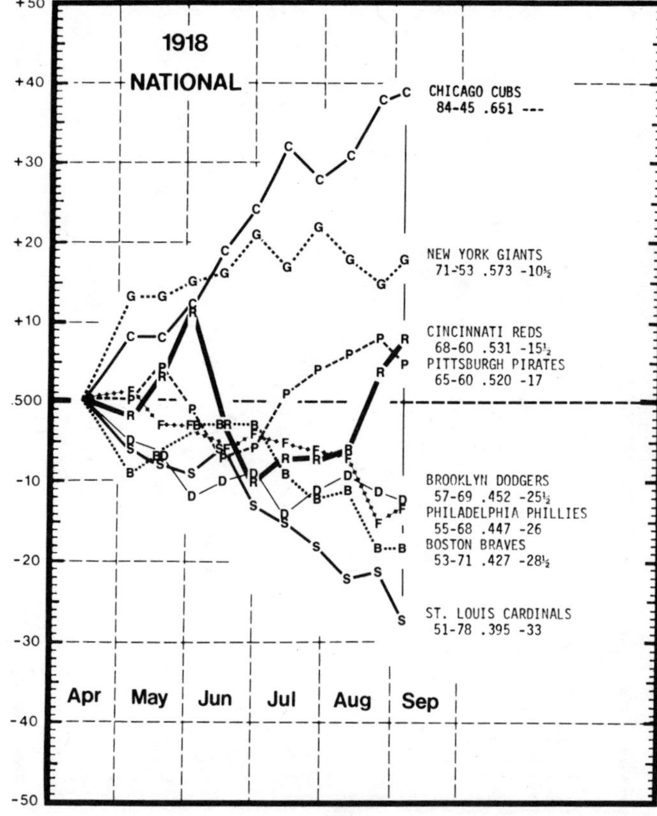

stead (.331), and still had Cobb (.384) and Veach (.355).

Virtually the only cheering in Boston was for Babe Ruth, who set a new major league home run record with 29, led the league with 114 RBIs, and batted .322, while winning eight of 13 pitching decisions. McInnis and Schang also hit over .300, but otherwise the Red Sox behaved quite unlike world champs. Three months after the season, the gloom of the Boston fans became mixed with fury when the Red Sox owner, Harry Frazee, sold Ruth to the Yankees under dire financial pressure, much of which stemmed from Frazee's greater interest in financing his theatrical productions on Broadway than in rebuilding a winner at Fenway Park. The loss of Ruth and Mays, it turned out, was only the beginning of the Rape of the Red Sox—over the next three years, the Boston-to-New York shuttle set up between Frazee and Yankee co-owner Jake Ruppert carried catcher Wally Schang, eventual Hall of Famer Waite Hoyt, shortstop Everett Scott, third baseman Joe Dugan, and pitchers Herb Pennock, Sad Sam Jones, Bullet Joe bush, and George Pipgras. In the process, baseball history was changed as drastically as it had been in the plunderage of the Baltimore Orioles in 1902.

For Cincinnati fans, on the other hand, 1919 was the most joyous year since they last had a winner in 1882. The Reds were lagging behind the Giants in May and June, caught up to them in July, and pulled away cleanly in August. Ironically, it was an ex-Giant, Slim Sallee (21-7), who led Cincinnati's hurlers, with strong support from Hod Eller (20-9) and Dutch Ruether (19-6). The Reds also had the great outfielder Edd Roush, who won his second NL batting title, and third baseman Heinie Groh, who, like Roush, hit over .300 for the third consecutive season.

In a context of puzzlingly poor mound performances by Eddie Cicotte and Lefty Williams, other oddities on the playing field, and attendant rumors and suspicions, the Reds surprisingly beat the favored White Sox in the 1919 World Series, five games to three. Heroically, but not fully appreciated as such until a year later, a rookie White Sox pitcher named Dickie Kerr had two complete-game victories.

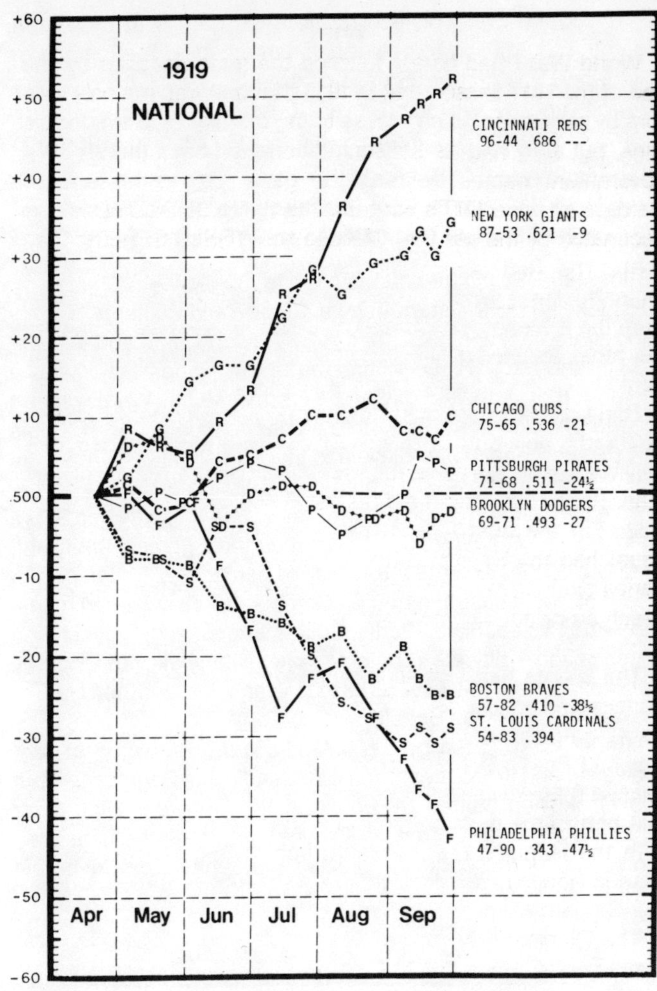


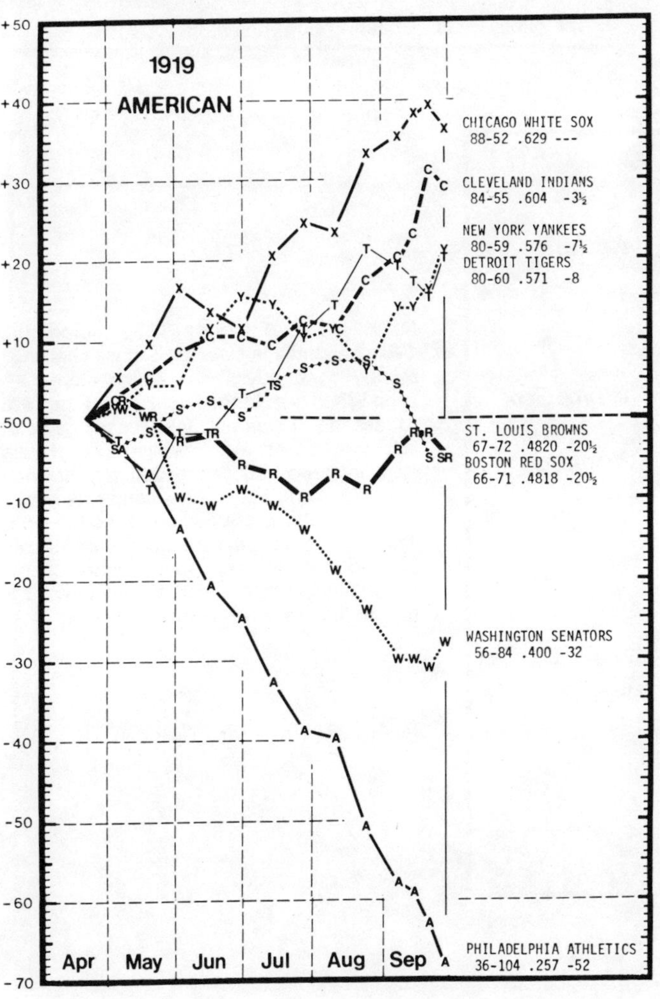


## 1920

The 1920 White Sox were, if anything, stronger than their 1919 edition. They won eight more games, batted .294 as a team, and had four 20-game-winning pitchers—Cicotte, Williams, Faber, and Kerr. In August they jumped past the Indians and Yankees into first place, and a torrid three-team race was on. Both the Yankees and Indians regained the lead in early September, but the three teams stayed within a 2½-game range through the middle of the month. On the 17th and 18th, the Yankees were effectively knocked out of the race by losing twice to the White Sox. The latter kept matching wins by the Indians right up to their scheduled showdown series in Cleveland, starting on Thursday the 23rd. The previous day, a grand jury had convened in Chicago to take up the matter of alleged fixing of major league baseball games.

The White Sox won two of the three games at Cleveland, bringing them back to only a half-game behind the Indians on Saturday, September 25th. Two more wins by Chicago, over Detroit, and by Cleveland, over St. Louis, left them with the same separation on Monday the 27th. The next afternoon, the shocking headlines appeared:

EIGHT WHITE SOX PLAYERS ARE INDICTED
ON CHARGE OF FIXING 1919 WORLD SERIES

Immediately suspended by White Sox owner Charles A. Comiskey were the star pitchers, Cicotte and Williams; the hitting stars Jackson (.382 that year), Felsch (.338), and Weaver (.333), shortstop Risberg, first baseman Gandil (who was a holdout that year), and utilityman Fred McMullin. What was left of the Chicago team had three games remaining, at St. Louis on the weekend, while Cleveland still had six left. As many as two losses in those six would give Chicago a chance to tie. While unlikely with such a huge loss of talent, it was hardly unthinkable for the White Sox to win their three games—they still had Dickie Kerr and the future Hall of Famer, Red Faber. And in the first post-scandal game on October 1st, they fielded a lineup with two regulars (Eddie Collins and Shano Collins) and three reserve players (Eddie Murphy, Bibb Falk, and Harvey McClellan) who hit over .300 that year, plus another Hall of Famer, catcher Ray Schalk.

Faber was beaten by the up-and-coming Browns that day, however, and in the meantime Cleveland's Jim Bagby and Stan Coveleski had beaten St. Louis on the 28th and 29th. After splitting a pair at Detroit on October 1st, the Indians needed only one more conquest to kayo the White Sox. In heroic

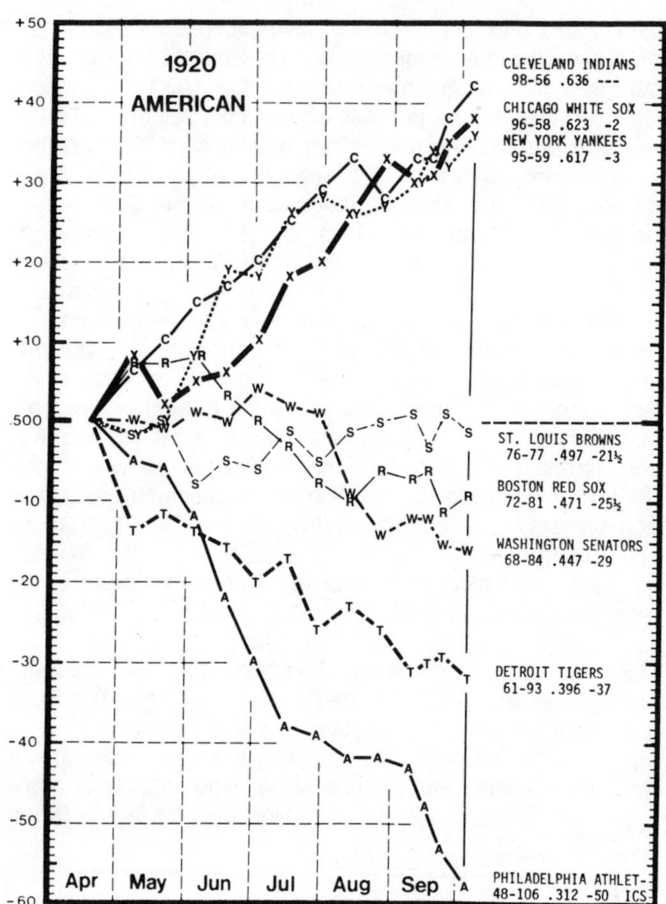


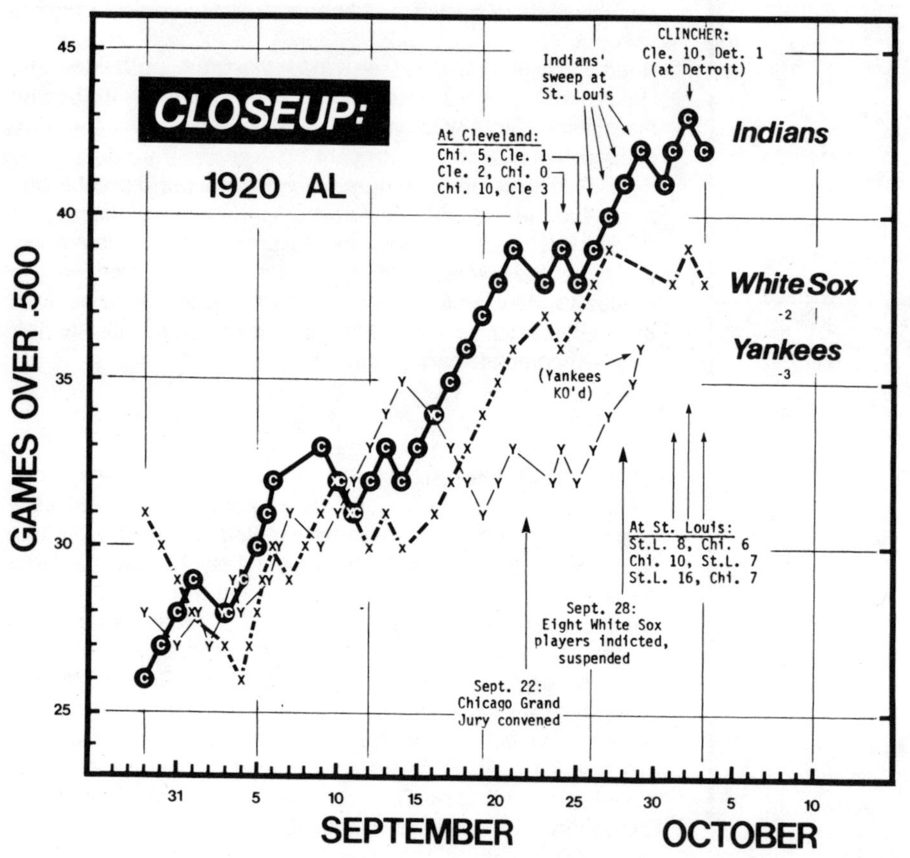


**NICE GUYS FINISH FIRST when the Cleveland Indians stave off a close challenge by the "bad guys," the scandal-torn Chicago White Sox, in the final week of the 1920 AL season. It was not until Tuesday of that last week that eight White Sox players were indicted and suspended for throwing the 1919 World Series; Cleveland was only a half-game ahead of Chicago at the time, but Jim Bagby, Stan Coveleski, and Duster Mails pitched the Indians to an uncatchable position while the Browns held down the decimated White Sox team.**

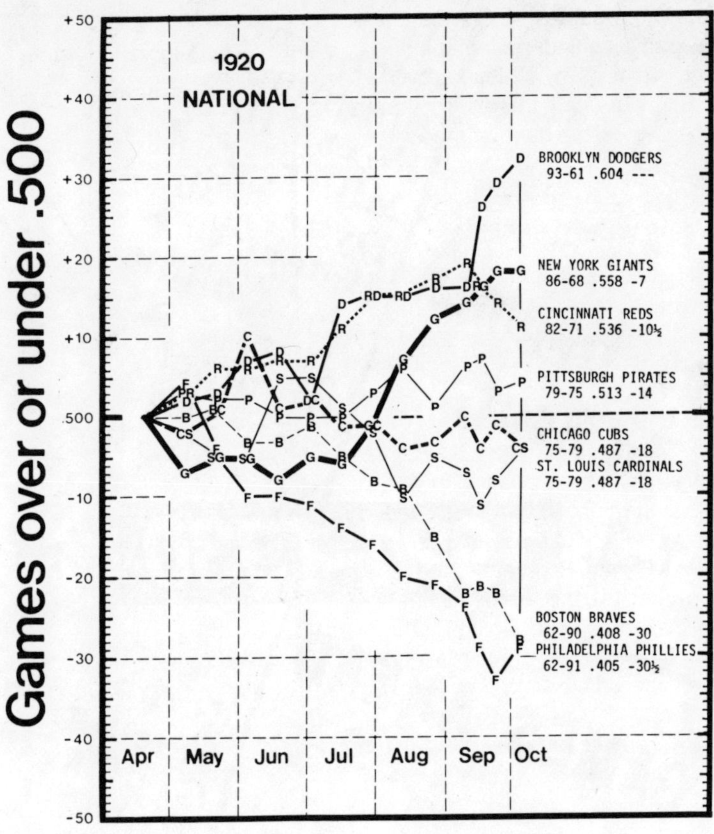


fashion, they did just that on Saturday the 2nd, when Bagby beat the Tigers for his 31st win of the year.

The country sighed with relief, spared the injustice and awkwardness of a pennant by a scandal-ridden team. Besides gratitude, many fans felt admiration for the Indians when they recalled that the Cleveland players had also had to overcome the shock of losing their star shortstop, Ray Chapman, who was killed by a fastball from Carl Mays on August 16, 1920.

The Yankees had been propelled into the heated race by Mays (26-11), along with Bob Shawkey (20-13), but most of all by Babe Ruth. In his first season in a Yankee uniform, Ruth hit an electrifying 54 home runs. That statistic, George Sisler's league-leading average of .407, and the general increase in team BAs supplied evidence that the AL's new ball in 1920 (introduced a year later in the NL) was livelier and a new baseball era had begun.

Cincinnati did its utmost to repeat in the National League, but Brooklyn foiled the attempt. Added to such Robin mainstays as Zack Wheat, Jeff Pfeffer, and Hy Myers were the ace righthander Burleigh Grimes, who won 23 games, and the veteran first sacker Ed Konetchy. In September the Reds and Robins were joined in a red-hot race by the Giants, who were threatening to duplicate the 1914 Braves' turnaround, but suddenly Brooklyn leaped free and clear of the other two by winning 16 out of 18 games starting the day after Labor Day. As in 1916, the strong finish by McGraw's club had most people predicting another pennant for the Giants in 1921.

The World Series went to Cleveland, five games to two, with Coveleski's three complete-game victories and Bill Wambsganss's unassisted triple play as the dramatic features.

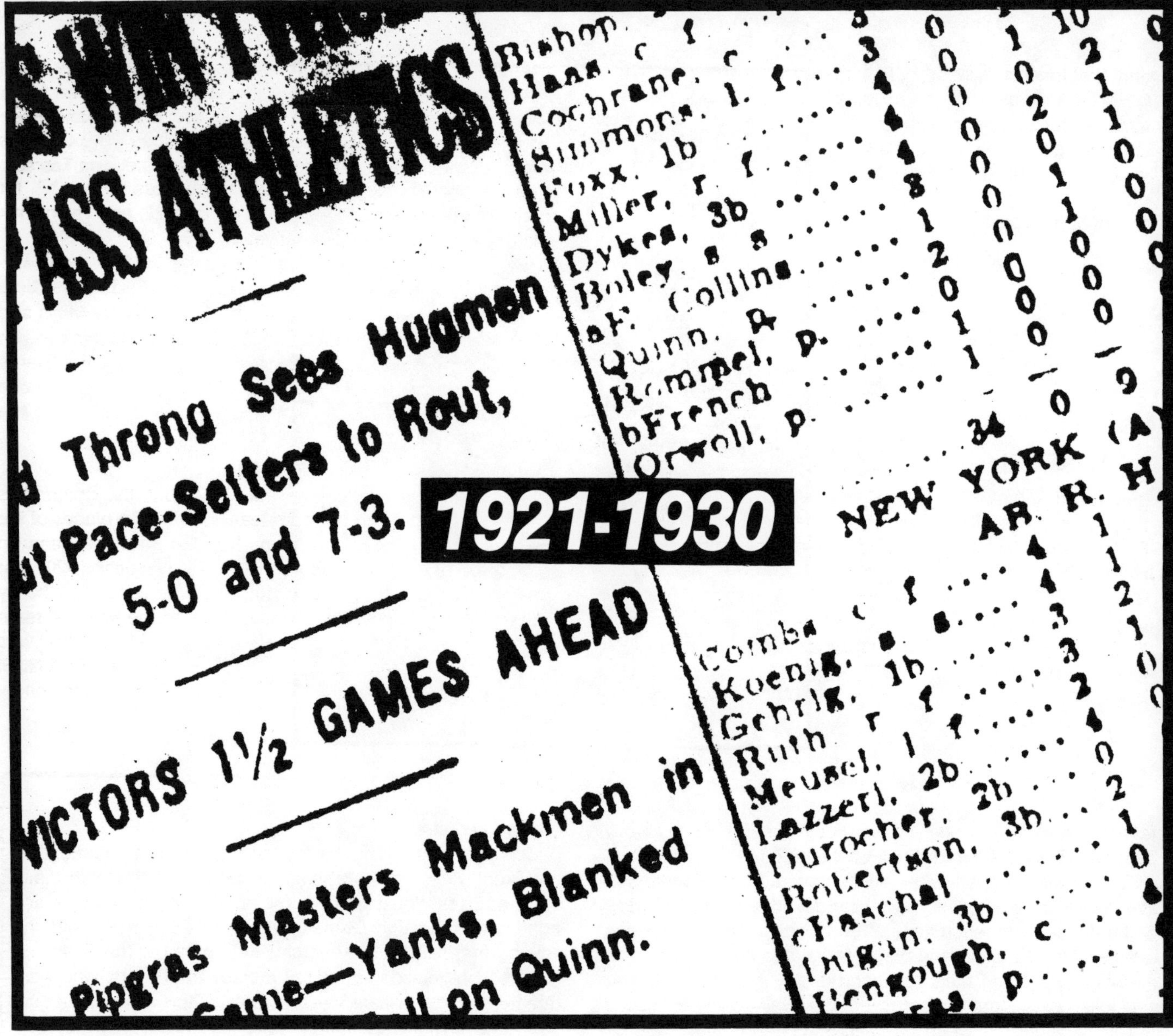


# 1921-1930

By 1921 both major leagues were playing with a lively ball, marking the onset of what is sometimes called "the really modern era" of baseball. Suddenly there were 70 .300 hitters instead of the usual 20, and several team batting averages above .300—it would be many years before the pitchers caught up to the batters. The sensational slugging by Babe Ruth was turning out the fans as had nothing else in the game's history, at the very time when the fans had reason to shun the whole sport and boycott the turnstiles. As a natural result, many other batters began swinging for the fences instead of the gaps. Whereas batting averages increased by around 25 points, home run totals showed a tenfold increase from the midteens to mid-Twenties.

After two decades, there were only four clubs in the majors which had never won a pennant—the St. Louis Cardinals in the National League and in the younger league, the St. Louis Browns, the Washington Senators, and (incredibly) the New York Yankees. And all four seemed to be on the upswing.

## 1921

Since their darkest days of 1912-14, the Yankees had gone through several seasons of early promise and late-summer wilting, but in 1919 and 1920 they had finished strongly. In the 1921 season, with both the White Sox and Red Sox stripped of talent and doomed to the second division, the Yankees' remaining obstacle was Cleveland, the world champion.

With the same lineup as in 1920, save for a superb new shortstop, Joe Sewell, in the late Ray Chapman's place, the Indians left the gate ahead of everyone in April and made an elusive moving target for New York. The Yankees, who by now had gotten a new battery from Boston, Waite Hoyt and Wally Schang, took until the middle of May to get in gear. The two teams staged an exciting chase scene thereafter, leaving the rest of the league in the dust. From the end of July to mid-September, there was seldom more than a two-game separation between them, and the lead went back and forth several times. Besides Hoyt, Carl Mays and Bob Shawkey provided mound strength for the Yankees, and Babe Ruth had the most prodigious batting output a hitter has shown in a season—59 home runs, 170 RBIs, and .378 (third best in the AL) for average. New York also got 135 RBIs from young outfielder Bob Meusel and 97 more from first baseman Wally Pipp. For Cleveland, on the other hand, Jim Bagby was showing an early decline at age 31 (14-12, 4.69 for the season), and the Indians lost both Tris Speaker and catcher Steve O'Neill to injuries late in the season. The effects of these problems surfaced abruptly in September in a brief but fatal collapse, giving the Yankees their first pennant. Remembering what a long struggle to the top it had been for Miller Huggins and his men, nobody dreamed that it would be only the first of 32 Yankee flags.

The Pittsburgh Pirates, from whom little had been heard through the teens, got the jump on the New York Giants in the spring of 1921, but the two teams were on a collision course through the summer. When they did meet head-on near the end of August, McGraw's crew swept the five-game series, and sent the Bucs reeling. Once again, the NL flag flew at the Polo Grounds.

This was McGraw's fourth pennant-winning combination, after the 1904-05, 1911-13, and 1917 flagwinners, basically a new and different roster from what the Giants fielded before the turn of the decade, except for outfielders George Burns and Ross Youngs. Not only were Benny Kauff, Jeff Tesreau, Buck Herzog, and Art Fletcher gone, but Heinie Zimmerman and Hal Chase (who was with the Giants in 1919) had been declared ineligible for life, even before the White Sox indictments, for their involvements with gambling interests. The new Giants included infielders Frankie Frisch, George Kelly, and Beauty Bancroft (joined by Heinie Groh in 1922), Irish Meusel out with Burns and Youngs, and catcher Frank Snyder, nearly all of whom had consistent .300 bats in the early twenties. New faces on the mound staff were Art Nehf, Jesse Barnes, and Rosy Ryan. Though less well remembered than their Polo Grounds predecessors Mathewson, McGinnity, Marquard, and Tesreau, these hurlers combined with their teammates on the hill for the NL's best team ERA (a lofty 3.45) in 1922, and Ryan took individual honors with 3.00 that year.

Since the Polo Grounds was the home field for both winners, the World Series was all in one place for the first time in 1921 (and again in 1922). After being shut out by Mays and Hoyt in the first two games, the Giants bounced back to win the '21 classic, five games to three. The next year, the Giants beat the Yankees more handily, four games to none, with one tie, and held Babe Ruth to a single and a double over the five games.

## 1922-23

In 1922 the winners were the same, but the contenders changed, with the two St. Louis teams taking the places of the Indians and Pirates. The Browns had the strongest team in their 1901-1953 history. George Sisler hit his peak (.420) that year, outfielder Ken Williams hit 39 home runs, and heavy stick work by the rest of the lineup brought the Browns' team BA up to .313 (only at Detroit, where Ty Cobb hit .401, was there another AL team over .300). The Browns' team ERA (3.38) was also the league's best; Urban Shocker (24-17) led the pitch-

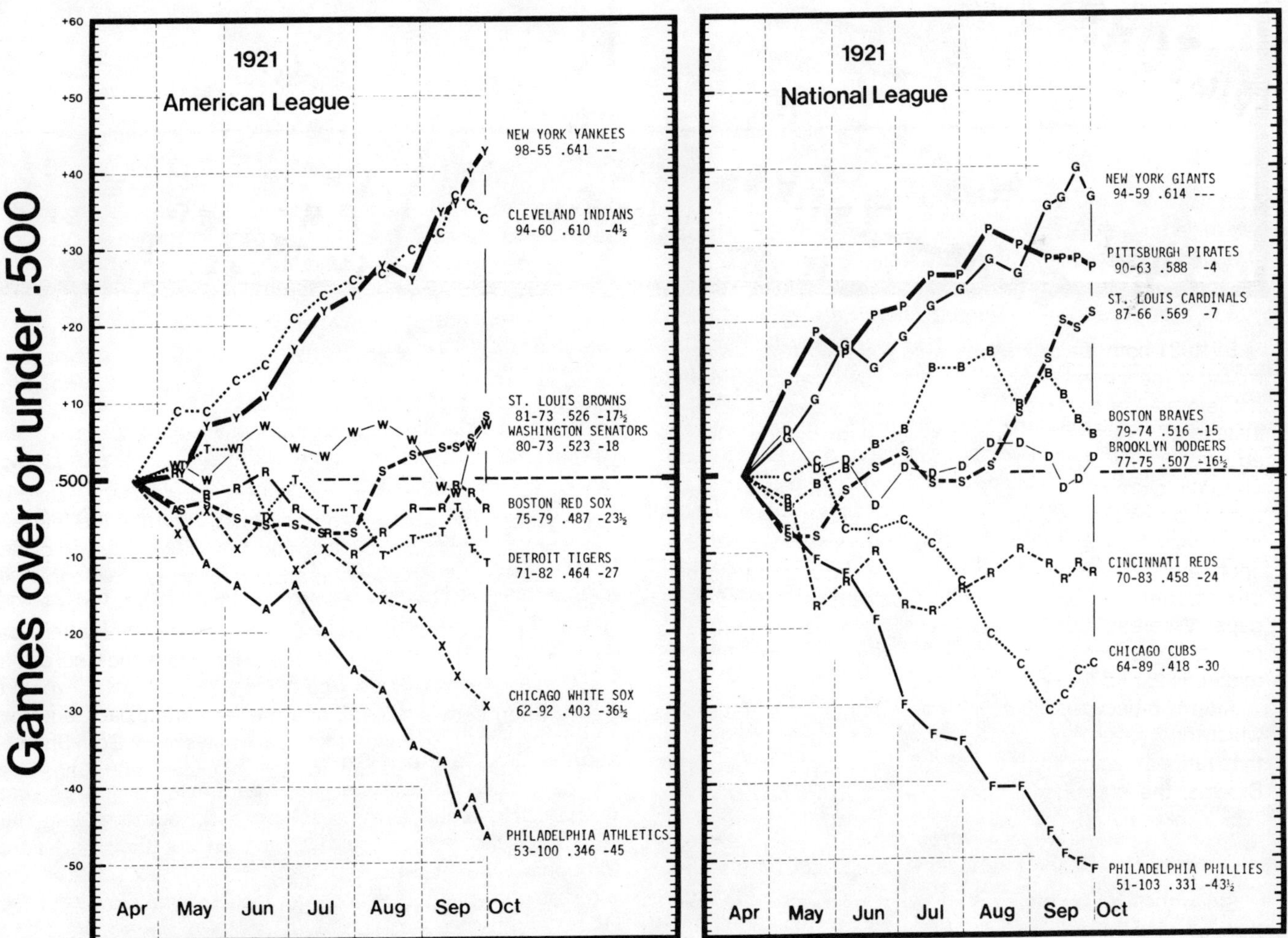

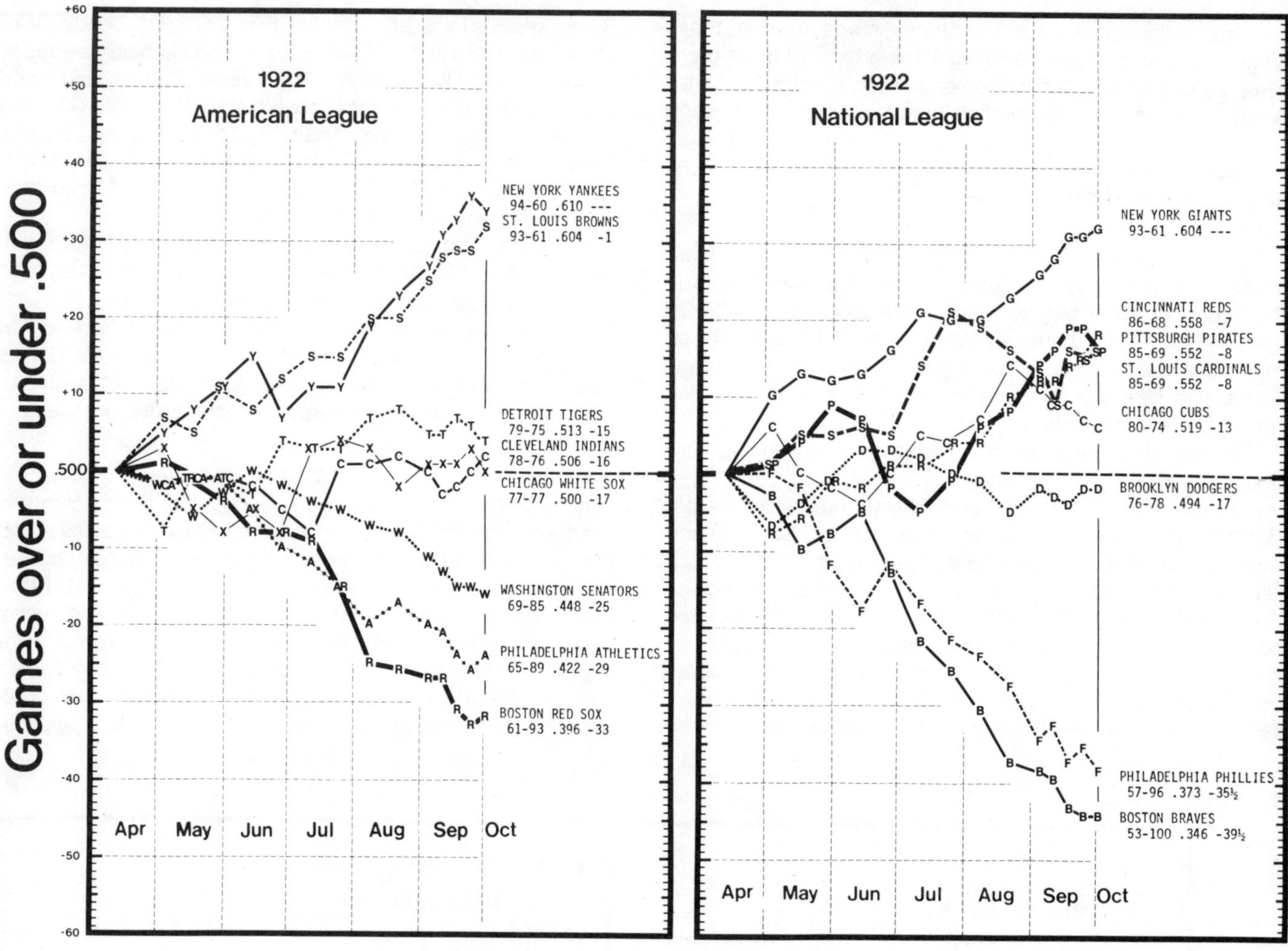


ing staff.

Managed by Lee Fohl, this St. Louis team had looked sharp in the last two months of the 1921 season, and in 1922 they were tooth-and-nail with the Yankees all season long. The latter took a tiny lead in mid-August when the two faced each other in St. Louis, and held it the rest of the way, beating the Browns by only a single game. Sadly, for St. Louis fans, this proved to be the Browns' one big chance for a pennant in over 40 years—the following year, they lost Sisler for the whole season because of an eye ailment, and never contended seriously thereafter until the Second World War years.

1922 was also a sad year in Boston, where the Red Sox settled into last place around the end of July. The Yankees, who were sometimes called the New York Red Sox by bitter Bostonians, had the problem of staying close to the powerful Browns without Babe Ruth and Bob Meusel in the first month of the season because of their suspension by Commissioner Landis for barnstorming after the previous season, and there was a problem with pitching depth on the New York team also. But the villainous Harry Frazee had peddled Boston's top two pitchers of 1921, Bullet Joe Bush (26-7 for the Yankees in '22) and Sad Sam Jones, to Yankee co-owner Jake Ruppert beteween seasons, and the Yankees also got infielders Joe Dugan and Everett Scott from Frazee in 1922 to replace the declining Home Run Baker and Roger Peckinpaugh. By the time Pennock and Pipgras joined the Boston-to-New York procession the next spring, four of the eight Yankee regulars in the field and six of the eight pitchers on the Yankee roster were ex-Red Sox players. The easy pennant victory in 1923, when the Yankees won by a 16-game margin, was in fact mainly due to the mound skills of Jones, Pennock, Bush, and Hoyt, since the Yankees were outhit that year by the Tigers (for whom Heilmann hit .403) and the Indians.

Under Branch Rickey's managership, which started in 1919, the St. Louis Cardinals were gradually emerging from their habitual buried position in the National League's first two decades. Like the Browns, the Cards had shown an impressive finish in 1921, led by Hornsby's .397 hitting performance. In 1922, they made it all the way to the top of the standings, taking first place away from the Giants in a midseason hot streak. This time Hornsby was even more obviously the man on whom the team's fortunes depended—in game after game it was his sensational batwork that brought victories to the Cardinals; by the end of the season he held the NL's first modern-era Triple Crown with a .401 average, 42 homers, and 152 RBIs. But he couldn't hold up his team singlehandedly, and the Cardinal's occupancy of the top spot lasted only a few days; they were, in fact, four years away from their first pennant. No other team presented a serious threat to the Giants for the rest of the 1922 season, for that matter, or throughout the 1923 season. With a rather odd collection of veterans and youngsters, however, the Cincinnati Reds cut the Giants' winning edge in 1923 to only 4½ games. Veterans

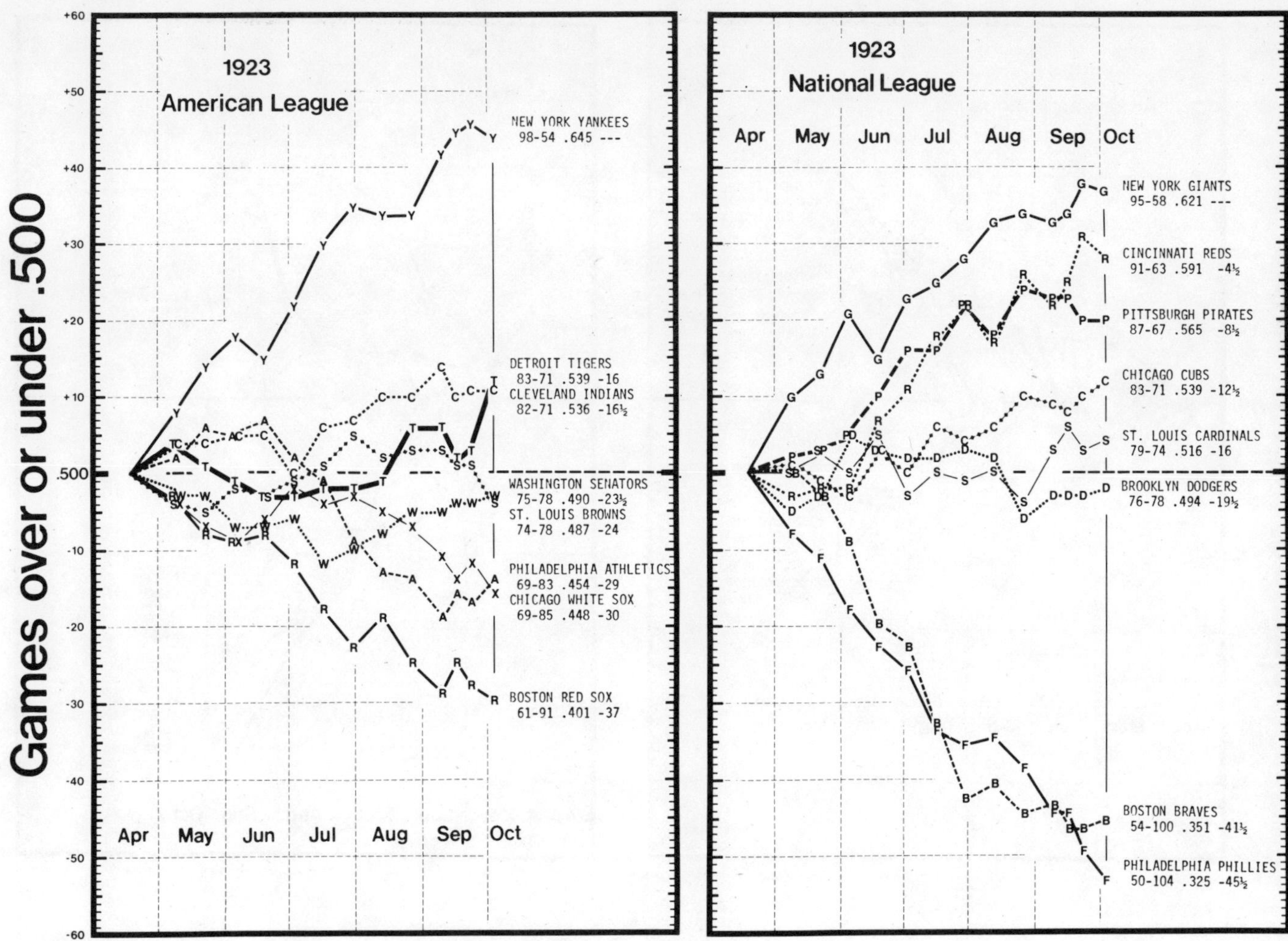


Dolf Luque (27-8) and Eppa Rixey (20-5) combined with 22-year-old Pete Donahue (21-15) and 36-year-old ex-Giant Rube Benton to give the Reds the NL's best pitching, and their batting lineup included 39-year-old Jake Daubert (.292) along with mainstays Edd Roush, Pat Duncan, and Bubbles Hargrave. As might be expected from this sort of mixture, the Reds proved to be a team on the way down during the twenties, rather than one building toward another championship.

In contrast, the Pirates were headed upward, but by a tortuous route. In 1922 Pittsburgh led the NL in hitting with a .308 team BA, but had a tumultuous season featuring a sizable midseason slump, during which the managerial reins passed from George Gibson to Bill McKechnie. Thereafter the Pirates displayed the best second-half record of any team in the league, finishing in a tie with the Cardinals just behind Cincinnati, and the Bucs maintained a winning record the rest of the decade. In the early 1920s the Pirates were heavily dependent on perennial 20-game-winner Wilbur Cooper for their pitching, and made up for their lack of pitching depth with heavy hitting from third baseman Pie Traynor, first sacker Charley Grimm, and outfielders Max Carey and Carson Bigbee, plus sparkling defensive work in the field by Traynor, Grimm and ex-Brave Rabbit Maranville.

The Yankees' big win in 1923 came in the new House That Ruth Built, and Yankee Stadium's first year was also when the first world championship came to Miller Huggins and his men. With three homers from Ruth, and strong hurling by Pennock, Bush, and Jones, they beat the Giants in six games in the '23 Series.

## 1924

After disappointing seasons in 1922 and 1923, the Washington Senators found a combination that clicked in 1924, and won the first pennant in the club's history. It was no breeze. After startling the league with a leap into first place in June, the Senators had to exchange leads several times with the Yankees and a heavy-hitting Detroit team through July and August. They held onto a slim lead over New York through September but didn't clinch the pennant until the closing day.

The Washington lineup was not a collection of household names, but the Senators had strength at every position: Muddy Ruel behind the plate, Joe Judge at first, "boy wonder" manager Bucky Harris at second, ex-Yankee Roger Peckinpaugh at short, and Ossie Bluege at third, plus an outfield consisting of lifetime-.322 hitter Sam Rice, sophomore .344-batting Goose Goslin, and Nemo Leibold or Earl McNeely. Their centerpiece was Walter Johnson, as had been the case for 16 years, and he was still in fine condition with a 23-7 record and a league-leading ERA of 2.72. Unlike many previous years, the Big Train didn't have to carry the whole load by himself in 1924—Firpo Marberry contributed 11 wins and 15 saves primarily in a reliever's role, and the Nats also got

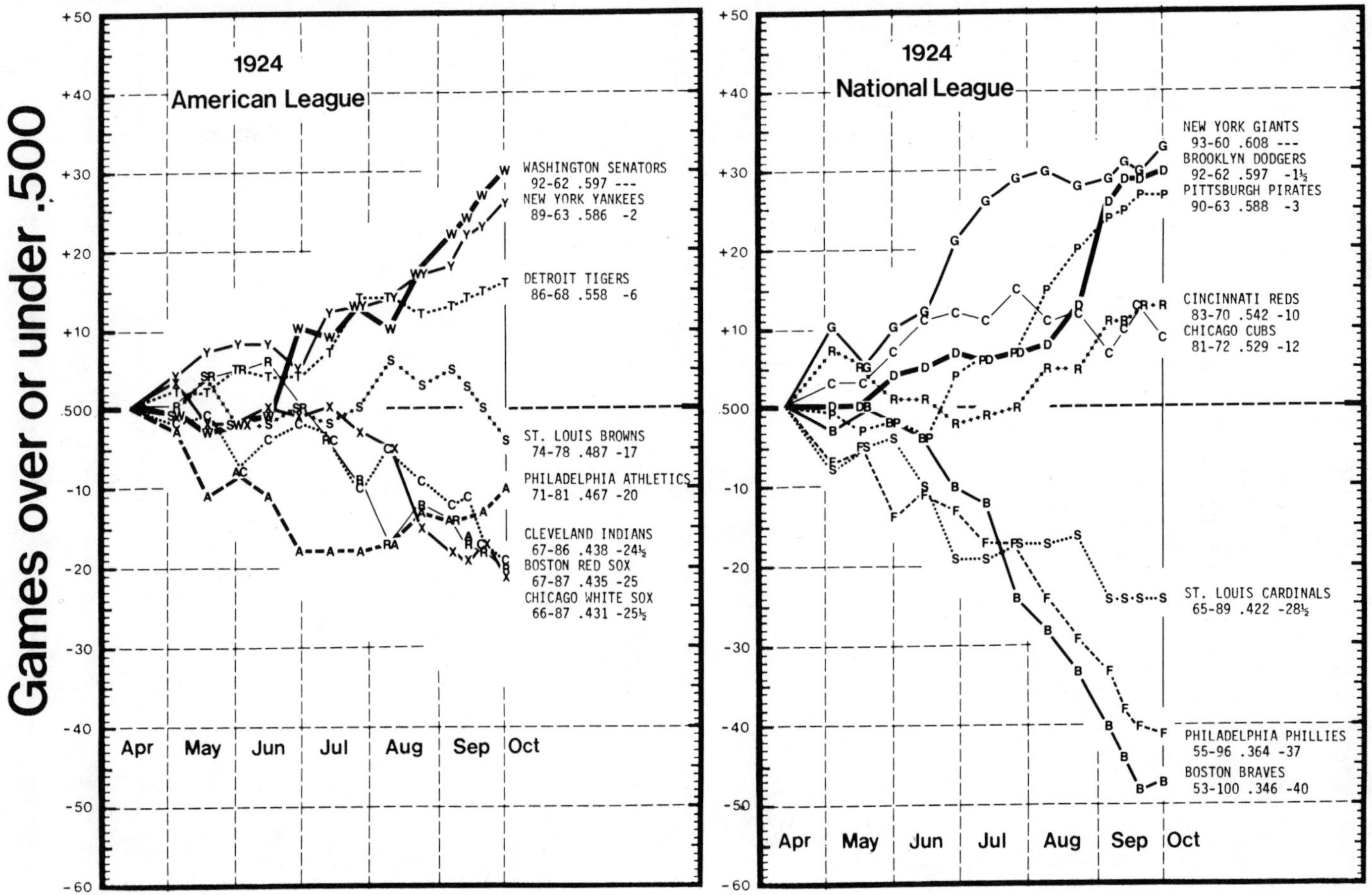


many good turns on the hill from George Mogridge and Tom Zachary.

The Red Sox, who repeated their last-place finish in 1923, were almost as amazing as the Senators when they pulled up to a near-tie with the Yankees in June. This was a brief renaissance, however, as Boston's hitting and pitching—both weakest in the league—let them down sharply in the middle part of the season; in the final week the Red Sox were barely saved from a third straight year in the cellar by the White Sox.

The occupants of the AL cellar had been the Philadelphia Athletics, which was certainly nothing new, but at midseason the A's started a gentle upswing, eventually finishing fifth. The turn in their curve in the 1924 graph, at the end of July, marks what proved to be another historic turning point for Connie Mack's team quite clearly, and a glance at the roster provides some explanation: newcomers Jimmy Dykes and Max Bishop in the infield, Al Simmons and Bing Miller in the outfield, and Eddie Rommel on the mound.

As late as August 15th, the New York Giants seemed to be headed for the easiest of four consecutive pennants. They had broken away from the Cubs in June and come into August safely ten games ahead of Pittsburgh. McGraw's pitching staff wilted in the hot weather, however, and the Pirates' strong drive that month put them only one game behind the Giants on Labor Day, September 1. But that was as close as the Bucs could get; a month later they completed their schedule three games out.

Meanwhile, out of nowhere came the Brooklyn Robins, led by the brilliant late bloomer, Dazzy Vance (28-6 at age 33 that year), and another veteran moundsman, Burleigh Grimes (22-13); Zack Wheat, now 38, was still pounding the ball (.375) for the Dodgers, and manager Robinson also had the NL's home run leader, ex-Cardinal Jack Fournier, and the consistent keystoner, Andy High, on his '24 team. Twelve games behind the Giants as late as August 10th, Brooklyn won 24 of 28 games, sweeping three-game sets from both Pittsburgh and New York in the process. The last 15 of the 28 were consecutive victories which included four straight doubleheader sweeps starting on Labor Day. (In one seven-day period, August 29 through September 4, the Robins won 11 and lost none, which must be the best week a major league has ever had.) At the end of their streak, they were actually in the league lead alone, but this was only for a couple of hours during another doubleheader which they split in Boston on September 6th. Nonetheless, it had taken only 26 days for the Giants' 12-game lead over Brooklyn to evaporate.

From then on, the Robins and Giants were in a torrid struggle, seldom more than a game apart. On the Friday before the final week, McGraw lost Frankie Frisch and Heinie Groh to injuries for the remainder of the season, and the following Monday found the Dodgers and Giants both at 30 games over .500. The Giants did not panic, and they had little reason to—they had some bright new talent in the form of infielders Bill Terry, Fred Lindstrom, and Travis Jackson and a rookie outfielder named Hack Wilson. On Tuesday, Wednesday, and Thursday, New York won three straight from the Pirates at the Polo Grounds, knocking them out of the race with the Wednesday victory. In the meantime the Dodgers lost a critical

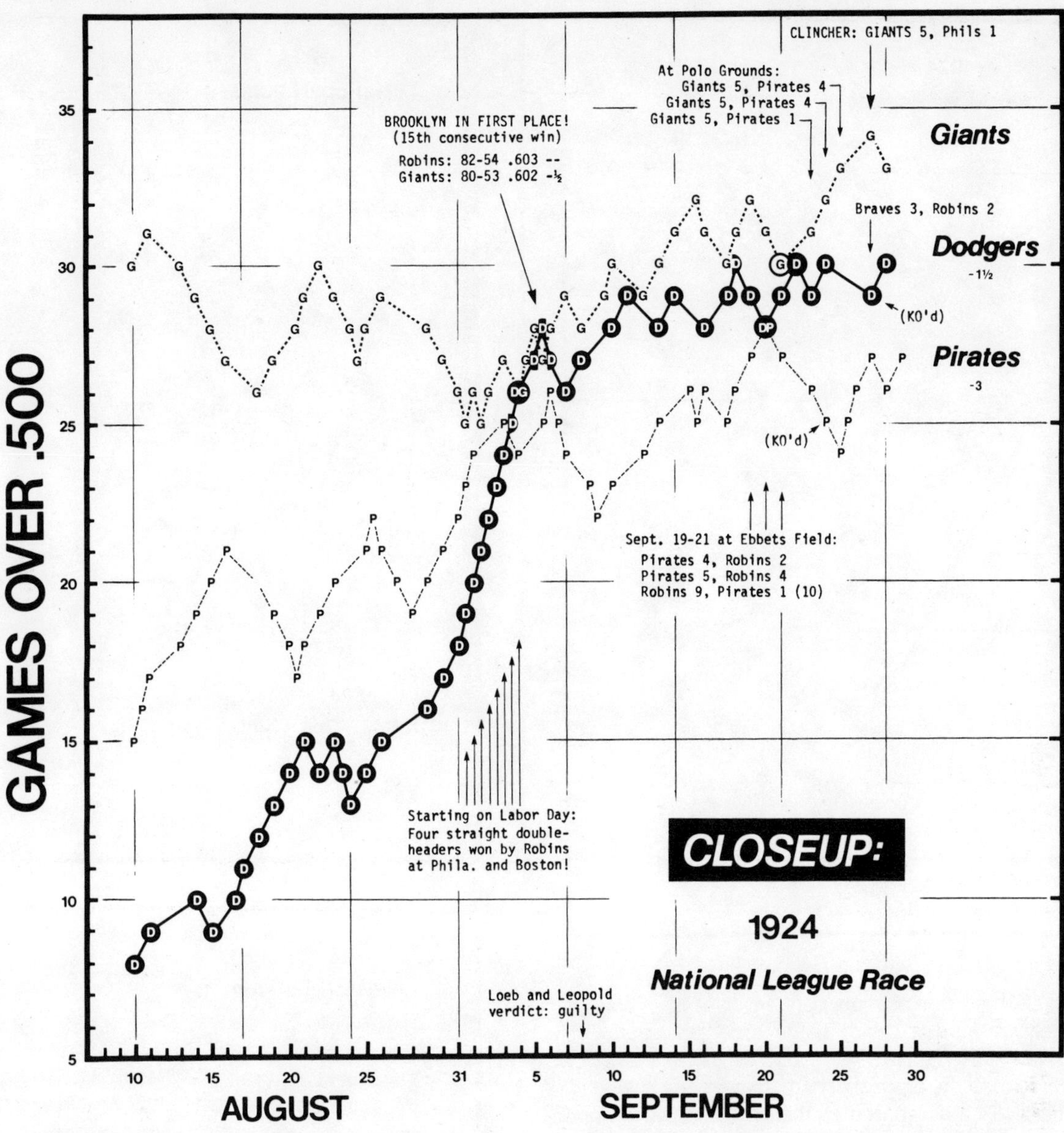


**FLY ROBINS FLY! could have been the chant in Brooklyn in 1924, when "Uncle Robby" Robinson's flock suddenly flew up to join the Giants and Pirates in a torrid race for the flag. The Robins were even in first place by themselves momentarily on September 6th, after winning 11 games in a single week. It all ended with gloom in Flatbush when Brooklyn failed to stop the Giants' bid for a fourth straight pennant.**

game (to the Cubs) by a single run at Ebbets Field on that Tuesday, and when this happened again, in a 3-2 loss to the Braves on Saturday, the Giants clinched the pennant with a win over the Phils on the same day. It was a bitter shortfall for the Robins; their only consolation was that they had made the Giants' unprecedented fourth straight pennant the toughest of the four to achieve.

The '24 Series went the full seven games, and the seventh game went 12 nearly-full innings. And after all that work, which included two losses to the Giants by Walter Johnson, the classic was decided on a bad-hop grounder, in Washington's favor.

## 1925

The Senators won a second pennant the next year. They had an easier September this time, but before that month had to wage a fierce battle with a much-revived Philadelphia team. Again Washington got 20 wins from Johnson and 15 saves from Marberry, and the Nats also got 38 pitching victories from two newcomers to the roster, Stan Coveleski and Dutch Ruether. Johnson was no slouch at the plate, either—he stung the ball at a .352 clip in 210 times at bat over the '24 and '25 seasons combined.

The 1925 AL season is probably better remembered for the Yankees' thundering crash, to seventh place, due in no small way to that team's Ruthlessness. The Bambino had to undergo intestinal surgery in April, and in the 98 games he played between the recuperation and his suspension in September (by manager Huggins, for insubordination and repeated violations of training rules) he only vaguely resembled the Sultan of Swat. Combined with Bob Meusel's AL-leading 33 homers and rookie

Games over or under .500
1925
American League
WASHINGTON SENATORS
96-55 .636 ---
PHILADELPHIA ATHLET-
88-64 .579 -8½ ICS
ST. LOUIS BROWNS
82-71 .536 -15
DETROIT TIGERS
81-73 .526 -16½
CHICAGO WHITE SOX
79-75 .513 -18½
CLEVELAND INDIANS
70-84 .455 -27½
NEW YORK YANKEES
69-85 .448 -28½
BOSTON RED SOX
47-105 .309 -49½
Apr
May
Jun
Jul
Aug
Sep
Oct

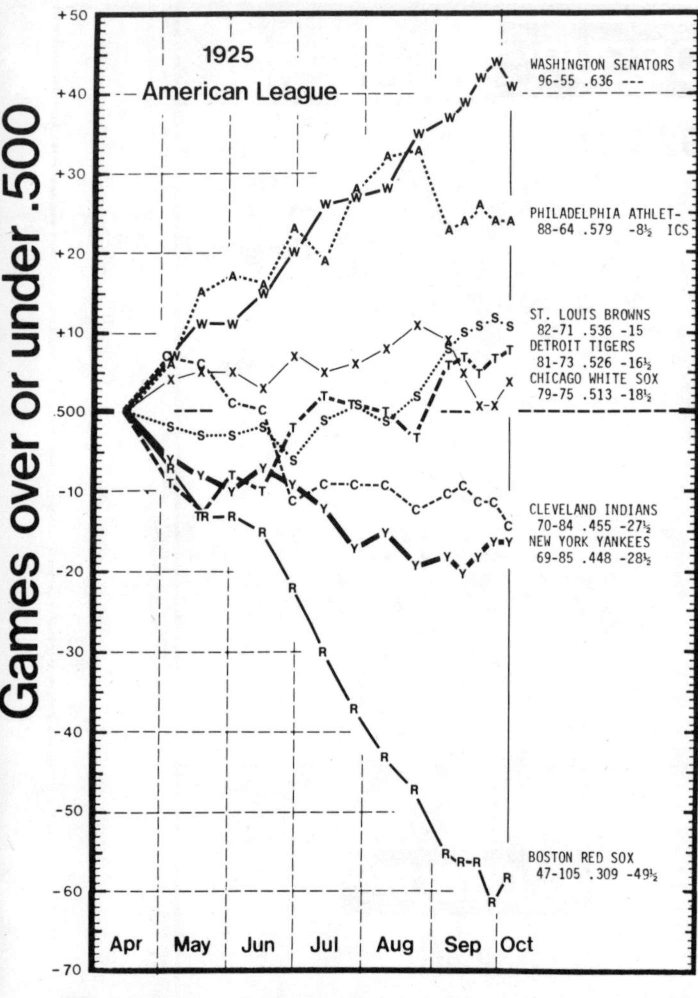

1925
National League
PITTSBURGH PIRATES
95-58 .621 ---
NEW YORK GIANTS
86-66 .566 -8½
CINCINNATI REDS
80-73 .523 -15
ST. LOUIS CARDINALS
77-76 .503 -18
BOSTON BRAVES
70-83 .458 -25
BROOKLYN DODGERS
68-85 .444 -27
PHILADELPHIA PHILLIES
68-85 .444 -27
CHICAGO CUBS
68-86 .442 -27½
Apr
May
Jun
Jul
Aug
Sep
Oct

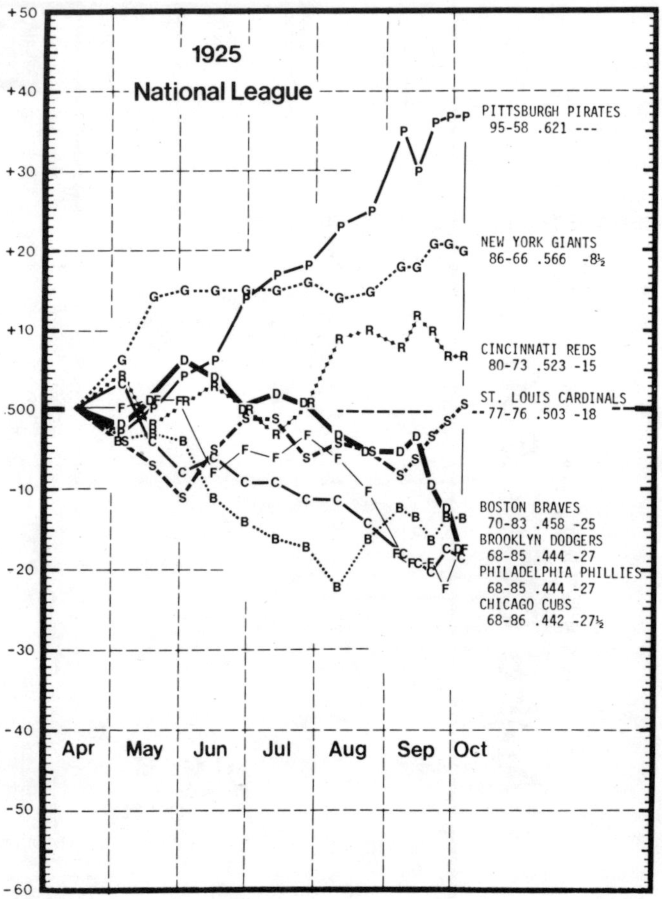

Lou Gehrig's 20, the Babe's 25 four-baggers gave the Yankees their usual league lead in team home runs, however. Off-years by the New York pitchers seemed to be more of a factor in the big tumble than the dropoff in batting averages.

The Pittsburgh Pirates soared to their first pennant since 1909, displacing the Giants, who started very well but in mid-May switched to only a break-even pace for most of the remaining schedule—they too had a pitching shortage. Except for second baseman Eddie Moore's .298, every Pirate regular batted over .300, and new faces in the Pittsburgh lineup included catcher Earl Smith, first baseman George Grantham, shortstop Glenn Wright, and outfielders Kiki Cuyler and Clyde Barnhart in addition to Moore. A very old face, on the pitching staff in 1925 and 1926, was Babe Adams, the Pirates' hero in the 1909 World Series, now approaching his mid-forties. Other pitchers, however, deserved more credit for the pennant win in 1925, namely, Lee Meadows (19-10) and three 17-game-winners, Ray Kremer, Emil Yde, and Johnny Morrison.

Once again the Senators were taken to the seven-game limit in the World Series, and this time they lost, the Pirates beating Walter Johnson in the final game after two earlier Series victories by The Big Train.

## 1926

In 1926 the Cards finally captured their first flag, and this marked their transition from being, on average, the NL's weakest club in the first quarter of the century to its strong-

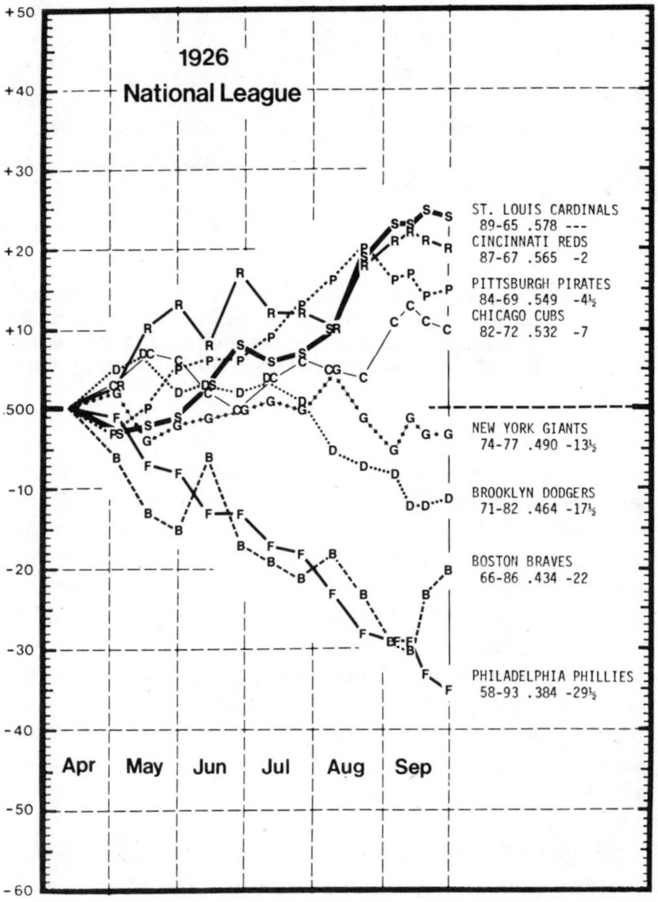

1926
National League
ST. LOUIS CARDINALS
89-65 .578 ---
CINCINNATI REDS
87-67 .565 -2
PITTSBURGH PIRATES
84-69 .549 -4½
CHICAGO CUBS
82-72 .532 -7
NEW YORK GIANTS
74-77 .490 -13½
BROOKLYN DODGERS
71-82 .464 -17½
BOSTON BRAVES
66-86 .434 -22
PHILADELPHIA PHILLIES
58-93 .384 -29½
Apr
May
Jun
Jul
Aug
Sep

**BEWARE THE BRAVES, who made life miserable for the St. Louis Cardinals just before mid-September of 1926, then helped them win their first pennant by treating the Redbirds' competitors in the four-team race just as rudely. Thinking they had finally broken free with a three-game lead, the Cardinals started a four-game series at Boston on September 10th, but by the time they left town, three losses to the Braves had knocked them down to a tie with Cincinnati. Then the Cubs, who still had faint hopes from their position only 4½ games behind at that point, were kayoed by losing five to the Braves while the Cards won five of six at Philadelphia. Then the Braves made the Reds their next victim, all but eliminating them in a three-game sweep. Finally, the Pirates lost two games at Boston as well, but by then the Bucs had already been put away by Brooklyn. The actual clinching by Rogers Hornsby's crew came on the 26th, when they beat the Giants at the Polo Grounds while the Reds were losing at Philadelphia.**

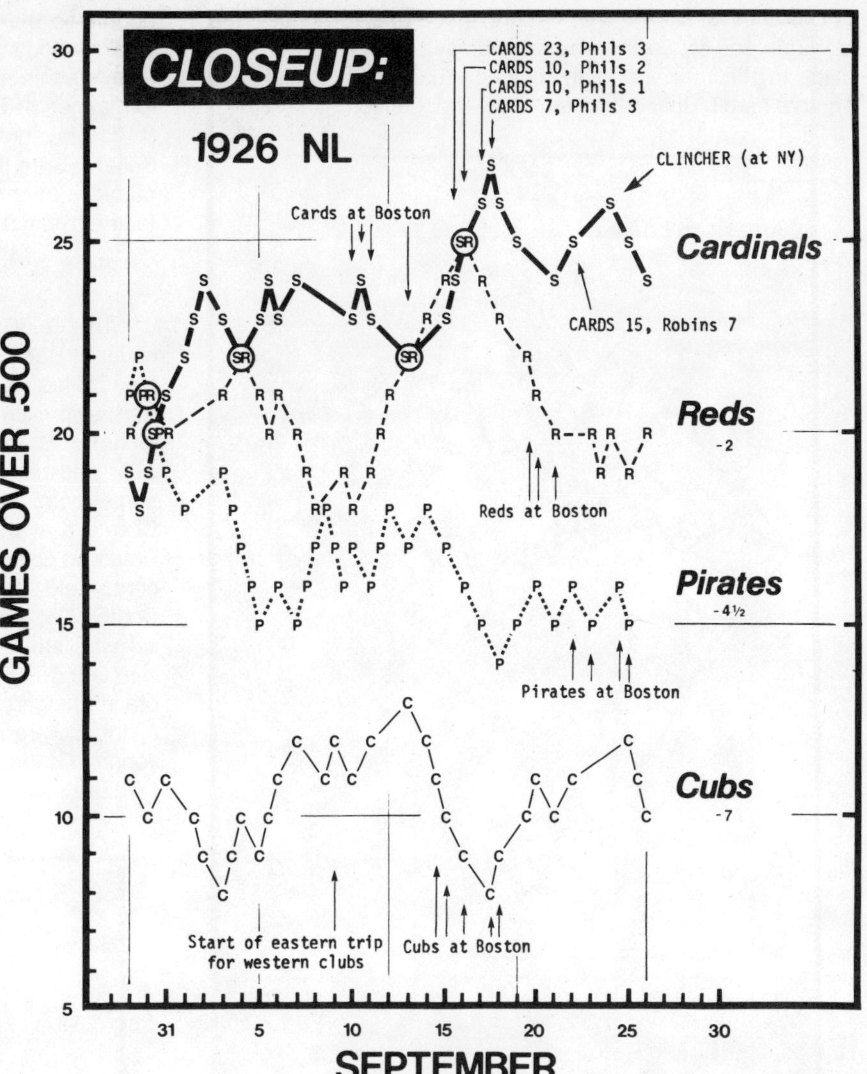


est over the next quarter—St. Louis would come in first or second in 17 years of the 1926-1950 span.

The architect of the Cadinals' 1926 triumph was second baseman-manager Rogers Hornsby. The Rajah had established himself as the NL's greatest hitter with batting-title figures of .370, .397, .401, .384, an incredible .424, and .403 in the previous six seasons and had won the Triple Crown not only in 1922 but again in his first year as manager in 1925. St. Louis's victory was by only a two-game margin, and had called for careful steering by Hornsby through some treacherous waters in September, when all four western clubs of the National League were in contention and on the road in the eastern cities.

The waters were especially treacherous in Boston, where the lowly Braves enjoyed perhaps the most influential role a seventh-place team has played in a tight, crowded pennant race (see closeup).

Hornsby's own output that year was, by his standards, modest—.317, 11 home runs, and 93 RBIs. But he had abundant help from his neighbor at first base, Sunny Jim Bottomley, who led the league in RBIs, his slick double-play partner at short, Tommy Thevenow, and his .325-hitting third sacker, Les Bell, plus the all-.300 outfield of Billy Southworth, Taylor Douthit, and Ray Blades. Flint Rhem (20-7) and Bill Sherdel (16-12) led the Cardinal pitching corps, and during the season Hornsby acquired 39-year-old Pete Alexander from the Cubs. Alexander had reached his declining years, but besides winning nine games for the Cards in the regular season, he had two wins over the Yankees in the '26 World Series. He also got an even more famous save in which he came in from the bullpen to strike out Tony Lazzeri with the bases loaded, preserving a 3-2 lead for the Cards in the deciding seventh game.

Hornsby's thank-you for the world championship was to be traded to the Giants for Frankie Frisch, so strained were the personal encounters between the Rajah and Cardinal owner Sam Breadon, but the chemistry between Hornsby and John McGraw quickly proved to be, if anything, even worse; by April of 1928, McGraw had dealt him to the Boston Braves, who in turn shuttled him to the Cubs in 1929.

The Reds' temporary uprising in 1926 was attributable to good years by Bubbles Hargrave, their catcher, who won the batting title (.352) with only 326 at-bats, the usual lusty hitting by Edd Roush (.323), strong pitching by Pete Donohue (20-14), and continued good mound work also from ex-American Leaguer Carl Mays (19-12). The Pirates had basically their '25 flag-winning roster, augmented by a sparkling rookie in the outfield, Paul Waner. The Cubs' fourth-place position under new manager Joe McCarthy was an impressive rebound from last place in the previous year; they now had Hack Wilson and another hard-hitting outfielder, Riggs Stephenson.

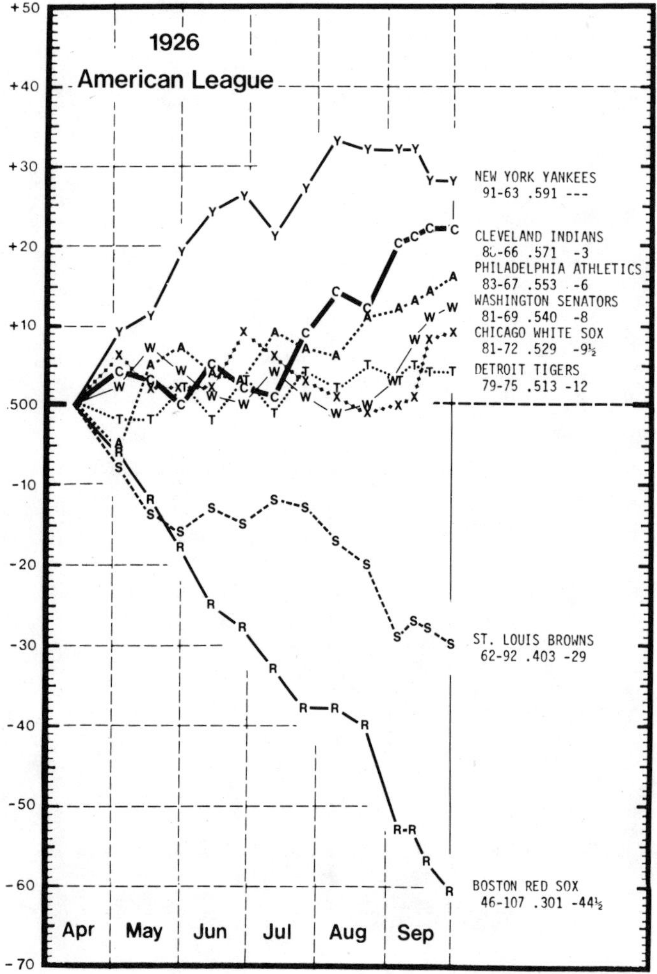


The Yankees' recovery from their various ailments of 1925 was even more impressive, and they did it without any important changes in their pitching staff—Pennock, Shocker, and Hoyt won 23, 19, and 16 games, respectively. The big change, still to be fully realized, was that they were building a more powerful offensive machine than their 1921-23 team, with the arrival of Gehrig, Lazzeri, and outfielder Earle Combs. And Babe Ruth made it clear in 1926 that he would still be the kingpin, returning to his usual productivity with 47 homers, 155 RBIs, and a .372 average. We should note, however, that the '26 Yankees played only slightly above .500 ball in the second half of the season, one of the few pennant-winners to get away with that dubious stunt.

The surprising runnerup team was Cleveland. Led by George Uhle's excellent (27-11) pitching, the Indians were also boosted from their sixth-place finish of the year before by Tris Speaker, who was still manager and now into his late thirties; the remarkable Joe Sewell, who as usual struck out only six times in 578 AB; and one of the less-remembered lifetime-.300 hitters of the period, outfielder Homer Summa. With the Yankees slumping and the Indians surging in the last two months, the winning edge was down to only three games at the end, and doubtless the Clevelanders were wishing for a couple more weeks in the schedule.

In Washington, aging effects began to show in the performances of Senator Johnson (15-16) and Senator Coveleski (14-11), but not in Senator Marberry (12 wins and 22 saves), Senator Sam Rice (.337), or the team's overall hitting. But the falloff in pitching alone was enough to account for the Nats' failure to win three pennants in a row.

## 1927

When Lou Gehrig got a little older, he proved to be the near-equal of Babe Ruth as a hitter. In 1927 the Yankee first baseman drilled 47 home runs, knocked in an unprecedented 175 runs, and averaged .373, the same year that Ruth hit his new record of 60 homers while driving in 164 runs and averaging .356. And here were these two mighty sluggers both on the same team, a one-two punch more powerful than Cobb and Crawford at their peak, or any other pair of teammates. But Ruth and Gehrig were only part of the '27 Yankee offense—in centerfield New York had the league leader in hits, Earle Combs (231 hits, .356) and in left field the veteran Bob Meusel was still in his prime (.337). Another slugger, Tony Lazzeri (.309, 18 home runs, 102 RBIs) was at second base, and the other infielders, Mark Koenig at short and Jumping Joe Dugan at third, were not weak hitters, either. Pat Collins (.275) and Johnny Grabowski (.277) did most of the catching that year. On the mound, the usual skills of Waite Hoyt, Herb Pennock,

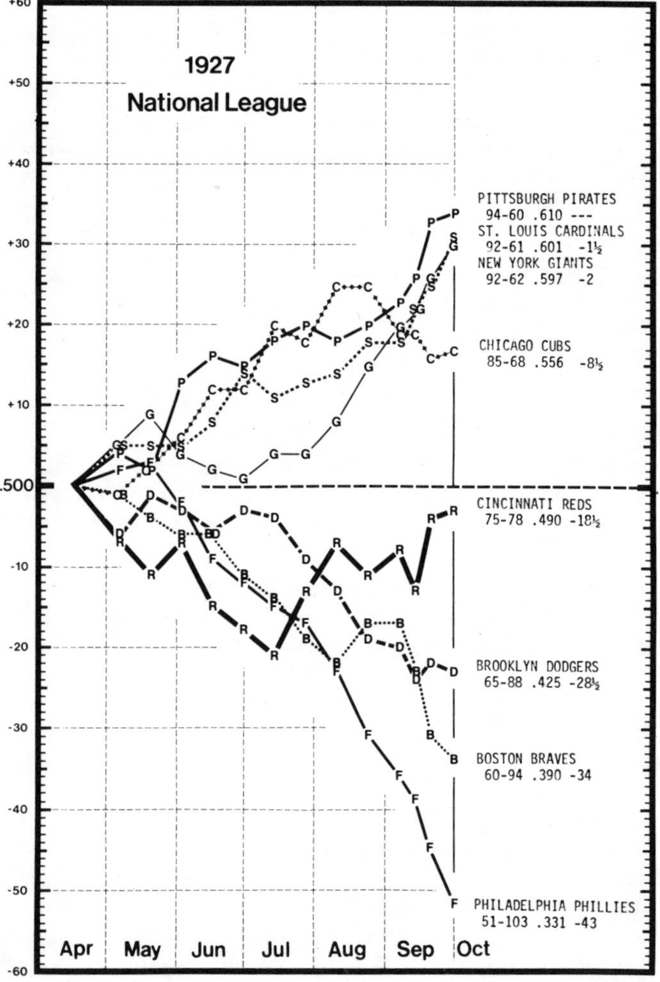

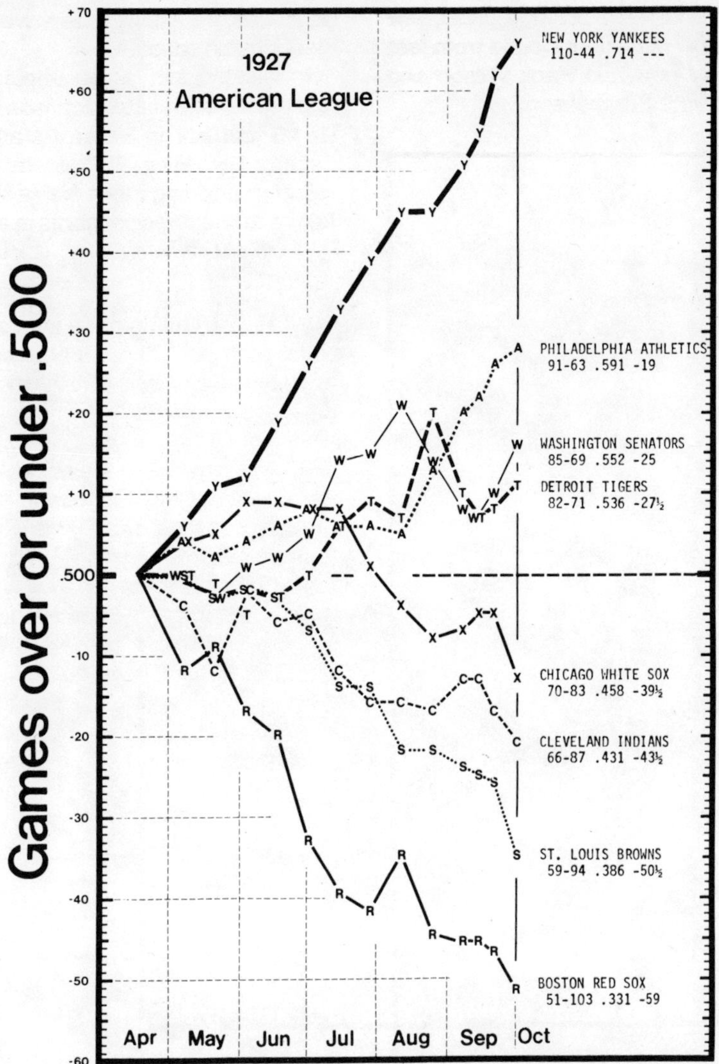


and Urban Shocker were complemented by two pleasant surprises, 30-year-old rookie Wilcy Moore (19-7, league-leading 2.27 ERA) and ex-Senator Dutch Ruether (13-6).

Little wonder, then, that the '27 Yanks took off like a rocket, clinched the AL pennant on September 13th, and set new league records of 110 wins and a 19-game winning margin. Everyone agreed in October that this was the best team the American League had ever seen and certainly the most powerful in its offensive weaponry the major leagues had seen. Today, many still feel that it was best—The Finest Crop—of all time in both leagues.

The Yankees' team batting average of .307 was nearly matched by Pittsburgh's .305 in the other league that year, the Pirate offense being boosted by Paul Waner's .380, his younger brother Lloyd's .355, Pie Traynor's .342, and ex-Senator Joe Harris's .326, but there was a big difference in slugging—no Pirate hit more than nine homers and the team total was only 54. With their pitching staff led by Carmen Hill (22-11, ERA leader with 2.42), they battled the Cubs and Cardinals all season long, and the Giants charged up in August to make it a four-team race. After trailing the Chicago Cubs throughout August, the Pirates recaptured the lead with a 4-3 victory over the Cubs at Pittsburgh on September 1st, and were never headed thereafter. The pennant clinching, however, didn't occur until the next-to-last day of the season.

The Yankees swept the World Series without any awesome display of power (only two home runs, both by Ruth, in the four games) except, according to legend, in batting practice the day before the first game in Pittsburgh, which the Pirate players made the mistake of watching.

## 1928

The almighty Yankees won 39 of their first 48 games in 1928, putting them 30 games over .500 on June 10th—the best start in the first third of a season any team in the modern era has had. With a 12-game lead over the Athletics just after the Fourth of July, the Hugmen were a foregone conclusion to win their sixth pennant in eight years. But incredibly, Connie Mack's new powerhouse turned the race into a squeaker by staging a come-from-behind rivaling any (even 1951's or 1978's) in its graphic and dramatic proportions.

Mack's '28 team had a nucleus of young players, including Lefty Grove, Al Simmons, Jimmy Foxx, Mule Haas, Mickey Cochrane, and Max Bishop, that would bring three more pennants to Philadelphia starting the next year. In addition, there were three 40-year-old superstars on the club who were completing their careers—Ty Cobb (.323 in 95 games in 1928), Tris Speaker (.267 in 40 games), and Eddie Collins (.303

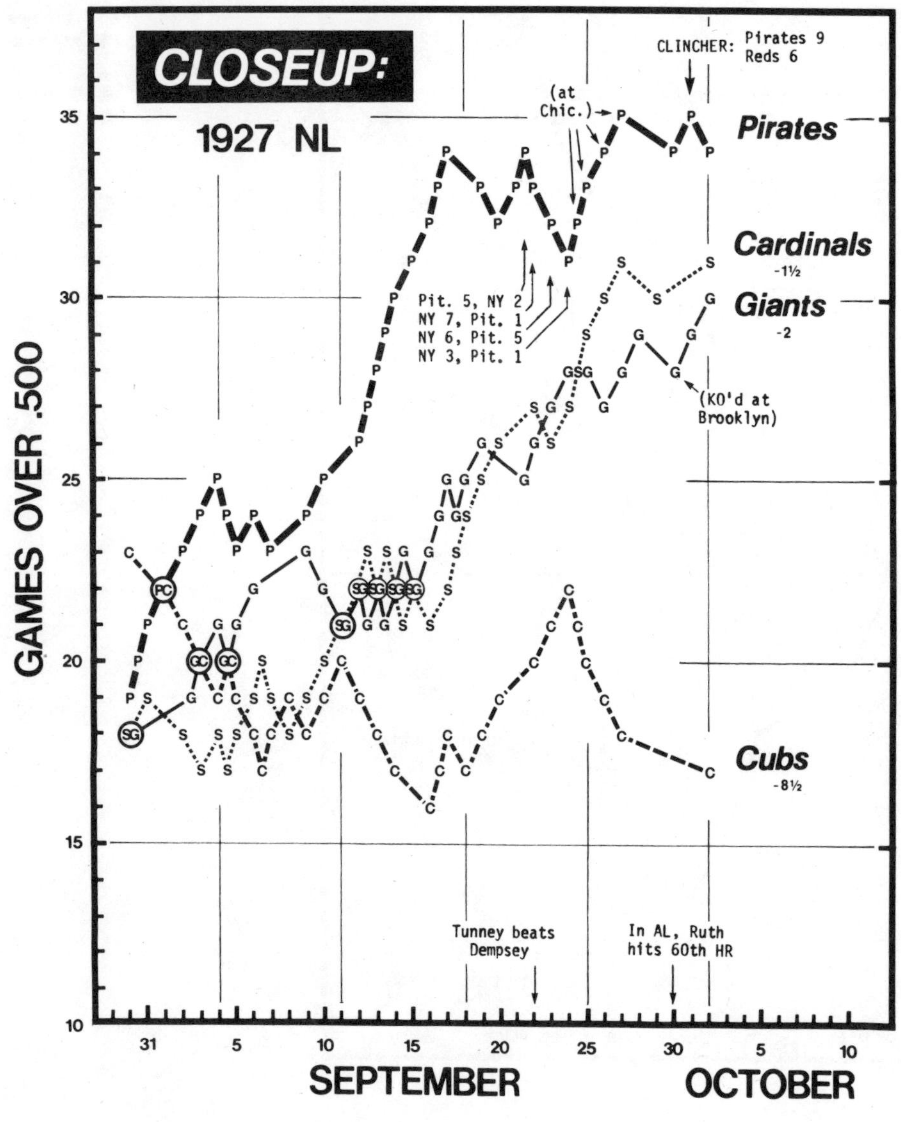


**WANER, WANER, & TRAYNOR, not a law firm, but a batting trio mainly responsible for the Pittsburgh Pirate's 1927 pennant triumph. Paul Waner, his brother Lloyd, and third sacker Pie Traynor contributed batting averages of .380, .355, and .342 to the victorious cause. The Pirates thought they had firm control of the league lead after an 11-game winning streak on September 9-17, but the Giants and Cardinals kept up their pursuit. Three victories by the Giants at Pittsburgh the next week reduced the spread of the top three clubs to 1½ games, but the Bucs recovered with a four-game sweep at Chicago and a final clinching at Cincinnati on October 1st.**

pinchhitting in 36 games). While some of the youngsters as well as the oldsters were only part-time players that year, this was the largest number of Hall of Famers ever clustered together on one club's playing roster—seven (all but Haas and Bishop of those just named).

In July the A's won 25 games, and by August 5th they had chopped the Yanks' lead down to 3½ games. On September 7th the Mackmen caught the Yankees at 40 games over .500, and a day later, completing a four-game sweep over the woebegone Red Sox, they went ahead of New York by half a game. On Sunday the 9th, Yankee Stadium managed to accomodate 85,265 fans, who joyfully watched the Bombers beat the A's twice, first on a 5-0 shutout by George Pipgras and then on a 7-3 shellacking in which Bob Meusel drove in four runs.

That was the season's most dramatic day, but the twin victory didn't really settle the pannant race, because the Athletics salvaged game #4 of the series and got right back to within a half-game of the Yankees the following weekend, when both clubs started western road trips. The critical difference occurred in Detroit, where the A's lost two they could not afford to on the 21st and 22nd, and where the Yanks beat the Tigers in four games out of five in their season-ending series.

There were no other true contenders in the American League in 1928, but the St. Louis Browns had one of their best years, thanks to topnotch pitching by Alvin "General" Crowder (21-5) and Sam Gray (20-12), and to their one superb hitter, Heinie Manush (.378, 241 hits). Cleveland went the other way, sagging almost to the Red Sox' lowly position, when the Indians' ace George Uhle developed a sore arm and nobody else on the mound staff could be found to take up the slack.

Pipgras (24-13) and Waite Hoyt (23-7) were Huggins's preeminent hurlers in the Yankee victory, making up for a mediocre (4-4) year by '27 hero Wilcy Moore and Urban Shocker's fatal illness (he died on September 9, 1928). Ruth and Gehrig were in their customary form, sharing the league lead in RBIs with 142, while Ruth hit 54 homers and Gehrig batted .374. The batting lineup was about the same as in the previous year, except that Huggins played rookie Leo Durocher regularly at second base after Tony Lazzeri injured his shoulder in August. Another rookie, who promised to solve the Yankees' one weakness behind the plate and did so in fine fashion starting the very next year, also got a brief trial; his name was Bill Dickey.

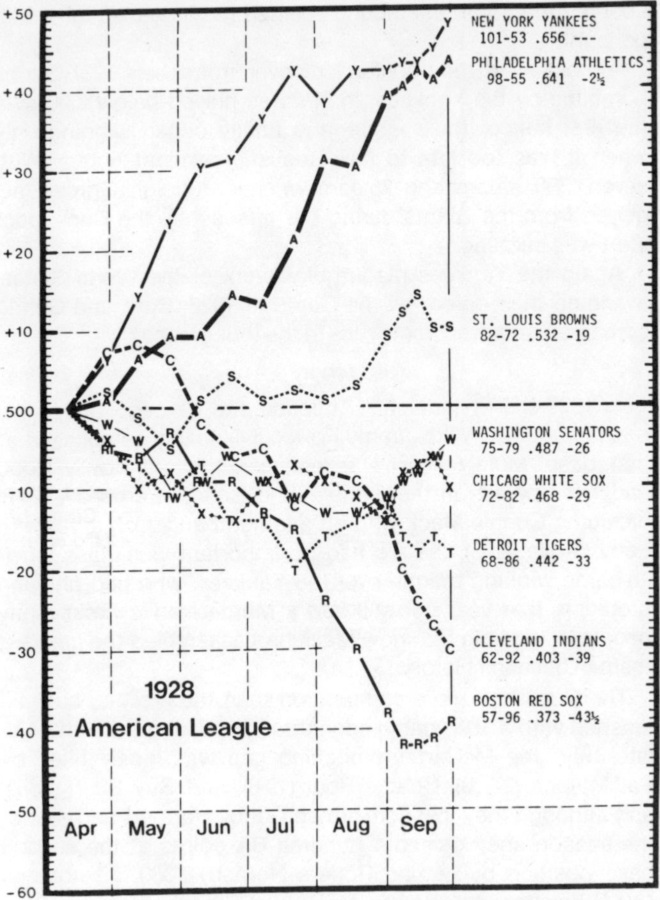


In the National League, the St. Louis Cardinals climbed back to the pinnacle, winning a tight race under a new manager, BIll McKechnie. Since their 1926 world championship, the Cards had made quite a few lineup changes: besides Frisch at second base, they now had Rabbit Maranville at short and Wattie Holm at third, and outfielder Chick Hafey was the team batting star (he hit .337 in 1928). Jim Bottomley, league leader in home runs (31) and RBIs (136), was still at first base. Bill Sherdel (21-10), Jesse Haines (20-8), and the amazing Pete Alexander (16-9 at age 41) provided first-rate pitching.

John McGraw was now without Hornsby or another Hall of Famer, Ross Youngs, whose career was tragically ended near its midpoint by a fatal illness in 1927. But as usual, impressive newcomers kept appearing in the Giant lineup. In 1928 they included outfielders Mel Ott (.322 in his first full season), Lefty O'Doul (.319), and Jim Welsh (.307), catcher Shanty Hogan (.333), and pitchers Larry Benton (25-9) and Carl Hubbell (10-6). McGraw still had Terry, Jackson, and Lindstrom in the infield, and third-year-man Freddie Fitzsimmons (20-9) on the mound, as well. With all this talent, it should come as no surprise that the Giants were in the pennant fight right up to the day before closing day; indeed, some would say that it was surprising the Giants didn't win the pennant.

One reason they did not was the Chicago Cubs' increasing strength. This was manifested decisively in the season's final week, when the Cubs whipped McGraw's men in three games out of four at the Polo Grounds while the Cardinals swept a three-game set in Boston (see closeup). The Cubs now had their outfield set, with Wilson, Stephenson, and Cuyler, and had developed a stellar backstop in Gabby Hartnett; only some

**A PAIR OF THOROUGHBREDS—Miller Huggins's New York Yankees and Connie Mack's Philadelphia Athletics—had a dramatic meeting in Yankee Stadium before more than 85,000 fans on September 9, 1928, near the time when each team was said to be the greatest in baseball history. The Yankees won the doubleheader that day and the AL pennant three weeks later, but the A's had served notice that summer that they were taking over the league for the next three years.**

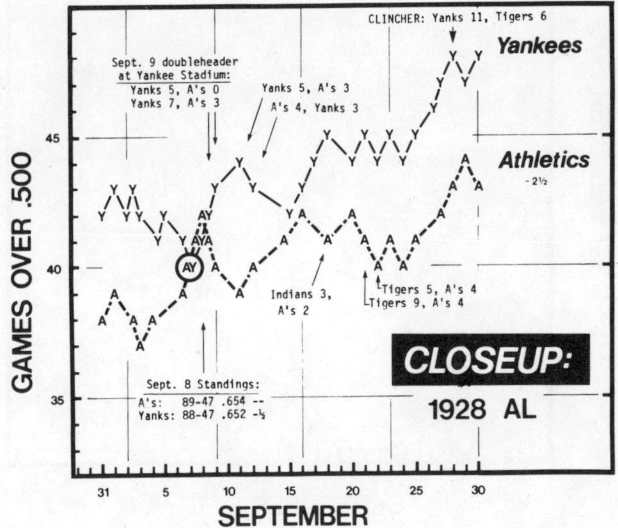


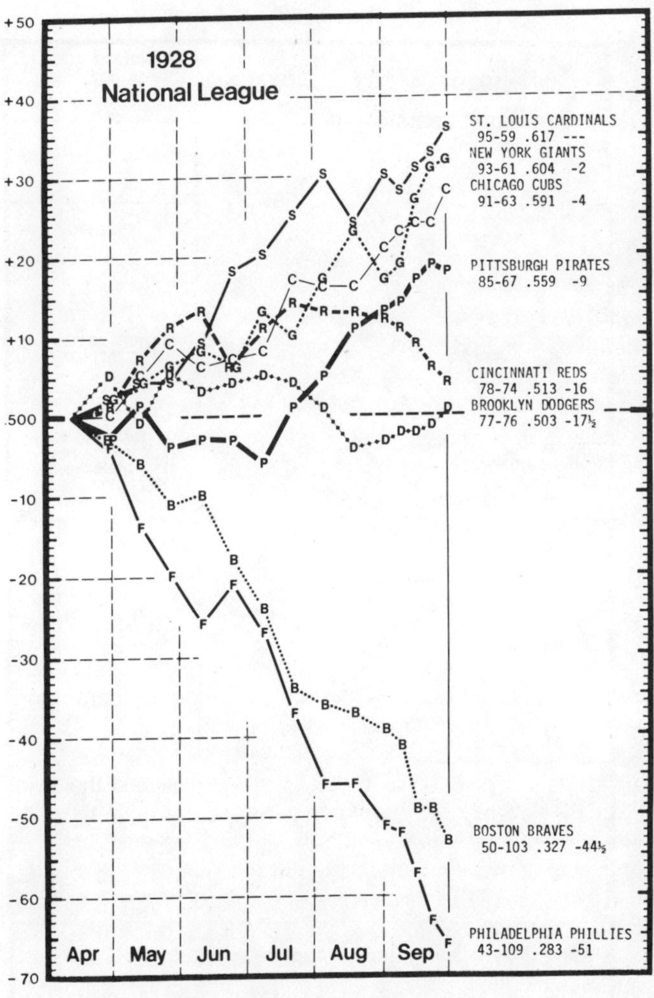

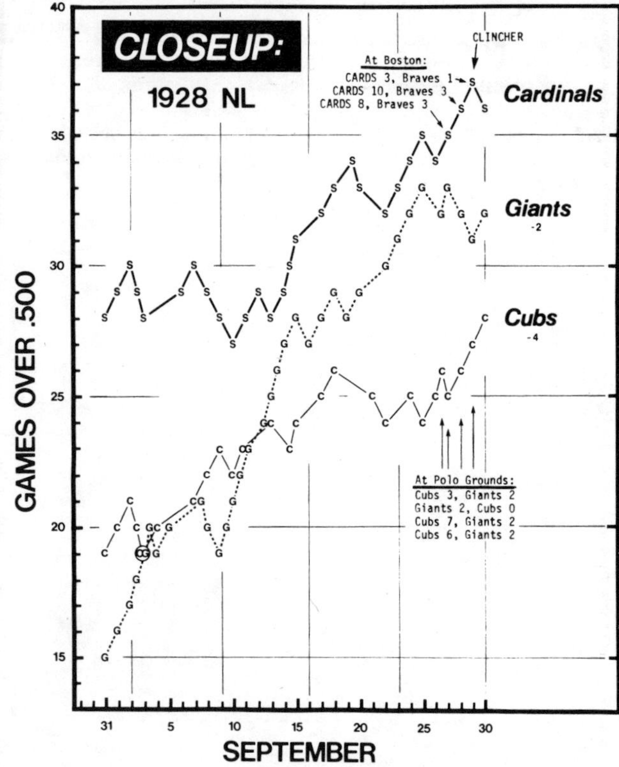


added strength on the mound seemed to be needed for a Cub pennant.

Almost as if they couldn't recover from their 1927 Series humbling by the Yankees, the Pirates played below .500 over the first half of the season, and finally began winning only when it was too late to have realistic pennant hopes. With seven .300 hitters and 25-game-winner Burleigh Grimes (acquired from the Giants during the offseason), the Bucs' poor start was puzzling.

Again the Yankees made quick work of the World Series, avenging their defeat by the Cards in 1926; Ruth and Gehrig combined for seven home runs in the four games.

## 1929

In 1929 the Philadelphia Athletics and Chicago Cubs won pennants easily. With Jimmy Foxx (.354) solidly established at first base, Mule Haas (.313) replacing the retiring Ty Cobb and Tris Speaker in the outfield, and George Earnshaw (24-8) providing Connie Mack with an ace righthander on a par with Lefty Grove (20-6), the A's had no important weakness. Their 18-game winning margin over the Yankees, who had pitching problems that year but still had a Murderers Row, set many people to thinking that now Mack had assembled the greatest team in baseball history.

The Cubs had more competition than the A's did, but still finished with a 10½-game edge after overtaking the Pirates in late July. Joe McCarthy's pitching gap was nicely filled by Pat Malone (22-10), Charlie Root (19-6), and Guy Bush (18-7), and although they lost sore-armed Gabby Hartnett for most of the season, they gained a hundred BA points at the second base position by getting Rogers Hornsby (.380, 39 homers, 149 RBIs) from the Braves to replace Freddie Maguire. Cuy-

Games over or under .500

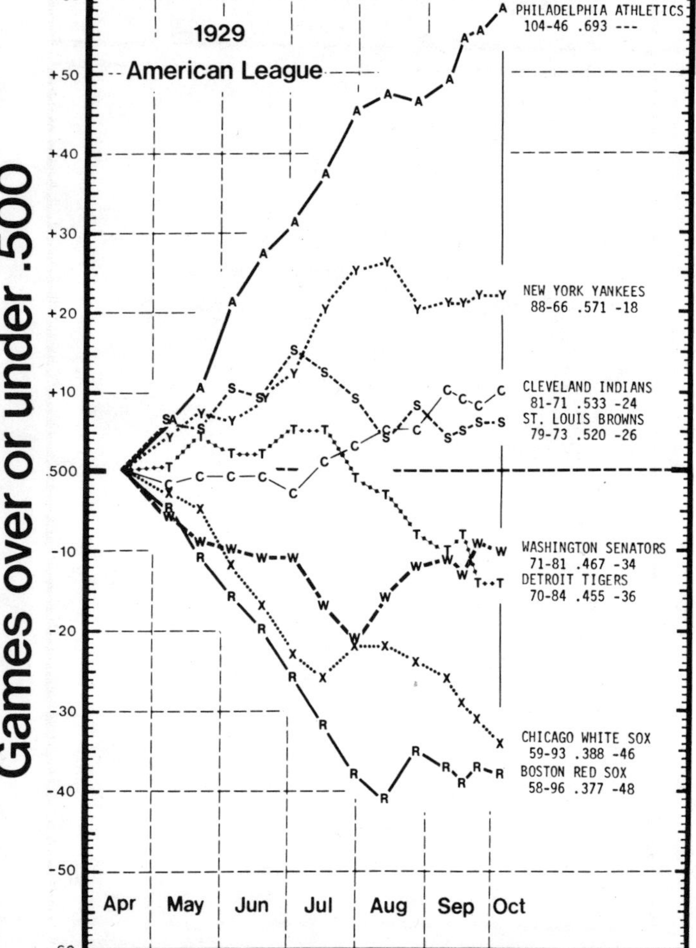


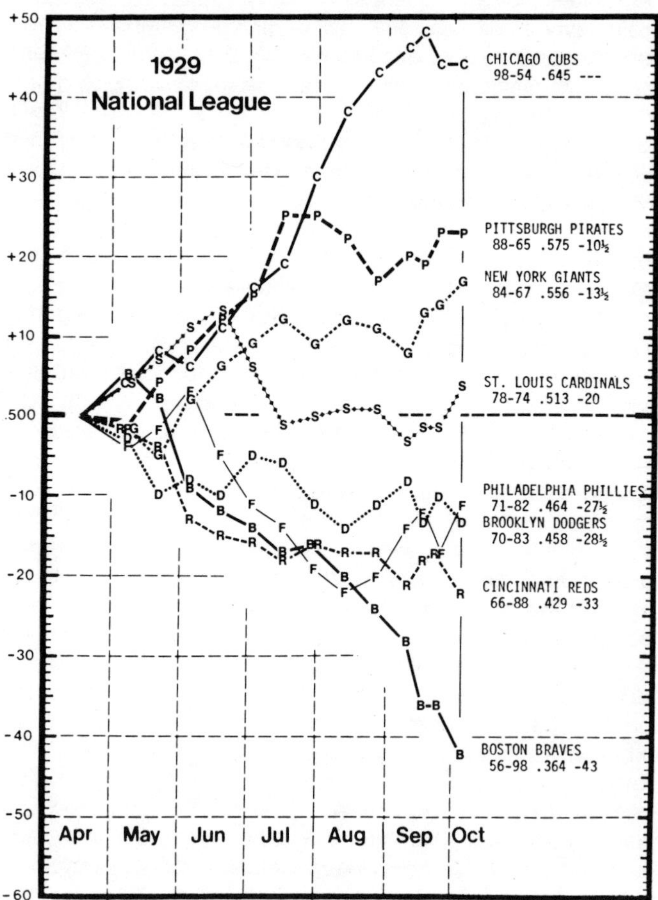

ler, Wilson, and Stephenson supplied the rest of the power, the three combining for an average over .350.

As further evidence of their supremacy, the Athletics beat the Cubs handily in the World Series, four games to one; the Series highlight came in the fourth game when the A's overcame an 8-0 Cub lead with ten runs in the bottom of the seventh inning.

## 1930

The 1930 American League season was almost a carbon copy of 1929 except for a striking improvement by the Washington Senators, who reduced the Athletics' winning margin to eight games. Five 15-game winners on Manager Walter Johnson's mound staff—Lloyd Brown, Sad Sam Jones, General Crowder, Firpo Marberry, and Bump Hadley—combined for the only team earned run average under 4.00 in the major leagues, and the Washington offense returned to the .300-plus level of the Senators' 1924-25 pennant years with the advent of youngsters Joe Cronin, Buddy Myer, and Sammy West.

Connie Mack's "million dollar infield" of Jimmy Foxx, Max Bishop, Joe Boley, and Jimmy Dykes was now set, and he had power, in Foxx, Al Simmons, and Mickey Cochrane, that was nearly equal to New York's Ruth, Gehrig, and Combs. And in pitching, the A's were in better shape than any other team in the majors, with Grove (28-5, and 2.54, only ERA under 3.00 in the AL) and Earnshaw (22-13).

Other AL clubs were not only less fortunate, but in one glaring case—the Boston Red Sox—mired in depths of despair. As if there weren't enough to feel down in the dumps about in the summer following the collapse of Wall Street, the Bosox struggled to their sixth straight finish in last place. To some Boston fans, then, it seemed downright fiendish when the Yankees raised the ghost of Harry Frazee on the 1930 closing day at Fenway Park by putting Babe Ruth on the mound against the Red Sox; pitching his first full game in nine years, Ruth dealt the Sox their 102nd loss of the season.

Like some other great baseball organizations, the St. Louis Cardinals were beginning to find new ways of winning. In 1930, they employed the dramatic come-from-behind method, bringing overwhelming success and joy to the St. Louis fans. Those fans had rightfully given up on pennant thoughts in early August, when the Redbirds were more than ten games behind an upstart Dodger team and pretty far behind Chicago and New York as well.

Brooklyn at that point had eyebrows raised all around the league. Led once again by the imperishable Dazzy Vance, and with Babe Herman's near-.400 batting, Uncle Robby's men were hitting over .300 as a team. But in 1930 that was nothing—every NL club except the Braves and Reds hit over .300 that crazy year, when an even livelier ball was temporarily in use. A little later in August, the Brooklyn bubble seemed to burst when the Robins fell beneath the Cubs and Giants in a terrible slump, but they recovered in September. On September 9-11, they met the leading Cubs in a three-game series at Ebbets Field that proved to be an important part of the 1930 plot. In that confrontation, the Cubs were limited to one run and 15 hits in the three games by Brooklyn's Ray Phelps, Dolf Luque, and Vance—this being the Cub team that had its star slugger, Hack Wilson, threatening Babe Ruth's 60-homer mark. (Wilson did set the NL home run record of 56 and the even less approachable major league record of 190 RBIs that year.) Two days after this sweep, the Cubs found themselves in third place, reeling to the point where they had trouble beat-

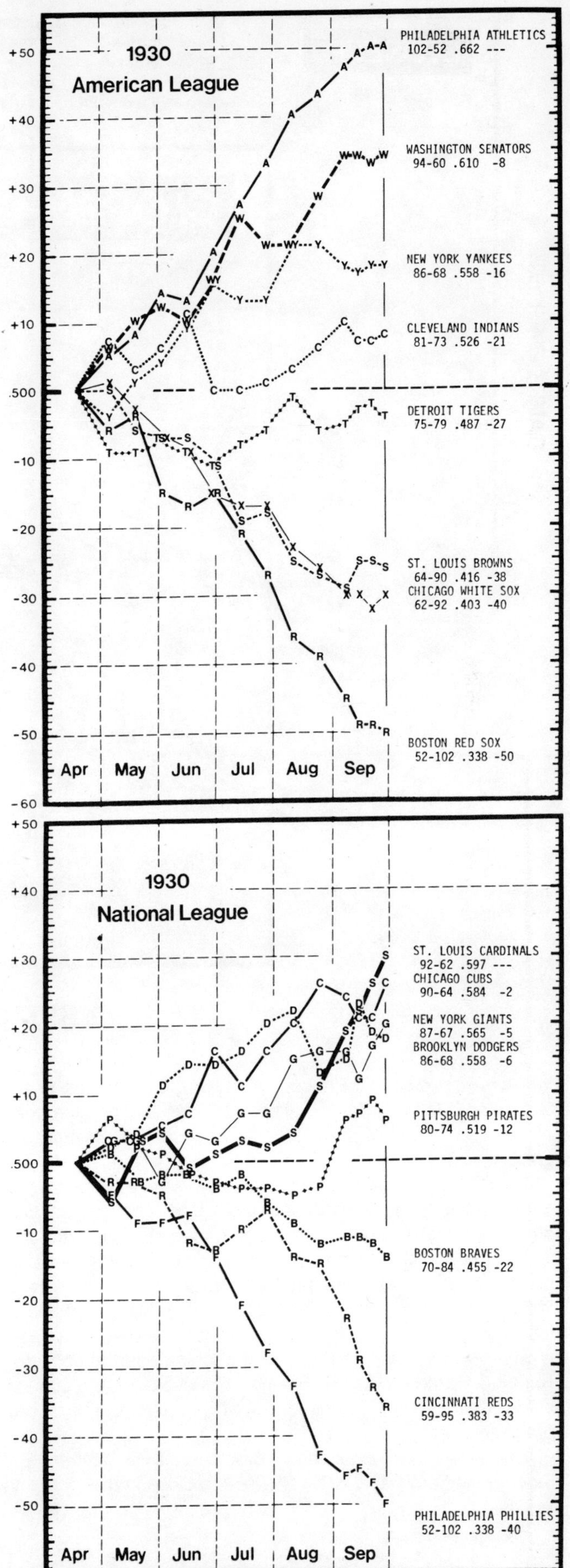

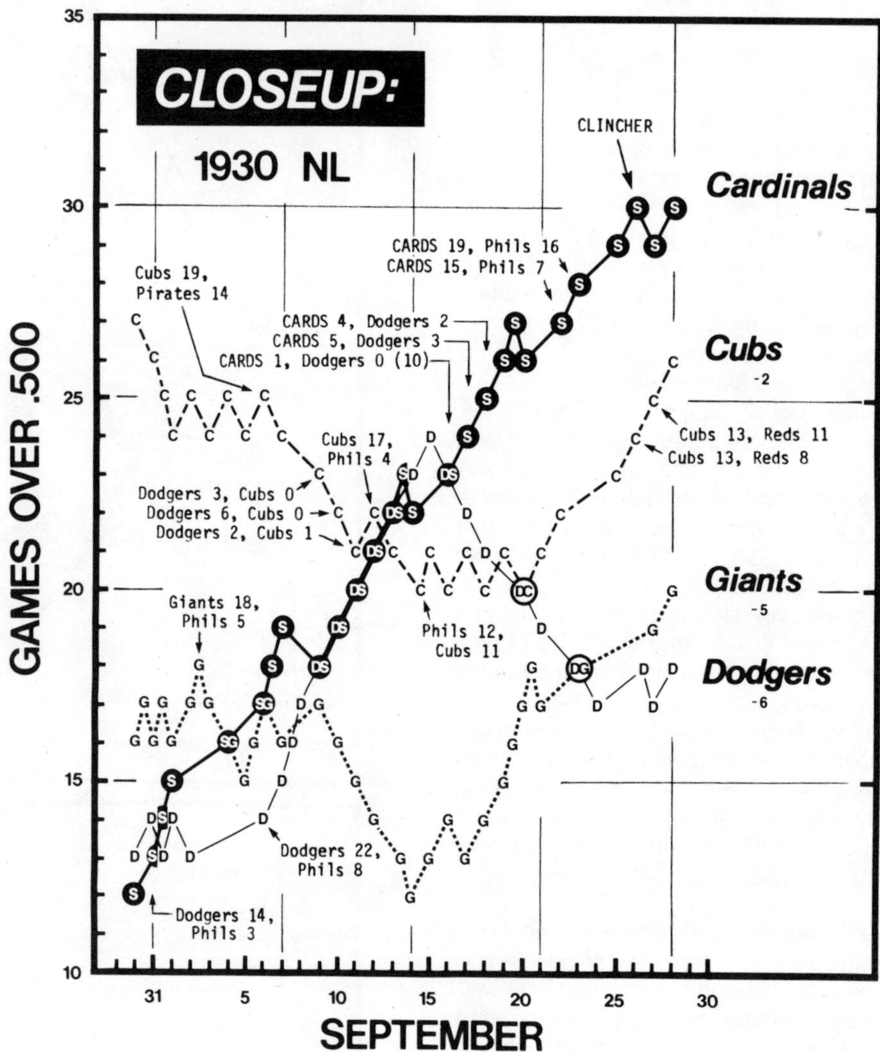


**REDBIRD RAMPAGE. Losing only four games in September, the 1930 St. Louis Cardinals smashed through the Giants, Cubs, and tenacious Dodgers in a thriller. Notice the scores of some of the games—that was the year of the extra-lively ball, when the futile Phillies batted .315 as a team but had a team ERA of 6.71.**

ing even the pathetic Phillies; with additional losses to the Giants and Braves later that week, Chicago reached the point of no return (to first place) even though it won its final six games.

The Robins did return to first place, just after the Cub sweep, but only briefly, because it was about that time that the Cardinal juggernaut passed through on its way to the pennant—St. Louis was in the process of winning 36 of its last 46 games, after having been only four games over .500 on August 10th. With Gabby Street as manager and a dozen .300 hitters led by Hafey and Frisch, the Cardinals became unstoppable when they got some badly needed pitching help by acquiring Burleigh Grimes from the Braves at midseason; the 36-year-old spitballer won 13 games for the Cards over the latter half of the season.

When the Cardinals invaded Brooklyn on September 16th, they had already passed the Giants and Cubs in the race, and were a game behind the Robins after having been tied with them most of the previous week. In this confrontation, the Brooklyn pitchers were overmatched by Grimes and his colleagues, the Cards taking 1-0, 5-3, and 4-2 victories that put them ahead in the race to stay. The Cubs' terminal winning streak delayed the clinching to the final Friday of the season, but the Cards had left little doubt about the outcome as they departed from Flatbush on the 18th. After all their strenuous efforts in the exciting race, the valiant Robins wound up in fourth place as a result of a hot streak in the final two weeks by the Giants.

Although the Cardinals had a team batting average of .314 (after the Giants' .319 and the last-place Phillies' .315), their bats were effectively silenced by Grove and Earnshaw in the 1930 World Series, hitting only .200. The Athletics had an even lower average, 197, but won the Series in six games on their superior hurling.

# 1931-1940

## 1931

In 1931, the Yankees, now managed by Joe McCarthy, still had Ruth and Gehrig's home run show (46 apiece) and led the American League again in team batting, but the Athletics' pitching superiority became even more obvious. At age 31 in 1931, Lefty Grove won 31 games while losing only four and compiling a stunning 2.05 ERA. George Earnshaw (21-7) was in his usual fine form, and now Mack had a third mound artist, Rube Walberg (20-12), plus Roy Mahaffey (15-4). The Yankees also had a new ace, Lefty Gomez (21-9 and holder of the only other ERA below 3.00) and an effective workhorse named Red Ruffing (16-14), but little more to compare with the A's staff. The Senators also remained strong, having acquired Heinie Manush from the Browns during the 1930 season, and still getting some offensive punch from Sam Rice (.310 in 413 AB) at age 41. It was again very impressive, then, that the Athletics beat these two teams handily—the Yanks by 13½ and the Senators by 16 games—in the 1931 AL pennant race.

Much the same could be said for the Cardinals' repeat victory in the NL race. This fourth win in six years for St. Louis was by 13 games over the Giants and 17 games over the Cubs. The Cards were again led by Chick Hafey's hitting (he beat Bill Terry for the batting title, .3489 to .3486), and got almost as much bat production from Jim Bottomley (.348) and Frankie Frisch (.311 and MVP). They also got good pitching from Wild Bill Hallahan, rookie Paul Derringer, and Burleigh Grimes.

Besides Terry, who had batted .401 in 1930, the Giants had Mel Ott, Travis Jackson, Fred Lindstrom, Freddy Leach, and Shanty Hogan still pounding the ball, and the Cubs were still a powerhouse with Hornsby, Charlie Grimm, Kiki Cuyler, Gabby Hartnett, and young Woody English. Injuries, and perhaps morale problems stemming from John McGraw's increasingly rigid and cantankerous ways, slowed the Giants' pennant push, and the Cubs were hurt by Hack Wilson's sharp drop in hitting (.261, 13 homers, 61 RBIs).

The Athletics were heavy favorites to win the World Series for an unprecedented third straight time, which might have clinched the case for the many who argued that Connie Mack had the greatest team of all time, but things didn't work out that way. The A's and Cards battled for seven games, in most of which the batting, baserunning, and fielding exploits of the Cardinals' young centerfielder, Pepper Martin, have become legendary, and these made St. Louis the surprise winner.

## 1932

The Athletics and Yankees swapped roles in 1932, Philadelphia becoming the AL slugging leader with 58 home runs by Jimmy Foxx and New York taking over the league's pitching leadership. As a result, the Yankees also took over the top spot in the standings, easily winning the pennant with about the same margin as the Mackmen's in 1931. The Yankees were still Bombers at the plate with Ruth, Gehrig, Lazzeri, Combs, and Dickey, but with recent additions—Frankie Crosetti at shortstop and ex-Indian Joe Sewell at third base—Joe McCarthy was emphasizing defensive abilities as well. The important change in New York's overall strength was the continued development of Lefty Gomez (24-7) and Red Ruffing (18-7) and the uncovering of rookie Johnny Allen (17-4). The Athletics' team ERA increased from 3.47 in '31 to 4.45, but Grove was still superb with 25-10 and 2.84 marks.

Boston Red Sox fans thought their low point had come in 1930, since the Bosox managed to climb out of the cellar with a winning spurt in September of 1931, but in 1932 the team's fortnightly won-lost records ran 3-11 (.214) on May 1, 4-20 (.167) on May 15, 7-30 (.189) on May 29, 10-41 (.196) on June 12, and 12-51 (.190, or 39 games below .500) on June 26—the worst start of any major league team in the modern era. Their final 43-111 record was not the worst of the century, thanks to the 1916 A's, but finishing 64 games behind the Yankees was, for Bostonians, total disgrace. In team averages the Red Sox were the AL's worst in hitting and pitching, yet, oddly, they had the league batting champion in first baseman Dale Alexander (.367 in 392 AB).

The team with the best record in the American League in the last two months of the '32 season was Washington. The Senators won 34 games while losing only 12 after August 7th, and once again a pennant-race curve that steep in August and September was predictive of an impending flag win. Monty Weaver's good rookie year (22-10) on the mound was a factor in the Senators' upswing in 1932, but much less a factor in later years. The Cleveland Indians, now managed by Roger Peckinpaugh, also were displaying a new wave of strength, and had some new talent to account for it, including pitcher Wes Ferrell (23-13) and hitters Joe Vosmik, Earl Averill, and Dick Porter. And wherever Cleveland went, Detroit was sure to follow (or vice versa)—the Tigers were on the rise again.

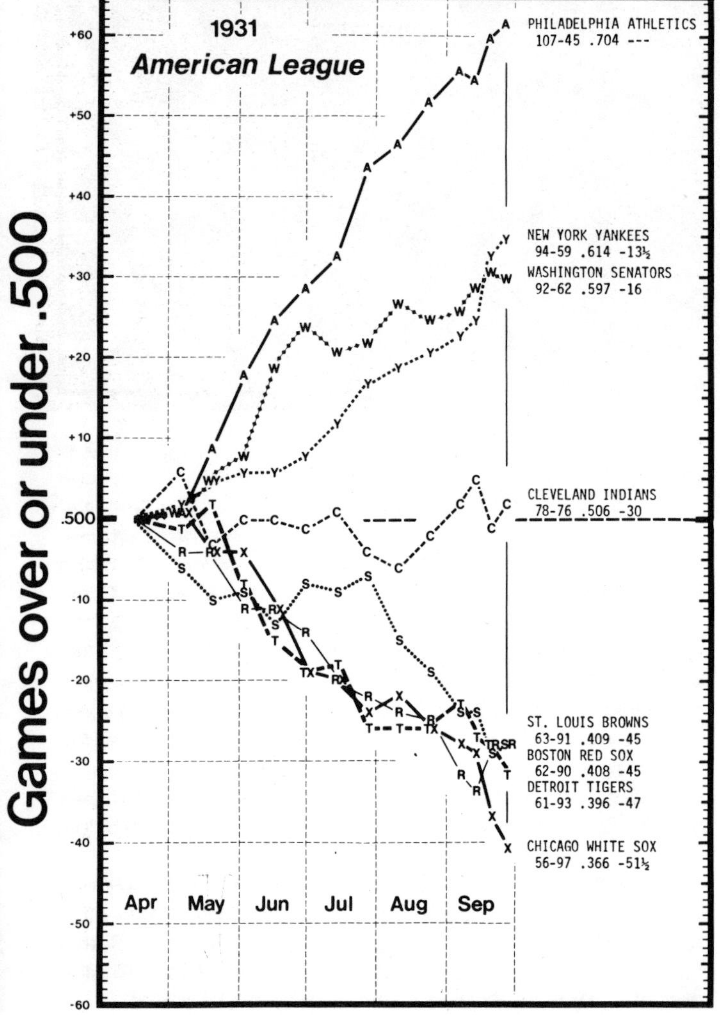


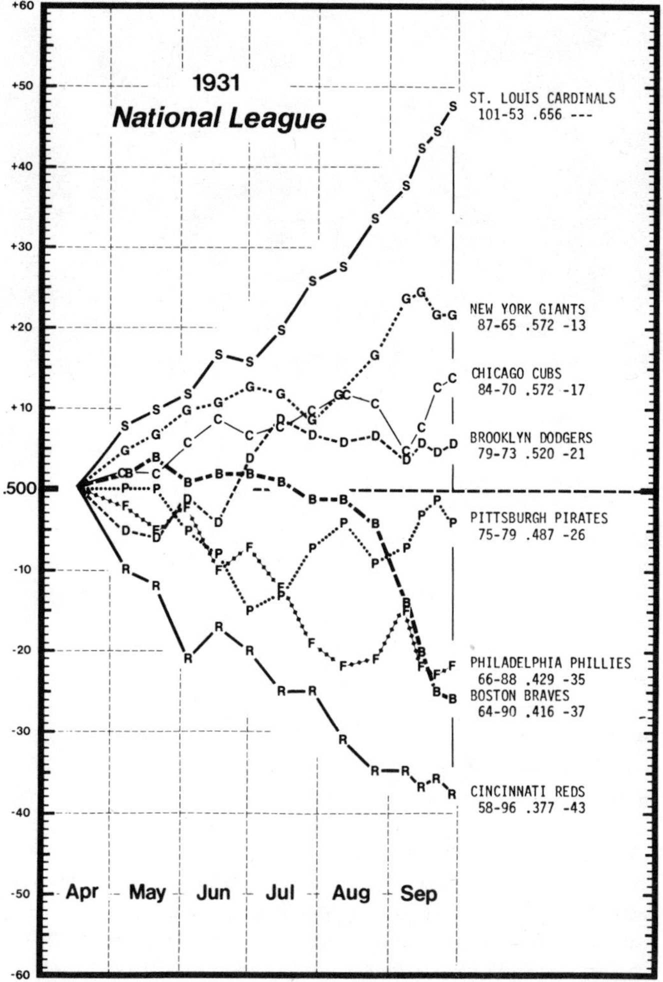

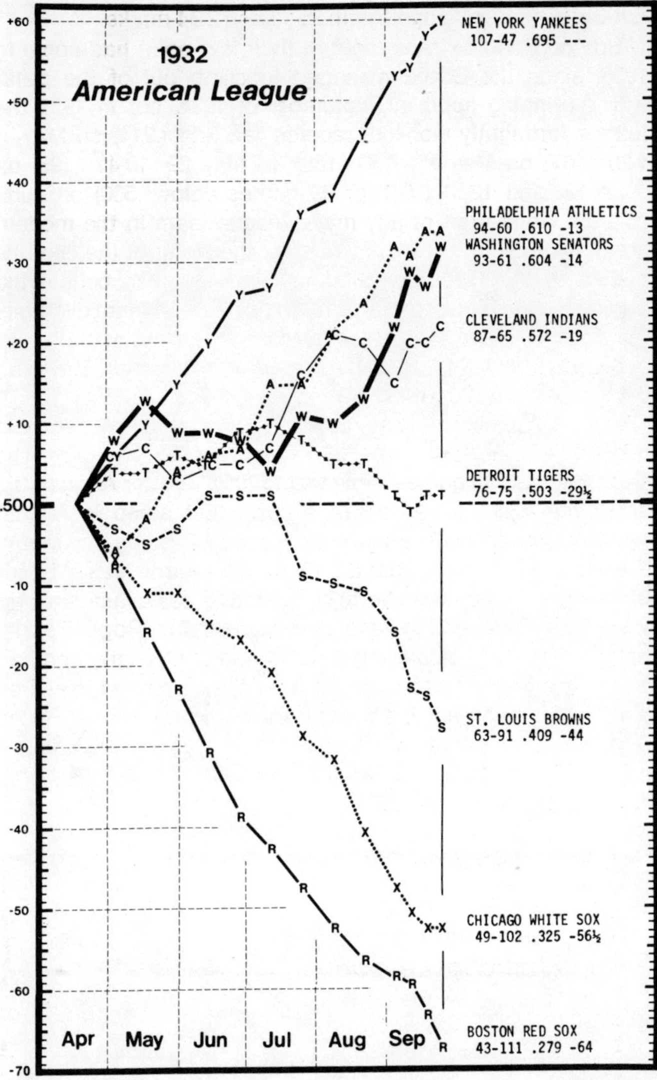


The National League had two important managerial changes in 1932. One was at New York, where after 30 years and ten pennants—but none since 1924—John McGraw stepped down in favor of Bill Terry. This was not a case of quit-while-you're-ahead—the Giants had sunk to last place around Memorial Day, and McGraw's relationships with his players were a shambles. The once-mighty Giants barely eked out a sixth-place finish that year, and when they did, it was a tie with—of all teams—the world champion St. Louis Cardinals. The Cards were racked with injuries and also suffered a team slump in hitting, partly from the aging of their veterans, and their only pitcher to win more than a dozen games was a 21-year-old freshman named Dizzy Dean (18-15).

The other passing of the reins was at Chicago, where on August 7th Charlie Grimm took over from Rogers Hornsby after a row between The Rajah and Cub owner William Veeck (Bill's father). The negative vibrations between the two stemmed from conflicts about the running of the team, but matters were not helped by the fact that the Cubs had lost their league lead to the Pittsburgh Pirates in late June. The Pirates, who were still getting great run production from the Waner brothers and Pie Traynor, and now had a rookie shortstop, Arkie Vaughn, hitting near the level of those veterans, were having a season of ups and downs—two ups and two downs, to be more precise. They were in a losing streak, their second down period of the year, when Grimm took charge of the Cubs.

Many of the '29 Cub players were on the '32 roster, among them Cuyler, Stephenson, Hartnett, Root, Rush, and Grimm himself. To fill gaps left by Hack Wilson, now with Brooklyn, and Hornsby, only an occasional player at age 36, Chicago had Johnny Moore and Billy Herman, both .300 hitters but not heavy sluggers, and more importantly, Lon Warneke, the NL's best pitcher in his rookie year (22-6, 2.37). Further aided by ex-Yankee Mark Koenig's .353 clip in the late stages, the Cubs jumped to a commanding lead around Labor Day under Grimm, and captured the flag with relative ease despite pressure from Pittsburgh's second upsurge.

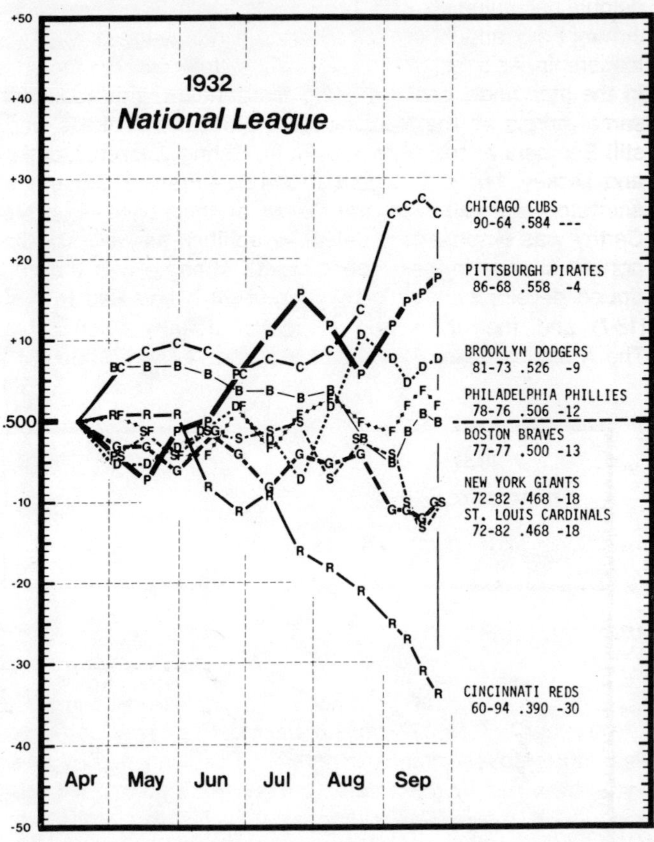


The Boston Braves had their best spring since the 1890s, actually challenging for the lead into July, but a succession of injuries brought them down to a .500 finish. The Dodgers, who said goodbye to Uncle Robbie after the 1931 season and installed Max Carey as manager, got a sizzling drive going in August after sagging to seventh; just before the Cubs' leap, Brooklyn passed Pittsburgh and came to within 1½ games of the league lead, eventually finishing third. The Phillies were also a surprise, having a winning record at season's end for the first time since 1917. As in most recent years since the mid-twenties, they had several .300 hitters, headed by the prodigious slugger Chuck Klein, but this was more meaningful in a year like 1932, when the less-lively ball reduced all team batting averages in the major leagues to below .300.

The 1932 World Series amounted to a slaughter of the Cubs by the Yankees in four games, 12-6, 5-2, 7-5, and 13-6. Among eight homers blasted by New York was Babe Ruth's fabled (and perhaps mythical) "called shot" off Charley Root in the third game, the last Series home run by the Bambino.

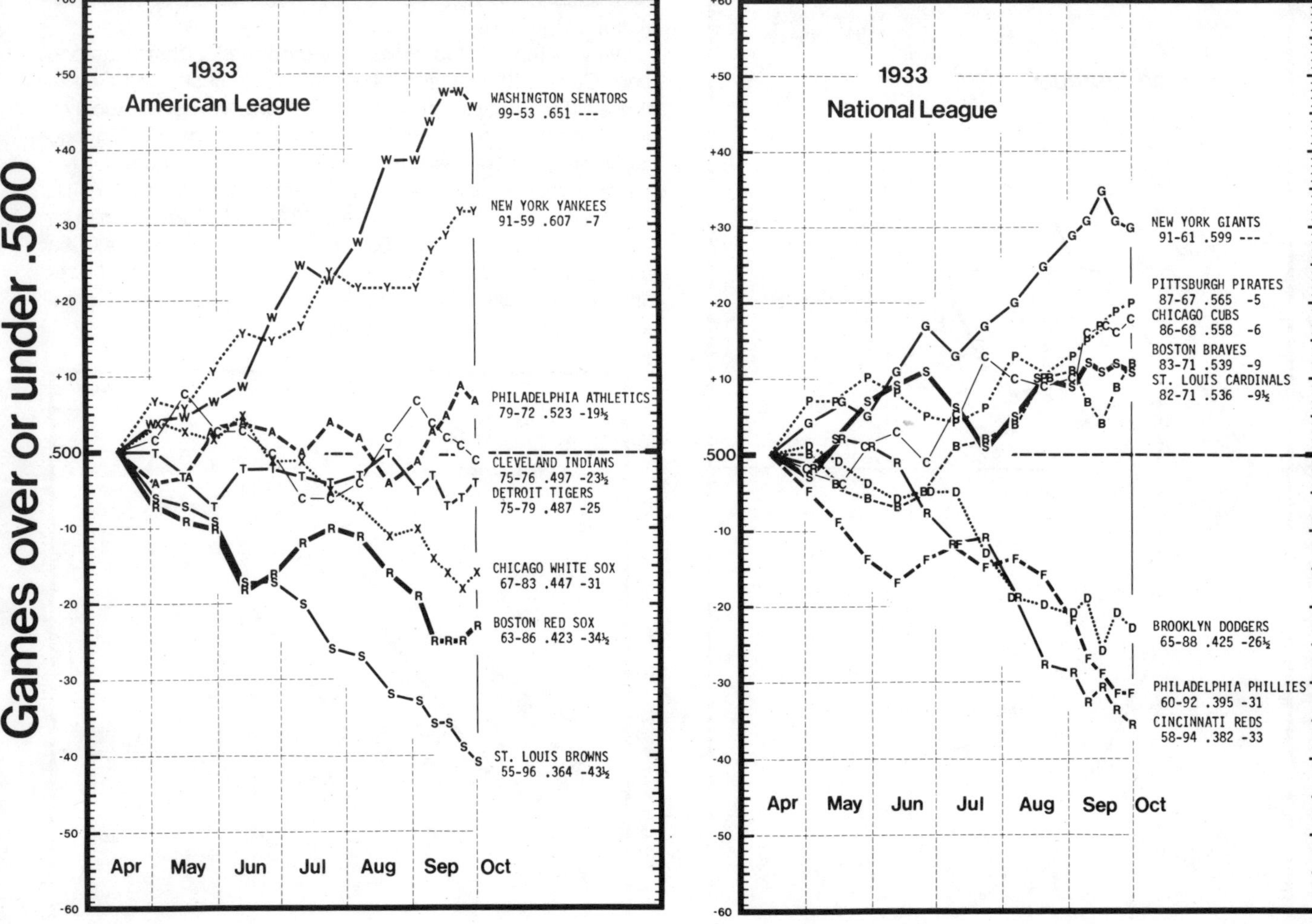


## 1933

In January of 1933, Franklin Delano Roosevelt came to Washington to lead the country out of the Depression, and a month later Tom Yawkey came to Boston to lead the Red Sox fans out of theirs. The millionaire from South Carolina intended to give Boston the best team money can buy, the way Jake Ruppert had done it for the Yankees in 1921, and only 13 short years and another whole world war after Yawkey purchased the Red Sox, his efforts were rewarded by the raising of the 1946 AL flag in Fenway Park. The first acquisitions of any consequence by Yawkey in 1933 were catcher Rick Ferrell and infielder Bill Werber, who helped the Red Sox climb out of last place; as the graph shows, this happened in June and marked an important turning point for the Boston club even though it moved up only one notch in the standings that year.

Not only FDR, but also the American League pennant came to Washington, the Senators' third and last in that location. The veteran pitchers General Crowder (24-15), Earl Whitehill (22-8), and Lefty Stewart (15-6), all in their thirties, led the Nats' drive, and were supported by outfielders Heinie Manush and Goose Goslin and infielders Joe Cronin, Joe Kuhel, and Buddy Myer. The Senators went ahead for keeps in August when the Yankees experienced a falloff in their pitching and some decline in hitting—Babe Ruth was now 38, and for him the figures of .301 and 34 homers represented signs of aging.

Under severe financial pressures again, Connie Mack once more dismantled the Athletics. Before the '33 season, he had traded Al Simmons, Mule Haas, and Jimmy Dykes to the White Sox, and after the season he sent Lefty Grove, Max Bishop, and Rube Walberg to Yawkey at Boston. With a great season from Jimmie Foxx, who won the Triple Crown, as well as from Grove (24-8), and strong hitting also from Mickey Cochrane and freshman infielder Pinky Higgins, the A's came in third. Sitting behind them in fifth place at the end of the season were the Detroit Tigers, giving out very few clues as to what they were about to do the next year.

Bill Terry got a whole new spirit going in the Giants' clubhouse, and he also had a new star on the mound, Hal Schumacher, to complement the hurling of Carl Hubbell and Freddie Fitzsimmons. Of the three, Hubbell's numbers were most impressive (23 wins, ten shutouts, and 1.66 ERA, all league-leading), but Schumacher's development into a 19-game-winner was the main factor in accounting for the Giants' transformation from a second-division club in 1932 to a pennant winner in 1933. Offensively, Terry himself and Lefty O'Doul, the 1932 NL batting titlist whom the Giants got in a trade with the Dodgers in June, were the only .300 hitters, but Mel Ott led the club with 23 homers and 103 RBIs. Hubbell and Ott were the World Series heroes when the Giants surprised the prognosticators by beating the Senators easily, four games to one.

## 1934

The Giants themselves became victims of a more stunning surprise the next year, when they lost the National League pennant to the Cardinals in the last weekend of the season after leading the league for 127 days. Up to September, the 1934 NL race was remarkably similar to 1933's, from the Giants' six-game lead at the top to the sad-sack performance at the bottom by the Reds, who were in the cellar for their fourth straight year. With Jo-Jo Moore (.331 for the year) joining Terry and Ott as major offensive guns, and fine mound work again by Schumacher, Fitzsimmons, and Hubbell (that was the year Hubbell struck out Ruth, Gehrig, Foxx, Simmons, and Cronin in succession in the All-Star Game), New York had forged into the lead on the 6th of June and seemed in no trouble.

But at St. Louis, where Frankie Frisch was now manager, an aggressive and colorful bunch of players known as the Gashouse Gang had formed and by mid-August had turned into a steamroller like the 1930-31 Cardinal team. The Gang was made up of a few veterans from that team—Frisch himself, first baseman Rip Collins, and Pepper Martin (now at third base)—and several newcomers, shortstop Leo Durocher, outfielders Joe Medwick, Ernie Orsatti, and Jack Rothrock, a lifetime-.308-hitting catcher from the Phillies named Spud Davis, another good catcher (rookie Bill DeLancey), pitcher Tex Carleton, and most important of all in their contributions—Dizzy Dean and his 20-year-old brother Paul. Dizzy was a 30-game-winner that year, and Paul, after a slow start, became nearly as effective as Dizzy in September, ending the season with 19 victories.

The Dean brothers led the Cardinals to a 33-12 record over the last month and a half, while the Giants slowed to a 23-21 pace and the erstwhile-challenging Cubs were 20-22 for the same period. In the last ten days of the season, seven of the nine games won by Cards were complete-game victories by either Dizzy or Paul. This remarkable string began with a fabled doubleheader win at Brooklyn in which Dizzy tossed a 3-hit shutout in the opener and Paul pitched a no-hitter in the nightcap. Two more victories by the pair on the 24th and 25th brought the Cards to within one game of the Giants.

Terry's men were displaying signs of exhaustion as well as worry as they dropped two games to the Phils at the Polo Grounds on the 25th and 26th, and when Dizzy shut out the Reds at St. Louis on the final Friday, the Cards and Giants were deadlocked at 93-58. The Cards won the pennant on the weekend with another win by Paul and another shutout by Dizzy, while the Dodgers whipped the Giants twice at the Polo Grounds. For the Dodgers, and Brooklyn fanatics, it was sweet revenge for Terry's famous put-down the previous January when he was asked to assess the Dodgers' 1934 outlook: "Are they still in the league?" That September weekend, he found out.

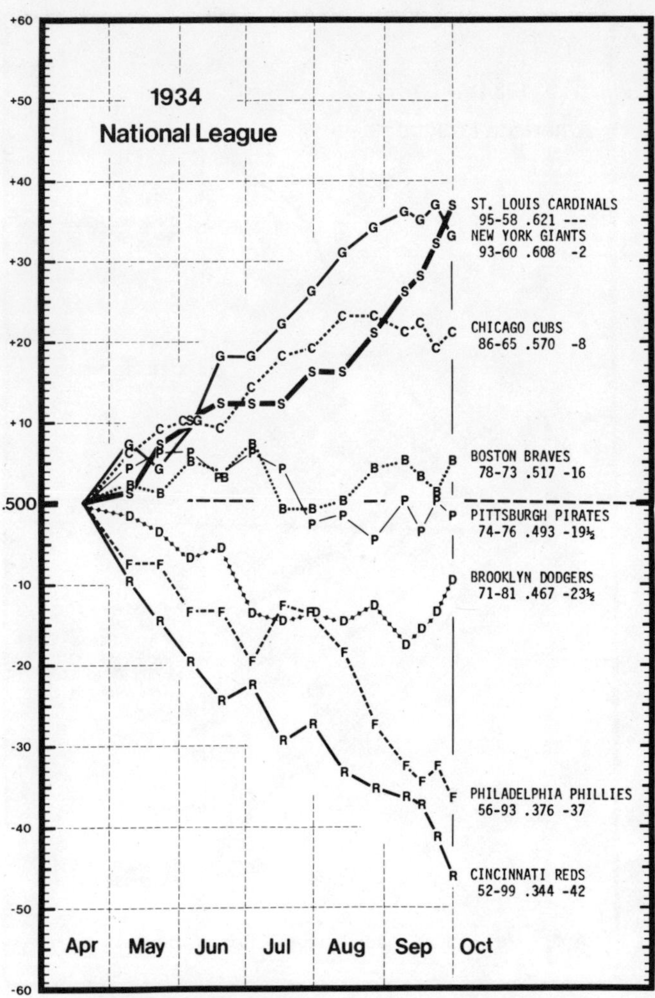


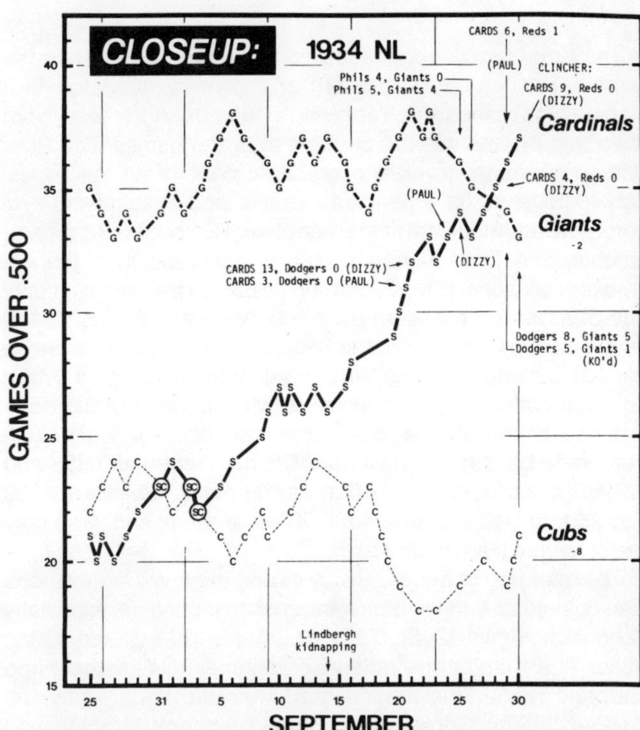


**DEAN BROS. CIRCUS. Led by Dizzy Dean (30-7) and his younger brother Paul (19-11), the 1934 St. Louis Cardinals became a juggernaut like the '30 and '31 Redbird teams. After Dizzy and Paul shut out the Dodgers (with a no-hitter by Paul) on September 21st, they paced the Cards in a pair of wins over the Pirates. Next on the Deans' list was Cincinnati, beaten four straight at St. Louis with two shutouts by Dizzy, while the Giants slumped in their final week. Between Dizzy's two shutouts, the Cards clinched a tie for the pennant on the final Saturday when Paul held the Reds to a single run while Brooklyn's Van Lingle Mungo did the same to the Giants at the Polo Grounds. The Dean brothers kept sailing on after the pennant clinch on Sunday, winning two games apiece over the Detroit Tigers in the '34 World Series.**

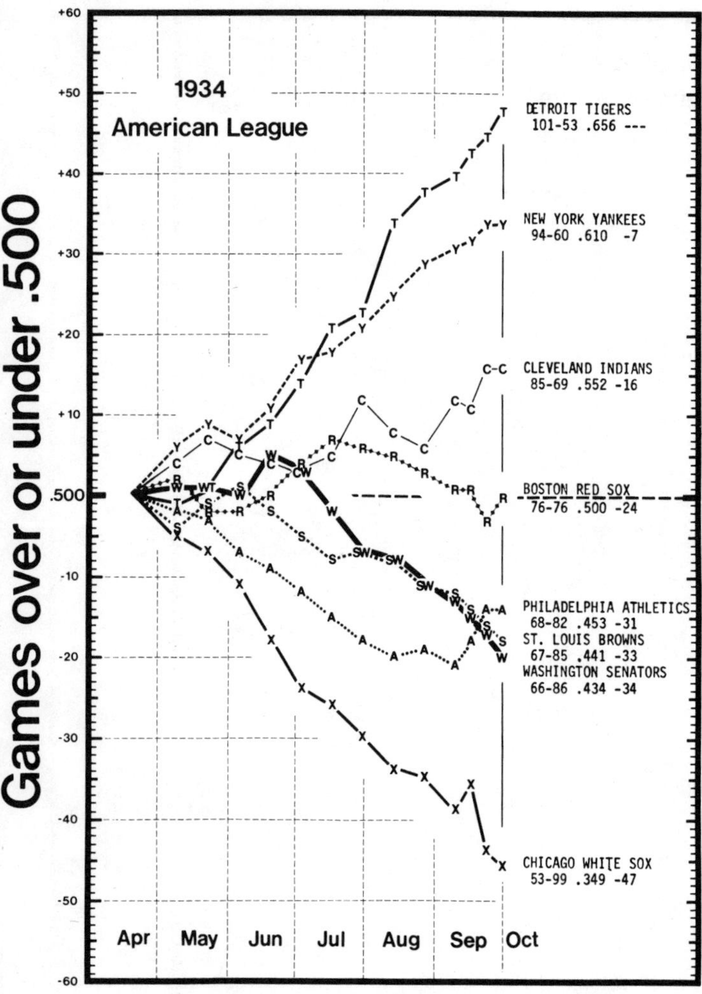


The American League breathed fresh air in 1934, when the Detroit Tigers came from out of nowhere (actually, fifth place) to challenge the Yankees in June, take the lead from them in July, and win the pennant by seven games. The Tiger victory seems to have been a classic case of all the necessary ingredients for a pennant materializing in satisfying synchrony. One important ingredient was Detroit's purchase of catcher (and Tiger manager) Mickey Cochrane from the A's between seasons. His .320 batting average, however, was only one of seven on the team over .300. Another acquisition, left fielder Goose Goslin, from the Senators, hit .305, and others on the list included suddenly-improved outfielders Jo-Jo White and Gee Walker and third baseman Marv Owen. But the heaviest part of the offense came from two home-grown Hall-of-Famers-to-be, second baseman Charlie Gehringer (.356 and 127 RBIs) and sophomore first sacker Hank Greenberg (.339 and 26 homers). The Tigers hit .300 as a team, and were only major league team to do so.

The maturing of the young Tigers and their new acquisitions also coincided with the blossoming of their pitchers, especially Schoolboy Rowe (24-8), Tommy Bridges (22-11), and Eldon Auker (15-7), and the addition of another ex-Senator, Firpo Marberry (15-5). This mound staff was still bettered by the Yankees' Lefty Gomez, Red Ruffing, Johnny Murphy, and Johnny Broaca, but the New York batting order no longer packed its usual wallop, even though Lou Gehrig won the Triple Crown.

Faced with a can-you-top-this? situation in the World Series, the Dean brothers did. Although the Tigers gamely strung the Series out to the seven-game limit, Dizzy and Paul each won two games, the deciding-game victory being a six-hit, 11-0 win by Dizzy.

## 1935

With one very noteworthy exception, the Tiger and Yankee lineups in 1935 were essentially unchanged from those of 1934, and so was the '35 AL pennant race. Detroit again grabbed the league lead in July, and pulled out to a seven-game lead over the Yankees; at the end, this was diminished to a three-game margin by an inconsequential late-September fade by the Tigers. The next week, in a six-game World Series against the Cubs, the Tigers won their first world championship.

The significant lineup change was the Yankees' release of Babe Ruth, who at age 40 closed out his magnificent career as both the league's best pitcher for a brief period and the game's greatest hitter of all time. Ruth's final at-bats, in which he hit six home runs in 72 official trips to the plate, were with the Boston Braves, who once again sank to the National League's lower depths, this time to the lowest won-lost percentage in the league's modern period.

The third- and fourth-place teams in the American League were also the same as in 1934—Cleveland and Boston. The Indians were persisting in their habit of playing respectably without seriously threatening the clubs they trailed. Nearly every

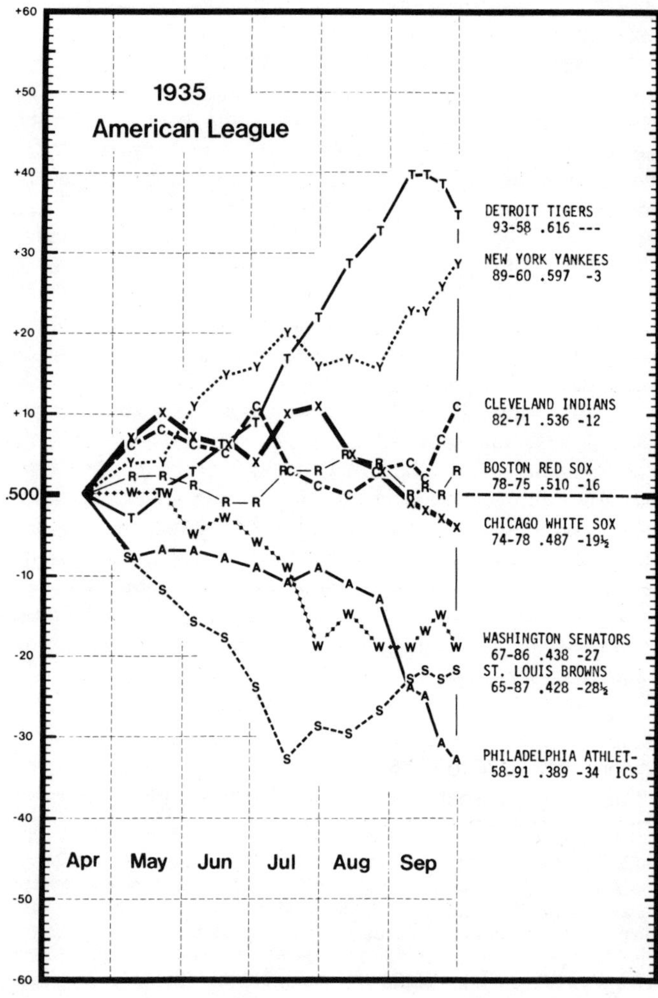

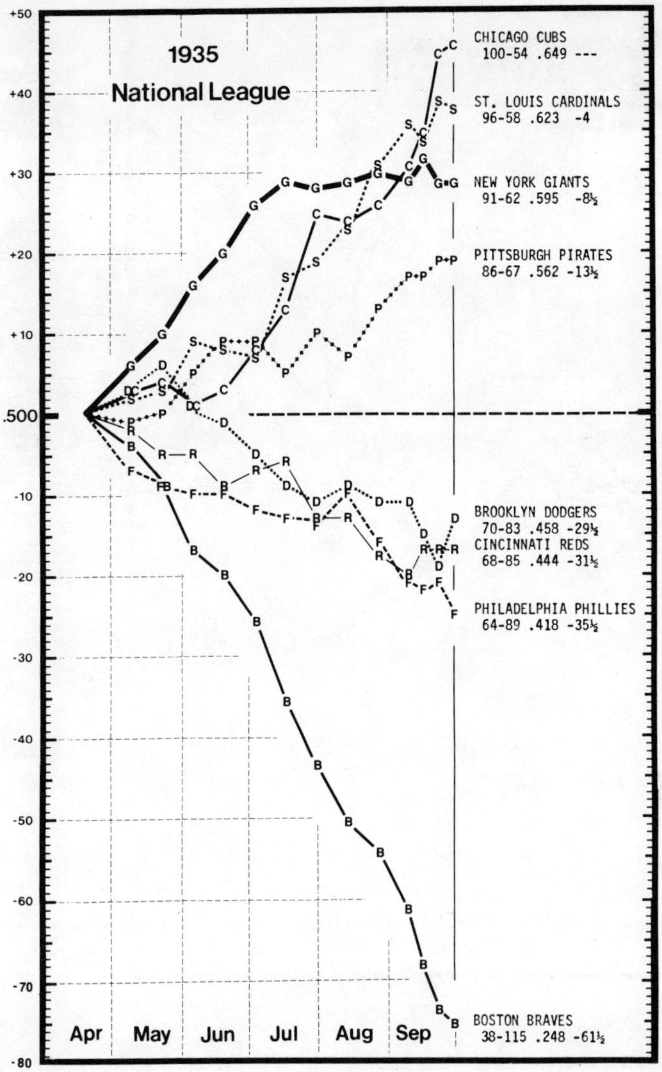

**RECORD LOW won-lost percentage in the National League's modern period is the 1935 Boston Braves' .248, .002 below the 1962 New York Mets' percentage although those Mets set the major league record for losses in a season—120.**

year Cleveland's hitting was among the league's best—they now had Hal Trosky and Odell Hall as well as Averill and Vosmik—but they kept coming up short on pitching talent.

It didn't help matters when they lost Wes Ferrell, to a sore arm in 1933, and then to Tom Yawkey's wallet in 1934. The latter year Ferrell helped the Red Sox climb to a fourth-place, break-even record, with support from .300 hitters Bill Werber, Roy Johnson, and Carl Reynolds and his brother Rick behind the plate. When Yawkey also bought Lefty Grove before the '34 season, hopes naturally leaped higher than .500 in Boston, but a sore arm reduced the great southpaw to an 8-8, 6.52 ERA performance. In 1935, Grove and Ferrell together won 45 games, and Yawkey brought in Joe Cronin from Washington, in exchange for a cool quarter-million, to be the new shortstop-manager. These happenings improved the Red Sox' record from 76-76 to 78-75.

Just behind Boston in the final 1935 standings were the Chicago White Sox. The Pale Hose had not finished in the first division since their big scandal, although they had completed two seasons over .500 when their ace hurler of the mid-twenties, Ted Lyons, had his best years. Now managed by Jimmy Dykes, who still played in the infield, they were returning to first-division status and signaled this by leading the AL in April and May, and staying in contention until August. In 1935 the White Sox uptrend still reflected the good efforts of Lyons and the ex-A's (Dykes, Haas, and Simmons) but also the development of such new lights as Luke Appling, Zeke Bonura, Mike Kreevich, and Vern Kennedy, who would keep the team competitive later in the decade.

In pennant-race drama the National League clearly held the edge in 1935. The Cardinals, Giants, and Cubs were at it again, and the Cubs lagged behind the Giants, and usually behind the Cards as well, over the first five months of the season despite leading the league in both team batting and team ERA. By Labor Day, the three clubs had converged to a 2½-game range with Chicago still in third. The Cubs had been winning consistently since the middle of August, but now they carried that pattern to the ultimate by winning every game for three weeks and two days—a 21-game winning streak, second only to the 1916 Giants' 26-game streak in the 1901-1980 period. Victories over Paul and Dizzy Dean at St. Louis near the end of the streak captured the flag for the Cubs, and their eventual winning edge was four games over the Cadinals. The Giants, who had gone flat (literally, in the graph) in mid-July, finished 8½ games in back of the Cubs.

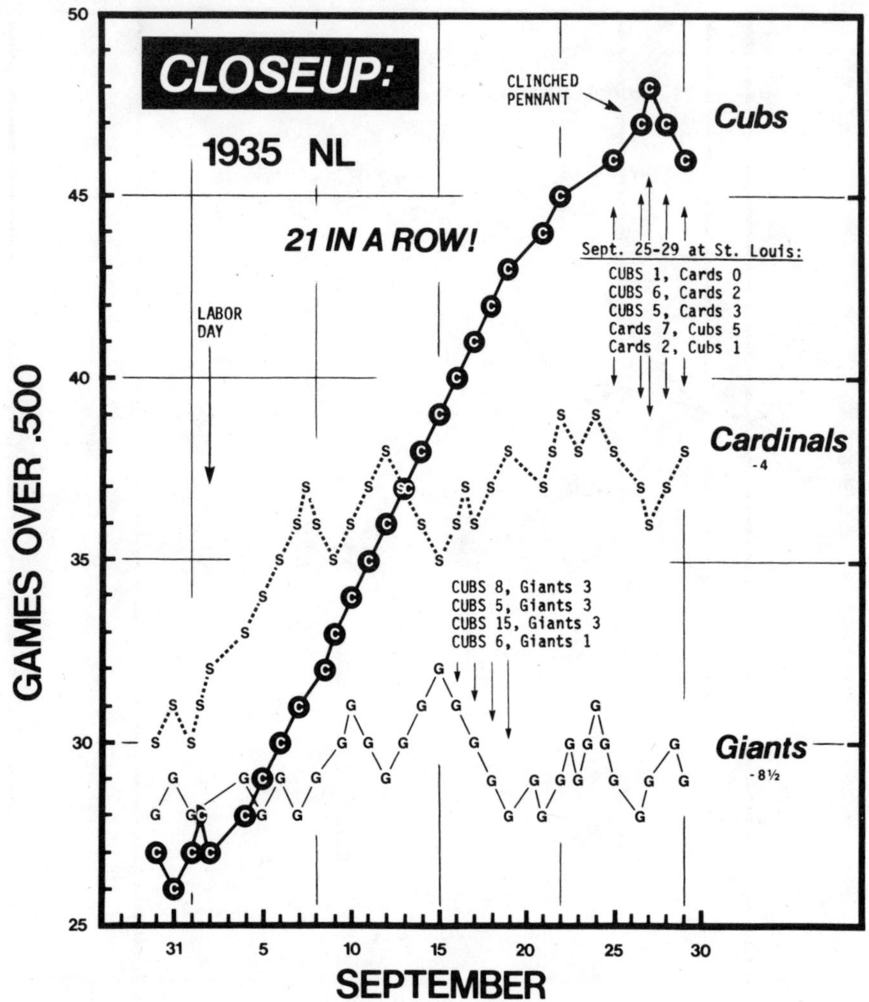


**COMMAND PERFORMANCE.** The 1935 Chicago Cubs entered the month of September leading the NL in batting and pitching but in the standings they were in third place. It was about that time that a Cubs' play-by-play announcer, Dutch Reagan, a versatile man who left radio for other occupations in Hollywood, Sacramento, and Washington, D.C., issued a Labor Day proclamation. If the Cubs want to win the pennant, he said, they will have to win all the rest of their games.

Which is just what the Cubbies did, save for two games at the end, after the pennant was clinched. Starting with the first game after Labor Day, they swept four games each from the Phillies, Braves, Dodgers, and Giants, and two more from the Pirates, at Wrigley Field, then won three more games at St. Louis—21 straight! They passed the Giants with the second of the 21 consecutive wins, the Cards with the 11th, clinched a tie for the pennant when Lon Warneke beat Paul Dean in the 19th, and took the pennant outright in a 6-2 victory over Dizzy Dean in the 20th victory of the string.

Lon Warneke and another young bloomer, Bill Lee, both 20-game winners, led the strong pitching of the Cubs. Several new faces, primarily off the Cub farm teams, were regulars in Charlie Grimm's lineup, including 18-year-old Phil Cavaretta at first base, Stan Hack at third, and Augie Galan and Frank Demaree in the outfield. The Cubs also had the slugging ex-Phillie, Chuck Klein, that year and the year before, but he was already in decline as a hitter at age 30. Gabby Hartnett, on the other hand, seemed to be getting better every year as he approached his mid-thirties; he led the '35 club with a .344 average.

Another significant change in the NL curves that year was Cincinnati's emergence from the cellar. With excellent mound work by Paul Derringer, who won 22 games, and high-average hitting by Babe Herman and Ernie Lombardi, the Reds rose to sixth place.

## 1936

The New York Yankees became baseball's superpower again in 1936, and won the American League pennant four years in a row, by margins of 19½, 13, 9½, and 17 games. In the first three of these years, Lou Gehrig, still dynamite in his thirties, overlapped with Joe DiMaggio, who hit .323 with 29 homers in his rookie season of 1936 and even more prodigiously in later years. Tony Lazzeri, the only other holdover from the powerhouse '27 team, was still a regular at second base in 1936 and 1937, but was replaced by Joe Gordon in 1938. The other infield spots were filled by Frankie Crosetti and Red Rolfe; the latter had become a .300-hitting mainstay at the hot corner in the latter part of 1934. Other good hitters, George Selkirk, Myril Hoag, Jake Powell, Tommy Henrich, and (by 1939) Charlie Keller played the outfield with DiMaggio. Behind the plate all four years was Bill Dickey, a tower of strength, as a catcher, slugger, and team leader. Another Hall of Famer, Red Ruffing, headed the Yankee pitching corps, and he won at least 20 games in each of the four years. For other pitchers, the Yanks had Lefty Gomez, past his prime but still very effective, Monte Pearson, Bump Hadley, Atley Donald, and the brilliant relief man, Johnny Murphy.

At the end of the 1936 season, the Yankees and the second-place Tigers were about as far apart as FDR and Alf Landon that November. McCarthy's club had no competition after the Red Sox hit their peak level in mid-June. The Red Sox had begun to strengthen their farm system, too, but Tom Yawkey was still at the stage of trying to buy a pennant. His failure to do so in 1936 was one of the year's biggest stories. Before the season he had acquired 34-year-old Heinie Manush from Washington and four more A's from Connie Mack—pitcher John Marcum, infielder Eric McNair, .300-hitting outfielder Doc Cramer, and one of the league's top three sluggers, Jimmie Foxx. These moves raised hopes to dangerous heights in Boston, hopes which were sadly dashed when the

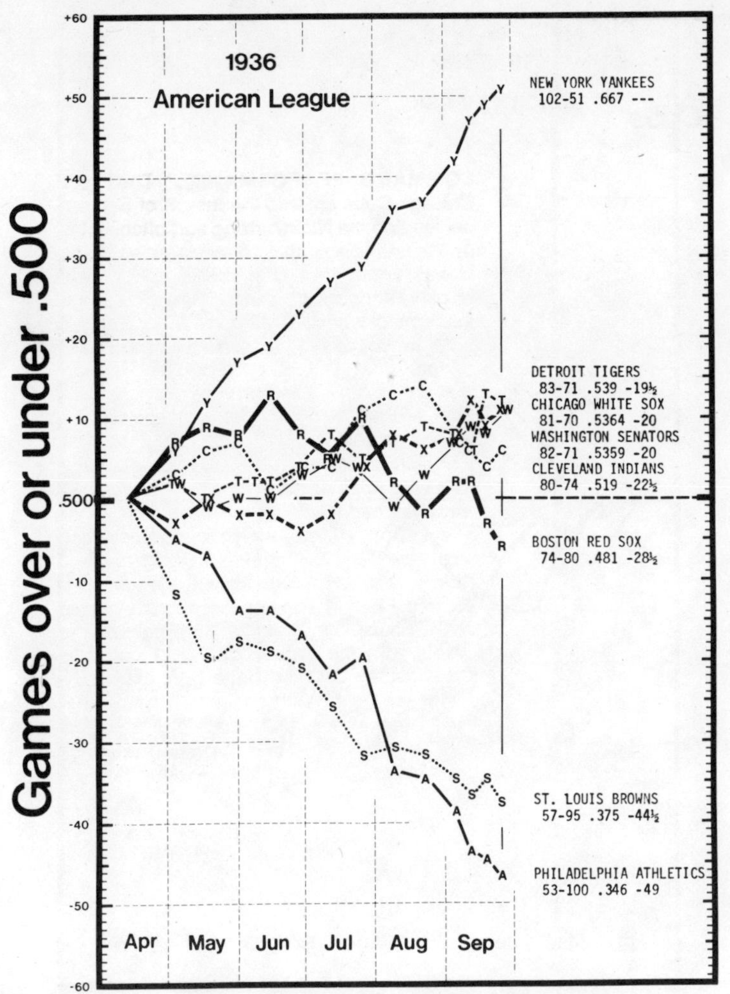


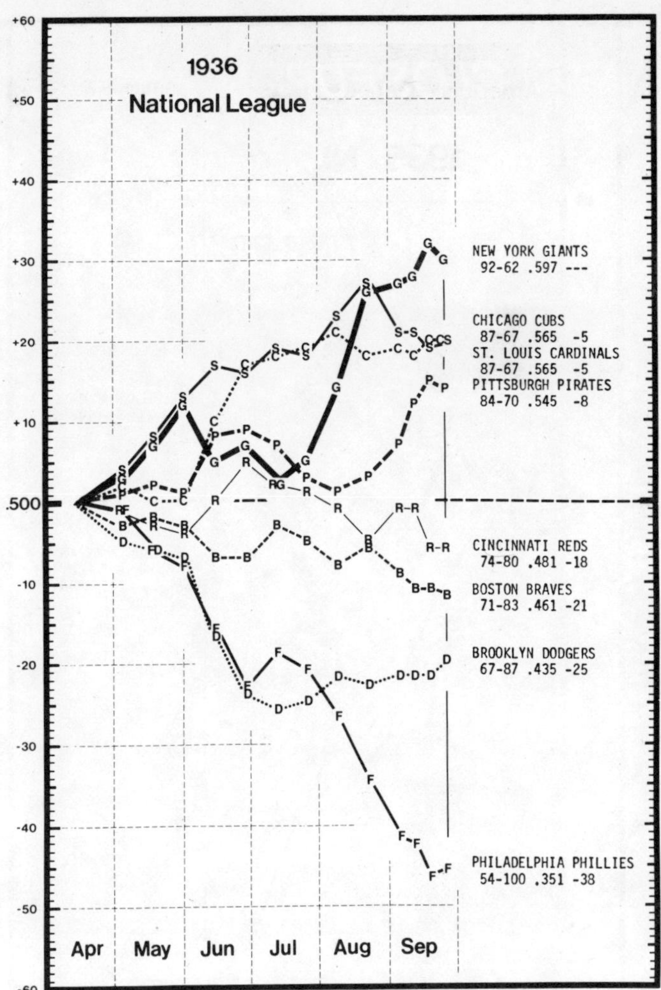


Red Sox faded to a sixth-place finish. The fizzle was partly due to the sidelining of Cronin and Manush by injuries, but generally taken as proof that you can't buy a pennant, a conclusion that was both emphatically supported and disproved in the later 1970s.

The downfall of the world champion Tigers was another big story in 1936. Two reasons for their poor-second season were clear: the loss of Hank Greenberg for all but 12 games because of a broken wrist, and Mickey Cochrane's psychiatric crisis in June, associated with an overactive-thyroid condition. But the team batted .300, ten points higher than in 1935, even without their bats, so another reason counts for more than these—the Tiger mound staff's combined ERA rose from 3.82 to 5.00.

In the 1936 National League season, the Giants won the first of two consecutive pennants. Bill Terry's '36 victory came as quite a surprise to the Cubs and Cardinals, from whom the Jints snatched the flag in the final six weeks, because New York was only a few games over .500 near the end of July. But Carl Hubbell went on a tear, winning his last 16 games of the season, leading a 15-game winning streak by the Giants in August. He ended up with 26-6 for the season, leading the NL in ERA with 2.31. Others who starred for Giants were Mel Ott, league leader in home runs with 33, Jo-Jo Moore, who hit .316 and dazzled in his outfield play, Gus Mancuso (.301) at the backstop position, and the sharp double-play combination of Burgess Whitehead and Dick Bartell.

The Cubs also had a 15-game winning streak, earlier in the year, that put them into first place in late June and also into head-and-head running with the Cardinals for several weeks before the Giants took over the race. All three clubs were behind the improving Pittsburgh Pirates in team batting figures.

The Giants were clearly outclassed by the powerful Yankees in the '36 World Series; two of the Yankee wins were by 18-4 and 13-5 scores. Most people thought the Giants did well to win two of the six games.

## 1937

It must be conceded that the 1936 and 1937 seasons bore a striking resemblance to each other, and "bore" is the right word, many would say. The Yankees and Giants won the pennants again, the Giants lost the World Series again (in five games this time), the Browns and A's fought it out for last place again, the Red Sox failed again after getting still more players from the A's and Senators, the Tigers led the AL in hitting again and repeated a far-back runnerup finish, the rest of the NL's first division was filled out by the Cubs, Cards, and Pirates again, the Dodgers and Phillies had poor years once more, and the Boston Bees (temporarily preferred over "Braves") again show some recovery from their 1935 disaster.

Did anything change? Yes, the Cincinnati Reds flopped back to the cellar, a move that was both unpredicted and unpredictive. But with the Phillies' Bucky Walters only recently con-

Games over or under .500

1937
American League
NEW YORK YANKEES
102-52 .662 ---
DETROIT TIGERS
89-65 .578 -13
CHICAGO WHITE SOX
86-68 .558 -16
CLEVELAND INDIANS
83-71 .539 -19
BOSTON RED SOX
80-72 .526 -21
WASHINGTON SENATORS
73-80 .477 -28½
PHILADELPHIA ATHLETICS
54-97 .358 -46½
ST. LOUIS BROWNS
46-108 .299 -56
Apr
May
Jun
Jul
Aug
Sep
Oct

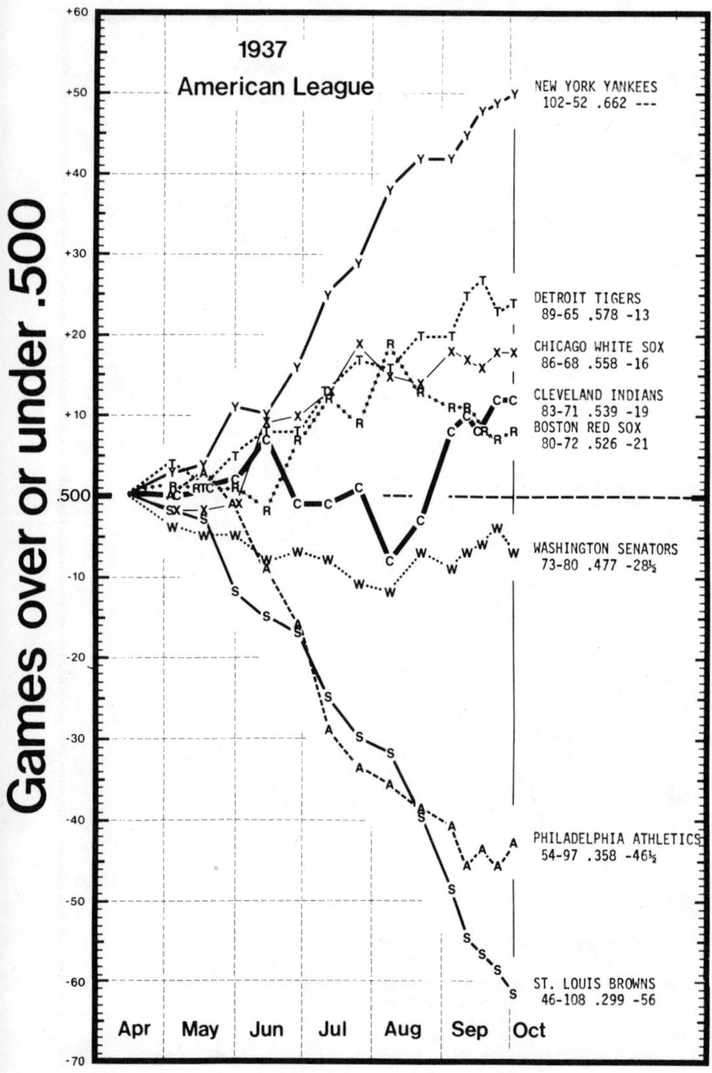

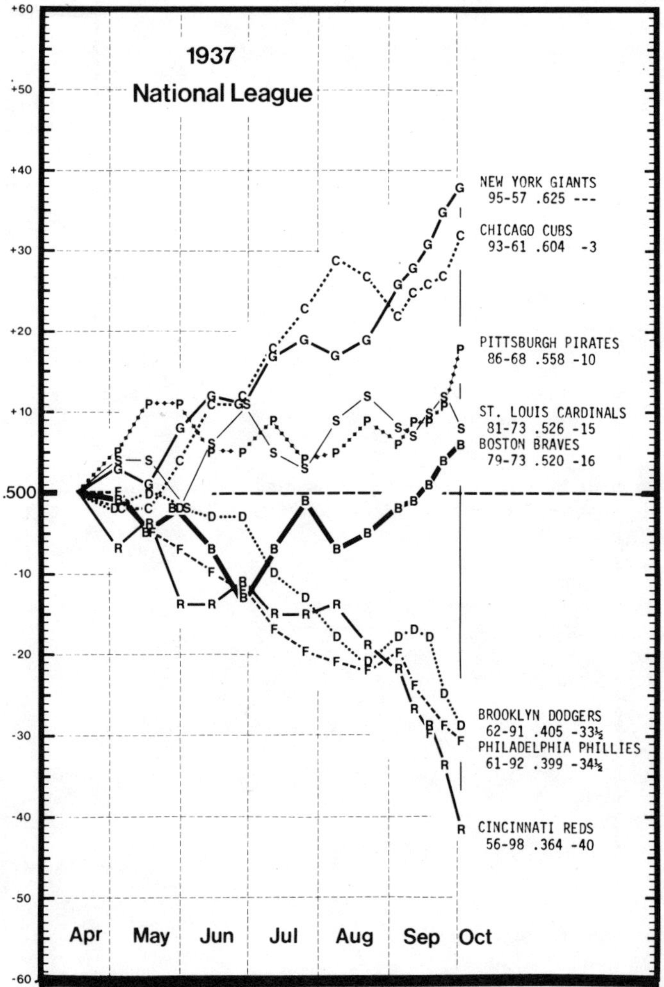

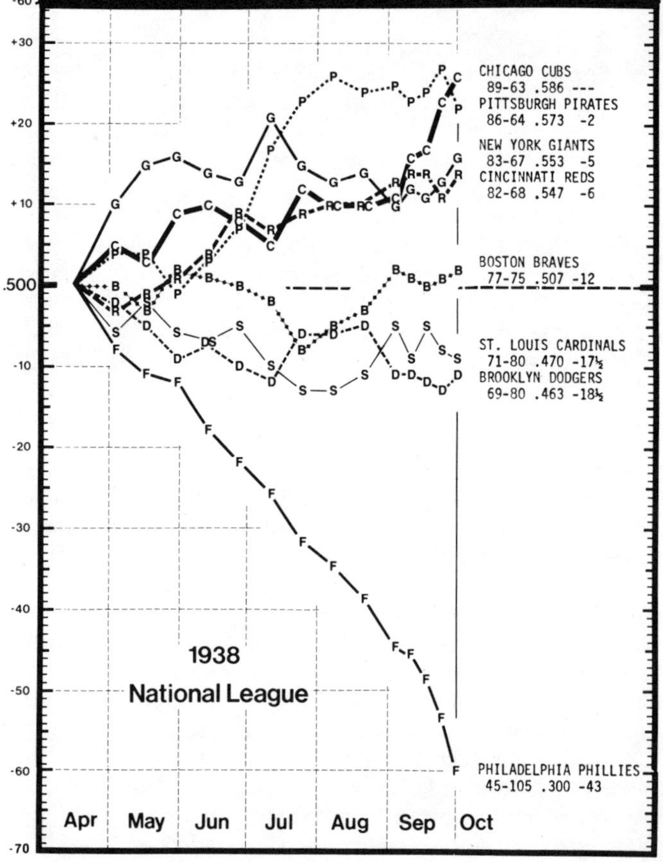

1937
National League
NEW YORK GIANTS
95-57 .625 ---
CHICAGO CUBS
93-61 .604 -3
PITTSBURGH PIRATES
86-68 .558 -10
ST. LOUIS CARDINALS
81-73 .526 -15
BOSTON BRAVES
79-73 .520 -16
BROOKLYN DODGERS
62-91 .405 -33½
PHILADELPHIA PHILLIES
61-92 .399 -34½
CINCINNATI REDS
56-98 .364 -40
Apr
May
Jun
Jul
Aug
Sep
Oct

1938
National League
CHICAGO CUBS
89-63 .586 ---
PITTSBURGH PIRATES
86-64 .573 -2
NEW YORK GIANTS
83-67 .553 -5
CINCINNATI REDS
82-68 .547 -6
BOSTON BRAVES
77-75 .507 -12
ST. LOUIS CARDINALS
71-80 .470 -17½
BROOKLYN DODGERS
69-80 .463 -18½
PHILADELPHIA PHILLIES
45-105 .300 -43
Apr
May
Jun
Jul
Aug
Sep
Oct

verted from a third baseman to a pitcher before his trade in 1938 to Cincinnati, and with hitters such as Frank McCormick just breaking in, nobody could be blamed for failing to forecast what the Reds did in the next three years.

Other changes: Joe DiMaggio's figures went up to .346, 46 homers, and 167 RBIs, and he would have won the Triple Crown as a sophomore if his average had been higher than Gehringer's .371 and Gehrig's .351 and if his RBI total had been up to Greenberg's 183; a rookie named Cliff Melton won 20 games for the Giants; the Bees outdid the Giants in that department (but in no other way) by bringing up two rookies who won 20, Jim Turner (NL ERA leader) and Lou Fette; the Tigers lost Mickey Cochrane as a catcher permanently when he was nearly killed by a pitched ball, but he was able to return to his managerial role; Detroit also lost Schoolboy Rowe to injuries, as did the Cards in the case of Dizzy Dean.

Still, not very many changes, considering 16 teams, and two or three dozen players for each, over a six-month season. Perhaps some of the yawns were justified.

### 1938

The 1938 Pittsburgh Pirates had, in their first-string lineup nearly all season long, such mortals as Al Todd (.265), Lee Handley (.268) and Pep Young (.278), and no pitcher who won more than 15 games. Yet in July they bounded past a slumping

**HURRICANE, HARTNETT, AND HAPPINESS marked the Chicago Cubs' triumph in 1938. When the huge '38 Hurricane washed out the whole NL schedule in the eastern cities of the circuit on September 18-21, the Cub pitchers got a chance to rest their weary arms. The break seemed to do wonders for them, because when fair skies returned, the hurlers squelched the Phillie and Cardinal batters in seven straight victories. That brought the Cubs to within 1½ games of the leading Pirates, who came to Wrigley Field for a three-game showdown series on September 27-29. In the middle game of that series, with twilight descending, Gabby Hartnett came to the plate with the score tied and two out in the bottom of the ninth, and slammed his famous "Home Run in the Dark" to put the Cubs into first place. The Cubs went on to sweep the series and clinch the NL flag on the following Saturday.**

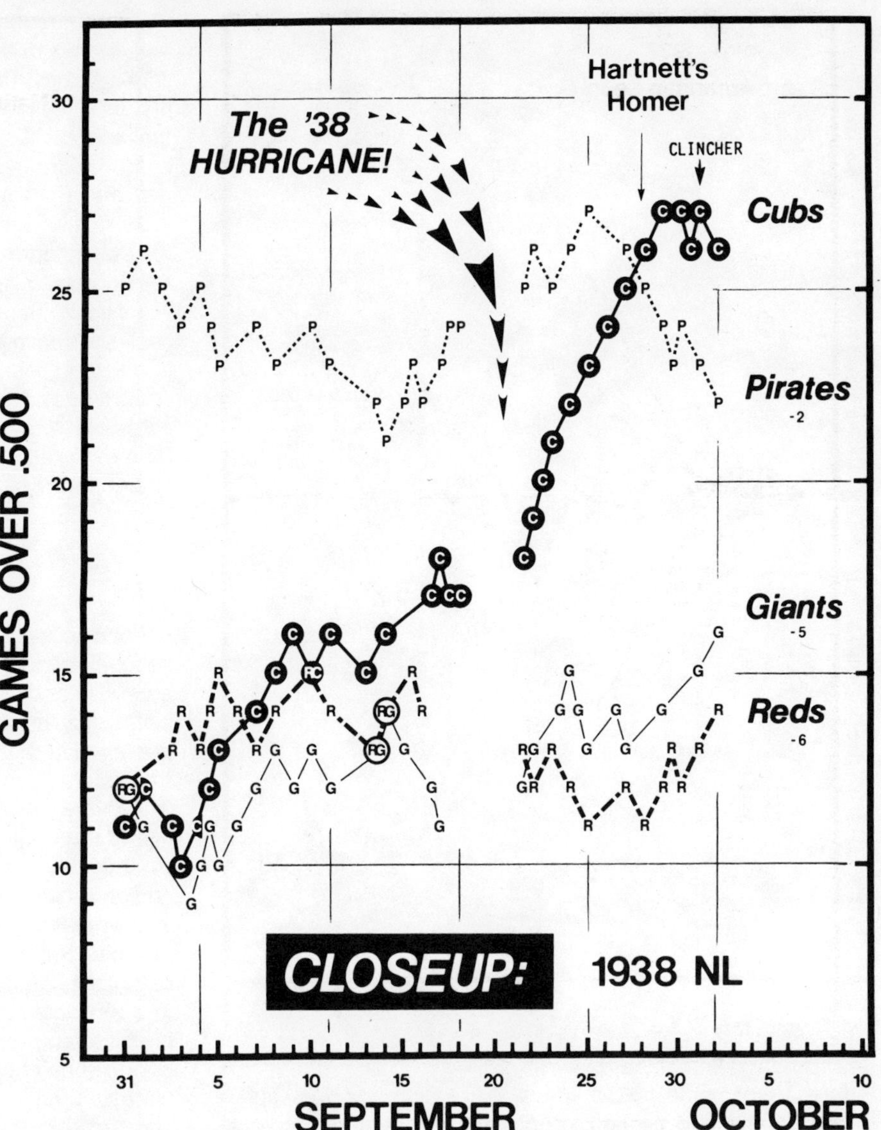


Giant team into first place, lengthened their lead to around seven games by Labor Day, and came within a few days of winning the NL pennant.

In fairness, we should note that the Pirate offense still contained the potent bats of Arky Vaughn and Paul and Lloyd Waner, but by 1938 all three were waners in comparison to their batting feats of younger years. What may account for the Bucs' lofty position through the hot months is the fact that their roster was like a bridge hand that is rather short on aces or kings but has plenty of tens and jacks for trapping queens and winning the close tricks. And among the jacks they had the veteran first baseman Gus Suhr, rookie outfielder Johnny Rizzo, in his only .300 season, and middling pitcher Mace Brown.

In August and September the Pirates engaged in the dangerous practice of winning no more games than they lost, and it was only a matter of time before someone would take advantage. The Giants, plagued by injuries and off-years, couldn't, especially after Carl Hubbell had to have a bone chip removed from his elbow in August. The Cubs, after they named Gabby Hartnett as manager in Charlie Grimm's place in July, did take advantage, and in an astonishing manner.

Up to Labor Day weekend, the Cubs and the other first-division trailers were coasting about as horizontally as Pittsburgh. Then on Labor Day itself, the Chicagoans swept a doubleheader at the Pirates' Forbes Field and found their momentum. By the end of the next week they had disentangled themselves from the Giants and surprising Reds, and all four western teams were into their final road trip in the east.

About that time, the enormous Hurricane of '38 roared up the Atlantic coast and swept through Philadelphia, New York, and New England, knocking out all National League play for half a week. (Two tied games were literally stopped in their midst by the storm on the 18th.) Having just played doubleheaders on two consecutive days, the Cubs were in dire need of a rest, especially their pitchers, Bill Lee, Clay Bryant, and Larry French.

The three-day break provided just that, and when the winds and rains abated, the Cubs swept two doubleheaders at Philadelphia by scores of 4-0, 2-1, 3-2, and 7-6 on the 22nd and 23rd. They made it seven in a row in three more games back in Chicago against the Cards, 9-3, 7-2, and 6-3, then waited in ambush for the arrival of the Pirates at Wrigley for three games starting on the 17th. To retain their lead, Pitt needed to take only one of the three contests, but the Cubs denied the Bucs even that, running the winning streak to ten

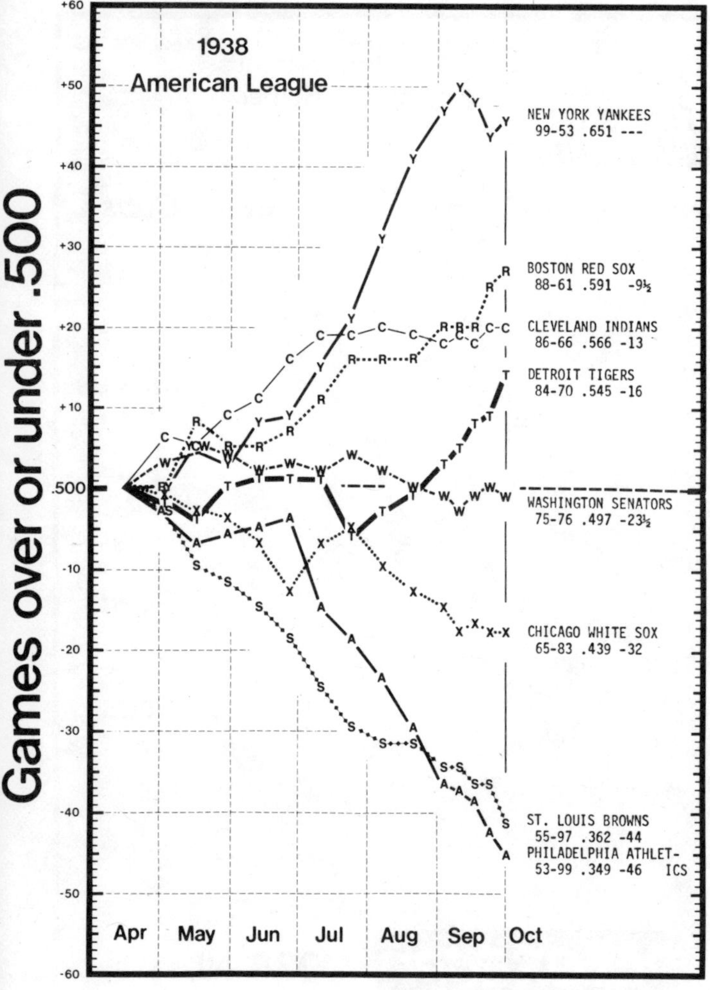


and capturing first place.

In the first game of the series, Dizzy Dean, who because of a sore arm had pitched in only a dozen games since his purchase for $200,000 from the Cardinals the previous winter, held Pittsburgh to one run and seven hits before relief by Bill Lee in the ninth, in a 2-1 victory by the Cubs. The next day, Hartnett moved his team into the lead with an historic home run that broke up a 5-5 deadlock in the last half of the ninth inning. The third game went to Chicago when Iron Man Lee, pitching for the fourth straight day, set down the Bucs in a 10-1, complete-game win. The Pirates had come to town a game and a half ahead, and they left a game and a half behind. The Cubs won only one more game that season, the clincher on Saturday, October 1st, but that was enough because the Pirates lost three of their last four games to Cincinnati after their debacle in Chicago.

In the American League, there were again few changes in the standings from the previous year, but a notable shift was Boston's move into second place. Jimmie Foxx recovered from an off-year in '37 to lead the AL with a .349 average and 175 RBIs, and his 50-homer total was second only to Hank Greenberg's 58. With five other regulars also hitting over .300, Boston led the league in team batting (with .299) for the first time since the 1903 Pilgrims' pennant year. As usual, however, their pitching didn't compare with that of the Yankees, especialy after 38-year-old Lefty Grove (14-4, league-leading 3.07 ERA) developed a sore arm in July.

Similar trouble frustrated the pennant bid of the Cleveland Indians, when Johnny Allen injured his arm after compiling a 14-8 record. The sensational fireballer Bob Feller, already in his third season at age 19, won 17 games for the Tribe that year, as did the more experienced Mel Harder. With those contributions and some new clouters, Jeff Heath, Ken Keltner, and Frankie Pytlak, to help out Trosky and Averill, the Indians might have maintained their threat to the Yankees if they had gotten a whole season from Allen. Injuries to Luke Appling and reliever Clint Brown, who had 18 saves the previous year, crippled the White Sox; after the season, Chicago's best starting pitcher of 1937 and 1938, Monty Stratton, lost his leg (and baseball career) in a hunting accident.

Further evidence that the Yankees may have had the strongest team in their history, or any club's before or since, came forth in the '38 World Series—the Yanks beat the Cubs in four straight, as they had done in 1932.

## 1939

For two weeks in April, 1939, the careers of two titans in baseball history overlapped. In the opening week of the season, 20-year-old Ted Williams had his major league debut, and on April 30th, 36-year-old Lou Gehrig played the last of his phenomenal 2,130 consecutive games. Batting only .143 in the first eight games, and fighting some disturbing motor symptoms, Gehrig took himself out of the lineup, and soon received the tragic news from the Mayo Clinic that he was dying of the rare and incurable neuromuscular disease called amyotrophic lateral sclerosis; he died on June 2, 1941.

Beyond the personal impacts of this tragedy, the loss to baseball could be measured in terms of what Gehrig's career batting statistics might have been had he continued playing in good health to the normal retirement age for a hitter or his style and aging pattern. Assuming he was already up to 80% of such hypothetical totals when he was forced to quit, his actual career total of 1,991 runs batted in might have become the highest ever (2,389 vs. Hank Aaron's 2,297 and Ruth's 2,204), his total-bases count of 5,059 might have advanced him from ninth to third (to 6,071 behind Aaron and Stan Musial) on that measure, his hits total would have easily have made the 3,000-Hit Club (3,265, about 9th), and his home runs might have totaled 592 (4th, behind Aaron, Ruth, and Mays). And some baseball historians would call this figuring conservative—Gehrig was actually a month under the age of 36 when he had to step out of the lineup, had played only 14 seasons as a regular, and might well have had five more full seasons before normal retirement.

Williams began his career with a .327 average for the 1939 season, hitting 31 homers and leading the league with 145 RBIs. Another fine product of the Boston farm system had come up the year before—second baseman Bobby Doerr (.318 as a sophomore)—and when Lou Finney came from the A's in 1939, he became a .300 hitter for the Red Sox. But neither the farms nor Yawkey's checkbook brought them any pitchers of consequence, so the Red Sox once more played second fiddle to the Yankees. There was a brief period of euphoria for Boston fans, however, when the Red Sox went on a 12-game winning streak in July. The streak included a five-game sweep of the Yankees at Yankee Stadium, which accounts for the July crimp in the steeply rising curve for the Yanks in the graph.

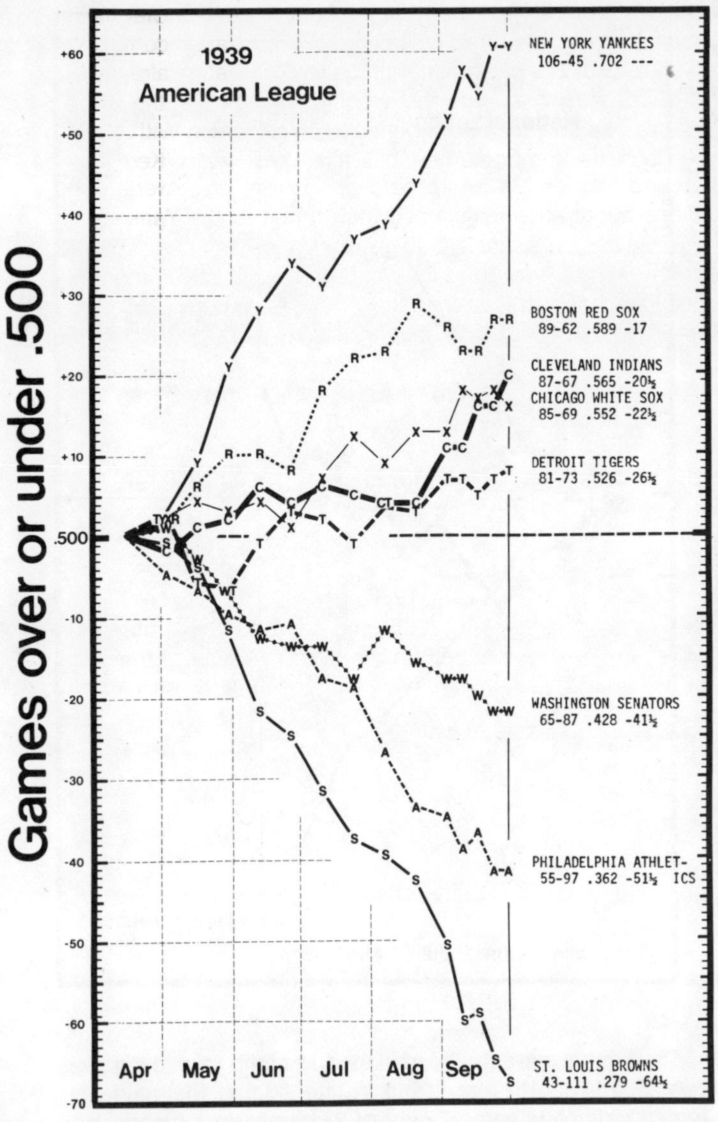


Much bigger news in 1939 was the sudden success of the Cincinnati Reds. In just two years, the Reds had jumped from last place to first, stopping at fourth on the way in 1938. Like the Giants of 1902, or the Braves of 1912, the Reds' rock-bottom finish in 1937 stands as a reminder to fans of all teams never to give up hope. As the graph shows, Cincinnati's victory in '39 was not only surprising, but a surprisingly easy one, save for some late-season threats by St. Louis.

The heroes in the Reds' achievement were Bucky Walters and Paul Derringer. The previous year, Walters had come to Cincinnati in midseason after a poor start (4-8, 5.20 ERA) with the Phillies, and then turned out to be a major reason why the Reds stayed in the '38 race until after Labor Day, winning 11 games for them. In 1939, he led the league with a 2.29 ERA and 27 wins. Derringer, in his sixth full season with the Reds, took league honors in winning percentage with a 25-7 record, and it was his victory on September 29th that clinched the pennant. Offensively, first baseman Frank McCormick had the loudest bat with .332 and a league-leading 128 RBIs. Outfielder Ival Goodman hit .323, and the Reds got some hefty hitting out of the catchers, Ernie Lombardi (20 homers) and Willard Hershberger (.345 in 174 at-bats). Bill McKechnie had taken over as the Reds' manager before the previous year, when Johnny Vander Meer made big headlines by pitching two consecutive no-hitters for the Reds (he won 15 games that year, but only five in 1939).

The St. Louis Cardinals, building still another winner, had a much stronger attack than Cincinnati's, thanks to Johnny Mize, the '39 batting-average and home run titlist; Enos Slaughter, who hit .320 as a second-year player; and another pair of backstops, Mickey Owen and Don Padgett, who combined for a .315 average.

Beyond Cincinnati's triumph and the Cards' return, there were other signs of a power shakeup in the NL. Brooklyn, in Leo Durocher's first year as manager, jumped to third place from its customary sixth or seventh, exchanging places with the aging Pittsburgh Pirates. The Cubs and Giants were also in need of new young talent, and showed this by fading to the second division.

As with several previous victims, the Yankees defeated the Reds in the World Series in another four-game sweep. That made it four straight world championships for McCarthy; no other team had managed to win more than two of these consecutively.

## 1940

There was one gigantic clue in mid-May that the 1940 AL season was going to be different—the Yankees were in last place. The Bronx Bombers often started slowly, even in their

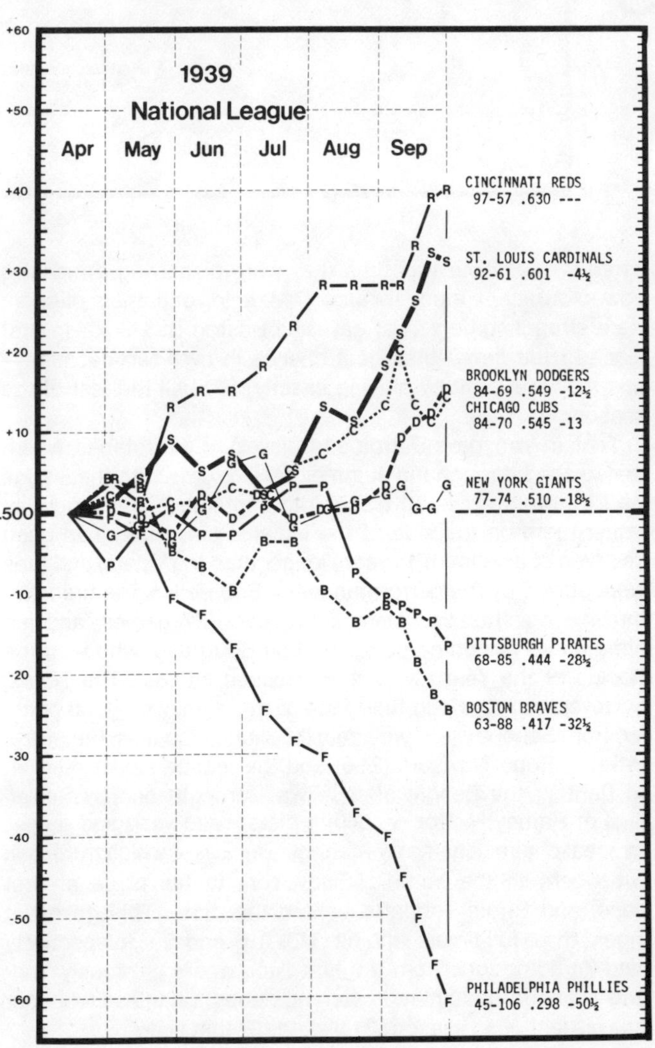

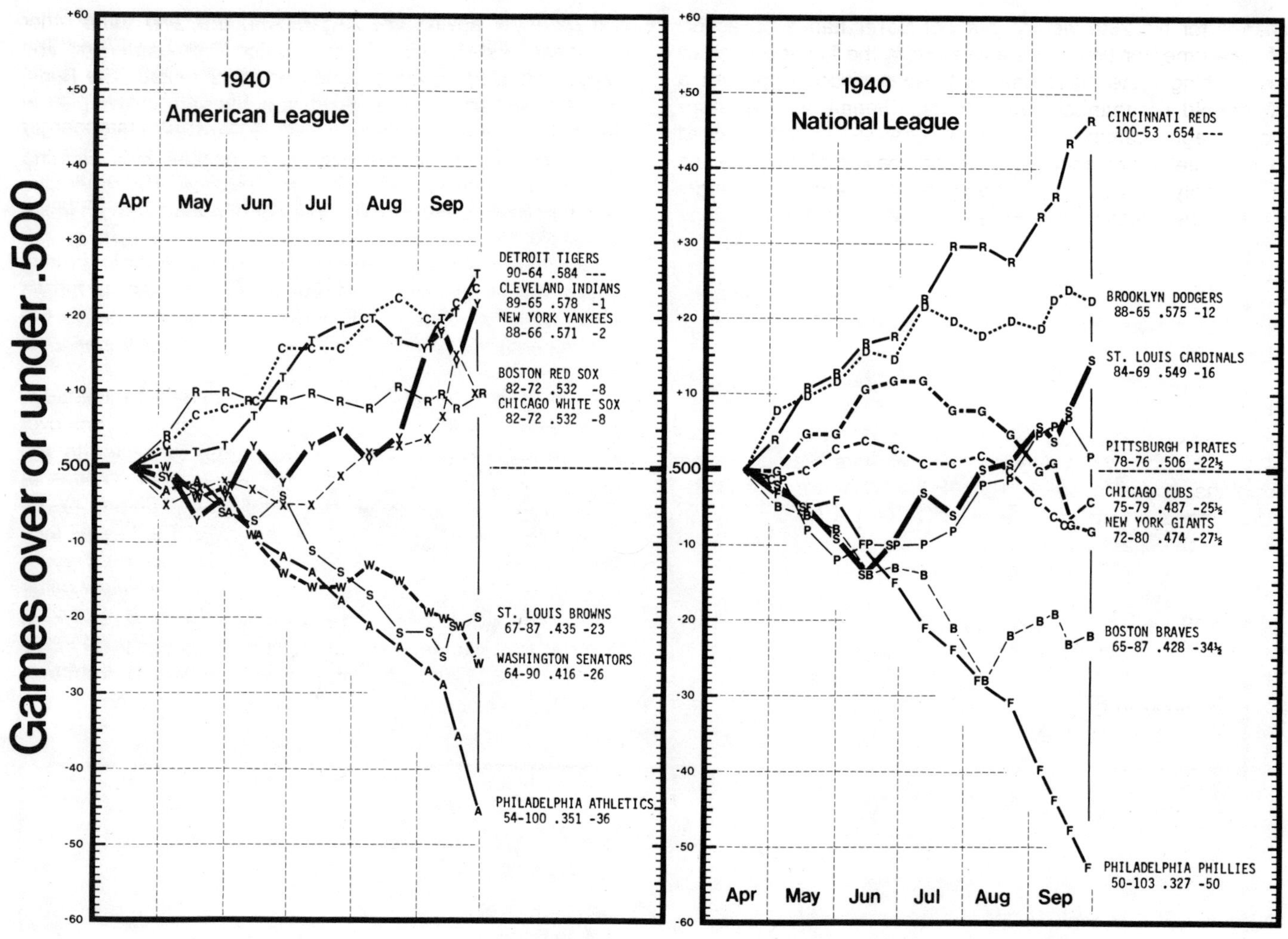


pennant years, but this time they were displaying a massive power outage, except for Joe DiMaggio, and their pitchers were struggling, too. That gave the Boston Red Sox—in first place at the time—their best chance in over two decades—and they muffed it by playing exactly .500 ball the rest of the season.

That, in turn, gave Detroit and Cleveland advantages, which they reaped through the summer, taking turns with the league lead in a tooth-and-nail tussle into September. Cheering was rather more on the side of the Indians, since they had been deprived of a pennant 15 years longer than the Tigers, and fans were stirred by the performances of Bob Feller. The fireballer threw a no-hitter on Opening Day, won 27 games, and led almost every pitching category. Lou Boudreau, who won the Rookie of the Year award also aroused interest. The Tigers, however, had regained their 1934-35 strength, with good pitching from Schoolboy Rowe again (16-3) and also from the much-traveled Bobo Newsom (21-5) and the league's best reliever, Al Benton; the Bengal offense was strengthened by the arrival of Barney McCosky (.340 in his second year) and a neat musical-chairs scheme by Manager Del Baker which put Hank Greenberg in the outfield, Rudy York in his place at first base, and Birdie Tebbetts behind the plate. This gave the Tigers three full-timers who hit .340, .316, and .296, respectively (and 74 home runs from the first two), where previously York and Tebbetts had shared catching duties. Charlies Gehringer had his last good season (.313) at age 37 that year.

The Yankees eventually managed to climb to a few games over .500 in fourth place, and in late August they suddenly turned red-hot, winning 19 out of 23 games in a manner and timing that was reminiscent of the 1924 Brooklyn team's upsurge. They completed that run just after the Indians had dropped an important Labor Day doubleheader to the Browns and three more games to the Tigers, with the result that there was a virtual three-way tie for the league lead on September 9-11. But a western road trip abruptly put an end to the Yankees' scary threat—they split a twin bill at Cleveland on the 11th, lost two of three at Detroit, and then lost three straight to the Browns at St. Louis, by 10-5, 2-1, and 16-4 scores.

Recovering with a nine-game winning streak on September 18-26, the Yanks were not mathematically eliminated until the final Friday, and a sudden uprising by the White Sox put that team also in theoretical contention on the 16th, when they were briefly only 3½ games out of first place. But the race had really reduced to a Tiger-Indian battle by mid-September. The Indians sought to avenge their three defeats of September 4-6, when the two clubs met again in Detroit on September 20-22, tied at 24 games over .500. The Tigers once more prevailed, however, in the first two games of the set, and the Tribe could only get a salvage win by Feller in the third contest on Sunday, the 22nd. That helped keep their pennant bid alive until the final weekend, when the Tigers came to Cleveland for still another three-game return match.

By that time, Bob Feller was rested and revved up for the

chance for his 28th victory, but Del Baker had a collection of sore-armed or tired-out starters. From the lower depths of his pitching roster he chose as Feller's mound opponent a 30-year-old righthander named Floyd Giebell, whose entire major league career to that point consisted of a 1-1 record in nine relief appearances in 1939 and one complete-game win in his only previous 1940 appearance. Giebell stunningly blanked the Indians, while Feller allowed a home run by Rudy York with Gehringer on base, and the 2-0 victory clinched the pennant for the Tigers. Strangely, that historic shutout was Giebell's last major league win, or decision of any kind—the next year (his last) he was 0-0 in 17 appearances, giving up 45 hits and 26 walks in 34-plus innings.

During the exciting '40 race, relations between the Cleveland manager, Ossie Vitt, and his players deteriorated so badly that all 25 on the playing roster signed a petition to the Indian brass calling for Vitt's dismissal. Owner Alva Bradley turned down the request of the "crybabies," as they were called by Indian management and the press, although he did release Vitt after the season was over.

In the 1940 NL race, the Brooklyn Dodgers chased the Reds and stayed close until a Dodger fade in July, and when Brooklyn's young infielders Pee Wee Reese and Cookie Lavagetto were sidelined in August, the Reds were home free. Walters and Derringer again were 20-game-winners, and three other Cincinnati hurlers—Jim Turner, Junior Thompson, and Joe Beggs—chipped in with a combined 42-19 record. The Reds' mound crew had batting support from the same players as in '39, with the tragic exception that .309-hitting Hershberger committed suicide on the evening of August 2nd, blaming himself for a loss by the Reds that afternoon. The other Cincinnati catcher, Lombardi, was put out of action with an ankle sprain the next month, after leading the club with a .319 average. The Reds brought their third base coach, Jimmie Wilson, out of retirement to fill in as catcher, and he turned out to be a .353 hitter as well as a first-rate catcher in the closely-contested World Series. The Reds won that Series, over the Tigers, four games to three.

The St. Louis Cardinals enjoyed the eighth-best midseason turnaround of the modern era after Billy Southworth took over as manager. Under Ray Blades and Mike Gonzalez in the spring, the Cards sank to a 15-29 record, scraping bottom in June, but under Southworth they were 69-40, running nearly parallel, but over 15 games behind, the Reds. The Pirates also had a new manager, Frankie Frisch, who replaced Pie Traynor between seasons, and after beating the Cardinals for the cellar in May, the Bucs followed the Redbirds' turnaround in striking similarity until mid-September. Together, the Cards and Pirates consigned the weakened Cub and Giant teams to the lower division.

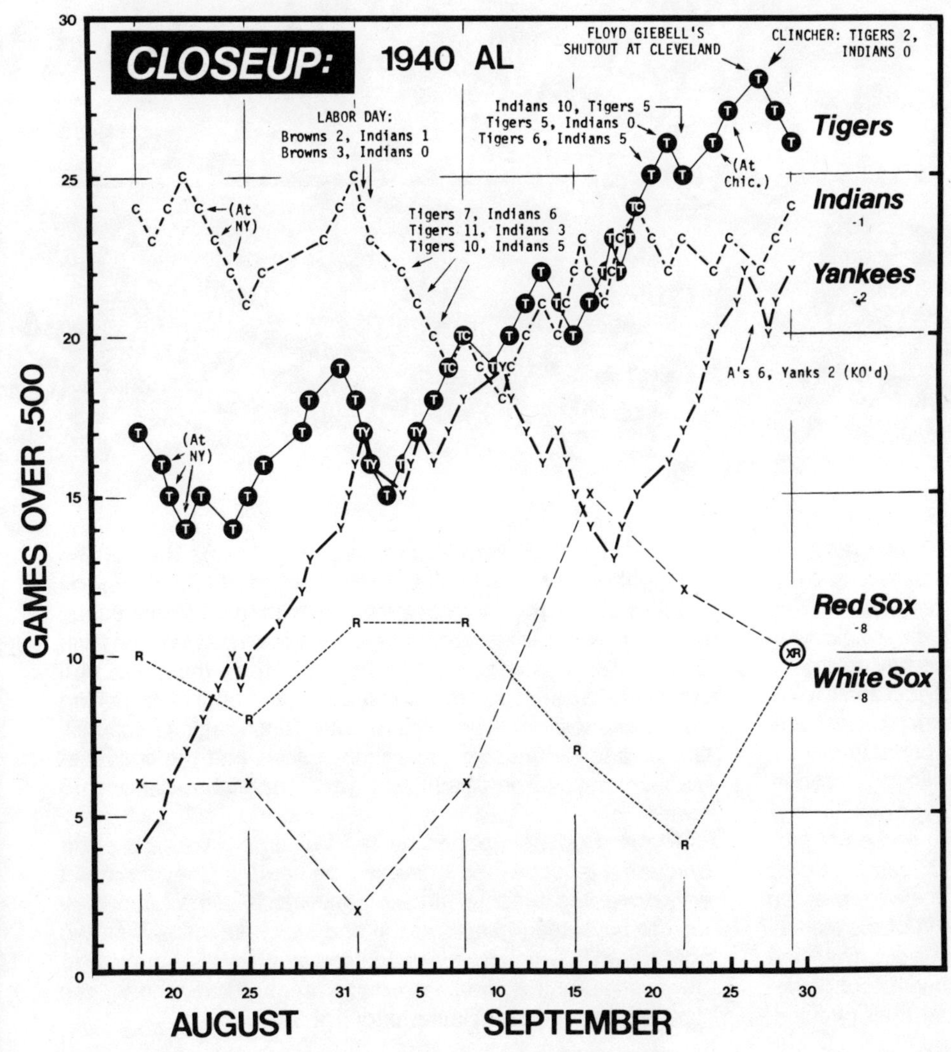


**GIEBELL'S GLORY came at Cleveland on Friday, September 27, 1940, when the Detroit Tigers put unknown Floyd Giebell on the mound against Bob Feller. Giebell shut out the Indians, clinching the pennant for Detroit in a dramatic resolution of one of the century's most exciting pennant races. The victory was only the third in Giebell's brief major league career, and it was his last.**

# 1941-1950

## 1941

The 1941 Cleveland Indians, with Roger Peckinpaugh replacing the besieged Ossie Vitt, started the season looking for all the world like a pennant winner. Thirteen games over .500 in mid-May, the Tribe seemed to have a clear field, with only Chicago among the other 1940 contenders having a good spring. Across Lake Erie, the Tigers had just lost their MVP, Hank Greenberg, to military service (the first major leaguer to be taken by World War II, although Pearl Harbor was still six months in the future), and were floundering, like the Yankees, whose pitchers were getting along in years.

But that was when baseball's most thrilling and most publicized individual feat—Joe DiMaggio's 56-game hitting streak—began, and by the time those 56 games were over, on July 17th, the Yankees had taken full command of the league. Then the Indians went into a second-half tailspin, from the loss of Hal Trosky, who broke his finger in July, a sophomore jinx on Lou Boudreau (.257), and a collapse of their pitching, outside of Bob Feller (he was 25-13 that year). This left no competition for the Yanks, who clinched the pennant on September 4th, the earliest clinch date in modern major league history. Besides DiMaggio, the Yankees got heavy lumber from Charlie Keller and Tommy Henrich (each of the three outfielders hit at least 30 home runs), and also from sharp-fielding infielders Joe Gordon and Phil Rizzuto. Those "aging pitchers," Gomez and Ruffing, won 15 games apiece, and the ace relief man, Johnny Murphy, had a fine year with eight wins and 15 saves.

The Red Sox, supported by Ted Williams' .406 hitting and untouchable-record .551 on-base percentage (he drew 145 walks over the season), cut the Yankees' 20-game Labor Day lead to seventeen games at the end, but September was the only month in which Boston won consistently. Had not the Red Sox done so, the final standings might have shown the Yankees the only team in the league above .500.

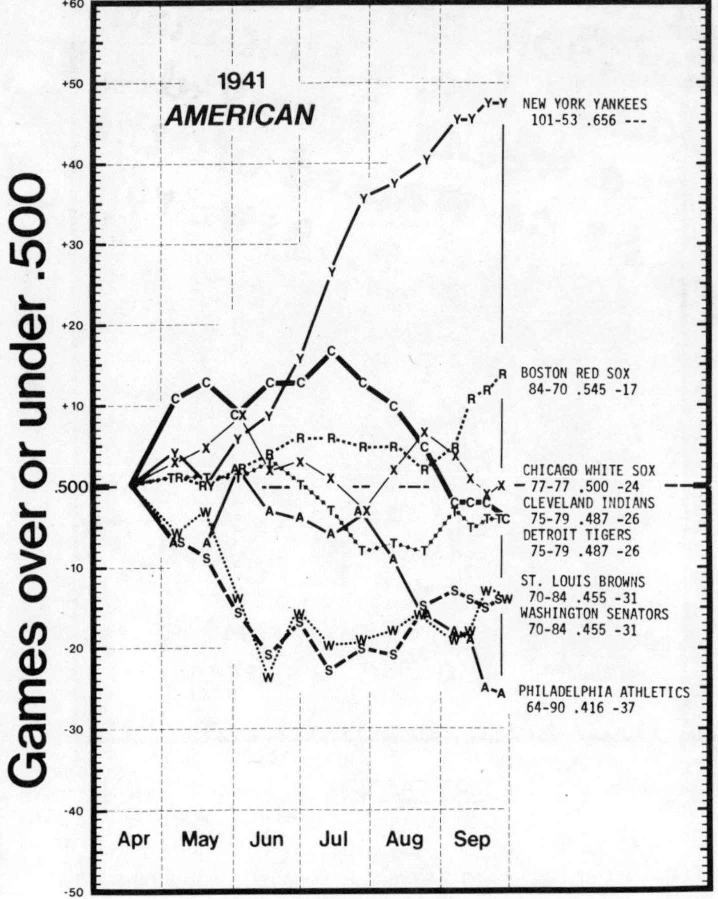


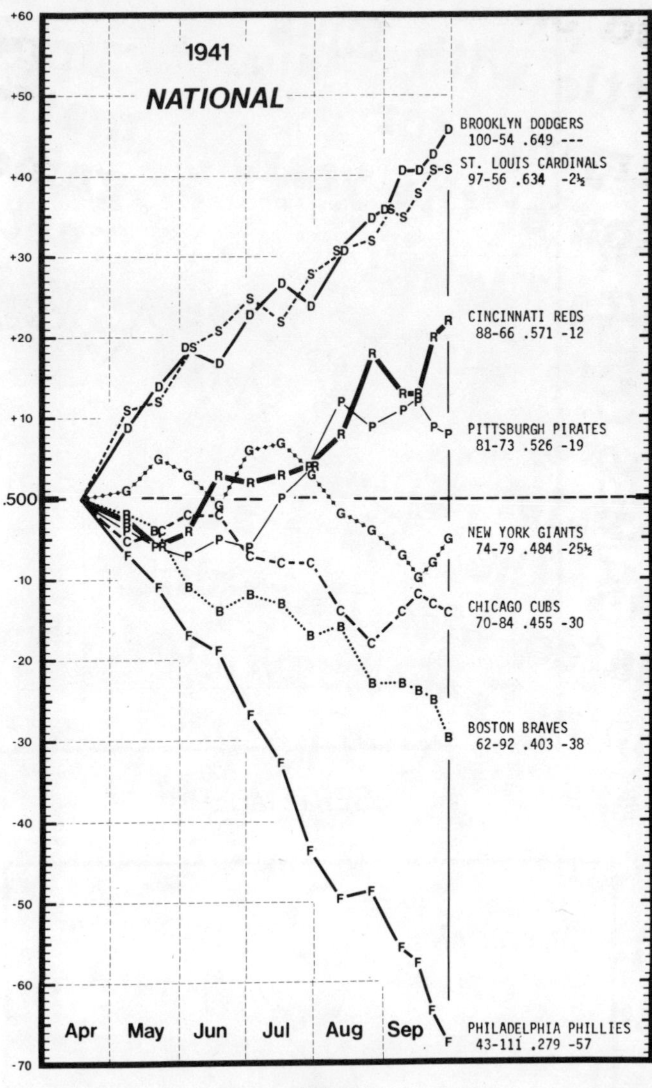


In the National League, the Dodgers and Cardinals launched a close race for the pennant on Opening Day, and kept it going all season long. By the time it was decided, in the Dodgers' favor, there were only two games left in the season. Remarkably, no other NL teams have staged such a long-duration battle for the lead in the modern era, but these same two teams repeated the stunt in 1946 and 1949. (In the AL, the 1922 Yankees and Browns had carried on in similar fashion.)

Leo Durocher's winning combine featured a trio of hard-hitting outfielders, 22-year-old Pete Reiser (.343, best average in the NL), veteran Dixie Walker (.311), and ex-Cardinal Joe Medwick (.318), and two 22-game-winners on the hill, Whit Wyatt and Kirby Higbe. Mickey Owen was the first-string catcher, and from first to third were Dolph Camilli, Billy Herman, Pee Wee Reese, and Cookie Lavagetto. Brooklyn's team batting and earned run averages led the league, but the Cards were a close second in both categories. Johnny Mize, in his last year with St. Louis before being surprisingly traded by Branch Rickey to the Giants, led the attack with .317 batting, and 17-game-winners Ernie White and Lon Warneke headed the Redbirds' pitching staff.

The Cincinnati Reds' try for a third consecutive pennant was stymied by weak hitting—Mike McCormick's club-leading .287 was their only individual BA over .270. Bucky Walters and Elmer Riddle both won 19 games, but in Walters' case the lack of offensive support also resulted in 15 losses; the other starters, Johnny Vander Meer (16-13) and Paul Derringer (12-14), had similar misfortune. The Cincinnati team BA dropped to .231, worst in the NL, in 1942.

## 1942

What holes existed in the Cardinal lineup were rapidly being filled by Rickey's farm system, and this made the difference in the rematch of Brooklyn and St. Louis the next year. Late in the '41 season, the Cards had their first look at 20-year-old Stan Musial, and he brought smiles with a 20-for-47 (.426) major league debut; the next spring he became a fixture in their lineup for 21 years. This was also about the time that Walker Cooper came up to take over Gus Mancuso's catching job, that Whitey Kurowski returned the .300-hitting Jimmy Brown to a utility-infielder role by capturing the hot-corner position as a rookie, that Johnny Beazley became an ace right-hander on the mound in his first season, and that Walker Cooper's older brother, Mort, also blossomed into an ace. With Mize gone, Billy Southworth moved outfielder Johnny Hopp, who hit .303 in 1941, to first base. The shortstop position had already been nailed down by The Octopus, Marty Marion, in 1940, as had the other two outfield slots by Enos Slaughter and Terry Moore earlier.

But when the spring of 1942 rolled around, it was Brooklyn who started strongly, while the Cardinal machine sputtered well into May. The Dodgers kept their hot pace going into the dog days, winning 70 of their first 100 games and reaching the thin air of 51 games over .500 on September 3rd. Then they looked over their shoulder and saw the onrushing Cardinals.

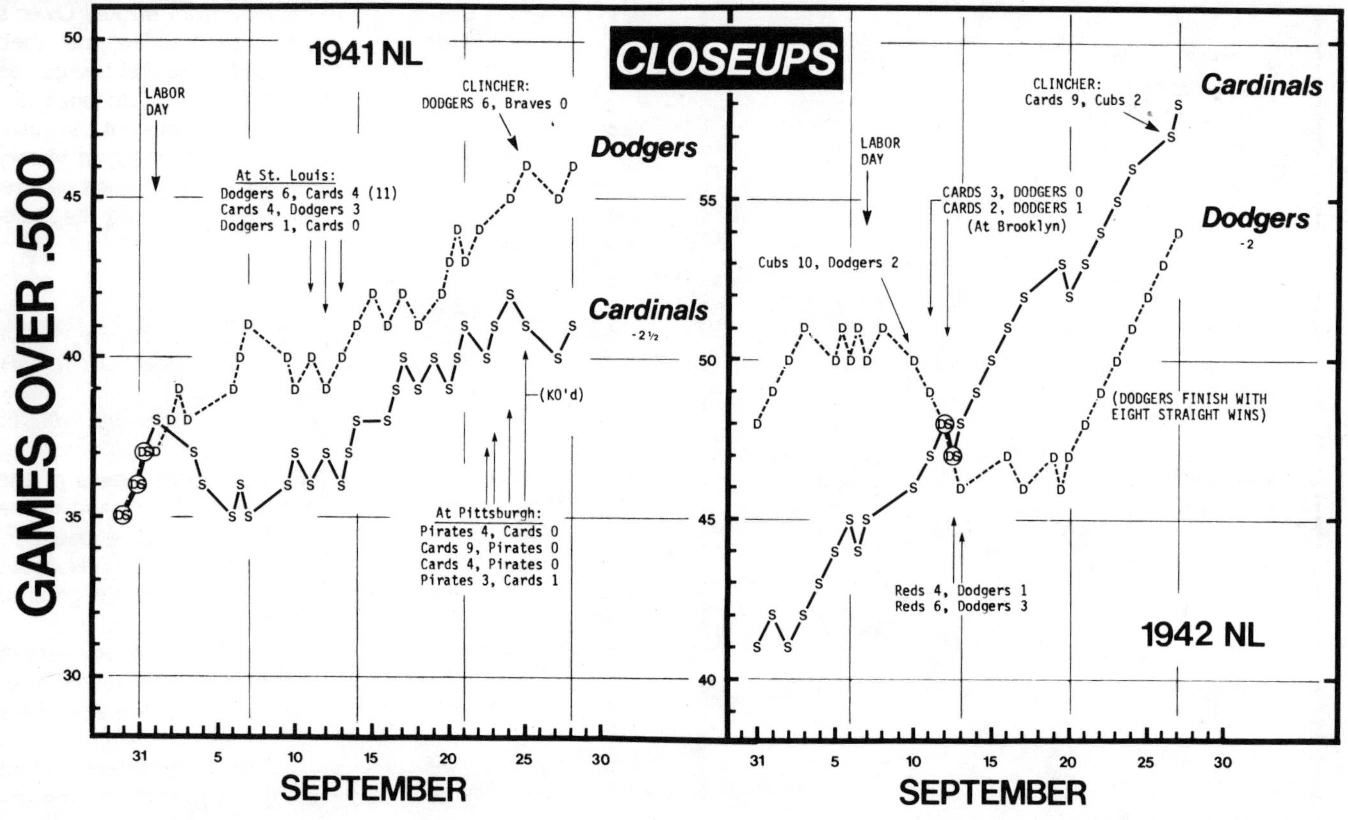


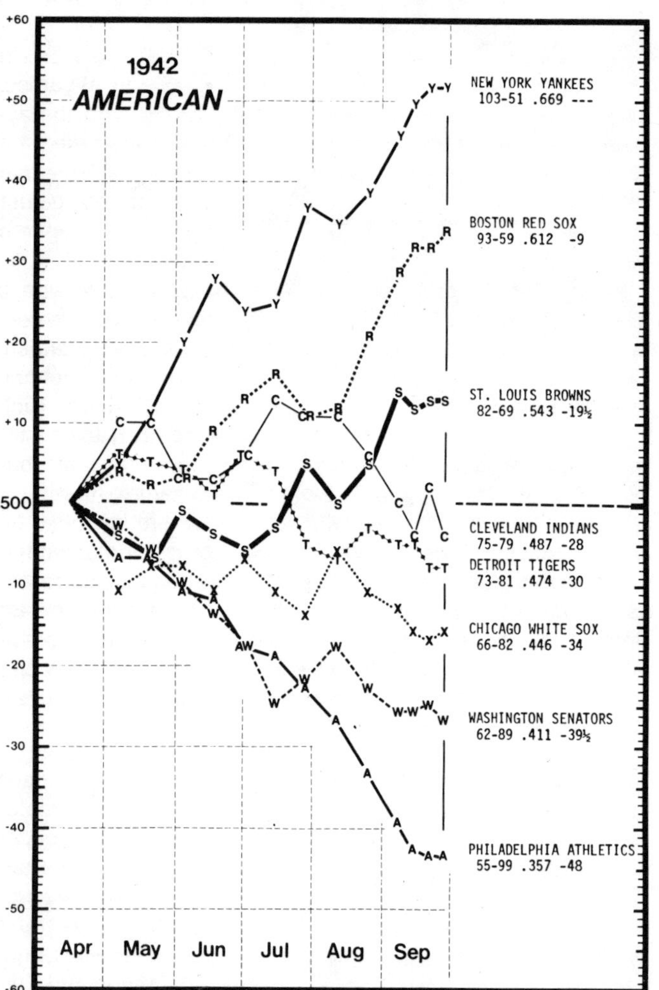


The latter had been keeping a parallel pace since May, except for a brief slump in August which had dropped them to 10½ games behind, but after that had shifted into overdrive, and now were only four games to the rear. In the next ten days the Dodgers lost the pennant—simply because they couldn't stop the sizzling Cards. St. Louis lost only four games in the whole month of September.

After stumbling over Labor Day weekend, Leo Durocher's squad saw their margin drop to two games when they were pelted by the Cubs at Ebbets Field on September 10th. The Cards themselves cut it to zero, stunning the Flatbush citizenry with 3-0 and 2-1 victories over the Dodgers on the 11th and 12th. The quick end for Brooklyn came on Sunday the 13th, when they dropped a doubleheader, again on their home turf, to the Reds, while the Cardinals won the nightcap of a twin bill at Philadelphia. Thereafter, the Dodgers lost only two more games the rest of the season, ending with an eight-game winning streak, but even that was futile because St. Louis won 12 of its last 13 games.

The Cardinals' blazing finish featured some strong hitting by Musial (.315) and Slaughter (.318), but it was clearly their mound corps that won the pennant. Mort Cooper and Johnny Beazley had phenomenal years, Cooper (22-7 and MVP) leading the NL in ERA (1.77) and shutouts (10) as well as wins, and Beazley (21-6, 2.14) having his one brilliant season before a war injury cut short his pitching career. Righthander Howie Krist (13-3) and lefty Max Lanier (13-8) also played important roles in the Cards' success. With the addition of Larry French (15-4) and excellent relief work by Hugh Casey, the Dodger pitching staff was nearly as strong, and with the same lineup as in 1941, the overall batting strength of the Brooklyn club came close to matching St. Louis's.

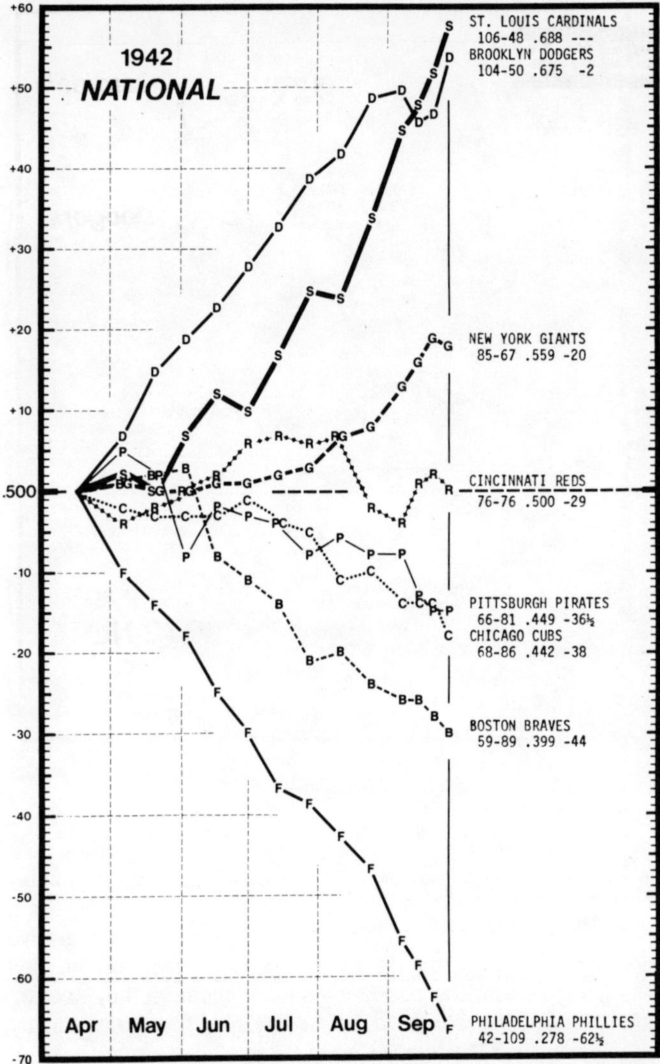


The American League race in 1942 was over, psychologically, by Memorial Day. The Yankees by that time were running away from the Indians, Tigers, and Red Sox, and only the latter were making any threatening noises. Boston displayed more good-looking youngsters from its farms, 22-game-winner Tex Hughson on the mound and shortstop Johnny Pesky (.331, 205 hits), and with Ted Williams winning the Triple Crown (.356, 36 home runs, 137 RBIs), the Red Sox led the league in hitting for the fifth year in a row. But Yankee pitching, headed by Ernie Bonham (21-5, 2.27), Spud Chandler (16-5, 2.37), and Hank Borowy (15-4, 2.53), made the difference again, holding Boston to its fourth runnerup finish in five years.

The St. Louis Browns showed a striking departure from their customary losing ways by nearly matching the New York and Boston won-lost records over the last three months of the season. Luke Sewell had taken over from Fred Haney as manager of the Browns during the '41 season, and seemed to be working miracles with limited roster talent in '42. He had some punch at the plate, from Walter Judnich (.313 17 homers), Chet Laabs (27 homers), and rookie shortstop Vern Stephens (.294, 14 home runs), but for pitching he had a motley collection of lackluster hurlers in their thirties, the oldest of whom, 38-year-old Johnny Niggeling, was the king of the staff with a 15-11 record.

The Yankees, who had beaten Brooklyn in five games in the 1941 World Series with a little help from Mickey Owen's fabled fumble of Tommy Henrich's third strike, met their masters in the 1942 classic. After a split of the first two games in St. Louis, the Cardinals' Ernie White, who had been disabled with a sore arm much of the season, shut out the Yankees on six hits at Yankee Stadium. A 9-6 slugfest victory by the Redbirds and Johnny Beazley's second Series win followed in rapid succession at the Stadium, giving the Cardinals the world championship.

## 1943

Baseball had survived the first year after Pearl Harbor remarkably unscathed. Of 71 players on major league rosters who had missed the whole 1942 season because of military service, only nine had been regulars in 1940 or 1941, and of these the only stars were Hank Greenberg of the Tigers, Bob Feller of the Indians, Cecil Travis and Buddy Lewis of the Senators, and Cookie Lavagetto of the Dodgers. And unlike 1918, baseball had been given a healthy wartime boost by President Roosevelt in January of 1942, when he advocated the continuation of normal playing schedules for the good of the country's morale.

By April of 1943, however, over 200 major leaguers were in military uniform, and the starting lineups of most teams were gutted. Joe DiMaggio, his brother Dom, Ted Williams, Pete Reiser, Pee Wee Reese, Johnny Mize, Enos Slaughter, and Johnny Beazley were among the departed. Replacements had to come from the minor leagues, and it quickly became obvious that those franchises with the strongest farm systems would fare best in the pennant races.

Unsurprisingly, then, the Yankees and Cardinals again dominated their leagues, winning flags by 13½ and 18 games, respectively. The lack of competition combined with the absence of batting stars to produce what many have called the dullest major league season of the modern era. The ennui was not diminished by the Yankees' turning the tables against the Cardinals in the 1943 World Series, another five-game affair.

Spud Chandler led the Yankees, and AL pitchers, with a 20-4 record and an ERA (1.64) which was the league's lowest since the dead-ball years. In place of DiMaggio, Henrich, Rizzuto, and first sacker Buddy Hassett, the Yanks had Johnny Lindell, Bud Metheny, Snuffy Stirnweiss, and ex-Phil Nick Etten, none of whom hit over .271; Joe Gordon, Frankie Crosetti, Charlie Keller, and Bill Dickey were still with the team, but only Keller (31 homers) and Dickey (.351 in 85 games) hit well.

For the Philadelphia Athletics, still owned and managed by Connie Mack, it was a case of the poor getting poorer—by the end of the '43 season Mack had lost 34 players to the war. The Washington Senators had lost 26, but in contrast to the miserable A's, had managed a respectable second-place finish, primarily on the pitching of 23-year-old Early Wynn and the offensive contributions of outfielder George Case (.294, 61 stolen bases).

Mort Cooper had another 20-win season for the Cardinals, and he was only one of ten pitchers on the St. Louis roster who would be rated as good in war or peacetime. The Cooper brothers battery remained intact,and Walker batted .319. Stan Musial, with 220 hits and a .357 average, spearheaded the Cards' batting. Filling in for Slaughter, Terry Moore, and second baseman Creepy Crespi were Harry Walker, Ray Sanders, and Lou Klein; the left side of the infield, Marion and Kur-

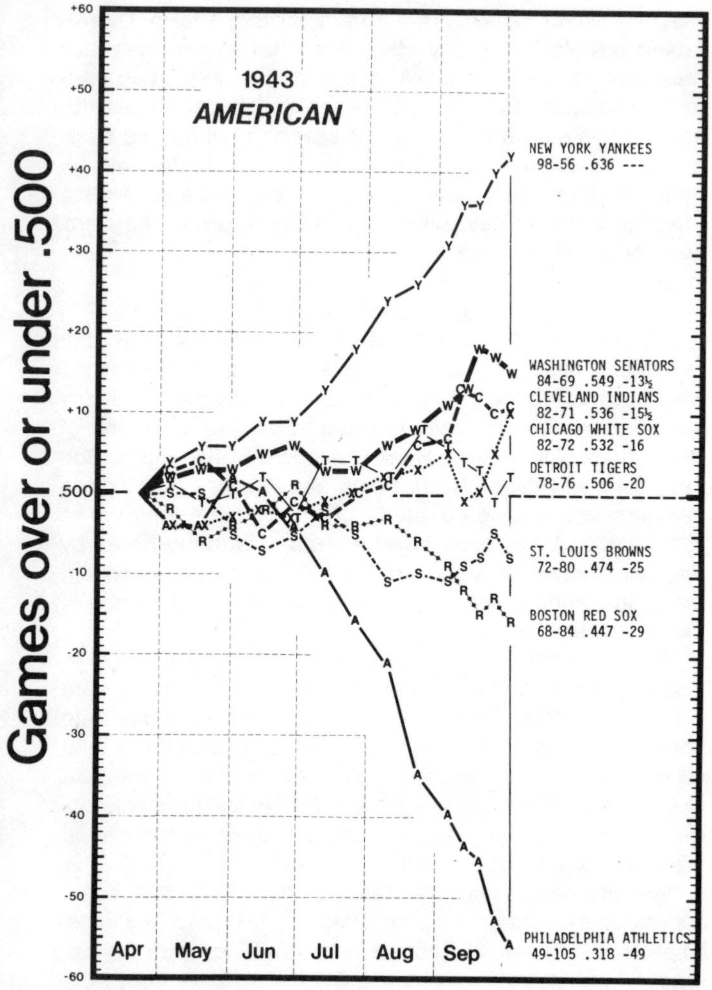

Games over or under .500
1943
AMERICAN
NEW YORK YANKEES 98-56 .636 ---
WASHINGTON SENATORS 84-69 .549 -13½
CLEVELAND INDIANS 82-71 .536 -15½
CHICAGO WHITE SOX 82-72 .532 -16
DETROIT TIGERS 78-76 .506 -20
ST. LOUIS BROWNS 72-80 .474 -25
BOSTON RED SOX 68-84 .447 -29
PHILADELPHIA ATHLETICS 49-105 .318 -49
Apr May Jun Jul Aug Sep
+60 +50 +40 +30 +20 +10 .500 -10 -20 -30 -40 -50 -60

Games over or under .500
1944
AMERICAN
ST. LOUIS BROWNS 89-65 .578 ---
DETROIT TIGERS 88-66 .571 -1
NEW YORK YANKEES 83-71 .539 -6
BOSTON RED SOX 77-77 .500 -12
CLEVELAND INDIANS 72-82 .468 -17
PHILADELPHIA ATHLETICS 72-82 .468 -17
CHICAGO WHITE SOX 71-83 .461 -18
WASHINGTON SENATORS 64-90 .416 -25
Apr May Jun Jul Aug Sep Oct
+40 +30 +20 +10 .500 -10 -20 -30 -40

owski, was unchanged from the previous year.

The biggest change in the National League was the plummeting of the New York Giants to last place. With Mel Ott (now manager) declining to a .234 average, Johnny Mize off

1943
NATIONAL
ST. LOUIS CARDINALS 105-49 .682 ---
CINCINNATI REDS 87-67 .565 -18
BROOKLYN DODGERS 81-72 .529 -23½
PITTSBURGH PIRATES 80-74 .519 -25
CHICAGO CUBS 74-79 .484 -30½
BOSTON BRAVES 68-85 .444 -36½
PHILADELPHIA PHILLIES 64-90 .416 -41
NEW YORK GIANTS 55-98 .359 -49½
Apr May Jun Jul Aug Sep Oct
+60 +50 +40 +30 +20 +10 .500 -10 -20 -30 -40 -50 -60

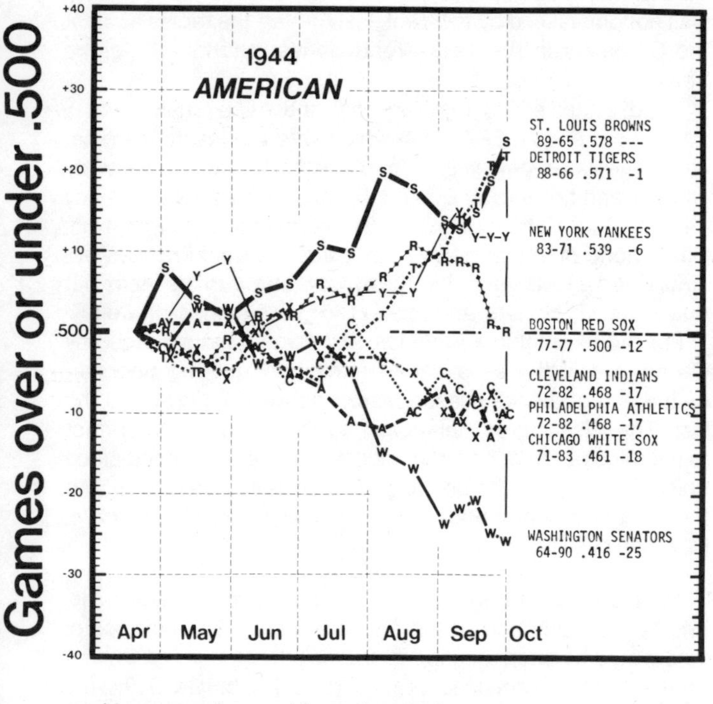

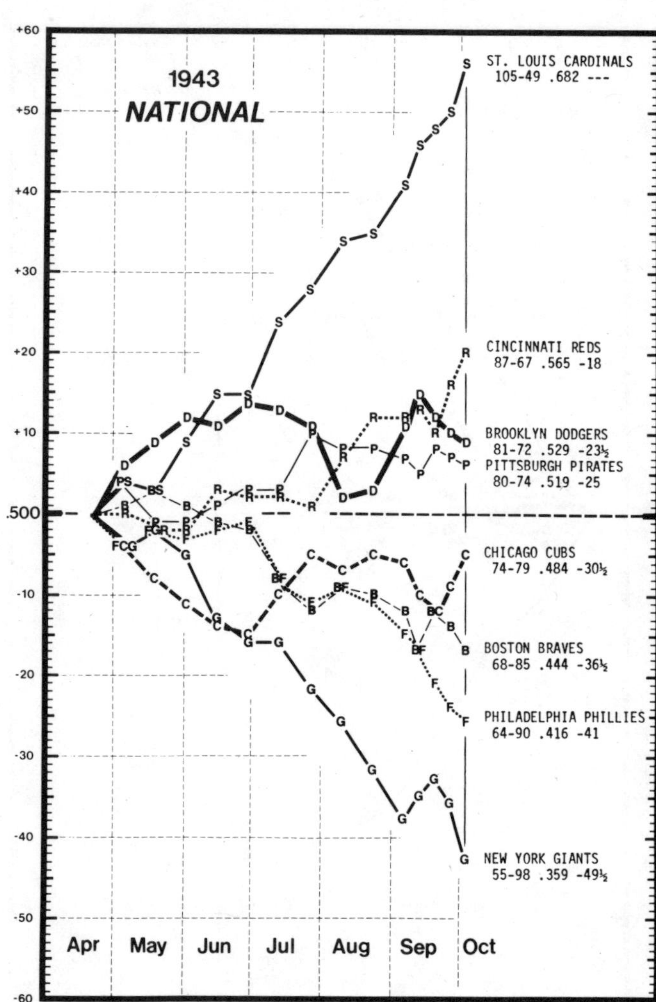

to war, and only one strong pitcher, reliever Ace Adams, the Polo Grounds in 1943 was a quiet and gloomy ballpark.

## 1944

The first of several surprises pulled by the 1944 St. Louis Browns was to win the first nine games they played in April, at the time a new American League record for consecutive wins at the start of a season. Before that feat, nobody had given serious thought to a Browns pennant, much less the Browns themselves. But now it occurred to many observers that Luke Sewell's team was not only leading the league but also leading the major leagues in the number of 4-F players on its roster. Whereas other teams were still losing their regulars to the war—the Yankees lost Spud Chandler after only one game, and the total for all 16 teams was now approaching 350 players—the Browns had 13 men, including most of their first-stringers, who were protected from the draft by their physical unfitness. As Bill Mead said in his entertaining and informative book *Even the Browns,* their strength was in superior weakness.

The Brownies slumped in May, letting the Yankees take over, but in June the latter had an even worse slump. In mid-June, all eight teams were within a 4½-game range, and out of the mass of mediocrity came the Browns, pulling away to 20 games over .500, and 6½ games ahead of the Red Sox, by early August. They were clicking on good pitching by starters Nels Potter, Bob Muncrief, Jack Kramer, and Sig Jakucki, and relief man George Caster, and on good batwork from Vern

**BROWNS SWEEP YANKS, WIN PENNANT was the unlikely headline in 1944, a clear measure of how World War II had turned the American League upside down. The clinching victory for Luke Sewell's team did not come until the final day, when Sig Jakucki pitched a six-hitter and Chet Laabs hit two home runs for a 5-2 win over the Yankees at St. Louis, while Washington's Dutch Leonard handcuffed the Tigers at Detroit.**

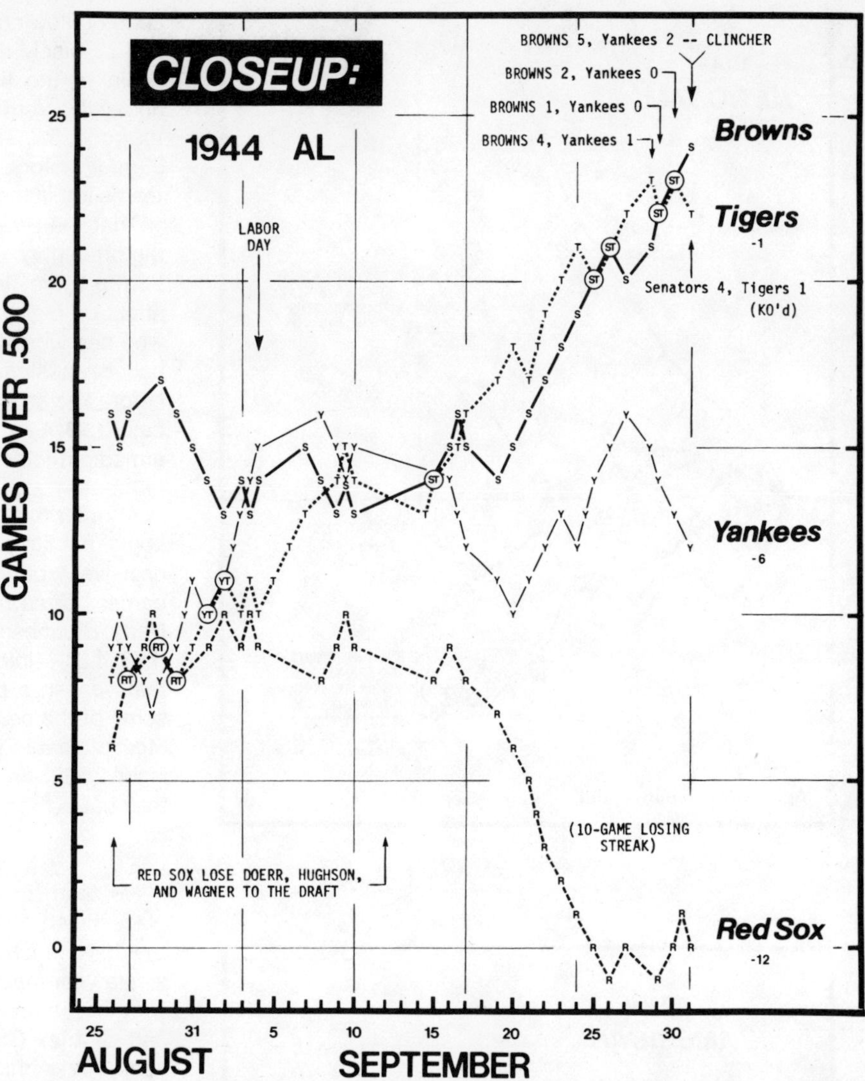


Stephens, Mike Kreevich, Milt Byrnes, and Al Zarilla.

Then came another tumble, from fatigue and complacency according to Sewell, and suddenly, two days before Labor Day, they were only a game ahead of the Yankees and Tigers and 1½ games in front of the Red Sox. When the Yanks beat the A's 10-0 and 14-0, on Labor Day, the Browns lost their lead of three months, and the free-for-all was on.

Boston was first to drop out, and the Red Sox did so spectacularly, as a result of the draft taking Tex Hughson, their best pitcher, and Bobby Doerr and Hal Wagner, their two best hitters, all in the same fortnight around September 1st. New York was next, losing a three-game series to the vengeful A's at Philly on September 16-17, and two of three at Detroit right after that, giving the lead to the Tigers in the process.

In the last eleven days of the season the surviving Tigers and Browns were never more than a game apart. On the final weekend, the Browns hosted the Yankees for four games at Sportsman's Park while the Tigers faced the Senators in Detroit. The rest of the country seemed more caught up in the race than St. Louis fans—only 6,172 showed up for Friday's doubleheader, when Kramer and Potter muffled the Yanks in 4-1 and 1-0 victories. The Tigers took the opener of their doubleheader that day, 5-2 behind Rufe Gentry, but Dizzy Trout got clobbered in the nightcap, 9-2, putting Detroit back into a tie with St. Louis. On Saturday, 12,982 watched Denny Galehouse shut out New York again, while MVP Hal Newhouser notched his 29th win of the season in a 7-3 Detroit victory. By now, with the two teams tied going into the closing day, the fans had perked up, and both Detroit and St. Louis filled their seats that Sunday afternoon.

Washington's Dutch Leonard faced Trout, who was after his 28th win as well as the pennant. A fourth-inning homer by Stan Spence with Joe Kuhel aboard gave the victory to Leonard, 4-1, and after the game thousands of dejected Tiger fans sat in Briggs Stadium watching the scoreboard's posting of the half-inning scores from the New York-St. Louis game, which had started an hour later. Luke Sewell had selected the rambunctious 34-year-old Jakucki, whose sole major league experience before 1944 had been 20.7 innings for the 1936 Browns, earning him no wins and three losses. The selection was final only after some careful mental estimates of Jakucki's blood alcohol level by his teammates, as he was known to imbibe on nights and even mornings before his turns on the mound.

Early in the game, Yankee outfielder Herschel Martin got to Jakucki for a double and triple, and combined with three Brownie errors, these put New York ahead, 2-0. But after the third inning Jakucki let only one Yankee get as far as third base, and the St. Louis bats began to boom. A homer by Chet

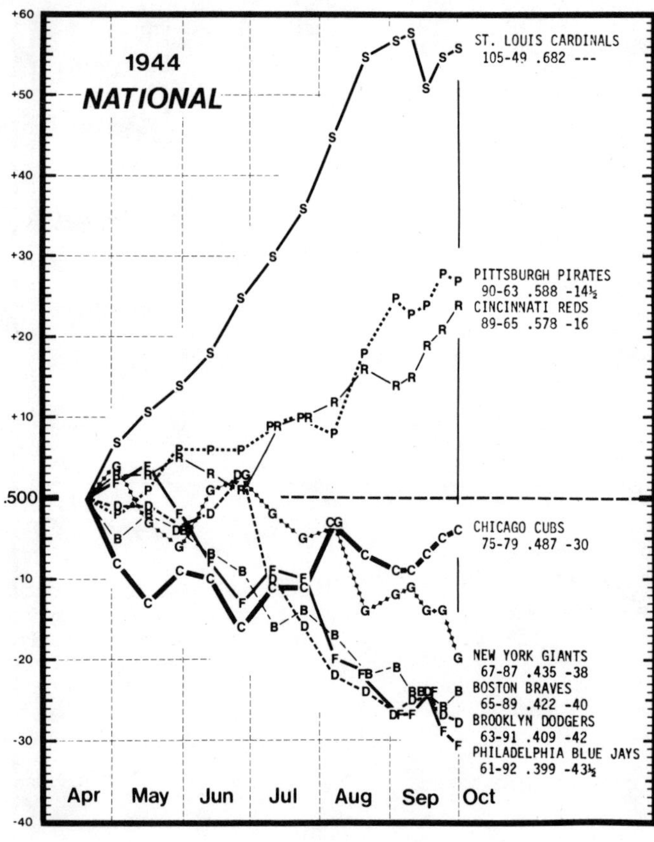


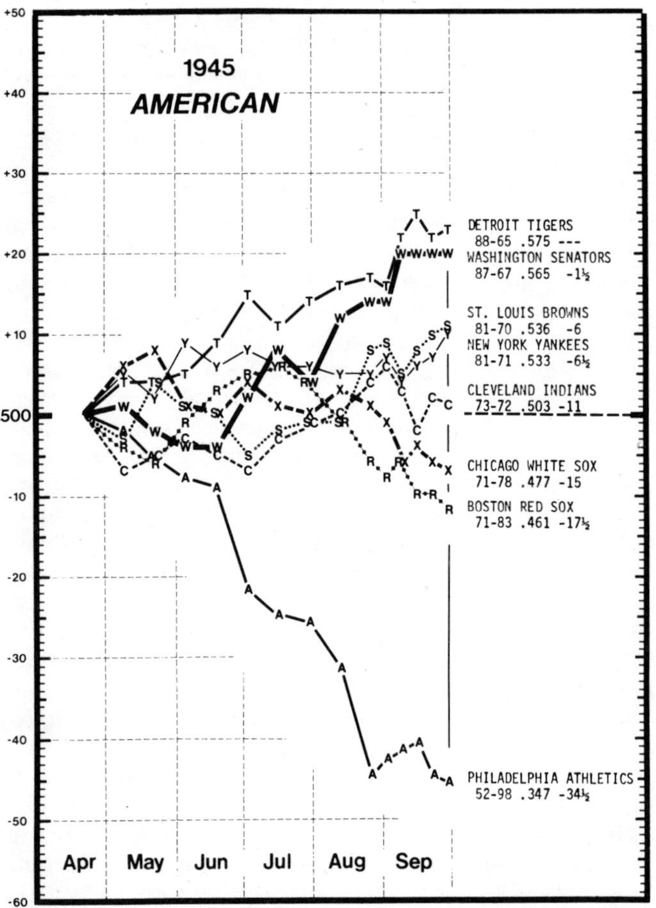


Laabs following Mike Kreevich's single tied it up in the fourth, and precisely the same combination by Kreevich and Laabs again in the fifth sent the Browns ahead by two. A solo homer by Vern Stephens in the eighth put the Yanks away for good, 5-2. The first, last, and only pennant in the Browns' 53-year history was captured, and now there were no flagless teams left in the major leagues.

That the Browns' pennant-clincher came at the expense of the oft-mighty Yankees only made St. Louis's triumph of 1944 all the more fitting as a barometer of the war's deforming effect on major-league baseball. And individually, Sig Jakucki, who had won 12 other games that year for his team and who had been signed right out of the semipro ranks in Texas before the season, made as good a symbol of wartime baseball in 1944 as the more famous Pete Gray, the Browns one-armed outfielder, did the next year.

Another big pennant victory for the Cardinals gave St. Louis a "Streetcar Series," which was won by the Cards decisively, but not as easily as many had expected, in six games. Three more products of the Cardinal farm system—Harry Brecheen (16-5), Ted Wilks (17-4), and George Munger (11-3, 1.34)—joined Mort Cooper (22-7) and Max Lanier (17-12) that year in a pitching staff that would have rated with the some of the best in peacetime years. Marty Marion was voted Most Valuable Player; heavy hitting was supplied by Johnny Hopp (.336) as well as Stan Musial and Walker Cooper in their usual form.

## 1945

No team in the modern period has jumped from a last-place finish to a pennant or division title the next year, but the 1944-45 Chicago Cubs went from last to first place in a single year measured from July to July. The Cubs got off to a wretched start in 1944, losing ten of their first 11 contests, and Charley Grimm was brought back to manage the club again that April. No instant miracle resulted from the change, but the Cubs did reverse the losing trend under Jolly Cholly, and got out of the NL cellar in July when four other teams fell beneath them. They were approaching the .500 mark when the season ended, and picked up where they left off in April of 1945. By the following Fourth of July, they had passed the Cardinals, Dodgers, and a flash-in-the-pan Giant team to take the league lead.

The spurt that put them into first place turned out to be a hot run of 26 wins in 30 games, producing what looked like a safe lead in August, but the Cardinals made a close race of it in September. With one week to go, only a game and a half separated the two contenders as they met head-on for a pair of games at Wrigley Field. Given the fact that later in the week the Cubs were scheduled to play their cousins, the Cincinnati Reds, whom they had already beaten 19 out of 20 times that year, the Cards figured their only hope for the pennant was to win both games. But in the first game Hank Borowy, who had become the stopper of the Cub pitching corps since he was surprisingly claimed on waivers from the Yankees in July, held the Cardinals at bay while the Cubs kayoed Harry Brecheen, giving the Cubs their season's climactic victory, 6-5. After a St. Louis win the next day, the Cubs swept twin bills from the Reds and Pirates to nail down the pennant. In the process, they set a record of 20 doubleheader sweeps in a season.

Besides Borowy, who ended up a 20-game-winner across

both leagues (10-5 for the Yankees and 11-2 for the Cubs), the Cubs also benefited from the mound work of Hank Wyse (22-10), Claude Passeau (17-9), and 38-year-old Paul Derringer (16-11), and had the NL's best team ERA. They also led the league in team batting, with 10-year veterans Phil Cavarretta (.355, MVP) and Stan Hack (.323) setting the pace and rookie Andy Pafko driving in 110 runs. Even without Musial or the Cooper brothers, the Cards remained a strong team by acquiring 23-game-winner Red Barrett from the Braves and bringing up rookie pitcher Ken Burkhart (18-8) and another freshman named Red Schoendienst.

The American League also had a tight race in 1945, and more than the National League's, one in which returning war veterans played prominent roles. The Detroit Tigers welcomed Hank Greenberg back on July 1st, by which time the Tigers already had a secure hold on first place in the standings. The Washington Senators had fallen to seventh place in early June, but an 18-and-6 spurt had suddenly made them second-place challengers. They slumped badly in July, however, obviously needing help, and got it when Buddy Lewis returned from service; his .333 batting, combined with effective pitching from the veteran knuckleballers Roger Wolff, Dutch Leonard, and Mickey Haefner, kept the Nats in the race to the season's final week.

Hammerin' Hank was Detroit's only .300 hitter that year, and

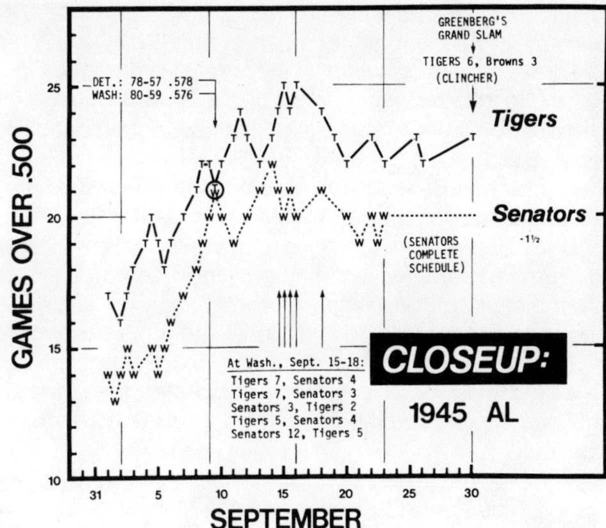


**COMING IN ON A WING AND A PRAYER. Like two flak-torn bombers barely able to make it back over the Channel, Detroit and Washington limped home in the last weeks of the 1945 AL season, neither seeming capable of winning a pennant. Hank Greenberg, back from the war, finally settled matters by clouting a grand slam home run in the ninth inning of the Tigers' last game at St. Louis when the Bengals were behind by a run. Detroit's won-lost percentage at the end was only .575, the lowest title-winning percentage until divisional play in the major leagues.**

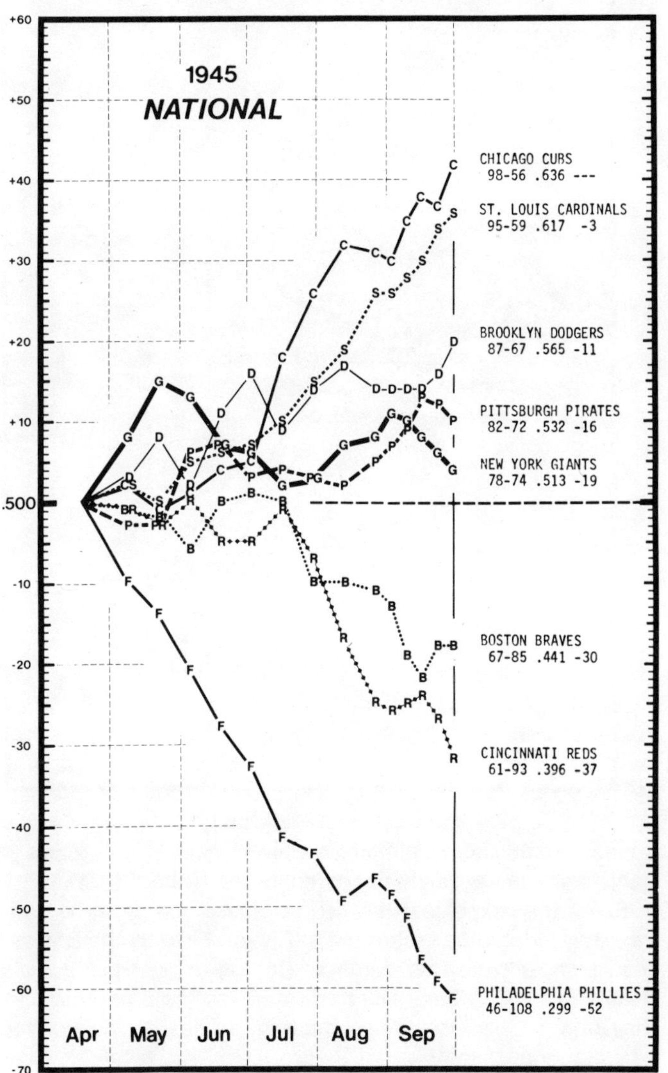


if the Tigers hadn't had Hal Newhouser, who won 25 games and was voted the MVP award for the second straight year, the Senators would have gotten the pennant by default. In September, Washington narrowed Detroit's margin to three percentage points—on the 10th, the two clubs were at 21 games over .500. When they confronted each other in Griffith Stadium on September 15-18, the Tigers took three of the first four games of the series, and that seemed to decide the race. But after a rainout on the 17th, the Senators rallied to salvage the fifth game, belting the Tigers 12-5, and thereafter each of the teams seemed to be trying to hand the pennant to the other. The Tigers dropped 2-0 and 6-1 decisions to the Indians at Detroit on the 19th and 20th, reducing their lead to a single game, but then the Senators returned the favor on the 20th and 21st by losing two games to the Yankees in New York. On Sunday the 23rd, when the Senators were back home completing their schedule early to make way for pro football at Griffith Stadium, the Tigers gave the Nats another opportunity to tie for the league lead by losing, 5-0, to the Browns at Detroit. But the Senators passed it up again, losing the first game of a doubleheader against the A's in the 12th inning on a mental error—outfielder George (Bingo) Binks of the Senators neglected to bring his sunglasses with him to the centerfield pasture after the clouds had lifted the previous inning. With two out, Binks lost Ernie Kish's routine fly in the sun for a double, and Philadelphia's George Kell quickly followed with a single to drive in Kish with the winning run.

The Senators won the nightcap, ending their regular schedule with an 87-67 record, and now all they could do is hope that the Tigers, at 86-64, would lose at least three of their last four games. One of those losses occurred in a doubleheader between the Tigers and Indians at Detroit on the 26th; the other two could have occurred in the Bengals' final pair of games at St. Louis. Rain forced these to be scheduled as a twin bill on the closing day, September 30th, and delayed the first pitch on that Sunday to the point where only one game would fit in the remaining daylight. When the showers stopped, Nels Potter of the Browns squared off against Detroit's Virgil Trucks, who had just gotten out of the Navy.

Tiger manager Steve O'Neill was holding Newhouser in reserve, and at the first sign of trouble, in the sixth inning, Prince Hal came in to snuff out a Browns rally, preserving a 2-1 Detroit lead. But the Brownies, who had proven to be no pushovers in the latter part of the season, inched ahead with single runs in the next two innings. In the top of the ninth, trailing 3-2, the Tigers loaded the bases with one out. Hank Greenberg then belted a 1-1 pitch into the left-field bleachers, and the grand slam finally gave the Tigers the one win they needed for the pennant.

Greenberg hammered two more home runs, and several other key hits, when the Tigers beat the favored Cubs in the World Series, four games to three.

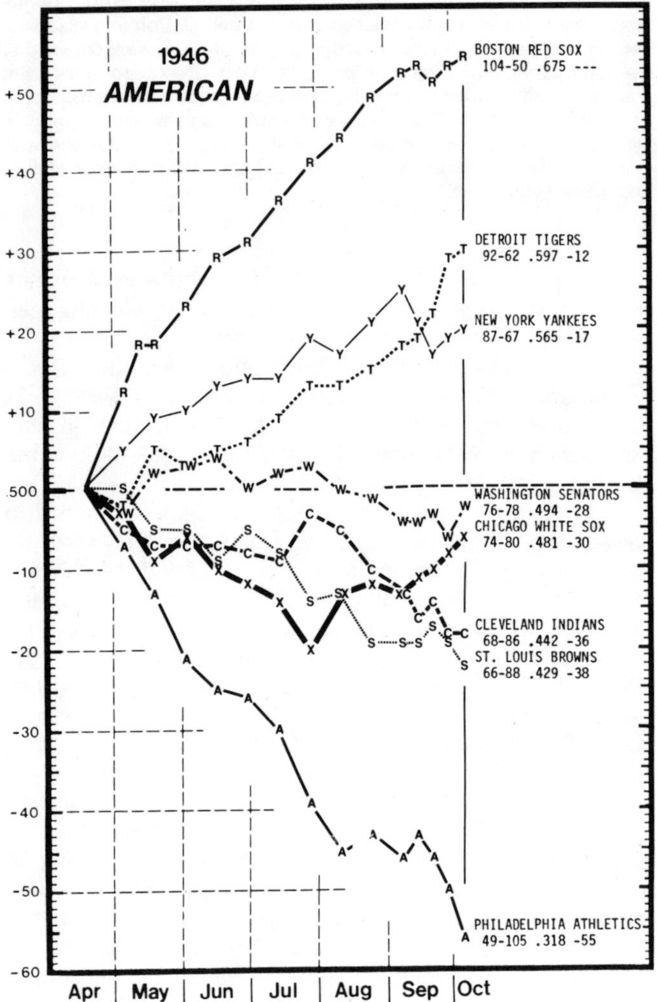


## 1946

The war was over, and they were *all* back: Ted Williams in left, Dom DiMaggio in center, Catfish Metkovich (or Leon Culberson, or Wally Moses) in right, Rudy York at first, Bobby Doerr at second, Johnny Pesky at short, Pinky Higgins at third, Hal Wagner behind the plate, and on the mound, Tex Hughson, Dave (Boo) Ferriss, Mickey Harris, and Joe Dobson. That was the lineup cemented into the memories of a million-plus New Englanders. By May 10th, these Red Sox were 21-and-3, by June 20th they were 30 games over .500, by mid-August they were 13 games ahead of the Yankees, and by the end, Boston had its first pennant since 1918. Temporarily at least, the demons and goblins of Harry Frazee's dynasty demolition, the dark dungeon days of the twenties, the maddening second-fiddle years before the war, and the nightmare war years themselves were replaced by pure euphoria. The 1946 season might have been dull for followers of other AL teams, but Red Sox fans savored every moment of it.

The major elements in the triumph by Joe Cronin's club were Ted Williams' MVP performance (.342, 37 homers, 123 RBIs) and the top-drawer pitching by Ferriss (25-6) and Hughson (20-11). Pesky (.335) and the neat-fielding DiMaggio (.316) were fine table-setters, as often driven home by York (119 RBIs) and Doerr (116 RBIs) as by The Thumper.

The 1946 National League race produced the first tie in major league history. The Cardinals and Dodgers returned to their pre-war habit of hounding each other all season long. In September, just when it appeared that the Cards, now man-

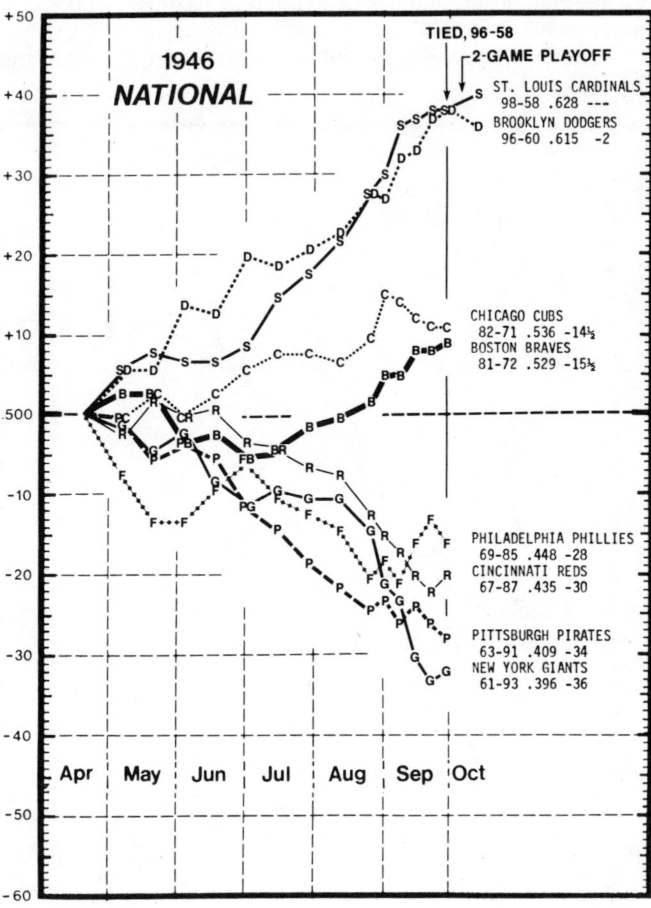


aged by Eddie Dyer, might pull away for good, Leo Durocher's gang went on an eight-out-of-ten binge, tying St. Louis at 96-57 on the next-to-last day of the season. On the final Sunday, the Dodgers were shut out at Ebbets Field by the Braves' Mort Cooper (who had come to Boston in the Red Barrett deal) and the Cardinals failed to capitalize, losing at home to the Cubs, 8-3. Under NL rules, the terminal deadlock called for a best-of-three playoff.

The next day, in the first pennant playoff game ever, the Cardinals went one up on the Dodgers when Howie Pollet, who took the league's ERA crown with 2.10 that year, outpitched a bright-looking Brooklyn rookie named Ralph Branca. Two days later, after the teams traveled to Brooklyn, St. Louis won the pennant with an 8-4 victory, Murray Dickson and Harry Brecheen sharing the pitching honors.

With Musial and Slaughter back, the Cardinals had been expected to sail to an easy flag win, but they were somewhat weakened by losses to the Mexican League. Their biggest loss was Max Lanier, lured by the higher salaries south of the border after pitching six complete-game victories for the Cards in the spring. The Mexican influence on the Cardinals was small, however, compared to the Giants' loss of eight players, including their relief artist, Ace Adams, a promising young pitcher named Sal Maglie, and regulars Danny Gardella and Nap Reyes. Mel Ott's team finished last even though they outhomered every other NL club by 40 clouts.

Brooklyn was probably hurt more by Pete Reiser's broken ankle three weeks before the playoff than by the Mexican raids, which lured away catcher Mickey Owen and outfielder Luis Olmo. While not yet back to his pre-war form at the plate (.277 in 1946), Reiser led the league in stolen bases and provided leadership for the Dodger club generally. Dixie Walker (.319, 116 RBIs) supplied the strongest bat, and Pee Wee Reese also displayed overall excellence. On the mound, Durocher had no superstar, but he did have nearly a dozen mostly young, low-ERA hurlers, the regular starters being Kirby Higbe, Joe Hatten, and Vic Lombardi. On balance and on paper, it was a tribute to Durocher's managerial skills that the Dodgers contended so well.

A surprise fourth-place finisher turned up in Boston, where Billy Southworth had moved from St. Louis before the season. Besides Mort Cooper, the Braves had a new mound ace, Johnny Sain, who won 20 games with a 2.21 ERA. They also had beefed up their batting order with the development of Tommy Holmes, who had set a new modern NL record of hitting safely in 37 consecutive games while batting .352 in 1945, and the acquisition of two other .300 hitters, Johnny Hopp and Billy Herman.

The 1946 World Series was a well-remembered one for Enos Slaughter's dash from first base to score the Series-winning run on a dying-swan hit by Harry Walker when Boston's Johnny Pesky paused a few milliseconds too long in relaying the ball to home plate. This storied base-running feat and Brecheen's three mound victories gave the Series to the Cardinals, but the Red Sox battled gamely enough over the seven games to avoid disgrace.

## 1947

In 1947 a gaping hole in the racial wall between organized baseball and black players was smashed by Jackie Robinson and by Branch Rickey, the Brooklyn general manager, who had the courage to put him in a Dodger uniform. This decades-overdue event started the racial integration of baseball, the lack of which had tragically deprived such great talents as Josh Gibson, Joe Williams, Buck Leonard, Pop Lloyd, Oscar Charleston, and Cool Papa Bell of the opportunity to show the world that they could hold their own with the likes of Ruth, Cobb, Johnson, and Grove. And when the hole in the wall was widened in the next few years by Larry Doby and Satchell Paige at Cleveland, Monte Irvin and Willie Mays with the Giants, and more Dodgers such as Roy Campanella and Don

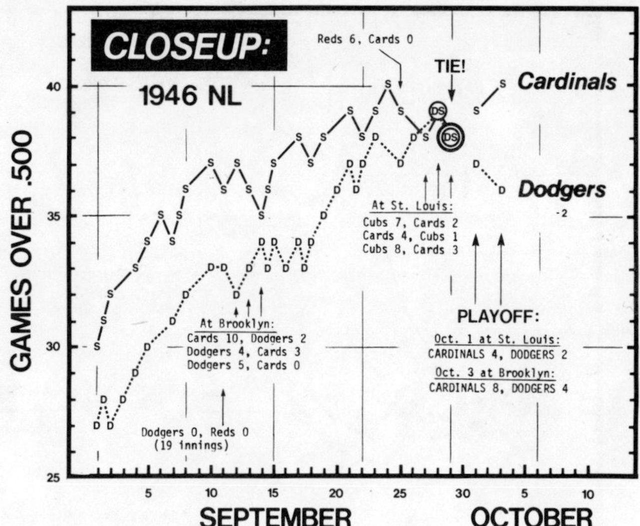


**DEAD HEAT #1. The first major league pennant playoff of the century took place after the St. Louis Cardinals and Brooklyn Dodgers completed their regular schedules with identical 96-58 records in 1946. If the Dodgers had won their final two games against Boston, it would have been a nifty come-from-behind pennant victory for them, but Brooklyn was thwarted by the Braves' Mort Cooper on the final Sunday at Ebbets Field. Two quick wins in the playoff gave the flag to the Cards instead.**

Newcombe, the white baseball world began to realize what its deprivation had been, too.

Although any selection for the historic role would have been a gamble for Rickey, in retrospect Jackie Robinson hardly

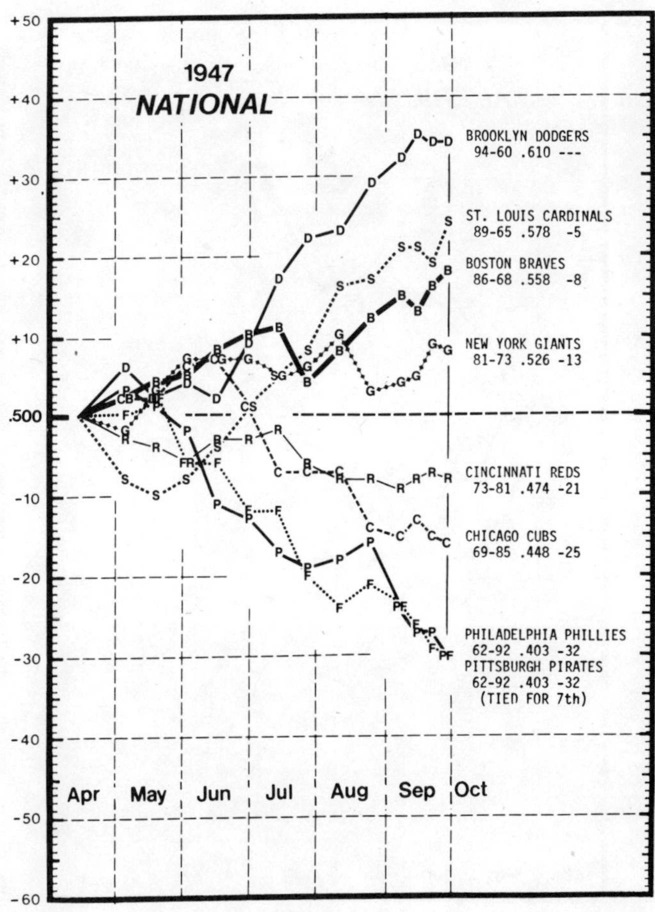

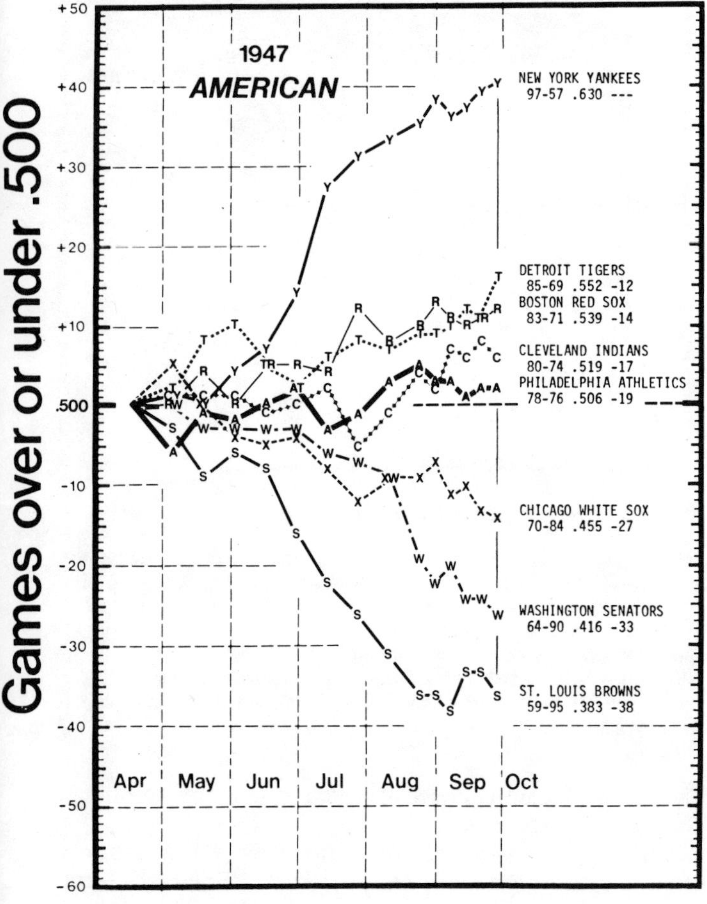


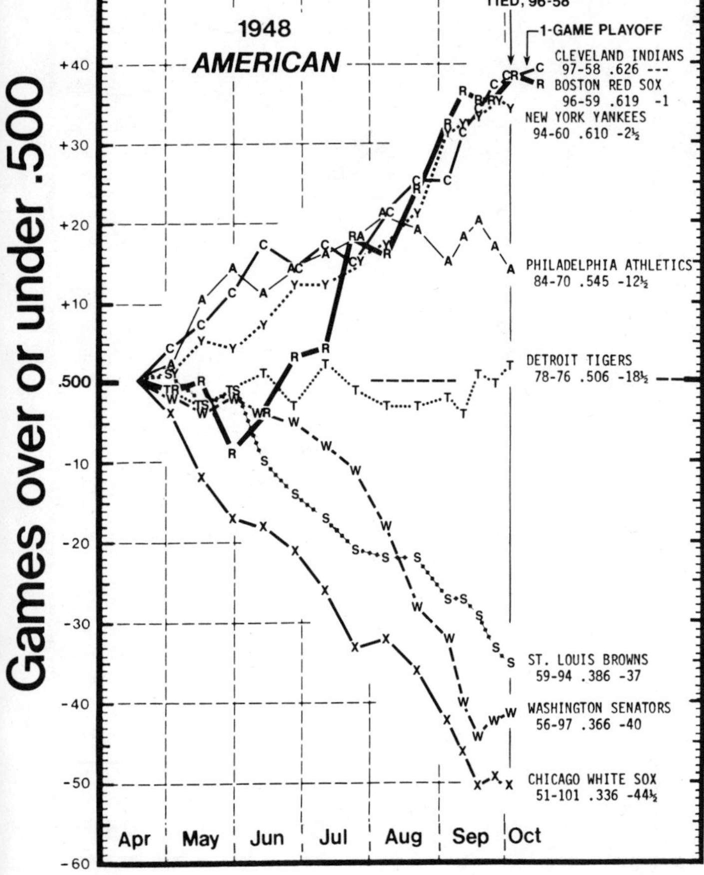


seems like one. Under tremendous, often infuriating pressure, he played nearly every game that season, batted .297, led the league with 29 stolen bases, and led the Dodgers to the pennant, for which he was voted the rookie of the Year award. His fine play was nearly matched by the pitching of Ralph Branca, who compiled a 21-12 record in his first full season, and reliever Hugh Casey, who won ten and saved 18.

The Boston Braves moved up another notch in the standings, again besting both Brooklyn and St. Louis in team batting, and displaying still another pitching star, Warren Spahn; Spahn and Sain both won 21 games. In fourth place, up from the cellar, were the Giants, who also found an ace, Larry Jansen (21-5), but whose elevation was also due to their thundering bats. The Polo Grounders set a new major league (and still NL) record for a team's home-run total in a season—221—to which the main contributors were Johnny Mize (51, league high), outfielder Willard Marshall (36), ex-Cardinal catcher Walker Cooper (35), and rookie Bobby Thomson (29).

In the American League, the Red Sox were favored to repeat and Ted Williams won his second Triple Crown, but Boston's three best pitchers of 1946—Hughson, Ferriss, and Harris—all developed arm trouble. Their combined total of 62 victories the previous year dropped to 29. The Yankees, on the other hand, had a new manager, Bucky Harris, a new pitcher, ex-Indian Allie Reynolds (19-8), and a new first baseman, veteran ex-Brownie George McQuinn (.305). Combined with near-typical performances by Joe DiMaggio, Tommy Henrich, and Phil Rizzuto at the plate and marvelous rally-squelching by Joe Page (14 wins, 17 saves), these factors were more than enough for an easy pennant for the Yankees.

Signs of life appeared in Philadelphia for the first time in a dozen years. Connie Mack got some good pitching from Phil Marchildon and Dick Fowler, and some batting punch from ex-Tiger Barney McCosky, Elmer Valo, and Ferris Fain, lifting the A's to a respectable fifth place in the standings.

The World Series, which was the second Yankee-Dodger contest, was won by the Yankees again, but not until after an unusually entertaining array of events spread over seven games. These included Bill Bevens' near no-hitter (he got the first 26 Dodger outs, but Lavagetto broke up both the no-hitter and the game with a double in the ninth), Al Gionfriddo's game-saving robbery of DiMag's near-homer, a pinch-hit home run by rookie Yogi Berra, and more bullpen dramatics by Joe Page.

## 1948

1948 was a year that belonged to Lou Boudreau, a rookie southpaw named Gene Bearden, and the long-deprived Cleveland Indians. But others—the Yankees, Red Sox, and even the A's for awhile—thought it was their year, and that provided the elements for a thrilling pennant race in the American League.

It began with much success by the Indians and A's in the spring, a decent start by the Yankees, and a disastrous slump by the Red Sox, for whom the venerable Joe McCarthy had replaced Joe Cronin as manager between seasons. On Memorial Day, Boston was in seventh place with a 14-and-23 record, and the Fenway fans were fuming.

In the next two months, however, the Red Sox won three-fourths of their games and caught up to the other three. On the 3rd of August, all four clubs were at 18 games over .500 (see closeup). The A's, showing further progress with much the same roster as in '47, fell out of the race later that month, while

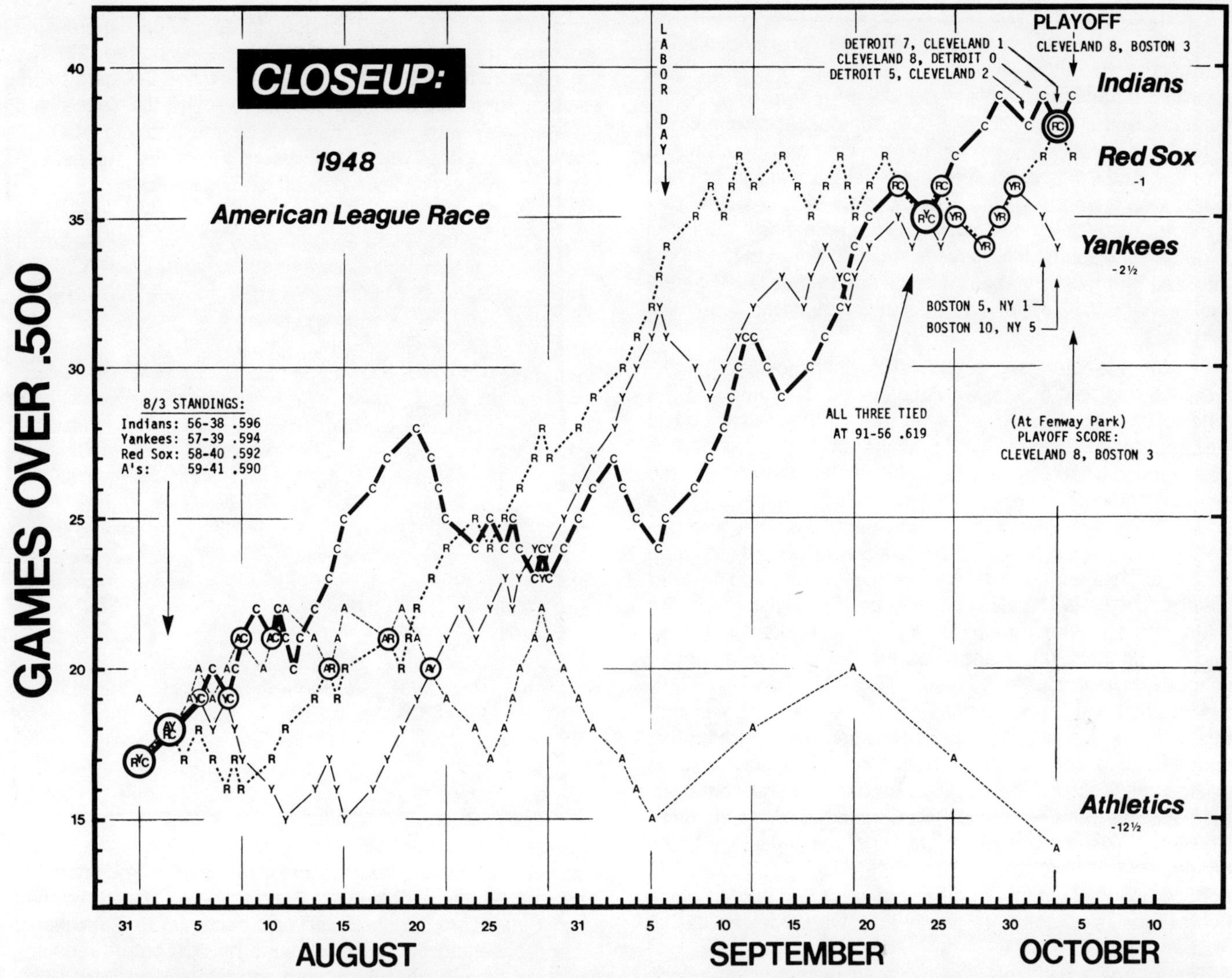


**THE BOUDREAU BOYS AND THE GALEHOUSE GANG met in the American League's first playoff at Fenway Park on Monday, October 4, 1948, and the Cleveland Indians beat the Boston Red Sox, 8-3, for the pennant. Three days earlier, after a 5-2 defeat of the Indians by Detroit and before New York's elimination by Boston, there had been seven possible outcomes of the three-team race: any one of the three — Cleveland, Boston, or New York — might have won the pennant outright on the final Sunday, or any two of the three might have wound up tied for first place, or there might have been a three-way tie. In their playoff victory, Lou Boudreau and other Indians pounded Boston's Denny Galehouse and a reliever, whacking several hard shots over and off the famed Green Monster, while rookie Gene Bearden held the Bosox to five hits.**

Boston, New York, and Cleveland continued a frantic pace the rest of the way.

All three eventual contenders were benefiting from some important personnel changes from the previous year. For the Red Sox, Tom Yawkey's purchase of shortstop Vern Stephens and pitchers Jack Kramer and Ellis Kinder from the financially-troubled Browns made a big difference, as did the maturing of lefty Mel Parnell and infielder Billy Goodman. The Indians were strengthened by Bearden's arrival (he won 20 games and led the AL with a 2.43 ERA), and the acquisition of outfielder Larry Doby and reliever Russ Christopher; with the development of outfielder Dale Mitchell (.366) and righthander Bob Lemon (20-14) added to the established skills of Bob Feller, manager Lou Boudreau, and sluggers Joe Gordon and Ken Keltner, Cleveland had, in fact, the best pitching and hitting in the majors. The Yankees now had Ed Lopat (17-11), acquired from the White Sox, and Vic Raschi (19-8) had become their best pitcher, but in general the Yankee mound crew was not up to the level of the previous year; their offense, however, did improve with .300 hitting by Yogi Berra and Bobby Brown. The superstars, Ted Williams and Joe DiMaggio, were up to their usual tricks, Ted leading the league with a .369 average and Joe with 44 homers.

The Indians took a three-game lead in August, then lost it to the Red Sox, who moved 3½ games out in front after Labor Day. Then Boston faltered on a western road trip, and the Indians tied the Red Sox for the lead when Feller beat them in Cleveland, 5-2, on September 22nd. Two days later, the Yankees joined them, and all three stood at 35 games over .500 with eight days left in the schedule. In the final week, the Yankees and Red Sox were tied for several more days, after a three-game series between them at Yankee Stadium proved to be indecisive, but the Indians pulled away with four straight wins over Detroit and Chicago. This string was broken by a 5-2 loss to the Tigers in Cleveland on Friday, October 1st, and with both New York and Boston winning the previous two days, the teams went into the final Saturday and Sunday with Cleveland leading the other two by only one game.

On those last two days, the Yankees and Red Sox faced each other at Fenway Park, while the Tigers and Indians were completing their three-game series in Cleveland. On Saturday, Bearden hurled a shutout and Doby went four-for-four, as the Indians smothered the Tigers, 8-0. In Boston, Jack Kramer outpitched New York's Tommy Byrne, allowing only one run and five hits, and Williams' homer with Pesky aboard in the first inning was enough, but the Sox added three tallies later. The 5-1 victory provided the Fenway fans the immensely satisfying experience of seeing the Yankees knocked out of the race, but they still had to worry about their own team helplessly losing the pennant to Cleveland if Bob Feller beat the Tigers on Sunday.

In both the Cleveland and Boston ballparks on Sunday, everyone had split brains, with one eye on the game and the other on the scoreboard (or an ear to a portable radio). Hal Newhouser, a 20-game-winner again for Detroit, was Feller's opponent, and proved to be his better that day, as the Tigers hammered Feller for a 7-1 trouncing. The news of this added to the pleasures of the Fenway Faithful as they watched the Red Sox overcome a 2-0 Yankee lead in the third inning on a pair of doubles by Williams and Doerr, followed in later innings by more heroics on the part of Williams, Dom DiMaggio, and Vern Stephens; after four Yankee and three Red Sox pitchers, the final score was 10-5, and the American League had its first tie.

McCarthy had Kinder with four days' rest, and Parnell with three, for the single-game playoff the next day. Perhaps because he had been called a "pushbutton manager" by the Boston press, or maybe because he had in mind some historic surprise pitching choices like Connie Mack's selection of Howard Ehmke in the opener of the '29 World Series, McCarthy handed the ball instead to 36-year-old Denny Galehouse to oppose Bearden, who was perhaps an equally dubious choice by Boudreau as a lefty in Fenway Park with only one day of rest.

Three batters past the third inning, it became clear which manager had made the better guess. After a homer into the left-field screen by Boudreau himself in the first which was promptly matched by a Red Sox run, the Cleveland manager led off the fourth with a single, Joe Gordon followed with another single, and Ken Keltner whacked another of Galehouse's servings over the left field wall. McCarthy brought Kinder in from the bullpen immediatley after that blow, but it was already too late—Bearden held Boston to three runs on five hits, Boudreau slammed another homer over The Wall, and the Indians won the pennant with an 8-3 victory. It was not the first or the last time that that fabled vertical surface called The Green Monster hurt the Red Sox more than their opponents. But why, wailed the Boston fans, did it have to happen at a time like this? Stay tuned.

The National League took a break from its domination by the Cardinals and Dodgers, the pennant going to the Boston Braves. Not since 1914 had the Braves tasted victory, and unlike that miraculous happening of 34 years earlier, the 1948 pennant was the predictable culmination of a smooth progression shown by the Braves since the middle of World War II. Another difference was that instead of a famous trio on the mound—Rudolph, James, and Tyler—the new Braves had only a famous duo, "Spahn and Sain and two days of rain."

Sain won 24 games for the Braves, nine more than Spahn, whose best years were still in the future and who actually was

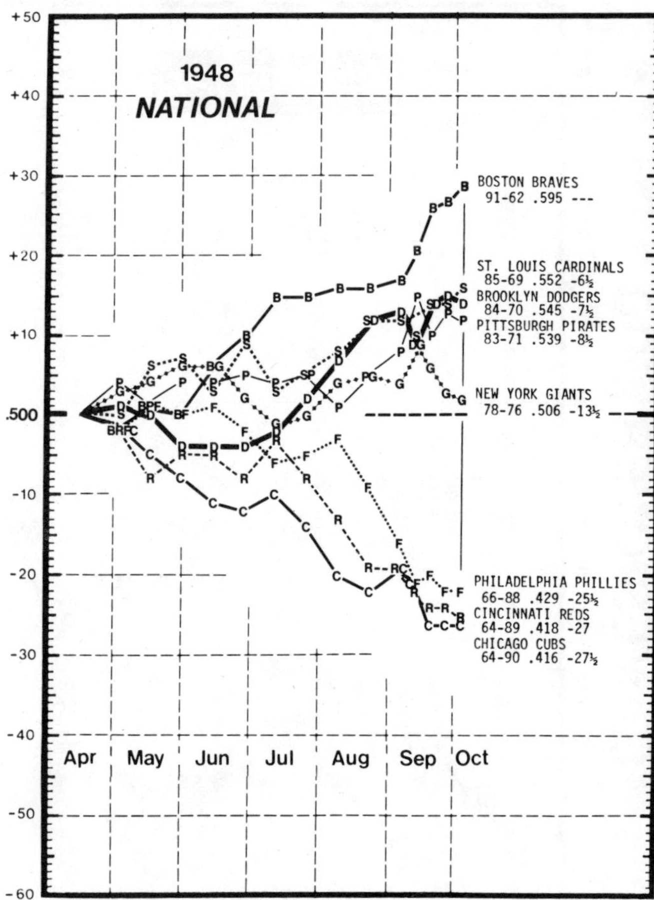


only a shade more effective that year than journeyman Bill Voiselle (13-13) and rookie Vern Bickford (11-5). The Braves had a very solid diamond crew with first baseman Earl Torgeson, second baseman Eddie Stanky (who hit .320 before breaking his ankle at mid season), rookie shortstop Alvin Dark (.322), slugging third baseman Bob Elliott and veteran Phil Masi behind the plate. In the outfield, Southworth had Tommy Holmes (.325), ex-Red Mike McCormick (.303), and ex-Indian Jeff Heath (who also batted over .300 before an ankle fracture). Considering the thinness of the pitching and the injuries, the pennant victory was another strong indication of Southworth's genius as a manager.

In the World Series, the Braves beat Bob Feller twice, but couldn't solve the slants of Lemon, Steve Gromek, and Bearden; the latter shut out the Braves on five hits in Game 3 and saved Lemon's 4-3 victory in the deciding sixth game.

## 1949

Another year, another melodrama. Being a Red Sox fan took its toll, but you couldn't complain about it being dull. This time, in just a two-team race, Boston staged one of the most stirring come-from-behind drives ever, took the lead in the last week of the season by beating the Yankees, and then lost the pennant on the closing day—to those same hated rivals.

The *dramatis personae* were much changed for the New Yorkers. Casey Stengel, a man of clownish reputation from his previous stints in charge of the Dodgers and Braves in the thirties, was in the dugout in place of Bucky Harris. Joe DiMaggio was out all spring with a foot injury, and the regular lineup was dotted with several new names: Jerry Coleman,

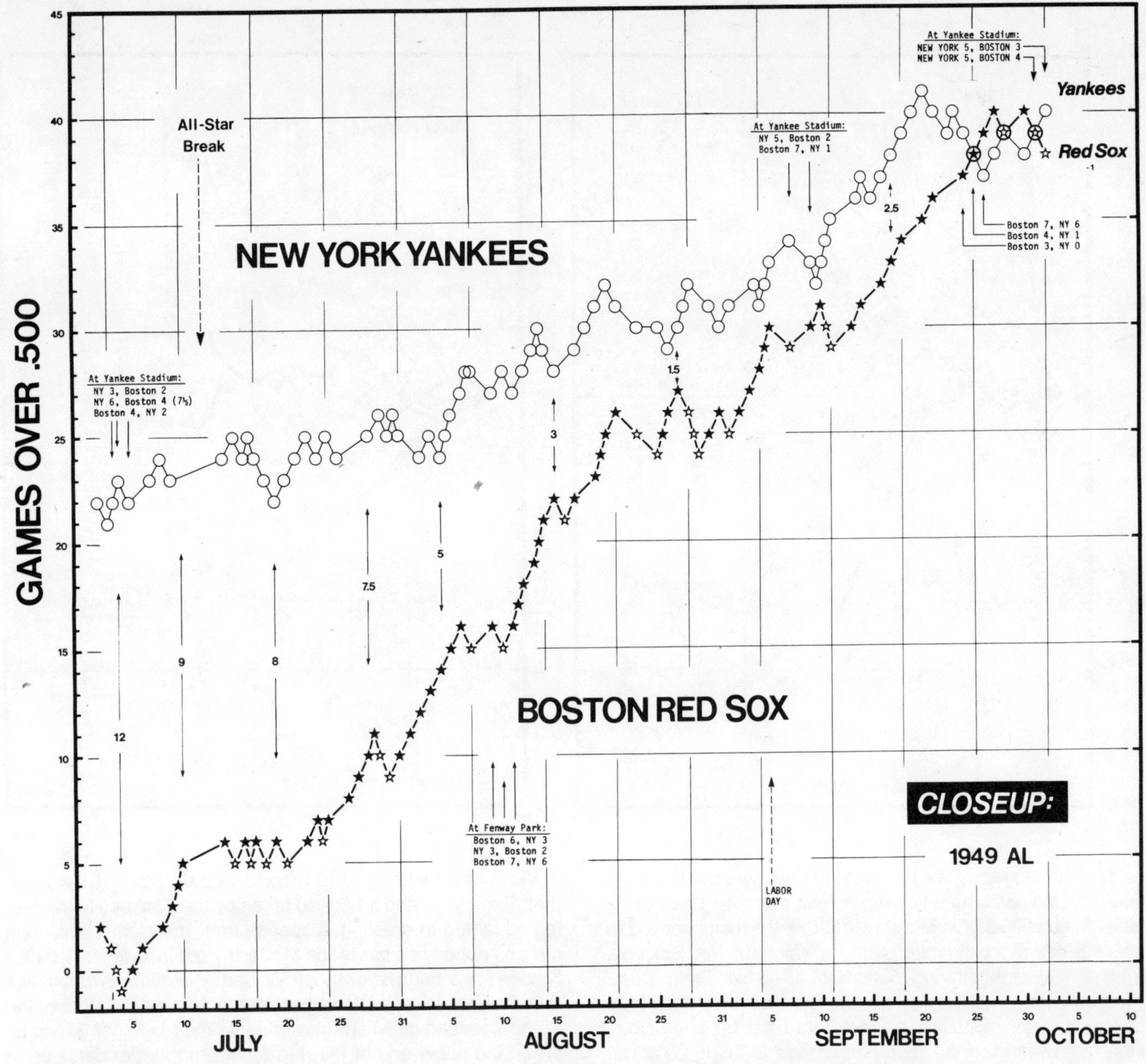


**THE STING, BY STENGEL. In 1949 the Boston Red Sox had to labor for twelve long weeks to overcome a dull start and catch Casey Stengel's New York Yankees. They finally did with a pair of victories over the Yanks at Fenway Park on September 24th and 25th. Then, almost as if Stengel meant to lure them into a trap, the Yankees yielded to the Red Sox in a 7-6 loss at Yankee Stadium on the 26th, and the Bostonians enjoyed a few days of heady experience as the frontrunner. On the Last Weekend, however, the New Yorkers struck with 5-3 and 5-4 stingings at the Stadium, killing the Boston pennant quest and avenging the previous year's knockout blows by the Bosox.**

Cliff Mapes, Gene Woodling, and Hank Bauer. Yogi Berra came in from the outfield to become a full-time catcher, except in the month when he was out with a broken finger, and Tommy Henrich came in to play first base. Nobody on the team batted .300 until the Yankee Clipper returned—DiMaggio hit .346 the rest of the way—and Charlie Silvera (.315) filled in for Berra. Fortunately for Stengel, he still had Vic Raschi, now ace of the staff, and the foursome of Reynolds, Lopat, Byrne, and Page on the mound.

The Red Sox, on the other hand, had an almost unchanged roster. Their changes were in performance—Mel Parnell became the league leader in wins (25) and ERA (2.78) and Ellis Kinder was right behind him with a 23-6 record. The Boston team BA rose, with Williams (.343, 43 homers, 159 RBIs, MVP) joined by Vern Stephens' 39 home runs and also-159 RBIs, and three other .300-hitting regulars, Doerr, Pesky, and Dom DiMaggio.

After another poor start, the Red Sox found themselves 12 games behind the Yankees on the Fourth of July. That day, in fact, the Yankees had beaten them twice at Yankee Stadium, sending them down to one game under .500. A victory at the Stadium the next day, however, started Boston on a seven-game winning streak, and after a better-than-.500 road trip following the All-Star break, the Bosox won 20 out of 23 in a long home stand and at Philadelphia and Washington. By Saturday, August 28th, the 12-game Yankee lead had shrunk to a game and a half. Then, for four weeks, it was a matching game, with Boston staying one to three games behind until the two met each for three games on September 24-26.

On the 24th, at Fenway Park, Ellis Kinder shut out the Yankees on six hits, Williams homering in the 3-0 victory. That was Kinder's thirteenth straight win, and it pared the Yankee

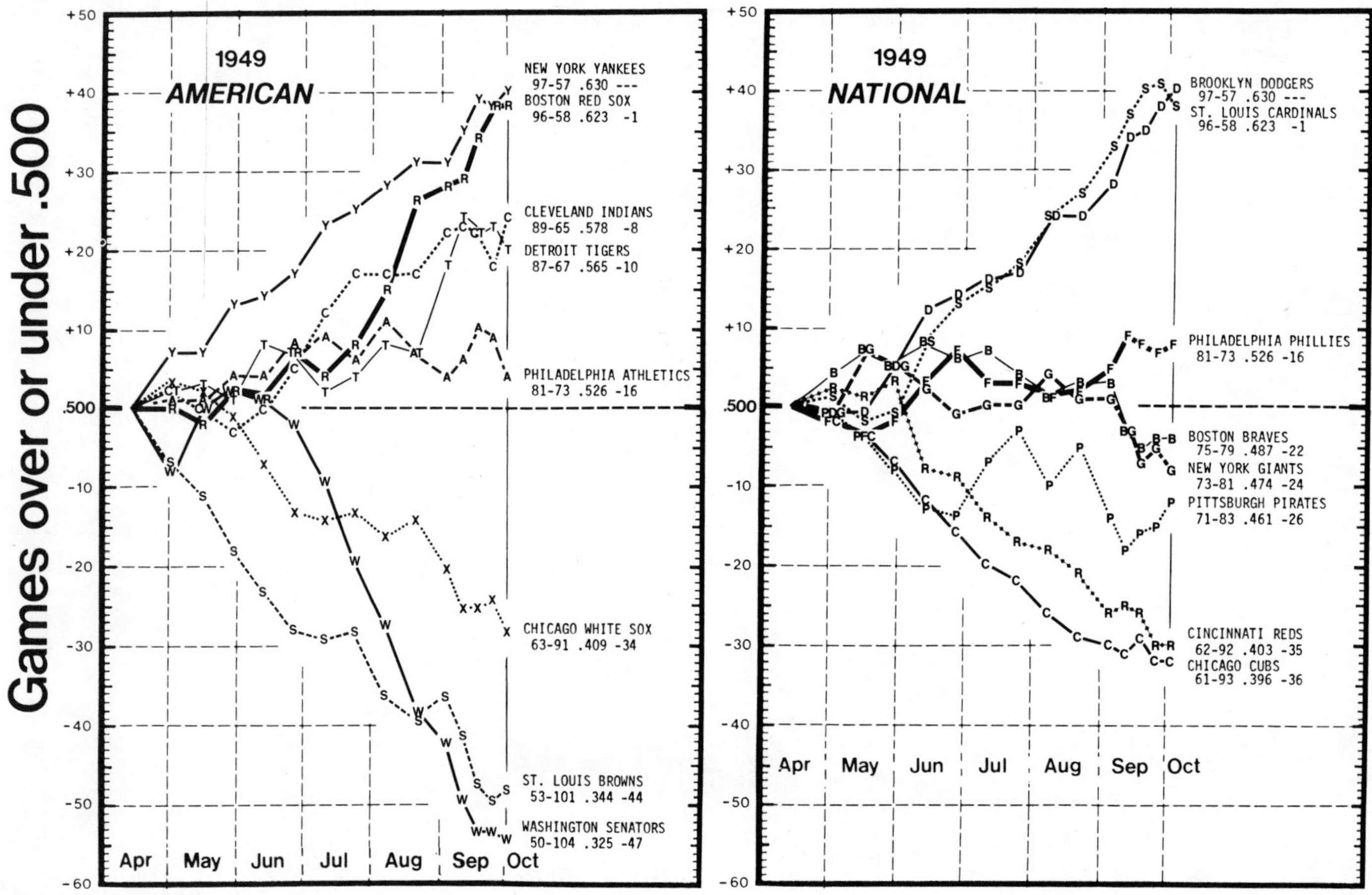


lead to a single game. The next day, Parnell held the Bombers to one run, Williams hit a two-run homer, and a 4-1 Sox victory made it a tie at 96-57. On Monday the 26th, the teams moved to Yankee Stadium for the third game, in which the Red Sox converted a 3-6, eighth-inning deficit to a 7-6 win with Doerr squeeze-bunting Pesky home with the seventh run in the ninth, a startling event made all the more dramatic by a ferocious rhubarb between the Yankees and umpire Bill Grieves about his call at home plate. Now Boston held the league lead for the first time all year.

When they lost at Washington on Wednesday, the Red Sox fell back into a tie, but two days later they recovered their lead in one of the strangest games of the decade—getting only five hits (but 14 walks), they outscored the Senators 11-9. Now all they had to do was win at least one of the two remaning games at Yankee Stadium on Saturday and Sunday.

New York's Allie Reynolds (17-6) faced Parnell in the Saturday Game. With one out in the third and already behind by a run, Reynolds walked the bases full, and then let Doerr drive in the second run with a short single. Stengel brought in Joe Page, who had already won 12 games and saved 27 that season, but he immediately walked in two more runs: 4-0. To the mortified Yankee fans, it looked as though the Red Sox were going to deprive them of a pennant for the second year in a row. But then Page did a complete about-face, shutting out Boston for 6⅔ innings, his longest relief duty of the year. Two Yankee runs in the fourth and two more in the fifth tied the game, and Johnny Lindell's first home run in exactly two months in the eighth inning gave New York a 5-4 victory. So now the Sunday winner would be the pennant winner.

Vic Raschi, with a 20-10 record, was up against Kinder in that final game, and a 1-0 lead taken by the Yankees in the first inning lasted in grueling suspense until the eighth. With one out and nobody on base, Joe McCarthy put in a pinch-hitter for Kinder—another one of those McCarthy decisions which, like the Galehouse selection the year before, would have the Boston second-guessers muttering in their beer for 30 years. When the heavy end of the Red Sox batting order came up in the top of the ninth, they got to Raschi for three runs, but that didn't put them ahead because in the previous half-inning Boston's relief pitching had been sieve-like: an exhausted Mel Parnell had been greeted by a Tommy Henrich homer, and the 33-year-old Tex Hughson, in his last major league appearance, had yielded a three-run double to Jerry Coleman. Raschi stifled the Red Sox rally in the ninth, and won, 5-3. Until recently, it was the bitterest moment in Boston Red Sox history.

The fourth cliffhanger of the decade between the Dodgers and Cardinals also went to the final day. Brooklyn, after having lost two of three to the Cards in the tussles of 1941, 1942, and 1946, made it even again (not counting their easier '47 triumph) by matching Cardinal victories all season long and hoping for a break. They got it in the last week when the Redbirds, leading by only a game and a half, lost four straight at Pittsburgh and Chicago. During the Cardinals' brief but fatal plunge, the Dodgers took the lead with a pair of pitching gems in Boston by rookie Don Newcombe and ex-Pirate Preacher Roe on September 29th. With a Brooklyn loss to the Phils on the final Saturday and a Cardinal win over the Cubs on the closing day, however, the Dodgers had to win their last game in order to clinch the flag, and the Phillies took them to the tenth inning before yielding, 9-7.

Burt Shotton, who had become Brooklyn's manager when Leo Durocher was suspended for the whole 1947 season and had stepped in again in mid-1948 when The Lip amazingly moved to the Giant managership, guided the '49 Dodger pennant victory. Jackie Robinson was the big hero, hitting .342 and winning the Most Valuable Player award, and Shotton had other holdovers from his 1947 team—Pee Wee Reese, Ralph Branca, and Carl Furillo. There were more changes than holdovers, however—infielders Gil Hodges and Billy Cox, catcher Roy Campanella, and outfielders Duke Snider and Gene Hermanski in addition to Newcombe and Roe. With so many newcomers, the Dodgers were underrated all year in relation to the Cardinals, still led by Musial, Slaughter, and Pollet.

In the 1949 World Series, the Yankees beat the Dodgers in five games.

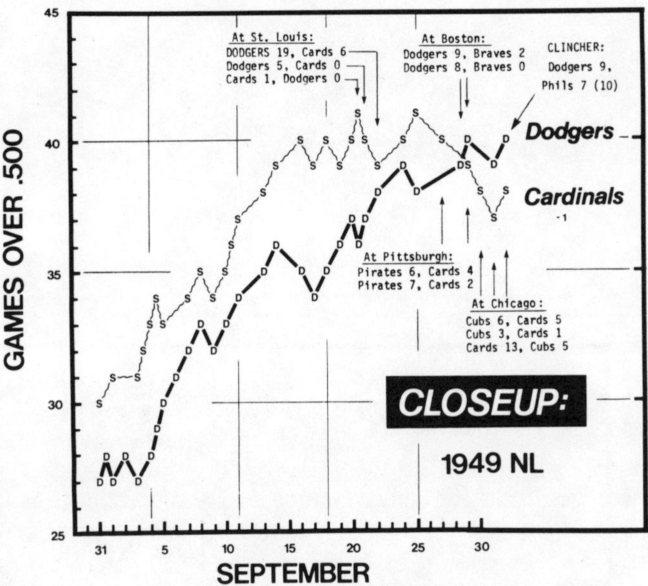


**FOUR BAD DAYS, after 95 victories, spelled doom for the St. Louis Cardinals on September 27 to October 1st, 1949, giving the Brooklyn Dodgers the little opening to the pennant they had been jockeying for all season. The Dodgers had come to within half a game of the Cards the previous week by whalloping them, 19-6, on September 22nd at Sportsman's Park, but the Redbirds got a 1½-game lead back by beating the Cubs twice at St. Louis on the next-to-last weekend while the Dodgers and Phillies split two games at Ebbets Field. When both of the contenders went on the road in the final week, everything turned in the Dodgers' favor — the Pirates and Cubs took four straight games from the Cards, and Brooklyn finally grabbed the lead with a doubleheader sweep at Boston.**

## 1950

Then came the Whiz Kids. They were a bunch of youngsters at Philadelphia who took over the National League for one year under the deft guidance of little-known manager Eddie Sawyer. For the first half ot the 1950 season they held their own with the Dodgers and Cardinals, and then astonished the baseball world by moving in front by nine games in August and September.

The youngest of the Kids were 20-game-winner Robin Roberts, 17-game-winner Curt Simmons, .303-hitting Richie Ashburn, and infielders Granny Hamner and Willie Jones, all between 21 and 24, and their tip slugger, outfielder Del Ennis (.311, 31 home runs, 126 RBIs) was 25 years old. The elders, 29-year-olds Andy Seminick and Dick Sisler (George's son) and 30-year-olds Eddie Waitkus and Mike Goliat, completed the regular batting lineup. But their most valuable player was a 33-year-old graybeard named Jim Konstanty, who was in fact voted the league's MVP honor for his 17 wins and 22 saves in 74 turns on the mound.

There was so much wondering in the press and around the league about how long the Phillies could keep "playing over their heads" that it may have undermined the Whiz Kids' belief in themselves by the middle of September. In the last two weeks of the season they lost nine games, and almost lost the pennant to the Dodgers. By then, the Phils had become darlings of fans all over the country, so their late slump elicited consternation as well as suspense. With heroics supplied by Sisler and Roberts (see closeup), however, they saved their pennant in the last few minutes of the season.

A hint of things to come appeared in the upturn of the New York Giants' curve from a seventh-place Memorial Day position to a third-place finish. Conversely, the end of an extremely rewarding quarter-century by the St. Louis Cardinals was marked when they fell from first place in June to a final fifth place record only three games above .500.

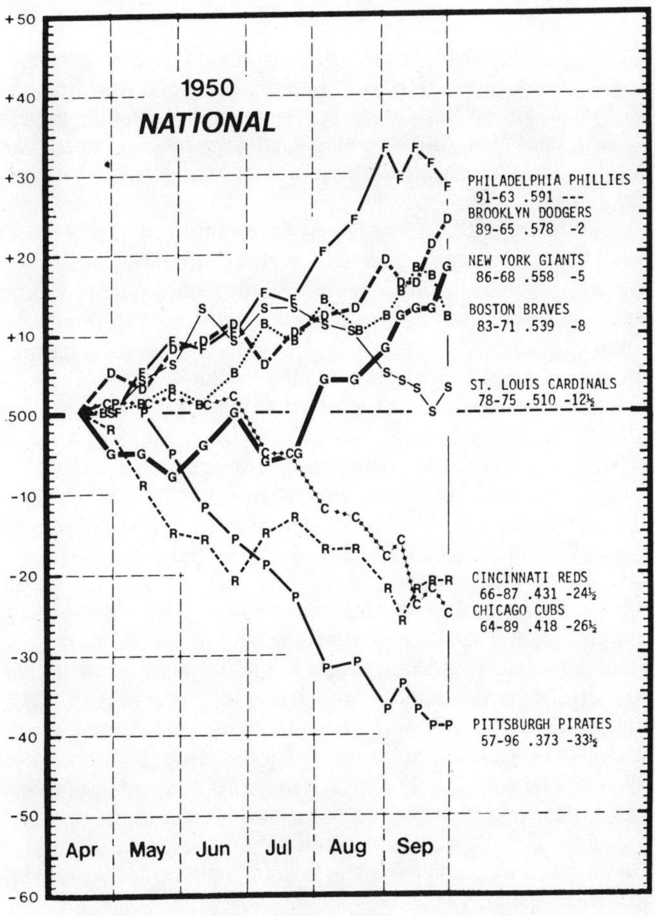

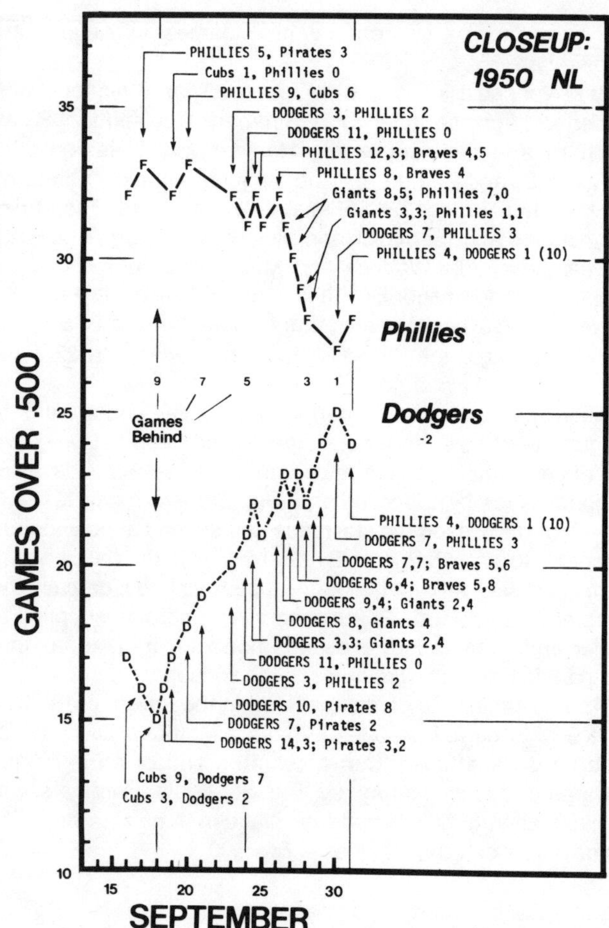


**WHIZ KIDS' SKID. The whole nation cheered the Philadelphia Whiz Kids' surprise takeover of the National League in 1950, but in the final fortnight the Phils tumbled, almost falling into a tie with the Brooklyn Dodgers. Philadelphia's nine-game lead on September 17th shrank to only a single game on the final Saturday, when Brooklyn's Erv Palica beat the Phils, 7-3, at Ebbets Field. On the closing day, Robin Roberts, starting for the third time in five days, battled the Dodgers' Don Newcombe into the tenth inning, and then Philadelphia's Dick Sisler broke a 1-1 tie with a three-run homer. Roberts, who had retired Carl Furillo and Gil Hodges with the bases full in the bottom of the ninth, set down the Dodgers in their half of the tenth, and the flag went to the Whiz Kids. A decade and a half later, it looked as though the Phils had been rehearsing for 1964.**

In the American League, four teams won over 90 games—the Yankees, Tigers, Red Sox, and Indians—and they finished in that order. All four were in a spread of only four games around Labor Day, but reversing what happened in the NL, the Yankees parted ways with their closest challengers after mid-September.

One reason for Casey Stengel's second straight triumph was the arrival of 21-year-old Whitey Ford, who won nine games in ten decisions after he was brought up in June and went on to help the Yankees sweep the Phillies in the World Series, pitching 9⅔ scoreless innings in the four games. Johnny Mize, who had come to the Yankees late in the previous season, was also a factor in the Bombers' success. With strong hitting also from Phil Rizzuto (.324, MVP) and Hank Bauer (.320), the Yanks' team batting average rose to .282.

That figure, however, was well below Boston's .302. The Red Sox, who had another hot streak in July and August, after Steve O'Neill replaced Joe McCarthy as manager, were the last major league team to hit over .300. They had seven regulars' averages in the .300 class, namely Billy Goodman's league leading .354, Dom DiMaggio's .328, Al Zarilla's .325, Rookie of the Year Walt Dropo's .322 (he also drove in 144 runs in 136 games and hit 34 home runs), Ted Williams' .317, Johnny Pesky's .312, and Birdie Tebbetts' .310. Bobby Doerr and Vern Stephens made up for their lowly .294 and .295 averages by clubbing 27 and 30 home runs, respectively. It has often been said that the Red Sox would have won the pennant that year if Williams hadn't broken his elbow in the All-Star Game, but they didn't need The Splinter's hitting—the problem was their team ERA of 4.88.

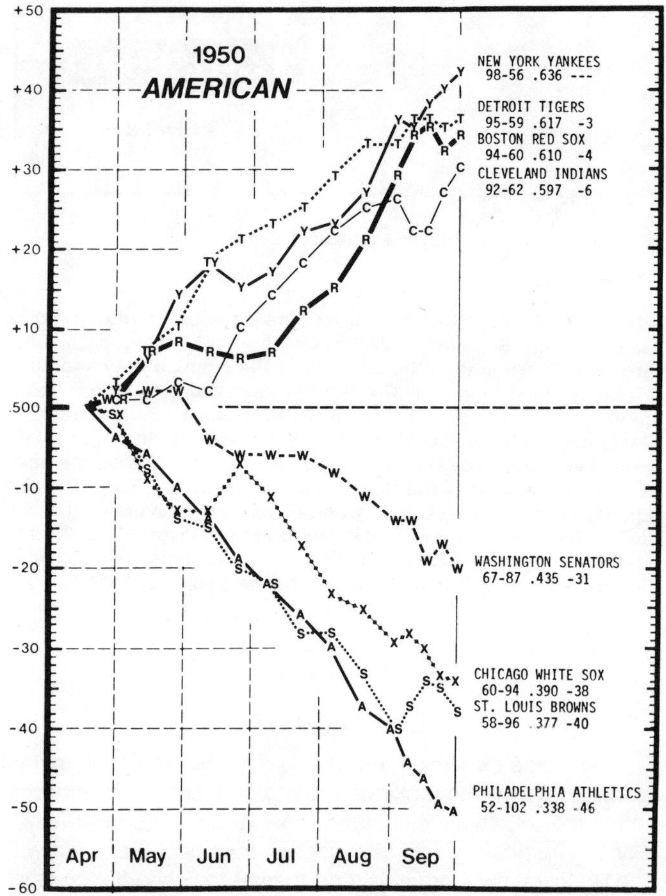

**A LITTLE HELP FROM THEIR ENEMIES** came to the New York Yankees in 1950. A close four-team race around Labor Day turned into a much tighter three-team race when the St. Louis Browns came to Cleveland the following weekend and beat the Indians four straight. But the Tribe came back with a winning streak starting on September 20th that started Boston's downfall and did even more damage to Detroit, the Yankees' only remaining opposition. After sweeping three games from the Tigers at Cleveland on the weekend of the 24th, the Indians mathematically eliminated them at Detroit with a 12-2 victory on the 29th. Result: #2 for Casey Stengel.

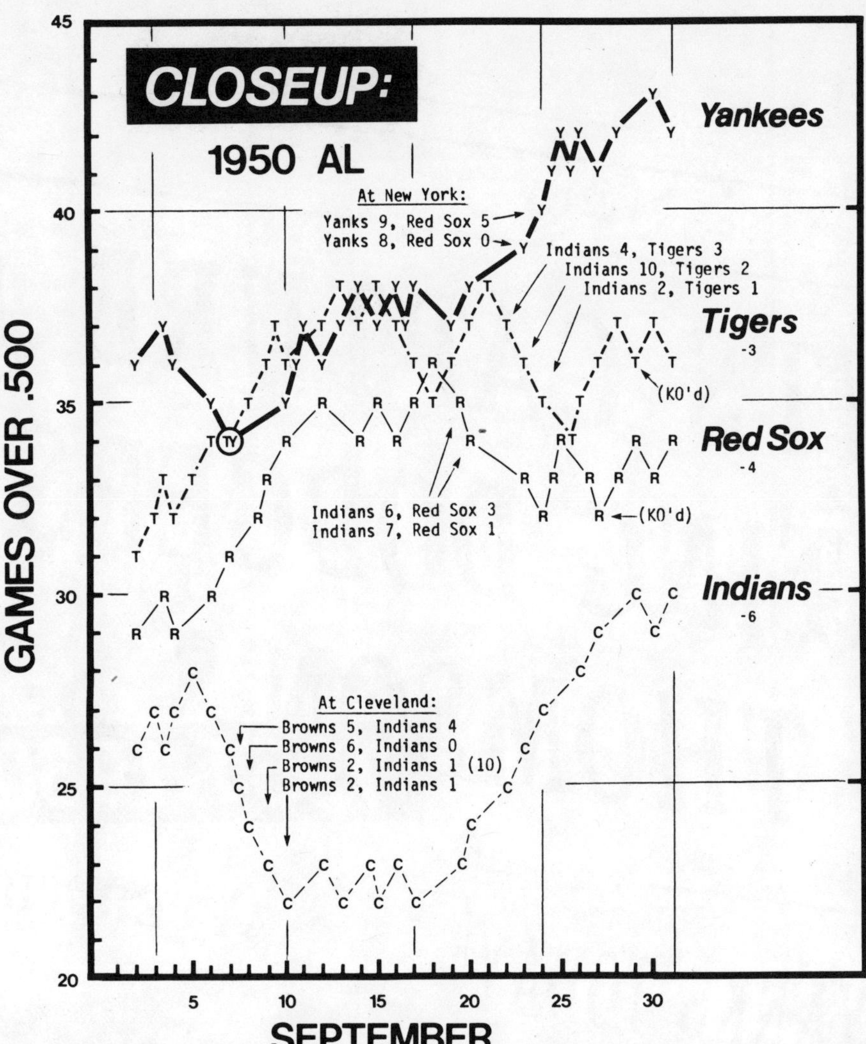


The Detroit Tigers, who held first place in the three warmest months, had a new crop of hitters, including George Kell (.340), Hoot Evers (.323), and Vic Wertz (.308. 27 HR), and some new mound strength with Art Houtteman and Fred Hutchinson, while still getting good innings from Newhouser and Trout. They were effectively eliminated from the race by the Indians, who despite having added armament in the form of Luke Easter and Al Rosen, were thrown for a loop by the Browns early in September.

The A's, after three straight over-.500 years, settled back into the basement of the league, and Connie Mack stepped down as manager at the age of 88 after 50 years of incredible highs and lows.

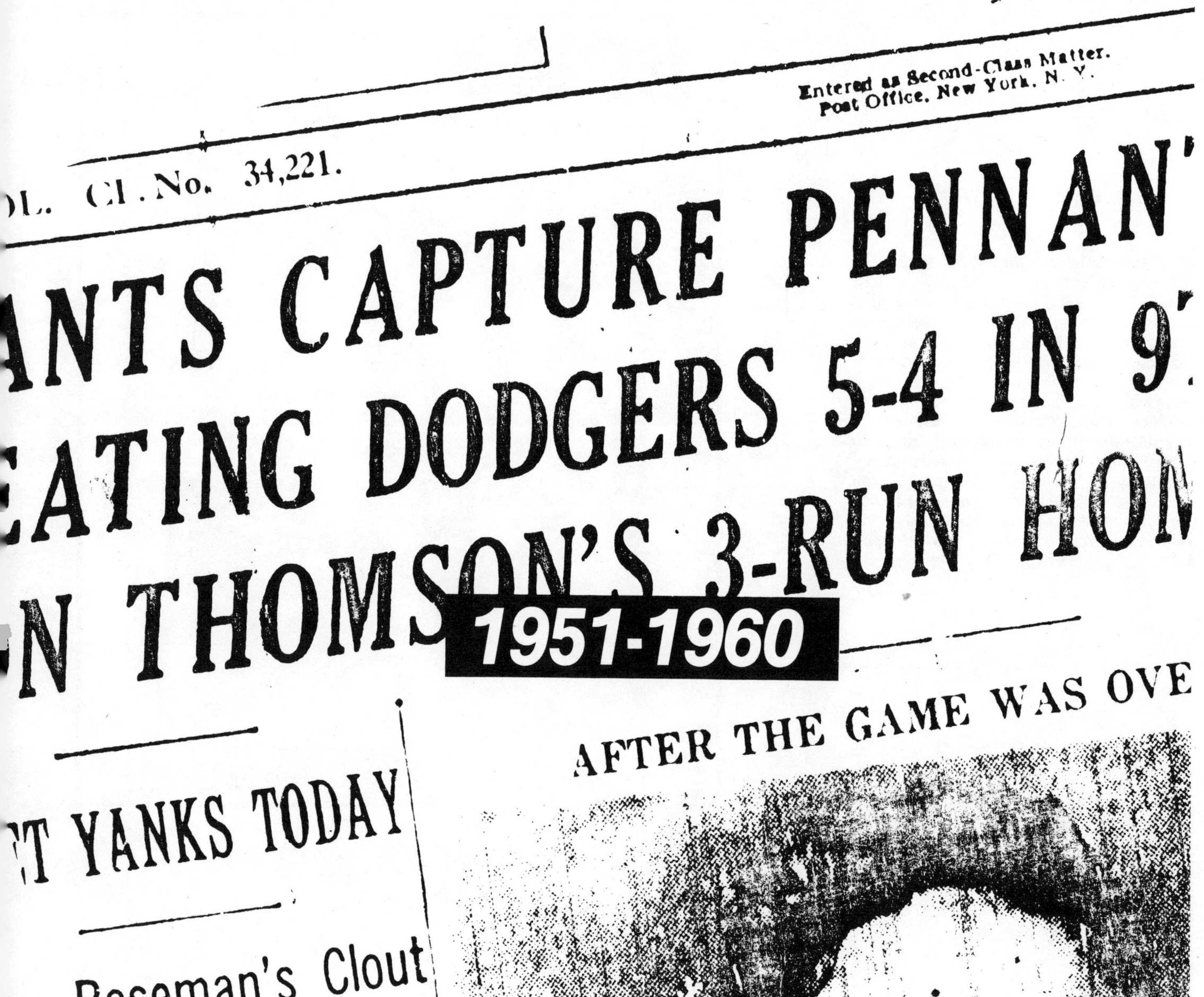

Entered as Second-Class Matter.
Post Office, New York, N. Y.

L. CI . No. 34,221.

NTS CAPTURE PENNAN

ATING DODGERS 5-4 IN 9

N THOMSON'S 3-RUN HOM

T YANKS TODAY

Baseman's Clout

AFTER THE GAME WAS OVE

# 1951-1960

## 1951

On Saturday, August 11, 1951, the Brooklyn Dodgers were playing a doubleheader at Ebbets Field against the Boston Braves, and across the East River at the Polo Grounds, the New York Giants were entertaining the Philadelphia Phillies. The Giants were still smarting from just having lost three in a row to their crosstown rivals at Ebbets. Combined with these defeats, this day's 4-0 shutout by the Phils rubbed salt into the wounds, dropping the Jints to only eight games over .500: they were lucky to be in second place—nobody else in the league but the Dodgers had a winning record. The Dodgers beat the Braves in the first game of their twin bill, which for a couple of hours until the Braves won the nightcap gave Brooklyn a 13½-game lead over the Giants.

Under their new manager, Chuck Dressen, the Dodgers looked utterly unbeatable. and with the recent infusion of talent developing so well—Campanella, Hodges, Snider, Newcombe, and others—they were threatening to become a dynasty like the 1936-39 Yankees. But the Giants themselves had been moving up in many departments since spiriting Leo Durocher across the river in 1948. Particularly their pitching: year after year, Larry Jansen was among the League leaders in wins, and now he was joined by 34-year-old Mexican League veteran Sal Maglie, who had achieved the NL's best won-lost percentage (18-4, .818) in 1950, andby Jim Hearn, who had won the ERA crown. The Giant offense wasn't up to Brooklyn's, but they had three men they could count on for over 20 homers a year—third baseman-outfielder Bobby Thomson, catcher Wes Westrum, and outfielder Monte Irvin. And maybe a fourth—a marvelous rookie outfielder named Willie Mays who had just been called up at the age of 20 after hitting .477 at Minneapolis. Getting Eddie Stanky and Al Dark from the Braves the previous year had strengthened the infield and the offense, too.

Durocher, looking at the 13-game deficit after that Saturday

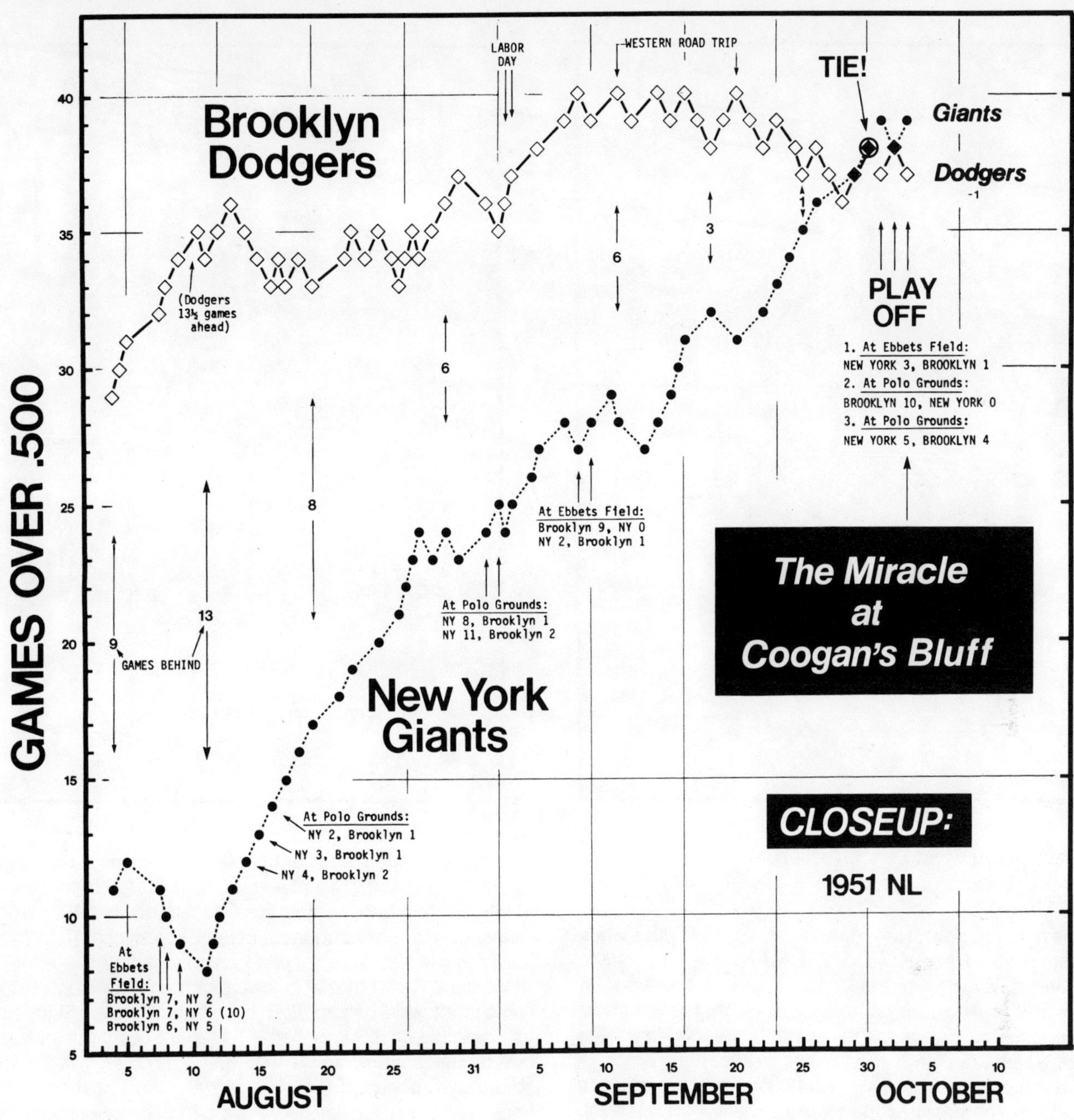


**ONE GIANT SWING, of Bobby Thomson's bat, climaxed The Miracle at Coogan's Bluff at the Polo Grounds on Wednesday, October 3, 1951, in the ultimate of pennant-race dramatics. Thomson's blow, a three-run homer off Brooklyn's Ralph Branca when the Giants trailed, 4-2, in the bottom of the ninth inning of the third playoff game, won the pennant for Leo Durocher's Giant club, but what led up to that stunning outcome, over the previous seven weeks, was a part of The Miracle that was no less theatrical. From mid-August the tension mounted daily as New York closed a 13½-game separation between the arch-rivals by playing at an .841 winning pace. For millions of fans, especially those within a 50-mile radius of the Bronx, there has never been a more thrilling pennant race.**

loss to the Phils, must have said, "Next week we've gotta get organized," because at that point his club started an historic upward climb. The Giants won their three remaining games with the Phils on Sunday and Monday, and then beat the Dodgers three straight at the Polo Grounds. Ten more wins, over the Phillies, Reds, Cardinals, and Cubs, made it 16 in a row, and now Brooklyn's lead was down to five games. If there had been any complacency in Flatbush, no trace of it could be seen now. Around Labor Day, the Dodgers spurted, holding the Giants six to seven games back. Significantly, though, the Giants momentarily broke the Dodgers' stride by beating them twice more at the Polo Grounds on the two days before Labor Day.

Toward the middle of September, Dressen's club began to sputter on a western road trip, and Giants, also out west, applied more pressure with a string of victories that cut the lead to three games by September 18th. The Giants' next game, a 3-1 loss at Cincinnati on the 20th, turned out to be their last defeat of the regular season and the only loss in their last 13 regularly-scheduled games. Meanwhile, the Dodgers came home to Ebbets Field on the 21st, and promptly lost two more games, 9-6 and 7-3, to the Phils. Then, on Tuesday the 25th in Boston, the Braves beat Ralph Branca, 6-3, and Carl Erskine, 14-2, and the stunned Flatbush Fandom saw their margin drop to only a single game. Two days later, the Braves beat Preacher Roe, 4-3, while the Giants were idle—now it was only

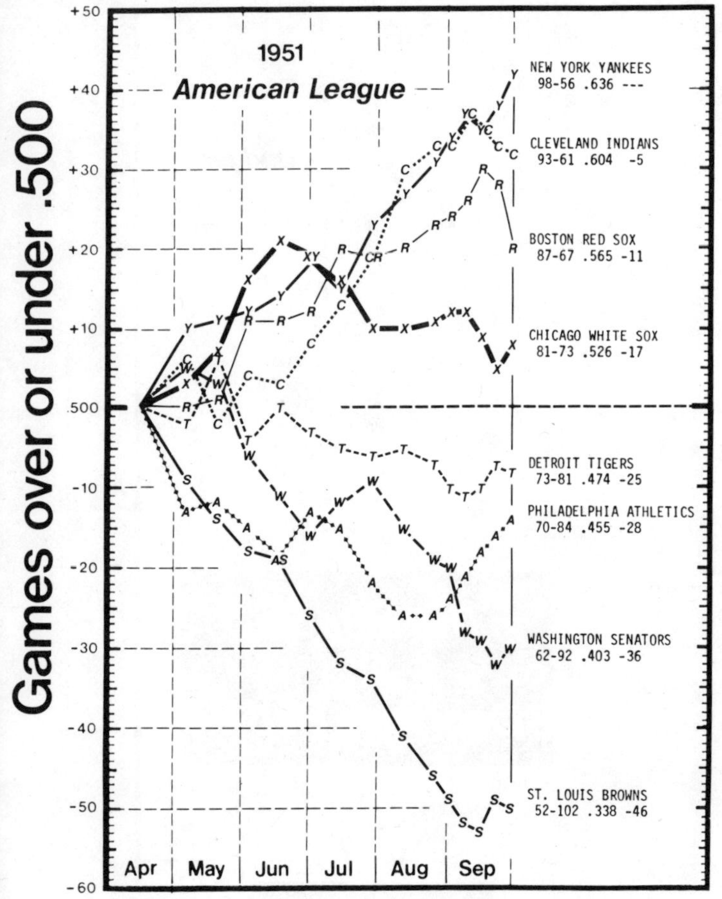


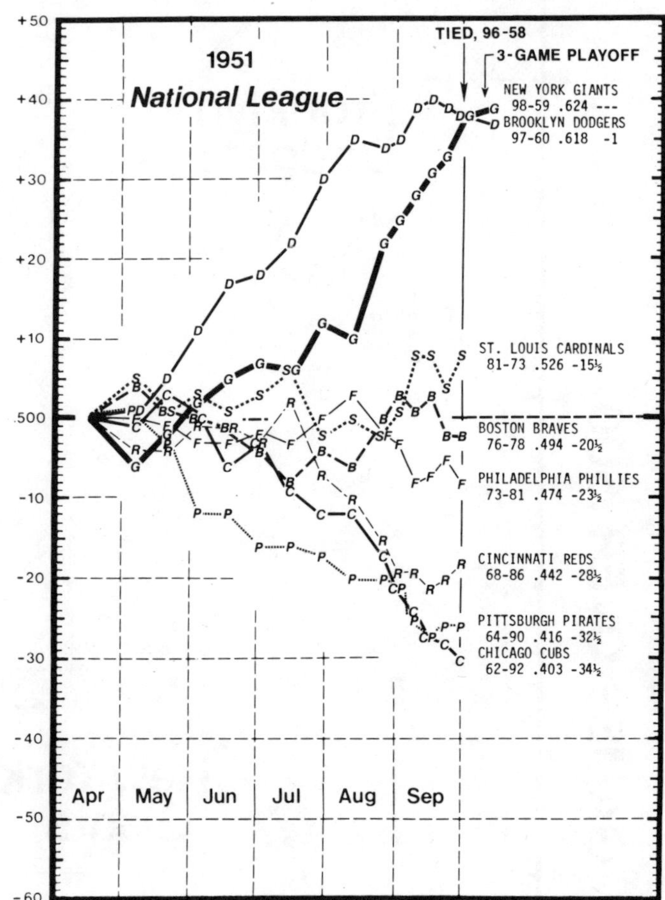


a half-game—and when Erskine lost again on Friday in Philadelphia, the Dodgers dropped into a 94-58 tie with the still-resting Giants.

On the final Saturday, Newcombe shut out the Phillies while the Giants blanked the Braves at Boston. And when Durocher's men cmae through with a 3-2 victory over the Braves on Sunday, their 37th win in 44 games (.841!), that was almost good enough for the pennant—about the same time, the Dodgers were taken into extra innings by the Phils. Brooklyn came up with a run in the top of the 14th inning, however, eking out a 9-8 win and finishing the regular schedule equal to the Giants at 96-58.

The NL's second pennant playoff started the next day at Ebbets Field. Jim Hearn (16-9) faced Branca (13-11) in the opening game. Hearn's only bad pitch of the day, which Andy Pafko blasted into the stands for a home run, gave the Dodgers a 1-0 lead in the second inning. Two innings later, a two-run homer by Bobby Thomson put the Giants ahead, and this less-remembered roundtripper by Thomson proved to be the game-winner in a 3-1 Giant victory. At the Polo Grounds the next day, the Dodgers drew even again with a 10-0 trouncing of the Giants; Clem Labine held them to six hits while Jackie Robinson, Rube Walker, Gil Hodges, and Pafko belted homers off three Giant pitchers.

In the finale at the Polo Grounds, Don Newcombe (20-9) took the mound against Sal Maglie (23-6). Robinson singled in Pee Wee Reese for a Dodger run in the first inning, and Newcombe held the 1-0 lead until the seventh, when the Giants squeezed out a tying run. But in the top of the eighth, Maglie weakened, and Brooklyn added three runs, on singles by Reese and Duke Snider, a wild pitch, an intentional walk, and two more singles by Pafko and Billy Cox. Larry Jansen (22-11) took over for Maglie in the ninth, setting the Dodgers down 1-2-3, and the Giants went into the bottom of the ninth, trailing 4-1.

Al Dark led off with a scratch single, only the fifth hit off Newcombe. Don Mueller followed with another single, to the same right side, where first baseman Hodges might have found a nice double-play ball if he hadn't been, questionably, over by the bag holding Dark on first. With Dark now on third, Monte Irvin popped up to Hodges at first, but then Whitey Lockman made the score 4-2 by banging an opposite-field double to left, and that was all for Newcombe. While Durocher was putting in Clint Hartung to run for Mueller, who had jammed his ankle sliding into third, Dressen waved in Branca from the bullpen.

Wearing his famous number 13 on the back of his jersey, Branca now had a chance to pay back Bobby Thomson for that homer on Monday, and he went right after him with two fastballs down the middle. The first was a called strike. The second came screaming off Thomson's bat as a high, sinking line drive into the left-field stands—quite simply, the most famous and most dramatic home run of baseball history. Better known as The Shot Heard 'Round the World which completed The Miracle at Coogan's Bluff, Thomson's blow ignited the most frenzied celebration by Giant players and fans ever seen at the Polo Grounds and nearly psychotic raving by Giant announcer Russ Hodges ("The Giants win the Pennant! The Giants win the pennant!), heard with absolute amazement by millions of radio listeners around the country. And for the sudden losers, it was the bitterest moment in Brooklyn baseball history, if not

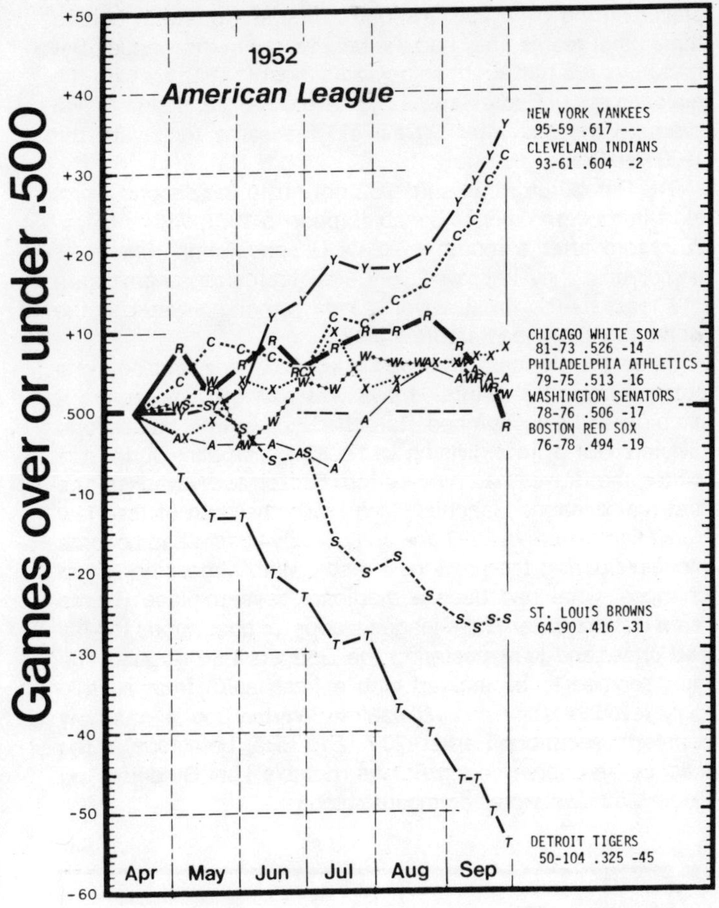


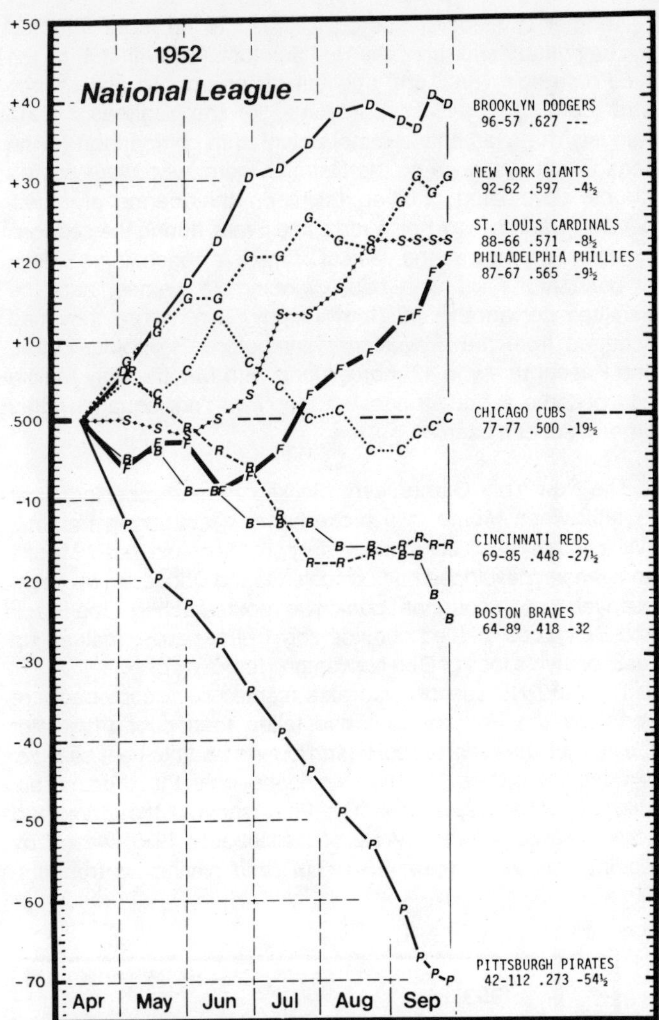


all of Dodger history.

For the first two months of the 1951 season, the American League also had what looked like a miracle in the making. The Chicago White Sox, one of the have-nots in the bifurcate standings of 1950, were leading the league, 21 games over .500 in mid-June, and pulling away from the Yankees and Red Sox. Paul Richards, onetime catcher for the Giants and Tigers, was Chicago's new manager, and his club's spring spurt announced a new era on winning baseball for the Hueless Hose, featuring starters such as pitcher Billy Pierce, keystoner Nellie Fox, fleet-footed outfielder Minnie Minoso, and first basemen Eddie Robinson and Ferris Fain. Although the White Sox slumped to fourth place in July, the 1951 season saw their first of 17 consecutive first-division finishes.

The Yankees won their third straight pennant, but only after a spirited battle with the Indians that delayed New York's clinching until their double victory over the Red Sox on Friday, September 28. The Yankees' batting was a shade behind the league-leading White Sox attack—the only Yankee regular to hit over .300, in fact, was rookie infielder Gil McDougald—and even with 21-win seasons by Lopat and Raschi, New York's pitching was not the equal of Cleveland's; Feller was in top form (22-8), having learned to get along without the fireball of his youth, Lemon was still pitching very well, and now the Indians had developed two more aces, Mike Garcia (20-13) and Early Wynn (also 20-13). But Casey Stengel's managerial magic prevailed in late September again. Out in the Yankees' centerfield, 36-year-old Joe DiMaggio played his last season, hitting ten homers in 116 games. His replacement, a much-ballyhooed 19-year-old named Mickey Mantle, hit 13 home runs in a half-season.

DiMaggio's final major league homer came in the '51 Series, which the Yankees won in six games. Two five-hit, complete-game victories over the Giants by Ed Lopat also helped the Bombers.

## 1952-53

The midpoint of New York City's Golden Age of Baseball was approaching. In 1920-24, the Big Apple had enjoyed eight pennants in five years, and in 1936-41, eight pennants in six years. But in 1949-56, New Yorkers were deluged with 12 pennants in seven years, the only interlopers being the 1950 Philadelphia Whiz Kids and the 1954 Cleveland Indians.

In 1952 and 1953, the Yankees won their fourth and fifth straight world championships under Casey Stengel. The Indians challenged again in '52, taking the lead away from the Yanks as late as August 22nd, and the Tribesmen had a favorable situation confronting them around Labor Day: trailing New York by only 2½ games, they had 20 of their 22 September games scheduled at home, whereas the Yankees had to play 18 of 21 on the road. It didn't matter—the Yankees won as usual, and the telling sign of the season came when they beat Mike Garcia in front of 73,609 fans in Cleveland on Sunday the 15th. Bob Feller's off-year (9-13, 4.73) spelled doom for the Indians even though they got 22 victories apiece from Wynn, Garcia, and Lemon. Despite losing Whitey Ford to the Korean War, the Yanks' team ERA was best in the league.

Another challenger, Boston, seemed to be more affected by the military situation; the Red Sox lost Ted Williams to the Air Force again in April, and fell off sharply to sixth place after coming to within four games of the Yankees in late August. That was only a minor downfall in comparison to the season-long collapse of the Detroit Tigers, who were having trouble developing pitching talent on their farms and desperately traded away Kell, Wertz, and Evers, during the season.

The next year was the easiest of the five consecutive Stengel pennants. Ford was back, winning 18 games, and the Yankees got another 13 from Johnny Sain, whom they had acquired from the Braves the year before. Reynolds, Lopat, and Raschi threw in 42 more. Along with Mantle, Billy Martin had become a first-stringer on the New York squad by this time, at second base.

The New York Giants were blocked from another pennant in 1952 when Monte Irvin broke his ankle in spring training, Willie Mays went on military duty in May, and both Maglie and Jansen developed back trouble. So the Dodgers, two years deprived, got the pannant back; two rookie pitchers, Joe Black and Billy Loes, helped considerably in the cause, making up for Brooklyn's loss of Don Newcombe to the war.

The 1952 NL season was also marked by a comeback, of sorts, by the Phillies, who had fallen to a poor fifth after the year of the Whiz Kids. Robin Roberts had his best season, winning 28 games in what would be only the third of six straight 20-game seasons. The Phils showed that they had come to a complete reversal of their absurd 1930 season by leading the NL in team ERA (3.07) and having no front-line player hitting over .290. Although they still came in behind three other teams, they had the best record in the league after mid-June; the turnabout coincided almost to the day with the replacement of Eddie Sawyer by Steve O'Neill, and almost two years to the day after O'Neill did the same trick with the 1950 Red Sox.

The Pittsburgh Pirates in 1952 got off to the second worst start in modern days of baseball (prior to 1981) with a 5-and-25 record after a month of play. Despite Ralph Kiner's 37 home runs, they improved very little thereafter, ending with 112 losses—the most abysmal year among several in the worst period of the Pirate franchise.

When the Dodgers won again in 1953, they had no competition from the Giants—Mays was still off to war, and a pitching collapse dumped Durocher's crew into the second division. Out of that division came a big surprise. During the winter, the Braves had moved from Boston to Milwaukee, the first major league franchise shift since the birth of the New York Highlanders in 1903 and Jolly Cholly Grimm had become manager during the previous season. With almost no lineup changes, what had been a mediocre seventh-place Braves team in 1952 became the league leader for brief priods in May and June, and kept pestering the Dodgers into August. The club seemed to be infused with a fresh spirit from a strikingly feverish fandom in Milwaukee. Warren Spahn was now a preeminent mound artist (23-7, 2.10 ERA, both tops in the league), and some young Braves, notably Lew Burdette and Eddie Mathews, were coming into bloom.

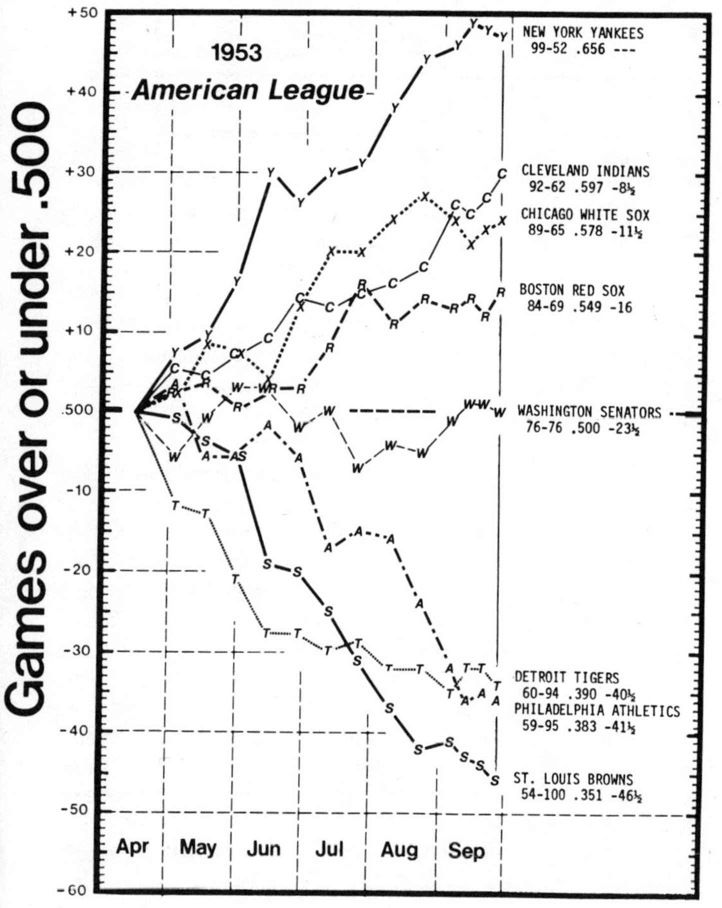


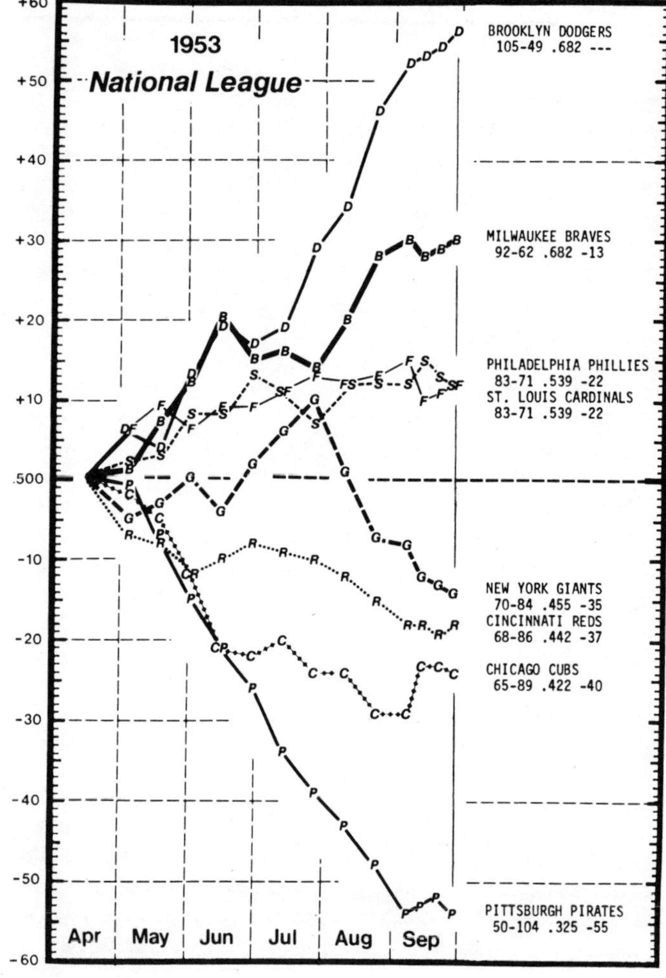

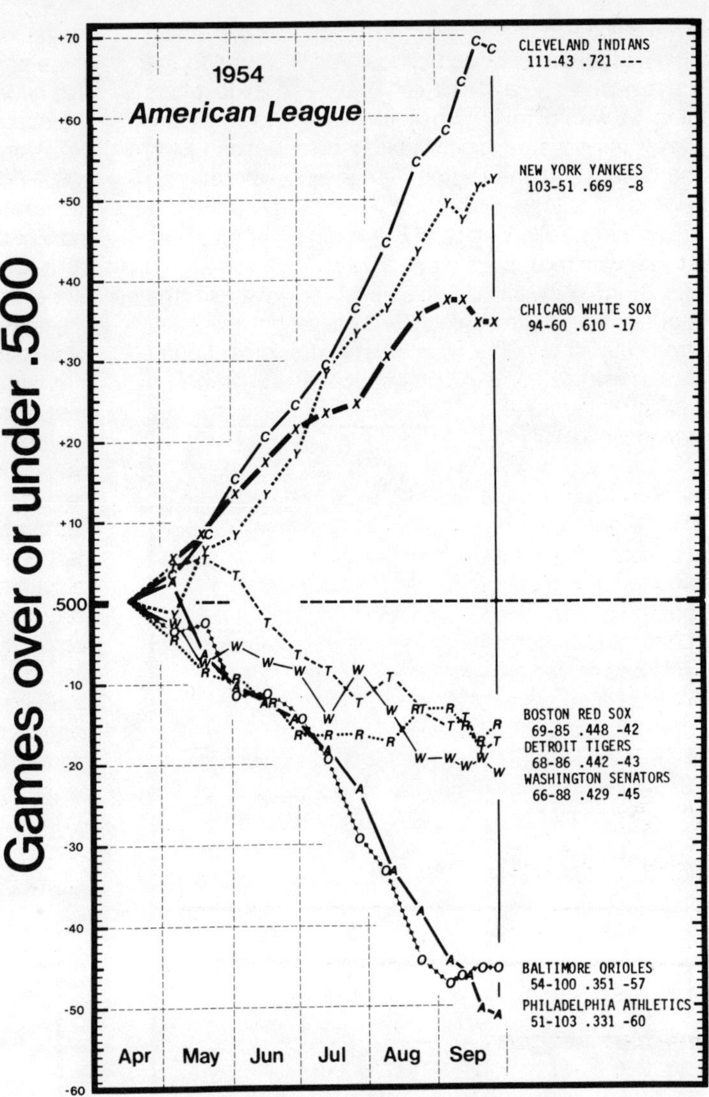


**AMERICAN LEAGUE RECORDS were set by the 1954 Cleveland Indians for wins (111), won-lost percentage (.721), and games over .500 (68). The Yankees' victory total of 103 was higher than in any of their five consecutive pennant-winning years under Casey Stengel, but only good for second place in 1954. The Indians had only two .300 hitters, Bobby Avila and Al Rosen, but they had eight good pitchers—Bob Lemon, Early Wynn, Ray Narleski, Bob Feller, Mike Garcia, Hal Newhouser, Don Mossi, and Art Houtteman.**

"Wait 'til next year" became the familiar refrain in Brooklyn as the Yankees disposed of the Dodgers in the '52 and '53 World Series. After seven pennants in 53 years, the Dodgers were still seeking their first world championship.

## 1954

1954 was to the American League what 1906 had been to the National League—a year in which one team played sensationally all season long and set a record for sheer success at winning baseball games. The '54 Cleveland Indians won 111 games, establishing the American League records for both games won in a season and won-lost percentage (.721). This performance was so stratospheric that the runnerup Yankees finished eight games behind even though they won 103 games, and the White Sox, who had their best season since 1920, finished 17 games behind with the same record (94-60) by which they would win the pennant in 1959.

Like the '06 Cubs, the Indians pulled off the stunt primarily with pitching. They had the AL's batting titlist, Bobby Avila (.341), and its home run leader, Larry Doby (32), and one other .300 hitter, Al Rosen, but this Cleveland club was 21 points below the 1948 flagwinner in team batting and outhit by the Yankees, White Sox, and Red Sox in 1954. The mound staff had a 2.78 ERA, the first team ERA below 3.00 in a peacetime year since the dead-ball era. Among the eight regular pitchers, the worst ERA was Art Houtteman's 3.35. Bob Lemon (23-7) and Early Wynn (23-11) were the biggest winners, followed by Mike Garcia (19-8), Houtteman (15-7), and Bob Feller (13-3). Whenever these starters faltered, Al Lopez usually got superb relief from Ray Narleski (three wins, 13 saves), Don Mossi (6-1, seven saves), or the ex-Tiger ace, Hal Newhouser (7-2, seven saves).

The Giants patched up their pitching in a hurry. They traded Bobby Thomson to the Braves for young southpaw Johnny Antonelli, and got a 21-game-winning pitcher with a league-leading 2.29 ERA out of the deal, whereas Milwaukee got an outfielder who broke his ankle and performed disappointingly for the Braves in later years. The ripening of sophomore Ruben Gomez and the return to form by Sal Maglie and Hoyt Wilhelm also helped, and during the previous year Durocher had also acquired 36-year-old reliever Marv Grissom from the Red Sox; Grissom was a pleasant surprise in 1954, earning ten wins and 19 saves. These changes gave the Giants a team ERA of 3.09, far superior to the Dodgers' 4.31, and enabled them to overtake Brooklyn for the NL pennant.

Although the Giants as a team did not outhit the Dodgers, Braves, or even the Phils and Cards, their pennant drive was

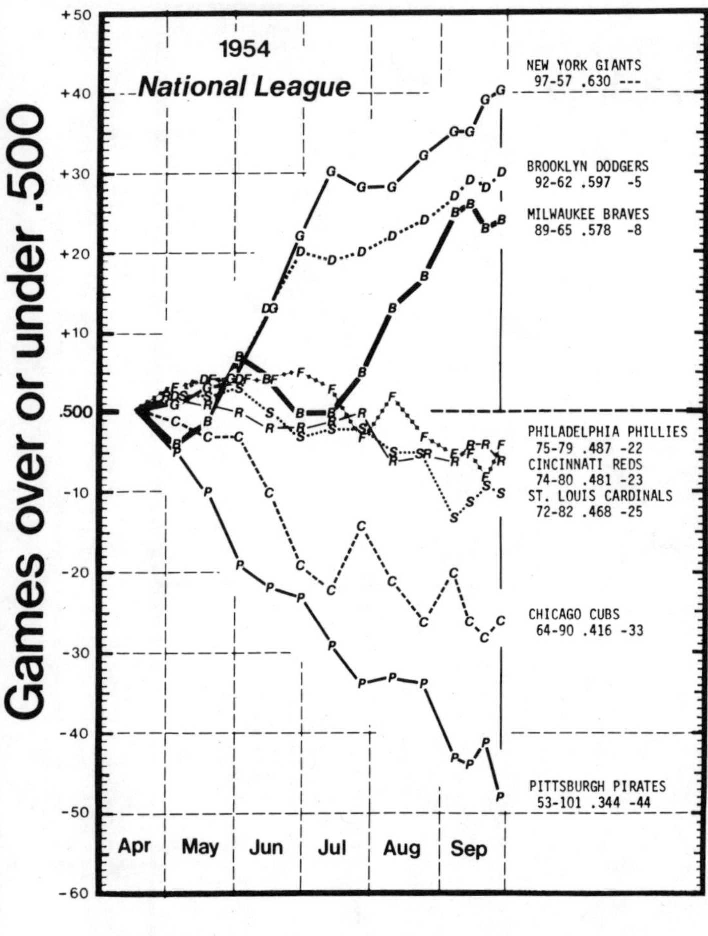


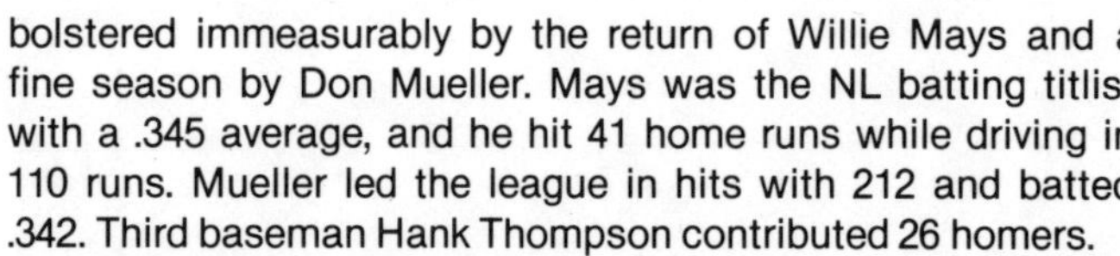
bolstered immeasurably by the return of Willie Mays and a fine season by Don Mueller. Mays was the NL batting titlist with a .345 average, and he hit 41 home runs while driving in 110 runs. Mueller led the league in hits with 212 and batted .342. Third baseman Hank Thompson contributed 26 homers.

The Braves stayed competitive with a strong mound corps that now included Bob Buhl and Gene Conley as well as Spahn and Burdette. The new Milwaukee had real gusto in Eddie Mathews' slugging (40 homers), increasing power from first sacker Joe Adcock (.308, 20 homers), and found a promising 20-year-old named Hank Aaron to occupy the outfield slot vacated by Thomson.

In another parallel with 1906, the record-setting Indians went down to defeat quickly in the World Series. The Giants put them away in four games, in fact, two games fewer than the Hitless Wonders took to overwhelm the Cubs back in the first decade. Despite its brevity, the '54 Series provided memorable thrills in the form of Mays's sensational catch of Vic Wertz's 460-foot liner to the Polo Grounds' deep center-field and Durocher's secret weapon—the pinch-hitting of reserve outfielder Dusty Rhodes; Rhodes had hammered 15 home runs in only 164 at-bats while batting .341 in the regular season, and in only six more at-bats in the Series, he hit a game-winning homer, a game-tying single, another two-run single that made the difference in Game 3, and an insurance homer.

## 1955

When a Brooklyn Dodger fan reminisces about the most ecstatic days in Flatbush, he savors the memories of 1955, when his team soared majestically to baseball's pinnacle of

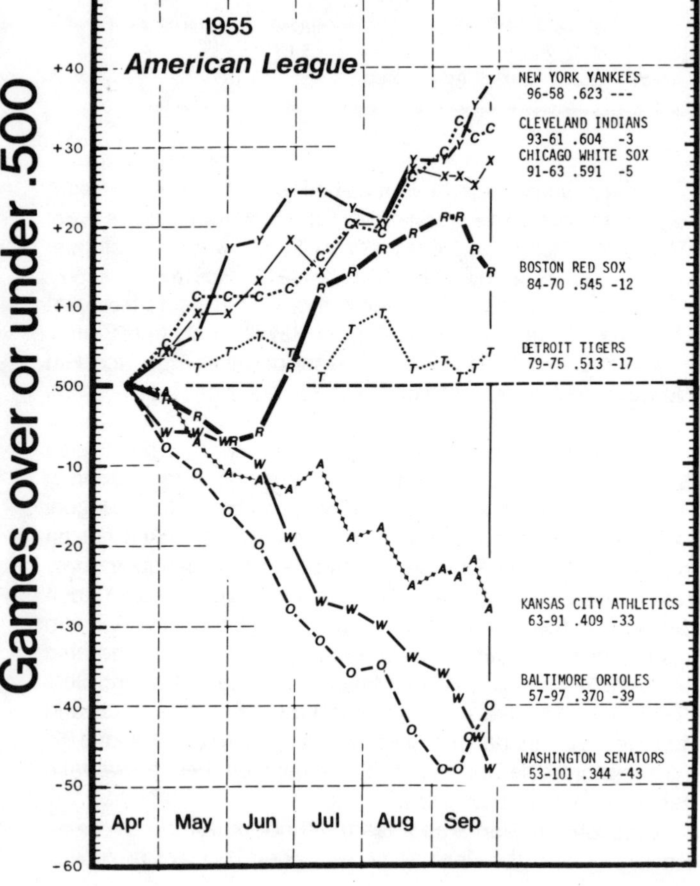


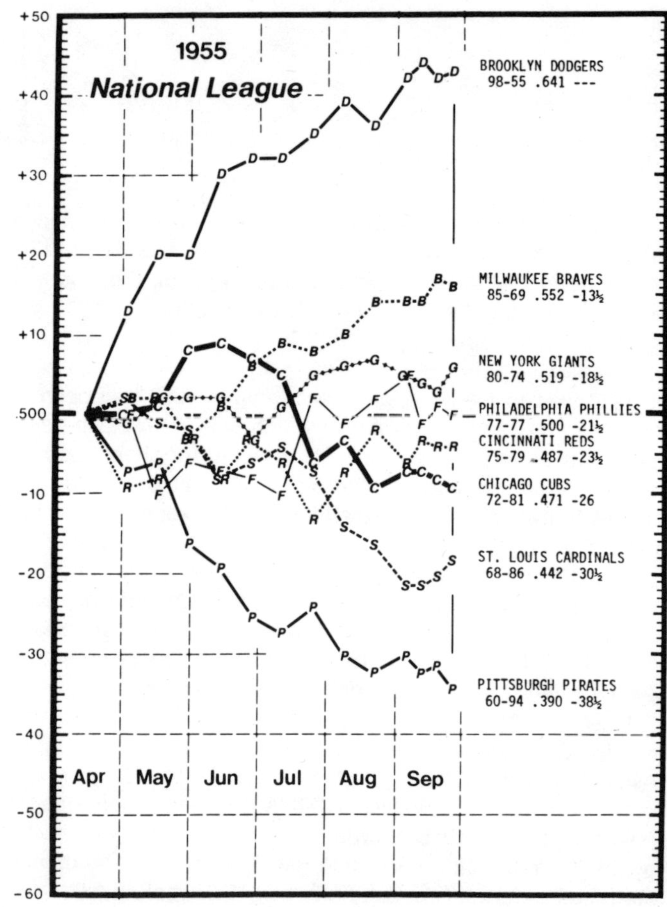

BACK ON THE TRACK after Cleveland's interruption in 1954, the 1955 Yankees had another of their many hot Septembers. Early in that month, the pennant race seemed to be turning into the tightest in the AL's history — even the Red Sox were only three games out of first place two days after Labor Day. Cleveland, Kansas City, and the Yankees themselves put Boston out of the race in short order, and the Yanks' three-game sweep of the Red Sox on September 16-18 put the Stengelmen back into the lead for keeps when the Tigers swept three from the Indians at Cleveland. New York sewed up the flag with another sweep at Washington and an official clinching in Boston on the final Friday.

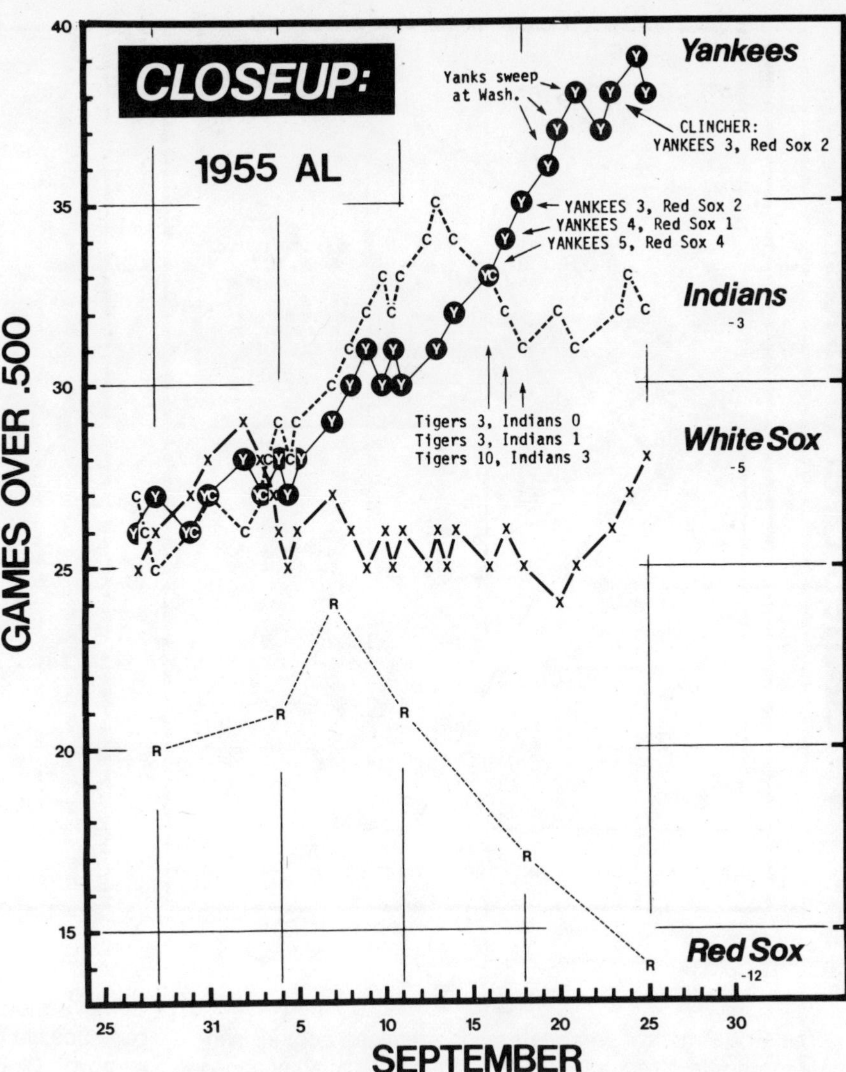


success—as defined by a Brooklynite of the fifties—a World Series victory over the Yankees. From the very first day of that season, things went well. The Dodgers won their first ten games, a feat that was unprecedented in modern times and has since been exceeded only by the Oakland A's when they won their first eleven games in 1981. After 24 games the Dodgers were 22-and-2, and they blazed on to a record that was more than 30 games over .500 by mid-June. Eventually their rate of climb tapered off, and they finished with only six more wins than in the previous year, but that was still a 13½-game margin of victory.

Under Walter Alston for the second year, the Boys of Summer had an infield of Gil Hodges, Junior Gilliam, Pee Wee Reese, and Jackie Robinson, with Robinson now at third and Gilliam at second, Roy Campanella at the backstop position, and an outfield of Duke Snider, Carl Furillo, and Sandy Amoros. Snider had a terrific season, bashing 42 homers and driving in 136 runs, and Campanella had 32 home runs and 107 RBIs. A third power source was Hodges, with 27 homers and 102 RBIs, and a foruth was Furillo, erstwhile singles-hitter, who was up to 26 roundtrippers.

After an off-year following his military stint, Don Newcombe was back in top form (20-5), and Carl Erskine, Billy Loes, and relievers Clem Labine and Ed Roebuck had decent years on the mound. A 19-year-old portsider named Sandy Koufax saw mound service in a dozen games.

The American League returned to business as usual, with the Yankees winning another pennant, but it had something resembling a suspenseful pennant race going until about September 20th. (see closeup) The top three clubs included the Indians and White Sox again, and they were joined by Boston for two months after the Red Sox won 23 out of 28 games near midseason. Boston was still struggling to come up with replacements for the retired Bobby Doerr, Johnny Pesky, and Dom DiMaggio, the departed Vern Stephens, the aging Mel Parnell and Ellis Kinder, and a .300-hitting first baseman named Harry Agganis, who died of a pulmonary emoblism in May at age 25; although the Red Sox had restaffed the outfield nicely with Jackie Jensen and the flashy-fielding temperamental Jimmy Piersall, it would be another dozen years before the Bosox could reverse a trend toward permanent second-division status.

In the World Series, the Yankees won the first two at the Stadium, but the Dodgers countered with three wins at Ebbets Field. After Whitey Ford pulled the Yankees even with a four-hitter in Game 6, Johnny Podres shut them out in Game 7, assisted dramatically by a fielding gem by Sandy Amoros. Finally, a world championship had come to Brooklyn, and glasses were raised on high in the borough for weeks thereafter.

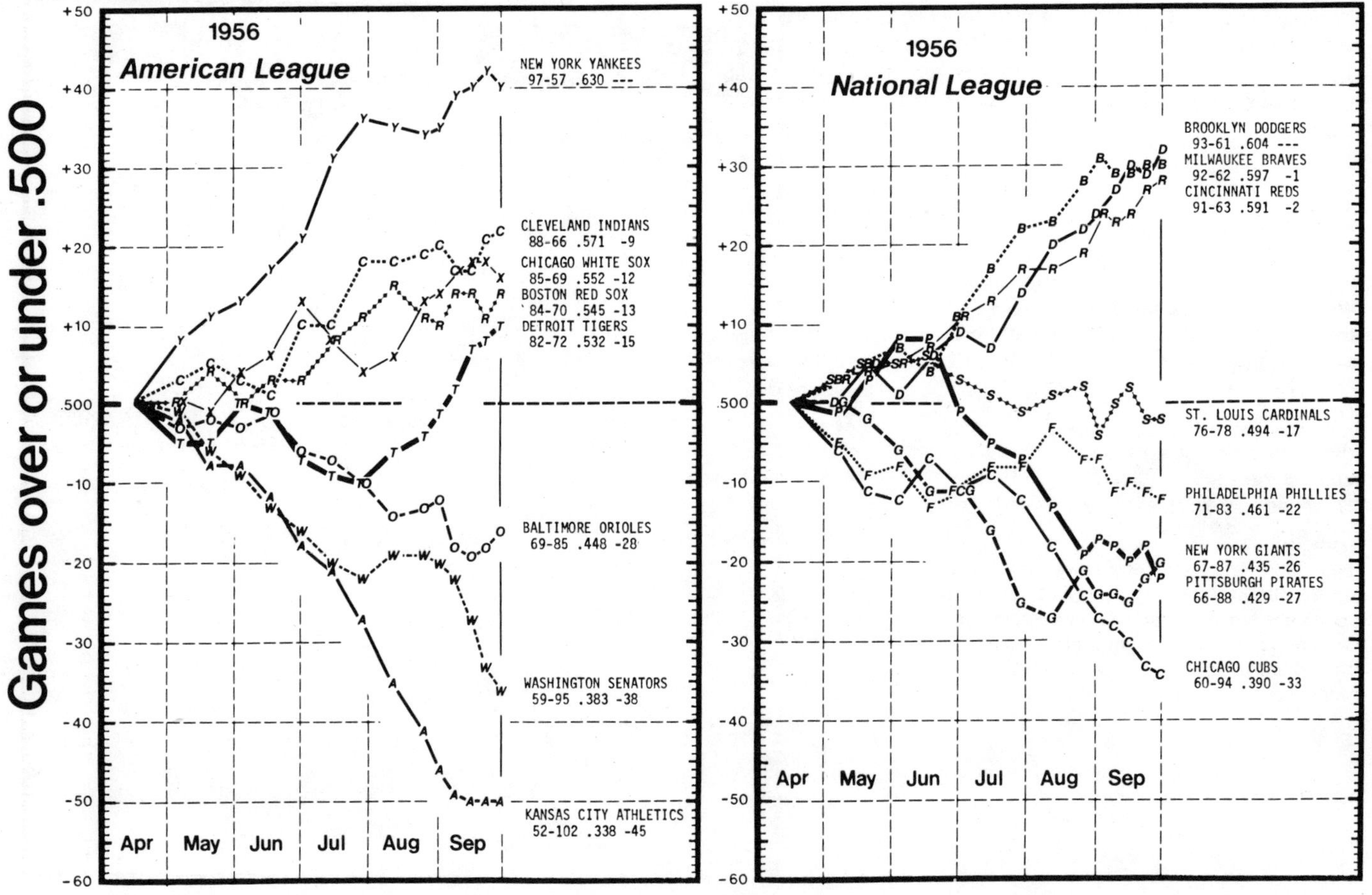


## 1956

The 1956 American League season produced another pennant for the New York Yankees, but some interesting changes were taking place in the lower half of the standings. The Detroit Tigers had been rebuilding, and now had two first-rate hitters in Al Kaline and Harvey Kuenn; Kaline had won the AL batting title at age 20 in 1955 with a .340 average. Three new pitchers, Billy Hoeft, Frank Lary, and Paul Foytack, also strengthened the Tiger roster The '56 Detroit team had the best second-half record in the league. A rebirth of the Baltimore Orioles franchise had taken place before the 1954 season, when the St. Louis Browns were purchased by an eastern syndicate, and under Paul Richards the Orioles began a voyage that would eventually take them to the winner's circle—and not just once like the Browns. Another change was the Philadelphia Athletics' shift to Kansas City in 1955; in this case, however, there was no upward trend, under either Lou Boudreau in 1955-57 or Harry Craft in 1957-59.

The Yankee win in 1956 was powered by Mickey Mantle, who won the Triple Crown (.353, 52 HRs, 130 RBIs) and MVP award after five previous seasons which had been excellent but less spectacular. Additional punch in the lineup came from first baseman Bill Skowron (.308, 23 homers), Gil McDougald (.311), and Yogi Berra (.298, 30 homers). The ace of the pitching staff, Whitey Ford, had a prime year with 19-6 and 2.47-ERA figures; he was backed up very ably by Johnny Kucks, Tom Sturdivant, and reliever Tom Morgan, showing once again how readily New York's farm system could replace retirees such as Reynolds, Lopat, and Sain.

The National League saw the Milwaukee Braves make a bona fide bid for the pennant that nearly succeeded, a sharply-improved Cincinnati team that also put in a strong bid, and an aging Dodger team that had to come from behind in September to win the pennant. The Braves had experienced a setback in Brooklyn's overwhelming win in 1955, but were fast approaching full strength—Aaron was turning into a superstar (he won the '56 batting title), Mathews and Adcock kept up their clouting, 35-year-old Warren Spahn was unfaltering, and younger pitchers such as Bob Buhl were progressing well. Fred Haney took over as manager of the Braves around Memorial Day. Cincinnati now had the most feared men at the plate, among them Ted Kluszewski, Wally Post, Gus Bell, catchers Ed Bailey and Smoky Burgess, and 20-year-old rookie Frank Robinson. These sluggers combined with their teammates to produce a total of 221 home runs, tying the 1947 Giants' team home run record. With one more good pitcher added to their staff regulars Brooks Lawrence, Joe Nuxhall, and Hersh Freeman, the Reds could have been a surprise pennant-winner in 1956.

These three teams had a lively fracas going all season, staying within five games of each other the whole way. After the three passed the boom-and-bust Pirates in June, Milwaukee stayed ahead of the other two in a nearly convincing manner throughout July and August, but the dog days turned into dogfight days around Labor Day. Milwaukee was enjoying a winning streak up to the holiday, but suddenly the Braves lost most of their lead when they dropped three in a row to the Reds at County Stadium and two more to the Cubs at

Wrigley Field. The Dodgers broke free from Cincinnati the same week with three wins over the Giants, and tied the Braves at 83-55 by beating them, 4-2, at Ebbets Field on September 11th. From then until the final week, Brooklyn and Milwaukee were in continual ties. A 7-1 win by the Braves (Spahn's 20th) at Cincinnati on the final Tuesday effectively removed the Reds from the race and put Milwaukee into the lead with a one-game edge over Brooklyn going into the last weekend.

But on Friday and Saturday at St. Louis, the Braves stumbled fatally, losing 9- and 12-inning games by the slimmest of margins; in Saturday's contest, the Cardinals' Herm Wehmeier outpitched Spahn, both pitchers going the whole 12 innings. Meanwhile, in Brooklyn, the Dodgers clinched a tie with a double victory over the Pirates; Sal Maglie, who had moved from the Giants to the Dodgers via Cleveland at age 39, won the first game, and Clem Labine, who had nine wins and 19 saves up to that point, won the second. Sunday, the Dodgers clinched the pennant when Don Newcombe hurled his 27th win in an 8-6 defeat of the Pirates.

The signs of fatigue in that final victory by Newcombe showed up more glaringly in the World Series, when he was kayoed by the Yankees in the second inning of Game 2 and the fourth inning of Game 7. The Yankees won those games by 13-8 and 9-0 scores, and tasted even sweeter revenge in Game 5, when Don Larsen set down the Dodgers 1-2-3 nine times in a row—the most perfectly stingy pitching of World Series history.

## 1957-58

Milwaukee's time had come, but it certainly didn't look that way to manager Fred Haney in the early months of the 1957 season. The Phillies and Cardinals were contending now as fiercely as the Dodgers and Reds, and the pennant race was shaping up as tougher than the previous year's heartbreaker. Spahn, Burdette, and Buhl were pitching well, but

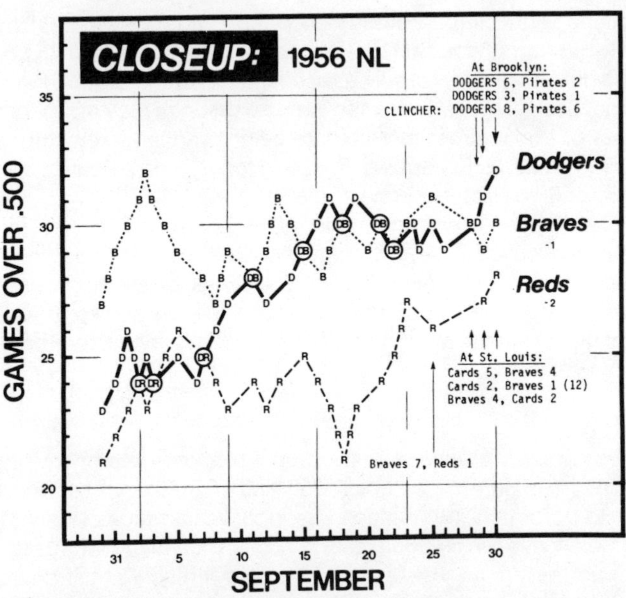


**NEW KID ON THE BLOCK, Milwaukee, got elbowed out of the NL pennant by the Boys of Summer in the final weekend of the 1956 season. A 2-1, 12-inning loss to the Cardinals in St. Louis on Saturday, September 29th, was the death blow for the Braves.**

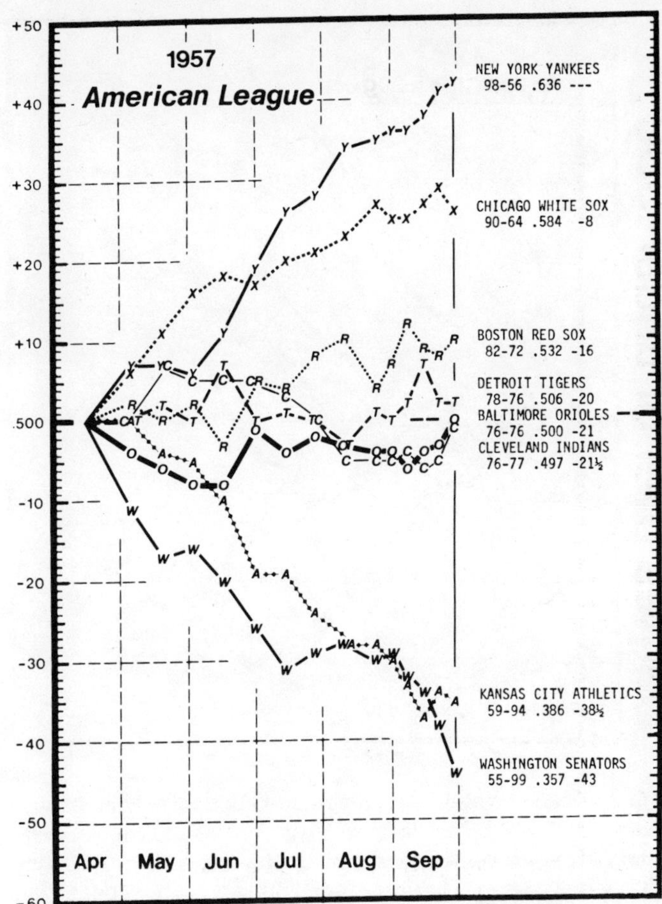


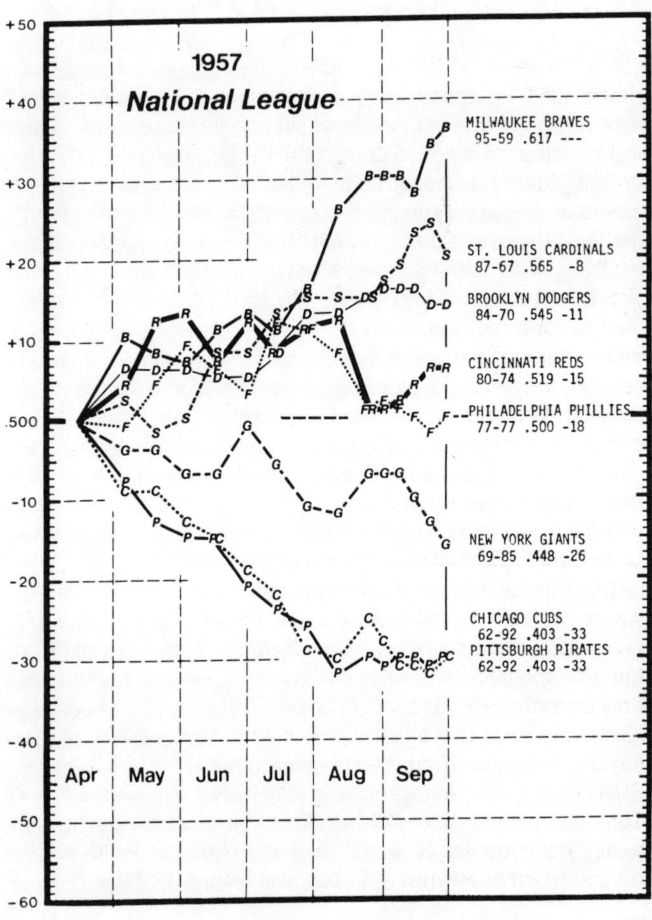

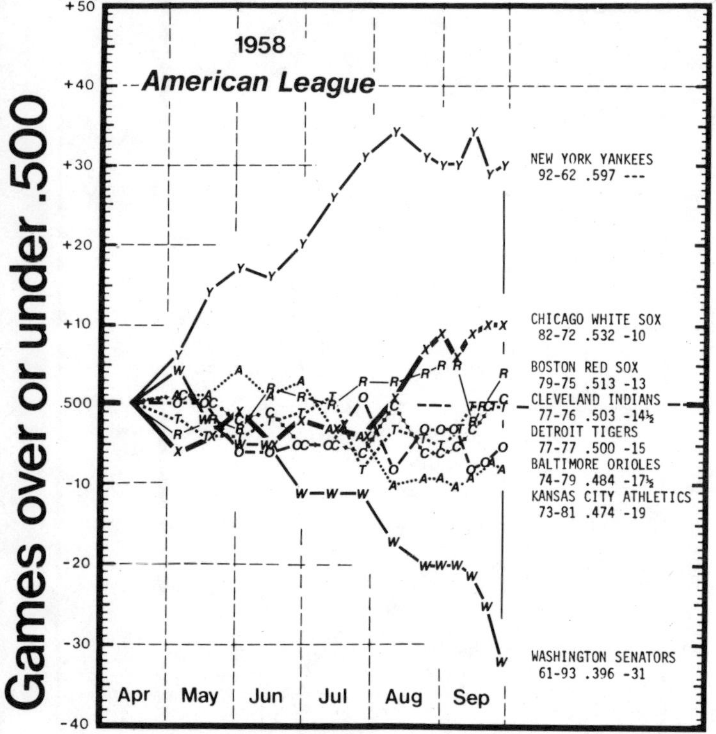


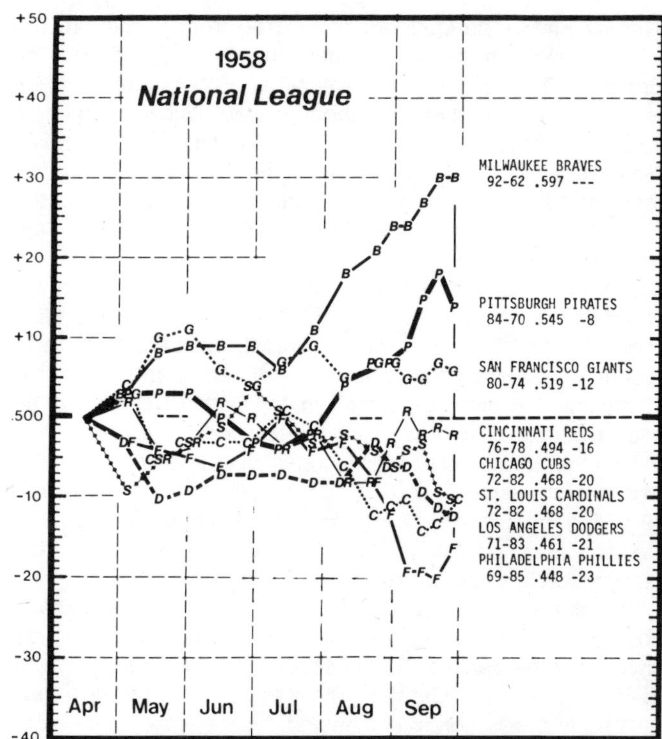


Haney needed a stronger bullpen. Joe Adcock had just broken a leg, and Bill Bruton was out with an injured knee. Aaron and Mathews were golden, but Bobby Thomson and Danny O'Connell weren't hitting—that hole at second base had needed plugging for several years.

So Haney shipped Thomson, O'Connell, and reserve pitcher Ray Crone to the Giants in exchange for 34-year-old Red Schoendienst, who patched up the second-base weakness by hitting .310 for the Braves and leading the league in hits. He put young Frank Torre in at first base in Adcock's place, and Torre handled the job ably. Other youngsters, Wes Covington and Bob "Hurricane" Hazle, filled the outfield vacancies, and handsomely—Covington blasted 21 homers in 328 at-bats, and Hazle, recalled from the Wichita farm later in the season, hit .403 in 41 games. Don McMahon also came up from Wichita to provide the needed relief help.

With these adroit maneuvers, Haney steered the Braves to a seven-game lead in August, and a fairly easeful pennant victory despite a mid-September slump. More surprisingly, they cruised on to the world championship, beating the Yankees, four games to three. Authentic heroism was displayed in the Series by Lew Burdette, who throttled the Stenelmen 4-2 in Game 2, 1-0 in Game 5, and 5-0 in the deciding game at Yankee Stadium—the first time a pitcher had tossed three complete-game Series victories since Stan Coveleski's triple-win feat for the Indians in 1920.

Hank Aaron won the MVP award and came close to winning the Triple Crown in 1957, with batting figures of .322, 44 homers, and 132 RBIs, but his batting average was behind Stan Musial's .351 and Willie Mays' .333. Musial, at 36, was still hammering the ball on a par with the younger batting leaders, and so was Ted Williams in the other league—at age 38, Williams won the AL batting title with a .388 average and did it again at age 39 with a .328 average. Otherwise, there wasn't much news to report from that league in 1957 and 1958, with the tragic exception that a brilliant pitching career was cut short when Cleveland's young Herb Score (20-9 in 1956) suffered a severe eye injury from a line drive off Gil McDougald's bat early in the '57 season.

The biggest news of the period came between the '57 and '58 seasons, when the Dodgers and Giants announced their moves to Los Angeles and San Francisco, leaving millions of New York City fans in stunned disbelief and anger, but triggering unbounded joy on the west coast.

The euphoria in the Bay area was further heightened the next spring, when the Giants jumped ahead of the Braves into first place, but neither the Giants nor a suddenly up-and-coming Pirate team could head off an impressive repeat by Milwaukee. In contrast to the Giants, the new-but-old Los Angeles Dodgers (an awkward-sounding name that took years to get used to) sank to the league's dungeon in May and spent most of the summer there before being outdone in ineptitude by the Phillies. Except for Snider, Hodges, and Podres, the Boys of Summer were done as well as gone.

The Yankees, who won the AL pennant in 1958 by ten games even after playing only .500 ball over the last nine weeks, beat the Braves in the '58 Series by winning three straight after spotting Milwaukee a 3-1 lead in games. It was Stengel's seventh world championship, after his ninth pennant, in ten years.

## 1959

Temporarily at least, the two major leagues were becoming rather homogenized. In both 1958 and 1959, the spread from top to bottom in the American League was a range of only 31 games and in the National League only 23 games. Within each league the teams were becoming more difficult to tell apart, in talent and style. And within most teams the batters were getting harder to distinguish, because there were fewer .300 hitters—batting averages were dropping steadily as pitchers improved and as the hitters swung more and more for the fences (home run totals were still rising).

Under these conditions it was easier for a team to move from a near-.500 record one year to a pennant in the next, as the 1959 White Sox did, or even from seventh place to a pennant, as the 1959 Dodgers did. There was nothing tainted about the White Sox triumph, however—the Go-Go Sox were an exciting bunch of players who led the league in base-stealing and like their ancestral Hitless Wonders of the first decade, eked out many victories of the one-and two-run kind, concentrating on defense more than hitting. Their manager, Al Lopez, had moved from Cleveland three years earlier, and he gambled successfully that the time was ripe for this good old-fashioned approach. Led by Early Wynn (22-10), Bob Shaw (18-6), and relievers Turk Lown and Gerry Staley, and with only one .300 hitter (MVP Nellie Fox, .306) in the lineup, the White Sox outfought a gamely contending Cleveland team and won the pennant with two more victories than the Yankees had achieved the previous year.

Besides Fox at second base, the Chicago infield had Earl Torgeson at first, Luis Aparicio (league-leader in stolen bases with 56) at short, and Bubba Phillips platooned with Billy Goodman at third. Catcher Sherm Lollar and outfielder Al Smith, with 22 and 17 homers, respectively, represented the only long-ball threat of the club. Three Jims—Landis, McAnany, and Rivera—also were regulars out in the pastures.

Cleveland's spirited competition revealed a 180-degree turn for the Indians since their victorious 1954 season—they were now the league's powerhouse, with Rocky Colavito (42 home runs), Woodie Held (29), Tito Francona (20), and Minnie Minoso (21), the latter coming to Cleveland in 1957 when Early Wynn moved to Chicago. Francona hit .363 in 399 at-bats; more typical of the statistical trends of that period were Colavito, Held, and Minoso's batting averages: .256, .251, and .302. The Indians' pitching, led by Cal McLish, was only fourth-best in the AL. The Yankees' only .300 batter was rookie infielder Bobby Richardson; Mantle and Ford were somewhat off their usual brilliance and age was showing in the performances of Berra, Bauer, and McDougald.

The 1959 NL race had a dramatic surprise ending, decidedly not a pleasant surprise for the San Francisco Giants. After leading from early July to mid-September, the Giants went into a brief tailspin and were suddenly overtaken by the Dodgers and Braves. The latter were glued together in the standings almost all of the final month, and ended up that way, forcing the National League's third pennant playoff. Two consecutive one-run victories by the Dodgers determined the flagwinner, the Braves carrying the final hame to 12 innings before yielding, 6-5.

Burdette and Spahn, both winners of 21 games, headed the Milwaukee pitching as usual, but the Dodgers were developing several new pitchers. Don Drysdale, a 22-year-old righthander, won 17 games in his sophomore year, to complement the usually-effective Podres and Labine, and two other recent farmhands, Roger Craig and Larry Sherry, promised future stardom. But another young pitcher, Sandy Koufax, was developing almost too slowly for the Dodger management to tolerate; Koufax won only eight games in 23 starts after records of 2-2, 2-4, 5-4, and 11-11 (cum 4.48 ERA) in the four previous seasons, and in 1960 he was 8-and-13.

The Giants, who were at the point of printing World Series tickets when they tumbled, had the NL's best pitching staff, still headed by Antonelli but also by the year's ERA titlist, Sam Jones (19-10, 2.82). They were also stronger at the plate: Willie Mays' output (.313, 34 homers, 104 RBI's) was now abetted by Orlando Cepeda (.317, 27 homers, 105 RBIs) Willie Kirkland (22 homers), and rookie Willie McCovey (.354 and 13 homers in 192 AB). The Pittsburgh Pirates were clearly getting stronger also, and had flashed this in both the '56 and '58 seasons; in 1959 they displayed a relief pitcher, Roy Face, who had the sensational record of 18-1 and ten saves in 57 appearances, and a starter, Harvey Haddix, who in one game set down the Braves in order 12 straight innings and then lost the game in the 13th.

Larry Sherry's stardom come sooner than he or anyone else had expected. In the '59 Series, his two wins and two

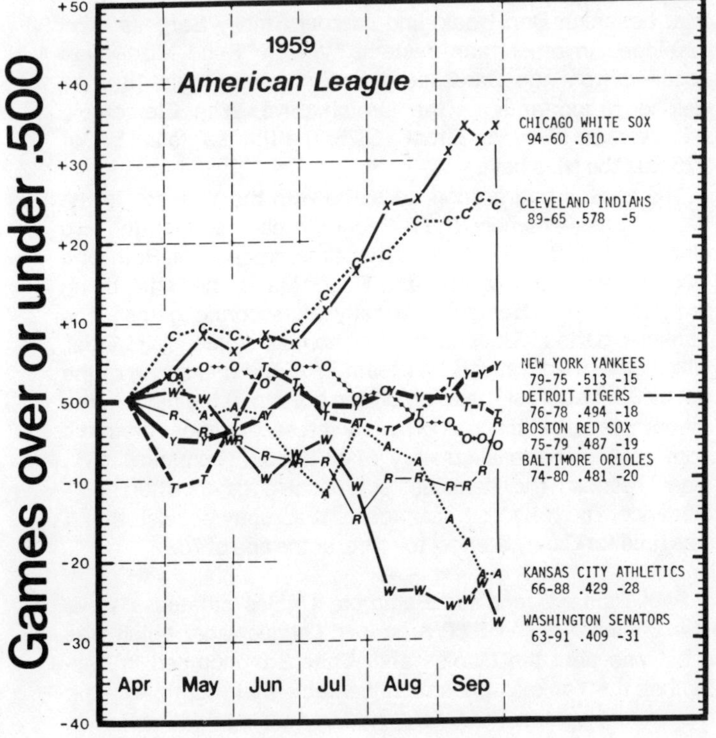


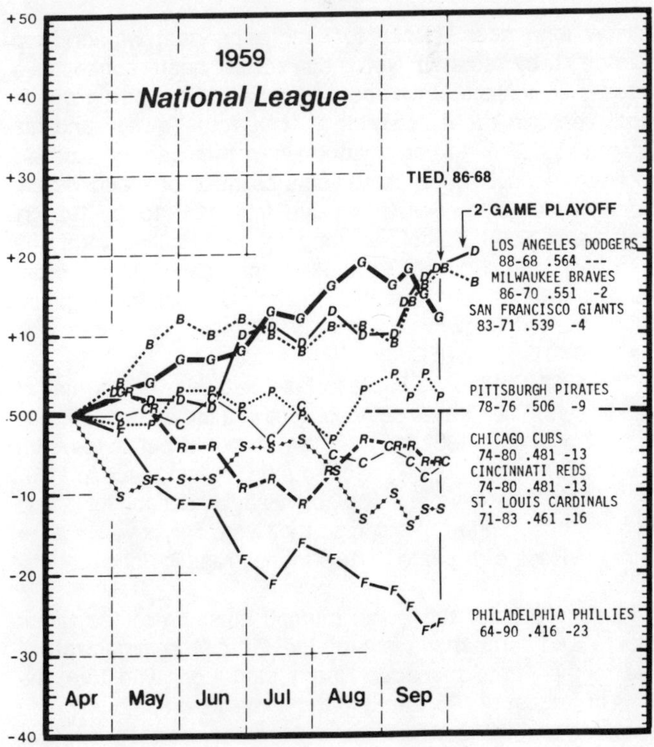

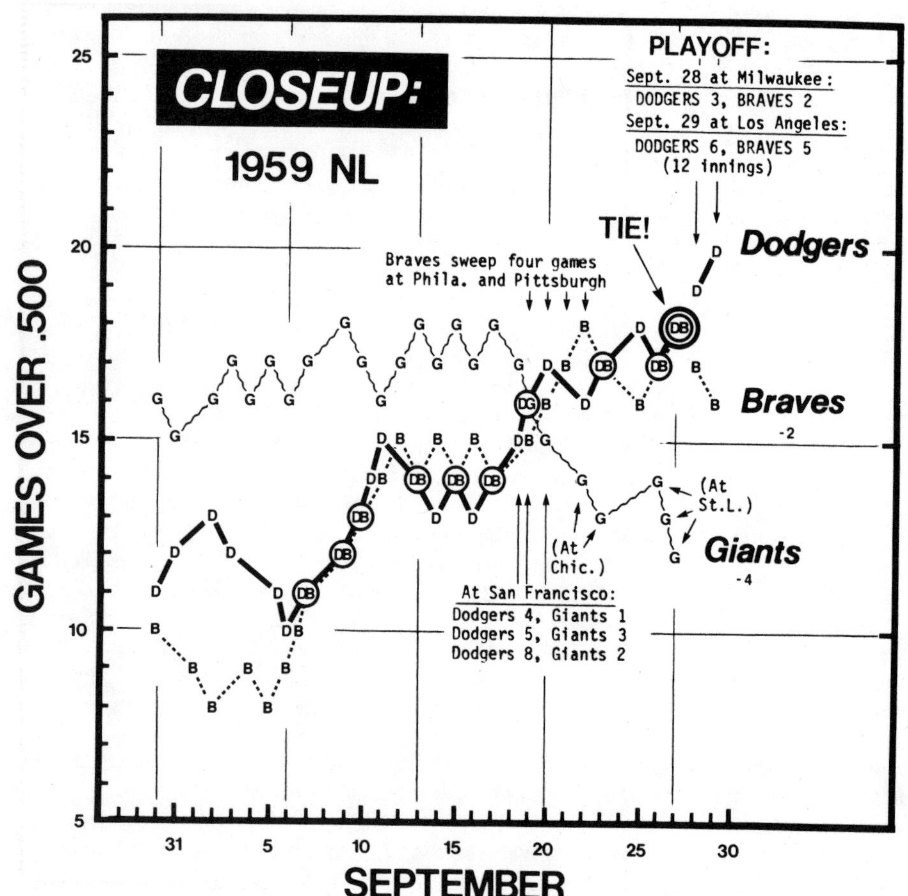


**STOP THE PRESSES! The San Francisco Giants were about to print World Series tickets when the Los Angeles Dodgers came to Seals Stadium on the weekend of September 20, 1959 and knocked Bill Rigney's club out of first place with a three-game sweep. Milwaukee also passed the Giants that weekend, and the regular season ended the next weekend with the Dodgers and Braves tied. Only 18,297 showed up for the first playoff game at Milwaukee on the 29th, when Johnny Roseboro's homer and Larry Sherry's seven-plus innings of strong relief brought a 3-2 victory to LA. Another good relief job — three scoreless innings by Stan Williams — made the difference the next day in Los Angeles, in a 12-inning, 6-5 Dodger triumph for the pennant.**

saves made him the hero for the Dodgers in a six-game affair.

## 1960

How long does it take to build a pennant winner from scratch? If by "scratch" you mean several nearly-consecutive years in last place, it can be a long haul. After seven out of eight years in the AL's cellar, it took Tom Yawkey and his Boston Red Sox 14 years, although in that case we should probably deduct two or three years because of World War II. Connie Mack also needed 14 years, from 1915 to the 1929-31 gravy days, and it took so long for the Phillies after the teen years that it's hard to figure in their case. On the other hand, we have some examples which by comparison might be called instant flagwinners—the 1914 Braves, of course, and the 1939-40 Cincinnati Reds.

The 1960 Pittsburgh Pirates could be added to the list of rapid risers. The Pirates seemed to have a life sentence in the NL's dungeon in 1952-55, then they crawled out to seventh place in 1956, but flopped back to a tie for last place in 1957. But in 1960 they were in first place nearly all season long, and won the title handily. In doing so they were only a year slower than the Reds of the late thirties in their rags-to-riches renaissance.

Major credit for the Bucs' triumph must go to the talent scouts and farm managers of the Pittsburgh organization, and to the Pirate manager, Danny Murtaugh, who took the reins in August of 1957. Among the home-grown products who helped bring the pennant—and even the world championship—to Pitt in 1960 were Face, Hall of Famer Roberto Clemente, 20-game-winner Vern Law, another strong righty named Bob Friend, batting titlist Dick Groat, outfielder Bob Skinner, first baseman Dick Stuart, and second sacker Bill Mazeroski. The frontlines also included outfielder Bill Virdon, third baseman Don Hoak, and catcher Smoky Burgess, who developed in other farm systems. Vinegar Bend Mizell was acquired from the Cards early in the season—his 13 wins weighed importantly in the stretch drive. With Clemente's .314 average following Groat's .325, the Pirates' team BA of .276 was the NL's best.

The Pirates had a score to settle with the Yankees in the World Series—namely, the 0-4 score in games when the two clubs met in the '27 Series. This time, instead of Ruth and Gehrig, they faced Mantle and Roger Maris, the latter being the AL's MVP. Over seven mostly high-scoring games, the Yankees batted .338 and hit ten homers (three by Mantle), which gave the Pirates a 7.11 team ERA. But one swing of the bat by Bill Mazeroski, leading off the bottom of the ninth in the seventh game, which was probably the second most dramatic home run in baseball history after Bobby Thomson's 1951 blast, reduced the Yankees' statistical edge to utter insignificance. The New York management abruptly decided that it was time for Casey Stengel to retire, at the age of 70.

Paul Richards and his Baltimore Orioles created a wave of excitement in the 1960 American League race, which was a hot one until the Orioles and White Sox slumped in September; the Yankees became unbeatable that month, winning their last 15 games. The Orioles had a sparkling third baseman,

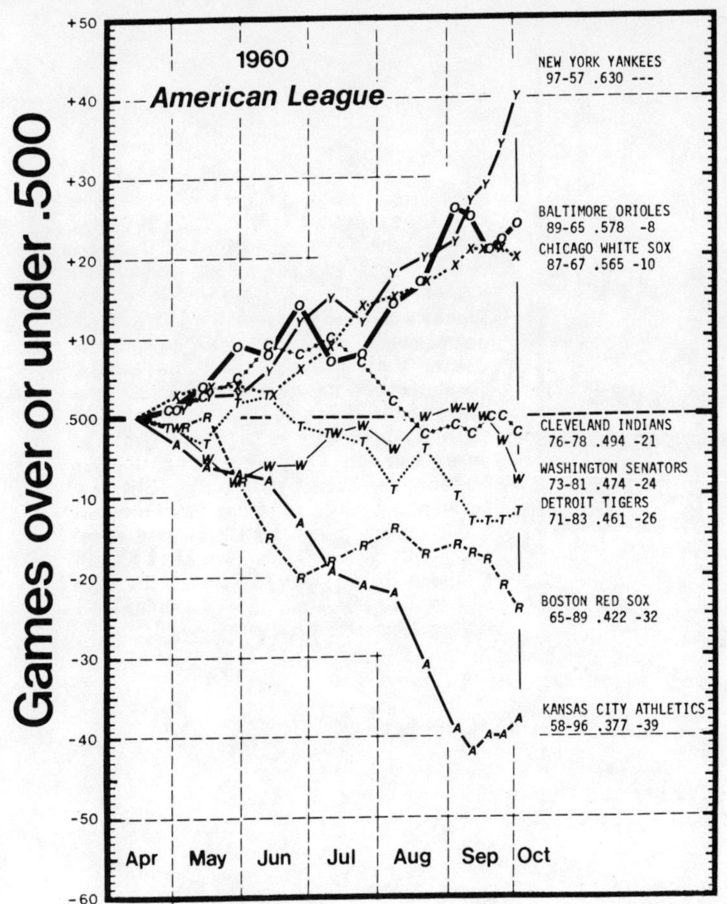


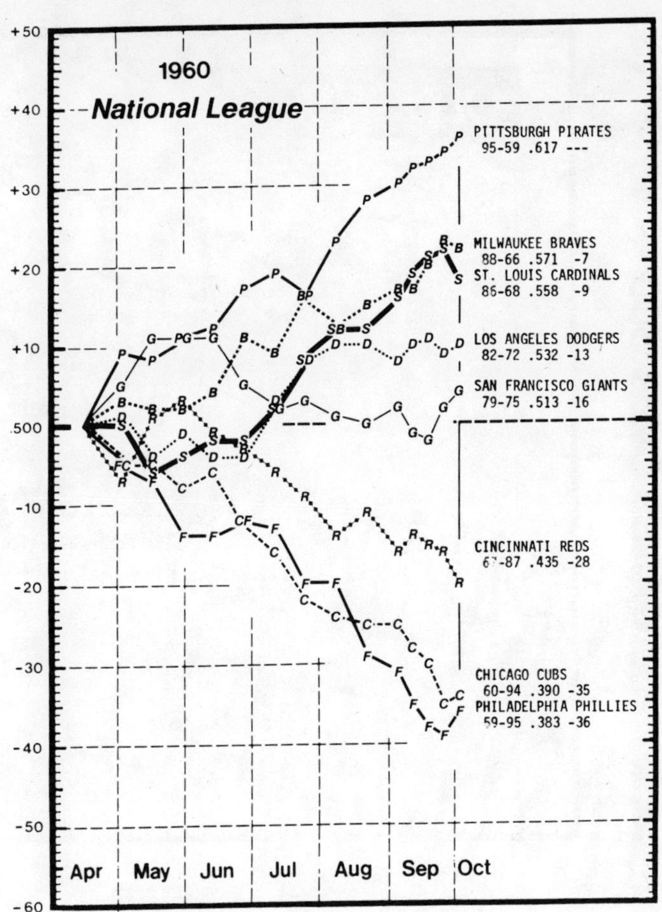


Brooks Robinson, already in his fifth year as a major leaguer at age 23, and several good young pitchers, including Chuck Estrada, Steve Barber, and Milt Pappas. In the lower echelons of the league were the Red Sox, back in last place again in the month of June and seventh at the end, wondering if there would ever be another pennant in the Yawkey Era. Late in the season, Ted Williams, still batting .316 at age 41, retired after spanning four decades of major league play. Filling his shoes fell upon a 21-year-old rookie named Carl Yastrzemski the next year.

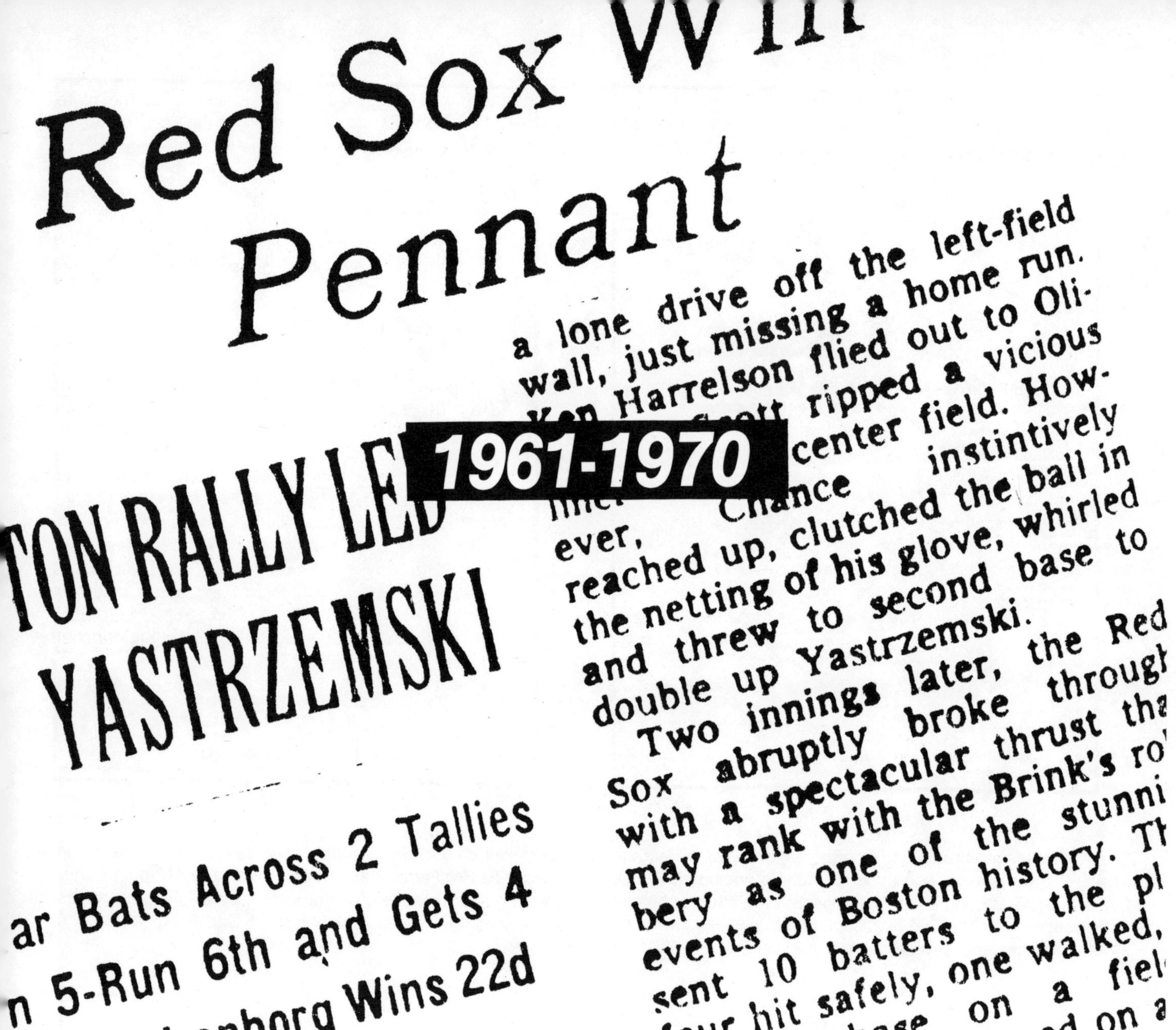


# 1961-1970

## 1961

Major league baseball's expansion era started in 1961, with the American League adding two teams. The Washington Senators moved to Minneapolis-St. Paul, becoming the Minnesota Twins, a new Senators franchise was created to replace the departees, and an outpost on the west coast was established—the Los Angeles Angels. With the ten-team lineup came a 162-game schedule in place of the 154-game season. The National League expanded to ten teams the following year.

The highlight of the '61 season was an unparalleled power display by the New York Yankees, the most flagrant example of which was Roger Maris's new seasonal record of 61 home runs. Mickey Mantle was also challenging Babe Ruth's old record of 60 most of the year; he hit 54. Four other Yankees hit over 20 homers—Bill Skowron, Yogi Berra, Elston Howard, and Johnny Blanchard—and the team set the modern major league record of 240 roundtrippers in a season.

This barrage and some nifty pitching by Whitey Ford (25-4), Luis Arroyo (15 wins plus 29 saves), Ralph Terry, and Bill Stafford almost carried the Yanks to a new AL record for games won. They finished with two victories under the 1954 Cleveland total, but on September 10th, when their record was 99-45 after an .804 pace since Memorial Day, it looked as if they were headed for at least a tie with the 1906 Cubs, who won 116 games. Ralph Houk, the new Yankee manager, got the maximum mileage out of his roster by putting Yogi Berra in left field, clearing the way for Howard (.348) and Blanchard (.305) to put in more time at the catcher's position. Besides its fearsome attack and strong pitching, Houk's squad had plenty of defensive strength, particularly with the keystone combination of Bobby Richardson and Tony Kubek and Clete Boyer at third base.

New York had to overtake a revitalized Detroit Tiger team to cop the pennant. The Tigers were led by first baseman Norm

Cash, whose marvelous season (.361, 41 homers, 132 RBIs) was hidden in the Maris and Mantle shadows. Al Kaline's .324 batting and Rocky Colavito's 45 home runs added to the Tiger offense, and Frank Lary (23-9) headed a strengthened mound staff. The '61 season was Detroit's second in which winning 100 games wasn't enough for a pennant, the first being 1915, when the Tigers came in second behind the Red Sox.

The National League had another unexpected winner, the Cincinnati Reds. The Rhinelanders were all the more surprising by starting off poorly, finding themselves in last place in early May. But Fred Hutchinson, manager since mid-1959, got his club turned around, and in six weeks they passed all seven of their competitors to take the lead in June. In the latter months, the Dodgers represented the only threat to the Reds, but after a ten-game losing streak suffered by Los Angeles in August, Cincinnati got home with the gonfalon without severe strain.

The Reds had acquired righthander Joey Jay from the Braves during the offseason, and his 21-10 performance, together with equally fine mound work by second-year lefty Jim O'Toole, gave Cincinnati what had been the Reds' major missing ingredients. Sixteen-game winner Bob Purkey, who went several better the next year (23-5), also made a valuable contribution to the pennant victory, as did relievers Jim Brosnan and Bill Henry. Frank Robinson, the league's MVP, and Vada Pinson, who hit .343, led the Reds at the plate. Cincinatti's hitting was no match for the Yankees', however, and this quickly became evident in the World Series, won by New York in five games.

The Pirates had the same batting lineup that had brought them the world championship the year before, and again led the NL in team batting, but the Bucs suffered such a drastic falloff in their pitching that they drifted to a sixth-place finish; a sore arm reduced Vern Law to a 3-and-4 record.

## 1962

For the umpteenth time in the century, the Giants were tooling up for another title win, this time under Al Dark as manager, and by the end of the '62 season they were, on paper, a loaded club which should have walked away with the pennant. Added to the reliable outputs of Willie Mays and Orlando Cepeda were those of Felipe Alou, Harvey Kuenn, Jim Davenport, and a developing Willie McCovey, good enough in aggregate for league-leading team-BA and team-HR figures (.278, 204). There was even more improvement in San Francisco's pitching: the 1962 mound corps included veterans Jack Sanford (24-7), Billy O'Dell (19-14), and Billy Pierce (16-6), a maturing superstar in 23-year-old Juan Marichal (18-11), and a fine reliever, Stu Miller (19 saves).

But most of the season the Giants trailed the Los Angeles

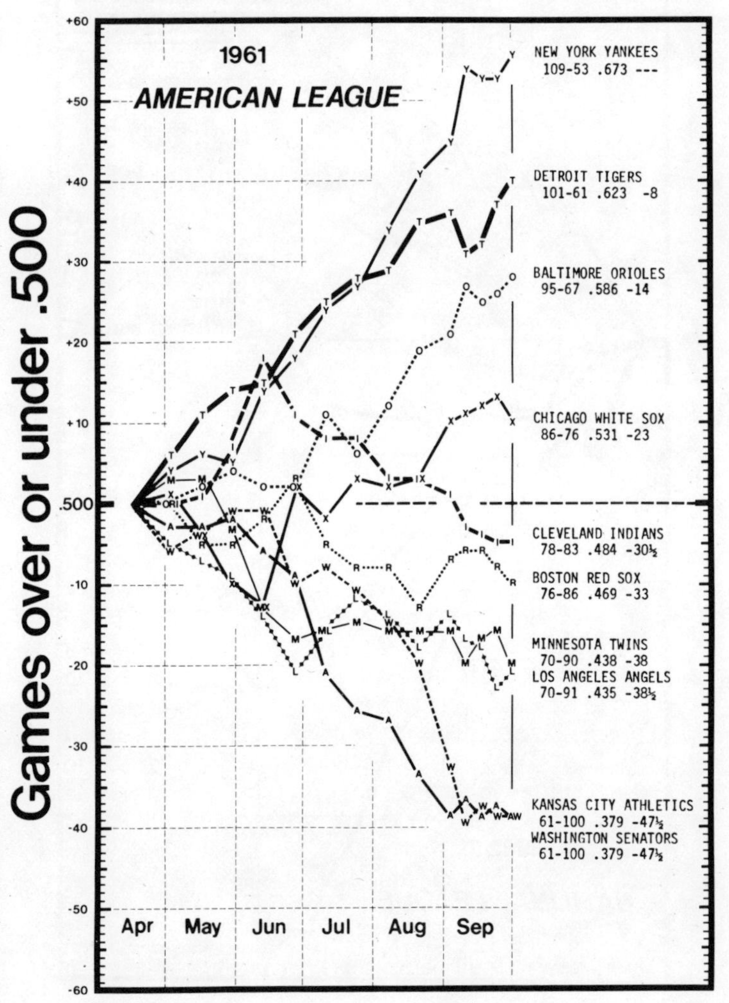


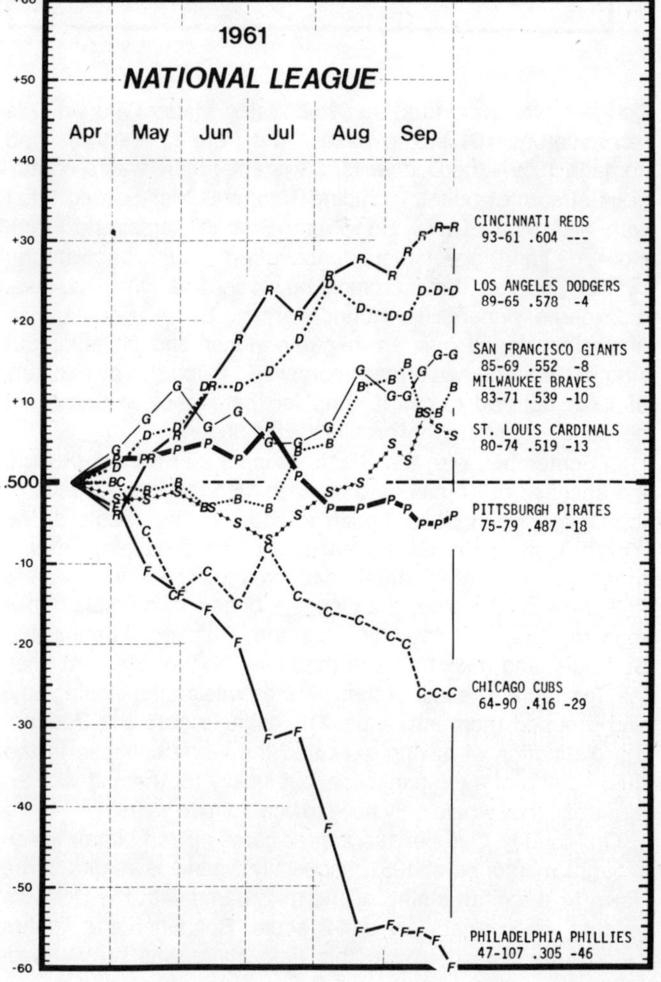

Games over or under .500

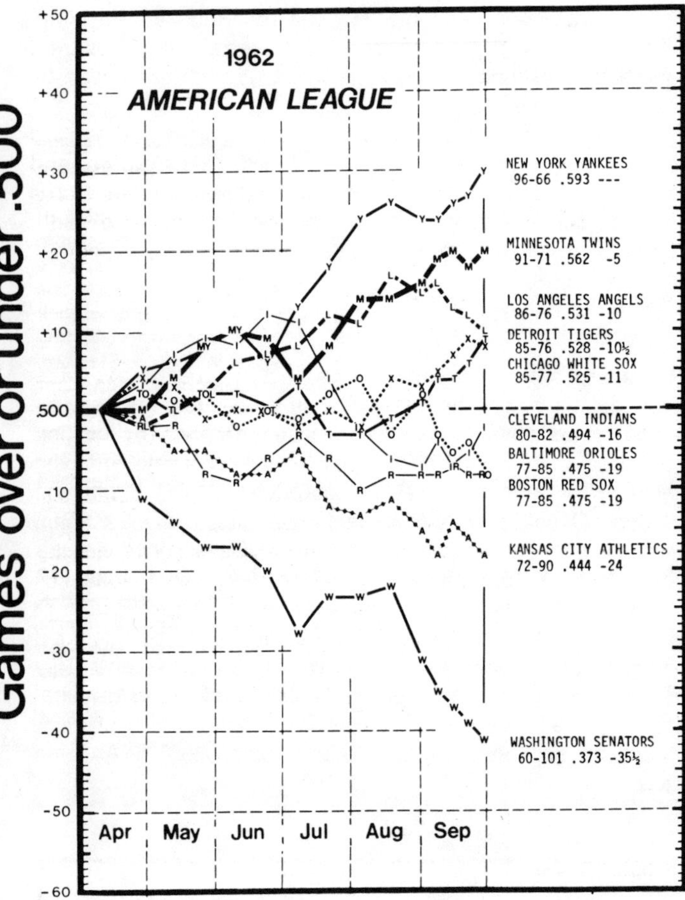


Dodgers, who were fired up by shortstop Maury Wills and his record-setting 104 stolen bases. And from where Wills had come in 1959—the Dodger farm system—there was a continuous stream of talent, including Tommy Davis, (batting titlist with .346), Willie Davis, Ron Fairly, Stan Williams, and Frank Howard. The biggest factor accounting for the pace-setting by the Dodgers that summer, however, was Don Drysdale, a 25-game-winner. His mound partner, Sandy Koufax, had finally developed into an 18-game-winner and NL strikeout king in 1961, and had already compiled 14 victories by mid-July of 1962, but had to call it quits for the season at that point because of a circulatory problem in his fingers.

In September, with the Giants keeping up their hot pursuit, the absence of Koufax, and perhaps also the inexperience of the Dodger youngsters, began to show. In the middle of the month, just as the Giants seemed to be collapsing after a seven-game winning streak had brought them to within a half-game of the lead, the Dodgers began to crumble. On a road trip they lost five out of nine at Chicago, Atlanta, and St. Louis, and back home in their new Dodger Stadium, they lost five more. The last of these losses was on the closing day, and dropped them into a tie. The debacle gave the Dodgers the distinction of having executed the worst collapse in the final stretch of a pennant race, but luckily for them, it was an albatross they would only have to bear for two years.

On Monday, October 1st, a three-game playoff began which brought memories of 1951, especially when the verdict come down to the ninth inning of the third game with the Dodgers leading, once again, by a 4-2 score. But when the Giants came from behind to win this time, there was no world-renowned home run. Instead, when the Giants had the bases full and the score knotted at 4-4, it was the yell of "ball four!" by umpire Dusty Boggess on reliever Stan Williams' last pitch to Jim Davenport that became the decisive event, before the stunned Dodger Stadium onlookers. The forced go-ahead run was followed by another run on a Dodger error, and Pierce came in to set the home team down in order in the bottom of the ninth, giving San Francisco the pennant.

Sixty and one-half games behind the victorious Giants were the futile New York Mets, guided to a record-shattering 80 games below .500 by the unpastureable Casey Stengel. Despite a roster containing such once-luminaries as Gil Hodges, Gus Bell, Gene Woodling, Roger Craig, and Marvelous Marv Throneberry (the latter's luminescence coming later in TV commercials), the Mets managed to win only 40 games out of 160. The other expansion team, the Houston Colt-45's, finished in a more respectable eighth position, having the handicap of that wretched nickname (changed to Astros two years later) to overcome as well as limited talent. The Phillies, who drew attention with an uprising to and over-.500 finish, were only too happy to relinquish the lower end of the standings to these two newcomers and the unhappy Cubs.

In the American League the Yankees' annual victory came

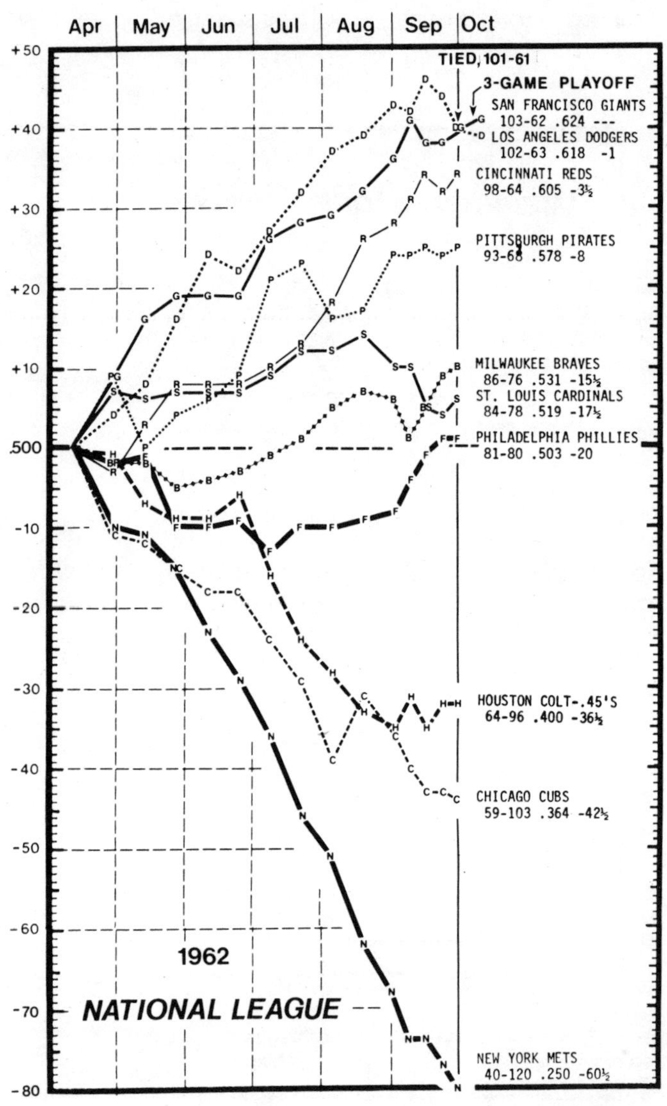

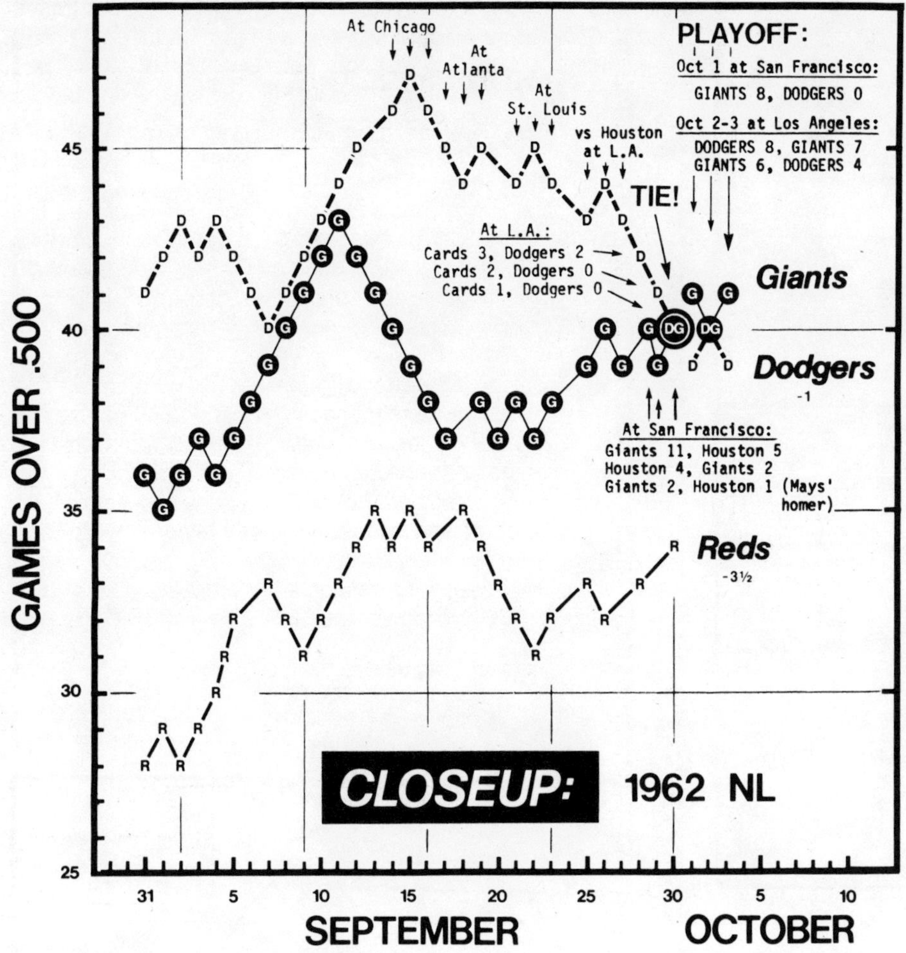


**TITANIC STRUGGLE.** When owner Walter O'Malley finally got his new Dodger Stadium afloat in 1962, the Dodgers' fortunes in the pennant race that year made one think of another maiden voyage that met disaster in the North Atlantic in 1912. Walter Alston's youngsters held a four-game lead over the Giants in mid-September, but lost ten of their last 13 games in the regular season, ending with four losses in a row in the new Stadium. On the closing day, September 30th, Curt Simmons of the Cardinals shut out LA while the Giants tied the Dodgers by beating Houston on a home run by Willie Mays, forcing the NL's fourth playoff series. Mays hit two more homers in the first playoff game, in which Billy Pierce handcuffed the Dodgers, 8-0, at Candlestick Park. LA's scoring drought ended the next day with an 8-7 Dodger victory, but in the third game the partisans at Dodger Stadium gasped in horror as their team sank for the final time—the Dodgers blew a 4-2 lead in the ninth (shades of '51!) and the Giants scored the pennant-winning run when LA's Stan Williams walked Jim Davenport with the bases loaded.

after some surprising competition from the Minnesota Twins and the second-year Angels. The Twins were getting powerful at the plate with the league's new home run champ, Harmon Killebrew (he hit 48 in 1962, 46 the year bafore, 45 the year after), and other strongmen including Bob Allison and Rich Rollins. Minnesota's pitching was also stronger, thanks to Camilo Pascual (20 wins in '62) and Jim Kaat (18 wins). The Angels trailed off in September after staying four to five games behind the Yankees for four months; Bill Rigney, the Angel manager, had a topnotch righthander in Dean Chance and some power hitting from Leon Wagner and Lee Thomas. The late-season falloff by Los Angeles was minor compared to Cleveland's collapse from first place in July; the Indians were repeating their 1961 performance, and as in that year they wound up in the second division.

The Yankees were still slamming the fences, hitting 199 homers; Mantle and Maris combined for 63 as opposed to the previous year's 115. Ralph Terry (23-12) was the premier hurler on the staff, with Ford (17-8) still in fine shape as he approached his mid-thirties; Marshall Bridges (eight wins and 18 saves) took over as the ace reliever. The Bombers won the World Series, four games to three, in a livley seesaw battle against the Giants.

**BIRTH TRAUMA.** The first year for a newborn expansion team is usually pretty rough, but the 1962 New York Mets played so poorly it became laughable—and the losing-can-be-fun spirit caught on, sustaining the Mets through several more seasons in the cellar. The '62 Mets set modern major league records by losing 120 games and finishing 80 games below .500.

## 1963

1963 was another Yankee-Dodger year, the eighth coincidence of their pennant successes. Despite injuries that limited action by Mantle and Maris, the Yankees won in a breeze; Whitey Ford was superb (24-7), and three relative newcomers to the New York pitching staff were of considerable help—Jim Bouton (21-7), Al Downing (13-5), and reliever Hal Reniff. For the Dodgers, Sandy Koufax reached full bloom, putting on a brilliant show of mound mastery with 11 shutouts, a 1.88 ERA, and a 25-5 record; in won-lost percentage he was exceeded only by teammate Ron Perranoski, who had a 16-3 (.842) record and 21 saves in 69 relief stints. The only threat Los Angeles faced after June was a momentary one when a rejuvenated St. Louis club won 19 of 20 games and came to within one game of the Dodgers on September 16th. After leading L.A. to the pennant, Koufax starred in the Dodgers' stunning sweep of the Yankees in the World Series. In the first game he beat Ford with 15 strikeouts and a six-hitter at Yankee Stadium, and in the Series finale at Dodger Stadium he outpitched Ford again with a two-hitter.

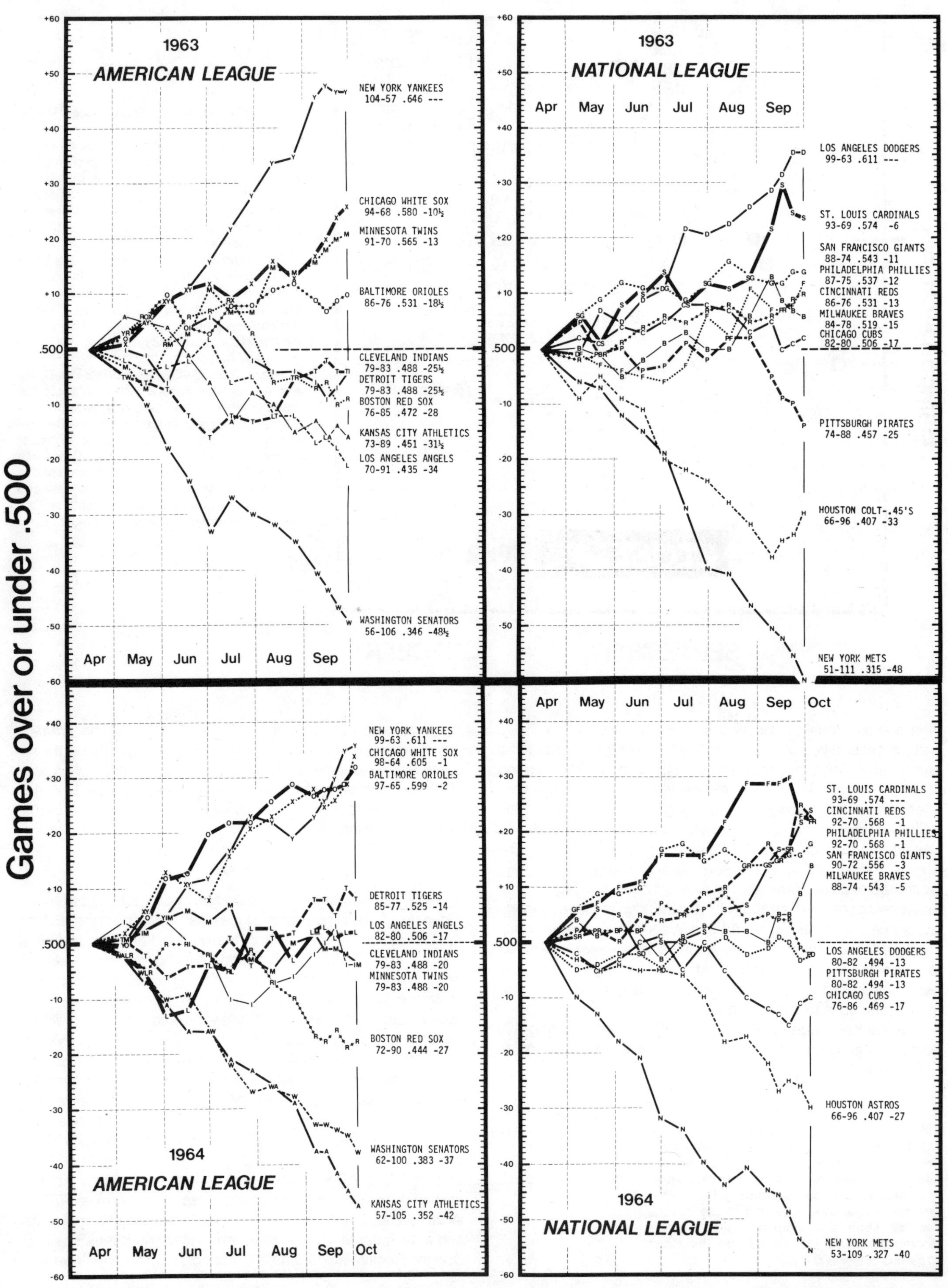
Games over or under .500
1963
AMERICAN LEAGUE
NEW YORK YANKEES 104-57 .646 ---
CHICAGO WHITE SOX 94-68 .580 -10½
MINNESOTA TWINS 91-70 .565 -13
BALTIMORE ORIOLES 86-76 .531 -18½
CLEVELAND INDIANS 79-83 .488 -25½
DETROIT TIGERS 79-83 .488 -25½
BOSTON RED SOX 76-85 .472 -28
KANSAS CITY ATHLETICS 73-89 .451 -31½
LOS ANGELES ANGELS 70-91 .435 -34
WASHINGTON SENATORS 56-106 .346 -48½
1963
NATIONAL LEAGUE
LOS ANGELES DODGERS 99-63 .611 ---
ST. LOUIS CARDINALS 93-69 .574 -6
SAN FRANCISCO GIANTS 88-74 .543 -11
PHILADELPHIA PHILLIES 87-75 .537 -12
CINCINNATI REDS 86-76 .531 -13
MILWAUKEE BRAVES 84-78 .519 -15
CHICAGO CUBS 82-80 .506 -17
PITTSBURGH PIRATES 74-88 .457 -25
HOUSTON COLT-.45'S 66-96 .407 -33
NEW YORK METS 51-111 .315 -48
1964
AMERICAN LEAGUE
NEW YORK YANKEES 99-63 .611 ---
CHICAGO WHITE SOX 98-64 .605 -1
BALTIMORE ORIOLES 97-65 .599 -2
DETROIT TIGERS 85-77 .525 -14
LOS ANGELES ANGELS 82-80 .506 -17
CLEVELAND INDIANS 79-83 .488 -20
MINNESOTA TWINS 79-83 .488 -20
BOSTON RED SOX 72-90 .444 -27
WASHINGTON SENATORS 62-100 .383 -37
KANSAS CITY ATHLETICS 57-105 .352 -42
1964
NATIONAL LEAGUE
ST. LOUIS CARDINALS 93-69 .574 ---
CINCINNATI REDS 92-70 .568 -1
PHILADELPHIA PHILLIES 92-70 .568 -1
SAN FRANCISCO GIANTS 90-72 .556 -3
MILWAUKEE BRAVES 88-74 .543 -5
LOS ANGELES DODGERS 80-82 .494 -13
PITTSBURGH PIRATES 80-82 .494 -13
CHICAGO CUBS 76-86 .469 -17
HOUSTON ASTROS 66-96 .407 -27
NEW YORK METS 53-109 .327 -40
Apr May Jun Jul Aug Sep Oct

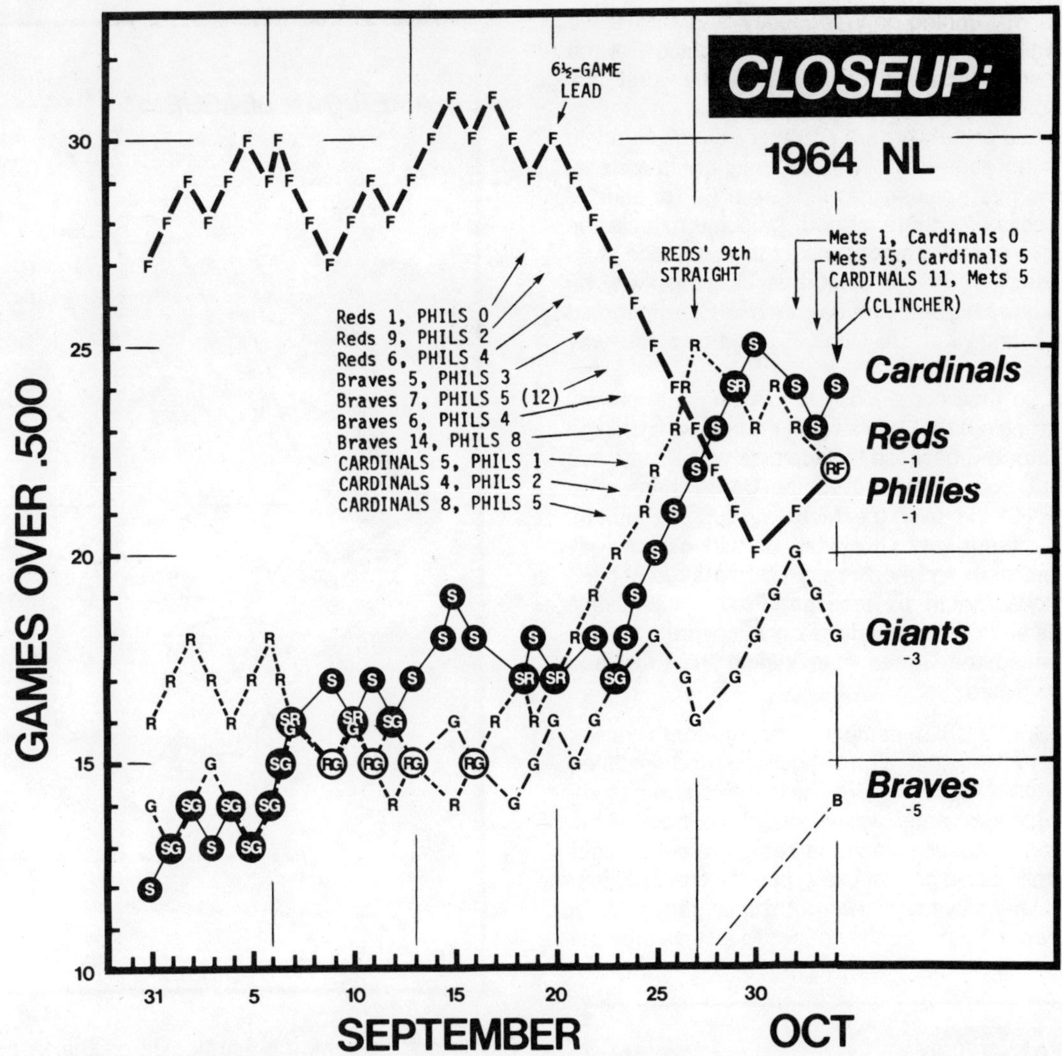


**PHILLIES' PHATAL PHLOP. When the Philadelphia Phillies headed into the fall on September 21, 1964, they had no idea that it would be the Humpty-Dumpty, rather than autumnal, kind of fall. From the 21st to the 30th, they lost ten straight games, the first seven at home. Unfortunately for Gene Mauch and his crew, their losing streak coincided with winning streaks by the Reds and Cards. The Phils' 6½-game lead vanished in seven days when the Reds took the league lead with their eighth and ninth straight wins on September 27th, and a day later the Cards started a three-game sweep of the Phillies at St. Louis which left the latter only a game above the fourth-place Giants. The spectacular collapse almost created a four-way tie for the pennant on the closing day, but Bob Gibson pitched the Cardinals to a flag-clinching triumph that afternoon as the Phils spoiled it for the Reds.**

## 1964

The Philadelphia Phillies, who had finished last in 1961, seventh (of ten) in 1962, and fourth in 1963, continued a lawful ascent to first place in 1964. Wide-eyed fans saw them grapple with the imposing Giants for the lead from Opening Day to well past the Fourth of July, and then move outs to a safe-seeming margin in August. Up to mid-September, the Phils' record was almost identical to that of the 1950 Whiz Kids from Philly, but there was less to explain the fine performance in '64. Their pitching, led by Jim Bunning and Chris Short, was only average, and their offense amounted to little beyond a pair of bombastic young hitters named Richie Allen and Johnny Callison. Gene Mauch managed the team—perhaps that was the explanation.

On Sunday evening, September 20th, the Phillies were 6½ lengths ahead of the Reds and Cardinals, 30 games over .500, and wondering who their World Series opponents would be—for a change, the AL had a close pennant race. Coming off a break-even road trip to Houston and Los Angeles, they started a seven-game home stand by getting blanked by the Reds on Monday. On the next two nights, Short and his teammate Dennis Bennett were beaten by the Reds, who now were only 3½ games behind. Thursday, the Milwaukee Braves came to town for a four-game series. In the first of these, they beat Bunning, 5-3; on Friday, they pulled out a 12-inning contest, 7-5; Saturday, the Braves came from behind with three runs in the ninth to beat Bobby Shantz, 6-4; and on Sunday they beat Bunning again, knocking him out this time in a 22-hit barrage, 14-8. By that time, the Phillies were in second place, a game bahind the Reds, who had won five more in a row over the Mets that weekend.

Then the staggering Phillies had to travel to St. Louis for three games against the Cards, who were also in a winning streak. Three more losses for the Mauchman: Bob Gibson beat Short on Monday, Ray Sadecki beat Bennett on Tuesday, and

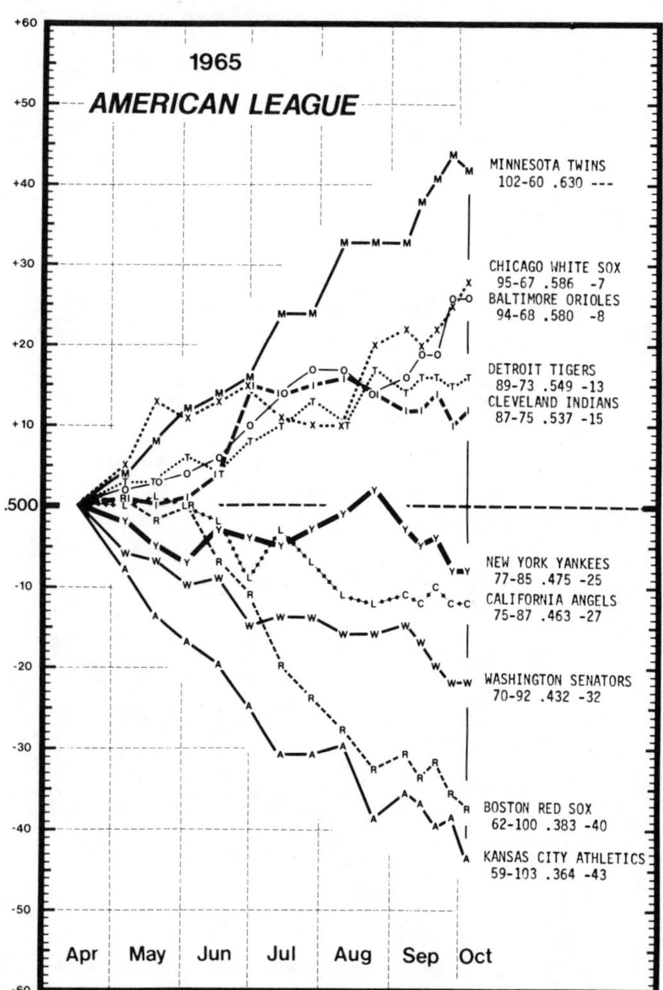


Curt Simmons beat Bunning on Wednesday, and with these victories the Cardinals put themselves into first place. For the bleeding Phillies, that ended what had become the worst late-season collapse by a frontrunner in the modern era.

The Phils still had some work left on Friday, October 2nd: in their two remaining games at Cincinnati, they could at least play the spoiler's role against the Reds, and tie for second place in the process. For that matter, if by some miracle the Cards lost all three of their games against the last-place Mets that final weekend, the Phillies could end in a three-way tie for first place, and if the uncomfortalby-close Giants should sweep their final series with the Cubs, it could be a four-way tie!

The Mets did, in fact, come close to creating a three-way deadlock by shutting out the Cardinals on Friday and creaming them, 15-5, on Saturday, because Philadelphia won its last two at Cincinnati. But Bob Gibson pulled the Cards through on Sunday in an 11-5 win over the Mets at Busch Stadium. Bunning's 10-0 shutout over Cincinnati of that closing day was the knockout blow for the Reds, who had already been jolted the previous month by manager Fred Hutchinson's cancer diagnosis and abrupt departure because of the illness. The Cubs prevented the Giants from joining the Phils and Reds in the second-place tie.

After Ralph Houk's third straight pennant, the Yankees moved him up to the general managership and installed Yogi Berra as the 1964 field manager. The transition from teammate-and-friend to taskmaster wasn't easy for a man of his temperament, and in August, when the Yanks were in danger of fading out of the heated pennant race, opinion mounted that Berra was too palsy-walsy to run the tight ship a pennant drive demanded. But when Yogi read the riot act to reserve infielder Phil Linz for playing his harmonica on the team bus around that time, the team discovered they had a boss after all, so goes the story, and they then made a concerted run for the title.

This account of how the Yankees snapped out of their doldrums and streaked past the Orioles and White Sox to win the '64 AL pennant is not the only possible explanation, and it doesn't tell us how the Yanks managed in July to sustain a winning pace equal to their 22-and-6 record of September. Other possibilities include the fact that a rookie pitcher, Mel Stottlemyre, came up from the minors in August to win nine games, and the fact that Mickey Mantle returned from a leg injury to provide more offensive punch in September. Whatever the case, Berra's severest critics were evidently in the Yankee management, and when his team lost the World Series to the Cardinals, he was dismissed in favor of Johnny Keane, who had masterminded those same Cardinals to the world championship.

The '64 White Sox, still managed by Al Lopez, may have been every bit as strong as the Go-Go flagwinners of '59. They had five regular pitchers with ERAs under 3.00, namely, 20-game-winner Gary Peters, 19-gamer Juan Pizzaro, 40-year-old reliever Hoyt Wilhelm, and the comparatively youthful Joe Horlen and John Buzhardt. Baltimore also had good pitching, led by Wally Bunker (19-5), Milt Pappas, ex-Phil Robin Roberts, and ex-Giant relief artist Stu Miller, and manager Hank Bauer's offensive capabilities were increased by the arrival of Boog Powell, who hit 39 homers.

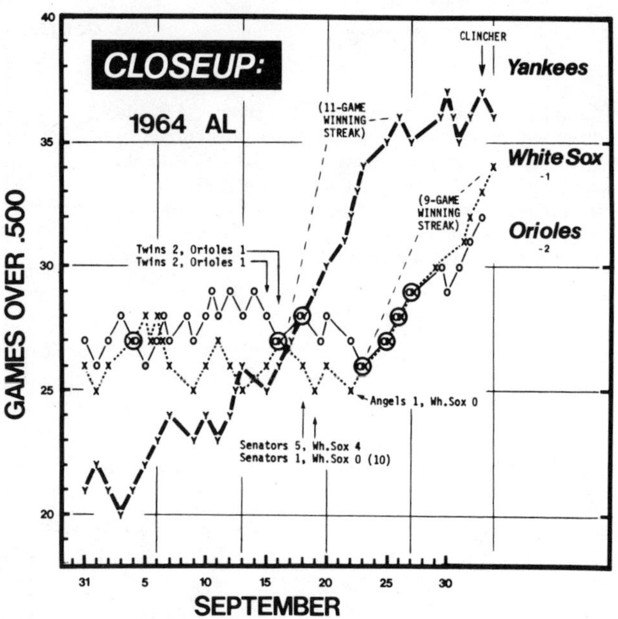


**BERRA'S BUDDIES. In his single year as manager of the Yankees, popular Yogi Berra was often accused of being too much a pal, and not enough a boss, of his players to earn their full respect. But in September of 1964 Berra's bunch swept to a typical Yankee flag victory with an 11-game winning streak. After key losses by the Orioles to the Twins and by the White Sox to the Senators and Angeles, Baltimore and Chicago couldn't catch New York even with finishing streaks of their own. The pennant win was the Yankees' 15th in 18 years, but it would be a dozen years until their next.**

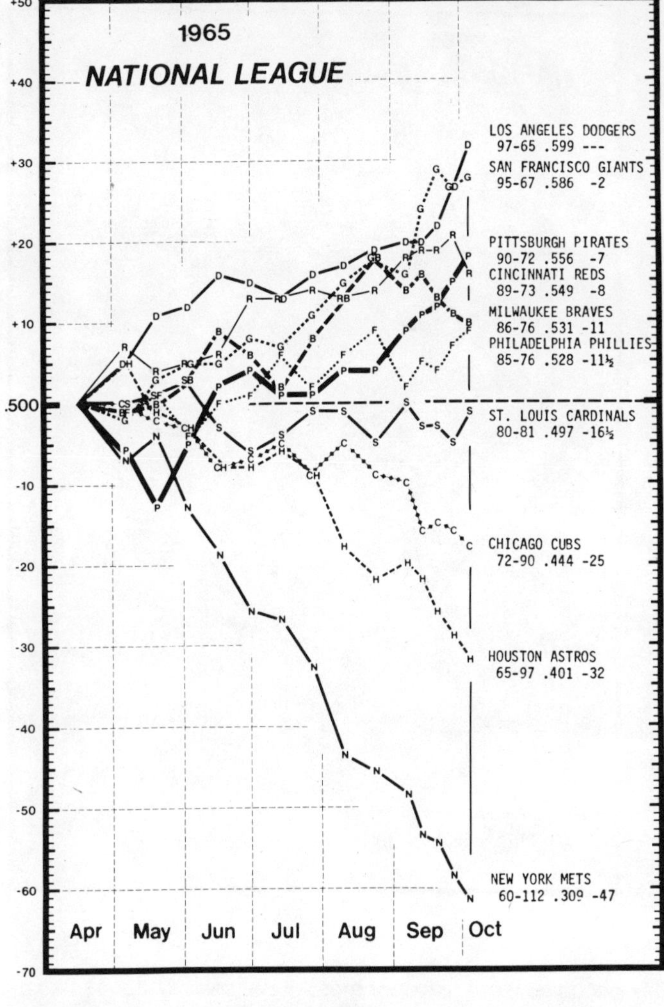


## 1965

When it came, the crumbling of the Yankee dynasty seemed sudden. As with some instant pennant-contenders who find all their regulars having good years together, everything can go in the reverse direction all at once. Johnny Keane's 1965 Yankees batted only .235, were only fifth-best in team ERA, had a slew of injuries and a weak bench, were hit by the ravages of age, and the New York organization even became ordinary in its farm system's productivity. Result: sixth place in 1965 and an unbelievable tenth place the following year.

The Minnesota Twins, piloted by Sam Mele, rushed into the room at the top vacated by the Yankees, and held a seven-game lead from early August to the season's end. Minnesota's long-ball output was well below their previous year's, when they socked 221 homers, partly because Harmon Killebrew was sidelined with an elbow injury for a third of the season, but with Tony Oliva's league-leading bat (.321) and other clouters such as MVP Zoilo Versalles, Bob Allison, Don Mincher, and Jimmie Hall, they didn't lack hitting. The team was well-balanced, with strong mound efforts by Mudcat Grant (21-7), Jim Kaat, and relief specialist Al Worthington.

In the National League, the main story was the scintillating mound duo of the Dodgers. The southpaw, Sandy Koufax, won 26 games, and the northpaw, Don Drysdale, won 23; Koufax also led the NL with his 2.04 ERA and record strikeout total of 382, and only one other hurler in the league, San Francisco's Juan Marichal (a 22-game-winner) pitched more shutouts. Marichal himself made headlines on August 22nd when he clubbed Dodger catcher Johnny Roseboro in the head with a bat. He drew a stiff fine and nine-day suspension for this misbehavior, and the one or two pitching victories which the Giants missed because of his suspension may have cost them the pennant, considering how close the Dodger-Giant battle became in September (see closeup).

Other headlines of the year were concerned with the Milwaukee franchise, whose management was at war with the local citizenry and city fathers in a public-relations disaster after the Braves announced their intention to move to Atlanta because of declining attendance. Amidst the year-long wrangling, the Braves' team played well, nearly taking the league lead in August, before a late-season fade. Pittsburgh was an equally Interesting Nonwinner, putting on a hitting show by Clemente, Virdon, and the younger Willie Stargell and Donn Clendenon that elevated the Pirates from last place in May to a surprise finish in third place. The Cincinnati Reds, nosed out of third by the Bucs in the final week, were even stronger at the plate with Pete Rose, Gordy Coleman, Vada Pinson, Frank Robinson, Deron Johnson, and Tommy Harper all displaying extra-base production.

After pitching the Dodgers to another pennant, Koufax and Drysdale carried them through a World Series victory over the Twins, but not until after they were both beaten by Minnesota in the first two games. Four-hit and three-hit blankings of the Twins by Koufax later made the difference in the seven-game struggle.

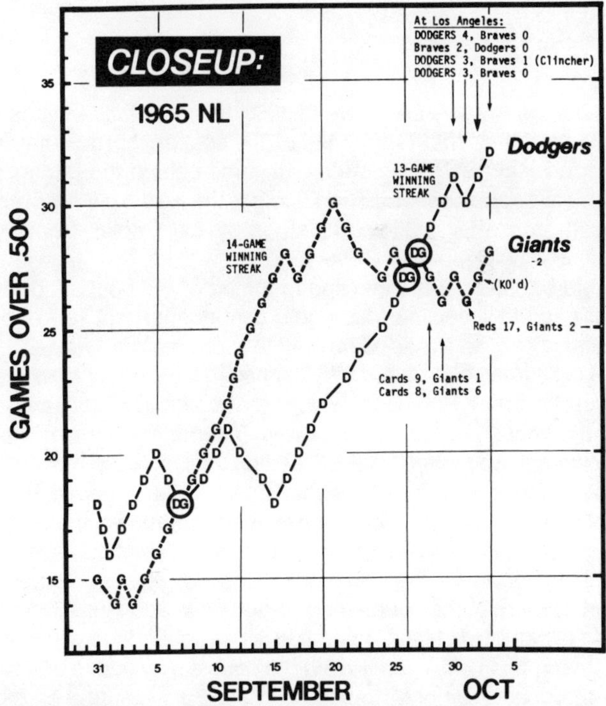


**A DODGER BLUE STREAK, 13 games long, in the last two weeks of September 1965 didn't quite match the 14-game winning streak by the Giants the week before, but it was better-timed for winning the pennant. While Sandy Koufax and Don Drysdale kept LA's streak going in the final week, the Giants dropped out of a tie with the Dodgers by losing two crucial games to the Cardinals and then getting slaughtered, 17-2, by the Reds in San Francisco on the final Friday. The next day, Koufax's 3-1 victory over the Braves in Dodger Stadium clinched the flag. Earlier, on the 9th of September, the great lefthander had pitched a perfect game against the Cubs.**

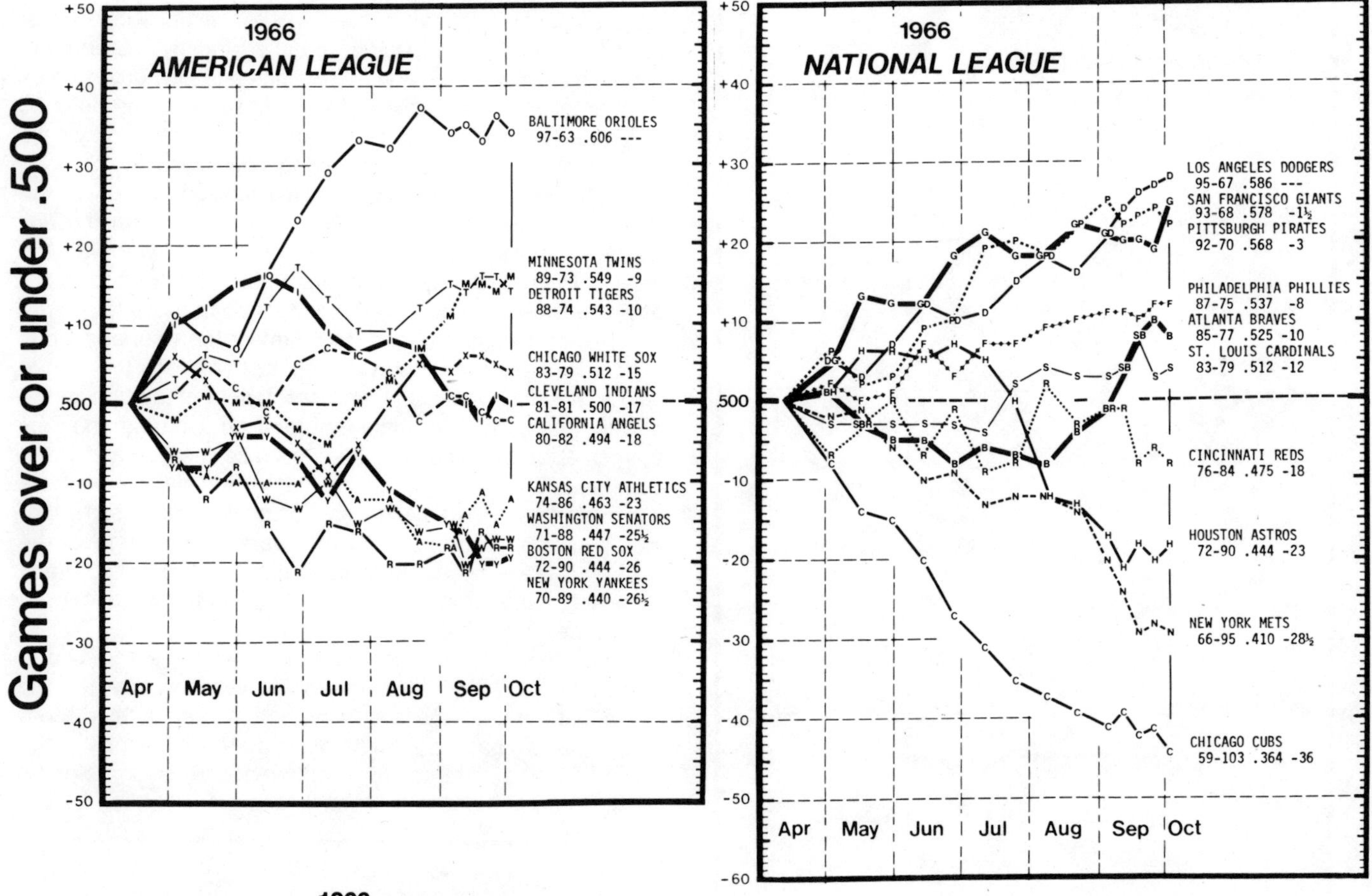


## 1966

Like the Brooklyn Dodgers of 1955, the Cleveland Indians of 1966 won their first ten games of the season, but two games later on May 1st, they were a half-game behind the Baltimore Orioles' 12-and-1 record. The Tribe got the lead back for over a month, but after a 35-and-12 surge by the Orioles from Memorial Day to July 9th, everyone knew who the flagwinner would be. Cleveland's fine spring turned out to be the Indians' last gasp in a decline that would continue (except for a brief moment of glory in mid-1974) until the spring of 1981.

The Orioles had traded Milt Pappas to Cincinnati in an even swap for Frank Robinson, which went down in history as one of the most uneven swaps when Robinson won the Triple Crown and was voted MVP for leading the Orioles to a pennant (Pappas was 12-11, 4.29 for the Reds and later traded to Atlanta). Besides Robinson, whose magic numbers were .316, 39, and 122, Baltimore had distance hitting from third baseman Brooks Robinson, first baseman Boog Powell, and outfielder Curt Blefary. Other outfielders, Paul Blair and Russ Snyder, also hit well, and Hank Bauer had an airtight infield with Dave Johnson and Luis Aparicio and the double-play duo in addition to the superb Brooks Robinson. Wally Bunker, Steve Barber, and Stu Miller still pitched well, but the mound staff was now headed by youngsters Jim Palmer (15-10) and Dave McNally (13-6), and was much strengthened in the latter part of the season by Eddie Fisher's move to the Orioles from the White Sox, This aggregation of mound skill amazed the baseball world in the '66 World Series by sweeping the Dodgers, allowing only two runs and 17 hits over the four games, and outpitching Koufax and Drysdale.

Down at the lower end of the AL standings, the Boston Red Sox occupied tenth place for most of the season, but as usual were beaten out by the Yankees in September, in the fourth-closest race for last place of the modern period. The Yanks did it in the aging of Mantle, Maris, and Howard (.288, .233, and .256); injuries to Kubek, Ford, and Bouton; and an off-year by Mel Stottlemyer, who lost 20 games after winning 20 the year before.

In the National League, Koufax's 27-9, 1.73-ERA season was nearly matched by Marichal's 25-6, 2.23 statistics, and another tight pennant race reflected this small difference, as the Dodgers finished only a game and a half in front of the Giants. Both clubs had excellent #2 starters, Claude Osteen (17-14) for LA (Drysdale dropped off to 13-16) and Gaylord Perry (21-8) for San Francisco, and relief aces, Phil Regan (14-1, 21 saves) for the Dodgers and Frank Linzy (7-11, 16 saves) for the Giants. Neither team hit much for average, but the Giants were far superior in slugging, as Mays, McCovey, and Jim Ray Hart each blasted over 30 homers. The league's best hitting was at Pittsburgh, where now the Pirates had batting leader Matty Alou (.342). Manny Mota (.332), and Gene Alley (.299) abetting the prodigious outputs of Clemente and Stargell; the Bucs' offense kept them in the thick of the pennant race all season long.

## 1967

In the spring, the American League's 1967 season contained few hints of its historic conclusion. At a time when most clubs in the league might have been in a buoyant mood now that

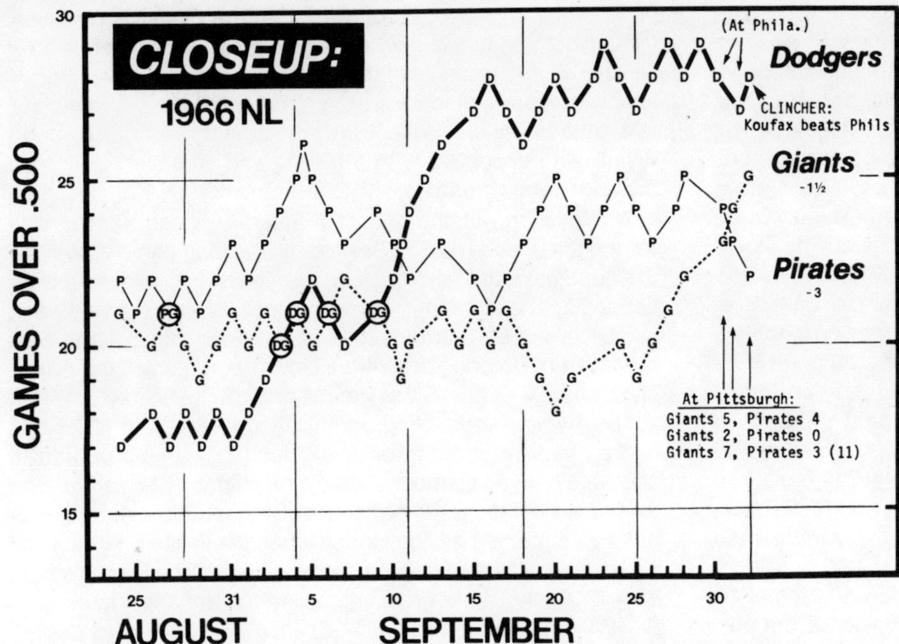


**SANDY'S SWAN SONG.** THe last regular-season game and last victory for Hall of Famer Sandy Koufax came on October 2, 1966, when he beat the Phillies, 6-3, at Philadelphia. That year Koufax led the Dodgers to the NL pennant for the third time in four years. The superb southpaw's win on the closing day was a crucial one for Los Angeles—if the Dodgers had lost that game, the Giants could have tied them for the title by winning a pending makeup game against the Reds. After one more appearance, in Game 2 of the 1966 World Series, Koufax was forced to retire at age 30 because of arthritis in his left elbow. In his last season he had won the league's ERA title for the fifth straight eyar.

the great weight of Yankee domination had been lifted, few teams seemed capable of winning over half their games, let alone a pennant. The new champions, the Orioles, suddenly had a severe shortage of pitching—Jim Palmer developed a sore arm, and nobody on the mound staff cvould win consistently—and Baltimore was off in its hitting as well. The previous winner, Minnesota, was spending the first month of the season in last place. Only the White Sox and Tigers had a good start, and by late June it looked as though Detroit was going to let Chicago have its pennant without a fuss.

Just before the All-Star break, though, the Tigers snapped out of their slump, and the Twins, who had acquired Dean Chance from the Angels over the winter, were up from tenth place, threatening to grab the runnerup position. The Angels

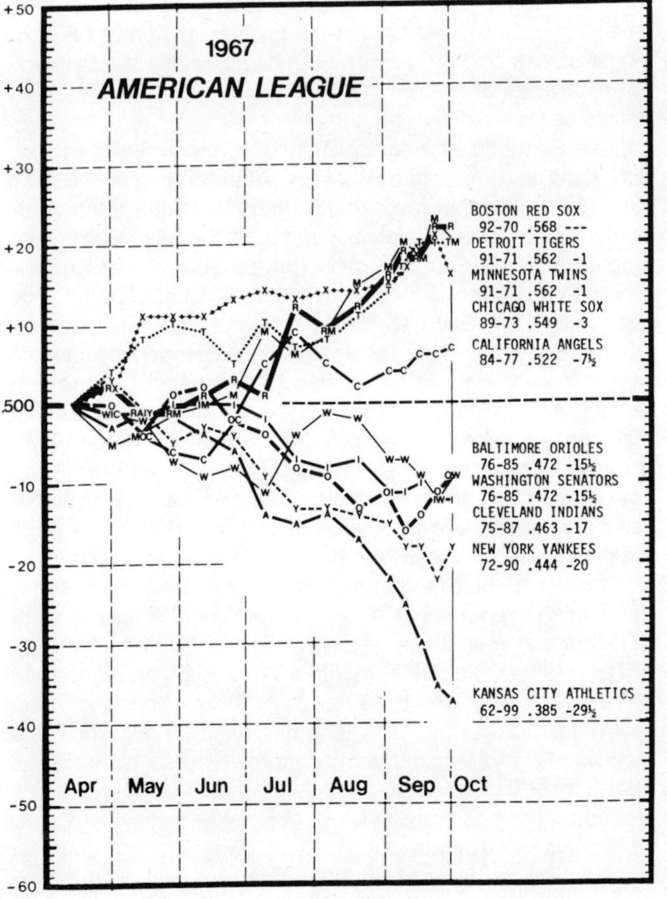


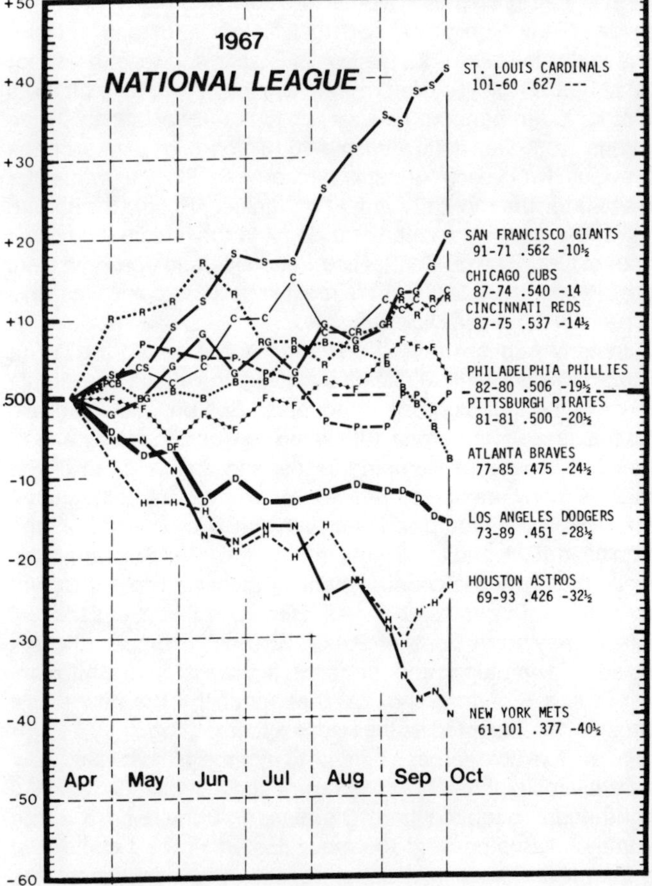

themselves had come alive also, vaulting from seventh to fourth. Detroit still had Kaline and Cash for muscle, now assisted by some able younger men, Dick McAuliffe at second, Willie Horton and Jim Northrop in the outfield, and Bill Freehan as catcher; Earl Wilson, Denny McLain, Mickey Lolich, Joe Sparma, and Fred Gladding made up the pitching core. Minnesota had the strong infield of Killebrew, Rod Carew, Versalles, and Rollins, and just as solid an outfield with Oliva, Allison, and Ted Uhlaender, plus good fill-in work by Cesar Tovar at several positions; besides Chance, Kaat and Worthington were still pitching well, as was 22-year-old Dave Boswell. The White Sox, as usual, were riding high on pitching, defense, and fielding—they had not a single regular who hit above .241 that season; on the hill, Tommy John had joined the regular rotation with Peters and Horlen, and the bullpen was stronger from Bob Locker's fine relief work added to Wilhelm's. By comparison to Chicago at least, California had some offense, with Jim Fregosi, Don Mincher, and Rick Reichardt, but as events proved, not enough else to stay in the race after July.

After the All-Star break, there was a sudden newcomer to the race—the Boston Red Sox, ninth-place finishers the previous year and 100-1 shots for the '67 pennant. On Sunday, July 23rd, the Red Sox capped a ten-game winning streak by beating the Indians twice in Cleveland. Stunningly, Boston was in second place, only a half-game behind Chicago. Who were these guys?

One of them was Carl Yastrzemski, who had shown he could fill Ted Williams' shoes in left field pretty well when he won the batting title in 1963 and was second in the league's batting in 1965; Yaz had not displayed a great deal of power hitting in his first six AL seasons, but in the Cleveland doubleheader he had just hit his 24th homer of 1967. Another Boston outfielder, Tony Conigliaro, had just hit his 16th and 17th, in line with his total of 28 the previous year and league-leading 32 at age 20 the year before that. One of the winning pitchers that day, Jim Lonborg, now was up to a 14-3 record; this marvelous work was following his 10-10 and 9-17 marks of the previous two years. Another pitcher, Lee Stange, would be 5-and-0 for the month of July. Two rookies, Reggie Smith and Mike Andrews, were clearly making it in the majors, and other youngsters, George Scott, Rico Petrocelli, and Joe Foy, were having good seasons. But the most important rookie was Boston's new manager, Dick Williams.

In early August the Red Sox sagged, but so did the White Sox and Tigers; with Minnesota winning, the effect was simply to bring the four clubs closer together. Boston lost Conigliaro for the season on August 18th when he was beaned by a fastball, but instead of slumping further and dropping out of the race as many predicted, the Red Sox won 12 out of 15 games and took over first place. As with the Braves in 1914, the Robins in 1924, and the Giants in 1951, new Red Sox fans were created all over the country, many of them turning out to root for the team in its road games. Hundreds and thousands of miles away from Fenway Park, "Go Sox!" bumper stickers could be seen along the interstate highways, and a hit number from a Broadway musical that summer, "The Impossible Dream," was adopted as the Red Sox theme song.

New Red Sox heroes seemed to emerge almost daily, too, as Williams plugged holes with new acquisitions. Gary Bell, a righthander, acquired from Cleveland in June, won a dozen games for Boston after the move. Elston Howard came over from the Yankees in August to steady things behind the plate, and Jerry Adair, purchased from the White Sox in June, filled in at three infield spots and delivered clutch hits one after another. Some more key hits were contributed by Ken Harrelson, who was signed as a free agent in August. Meanwhile, two other pitchers were turning into stars—reliever John Wyatt, who ended up with ten wins and 20 saves, and Jose Santiago, who wound up with a 12-4 record.

A mini-slump at the end of August, in which Yastrzemski went o-for-18 and the Red Sox lost a 20-inning game at Yankee Stadium, gave the lead back to the Twins. But two days after Labor Day the standings showed, amazingly, a four-way tie in games over .500 and only .001 separating Chicago and Minnesota from Boston and Detroit. Now it was official: the American League was having the greatest race in its history.

The Twins were getting another good year from Killebrew, had a pleasant surprise on the mound in young Jim Merritt, and were bouyed up most of all by the pitching of Chance, who tossed a no-hitter at Cleveland on August 25th. Another no-hitter was pitched by Joe Horlen when the White Sox beat the Tigers on the 10th of September; Horlen had the league's best ERA (2.06) that year. The biggest factor for the Tigers was Earl Wilson's hurling; he finished with a 22-11 record.

The race was not much closer to being resolved on September 18th, when Detroit, Minnesota, and Boston were tied and Chicago was only a half-game behind. It was a four-way free-for-all until well into the final week. in fact. The first drop-out finally came when the White Sox lost twice to the Kansas City Athletics on Wednesday the 27th, starting what proved to be a terminal five-game losing streak. Going into the last two days of the season, the Twins held a one-game lead with 91-69, over the Red Sox (90-70) and the Tigers (89-69). The Tigers had two doubleheaders against California left to play at Detroit. The Twins and Red Sox, in another theatrical flourish by the schedule-maker, faced each other at Fenway Park in single games on Saturday and Sunday. Besides the standing-room crowds at Fenway, millions more watched the two games on national television.

Jose Santiago started for Boston against 16-game-winner Jim Kaat in the Saturday game. After getting a 1-0 lead, Kaat had to retire in favor of Jim Perry in the third inning because of an elbow problem. In the fifth inning, Jerry Adair singled in Reggie Smith to tie the game, and Yaz drove in pinchhitter Dalton Jones with another single, putting the Sox ahead, 2-1. Each team got one more tally in the sixth, George Scott homering for Boston off reliever Ron Kline. Jim Merritt was brought in by Minnesota's manager Cal Ermer to replace Kline in the bottom of the seventh, after the Red Sox put two on with none out, and Yaz greeted Merritt with a three-run blast into the right-field bullpen. This blow, Yaz's 44th of the year, proved to be the game-winner when Harmon Killebrew delivered a two-run shot off Gary Bell in the ninth, making the final score 6-4. Killebrew's was also #44, tying Yaz for the home run championship but not depriving him of the Triple Crown, which he earned with a .326 average and 121 RBIs that year.

The Red Sox win put them into a 91-70 tie for first place with the Twins, going into the final day. Mickey Lolich shut out the Angels for Detroit, but Claifornia rallied for six runs in the eighth inning to win the second game of their twin bill, 8-6. That left the Tigers a half-game behind with 90-70, but still in a position to tie Sunday's winner at Fenway if they could beat the Angels twice on the closing day.

In Boston the fever of the fans rose to a pitch well beyond

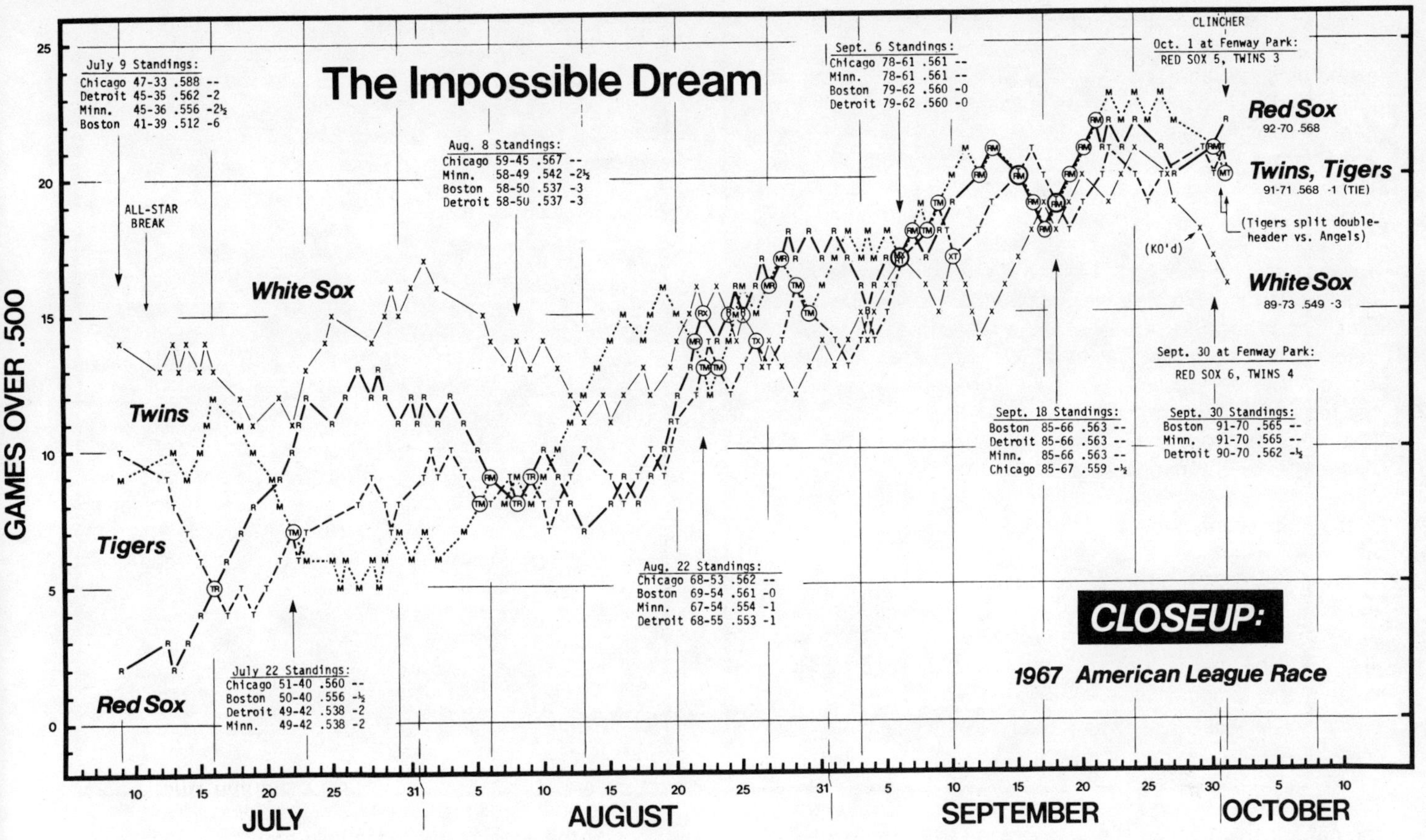


**THE LONGEST HOTTEST SUMMER. The ultimate mind-boggler of pennant races, the '67 AL chase became an exciting four-team affair with a win streak by the Red Sox right after the All-Star break, then incredibly grew tighter week by week. The winner was not decided until the final hour of the closing day, October 1st, when the Detroit Tigers lost the nightcap of a doubleheader to California, giving the gonfalon to the Twin-killing Red Sox.**

the levels of 1948 and 1949, and especially avid was a whole new generation of Red Sox fans who had never experienced a pennant victory. To enhance the already-electric atmosphere of the Sunday showdown, the American League's two best pitchers—Jim Lonborg and Dean Chance—faced each other, each having reached the charmed circle of 20-game winners. This final thriller began with Minnesota runs in the first and third, and Chance carried his 2-0 lead into the seventh. Lonborg led off with an astonishing bunt single, and two more singles by Adair and Jones loaded the bases for Yaz. He promptly drilled a two-run single over second base, tying the score. Then came another of those critical mental errors: shortstop Zoilo Versalles took Ken Harrelson's grounder and made a futile peg to home plate trying to nail Jones, who beat the throw for the go-ahead run. Ermer waved in Al Worthington to replace Chance, who might have survived the inning only one run behind, if Harrelson and Yaz had been rubbed out in a feasible double play. Yaz scored the fourth Boston run on two wild pitches by Worthington after Scott struck out, and Harrelson came in with the fifth on an error by Killebrew.

The Twins made a strong bid to tie up the game in the next half-inning. With two out and two on, Bob Allison lined safely into the left-field corner—Yaz's territory. The front runner, Killebrew, scored, but Yastrzemski pulled a surprise: instead of throwing home to head off a second score, he fired the ball to second base, where the unspeedy Allison was caught coming into the bag, ending the inning. In the ninth, Lonborg allowed a leadoff single, but got Rod Carew to hit into a DP, and Rich Rollins to pop up to Petrocelli. The verdict was Boston 5, Minnesota 3, and with that final out, the fans mobbed the field in total delirium and delight, hoisting Lonborg on high.

Meanwhile, at Detroit, the Tigers won their first game and were leading the Angels in the second. The Red Sox players in their Fenway clubhouse sat in suspense listening to Tiger announcer Ernie Harwell's play-by-play, and began mental preparations for a trip to Detroit for a playoff. But California came through for them again, rallying late in the game to knock off the Tigers, 8-5. The title, free and clear, went to the Red Sox, and it would be the St. Louis Cardinals traveling to Boston in three days to open the World Series.

Yastrzemski's batting output in those two final games had included four other singles and a double in addition to his game-winning homer on Saturday and game-tying single on Sunday—he was seven-for-eight over the two days—and this was just part of what he had done in the season's late stages to bring the pennant to Boston. Over the last ten games, he had gone 20-for-37 (.541) with 13 RBIs, and over the last month, 40-for-96 (.417) with 25 RBIs. In at least ten games won by the Red Sox in that month, he was the batting star or co-star. Probably no other batter in modern major league history has made so many clutch hits or played so decisive a role in the stretch run of a closely-fought pennant race as Yaz did in 1967.

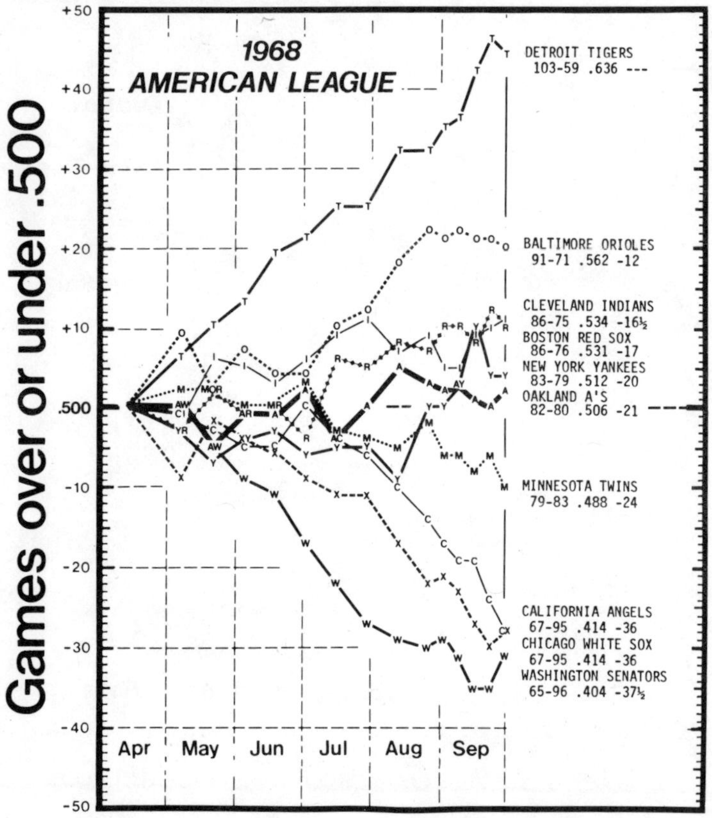

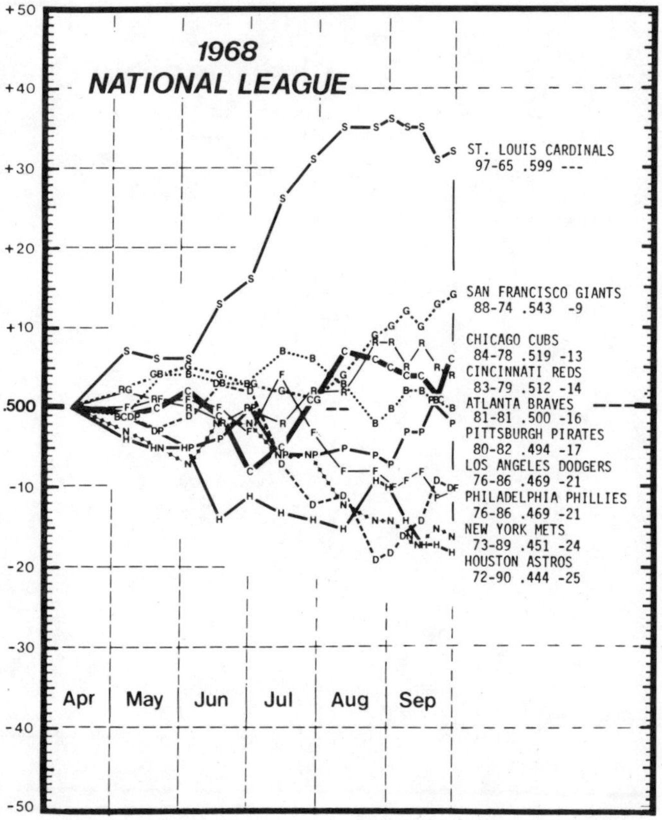

Games over or under .500
1968
AMERICAN LEAGUE
DETROIT TIGERS
103-59 .636 ---
BALTIMORE ORIOLES
91-71 .562 -12
CLEVELAND INDIANS
86-75 .534 -16½
BOSTON RED SOX
86-76 .531 -17
NEW YORK YANKEES
83-79 .512 -20
OAKLAND A'S
82-80 .506 -21
MINNESOTA TWINS
79-83 .488 -24
CALIFORNIA ANGELS
67-95 .414 -36
CHICAGO WHITE SOX
67-95 .414 -36
WASHINGTON SENATORS
65-96 .404 -37½
Apr
May
Jun
Jul
Aug
Sep

1968
NATIONAL LEAGUE
ST. LOUIS CARDINALS
97-65 .599 ---
SAN FRANCISCO GIANTS
88-74 .543 -9
CHICAGO CUBS
84-78 .519 -13
CINCINNATI REDS
83-79 .512 -14
ATLANTA BRAVES
81-81 .500 -16
PITTSBURGH PIRATES
80-82 .494 -17
LOS ANGELES DODGERS
76-86 .469 -21
PHILADELPHIA PHILLIES
76-86 .469 -21
NEW YORK METS
73-89 .451 -24
HOUSTON ASTROS
72-90 .444 -25
Apr
May
Jun
Jul
Aug
Sep

The diagram below (from *Baseball Graphics*) shows Yaz's day-by-day batting over the month in relation to Boston's wins and losses; the white-numbered black rectangles represent his home runs, the black-numbered and smaller rectangles indicate doubles, the shaded squares stand for singles, and the "O" symbols are for hitless days.

SEPTEMBER, 1967: YAZ!
TOTAL BASES
RBI
W L L L W W - W L W W - W W - L L L W W W W L W L W - L L - - W W ! !

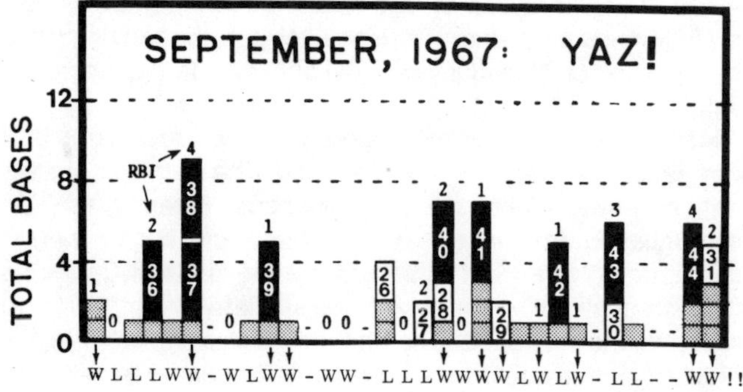

The National League had a change of leadership that year, as the period of domination by the Los Angeles Dodgers was over for awhile and the team to beat became the St. Louis Cardinals. Red Schoendienst had replaced Johnny Keane at the helm after the Cards' surprise pennant in '64, and spent two frustrating years ending in seventh and sixth places. But with Orlando Cepeda's move from the Giants to the Cards during the '66 season and the maturing of outfielders Curt Flood and Lou Brock, the keystone combination of Julian Javier and Dal Maxvill, and catcher Tim McCarver, Schoendienst had a good-hitting, slick-fielding club in 1967. He also had an abundance of pitching talent that had developed well, including Nelson Briles, Dick Hughes, Steve Carlton, and Joe Hoerner to back up the authentic superstar, Bob Gibson. This mound was strong enough, in fact, to withstand the loss of Gibson for the second half of the season, after he suffered a broken leg from a line drive hit by Roberto Clemente in July.

The Redbirds had little competition in the race after July, and with Cepeda's .325 and MVP performance leading the club, the Cards cruised to a 10½-game victory margin. Up until the latter part of July, however, they were challenged by a rejuvenated Chicago Cubs team. The Cubs, now under Leo Durocher's tutelage, had an aging superstar, Ernie Banks, who had led the club since the mid-fifties, a young pitcher, Ferguson Jenkins, who in 1967 was enjoying the first of many 20-game-winning seasons, and another veteran power hitter, Billy Williams.

Unfortunately for the Red Sox, Gibson's leg healed in time for him to pitch 2-1, 6-0, and 7-2 victories in the World Series, which sealed Boston's doom. Star performances were also turned in by Lou Brock, Yastrzemski, and Lonborg in the seven-game classic.

## 1968

The new world champs won an easier pennant in 1968, with the benefit of a full—and spectacular—season's work by Gibson. He pitched 13 shutouts, won 22 games, and had a sizzling 1.12 ERA, lowest in the majors since the marks of Dutch Leonard of the 1914 Red Sox and Three Finger Brown of the 1906 Chicago Cubs. Gibson and Detroit's Denny McLain, who with a 31-6 record became the first (and only) 30-game-winner since Dizzy Dean in 1934, were emblematic of what was called the Year of the Pitcher, when batting averages sank to the lowest level of the lively-ball era. McLain, joined by Mickey Lolich (17-9), led the Tigers to their first pennant in 23 years; Willie Horton was Detroit's main offensive

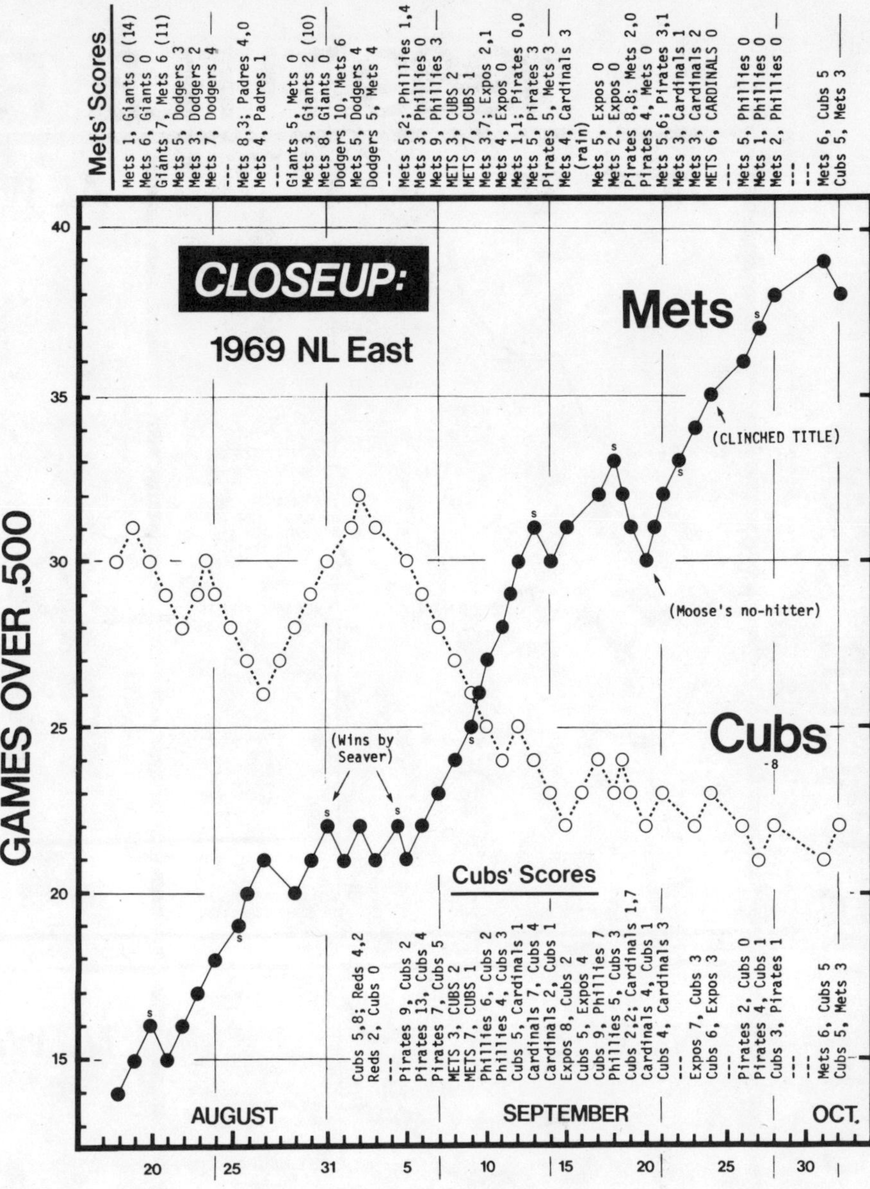


**THE MIRACULOUS METamorphosis shown by the New York NL expansion team in 1969 ranked historically with the 1914 Miracle Braves and outranked the 1967 Red Sox in the size of a come-from-behind. Led by Tom Seaver's superlative pitching, the '69 Mets not only overcame a 9½-game lead by the Chicago Cubs but won 100 games, finishing at 38 games over .500, after a 1968 season in which they ended up 18 games below .500 and many earlier seasons in the NL cellar.**

weapon with 36 homers. In the World Series, however, it was Lolich's three complete-game victories that led the Bengals to an unexpected defeat of the Cardinals.

The Tigers were the only 1967 contender that managed to win consistently in 1968. Although Yastrzemski's .301 average won him another batting title, the Red Sox got the bad news from the ski slopes between seasons that Jim Lonborg had broken his leg. The Twins' Jim Kaat developed a sore arm, and Tommy John's shoulder injury was part of Chicago's downfall in pitching. Cleveland, on the other hand, got above the .500 level on the fine pitching of Luis Tiant (21-9, 1.60 ERA) and Sam McDowell (283 strikeouts, 1.81 ERA). The Orioles benefited from good hurling by Dave McNally (22-10), and also got an apparent boost when Earl Weaver replaced Hank Bauer as manager at midseason.

The most interesting AL team was in Oakland, where Athletics owner Charlie Finley had moved his team during the winter. On the strength of 22-year-old Reggie Jackson's hitting (29 home runs), Bert Campaneris's basestealing, a league-leading team batting average (of only .240), and some good pitching by youngsters Blue Moon Odom, Catfish Hunter, and Jim Nash, the A's moved from tenth to sixth place.

## 1969

The two major leagues split into East and West Divisions in 1969, with the addition of four new franchises. The American League added the Kansas City Royals and Seattle pilots, the latter becoming the Milwaukee Brewers in 1970. The National League added the Montreal Expos and the San Diego Padres, the latter setting a new NL record for trailing the next-to-last team by finishing 29 games behind the fifth-place Houston Astros.

It was a summer of amazements—the Moon Landing, Chappaquiddick, Woodstock—and the Mets. The team that had been a subject of amusement rather than amazement in its first seven years became the Amazing Mets, in a theatrical setting that rivaled those of the Miracle Braves of 1914, the Giants of 1951, or the Impossible Dream Team of '67.

The Mets had finished last in their first four years, ninth in 1966, but back to tenth in 1967. In 1968, however, when Gil Hodges took over as manager, their return to ninth place came with a fairly respectable .451 winning percentage that was only 16 games below .500—a far cry from the 80 games below .500 of their first year in 1962. And while their .228 team batting average had been the NL's worst, their team ERA had im-

# 1969 TITLE RACES

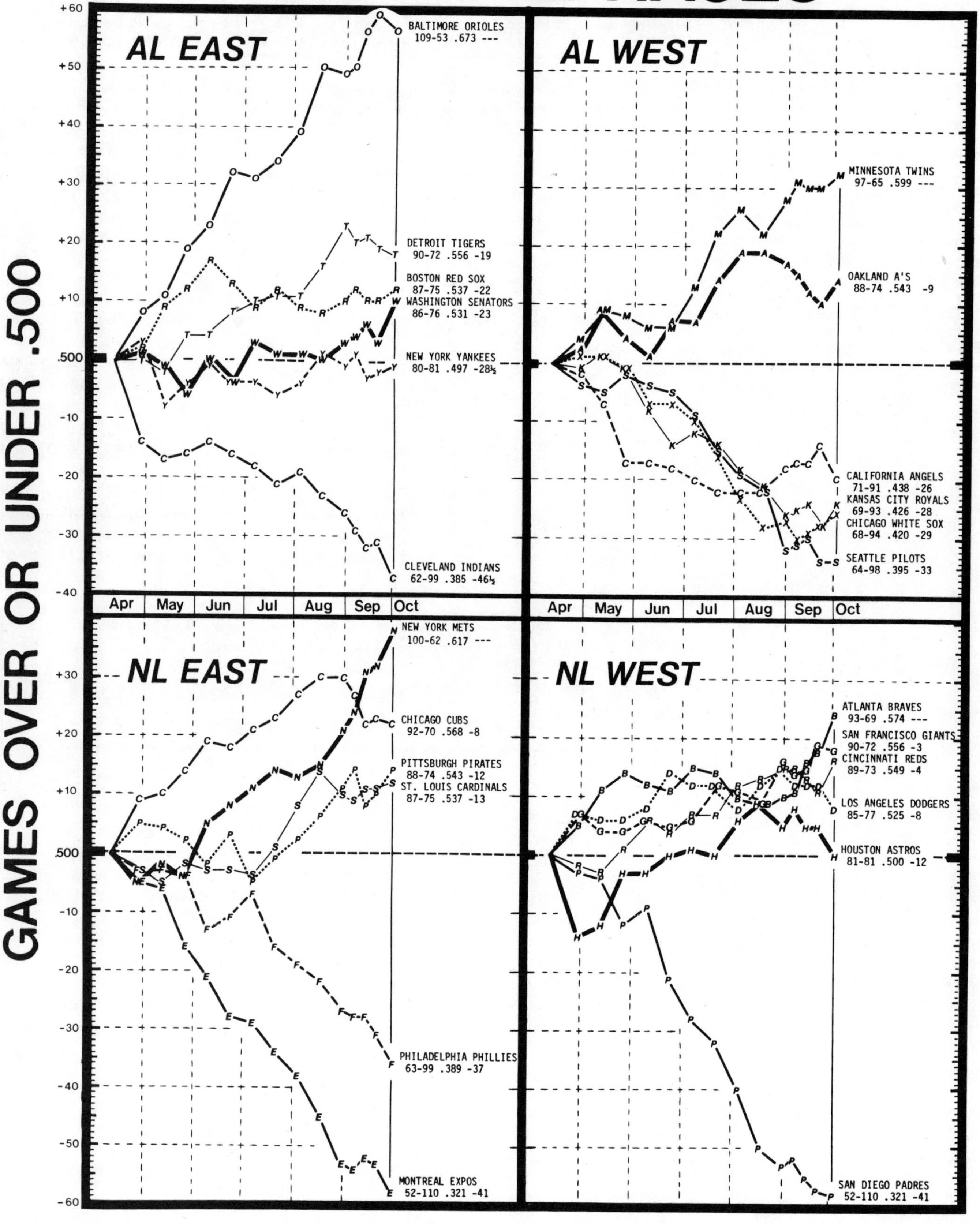

GAMES OVER OR UNDER .500

+60 +50 +40 +30 +20 +10 .500 -10 -20 -30 -40

## AL EAST

BALTIMORE ORIOLES 109-53 .673 ---

DETROIT TIGERS 90-72 .556 -19

BOSTON RED SOX 87-75 .537 -22

WASHINGTON SENATORS 86-76 .531 -23

NEW YORK YANKEES 80-81 .497 -28½

CLEVELAND INDIANS 62-99 .385 -46½

## AL WEST

MINNESOTA TWINS 97-65 .599 ---

OAKLAND A'S 88-74 .543 -9

CALIFORNIA ANGELS 71-91 .438 -26

KANSAS CITY ROYALS 69-93 .426 -28

CHICAGO WHITE SOX 68-94 .420 -29

SEATTLE PILOTS 64-98 .395 -33

Apr May Jun Jul Aug Sep Oct

+30 +20 +10 .500 -10 -20 -30 -40 -50 -60

## NL EAST

NEW YORK METS 100-62 .617 ---

CHICAGO CUBS 92-70 .568 -8

PITTSBURGH PIRATES 88-74 .543 -12

ST. LOUIS CARDINALS 87-75 .537 -13

PHILADELPHIA PHILLIES 63-99 .389 -37

MONTREAL EXPOS 52-110 .321 -41

## NL WEST

ATLANTA BRAVES 93-69 .574 ---

SAN FRANCISCO GIANTS 90-72 .556 -3

CINCINNATI REDS 89-73 .549 -4

LOS ANGELES DODGERS 85-77 .525 -8

HOUSTON ASTROS 81-81 .500 -12

SAN DIEGO PADRES 52-110 .321 -41

proved to 2.72, fourth-best, with excellent progress by young Jerry Koosman (19-12, 2.08) and Tom Seaver (16-12, 2.20).

In 1969 the Mets' hitting perked up with the blossoming of outfielder Cleon Jones, the reblooming of outfielder Tommy Agee, who had fallen into mediocrity after winning the AL's Rookie of the Year award in 1966, and the midseason acquisition of first baseman Donn Clendenon. And Seaver, at age 24, became a mound artist at the level of Gibson. The whole pitching staff, in fact, became better balanced with new bullpen strength added by rookie Tug McGraw (he wound up with nine wins and 12 saves, and the Mets' other main fireman, Ron Taylor, had nearly the same record). Perhaps most importantly, Hodges became a managerial virtuoso, working magic with platooning combinations, pinchhitting selections, and lineup changes, milking every drop from a roster of limited talent. He had a .215 hitter, Al Weis, and a .207 hitter, Ed Charles, sharing infield chores with Ken Boswell, Wayne Garrett, and Bud Harrelson (the latter becoming a regular shortstop later in the season). Art Shamsky, Rod Gaspar, and Ron Swoboda took turns in the outfield, and Ed Kranepool as well as Clendenon covered first base. Jerry Grote was the frontline catcher, frequently spelled by J.C. Martin.

In June, the Mets found themselves in second place, but well behind Durocher's Cubs, who looked like flagwinners this time. Besides Fergy Jenkins, Chicago now had another 20-gamer, Bill Hands, a third very able hurler in Ken Holtzman, and the ace reliever Phil Regan. Catching them was the sturdy Randy Hundley, and the Cubs now had a seasoned infield of Banks, Glenn Beckert, Don Kessinger, and the heavy-hitting Ron Santo. Besides the slugging BIlly Williams in the outfield, they had another long-ball hitter, Jim Hickman.

The Mets had reason to be encouraged, however, by their two meetings with the Cubs in July. In the first encounter, at Shea Stadium, Seaver set the first 25 Cub batters down in a row before losing the perfect no-hitter in the ninth, but nonetheless leading the Mets to a two-out-of-three edge in the series; in Chicago a week later they won another two of three, with Weis slamming two homers (his only two of the season). In early August the Cubs still led by 9½ games, but after the middle of that month the Mets turned into a steamroller. Seaver, at 15-7, became "Tom Terrific," launching a pitching streak in which he won his last ten starts, and he inspired the rest of the team members to play at their career-best. When the Cubs lost three straight to the Pirates at Wrigley Field on the weekend after Labor Day, the Mets drew to within 2½ games of the lead, as Durocher's crew headed for Shea Stadium for two crucial games.

The first of these, before 43,274 fans on Monday evening, September 8th, went to the Mets, 3-2, with Koosman beating Hands with a seven-hitter and Agee clubbing his 26th homer. The next evening, with 51,448 looking on, Seaver beat Jenkins with a five-hitter, 7-1, helped by Clendenon's 13th homer, and Shea became a scene of total bedlam. The Cubs' remaining half-game lead became a one-game deficit the following day, when Nolan Ryan, Jim McAndrew, and Ron Taylor pitched the Mets to a doubleheader sweep of the Expos. The following Saturday, Seaver completed a ten-game winning streak by the Mets with his 22nd victory at Pittsburgh, by which time the Cubs were 3½ lengths in arrears and psychologically beaten for the year. Except for a trio of losses to the Pirates at

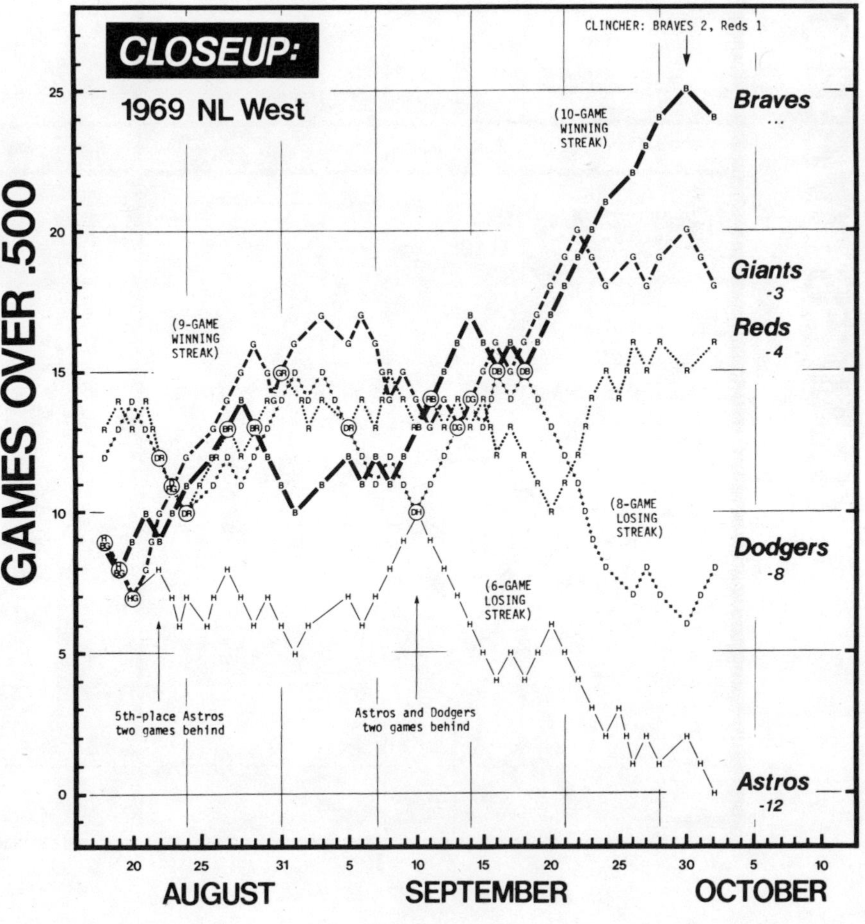


**HOW THE WEST WAS WON—by an easterner, the Atlanta Braves, in 1969. Five of the six teams in the newly-formed NL West division drew together into a virtual tie in August and September, creating the closest five-team race in the league's history to that point. But it was easily resolved in the final two weeks by Atlanta's ten-game winning streak, led by Hank Aaron, Orlando Cepeda, and Rico Carty.**

# 1970 TITLE RACES

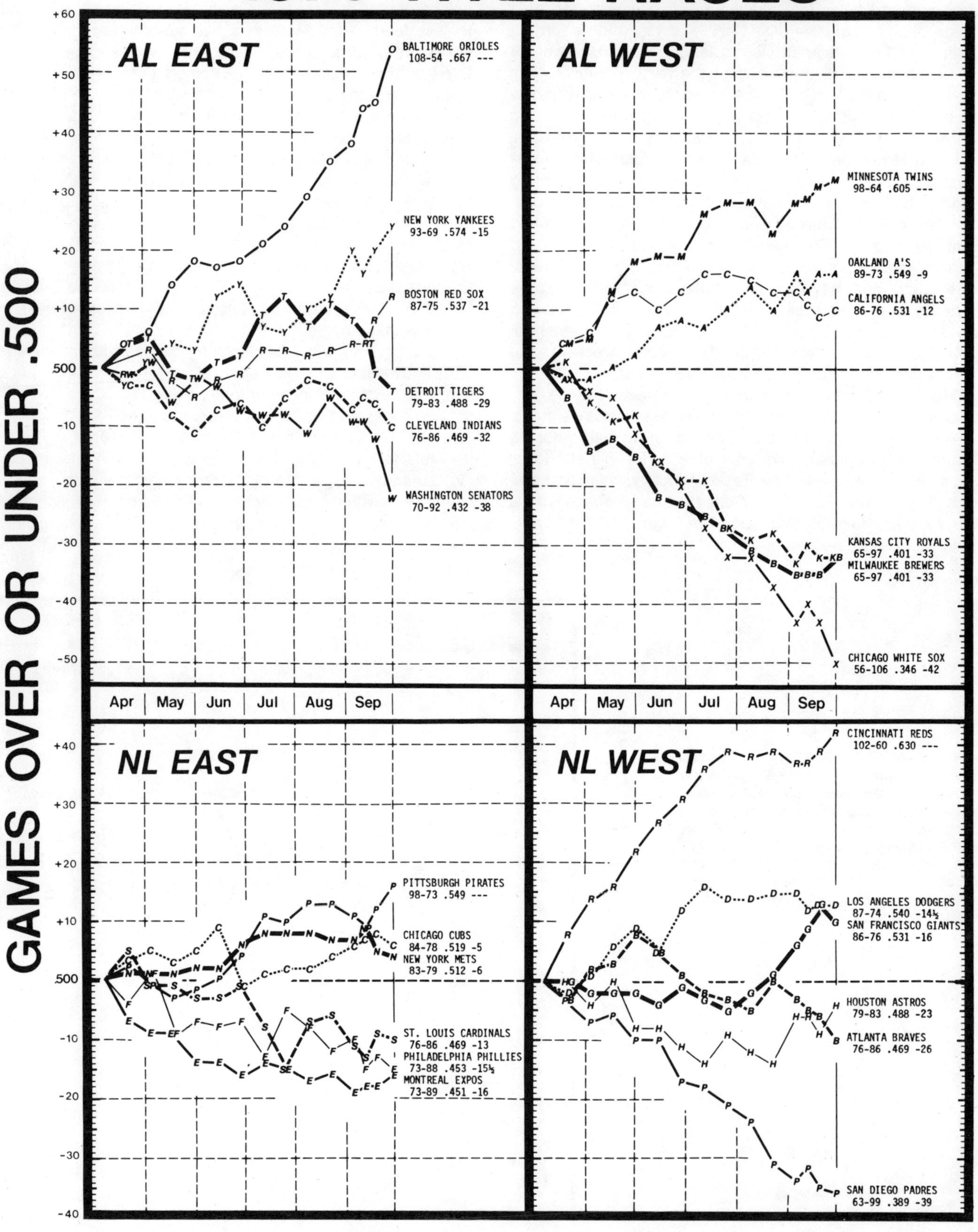

Shea on September 19th and 20th, in which Bob Moose threw a no-hitter, there was no letup by Hodges' men over the rest of the schedule.

Or, for that matter, through the postseason games. After winding up with an eight-game winning margin over the Cubs, the Mets outslugged the Atlanta Braves three straight in the NL's first championship series, and then mowed down the Baltimore Orioles four straight, following an opening-game loss, in the World Series. The four-game sweep ending the Series, which featured more heroics by Agee, Koosman, Seaver, and Swoboda, completed a long list of parallels between the Miracle Mets and the Miracle Braves of 1914.

The National League's West division had some amazing happenings that year as well. After what appeared to be a contest mainly between the Braves and Dodgers in the first half of the season, slumps by those teams and a spurt by the Houston Astros brought a quintet of teams close a five-way tie in mid-August. On the 18th of August, the Braves, Dodgers, Astros, Reds, and Giants were all within a two-game range, and no further apart on September 10th, when the Giants led the Braves and Reds by a half-game and the Dodgers and Astros by two games. In the last three weeks of the season, however, things became clarified in a remarkably systematic manner. The Astros dropped out of first with a six-game losing streak starting on the 11th. Then the Reds fell off, losing five out of six games between the 15th and 20th. A few days later, the Dodgers careened out of the race with an eight-game losing streak, starting about the same time that the Giants and Braves began winning streaks. The Giants, however, stopped winning on the 22nd, losing four games to the Padres in their last eight games. The Braves on the other hand ripped off a 10-game streak over the Padres, Astros, and Reds that ended with a title-clinching victory on Tuesday, September 30th. The Braves' win owed much to Hank Aaron (44 homers), Phil Niekro (23-13), and reliever Cecil Upshaw (27 saves).

Baltimore's victory in the AL East reflected the good works of Mike Cuellar (23-11), Dave McNally (20-7), Jim Palmer (16-4), and Tom Phoebus (14-7) on the mound; Frank Robinson, Boog Powell, Paul Blair, and Don Buford led the offense. The Orioles defeated the AL West winner, Minnesota, for the American League pennant in three straight contests, but the first two—4-3 in 12 innings and McNally's 1-0 shutout in 11—were not easy victories. The Twins that eyar had the home run champ and MVP, Killebrew, the batting titlist, Rod Carew (.332); and two 20-game winners, Jim Perry and Dave Boswell.

## 1970

The New York Yankees emerged from obscurity in 1970, winning 93 games, but they were no match for the Orioles, who nearly equalled their 1969 total of 109 wins. This time Earl Weaver got 24 wins apiece from Cuellar and McNally and 20 from Palmer. The Yankee revival was due to newcomers Roy White, Bobby Murcer, Thurman Munson, and Danny Cater at the plate, and good pitching by Stottlemyer, Fritz Peterson, and Lindy McDaniel. The Red Sox remained strong offensively, leading the league with 203 home runs, chief contributors being Yastrzemski with 40, a recovered Tony Conigliaro with 36, Petrocelli with 29, and Reggie Smith with 22.

Another repeater appeared in the AL West, where the Twins won handily over an improving Oakland team and a surprising California team. Two ex-Dodger relief men, Ron Perranoski (34 saves) and Stan Williams (10-1, 15 saves) made up for Dave Boswell's back injury, which limited his output to 3-and-7, and good hitting by Killebrew, Oliva, and Tovar made up for Rod Carew's knee injury, which forced him to miss two-thirds of the season. The Twins were overpowered by Baltimore in three straight games again, 10-6, 11-3, and 6-1, in the post-season playoff.

The Mets and Cubs battled again in the NL East, but both of them lost to the Pittsburgh Pirates after a near-three-way tie in mid-September. As usual, the Pirates were strong up and down their batting lineup, with Clemente (.352), Stargell, Bob Robertson, and Manny Sanguillen leading the attack. The offense fizzled, however, when it came up against Cincinnati's pitching in the championship series, the Reds winning by 3-0, 3-1, and 3-2 scores. The Reds, under rookie manager Sparky Anderson, equalled the Pirates' team batting average that year, with .300-plus efforts by Tony Perez, Pete Rose, and Rookie of the Year Bernie Carbo; they outhomered the Bucs by 61 blows, with a league-leading 45 circuit blows by MVP Johnny Bench, 34 by Lee May, and 40 more by Perez.

The Cincinnati bats, in turn, were quieted by Oriole pitching in the World Series, won by Blatimore in five games.

llies clinch East title

TREAL (AP) — Mike
t has hit 285 home runs in his
league career, but
ant, he says, than the one he hit
ay.
at was No. 1," said Schmidt,
is two-run homer in the 11th in-
gave the Philadelphia Phillies a
ctory over the Montreal Expos
he National League East title.
This will give me a heck of a lot
character for future pressure
ball," added the Phillies' third

Schmidt lined his home
left-field fence to snap a 4-
The victory sends Ph
against the winner of the W
Houston or Los Angeles, in
five series, starting in P
Tuesday night.

| PHILA | ab | r | h | bi | MONT |
|---|---|---|---|---|---|
|  | 5 | 2 | 3 | 1 | White |
| Rose 1b | 5 | 2 | 3 | 0 | RScot |
| McBrid rf | 5 | 1 | 3 | 2 | Office |
| Schmdt 3b | 4 | 0 | 2 | 2 | Daws |
| Luzinski lf | 0 | 0 | 0 | 0 | Carte |
| Reed p | 0 | 0 | 0 | 0 | Crom |
| Lyle p | 1 | 0 | 1 | 1 | Parr |
| Boone ph | 0 | 0 | 0 | 0 | Spei |
| Dernier pr | 1 | 0 | 1 | 0 | LeF |
| McCrmc c | 4 | 0 | 1 | 0 | Mar |
| Unser cf | 1 | 0 | 0 | 0 | Rog |
| LSmith lf | 4 | 0 | 0 | 0 | Mo |
| Morelnd c | 0 | 0 | 0 | 0 | Ta |
| Loviglio pr | 0 | 0 | 0 | 0 | Ra |
| Brusstar p | 1 | 0 | 0 | 0 | So |
| Aviles ph | 1 | 0 | 0 | 0 | Fr |
| McGraw p | 5 | 0 | 1 | 0 | W |

# 1971-1980

## 1971

The action moved to the west coast in 1971. In the American League, Oakland arrived, and in the National League, the Giants and Dodgers were at it again.

Now under Dick Williams, the Oakland A's began a five-year domination of the AL West with an easy divisional title win, 16 game sover the fast-rising Kansas City Royals. This was basically the same Oakland team that made noise in its first year on the coast in 1968 except for a major new ingredient—Vida Blue. Blue had made headlines in his major league debut in September of '70, when he pitched a no-hitter and another shutout, and he became even more of a phenomenon in the spring of '71 when he won nine of his first ten pitching decisions. He couldn't keep up that pace, of course, but his final 1971 figures were 24-7 and the AL's best ERA of 1.82. With his skills combined with those of Catfish Hunter (21-11), Chuck Dobson (15-5), and the young rally-killer Rollie Fingers, the A's had pitching nearly as good as Baltimore's, which brought the Orioles their third consecutive AL East title. The heavy hitters for Oakland were Reggie Jackson and third sacker Sal Bando, who hit 32 and 24 homers, respectively.

Earl Weaver had four 20-game winners, but he only needed three of them to vanquish the A's in the playoff. With two innings of help from sharp reliever Eddie Watt in the first game, McNally, Cuellar, and Palmer squelched Oakland while Pat Dobson (20-8) sat on the bench.

The San Francisco Giants had only a so-so batting attack in 1971, with 40-year-old Willie Mays showing decline, Willie McCovey out with an injury part of the year, and Bobby Bonds taking over the team batting leadership with 33 homers and a .288 average. But their pitching was good enough to hold off a close challenge by Los Angeles in the last three weeks of the season; Juan Marichal (18-11), Gaylord Perry (16-12), and Jerry Johnson (12 wins plus 18 saves) were the mound leaders. The Dodgers, who also lacked a potent offense but got strong pitching by Al Downing (20-9), Don Sutton (17-12), and Jim Brewer (22 saves), created plenty of excitement by surging from 8½ games behind on September 5th to within one game

# 1971 TITLE RACES

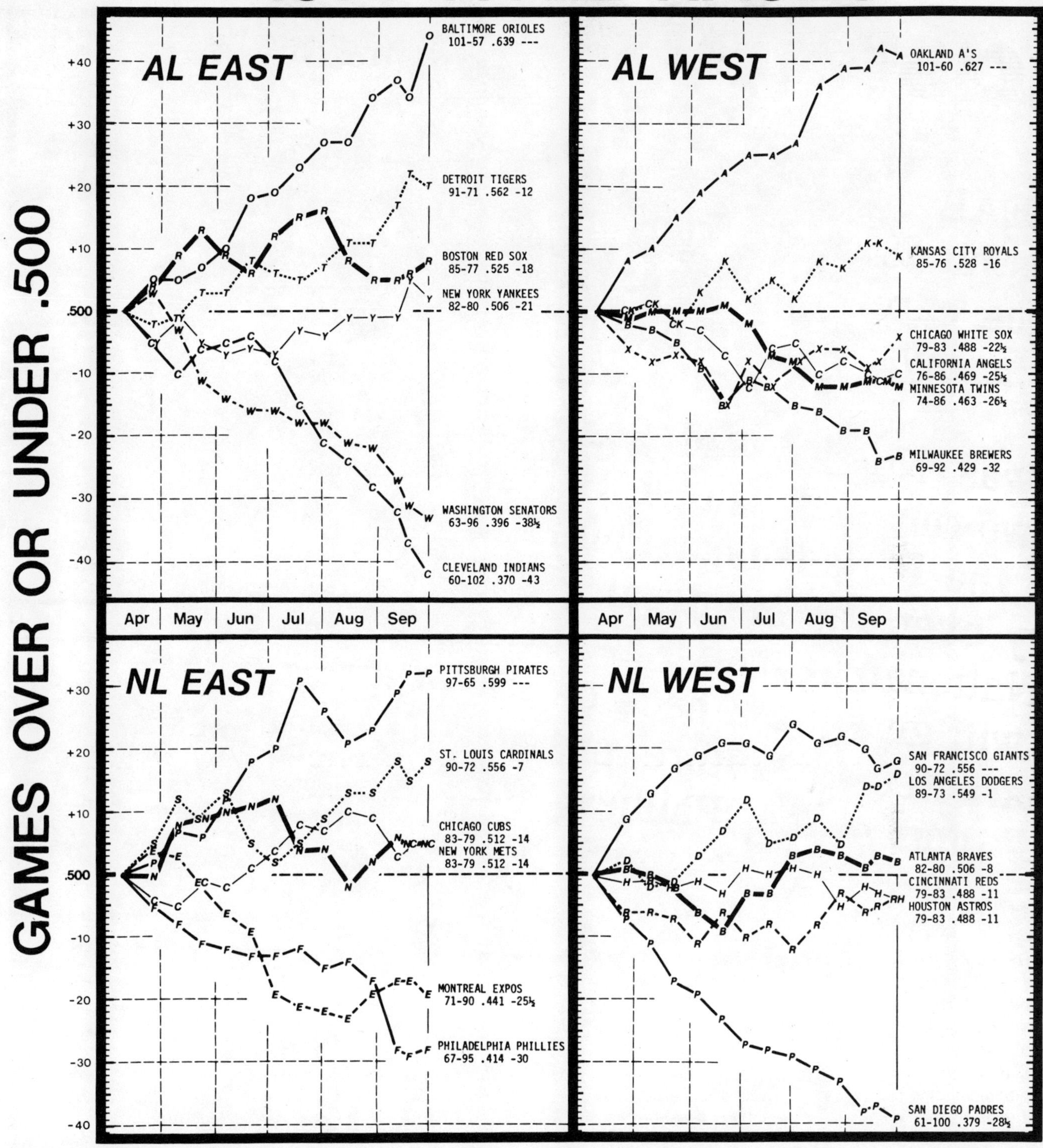


only nine days later. But the Giants kept their tiny lead the rest of the way, thanks mostly to Bonds's hitting and Marichal and Perry's pitching.

The Pirates won again in the NL East, soaring to a big lead in July, but then staggering badly, putting themselves in danger of a takeover by the Cardinals, and then finally recovering. The Bucs finished seven games ahead of the Cards, at 32 games over .500, but they had been 31 games over .500 in July. Clemente, Stargell, Sanguillen, and Robertson again had good years, and Pitt had better pitching then in the previous year, particularly from starters Steve Blass and Dock Ellis and reliever Dave Giusti, who won seven and saved 22. St. Louis's challenge was led by the league's MVP, Joe Torre, who batted .363, hit 24 homers, and knocked in 137 runs.

Blass had problems with the Giants in the NL playoff, which the Pirates nevertheless won in four games, but he was the pitching hero in the World Series, holding the Orioles to three hits in Game 3 and four hits in Game 7. Cle-

# 1972 TITLE RACES

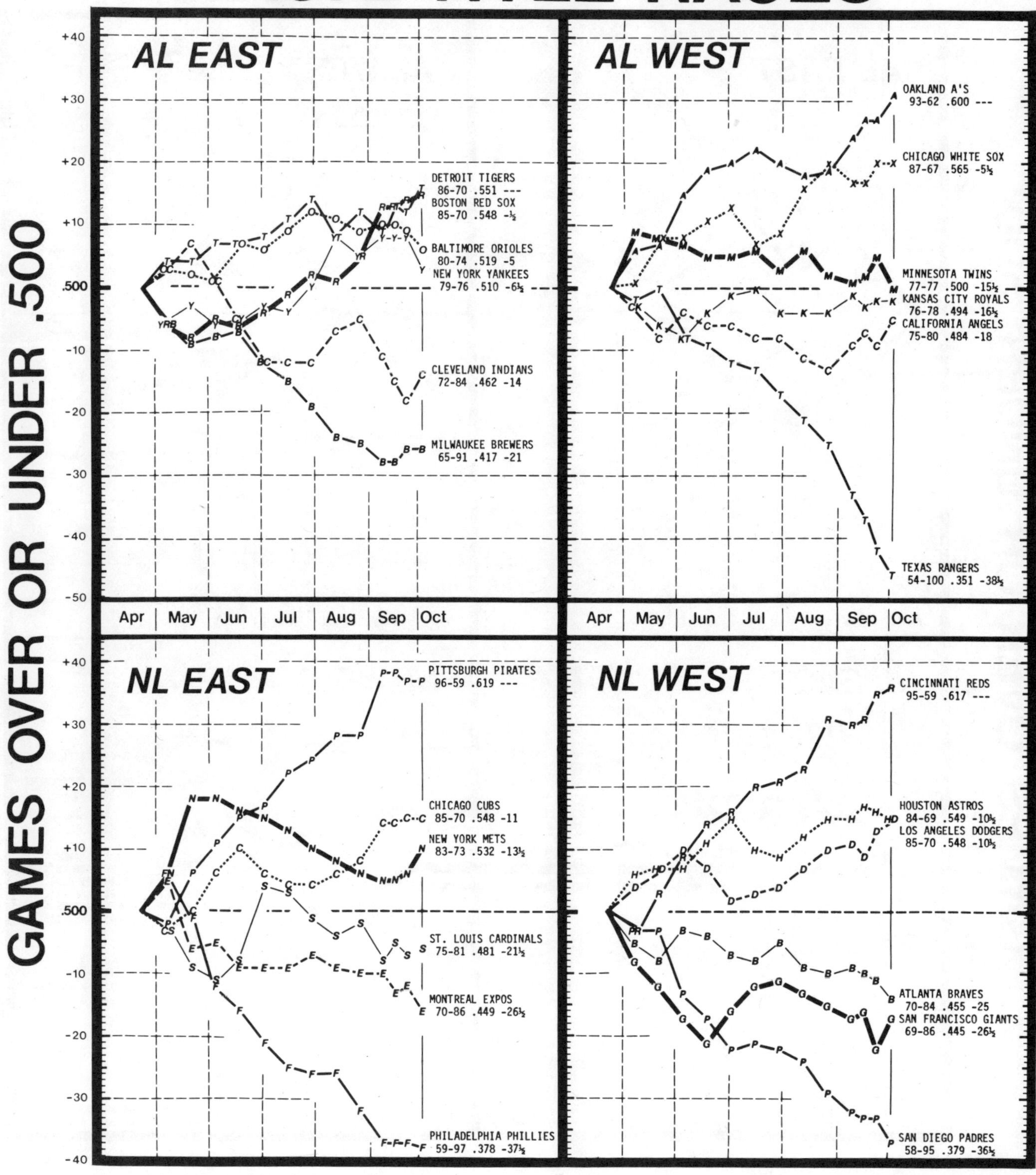


mente, with 12 hits including two homers, was the batting hero.

### 1972

The first 13 days of the 1972 major league schedule didn't happen—they were canceled by a players' strike. When the strike was resolved, the leagues ruled that the canceled games could not be made up even if they affected a title race, which they did in the AL East.

That division had a torrid four-team race going around Labor Day, the slow-starting Red Sox and Yankees having caught up to the Orioles and Tigers in August. The day after Labor Day, the four clubs were within a half-game spread, quite like the situation in 1967 at that time of the season. But unlike that year, two of the contenders dropped out with two weeks left, and the competition became a no-less-torrid two-team contest

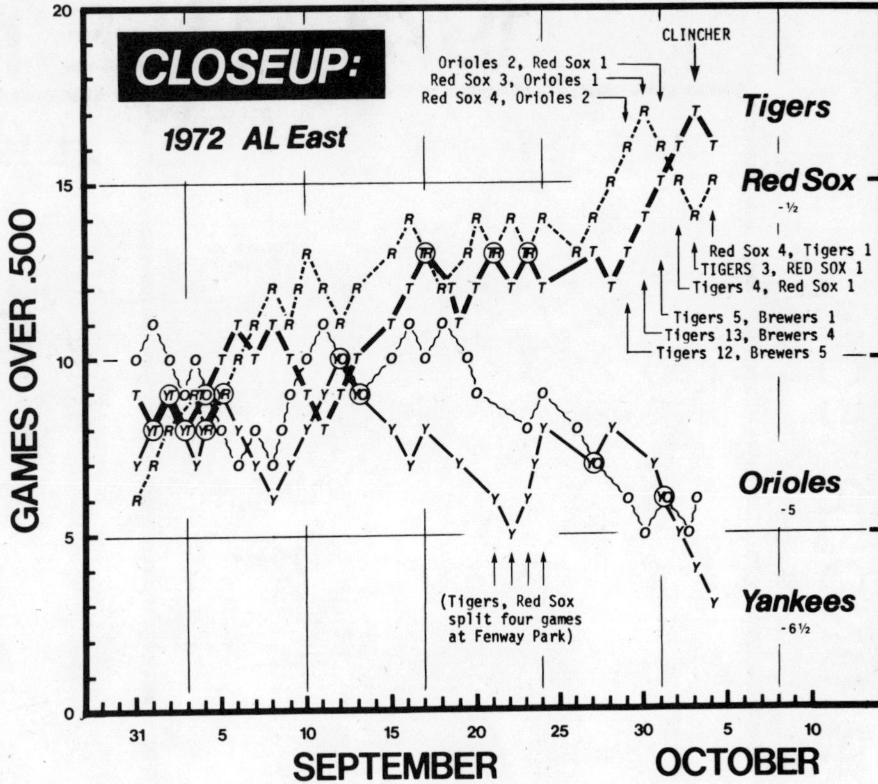


**FIFTY WAYS TO LOSE ANOTHER, and the Red Sox know them all. This time, it was the 13-day players' strike in April that helped bring Boston's downfall. The Bosox lost the 1972 AL East title to the Detroit Tigers by only half a game, after having had seven games chopped from their schedule by the strike as opposed to Detroit's six. Had the rules adopted at the end of the strike permitted the Red Sox to make up just one of their seven, they might have tied the Tigers and forced a playoff.**

between the Red Sox and Tigers. The demise of the Yankees began with a three-game sweep by Boston at Fenway Park on September 6-8, and was furthered by four more losses to Baltimore and Milwaukee at Yankee Stadium between the 15th and 21st. Twin victories by Boston's Marty Pattin and Luis Tiant on the 20th started the Orioles' downfall, and the O's lost five of their next six games, to the Brewers, Indians, and Red Sox; over these eight games, Baltimore scored a total of only 11 runs.

The Red Sox, managed by Eddie Kasko, had to travel to Detroit, where Billy Martin was in his second year as manager, for their last three games. By the eve of this series the Tigers had come up to within a half-game of Boston's lead by sweeping three from the Brewers. On Monday, October 2nd, Mickey Lolich won his 22nd game of the year by besting the Red Sox' John Curtis, 4-1, on a six-hitter and home runs by Al Kaline and Aurelio Rodriguez. On Tuesday, Tiant, later voted Comeback of the Year, with his catcher Carlton Fisk, who was Rookie of the Year, faced the veteran Woody Fryman, who had won nine games since coming to Detroit from the Phillies in August. Again the 37-year-old Kaline came through with a key hit, a game-winning single, and Fryman prevailed, 3-1, to clinch the title for Detroit. The Red Sox won the final game of the season the next day, finishing only half a game behind, and painfully aware of the fact that they had lost seven games to the strike in the spring as opposed to the Tigers' six.

In the AL's other division, the Chicago White Sox livened things up by displaying some power in the form of Dick (earlier, Richie) Allen, who was MVP and missed a Triple Crown only by coming in nine BA points behind Rod Carew, and by giving Oakland a good scare in August. The Unhued Hose not only challenged the A's, but snatched the lead from them momentarily in the latter part of that month, after trailing in July by nine games. Wilbur Wood (24-17) and Stan Bahnsen (21-16) were the chief moundsmen in Chicago's upbeat season.

Charlie Finley added Ken Holtzman (18-11) to Dick Williams' pitching staff in a deal with the Cubs, making up for a hold-out and subsequent offseason by Vida Blue. With a return to form by Odom and the usual fine hurling by Hunter and Fingers, the A's eventually rolled to a 5½-game victory margin. Odom's pitching and Matty Alou's .381 hitting led the Oakland club in the league championship playoff, a tightly-contested series won by the A's, three games to two.

The Pirates won the NL East title for the third year in a row, Al Oliver and Richie Hebner abetting fine performances again by Stargell, Sanguillen, and Clemente. Clemente's last hit of the season was his 3,000th and tragically proved to be the last of his career when he was killed on December 31, 1972 in a plane crash while attempting to bring aid to earthquake victims in Nicaragua; the next year he was voted into the Hall of Fame on a waiver of the five-year waiting rule.

The Big Red Machine at Cincinnati, which had sputtered from hitting slumps and pitching inconsistency in 1971, got rolling again in May of 1972. It became unstoppable, in fact, with the multifaceted contributions of second baseman Joe Morgan, acquired from Houston, and strong pitching by Gary Nolan, Ross Grimsley, and Clay Carroll. Reminiscent of the 1904 AL race, the NL championship was decided in the ninth inning of Game 5, in Cincinnati's favor, on a wild pitch by Pittsburgh's Bob Moose.

The World Series was also hotly contested, with six of its seven games decided by a single run. That only enhanced the importance of Oakland reserve catcher Gene Tenace's four home runs and nine RBIs, and relief whiz Rollie Fingers' victory and two saves in six appearances. Possibly, some felt, with such closely matched teams, the real deciding factor was the sporting of moustaches by all the Oakland players.

# 1973 TITLE RACES

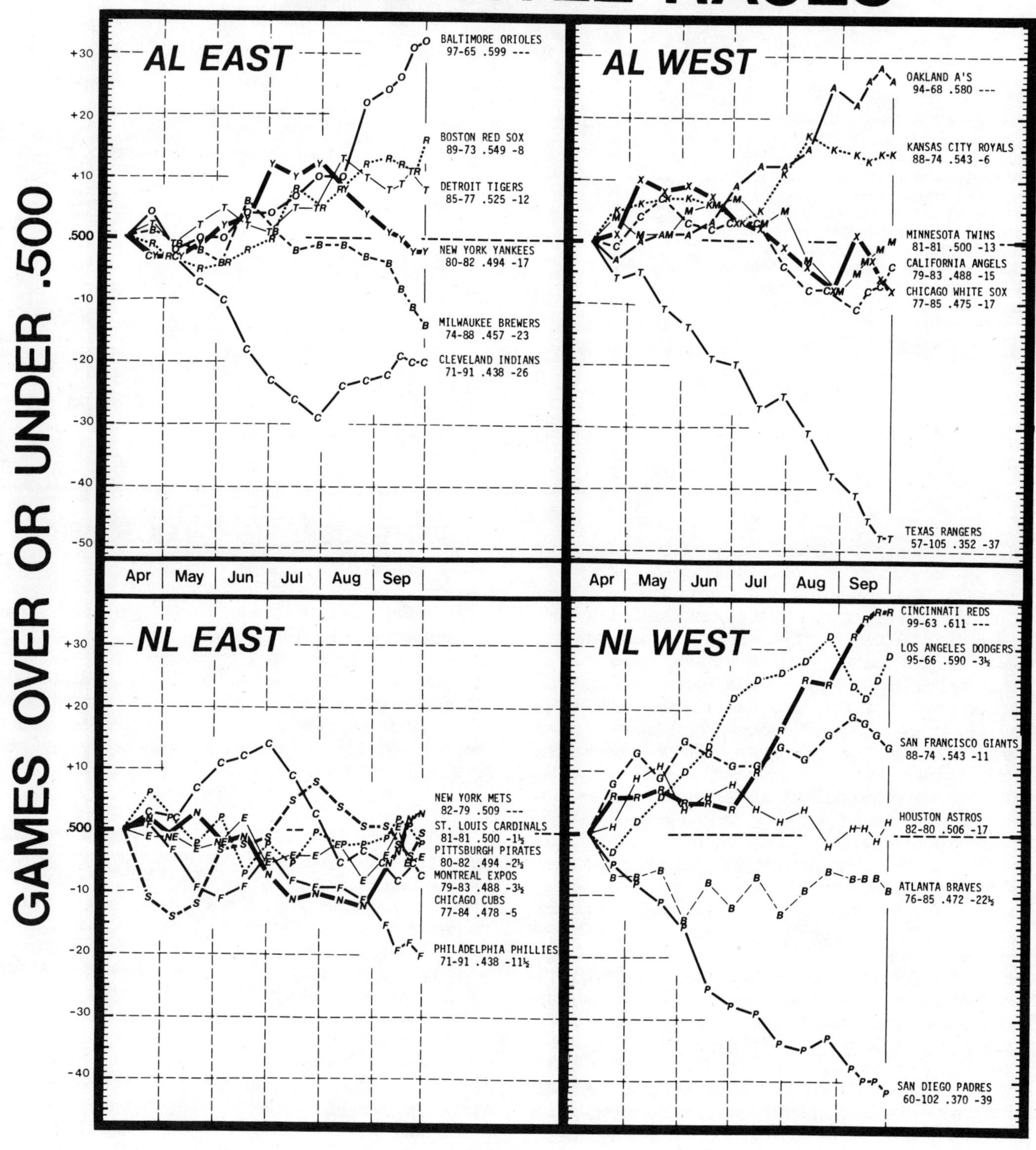


## 1973

In the 1973 season, the Baltimore Orioles returned to the top of the American League's East division, and the Oakland and Cincinnati clubs repeated their title wins in the two West divisions. More interesting than these victories were the waves of the future seen in the rise of the Kansas City Royals in the AL West and the resurfacing of the Los Angeles Dodgers in the NL West. Names such as Amos Otis, Hal McRae, John Mayberry, Paul Splittorff, and 20-year-old George Brett were becoming familiar in one case, and in the other, an infield of newcomers named Steve Garvey, Dave Lopes, Bill Russell, and Ron Cey. These and older Dodgers such as Willie Davis, Willie Crawford, Don Sutton, and ex-AL pitcher Tommy John, carried Los Angeles into first place for over two months during the summer before the Reds took over in September. Graph-

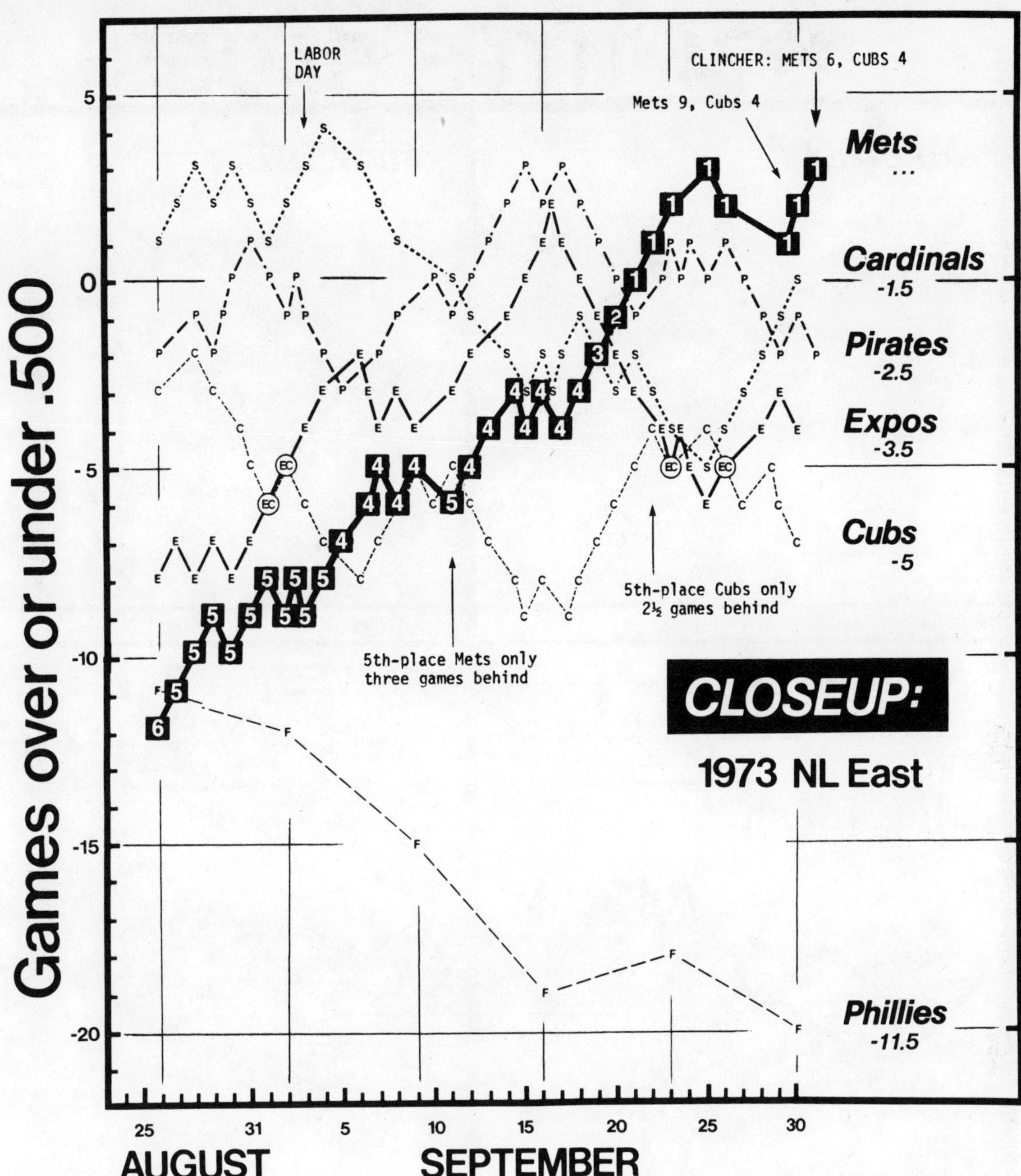


**RAGS TO RICHES, THE CHEAP WAY. The New York Mets won the NL East title in 1973 after being in last place as late as August 26th, and the spread of the division was so narrow that a gain of only 13 games re .500 by the Mets was enough to do the trick. This was the closest five-team race in modern major league history, but it was tarnished by the fact that the winning Mets ended up only three games above .500, and no other team in the division had a winning record.**

ically, Kansas City's challenge to the A's was almost identical to the threat by the White Sox in the previous year.

Far more interesting than the doings in these three divisions were the bizarre events in the NL East. At the end of the season, that division had the smallest spread—11½ games from top to bottom—of all 186 title races in the 1901-1980 period. Five weeks before the season's end, the range was even smaller, with the first-place St. Louis Cardinals only 6½ games ahead of the last-place New York Mets, and at the time those first-place Cardinals were only one game over .500. Most bizarre of all, those last-place Mets won the divisional title!

In 26 days, and without a winning streak longer than four games, the Mets moved from last on August 26th to first on September 21st. All it took was a shift from winning only half their games, which had been the best they could manage from mid-July to late August, to a pace just shy of winning three-fourths of their games—19 wins in 26 games (.731). Although it was indeed a jump from the bottom to the top, it is not to be compared with the 1914 Miracle Braves or the 1969 Miracle Mets, especially when we note that the '73 Mets wound up winning only three more games than they lost and we find three teams in the other division of the NL with much better records. But it was still very interesting, and it provided another great round of thrills for Met fans.

# 1974 TITLE RACES

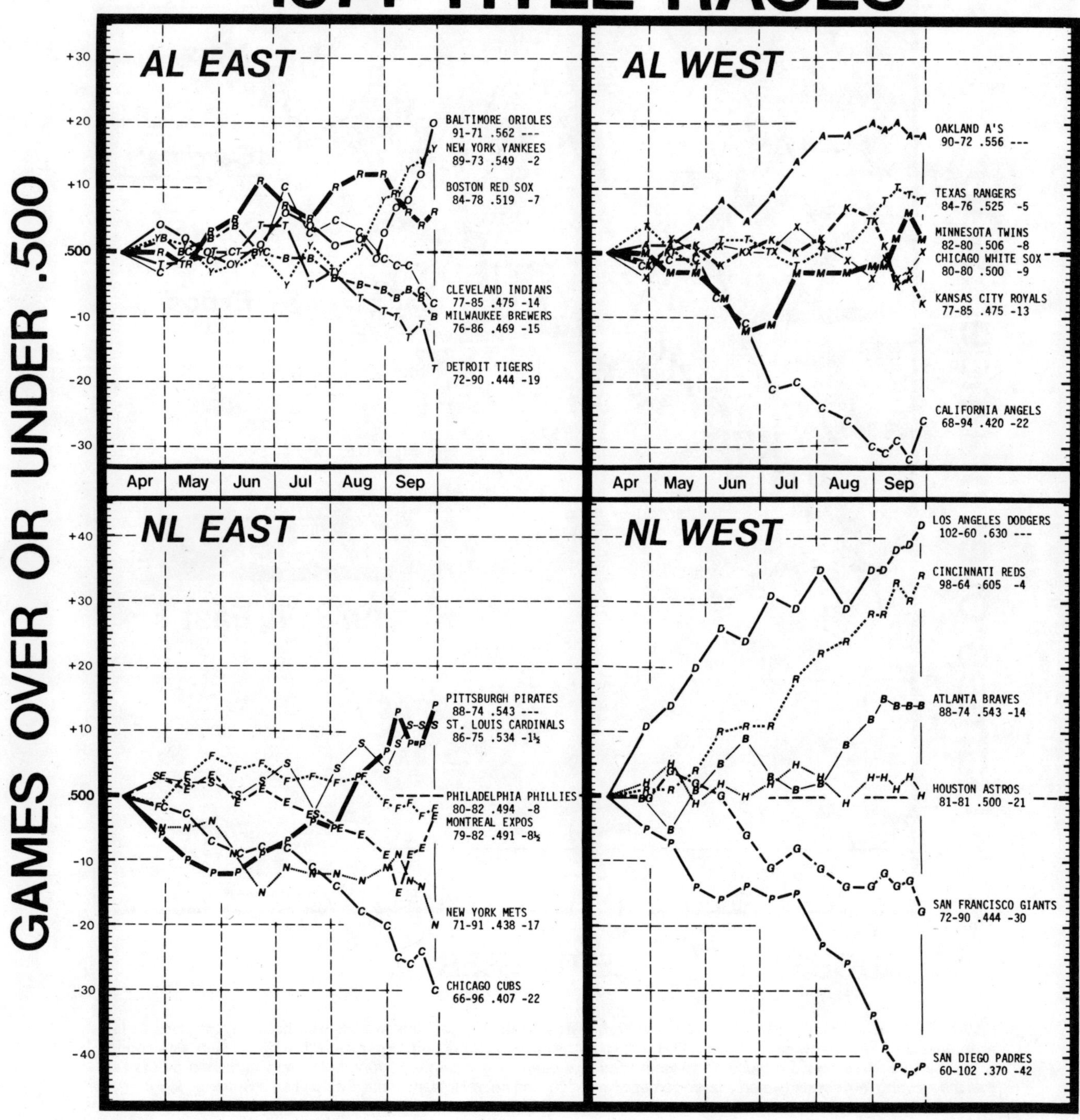


Almost every other team in the division had been in first place before the Mets during the season, and some had gotten there via off-course routes. The Cardinals had a disastrous spring, but righted themselves impressively, taking the Cubs' place at the top in late July; they were hurt in September when Bob Gibson was out most of the month with a leg injury. The Pirates were in the lead in the early weeks, then sagged until they discontinued an experiment with Manny Sanguillen in Clemente's place in the outfield; after they returned Sanguillen to the backstop position and gave Richie Zisk (.324) more playing time, they worked their way back to first place in mid-September. Even Montreal, with good hitting by Ken Singleton, Bob Bailey, Ron Fairly, and Ron Hunt, had a whiff of the top spot, when they tied the Pirates momentarily by winning the opener of a doubleheader on September 17th. The Phillies, on the other hand, stayed in the lower regions all year, in part because Steve Carlton, who had turned in the decade's best pitching performance the year before (27-10 with a last-place club), was a 20-game loser in 1973.

The Mets were held down in the summer months by injuries to catcher Jerry Grote, shortstop Bud Harrelson, first baseman John Milner, and outfielder Cleon Jones. Seaver, Koosman, and McGraw, now joined by Jon Matlack, were still pitching well, and the Met offense now included Rusty Staub and

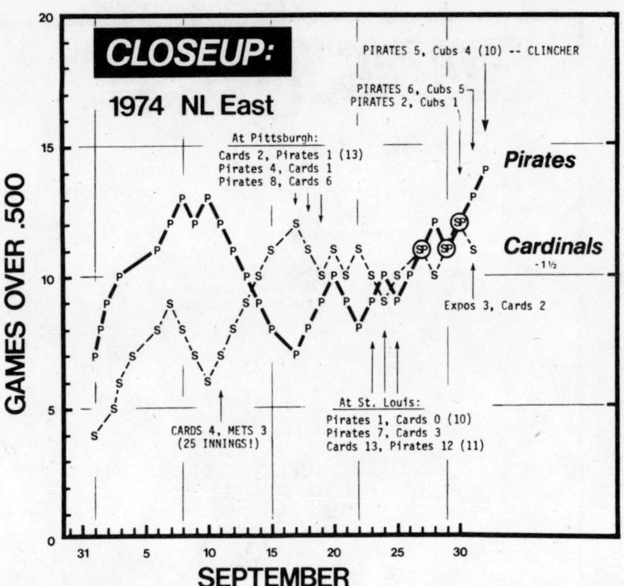


**PITTSBURGH PIRACY. In another rags-to-riches story, the 1974 Pittsburgh Pirates came out of last place in June to win the NL East title. They were tooth-and-nail with the St. Louis Cardinals in late September, beating the Cards in four of six meetings. Pitt broke out of a tie at the end of the month by edging the Cubs, 6-5, on Bob Robertson's two-run homer in the eighth inning at Three Rivers Stadium, while St. Louis lost at Montreal. The Pirates clinched the flag the next day, October 2nd, by tying the Cubs in the bottom of the ninth on a freak play—a two-out by Steve Swisher passed ball, on Robertson's third strike, after which Swisher's peg to first hit Robertson's shoulder and allowed Manny Sanguillen to score from third. In the next inning, Sanguillen's slow roller after a triple and two intentional walks brought in Al Oliver from third—an unintentional squeeze play—with the title-winning run.**

Felix Millan. It was when the injured came back to play that the club got up its steam in September. After taking the division lead on the 21st, the Mets went on to complete a seven-game winning streak, but continued pursuit by the Pirates and Cardinals, and some rainy days in Chicago, delayed the clinching to the final day of Monday, October 1st. In a 6-4 victory over the Cubs that day, Seaver won his 19th game of of the season and McGraw earned his 25th save. Yogi Berra, the Mets helmsman, became only the second manager (after Joe McCarthy) to win pennants in both leagues, when the Mets outpitched the Reds in NL playoff series.

Thanks mainly to Catfish Hunter's pitching, the A's prevailed over the Orioles in the AL championship series. The World Series, a suspenseful seven-game affair, also went to Oakland, which had the benefit of Reggie Jackson's clutch hitting and Rollie Fingers' repeat performance of two saves in six appearances.

## 1974

For the second straight year, the constricted NL East had a winner who had charged out of last place. Pittsburgh in 1974 was much slower about it than the '73 Mets, moving from sixth to fifth in June, passing the cellar-bound Cubs into fourth in early July, taking third from the Expos in early August, finally passing the Phillies and Cardinals into first place later that month. Except that it wasn't a final passing so far as the Cards were concerned—they retook the lead on September 14th and made a two-horse race out of it right to the finish line (see closeup).

The Cardinals had gotten Reggie Smith from the Red Sox during the winter, and he, along with Lou Brock, Bake McBride, and Ted SImmons, supplied the Cards with some good batwork; Brock stole an amazing 118 bases, setting the current major league record for a season. The Pirates had the edge in offense, however, with the hitting of Stargell, Zisk, Oliver, Hebner, and Rennie Stennett. Neither team had particularly strong pitching.

The Dodgers did—Andy Messersmith (20-6), Don Sutton (19-9), Tommy John (13-3), and Mike Marshall (15-12 and 21 saves in 106 relief stints). And with Steve Garvey's MVP performance and 32 homers from outfielder Jim Wynn, they outhit as well as outpitched their NL West competition. The imbalance of the East and West divisions again was evident, with the Pirates ending up with the same record as the third-place Atlanta Braves in the West division. Appropriately, the Dodgers disposed of Pittsburgh quite handily in the league playoff, three games to one.

The AL East had a 19-game spread at the season's end, but up to August this division had something resembling a six-way tie—only five games separated the leading Red Sox from last-place Detroit on July 23, 1974. This situation gave the Cleveland Indians a chance to shine in first place for a few days earlier in July, and the Red Sox to generate some pennant fever in Boston the following month, before both teams slumpted out of the race. It also gave the Yankees an opportunity to pull off a near-miracle title. Under Bill Virdon now, and with Ron Blomberg, Elliott Maddox, Graig Nettles, and Lou Piniella stinging the ball, the Yanks displayed a mirror-image of their 1973 flop and vaulted from last place in mid-July to first place right after Labor Day, tying the Red Sox on September 3rd and getting the top spot to themselves for nearly two weeks.

The real miracle-maker, however, turned out to be Earl Weaver and his uncanny Orioles, who were two games below .500 on the 28th of August and won the title five weeks later. The O's won all but six of their last 34 games, with a magnificent display of pitching by Cuellar, McNally, ex-Red Ross Grimsley, and Jim Palmer, who had been battling a sore arm most of the year. After five straight shutouts over the Red Sox and Indians, the Orioles passed Boston for good on September 14th, then invaded Yankee Stadium to sweep three from New York, passing the Yanks on the 24th with a terminal nine-game winning streak.

By that year, Bobby Grich and Mark Belanger had become mainstays in Weaver's solid infield with Boog Powell and Brooks Robinson, and Paul Blair had been joined in the outfield by Don Baylor, Rich Coggins, and Al Bumbry. The only Baltimore hitters above .265 were Baylor (.272), Robinson (.288), and Tommy Davis (.289), who was the American League's best designated hitter (DH) when that strange role was inaugurated by the league in 1973.

Although Oakland won again, there was news in the AL West division from Texas. The Rangers, in their third season since the transfer of the second Washington Senators franchise to the southwest, now had Billy Martin as manager and jumped from last place in the previous year to a very respectable second-place finish, only five games behind the A's. The Rangers also led the league in team batting, with .300 hitters Mike Hargrove, Lenny Randle, and Jeff Burroughs supporting ex-Cub Ferguson Jenkins' (25-12) fine pitching. The A's had the league's best pitching, with Hunter, Holtzman, Blue, and Fingers beating even the Oriole staff in the statistics. Pre-

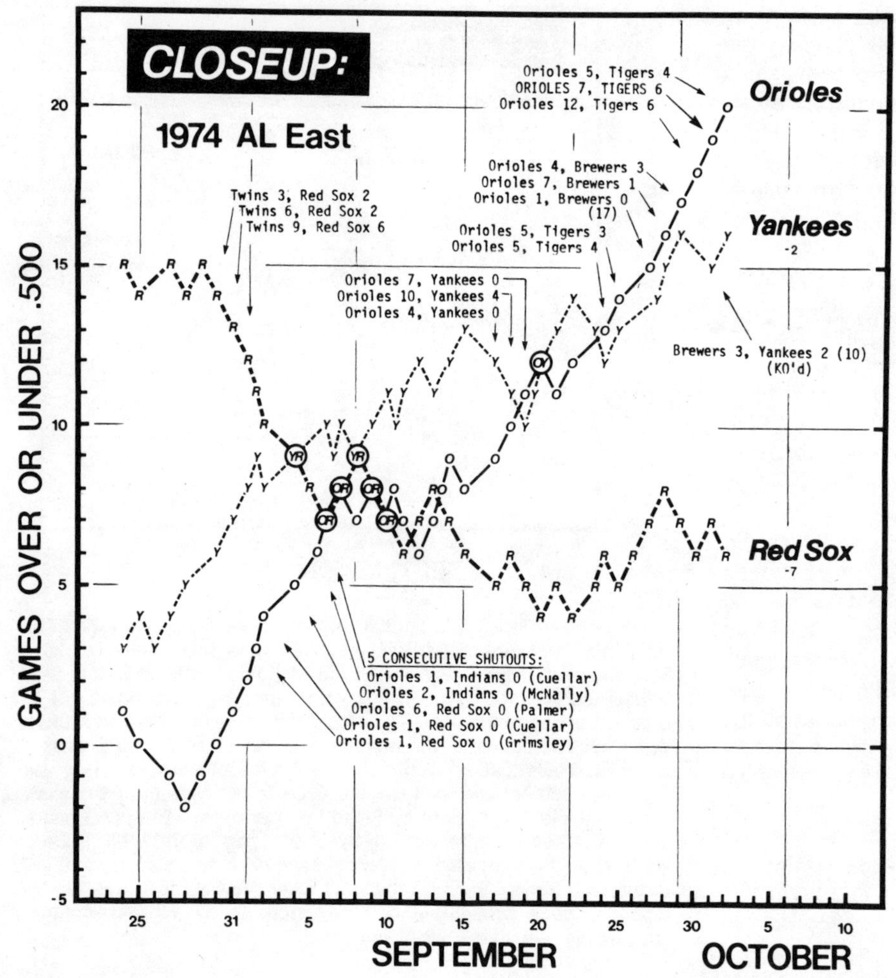


**THE BALTIMORE EXPRESS, fueled by sensational shutout pitching by Mike Cuellar, Jim Palmer, Ross Grimsley, and Dave McNally, roared through New York and Boston for a title triumph in the 1974 AL East race. The pennant fever in Boston died in one week when the Red Sox lost eight straight at the Twin Cities, in Baltimore, and in Fenway Park against the Brewers. Those same Brewers kayoed the Yankees on October 1st in Milwaukee to help the Orioles' cause. The O's won 28 of their last 34 games, before which they were two games under .500.**

cisely these same men beat McNally, Palmer, and Cuellar in the league championship series after Cuellar opened the series with a victory over Hunter. The change of managership at Oakland, from Dick Williams to Al Dark, after the '73 World Series made little difference in the outcome of the '74 Series—the A's won their third straight world championship, in five games over the Dodgers.

### 1975

In little more than half a decade, 1975 has already gone down in history as the year that produced the greatest World Series ever. Maybe it had to have the best Series—to make up for the lack of suspense in the pennant races.

Suspense and excitement can be two different things, however, and the fans in Boston didn't lack the latter. Rather unexpectedly, the Red Sox won the AL East title. The Boston farm system had been producing quite impressively since the mid-sixties—many players who starred on the '67 pennant-winner, plus Sparky Lyle, and others. Toward the mid-seventies it became a veritable cornucopia—Billy Conigliaro, Bill Lee, Roger Moret, Juan Beniquez, Carlton Fisk, Dwight Evans, Ben Oglivie, Rick Miller, Rick Burleson, and Cecil Cooper. The peak came with Fred Lynn and Jim Rice, who debuted with the Red Sox in September of 1974, and made the team in a flash (Lynn hit .419 in 43 ABs).

With the new muscle supplied by these two for the whole 1972 season (until Rice broke his wrist in September), the title came to Boston fairly easily after mid-July. Manager Darrell Johnson and his charges were pestered by the Yankees and Brewers near the end of June (Milwaukee was only .001 behind Boston as late as July 5th, after which the Brewers displayed one of the worst fades in modern history). After those threats, the only worry was Baltimore, which started a more sustained uprising than its pennant drive of the year before, but the closest the Orioles could get was 3½ games behind.

Lynn, on his .331 batting with 105 RBIs and 21 homers, plus fielding gems galore, became the first Rookie of the Year also to win the MVP award. Rice was only an inch behind, with .309, 102 RBIs, and 22 roundtrippers, making these two, many felt, the most phenomenal pair of rookies ever to land on one major league team at the same time. The Red Sox also got good hitting from an injury-plagued Carlton Fisk (.331), half-time-DH Cecil Cooper (.311), Carl Yastrzemski before a mid-season shoulder separation, and during the stretch drive, second baseman Denny Doyle (.310). Rick Wise (19-12), Luis Tiant (18-14), Bill Lee (17-9) and Roger Moret (14-3) provided Boston with uncustomarily strong pitching, and the relief star turned out to be Jim Willoughby, who was acquired during the summer.

Oakland, Pittsburgh, and Cincinnati won again in their respective divisions, with the Reds reminding many of the '27 Yankees or other great teams of the past. Oakland lost Catfish Hunter to free agency and thence to the Yankees, but still had enough good pitching to stay ahead of the Royals; the A's were surprisingly easy victims of the Red Sox in the AL playoff, a quick three-gamer. Similarly, the Reds put down the Pirates

# 1975 TITLE RACES

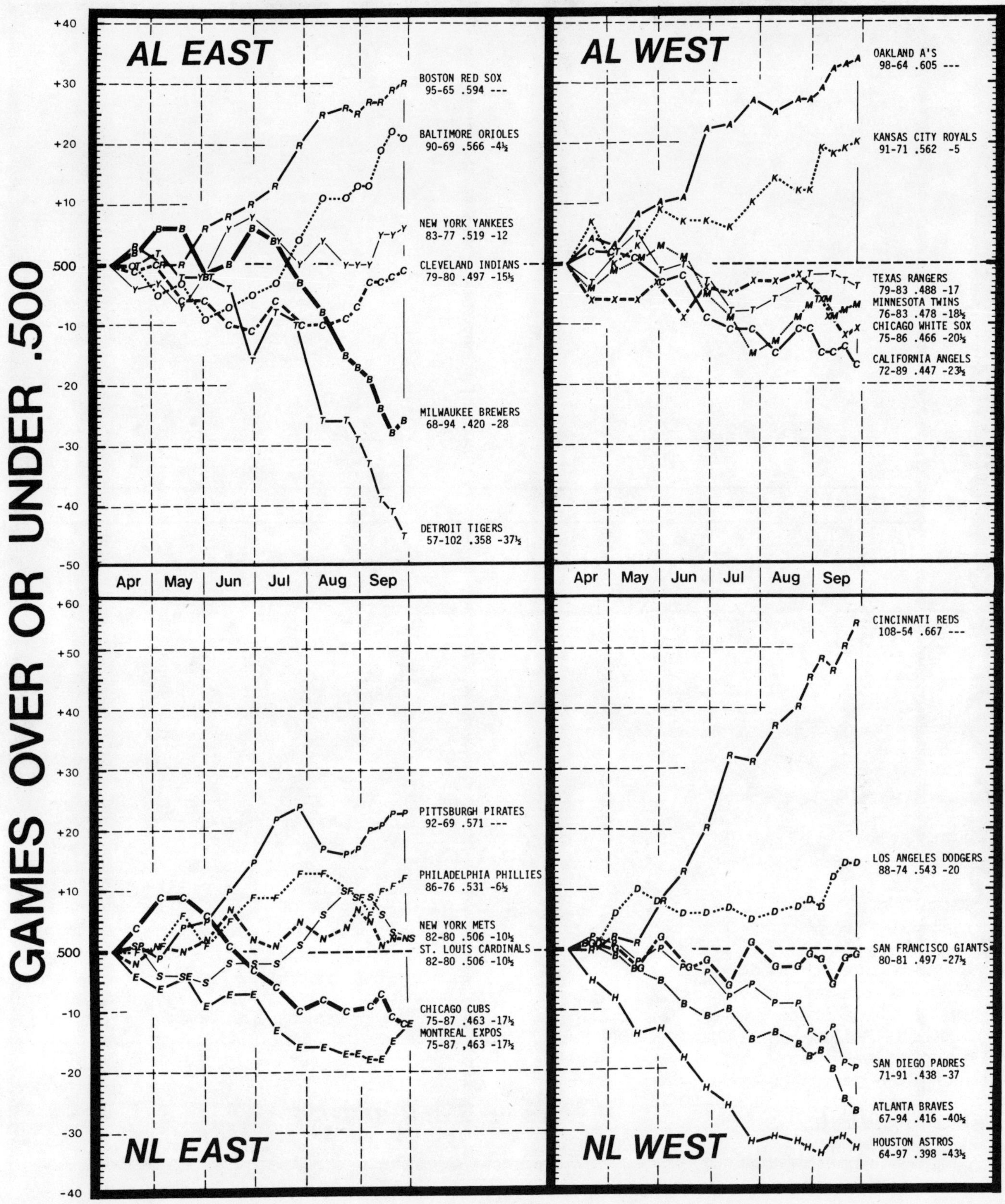


with dispatch, 8-3, 6-1, and 5-3.

The World Series turned into such a closely-contested, see-saw battle and generated so many heroic acts on both sides that it almost didn't have a loser—many wanted both the Reds and Red Sox to win by the end. But in actual fact, a 4-3 victory was eked out by Cincinnati in the anticlimactic seventh game that followed Carlton Fisk's 12th-inning, Series-tying home run off the left foul pole at Fenway Park in Game Six.

# 1976 TITLE RACES

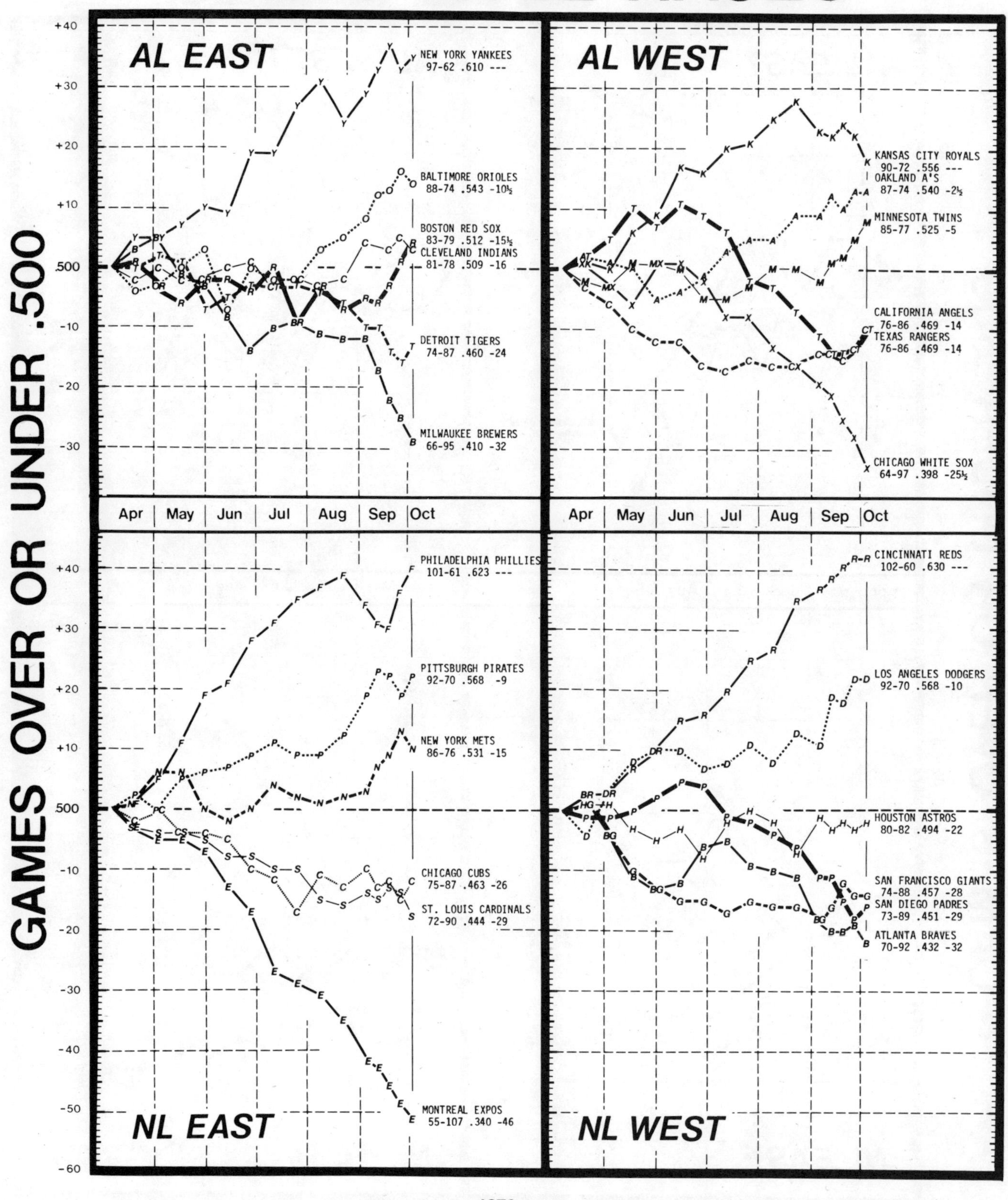


**1976**

Oakland's strength finally diminished in more obvious ways, mainly from continual conflicts between Charlie Finley and his players, and resultant departures and morale problems, giving the AL West a new winner in the 1976, the Kansas City Royals. Boston didn't come close to repeating its title win in the AL East, and replaced Darrell Johnson with Don Zimmer in July; owner Tom Yawkey's death added to the depressed atmosphere in Boston near the same time. Earl Weaver no longer

# 1977 TITLE RACES

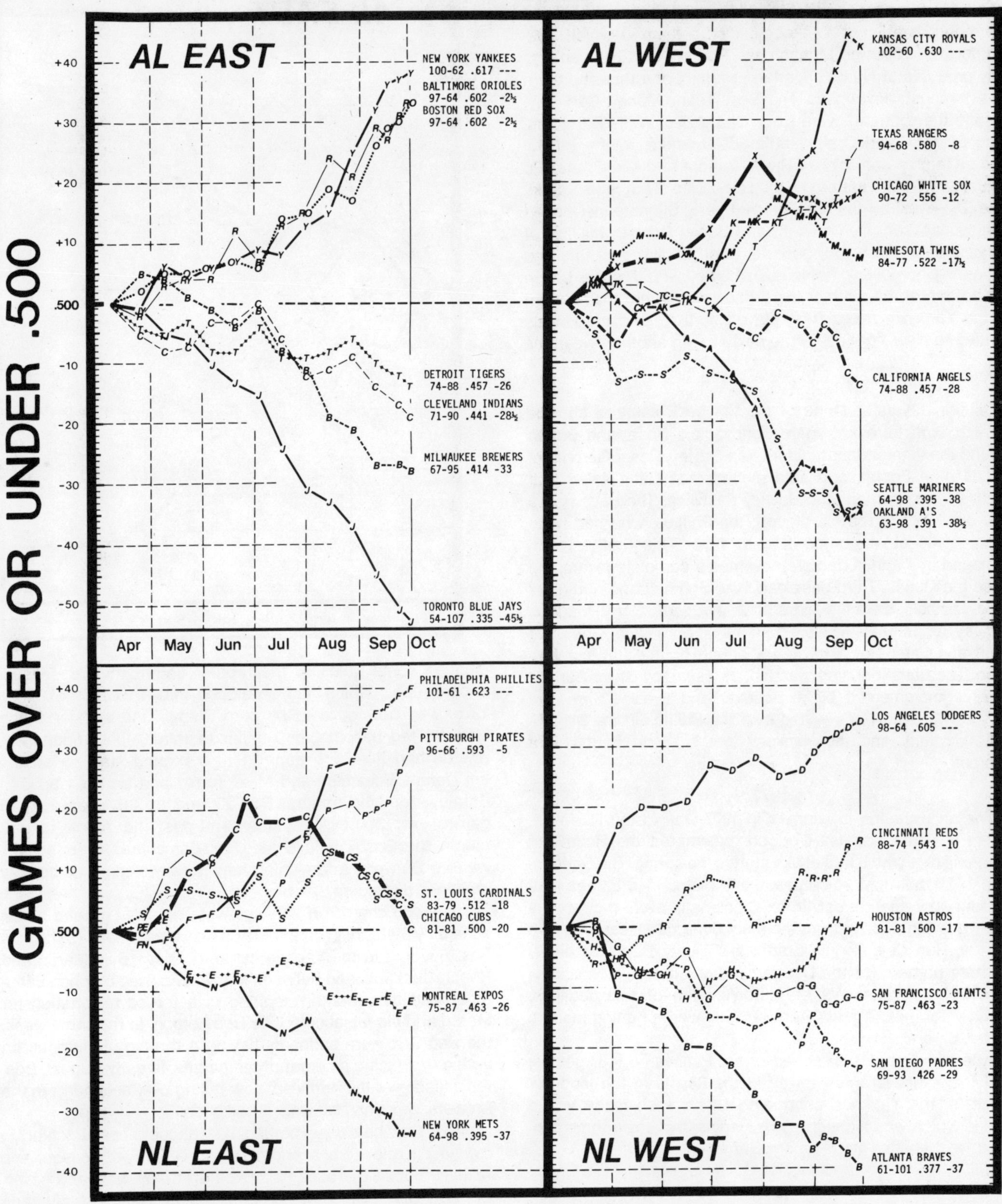


had McNally or Cuellar as reliable aces on the mound, and with a light-hitting team, Jim Palmer and Wayne Garland, both 20-game winners, weren't enough to bring the Orioles into contention, either. So the New York Yankees, now owned by George Steinbrenner and managed by Billy Martin, took over the division in a cakewalk.

Kansas City's winning combination, under manager Whitey Herzog, was an infield of John Mayberry, Frank White, Freddie

Patek, and George Brett, the latter taking the AL batting title with a .333 average, and an outfield-DH group of Al Cowens, Amos Otis, Hal McRae, and Tom Poquette. Dennis Leonard (17-10), Al Fitzmorris, and fireballing reliefer Mark Littell led the mound staff. The Yankees fielded a team in which .302-hitting MVP Thurman Munson and Roy White (.286) were the only products of New York's farm system, and thus the team was famously known as The Best Team Money Can Buy. Among the "bought" were Chris Chambliss, Willie Randolph, Fred Stanley, and Graig Nettles (32 homers) in the infield, Oscar Gamble and Mickey Rivers in right and center, and Ed Figueroa (19-10), Hunter (17-15), Dock Ellis (17-8), and Sparky Lyle (23 saves) on the hill. The next year, Steinbrenner added Reggie Jackson, Don Gullett, and Bucky Dent to his list of acquisitions, which was good for another divisional title and pennant. Chambliss's home run off Littell with th score tied in the bottom of the ninth of the fifth game brought the pennant to the Yanks in an exciting playoff in 1976, and the Royals yielded to New York again the next year in another five-game set.

Cincinnati was still one of the ten best teams of all time in 1976, with Perez, Morgan, Concepcion, Rose, and Bench around the diamond; outfielders Ken Griffey, Cesar Geronimo, and George Foster; and able moundsmen Gary Nolan, Pat Zachry, Fred Norman, and Rawley Eastwick. The Reds had a new opponent in the NL playoff, the Phillies, who had been Pittsburgh's chief competition in 1975. This Phillie team, managed by Danny Ozark, represented a complete revamping since the sixties. Third baseman Mike Schmidt and outfielder Greg Luzinski were its extra-base sluggers, Garry Maddox and Jay Johnstone also were hard-hitting outfielders, and Dave Cash and Larry Bowa formed a strong double-play combination. The Phils' pitching was led, as usual, by Steve Carlton (20-7), complemented by ex-Bosoxer and Brewer, Jim Lonborg (18-10). The Reds rolled over the Phillies in the playoff, three straight, and the Yankees in the World Series, four straight.

### 1977

The only change in winners in 1977 was in the NL West, where the Los Angeles Dodgers preempted the Reds and everyone else with a rocket-like start in the spring. The Dodgers won 17 of their first 20 contests, and maintained a huge lead without any real threat from Cincinnati, even though the latter got Tom Seaver from the Mets during the season. Steve Garvey, Ron Cey, Reggie Smith, and Dusty Baker all hit 30 or more homers for the Dodgers, whose manager was now Tom LaSorda after Walter Alston's reign of two decades. Tommy John (20-7) and Charlie Hough were pitching leaders for the Blue.

After the Dodgers disposed of the Phillies (in four games) and the Yankees again thwarted the Royals in the leagues' playoffs, the Yankees conquered LA in a six-game World Series which was highlighted by Reggie Jackson's three consecutive first-pitch home runs in Game 6.

### 1978

The Cleveland Indians' American League record of 111 wins in a season appeared to be in danger in the middle of the 1978 season. The Boston Red Sox, who had put on the most awesome display of home run hitting in baseball history during a brief period in 1977 (33 homers in ten games), had also

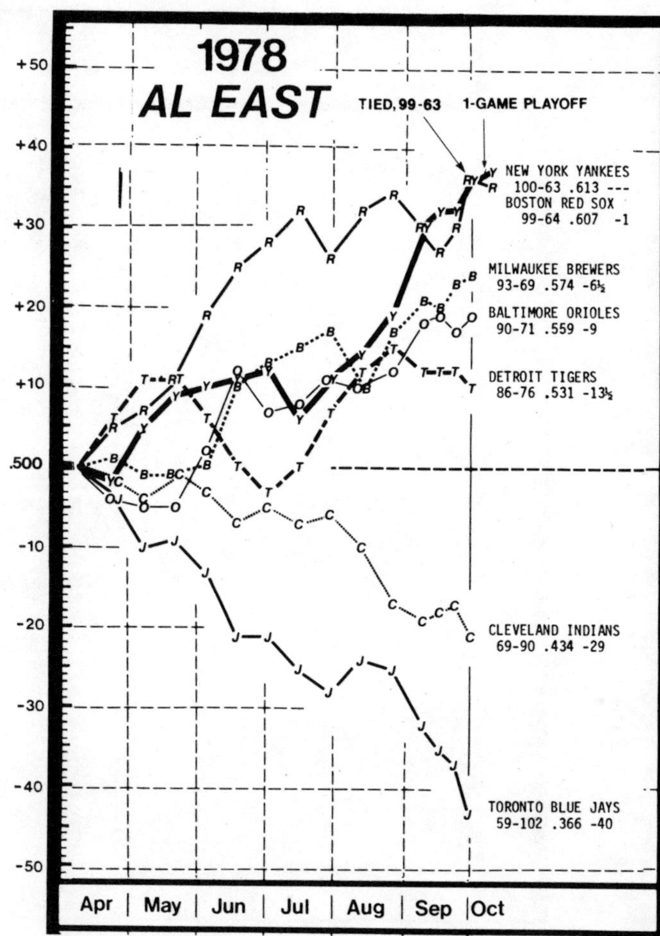


plugged some holes in their roster before the '78 season. Second base, which had developed into a weak spot since 1975, was now covered by Jerry Remy, and slugger Butch Hobson had become the regular at third. More importantly, Boston had filled the gaps in their mound staff by acquiring Dennis Eckersley and Mike Torrez and bringing up Bob Stanley from the minors. Don Zimmer's club soared to 30 games over .500 by early July, and past the middle of that month the Bosox held a safe, ten-game lead over the Milwaukee Brewers, a fast-rising new power in the division now managed by George Bamberger.

The world champion Yankees were not even in third place, as of July 19th; they were fourth, 14 games in back of the Red Sox. Feuding in the Yankee camp, between Billy Martin and Reggie Jackson, and between Martin and Steinbrenner, came to a head that month, resulting in a forced resignation for Martin and his replacement by Bob Lemon. In the same week, the Red Sox were suddenly having a famine of victories on a road trip, losing nine out of ten games. In early August, Boston's lead over the Yankees, now taking over second from the Brewers, was only half what it had been.

New York had been getting the league's best pitching in over a decade from sophomore Ron Guidry all season, and reliever Goose Gossage had piled up many wins and saves, but now Catfish Hunter and Ed Figueroa were also catching fire. A ten-out-of-twelve winning binge by the Bombers around mid-August didn't cut the Red Sox lead any further, but when that was soon followed by a 14-out-of-15 streak, it was calamitous for the Bosox, because they started another sharp losing trend near the end of August. Injuries, to Lynn, Yastrzemski,

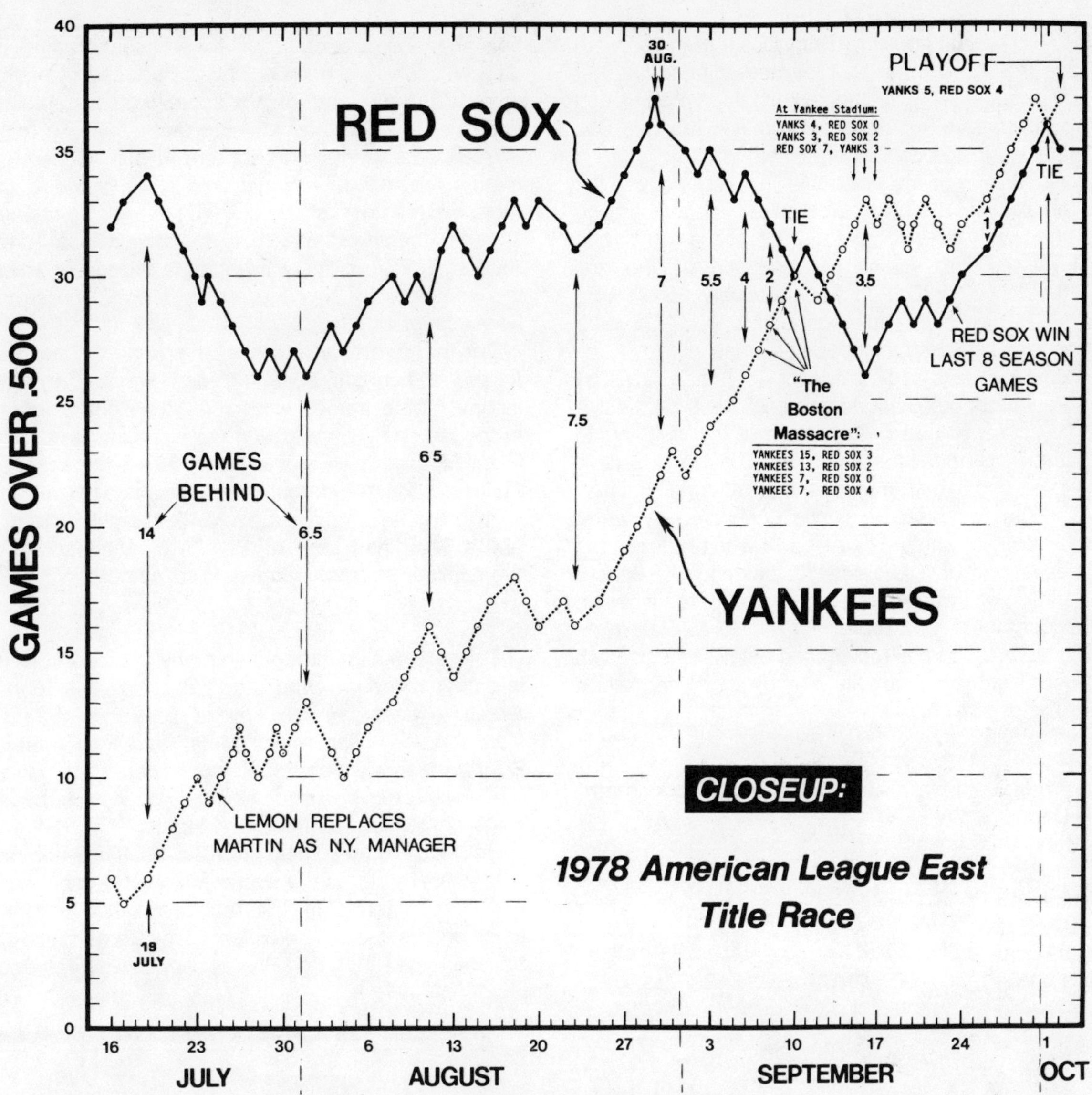


**FENWAY FIASCO. In 1978, the Boston Red Sox and New York Yankees, probably the two best teams in the majors that year, staged one of the great dramas of the century. Fourteen games ahead of the Yankees on July 19th, the Red Sox suddenly lost half of their lead with a bad road trip at the end of July, matched Yankee wins through August, then lost the other half of the lead in early September, completing what was, numerically, the worst fold in modern major league history. The collapse of the injury-riddled Bosox in September was climaxed by a four-game slaughter by the Yankees at Fenway Park called The Boston Massacre. Later that month, Boston removed part of the stigma of its disintegration by recovering remarkably, rallying from 3½ games behind to tie New York on the closing day. In the October 2 playoff game at Fenway Park, Bucky Dent's three-run homer over The Wall put the Yanks ahead in the seventh inning and another homer by Reggie Jackson gave them their winning run in a 5-4 thriller.**

Remy, Evans, and Hobson, hardly helped the team's cause at this critical time in the season. By the time the Yankees and Red Sox met in Fenway for four games starting September 7th, the margin was down to only four games, and there were signs of panic in Boston, if not in the players, certainly in the fans.

In what was quickly branded The Boston Massacre, the Yankees humiliated Boston in the four-game series, scoring 42 runs on 67 hits and 12 Red Sox errors. That cut the lead to zero—the Red Sox had blown a 14-game lead in little more than seven weeks. Their disintegration continued, to a point 3½ games behind the Yankees the next week, suggesting that even a 17½-game lead may not be a safe one sometimes. Finally, in the last of three games at Yankee Stadium, Boston put an end to the collapse with a 7-3 win by Eckersley and Stanley. Then a chase-in-reverse began, almost like a co-hit in a double feature that had been scheduled all along. The Yankees staggered a bit in September's third week, letting the Red Sox get back to within a game, and then the two matched consecutive wins on Sunday through Saturday of the final week, Boston getting brilliant pitching from Tiant and Eckersley. On Sunday, October 1st, the Red Sox shut out the Toronto Blue Jays while the Yankees lost to Cleveland, and the American League had the second tie in its history.

The showdown came the next day in Fenway Park, 30 years, minus one day, after Boston's Denny Galehouse had faced Cleveland Gene Bearden in the league's first playoff at the same ballpark. This time, it was Torrez vs. Guidry. And once again, The Green Monster turned its wrath upon its owners, converting what would have been a routine left-field flyout in many parks to a three-run homer by Bucky Dent in the seventh inning, to give the Yankees a lead they never lost. Another home run, by Reggie Jackson the next inning, represented New York's final margin in the game, because the Red Sox rallied for two runs in the bottom of the eighth. The gripping tension continued right to the last batter in the bottom of the ninth, Yastrzemski (who also had homered earlier), as the tying run was on third with the score 5-4. But Gossage got Yaz to pop up to Nettles at third, ending the game and the title race in another bitter defeat for the Red Sox—probably, considering how things had looked in July, the most painful in all the years a Boston American League franchise has existed.

The Red Sox-Yankee playoff game of 1978 was rated by fans in one survey as the greatest game of the seventies. A diagram of it (similar to that of Game Six of the 1975 World Series in *Baseball Graphics*) is presented here to provide a detailed view and also to demonstrate the advantages of a new form of box score for baseball games concocted by writer Bill James, the brilliant analyst of the sport who produces the annual *Baseball Abstract*. (P.O. Box 2150, Lawrence, KS 66044). In his 1979 edition of the *Abstract*, James illustrates what he calls the "account-form" box score with the '78 AL East playoff game and his box score is reproduced below. The diagram was constructed entirely from the play-by-play information contained in James's box score.

```
New York                  Boston
8Rivers   wsd 65Ws        6Burleso k 53D 63w
o8Blair          s        4Remy    7 7 5fD s
2Munson  k k k d'64       9Rice    k 63s'9 9
9Piniell 53s 8 9          7Yaz     H k 3 S'5
0Jackson 7 9 43H          2Fisk    7 8 w s
5Nettles 6 6 9 k          8Lynn    8 139 s'
3Chambli 3 63S 43         0Hobson  53s k 9
7White   k w S 43         3Scott   d k sak
7Thomass                  5Broham  2f7
4Doyle    4 43            o5Bailey     k
6Spencer      7           oEvans           7
4Stanley        43
6Dent     9 6 H"k

(1Guidry)9 9 9 1          (1Torrez)9 9 8
(1Gossag)        3        (1Stanle)    1 9 4
                 5 1      (1Hassle)
                   1      (1Drago)
New York.........0 0 0  0 0 0  4 1 0-5
Boston...........0 1 0  0 0 1  0 2 0-4
T: 2:52.  A-32,925.
```

James uses the conventional numbering of player positions (1 for pitcher, 6 for shortstop etc.) and these numbers are also used to indicate flyouts (e.g., "8" means "flied to centerfield") and groundouts (e.g., a groundout to third base would be "53"), as in scoring games. With a few letter symbols, he can indicate singles (s or S), doubles (d or D), triples (t or T), home runs (H), walks (w or W), and other ways of getting on base, using capitals if the batter scores, lower-case if not. Prime symbols for baserunners driven in (not including the batter, in the case of home runs) are also used, so d″ would be a double that drove in two runners and H″ would be a three-run homer (H! is a grand slam). A few other, mostly conventional, symbols are needed, such as "k" for strikeout. In the lower part of the box score, the number of batters faced by each pitcher is given. From this kind of box score, we can reproduce all the action of a game, and all-importantly, we can recapture the *sequence* of events, and still get all the nonsequential information that a conventional box score provides, (plus much more, such as who struck out whom), without taking any more space in the newspaper than the conventional form requires. As James insists, there are simply dozens of advantages of the account-form box score, but it would be surprising if it were accepted.

For the third year in a row, the Yankees beat Kansas City for the AL pennant, despite three home runs by George Brett in one of the games, in a four-game championship series. In the NL, the Dodgers, who were challenged by a surprising Giant team as well as the Reds during the season, beat the Phillies, who were almost caught by a late-blazing Pirate team. With great fielding plays by Nettles, eight RBIs by Jackson, and a combined total of 15 hits by Dent and Brian Doyle, the Yankees beat the Dodgers in six games.

## 1979

The 1979 season brought so many changes from 1978 that it is easier to count what didn't change—the four last-place teams, for example, were still the Toronto Blue Jays, the Oakland A's, the New York Mets, and the Atlanta Braves. But two teams which usually wallowed in the lower regions, the Montreal Expos and the Houston Astros, became legitimate contenders, almost winning titles. And the California Angels won a title, their first. So did the Baltimore Orioles, who appeared to be the supreme power of the major leagues, with 102 victories in the regular season and three more quick ones over the Angels, until they were licked in the World Series by the Pittsburgh Pirates. Conversely, the Dodgers, suf-

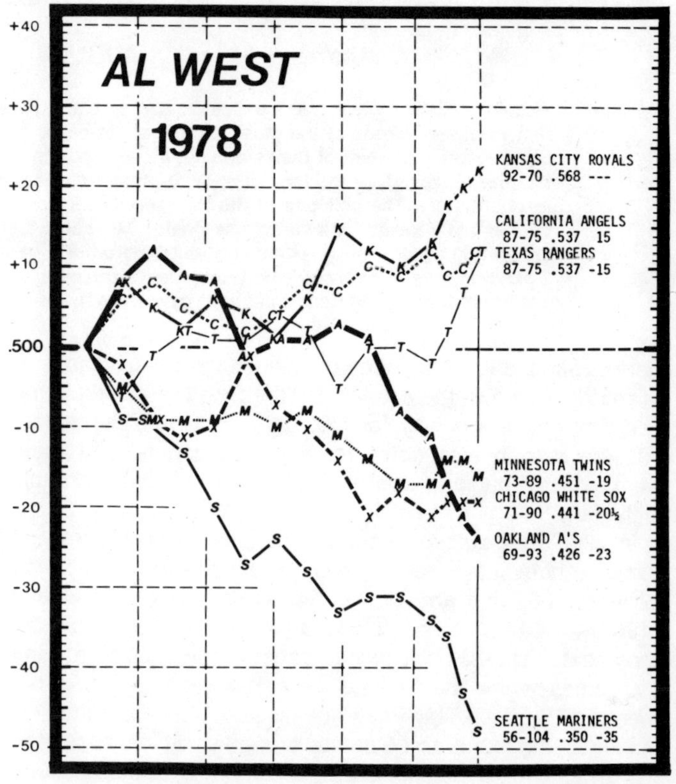

# 1978 AL East Playoff

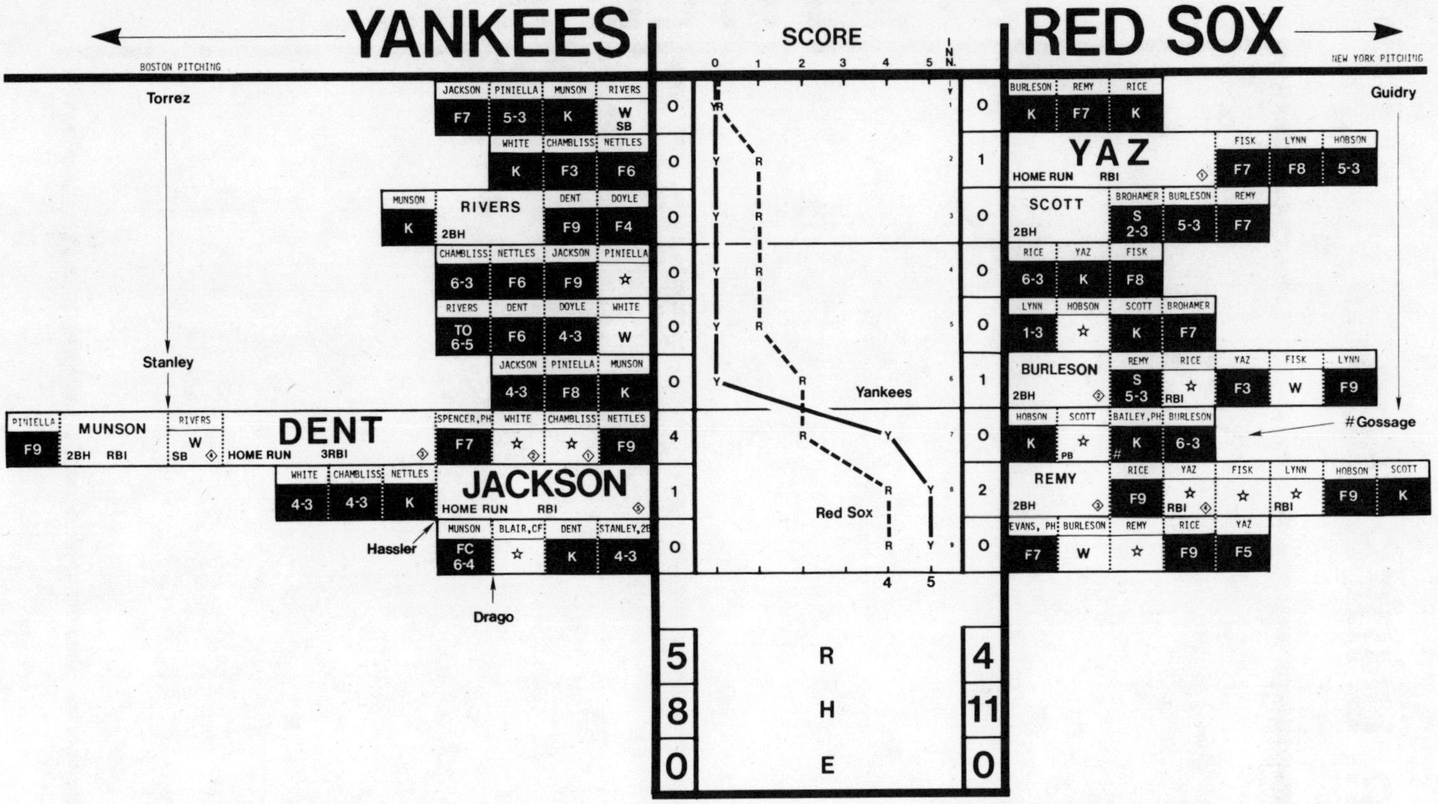

**YANKEES** ← BOSTON PITCHING | SCORE | **RED SOX** → NEW YORK PITCHING

Boston pitching: Torrez, Stanley, Hassler, Drago. New York pitching: Guidry, # Gossage.

| Inn. | Yankees (read right-to-left from center) | Yankees | Red Sox | Red Sox (read left-to-right from center) |
|---|---|---|---|---|
| 1 | RIVERS W SB; MUNSON K; PINIELLA 5-3; JACKSON F7 | 0 | 0 | BURLESON K; REMY F7; RICE K |
| 2 | NETTLES F6; CHAMBLISS F3; WHITE K | 0 | 1 | YAZ HOME RUN RBI ①; FISK F7; LYNN F8; HOBSON 5-3 |
| 3 | DOYLE F4; DENT F9; RIVERS 2BH; MUNSON K | 0 | 0 | SCOTT 2BH; BROHAMER S 2-3; BURLESON 5-3; REMY F7 |
| 4 | PINIELLA ☆; JACKSON F9; NETTLES F6; CHAMBLISS 6-3 | 0 | 0 | RICE 6-3; YAZ K; FISK F8 |
| 5 | WHITE W; DOYLE 4-3; DENT F6; RIVERS TO 6-5 | 0 | 0 | LYNN 1-3; HOBSON ☆; SCOTT K; BROHAMER F7 |
| 6 | MUNSON K; PINIELLA F8; JACKSON 4-3 | 0 | 1 | BURLESON 2BH ②; REMY S 5-3; RICE ☆ RBI; YAZ F3; FISK W; LYNN F9 |
| 7 | NETTLES F9; CHAMBLISS ☆ ①; WHITE ☆ ②; SPENCER,PH F7; DENT HOME RUN 3RBI ③; RIVERS W SB ④; MUNSON 2BH RBI; PINIELLA F9 | 4 | 0 | HOBSON K; SCOTT ☆ PB; BAILEY,PH K; BURLESON 6-3 |
| 8 | JACKSON HOME RUN RBI ⑤; NETTLES K; CHAMBLISS 4-3; WHITE 4-3 | 1 | 2 | REMY 2BH ③; RICE F9; YAZ ☆ RBI ④; FISK ☆; LYNN ☆ RBI; HOBSON F9; SCOTT K |
| 9 | STANLEY,2B 4-3; DENT K; BLAIR,CF ☆; MUNSON FC 6-4 | 0 | 0 | EVANS, PH F7; BURLESON W; REMY ☆; RICE F9; YAZ F5 |

| | Yankees | Red Sox |
|---|---|---|
| R | 5 | 4 |
| H | 8 | 11 |
| E | 0 | 0 |

Diagram of the 1978 American League East playoff game, based on Bill James's account-form box score of the game in his 3rd annual *Baseball Abstract* (1979). In the inning-by-inning rows of symbols, read left-to-right from the center of the diagram for Red Sox action and right-to-left for Yankee hitting. The black squares represent outs, with conventional abbreviations in white lettering for further identification ("F" for flyout or popout, "G" for groundout, "K" for strikeout, "S" for sacrifice, "FC" for fielder's choice, and "TO" for tag play). Stars are singles, and diamonds are runs scored, numbered ordinally. Other abbreviations: "W" = walk, "SB" = stolen base, "PB" = Passed ball, "2BH" = a double, and "RBI" = run(s) batted in.

# 1978 TITLE RACES

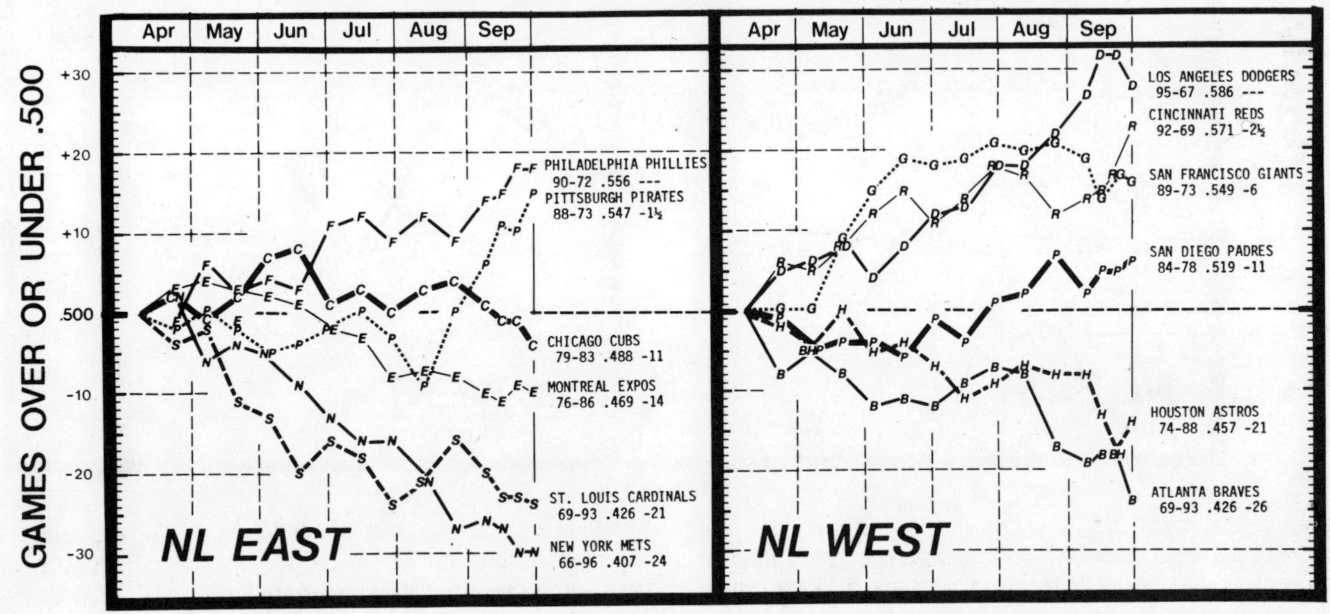

# 1979 TITLE RACES

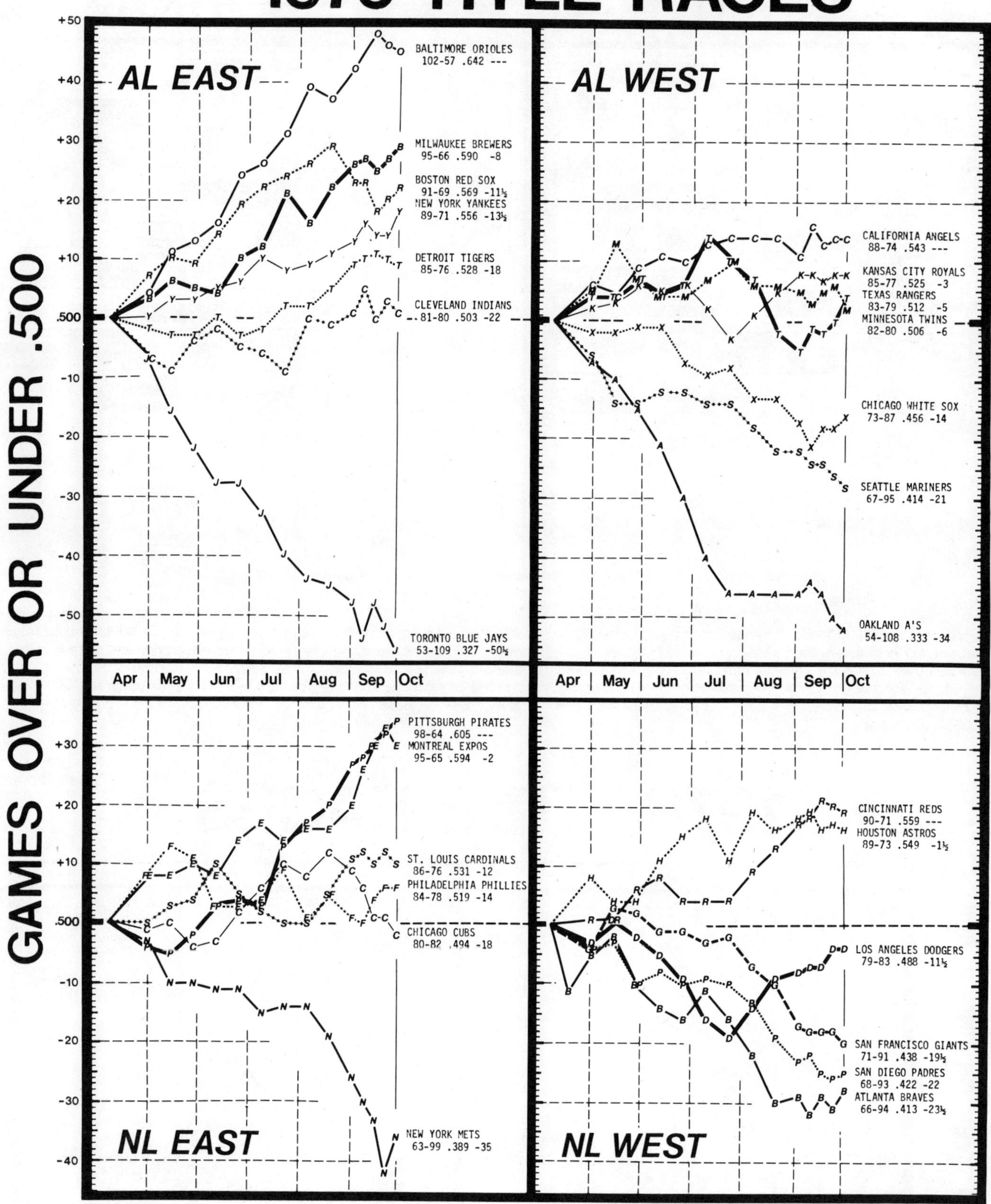


fering several key injuries, spent much of July in last place, and the Yankees were stuck in fourth place almost every week of the season. The best title races were in the NL East, where the Expos challenged the Pirates to the closing day, and the NL West, where Tom Seaver led the Cincinnati Reds to a narrow victory over the Astros (see closeups).

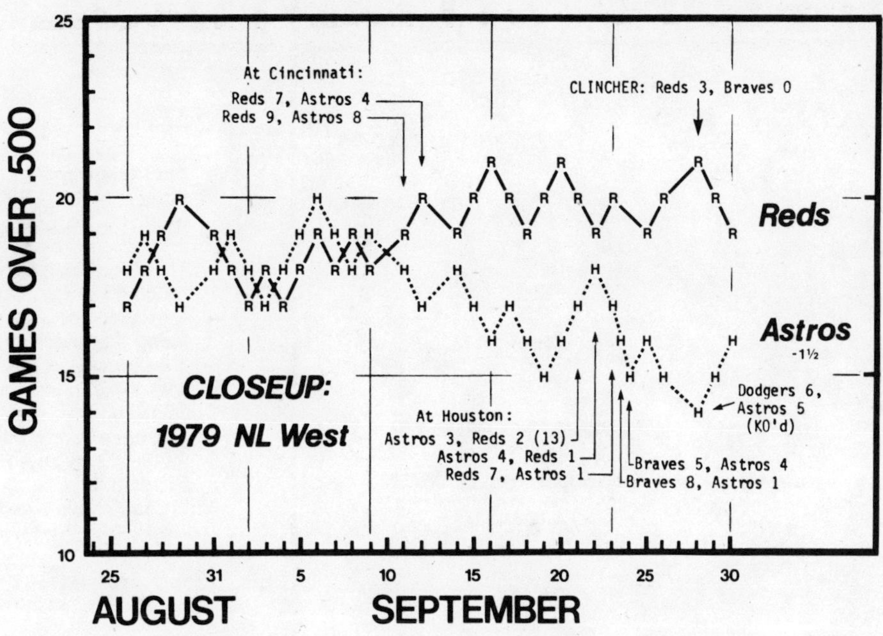


**IF AT FIRST YOU DON'T SUCCEED . . . In 1979 the Houston Astros rose out of obscurity and contended fiercely for the NL West title (upper graph). The Astros that year were "runless wonders," scoring only 583 runs in the season, but they were led magnificently by the pitching of J.R. Richard, Phil Niekro, and Joe Sambito. The Cincinnati Reds beat them in the last two weeks of the '79 title chase, but in 1980 (lower graph) Houston battled to a tie with the Dodgers, despite losing Richard midway through the season, and whipped LA, 7-1, in the National League's fifth title-playoff. First baseman Art Howe's four runs batted in and Niekro's six-hitter were the main elements in the divisional triumph.**

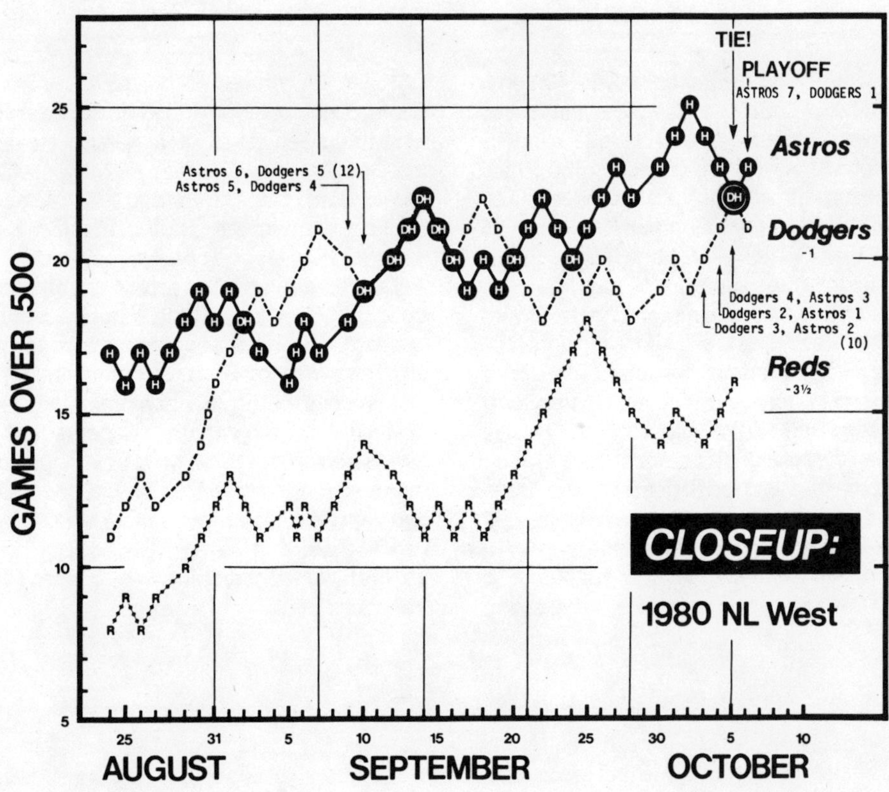

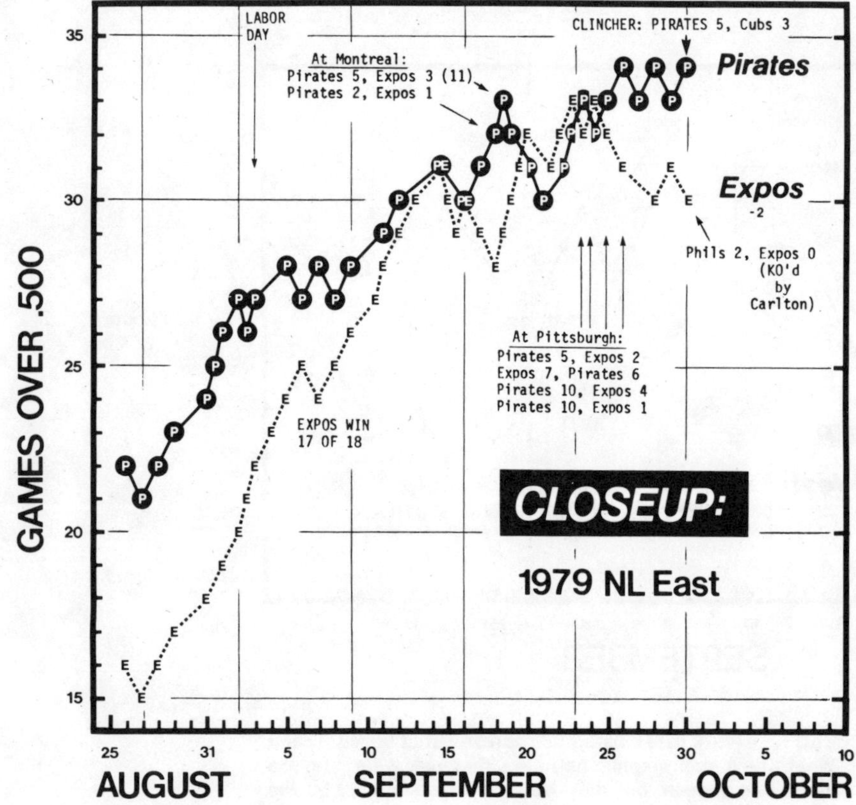


**IN A FAM-A-LEE WAY, with 39-year-old Willie "Pops" Stargell as the inspiring father figure, the Pittsburgh Pirates pulled together for a victory in the 1979 NL East title race, and went on to an upset come-from-behind World Series win over the Baltimore Orioles. The Montreal Expos had their first big-winning season, and created an exciting race with a red-hot pace around Labor Day, recapturing first place in mid-September. They did not fare well in their face-to-face encounters with the Pirates, however, who had somewhat superior offensive strength with Stargell, Dave Parker, Bill Madlock, Omar Moreno, Phil Garner, and Bill Robinson. The Bucs clinched the title on the final day, helped by Philadelphia's two defeats of the Expos that weekend in Montreal.**

## 1980

The 1980 season had two hot title races in the National League, a warm one in the AL East, and a cool walkaway by the Kansas City Royals in the AL West. Despite eventful doings in all four divisions, the year belonged to the Philadelphia Phillies, their freshman manager, Dallas Green, and three outstanding Phillie players—Mike Schmidt (MVP with 48 homers and 121 RBIs), Steve Carlton (24-9), and Tug McGraw (five wins, 20 saves, and an infectious spirit).

The Phillies, Expos, and world champion Pirates were hooked up in a splendid title chase all summer, until the Pirates took a surprising plunge starting in August. The Expos were strong again with good pitching by Steve Rogers, Scott Sanderson, Bill Gullickson, and 40-year-old Woody Fryman, and they were well-heeled offensively with catcher Gary Carter, first sacker Warren Cromartie, and outfielders Andre Dawson, Ellis Valentine, and ex-Tiger Ron LeFlore, who stole 97 bases. They carried the fight to the Phillies all the way to a dramatic confrontation in Montreal on the final weekend, in which Mike Schmidt's 11th-inning homer on Saturday night, October 4th, proved to be the title-clinching blow. In the NL championship series, the Phils conquered the Houston Astros, who had been taken to a tie and playoff in the NL West by the Dodgers (see closeup). But it took five games for the Phillies to down the Astros, and four of the contests were spine-tingling extra-inning affairs, making this set of games the most thrilling league championship series ever.

The Royals, who had prospered all summer under new manager Jim Frey from strong mound work by Larry Gura, Dennis Leonard, and relief ace Dan Quisenberry, and more dramatically from George Brett's assault on the magic .400 BA mark (he finished with .390), whipped the Yankees three straight in the AL championship. KC contested gamely in the World Series, which it was favored to win, but the Phils staged some more exciting comebacks to win, four games to two; Carlton's two victories, McGraw's victory and two saves, and Schmidt's two homers and seven RBIs paced the Philadelphia club to its first world championship in the 104-year history of the franchise.

# 1980 TITLE RACES

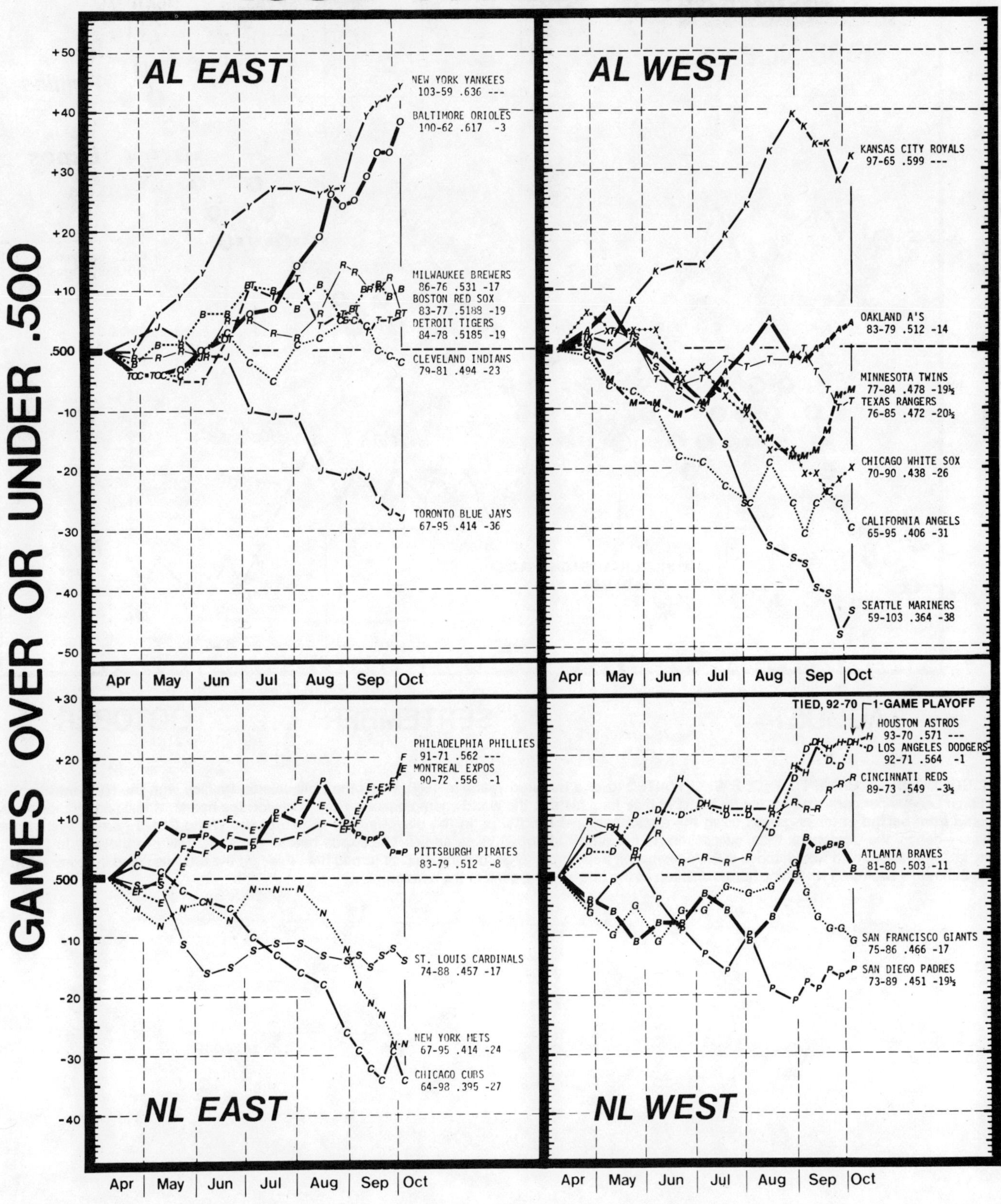

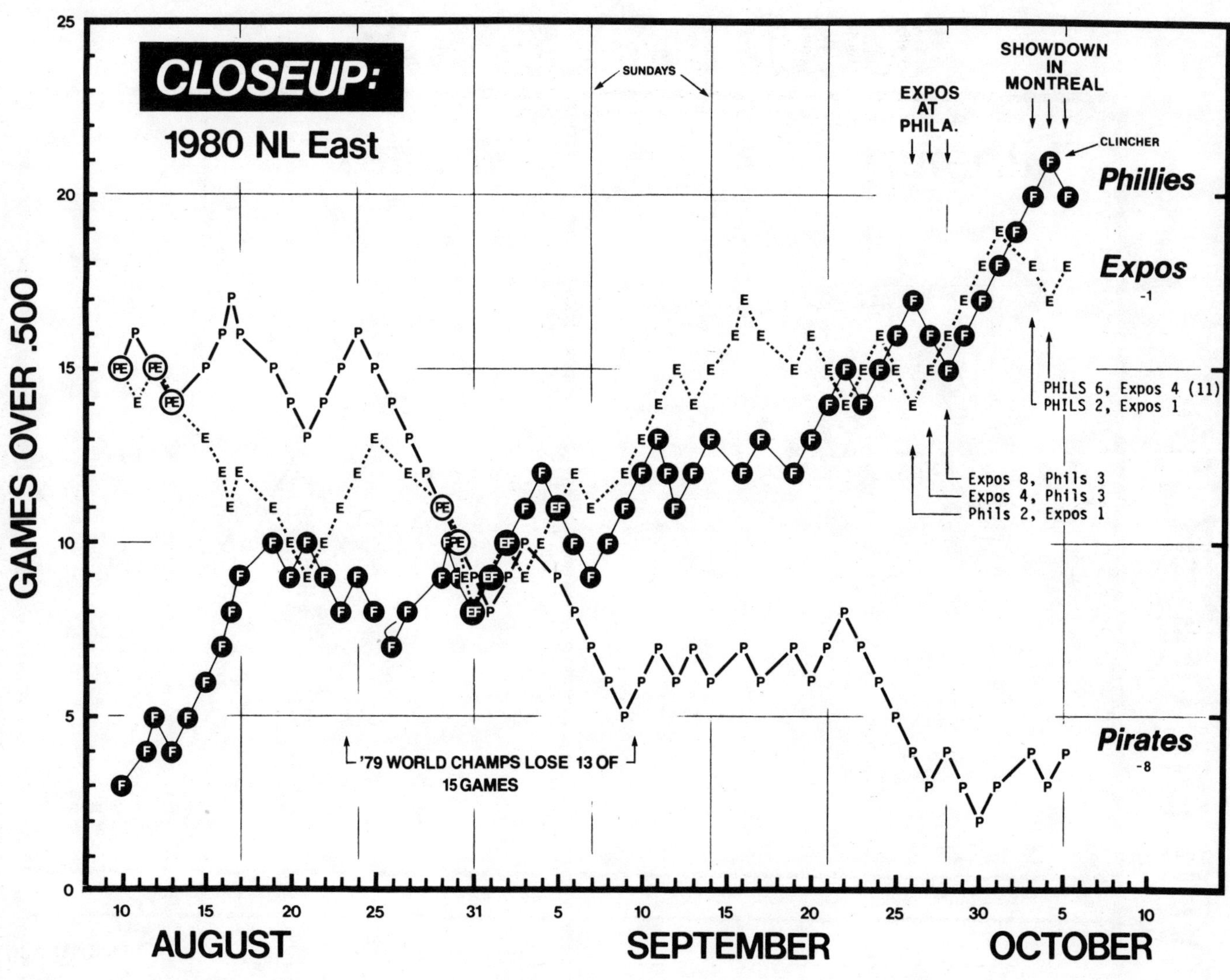


ALL GOOD THINGS CAME TO THOSE WHO WAITED (over a hundred years) in 1980, when the Philadelphia Phillies won the NL East title, the National League pennant, and for the first time in their long history, the world championship. They also won the hearts of millions by repeatedly coming from behind in tense games down the stretch, against the Astros in the playoffs, and in two of the World Series games against the Royals—hence, the Comeback Kids, successors to the Whiz Kids of 30 years earlier. The Expos battled the Phils down to the wire in the title race, taking the lead with two victories in Philadelphia on September 27-28, but the Phillies turned the tables on the final weekend in Montreal with Mike Schmidt's two-run, 11th-inning home run blast as the title-winning peak of the heroics.

# The Best and Worst

Out of all the pennant races we've had since 1900, which were the most dramatic? This is partly a matter of subjective judgment, of course, but if we measure pennant-race drama in terms of the amount of shouting and ink at the time and the number of historical citations in later years, we can at least attempt a listing. The first multigraph ("Six Dramas") presents some races which must be in the top ten, if not the top six; at any rate, these are certainly six of the most memorable, involving the Miracle Braves of 1914, the Coogan's-Bluff Miracle Giants of 1951, the Comeback Yankees of 1978, the Amazing Mets of 1969, the Impossible-Dream Red Sox of 1967, and the Phamous Phizzle of the Phillies (the Cardinals being the beneficiaries) in 1964. Other authors would doubtless prefer to include the 1908 fracas among the Cubs, Giants, and Pirates ahead of some of these selections, or perhaps the 1930 Cardinal, the 1935 Cub, the 1940 Tiger, or the 1948 Indian triumphs.

One glance at the first multigraph shows a common theme: the come-from-behind victory. In five of the six cases at least, the drama came not so much from how close the race was near the end of the season as how far behind the underdog winner was at some early point. For the '51 Giants and the '78 Yankees, that early point was near the middle of the season. But for the '69 Mets and '67 Red Sox, the early low point that operated psychologically was the previous year's next-to-last finishing position more than a poor midseason position the same year. In the 1964 NL case, the dramatic source was much less the come-from-

# SIX DRAMAS

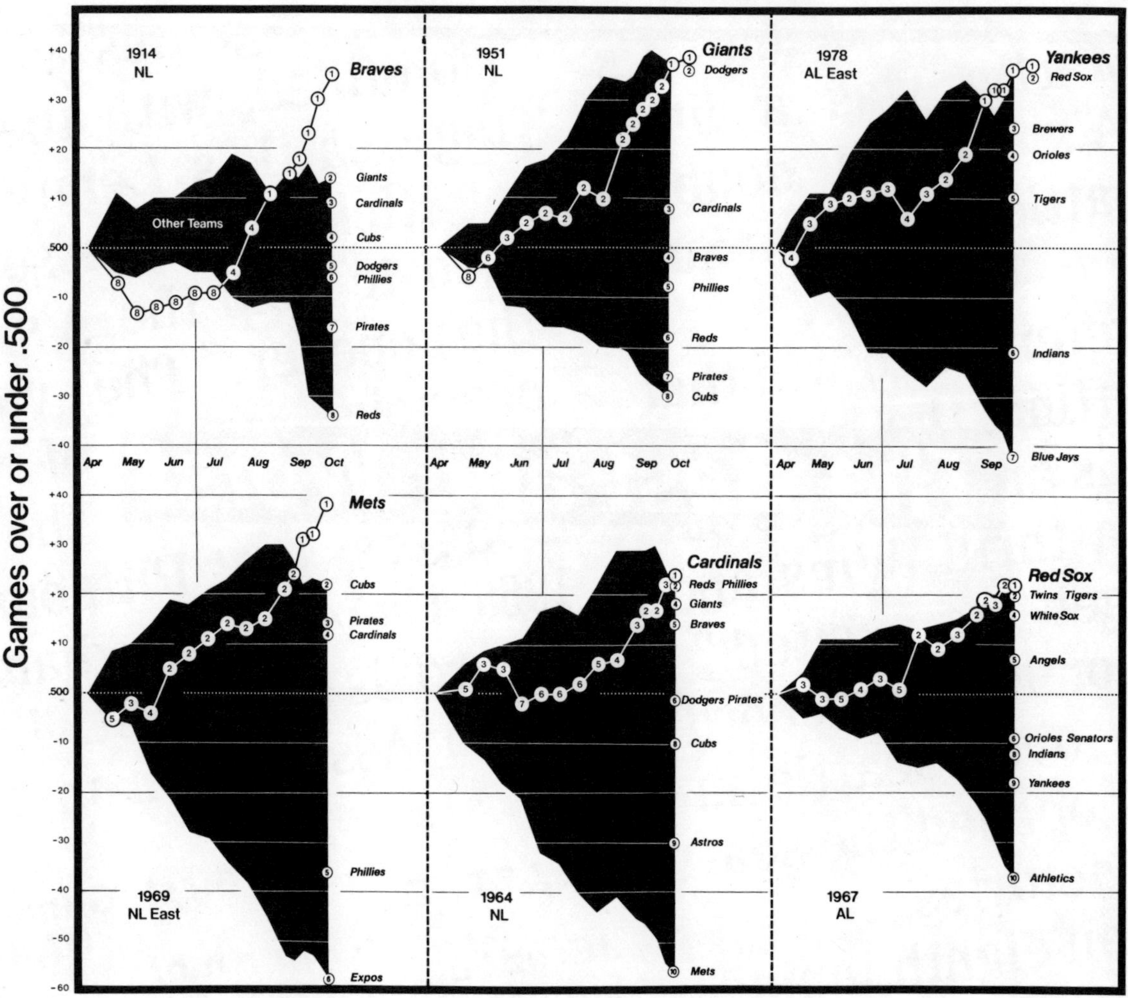


behind by the Cardinals as the Phils' flop, because the latter was so sudden and so late—too late for much buildup of suspense.

If we define another category, Greatest Heartbreakers, we will find some other races that may belong in the top ten of Most Dramatic, too. The four affairs shown in the second multigraph all involved thrilling come-from-behinds in which the challengers wound up still behind—the 1924 Robins (Dodgers), the 1928 Athletics, the 1948 Red Sox, and the 1949 Red Sox. In all four of these, the popular underdog did actually come from behind—far behind—to take the lead, at least momentarily, in the last month of the season, only to snatch defeat (if #2 must be called that) from the jaws of victory in the final days or hours.

Since baseball is a game of numbers, and we have zillions of them in our pennant-races data, there is no excuse for not pursuing these summaries and listings in more systematic and objective ways. So let us next examine the Closest Races, whether they were dramatic or not, mainly in terms of the number of games separating the contenders at the finish line. And where ties occurred at the finish, we can still order the races according to how long the close competition took place. If nothing else, we ought to be able to gauge how much closeness, by itself, relates to thrillingness and other forms of interest from this exercise.

We can also get a view of whether the number of contending teams makes a difference in how exciting a pennant race is, by separating the five-team fracases from the four-team frays, the three-team thrillers, and the two-team tussles. That is done in the next four multi-panel graphs. With few exceptions, how many teams were considered to be true contenders in a race was determined by whether a team was as close as five games behind the league or division leader at any point in the last four weeks of the season.

Starting with the most crowded races, we have four of the 186 races that qualify as five-team competitions—the 1973 NL East and 1969 NL West divisional races and, oddly, the only two Federal League races that took place. The FL races clearly became three-team (1915) and two-team (1914) contests in the final fortnights, suggesting that our criterion for defining the number of true contenders may be too lenient, but we have to keep it this liberal to cover cases like the 1973 NL East battle. In that crazy contest, all five

## We're Number Two!

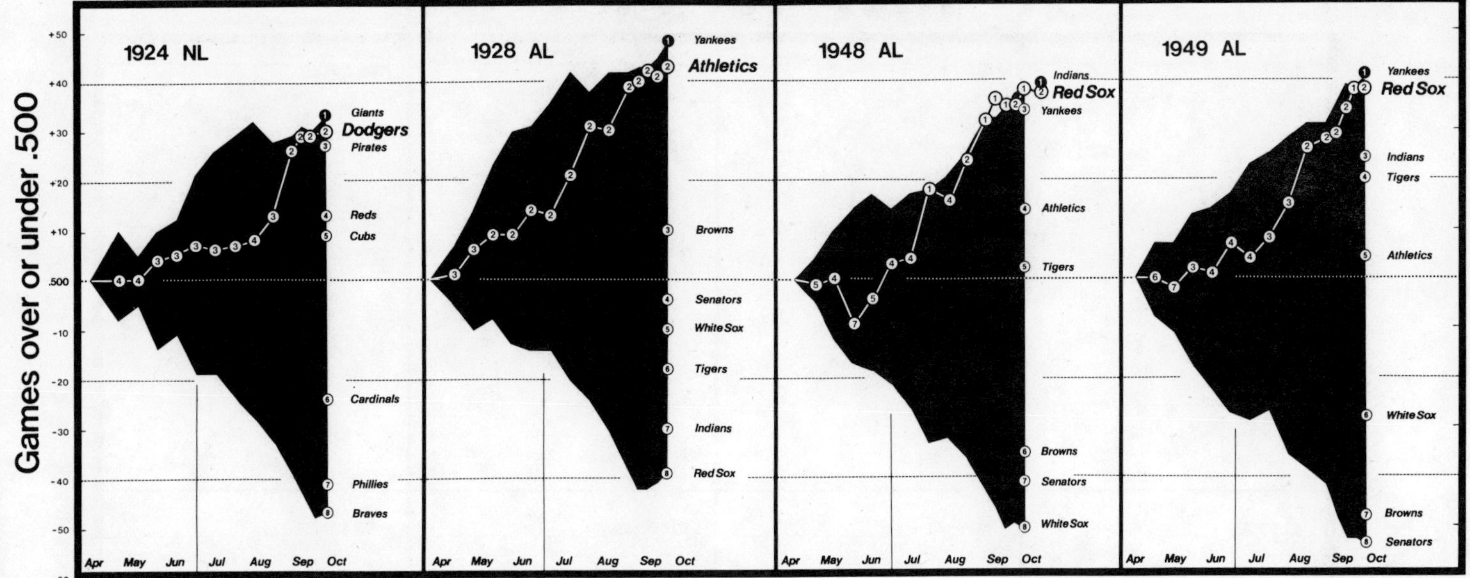


clubs were "in the race" to the late stages, even when they were four to five games behind the leader, since the New York Mets, who won, were behind the other four contenders as late as September 11th and the Cubs were in fifth place only 2½ games behind as late as September 22nd. Beyond question, then, the award goes to the 1973 NL East for the closest race having the most competitors. But considering the mediocrity of the teams (only the Mets finished above .500), was this race the most dramatic, or anywhere near that?

It didn't compare in thrills with the 1967 AL race, which leads the list of four-teamers in closeness. Many Red Sox fans would say that no pennant race of any size compared with that one. And objectively, it must be admitted, that '67 thriller was not only as close as any other four-team chase at the end, but excruciatingly tight for a far longer period before the finish.

Since teams can't get any closer than being tied, those races that ended in ties and required playoffs to decide winners have been put at the top of the multigraphs representing three- and two-team races (no four- or five-team races ended in ties). When the tied three-teamers are or-

## CLOSEST 5-TEAM RACES

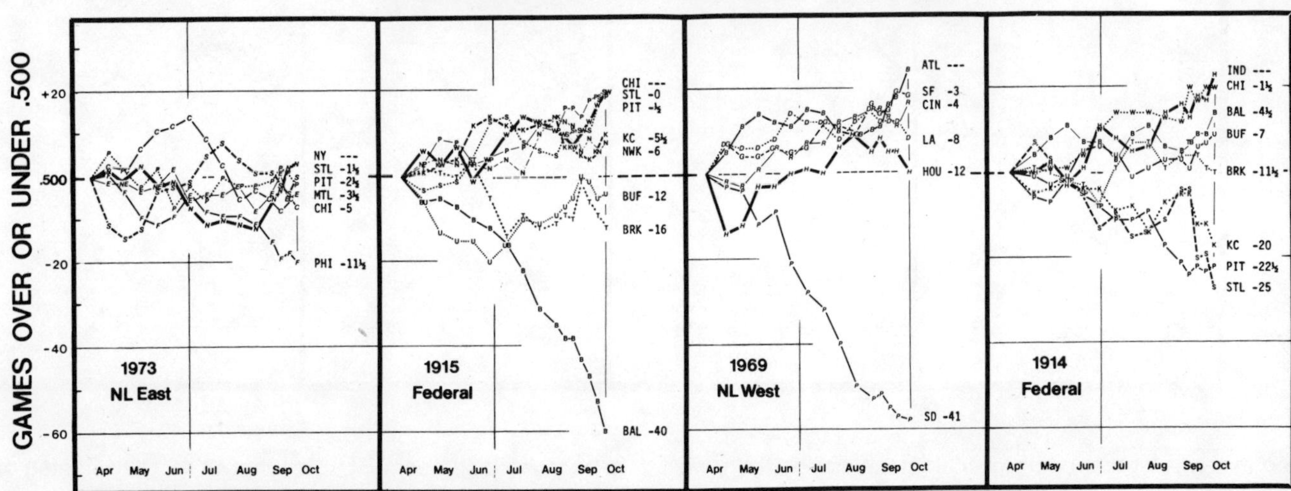


**CLOSEST FOR THE MOSTEST. The closest five-team title race of the modern era as the 1973 NL East free-for-all in which the New York Mets narrowly beat out the Cardinals, Pirates, Expos, and Cubs. Three other races are shown above in which five clubs were still in the running (within five games of the top) in the last four weeks. The succeeding multigraphs, for four-, three-, and two-team races, have with few exceptions the individual races ordered in terms of the closeness at the end of a season, of all of the teams considered to be contenders in the final month.**

# 4-TEAM RACES

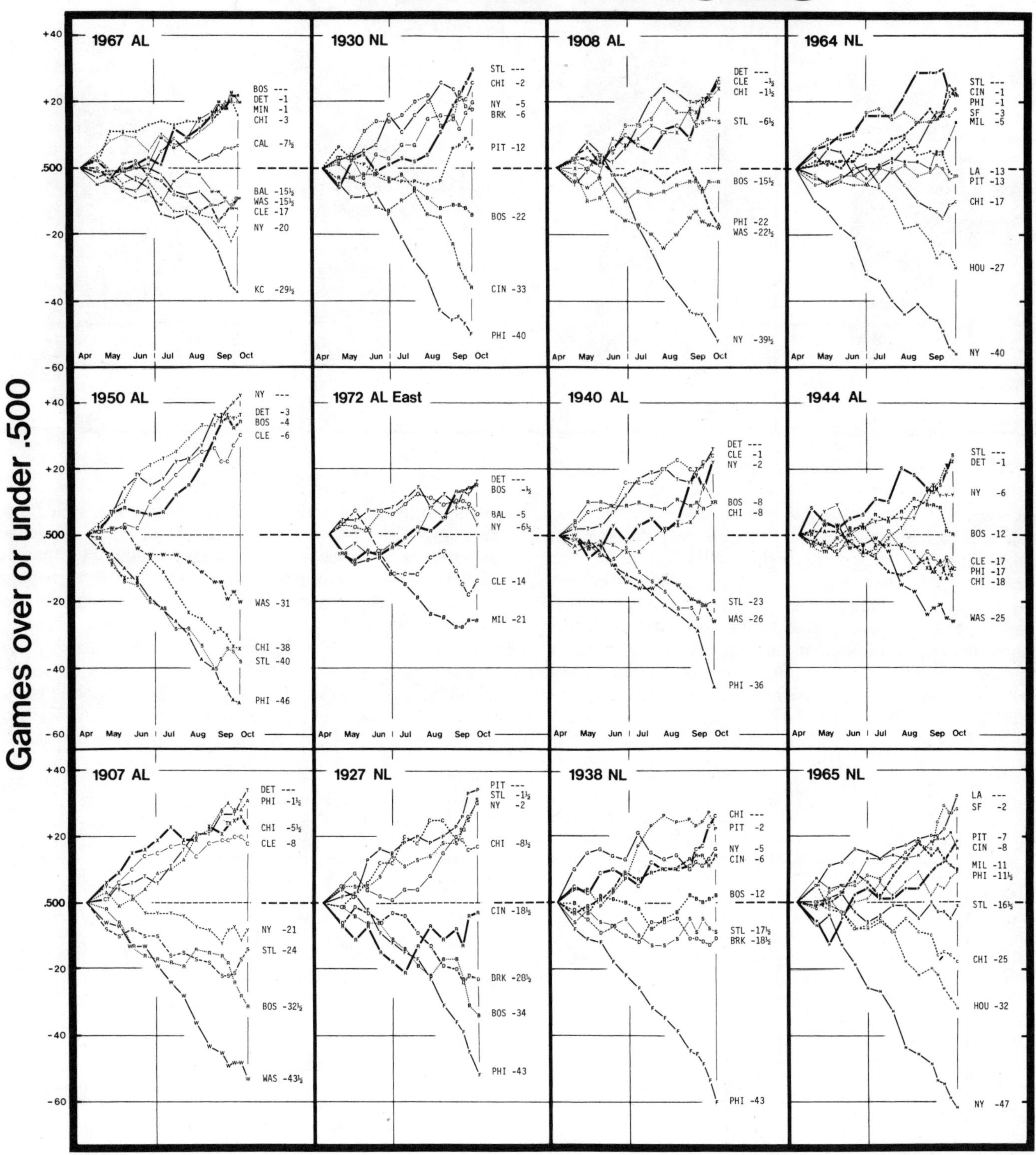


dered in terms of the length of their close competition, we find the 1948 AL race, won by Cleveland, in the first rank; the 1980 NL West race, won by Houston, second-closest; the 1959 NL race, won by Los Angeles, third (the front-running Giants in 1959 had a bigger lead in July and August than the Astros had in those months in 1980); and the 1962 NL race, won by San Francisco, fourth. There doesn't seem to be much disagreement about the '48 AL fracas being one of the most exciting, but several of the three-team races that didn't end in ties have been considered by many fans and writers to be more spellbinding than the 1980 (West or East), 1959, and 1962 contests. For examples, the 1908 NL race, with three superior clubs playing at a brilliant pace and Merkle's Boner for added spice, and the 1924 NL race, with

# 3-TEAM RACES

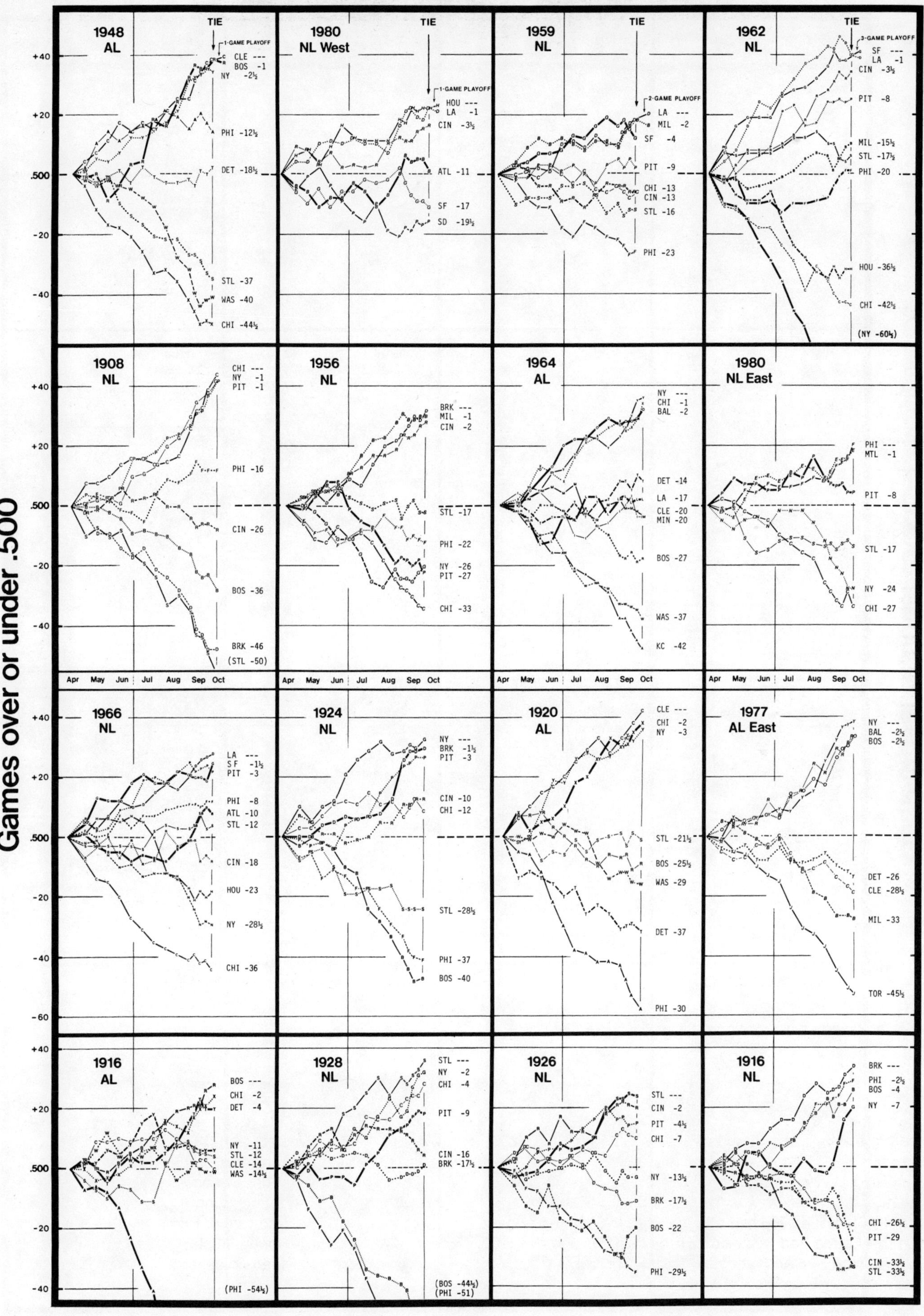
Games over or under .500
+40
+20
.500
-20
-40
-60
Apr May Jun Jul Aug Sep Oct
TIE
1948 AL
1-GAME PLAYOFF
CLE ---
BOS -1
NY -2½
PHI -12½
DET -18½
STL -37
WAS -40
CHI -44½
1980 NL West
1-GAME PLAYOFF
HOU ---
LA -1
CIN -3½
ATL -11
SF -17
SD -19½
1959 NL
2-GAME PLAYOFF
LA ---
MIL -2
SF -4
PIT -9
CHI -13
CIN -13
STL -16
PHI -23
1962 NL
3-GAME PLAYOFF
SF ---
LA -1
CIN -3½
PIT -8
MIL -15½
STL -17½
PHI -20
HOU -36½
CHI -42½
(NY -60½)
1908 NL
CHI ---
NY -1
PIT -1
PHI -16
CIN -26
BOS -36
BRK -46
(STL -50)
1956 NL
BRK ---
MIL -1
CIN -2
STL -17
PHI -22
NY -26
PIT -27
CHI -33
1964 AL
NY ---
CHI -1
BAL -2
DET -14
LA -17
CLE -20
MIN -20
BOS -27
WAS -37
KC -42
1980 NL East
PHI ---
MTL -1
PIT -8
STL -17
NY -24
CHI -27
1966 NL
LA ---
SF -1½
PIT -3
PHI -8
ATL -10
STL -12
CIN -18
HOU -23
NY -28½
CHI -36
1924 NL
NY ---
BRK -1½
PIT -3
CIN -10
CHI -12
STL -28½
PHI -37
BOS -40
1920 AL
CLE ---
CHI -2
NY -3
STL -21½
BOS -25½
WAS -29
DET -37
PHI -30
1977 AL East
NY ---
BAL -2½
BOS -2½
DET -26
CLE -28½
MIL -33
TOR -45½
1916 AL
BOS ---
CHI -2
DET -4
NY -11
STL -12
CLE -14
WAS -14½
(PHI -54½)
1928 NL
STL ---
NY -2
CHI -4
PIT -9
CIN -16
BRK -17½
(BOS -44½)
(PHI -51)
1926 NL
STL ---
CIN -2
PIT -4½
CHI -7
NY -13½
BRK -17½
BOS -22
PHI -29½
1916 NL
BRK ---
PHI -2½
BOS -4
NY -7
CHI -26½
PIT -29
CIN -33½
STL -33½

# 2-TEAM RACES

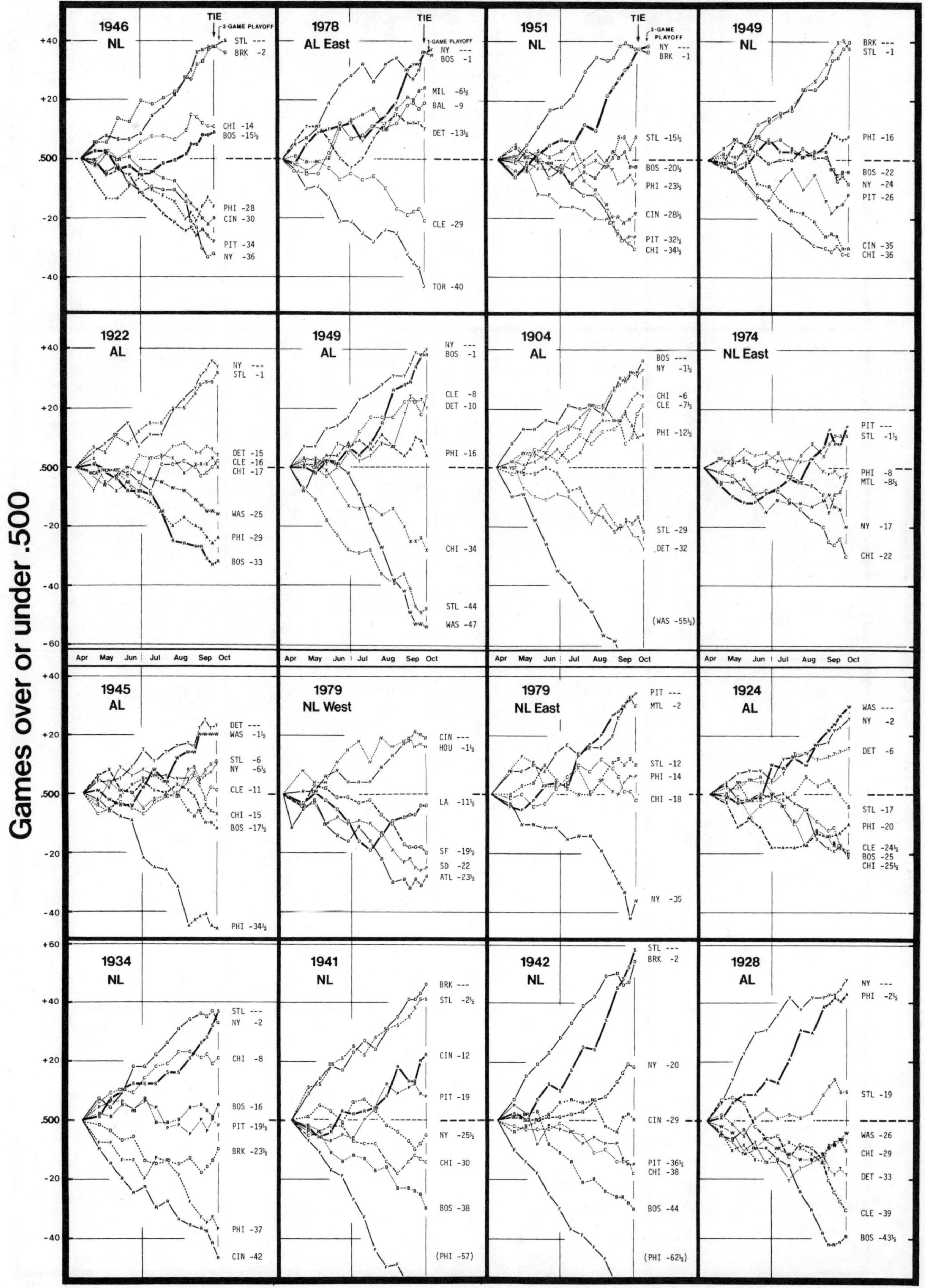

Games over or under .500
1946 NL
TIE
2-GAME PLAYOFF
STL ---
BRK -2
CHI -14
BOS -15½
PHI -28
CIN -30
PIT -34
NY -36
1978 AL East
TIE
1-GAME PLAYOFF
NY ---
BOS -1
MIL -6½
BAL -9
DET -13½
CLE -29
TOR -40
1951 NL
TIE
3-GAME PLAYOFF
NY ---
BRK -1
STL -15½
BOS -20½
PHI -23½
CIN -28½
PIT -32½
CHI -34½
1949 NL
BRK ---
STL -1
PHI -16
BOS -22
NY -24
PIT -26
CIN -35
CHI -36
1922 AL
NY ---
STL -1
DET -15
CLE -16
CHI -17
WAS -25
PHI -29
BOS -33
1949 AL
NY ---
BOS -1
CLE -8
DET -10
PHI -16
CHI -34
STL -44
WAS -47
1904 AL
BOS ---
NY -1½
CHI -6
CLE -7½
PHI -12½
STL -29
DET -32
(WAS -55½)
1974 NL East
PIT ---
STL -1½
PHI -8
MTL -8½
NY -17
CHI -22
Apr May Jun Jul Aug Sep Oct
1945 AL
DET ---
WAS -1½
STL -6
NY -6½
CLE -11
CHI -15
BOS -17½
PHI -34½
1979 NL West
CIN ---
HOU -1½
LA -11½
SF -19½
SD -22
ATL -23½
1979 NL East
PIT ---
MTL -2
STL -12
PHI -14
CHI -18
NY -35
1924 AL
WAS ---
NY -2
DET -6
STL -17
PHI -20
CLE -24½
BOS -25
CHI -25½
1934 NL
STL ---
NY -2
CHI -8
BOS -16
PIT -19½
BRK -23½
PHI -37
CIN -42
1941 NL
BRK ---
STL -2½
CIN -12
PIT -19
NY -25½
CHI -30
BOS -38
(PHI -57)
1942 NL
STL ---
BRK -2
NY -20
CIN -29
PIT -36½
CHI -38
BOS -44
(PHI -62½)
1928 AL
NY ---
PHI -2½
STL -19
WAS -26
CHI -29
DET -33
CLE -39
BOS -43½
+60
+40
+20
.500
-20
-40
-60

# Closest Races for Last Place

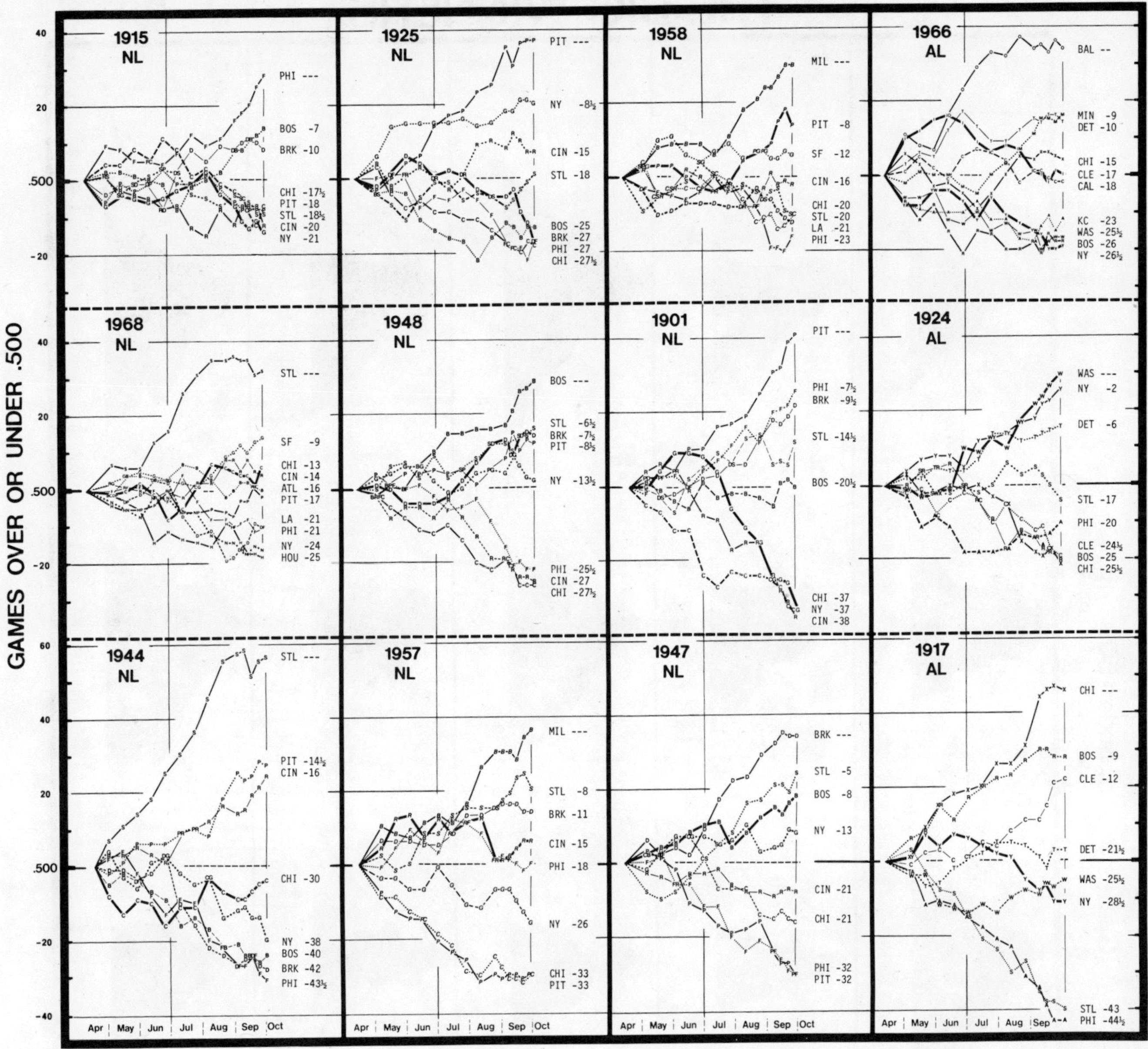


the stirring catch-up by the Brooklyn Robins, seemed to generate more excitement than these more recent races. Generally, the three-team races seem more interesting than the four-and five-teamers.

It is in the two-team category, though, where we find the theatrical quality most intense, with such famous shoot-outs as the Brooklyn Dodgers vs. the New York Giants in 1951, the Yankees and Red Sox in 1949 and 1978 (and by other names, in 1904), the Gashouse Gang's snatch from the Giants in 1934, the Ruth-and-Gehrig Yankees vs. the rebuilt Athletics in 1928, and countless Dodger-Cardinal confrontations. Uncluttered by other contestants, these one-on-one dramas take us right to High Noon, and often generate the highest theatre when the two teams in combat are *not* close to each other all season long but instead converge slowly from a large separation.

From one point of view (not a very popular one), there is nothing sacred about first place. As long as we are discussing the closeness of teams in competition, we might as well take a look at the historic happenings at the other end of the standings—the Closest Races for Last Place. Or to put it another way, the closest bunchings of teams trying to avoid finishing in last place. The multigraph for this category shows the 1916 New York Giants of John McGraw taking the dubious honors, with four other teams less than five games away from those Giants at the finish line. That was the only clearcut five-team race for the cellar. In four other seasons, there were four teams that finished within four games of the bottom spot, and in four more races, there were tight three-team groupings. Finally, there was the classic 1957 NL race, in which the Pirates and Cubs battled all season long to an absolute draw, and with no playoff deemed necessary, both teams ended the year 33 games behind the Milwaukee Braves. Ten years earlier, the Pirates and the Phillies did the same thing, and the Browns and Athletics went tooth-and-nail into the cellar in 1917.

# THE BIG WINNERS

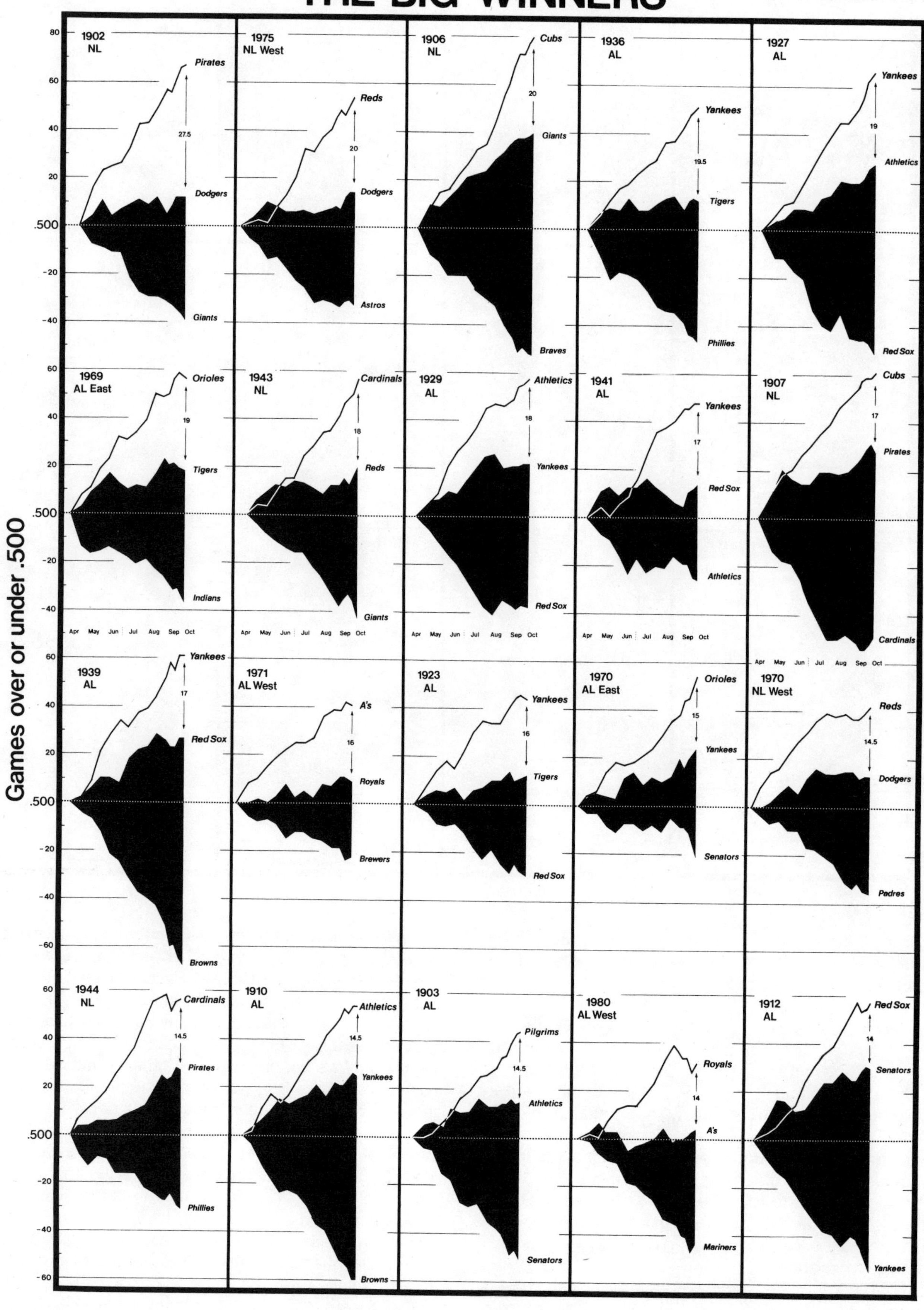

# THE BIG LOSERS

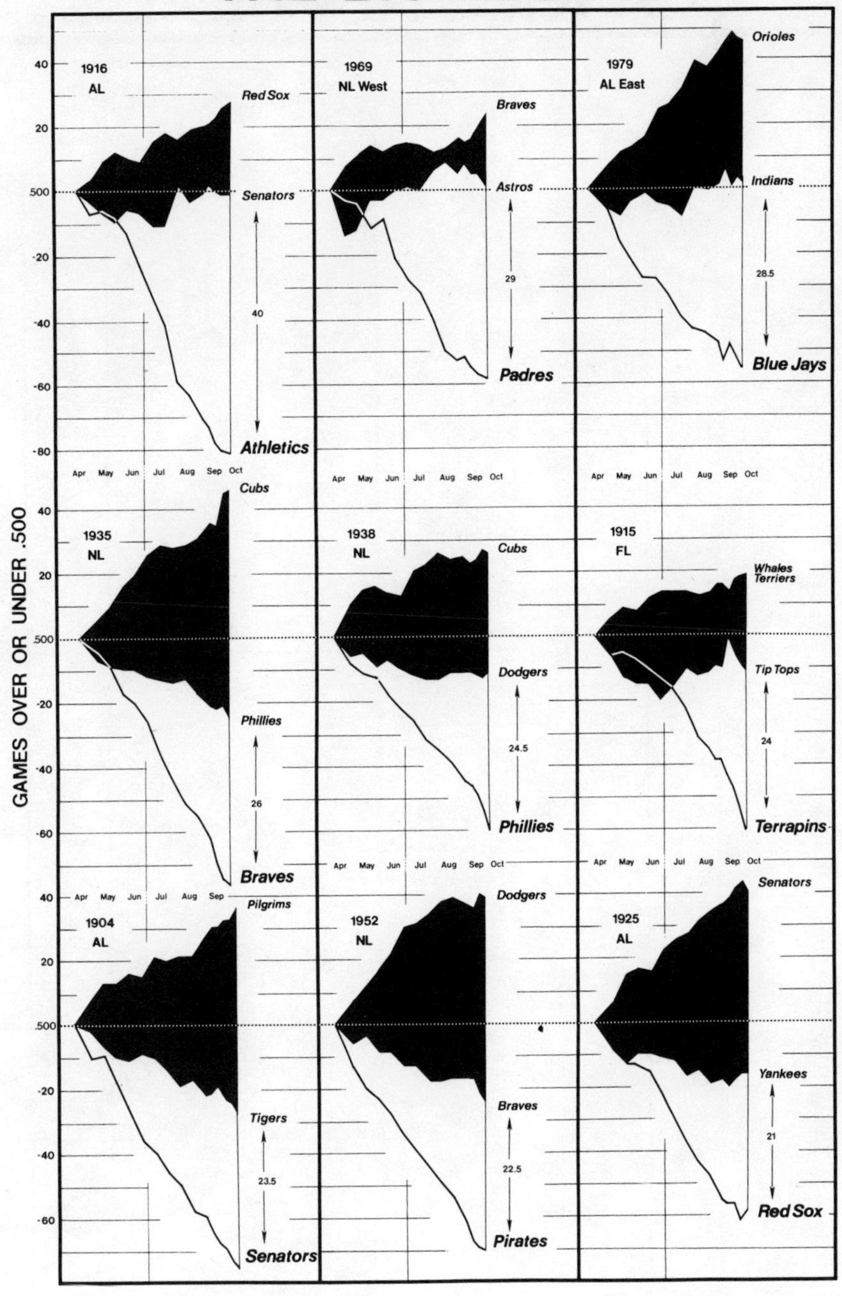


Our next comparisons involve the size of winning and losing margins, and here we are concerned with the opposite of closeness, at both ends of the standings. The 20 races in which the pennant winner finished with a margin of 14 games or more over the second-place team are displayed in one multigraph (entitled "The Big Winners"), with the 27½-game margin of the 1902 Pittsburgh Pirates taking the honors. The 1975 Cincinnati Reds and the 1906 Chicago Cubs come next, with their 20-game margins, but the Reds are placed ahead of the Cubs in the order because those Reds held a big edge for a greater proportion of the season (the area between their curve and the black shading representing the rest of the teams was greater) that that of the Cubs. Among other points of interest in this collection of graphs: the appearance in the top 20 of the 1980 Kansas City Royals, despite their losing record over the last five weeks of the season; had they kept up their earlier pace, the Royals would probably have made the #2 position right behind the '02 Pirates instead of #19.

As with the Big Winners, the Big Losers are distinguished not in terms of how far from the opposite end of the standings they finished but how far they were from their nearest competitor—that is, how far behind the next-to-last team in the standings these last-place teams wound up. So even though the 1935 Boston Braves had the worst winning percentage of the modern era, they are fourth in this category, because their trailing distance of 26 games (behind the seventh-place Phillies) was exceeded by the 1916 Athletics' 40, 1959 Padres' 29, and the 1979 Blue Jays' 28½ games. And the 1962 New York Mets, who lost a record 120 games,

# LARGEST SPREADS

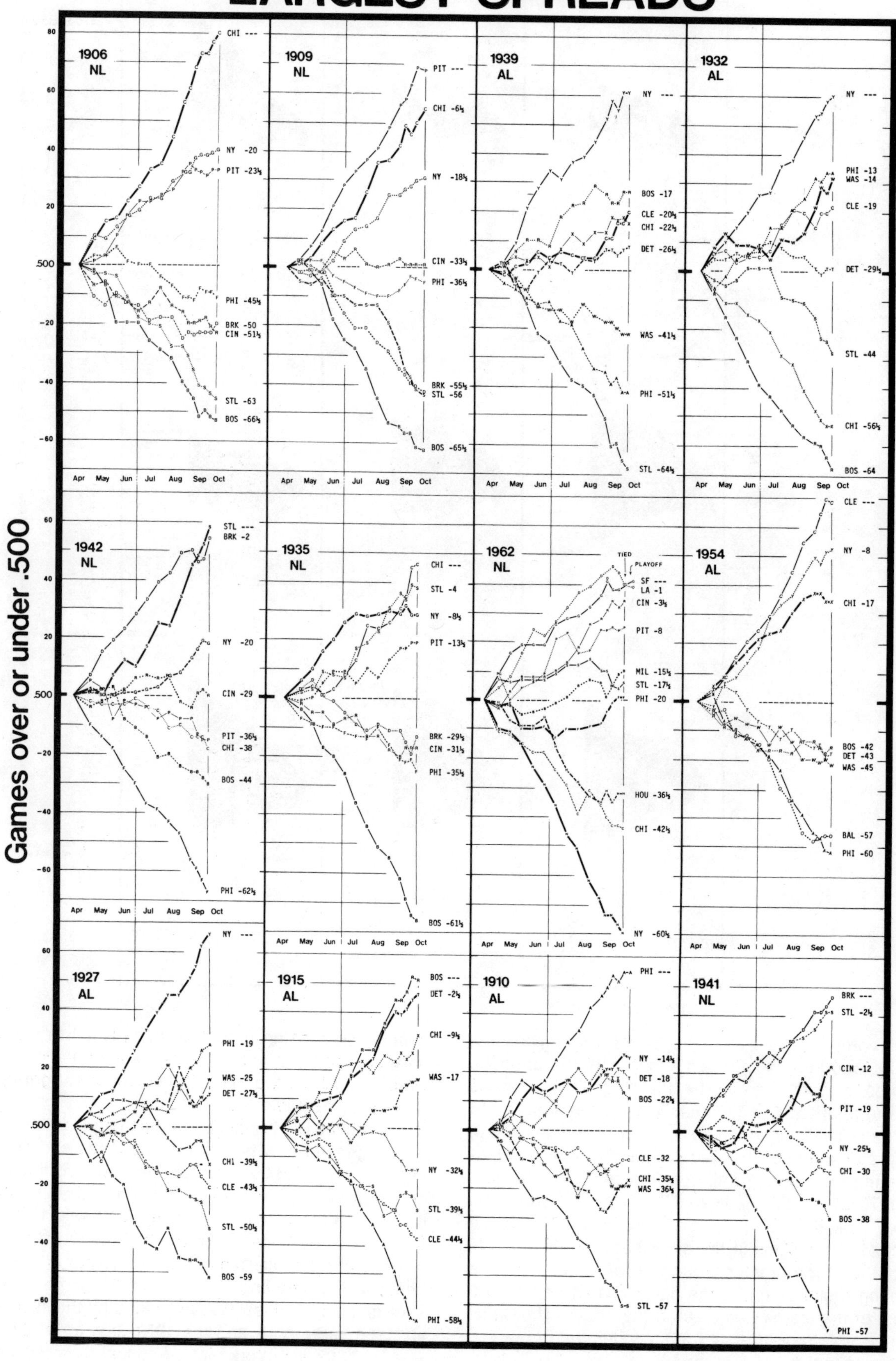

# SMALLEST SPREADS

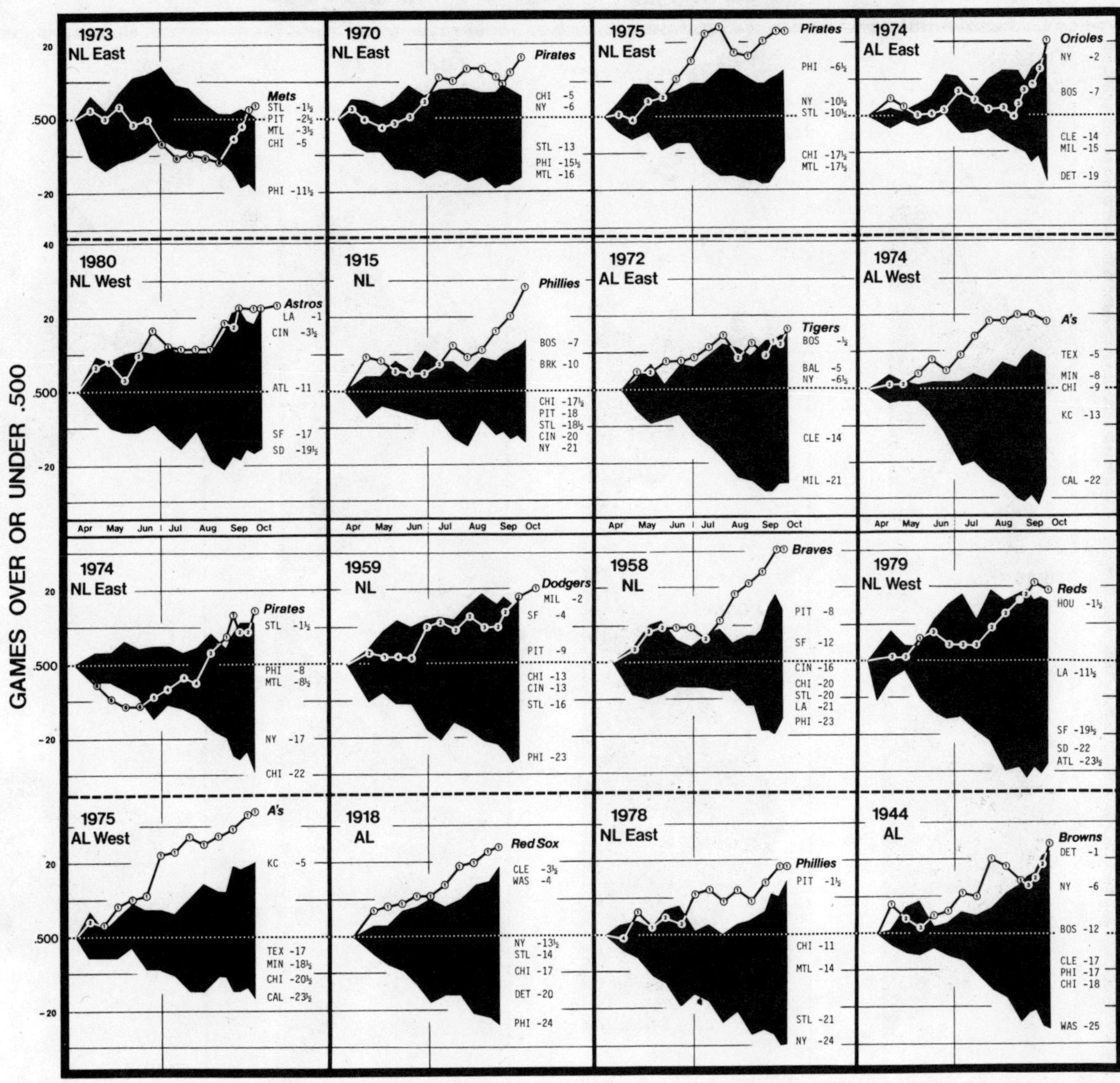


don't even appear in the first (worst) nine, or for that matter, in the worst 20, because the ninth-place Cubs lost 103 games that year. For those interested in the teams coming after the #9 Red Sox of 1925 in trailing distance, they were the 1972 Texas Rangers, the 1911 Boston Braves, the 1917 Pittsburgh Pirates, and the 1910 St. Louis Browns, who were tied with 20½ games separating them from their nearest neighbors in the standings; three other teams—the '73 Rangers, '43 A's, and the '19 A's—tied at the 20-game distance.

The next category, Largest Spreads, deals with the total range from top to bottom in the final standings of a season. This depends not only on how good the winner is but also on how terrible the trailing team is. So, although we have the 1906 NL season in first place (with a 66½-game range) when the older league had its winningest team ever (the Cubs, with 116 wins), the American League season with the record number of wins—1954, when the Cleveland Indians won 111 games—shows up in eighth place, because the trailing Athletics didn't do as badly as many cellar-dwellers. The multigraph shows 12 of the 13 races that ended with a spread of 57 games or more; beyond this cutoff, there have been eight more, or 21 in all, with a spread of 55 games or more, and 47 with a spread of 50 games or more.

The main purpose of this multigraph, however, is to provide the contrast for the "Smallest Spreads" array, when we have 16 of the 18 seasons in which the top-to-bottom range has been only 25 games or smaller. (The 1944 AL season was tied with the 1914 Federal and 1968 NL West season at the 25-game spread.) Here the winning team's curve is plotted separately from the black-shaded area representing the range of all the other teams in the league or division. This makes it easier to see how a team can worm its way from last place to first place with a few weeks of playing .750 ball, the way the 1973 New York Mets did when the final range was only 11½ games and the spread a month earlier was only six games. We also find here, naturally, the most modest or mediocre winners, such as those '73 Mets, whose winning percentage was .509, the '74 Pirates (.543),

# BEST STARTS

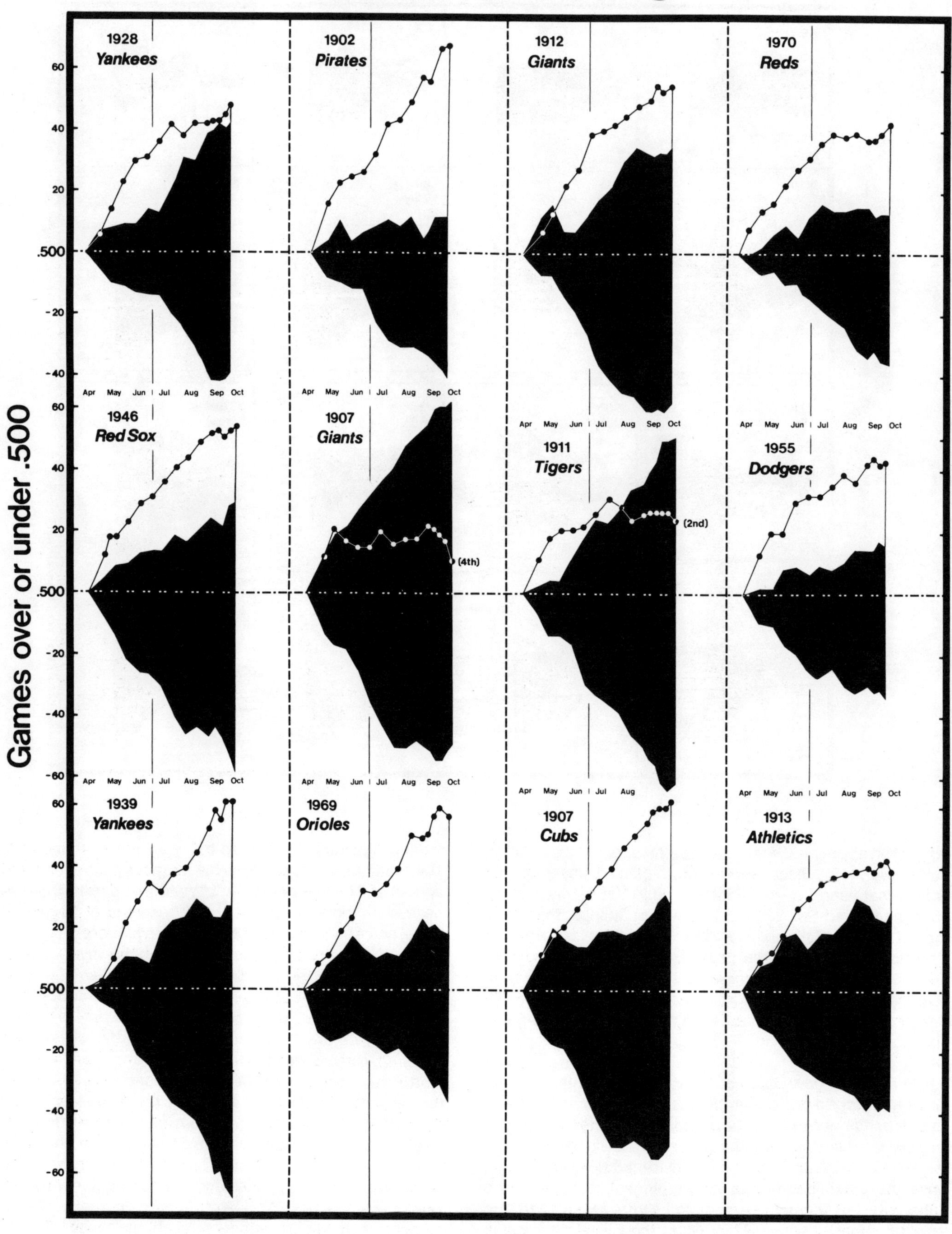

Games over or under .500
60
40
20
.500
-20
-40
-60
1928
Yankees
1902
Pirates
1912
Giants
1970
Reds
1946
Red Sox
1907
Giants
(4th)
1911
Tigers
(2nd)
1955
Dodgers
1939
Yankees
1969
Orioles
1907
Cubs
1913
Athletics
Apr May Jun Jul Aug Sep Oct

# WORST STARTS

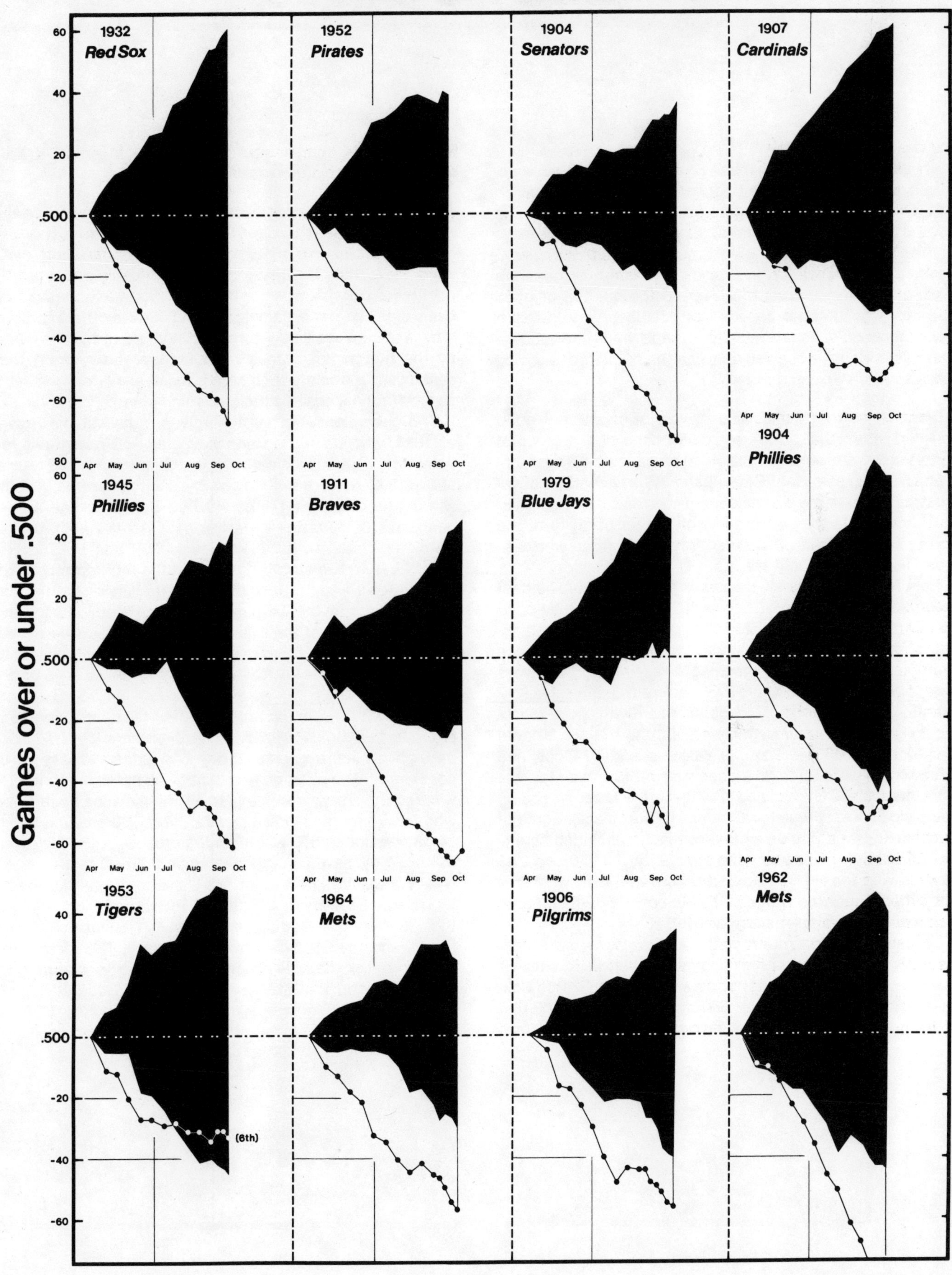

and the '72 Tigers (.551).

An ungodly number of these Smallest Spreads have occurred since divisional play began—two-thirds of them, in fact. This is no doubt an expression of the parity which the powers that be in professional sports strive to achieve as well as an effect of creating divisions, but these recent trends don't necessarily create more interest or generate more quality in the level of play. And the number of good title races in the past decade has not been very different from the pre-divisional decades; having four title races a year has certainly not given us twice the number of exciting races as when we had only two.

There is so much talk, nearly every spring, about good and bad starts that a look at some of the best and worst early-season performance seems to be called for. The multigraphs for these ("Best Starts" and "Worst Starts") show most of the extreme examples, but the reader is cautioned that these plots are concerned with longer portions of the spring schedule than the usual first two or three weeks in most discussions about starts.

Regarding Best Starts, the cases selected were the best records in terms of games above .500 in mid-May, the end of May, or mid-June, and these three cutoffs are mixed together rather unsystematically in the multigraph. We have examples here of teams reaching or exceeding 30 games over .500 by mid-June (the '28 Yankees, '02 Pirates, '12 Giants, '70 Reds, and '55 Dodgers) mixed with those reaching 20 games or more by the end of June but not 30 until mid-June (the '46 Red Sox, '39 Yankees, and '07 Cubs) and a few which were up to 20 games over .500 by mid-May (the '13 Athletics, '07 Giants, and '11 Tigers, the latter two being sputtering rockets which didn't land in first place). Some of the best-known starts on a briefer basis are included here—the '55 Brooklyn Dodgers, who jumped off to 10-0 and 22-2 records, and the '46 Red Sox, who were 21-3 early in May—but others, such as the '62 Pirates and '66 Indians, who also won their first ten games, are not.

The Worst Starts multigraph has the races more consistently ordered, according to how far below .500 teams were in mid-June. The worst of the worst, the 1932 Red Sox, were nearly 40 games under .500 by that time, and the rest of the top row had mid-June records of around 35 games below .500. By comparison, such famous losers as the '62 Mets were not so quick to fall into the abyss.

How a team makes up for a bad start, or a good one, is our next topic—Midseason Turnarounds. In the upper and happier half of this multigraph, we have the eight clubs which have done the best job of overcoming a poor start. To qualify for consideration in this category, a team must have been eight or more games under .500 after the middle of May, and how well they turned things around is measured by the number of games re .500 they gained from their season's low point to their high point at any later time in the season (not necessarily their finishing point).

The champions, not surprisingly, are the Miracle Braves of 1914, who gained an unbelievable +58 from their low point of 13 games below .500 to their finish at 45 games above .500. They are followed by six teams which didn't win a title or pennant—the '48 Red Sox (who had a +47 gain), the '65 Pirates (+31), the '75 Orioles (+30), the '40 Cardinals (+29), the '52 Phillies (+29), and the '55 Red Sox (+29). In the eighth position in the multigraph are the '74 Pirates (+26), who did win their division's title, and finding them in the elite company of these other teams which pulled out of their dives so handsomely makes Pitt's 1974 victory all the more respectable than the Mets' last-to-first turnaround the year before (that was only a +15 on the scale).

The downturns, in the bottom half of the Midseason Turnarounds, had similar qualifying requirements: a team had to be eight or more games above .500 after mid-May to be considered. The champion collapser, as noted much earlier, was the Braves' mirror-image in 1914—the Cincinnati Reds, who fell from first place, 11 games over .500 on June 1st, to 34 games under .500 at the end, a drop of −45. They were followed by seven teams that didn't finish last—the '01 New York Giants (−43), the '78 Oakland A's (−36), the '75 Milwaukee Brewers (−33), the '56 Pittsburgh Pirates (−30), the '66 Houston Astros (−28), the '24 Boston Red Sox (−26), and the '80 New York Mets (−26). The reader may wish to check the full-season graphs in earlier chapters for the next eight: the '53 Giants (−24), '15 Cubs (−23), '18 Reds (−23), '61 Indians (−23), '73 Cubs (−22), '77 Cubs (−22), '75 Cubs (−21)—ahem—and the '41 Indians.

# MIDSEASON TURNAROUNDS

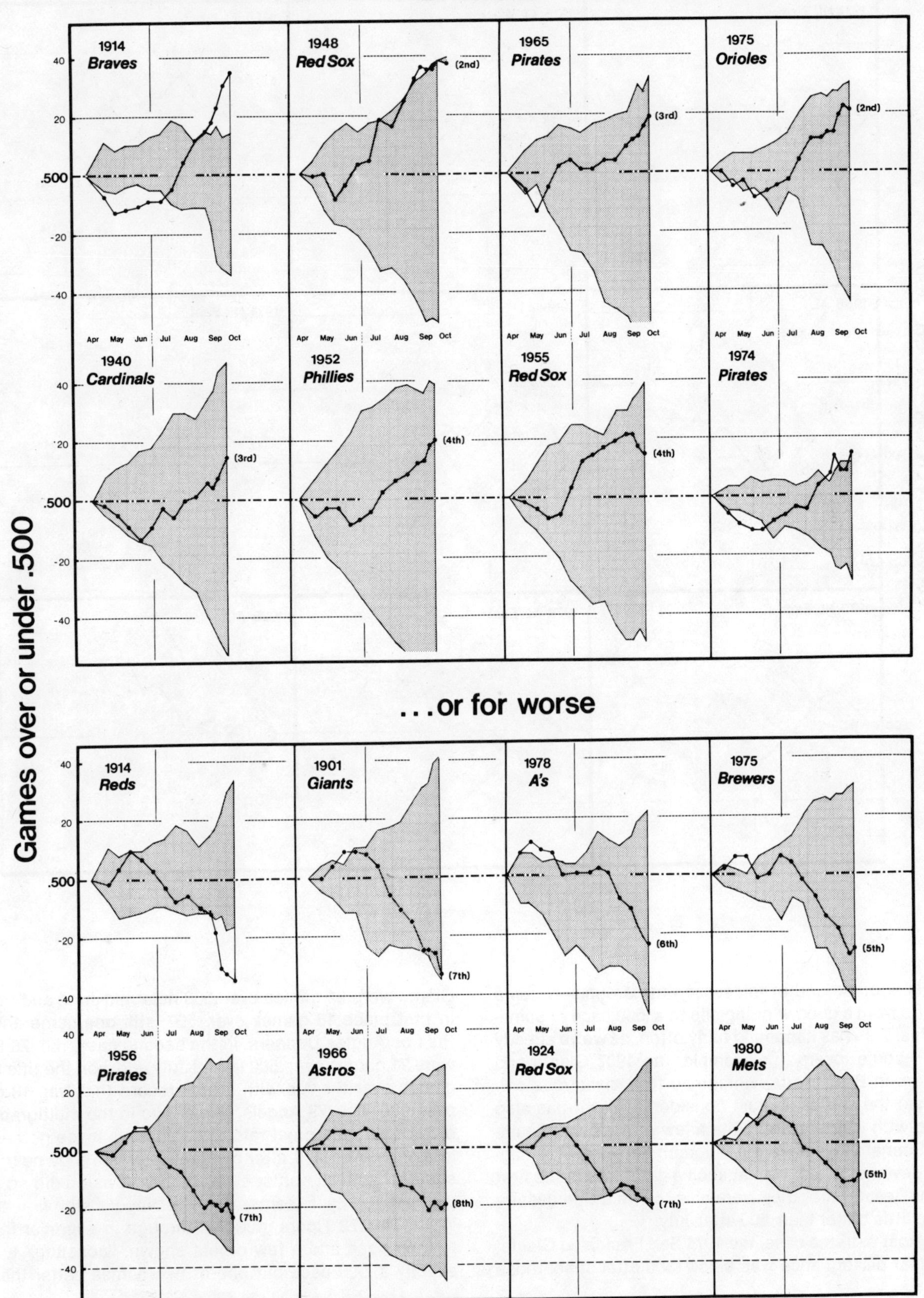

# COASTING TO A PENNANT

**WINNERS WHO PLAYED .500 BALL AFTER MIDSEASON**

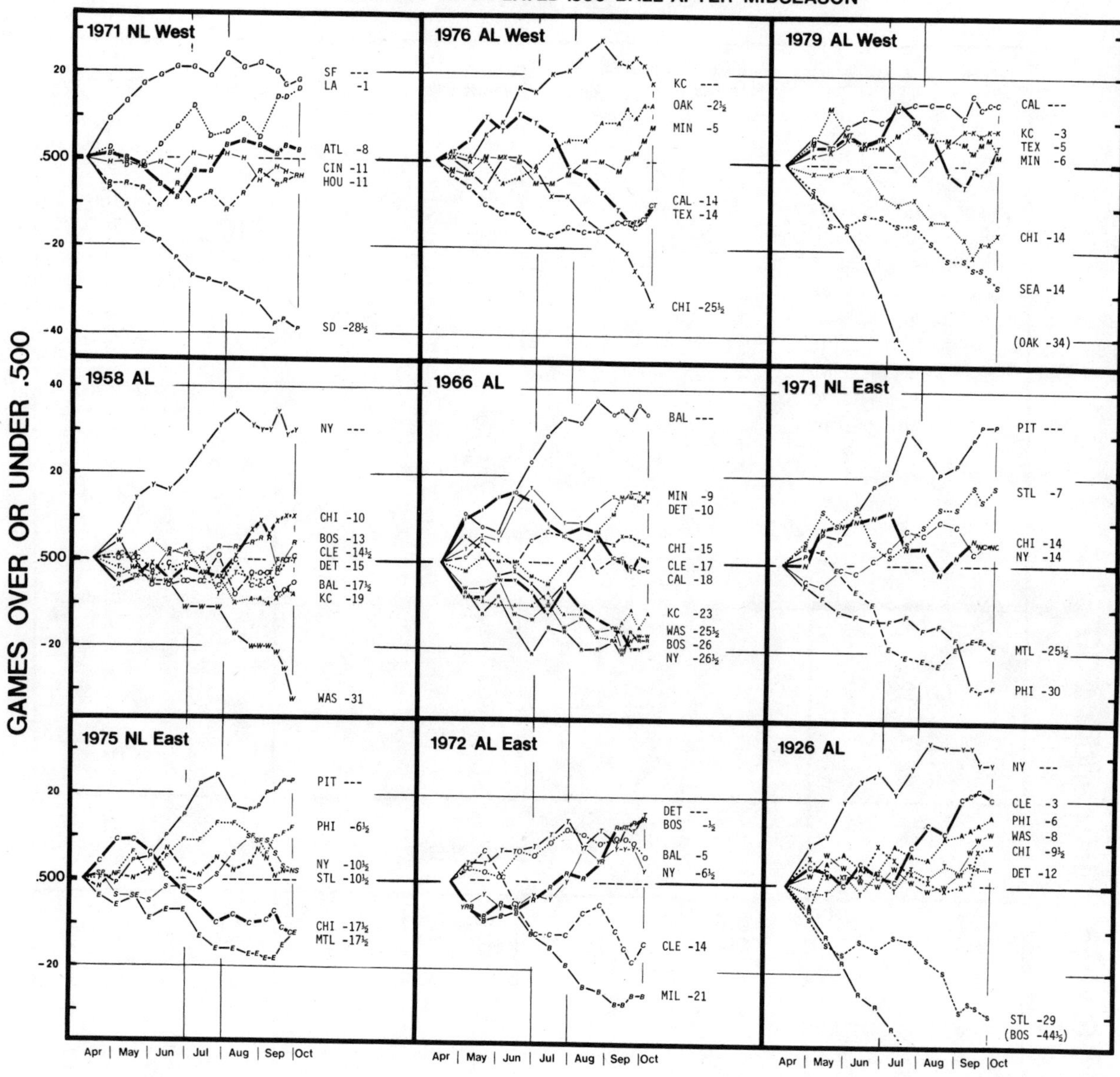


There is another kind of midseason turnaround—when a team shifts from a good winning clip to a .500 pace or somewhat worse. This has happened fairly often, as we've already seen with some losers (for example, the 1907 Giants and 1911 Tigers in Best Starts) which had less disastrous collapses than the sad cases just considered. But it has also happened with winners, and quite a few of them. In "Coasting to a Pennant" we have a multigraph showing nine flag-winners, seven of whom won at such a great rate in the first half of the season that they were able to win a title despite averaging little better than .500 after July.

In the most extreme case, the 1971 San Francisco Giants, the won-lost performance was below .500 after June; those Giants were 21 games over .500 near mid-June and finished in first place 18 games over .500, still one game ahead of the Los Angles Dodgers. In the second case, the '76 Royals were 21 games over .500 in mid-July and won the title by 2½ games over the A's with a final record that was 18 games over .500. The '79 Angels, one of two in the multigraph who did not win at a great rate to begin with, made no headway in games over .500 after midseason, when they held only a slim lead, but the other clubs in their division did so poorly (against AL East teams) that the Angels still won the AL West. The '72 Tigers muddled through in a similar fashion. In their case and a few others shown, "coasting" was not exactly a .500 pace but one or two games better than that over the latter half of the season. More often than these nine cases, we should be reminded, July leaders who have failed to maintain a winning pace have lost their lead and the pennant.

This raises questions about what we can predict about pennant-winners from the standings at various stages of a season. Tallies of all 186 races since 1900 show that the teams that were leading their league or division on Labor Day (after the teams played that day) have gone on to win titles 154 times and failed to do so 32 times, finishing second 23 times, third eight times, and fourth once. Fourth-of-July leaders have won 130 times and missed out 56 times, placing second 33 times, third 13 times, fourth seven times, and fifth three times. Leaders on Memorial Day have captured titles only 86 times, missing 100 times, with the misses being second 39 times, third 28 times, fourth 16 times, fifth nine times, sixth twice, seventh four times, and eighth (last) twice.

We conclude with two matters having to do with the overall shapes of pennant races rather than winners or losers. "Most Divisive Races" shows how a league or division can sometimes be rent in twine, especially by hard-fought races of the three-or four-team kind. It is probably true that in some red-hot multi-team races, the players and fans of the contending clubs get worked up into such a fever that these teams feast on the weaker clubs more than would happen if there weren't so much excitement. The haves win more than they otherwise would, and the have-nots get dumped on more. This seemed to be happening in the 1950 AL and 1977 AL East races, and perhaps also in some other cases of these "splits."

## MOST DIVISIVE RACES

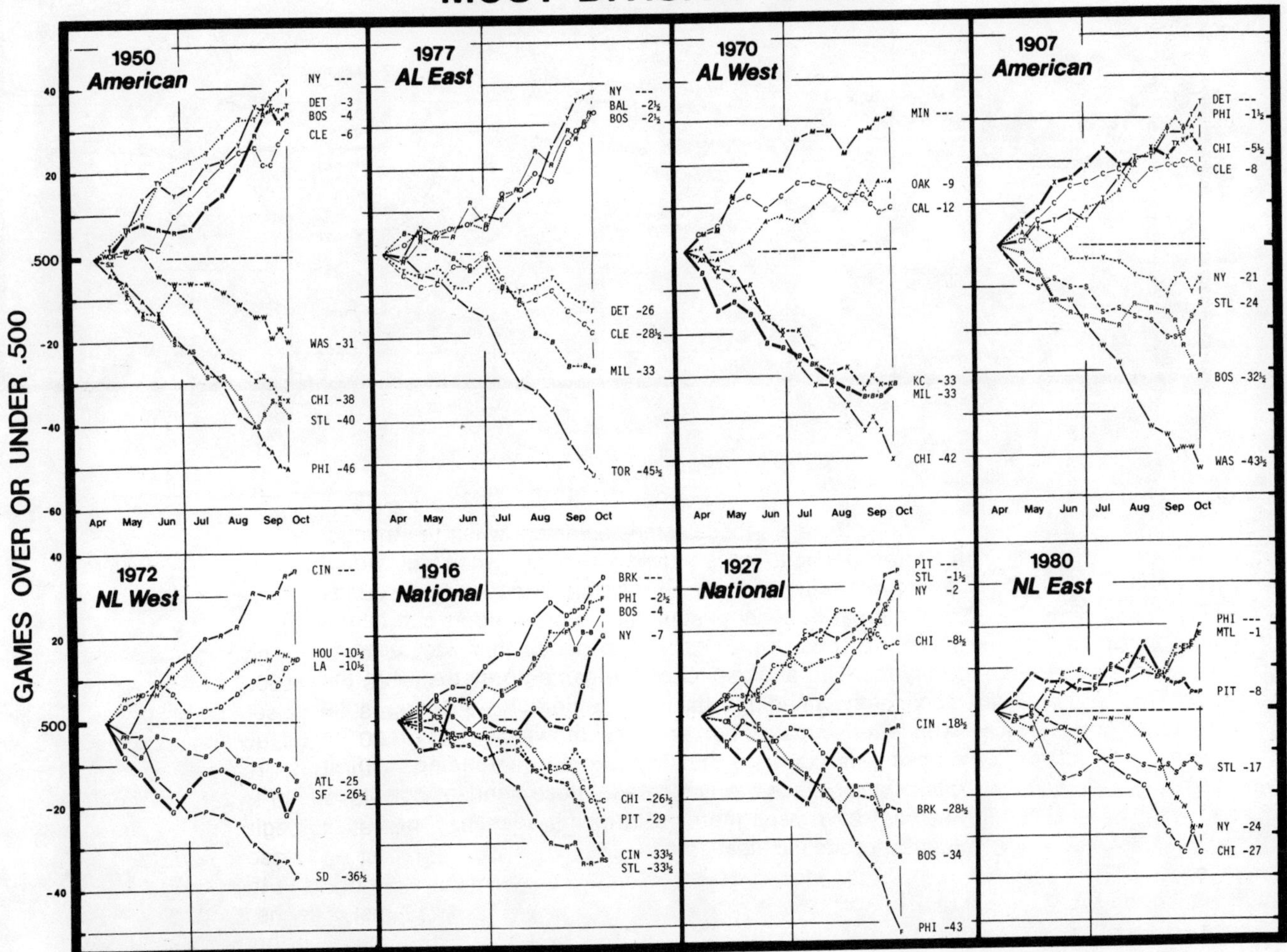

# BASEBALL'S PENNANT NON-RACES

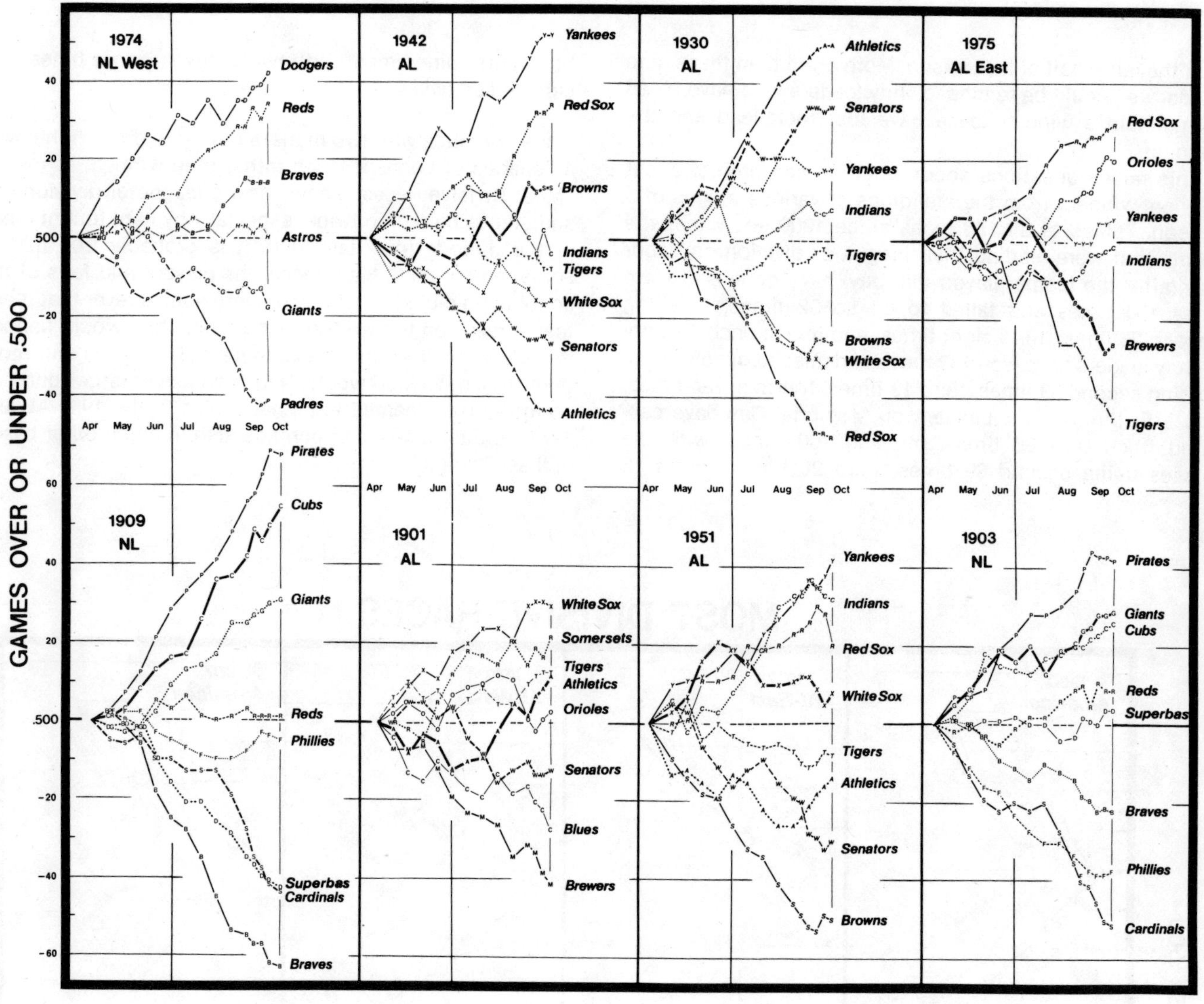


Finally, there are those serene summers when the thought of torrid pennant races seems wearying, when one would prefer, restfully, to savor all the quieter colors and sounds of the great national pastime as no other sport can be enjoyed. To those who like their baseball this way, adoring every moment and aspect of the game no matter what the score or the standings, the final multigraph—showing those wonderfully spaced-out seasons in which each team is tracking its course of destiny without contending for first place or anyplace—is dedicated. These pennant non-races may not have been the most gripping seasons, but graphically they are the most graceful.

# Appendix

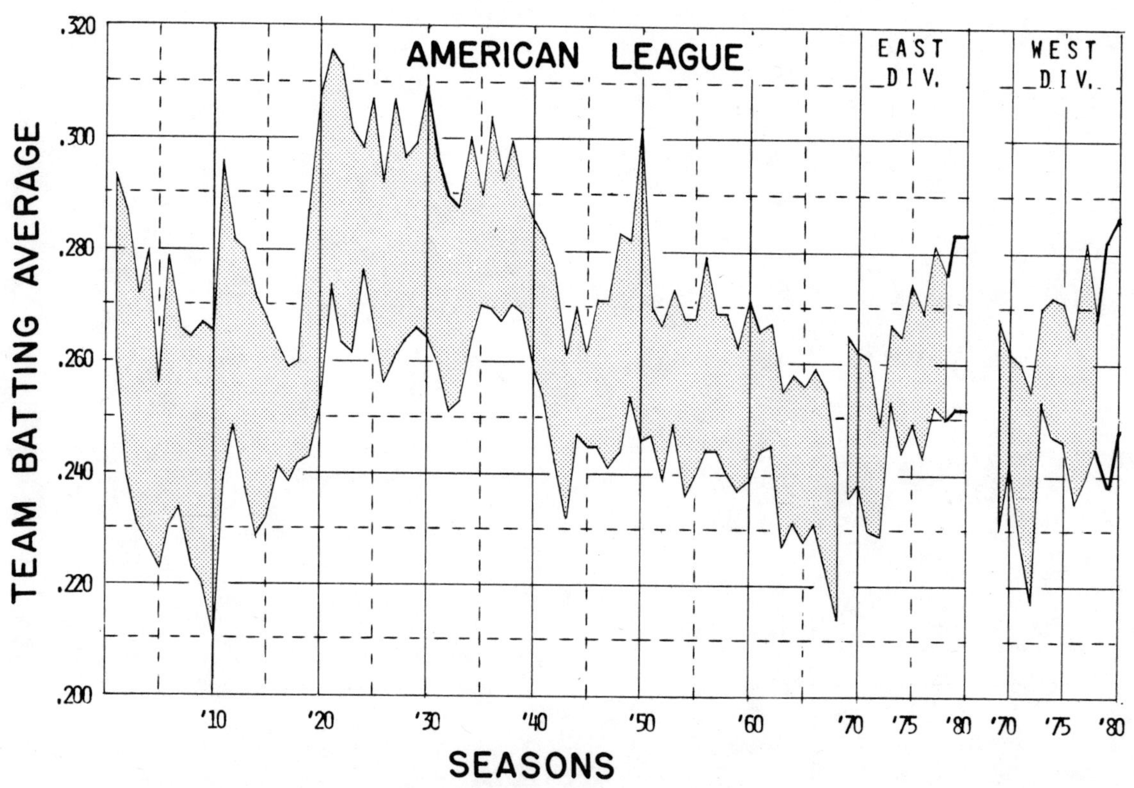


The range of team batting averages, from best to worst each year, since 1901 in the American League (shown separately for the East and West divisions after 1968).

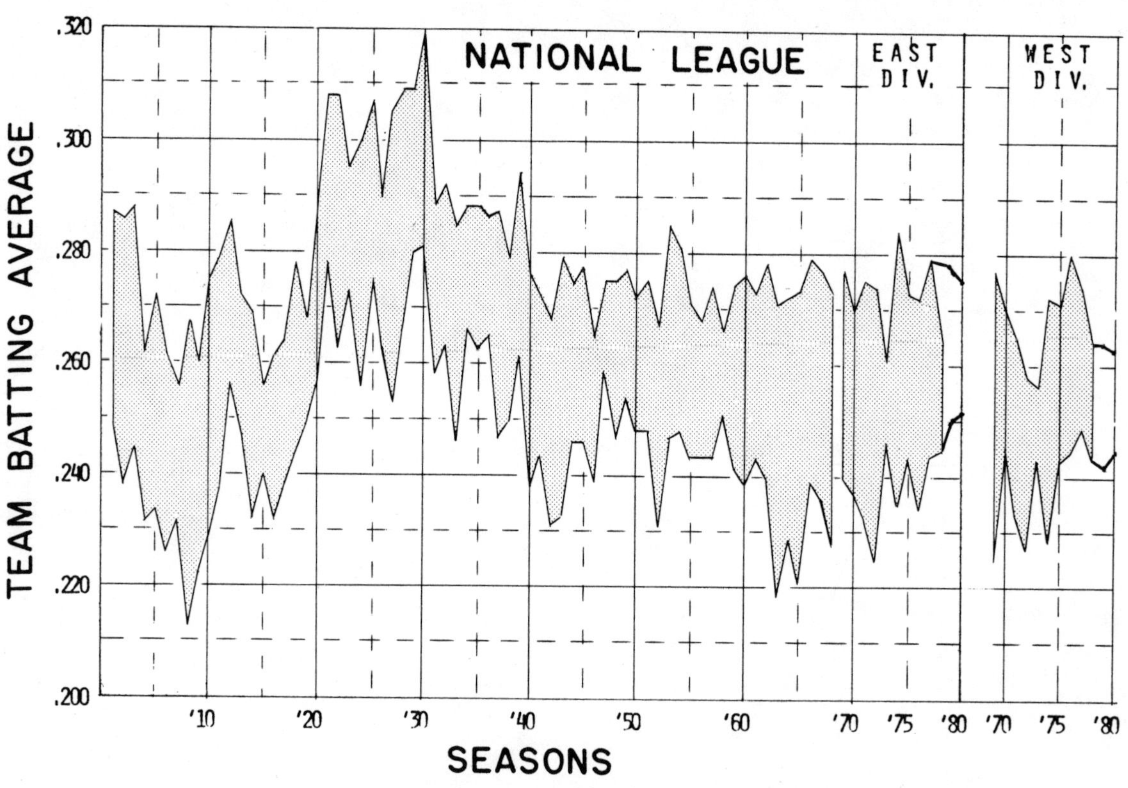


The range of team batting averages in the National League since 1901.

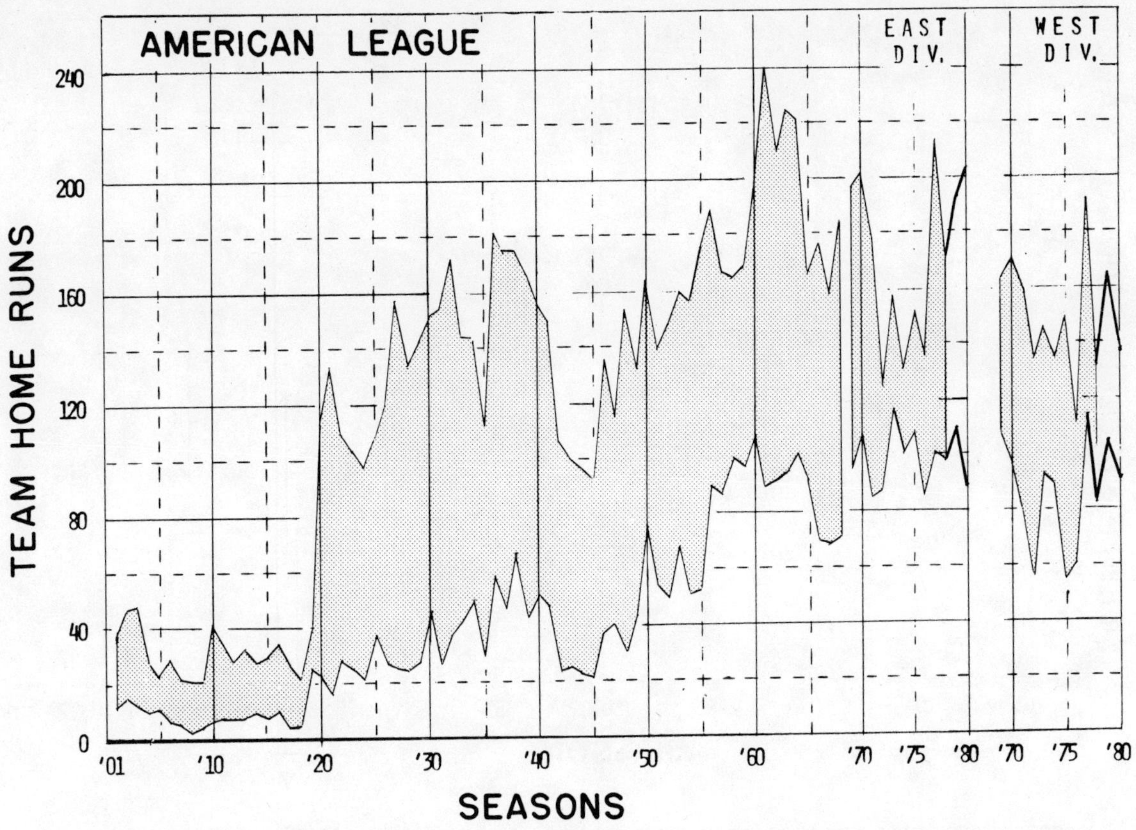


**The range of team home runs, from highest to lowest yearly totals, since 1901 in the American League.**

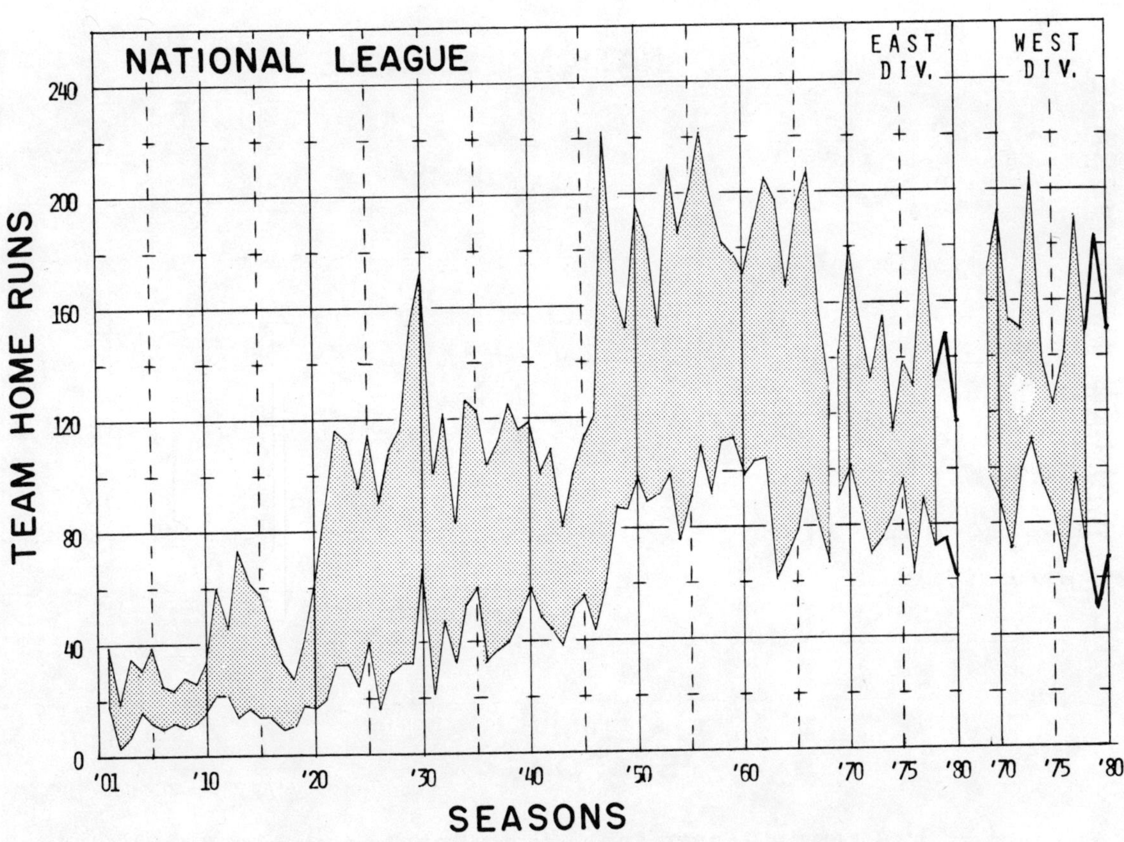


**Highest to lowest team home run totals in the National League.**

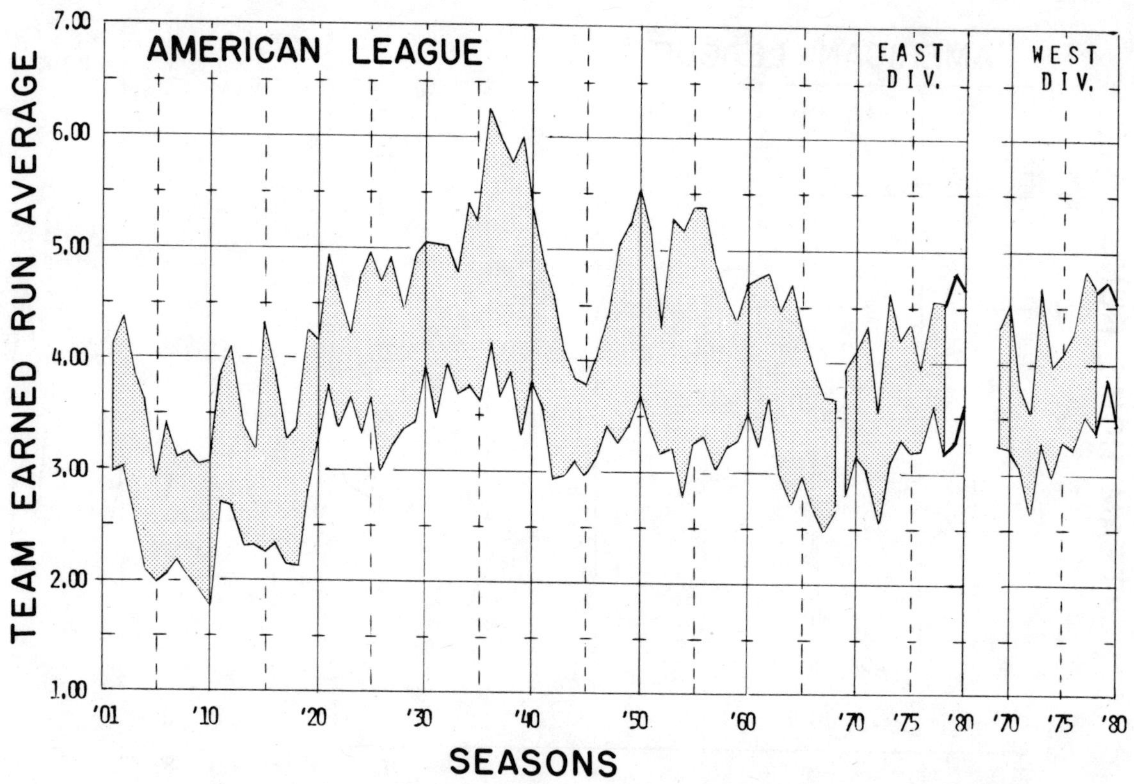


The range of team earned run averages, from lowest to highest each year, since 1901 in the American League.

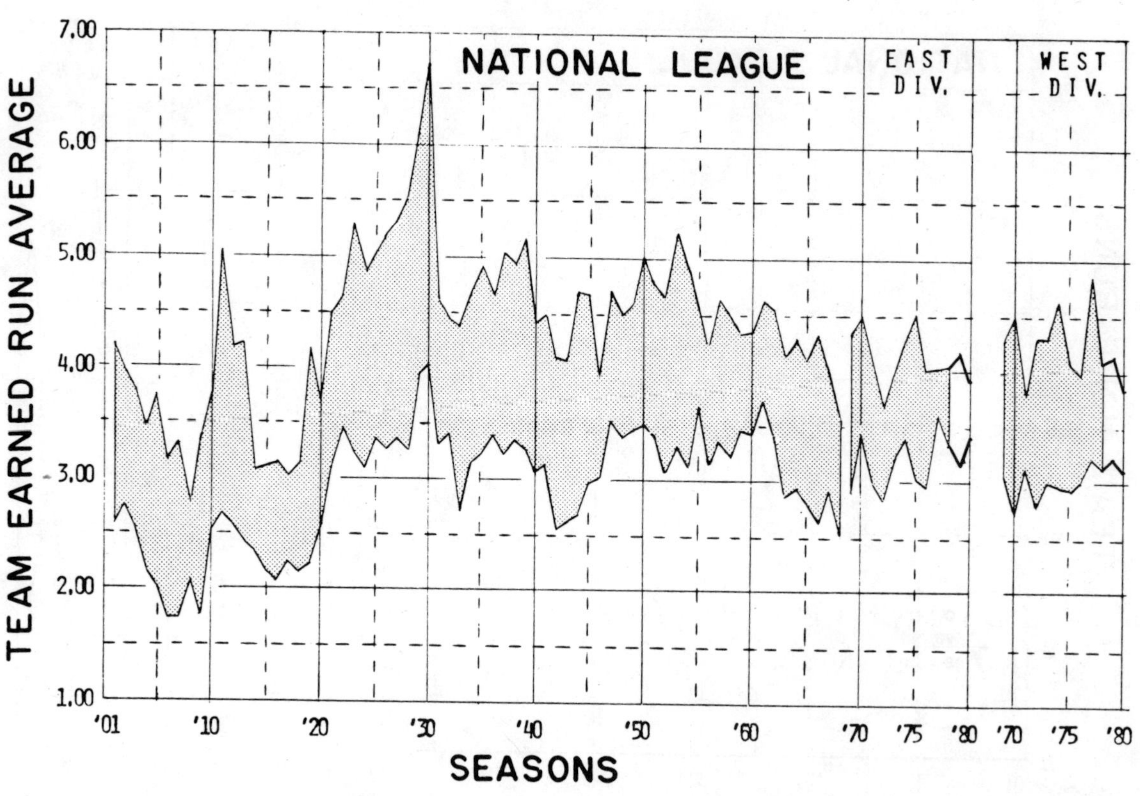


The range of team earned run averages for the National League.

# WORLD SERIES OPPONENTS AND OUTCOMES SINCE 1903

| AL \ NL | DODGERS | GIANTS | CARDINALS | CUBS | REDS | PIRATES | BRAVES | PHILLIES | METS | ASTROS | EXPOS | PADRES | |
|---|---|---|---|---|---|---|---|---|---|---|---|---|---|
| YANKEES | 1955 1963 / 1941 1947 1949 1956 1952 1977 1953 1978 | 1921 1922 / 1923 1936 1937 1951 1962 | 1926 1942 1964 / 1928 1943 | / 1932 1938 | 1976 / 1939 1961 | 1960 / 1927 | 1957 / 1958 | / 1950 | | | | | 32 |
| A'S | / 1974 | 1905 / 1911 1913 | 1931 / 1930 | | / 1972 | | 1914 / | | / 1973 | | | | 9 |
| RED SOX | / 1916 | / * 1912 | 1946 1967 / 1918 | | 1975 / | / 1903 | | / 1915 | | | | | 8 |
| TIGERS | | | 1934 / 1968 | 1907 1908 / 1935 1945 | 1940 / | 1909 / | | | | | | | 8 |
| ORIOLES | / 1966 | | 1944 / | | / 1970 | 1971 1979 / | | | 1969 / | | | | 6 |
| WHITE SOX | 1959 / | / 1917 | | / 1906 | 1919 / | | | | | | | | 4 |
| TWINS | 1965 / | 1933 / 1924 | | | | 1925 / | | | | | | | 4 |
| INDIANS | / 1920 | 1954 / | | | | | / 1948 | | | | | | 3 |
| ANGELS | | | | | | | | | | | | | |
| RANGERS | | | | | | | | | | | | | |
| BREWERS | | | | | | | | | | | | | |
| ROYALS | | | | | | | | 1980 / | | | | | 1 |
| BLUE JAYS | | | | | | | | | | | | | |
| MARINERS | | | | | | | | | | | | | |
| TOTALS: | 16 | 15 | 12 | 8 | 8 | 7 | 4 | 3 | 2 | | | | |

* BOSTON (AL) AND NEW YORK (NL) WON PENNANTS IN 1904, BUT THERE WAS NO WORLD SERIES THAT YEAR.

**THE PENNANT WINNERS** who have contended in the World Series since the first in 1903. For each pairing, the Series winner is indicated by placement of the year in the lower-left half of a square in the American League team won, upper-right half in the National League team won. 1901 and 1902, the Pittsburgh Pirates won the NL pennant and the Chicago White Sox and Philadelphia Athletics, respectively, won the AL pennant.

# Index




Earnshaw, George 58-61
Easter, Luke 93
Eastwick, Rawly 138
Eckersley, Dennis 138, 139
Ehmke, Howard 88
Elberfeld, Kid 14, 16
Eller, Hod 43
Elliott, Bob 88
Ellis, Dock 127, 138
English, Woody 61
Ennis, Del 91
Ermer, Cal 118, 119
Erskine, Carl 95, 96, 101
Estrada, Chuck 107
Etten, Nick 79
Evans, Dwight 134, 139
Evers, Hoot 93, 98
Evers, Johnny 15, 18, 22, 27

# Contents of BASEBALL GRAPHICS

First Impressions, P.O. Box 9073, Madison, Wisconsin 53715

### Chapter 1. One Season

A whole major league season summarized in graphs, with 1978 as the example. Includes: the '78 Red Sox-Yankee race and comparison of the Yankees with the "Miracle Braves" of 1914; the AL West, NL East, and NL West races in 1978; histories of the Yankees and Dodgers; World Series outcomes since 1903; the 1978 league championships and World Series; Ron Guidry's 25 wins and 3 losses; Jim Rice's 406 total bases, Rod Carew's position in the AL Top Ten since 1967; Pete Rose's 44-game hitting streak compared with Willie Keeler's; Rose's entry into the 3,000-Hit Club and approaches by Lou Brock and Carl Yastrzemski (page 21--Yaz predicted to hit his 3,000th on 9/12/79); Gaylord Perry's entry into the 3,000-K Club; individual batting and pitching statistics for 1978; and the rise of the San Diego Padres and Milwaukee Brewers.

### Chapter 2. Rainy Days at Fenway

A look at baseball graphics as a hobby. How a 12-year-old New Englander gets to be a Red Sox fan in 1943, and progresses from notebook stats and daily game logs in the 1940s to pennant-race graphs, team offense-defense charts, daily hitting and pitching plots, and graphic "wall hangings" in the 1970s. In this chapter, "you may get more than your fill of Red Sox marvels, miseries, and mania." Includes: graphic history of the Red Sox; daily game logs from 1943, 1946, 1975, and 1978; the 1972 and 1974 AL East title races; the 1977 Red Sox Rampage in home runs; daily batting by Burleson, Remy, Rice, Yaz, Fisk, Lynn, Scott, Evans, and Hobson in all 1978 games; home vs. road offense and defense by the '78 Red Sox; Fred Lynn's early-1979 hitting; and graphs of all 1978 Milwaukee Brewers games.

### Chapter 3. History, Hitting, and Hurling

Sweeping historical views of team statistics since 1901: batting averages, home runs, slugging percentages, and earned run averages, separately for the AL and NL; the leading individual career batting averages, home runs, and total bases over the 1901-78 period; the top pitchers in lifetime shutouts, hits and strikeouts per nine innings, and relief statistics.

### Chapter 4. Batters and Sluggers

Daily, seasonal, and lifetime hitting (and base-stealing) in graphs. Includes: a frame of reference for daily hitting graphs; Lyman Bostock's final season, day-by-day; Ted Williams' daily hitting in September 1941, ending at .406; Joe DiMaggio's 56-game slugging streak; Babe Ruth (1927) vs. Roger Maris (1961) in seasonal home runs; Lou Brock's record 118 stolen bases in 1974 and his record career SB total plotted yearly against Ty Cobb's; year-by-year batting and slugging averages for 18 all-time hitting greats and for the 24 current hitters having the highest lifetime slugging averages; and total bases by age plotted for Aaron, Ruth, Gehrig, Foxx, Hornsby, Cobb, Musial, J. DiMaggio, Williams, Mays, Mantle, F. Robinson, Yastrzemski, Rose, McCovey, Stargell, Carew, Jackson, Parker, and Rice. (In the last eight graphs and the "24 current hitters" graphs, space is left for the reader to plot 1979 figures.)

### Chapter 5. Pitching Plots

The creation of "pitching plots" and a frame of reference for interpreting them, with examples of perfect-to-poor pitching from 1978; starters vs. relievers; yearly pitching by Jim Palmer and Tom Seaver; Sandy Koufax's last four seasons--the greatest pitching ever?; and career pitching plots for Mathewson, Koufax, Waddell, Walsh, Johnson, Gibson, Alexander, Young, Plank, Grove, Ford, and Spahn.

### Chapter 6. Game Graphs

Minimum requirements for a "gamegram" (game diagram); examples from recent World Series; the 17-run inning in Boston (1953); Don Larsen's perfect game (1956), pitch by pitch; Mazeroski's Series-winning homer (1960); Reggie Jackson's one-man slugfest (1977); and the 1975 World Series games, with a closeup of Game Six.

### Chapter 7. Going for the Gonfalon

Ways of plotting pennant races; the races in the AL East (1975-78), AL West (1976-77), NL East (1976-77), and NL West (1976-77); the 1914 NL race ("Miracle Braves") and World Series; the Brooklyn Dodgers vs. New York Giants in 1951; the 1967 AL race and Yaz's daily hitting in that September; the Amazing Mets of 1969; and the four 1979 divisional races (through June 10--you plot the rest of the season).

### Chapter 8. Seventy-Eight Seasons

Team histories presented by graphs of won-lost percentage and finishing position in each season, for all major league franchises not presented in earlier chapters, including the Cleveland Indians, St. Louis Browns-Baltimore Orioles, Detroit Tigers, Chicago White Sox, 1st Washington Senators-Minnesota Twins, Philadelphia-Kansas City-Oakland A's, Kansas City Royals, Seattle Mariners, Toronto Blue Jays, California Angels, 2nd Washington Senators-Texas Rangers, New York Mets, Philadelphia Phillies, Pittsburgh Pirates, Chicago Cubs, St. Louis Cardinals, Montreal Expos, Houston Astros, New York-San Francisco Giants, Boston-Milwaukee-Atlanta Braves, and Cincinnati Reds (and a little surprise).

### Chapter 9. The Possible Dream

A whimsical view of baseball graphics hobbying and baseball graphics publications of the future; advanced baseball graphics, with the Triple Crown Index (for batting) and Triple Crown Index of Pitching as examples. Only a half-chapter, naturally.

PRAISE FROM THE PROS......

# "What a baseball book!

*. . . I was won over instantly. (These) graphs enlarge and illuminate my appreciation for the game . . . this is the perfect hot-stove dish. . . I predict great success for the book."*

— Roger Angell, NEW YORKER writer
and author of FIVE SEASONS and THE SUMMER GAME

**April 1980 Selection**
**Small Press Book Club**

***"BASEBALL GRAPHICS is a new book and a new hobby designed to enchant both baseball fans and closet statisticians. . . . .this is the book (they) would need on a desert island. . . . .It is well produced and attractively designed; the visuals are whimsical and delightful."***

**–SMALL PRESS REVIEW**

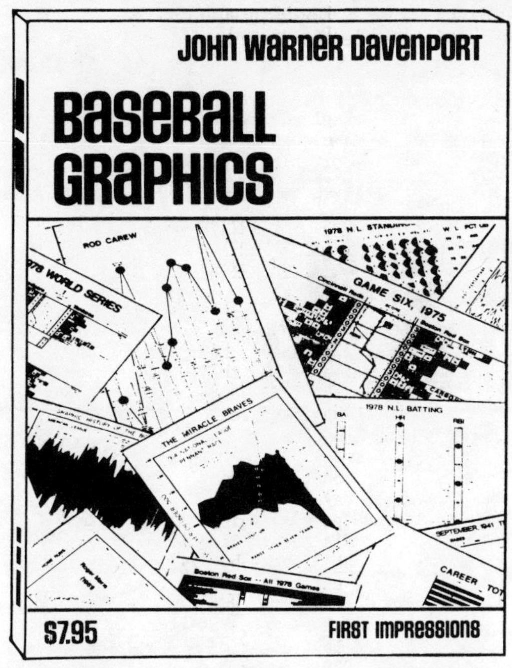


8½x11" paperback, 152 pp., $7.95 + $1.05 shpg., pub. 7-15-79

*"Davenport has . . . (taken) baseball stats one step beyond. Pitching and batting feats, pennant races, team histories, player ratings — all have been converted from gray columns of numbers into colorful charts and graphs . . . the book's biggest pleasure is the more than 200 graphic examples of his work."* --Randy Curwen, CHICAGO TRIBUNE

*". . . a tremendous amount of work. . . a valuable addition to our library."* --C.C. Johnson Spink, THE SPORTING NEWS

*". . . a fine job . . . Illustrating these things graphically is an interesting concept, which we intend to look at in more detail."* --Robert O. Fishel, Secretary, American League of Professional Baseball Clubs, New York

*". . . a book that is certainly marketable and the market is now ready for sports graphics . . . I find it a thing of beauty."* --James A. Barnes, SPORTOGRAPHY

*". . . baseball addicts. . . will rejoice in the sophistication and complexity of these statistical displays."* --Ben Reuven, LOS ANGELES TIMES

*". . . unique . . . For the statistics nut, this should be a grand slam."* --Wirt Gammon, Sr., CHATTANOOGA TIMES

*". . . an interesting concept . . ."* --SABR (Soc. Amer. Baseball Research) BULLETIN

---

ST. LOUIS — This month's motif centers on those dedicated writers who have ventured into the uncertain waters of self-publication. It is not often a reviewer comes across a unique approach to enjoying the history of baseball. John W. Davenport, a psychologist at the University of Wisconsin has provided this in his book **BASEBALL GRAPHICS**. His study is much more than a book . . . it is an art form. On a standard graph, Dr. Davenport has plotted every conceivable form of statistical comparison or analysis, including DiMaggio's hitting streak, Ruth vs. Maris, the miracle seasons of the 1914 Braves and the 1969 Mets, pennant races, the 3,000-hit club and a fascinating chapter, entitled "Seventy-Eight Seasons," a visual representation of every team history from 1901-1978. What the X-ray is to medicine, **BASEBALL GRAPHICS** should be to the history of baseball.

The book has over 200 scientifically accurate graphs and diagrams. If statistics are the bloodline of baseball, then Davenport has the keys to the blood bank. **BASEBALL GRAPHICS** might also open up a new hobby for those fanatics who wish to plot the entire course of their team's next season on a graph, or compare their favorite players with the greats, past or present. All you need is graphpaper, **THE BASEBALL ENCYCLOPEDIA** and an elementary knowledge of statistics. It promises to be more absorbing than "Rubin's Cube," the newest fad to hit this country.

—Bill Borst, *Baseball Bulletin,* May, 1981

***And now BASEBALL GRAPHICS has a "tenth inning" - - -➤***

The *'79 SAMPLER* -- a 16-page graphic review

*". . .Davenport has also issued a supplement, with the same detailed treatment of the 1979 season, including an interesting spread on Carl Yastrzemski . . . his light, wry style is a pleasure in itself."* --Brian Burns, SOUTHBRIDGE (Mass.) NEWS

8½x11" pamphlet, 16 pp., $1.75 + 25¢ postage, pub. 12-1-79

john warner davenport
BASEBALL GRAPHICS
'79 SAMPLER
Man of the Year
Willie Stargell
TOTAL BASES
AGE
$1.75 0-934794-01-4 first impressions

**first impressions, p.o. box 9073, madison, wis. 53715**

". . . the perfect hot-stove dish . . ." – *Roger Angell*

# BASEBALL GRAPHICS

**BASEBALL GRAPHICS, published in July 1979, is the first book to present major league pennant races, batting and pitching feats, team histories, and World Series heroics in graphic forms. In over 200 graphs and diagrams this creative work provides fascinating new views of 60 superstars' careers and many of baseball's most stirring moments — Joe DiMaggio's streak, Ruth vs. Maris, the 1914 and 1951 "miracles," Yaz in 1967, the Amazing Mets, the 1975 World Series, and the 1978 Yankee-Red Sox race. The book also shows what a marvelous new hobby baseball graphics can be, using player performances and games of the Boston Red Sox and Milwaukee Brewers in many examples.**

8½x11″ paperback, 152 pp., $7.95 + $1.05 shpg., pub. 7-15-79

**BASEBALL IN GRAPHS – FASCINATING! MAKES A GREAT HOBBY, TOO!**

These are the two main ideas of BASEBALL GRAPHICS, which has over 200 scientifically accurate graphs and diagrams of batting and pitching feats, pennant races, play-by-plays, career summaries, team histories, and player ratings – just about anything in baseball you can count or measure. Here you will find graphic renditions of the 1978 season's highlights, from the thrilling race between the Yankees and Red Sox to the glittering performances of Ron Guidry, Jim Rice, and Pete Rose. Besides reviewing the whole 1978 season, this innovative book presents a graphic history of every major league team, plots of team batting and pitching statistics since 1901, an overview of 60 famous stars' careers, and a new view of baseball's most cherished memories – Joe DiMaggio's 56-game hitting streak, Don Larsen's perfect game, the 1914 and 1951 "miracles," Yaz in 1967, the Amazing Mets, the 1975 World Series, and many others. Two chapters explain how baseball graphics as a hobby can double a fan's enjoyment of baseball as events unfold daily during the season, and also provide endless hours of fun with statistics from baseball encyclopedias during the offseason.

John Warner Davenport, the author, is a native New Englander who has followed the game closely for over 35 years. He has been a psychology professor at the University of Wisconsin-Madison since 1962, and previously taught at Rutgers and Amherst after schooling at Bates College, the University of Massachusetts, and the University of Iowa.

BASEBALL GRAPHICS

JOHN WARNER DAVENPORT

BASEBALL GRAPHICS

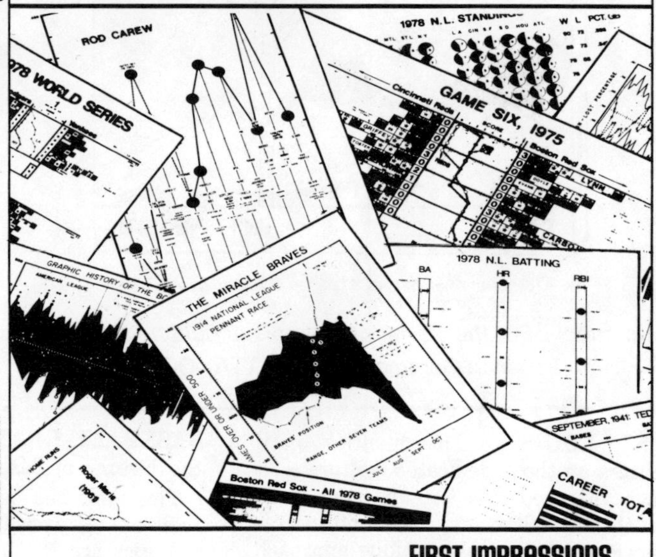


$7.95 ISBN: 0-934794-00-6

JOHN WARNER DAVENPORT

FIRST IMPRESSIONS

Quite the reverse is true of John Warner Davenport's **Baseball Graphics**, which is surely this year's most refreshing baseball book. Davenport is a professor of psychology at the University of Wisconsin in Madison, where he spends much of his time running rats through mazes and graphing the results. He obviously spends the rest of it turning baseball statistics into graphs, for this book contains no less than 136 of them—graphs of all sorts, illustrating statistics on pennant races, hitting, pitching, player comparisons, and individual games.

Now as everyone knows, baseball statistics are nearly as important to the game as the action on the field. In this, baseball is unique among all organized team sports: the true fan is always part computer. But Davenport goes even further, by expressing those statistics in graphic form. It's such a simple idea that one wonders, as the author does, why it hasn't been used more. If you're not scared off by the imposing look of 136 complicated-looking (but actually quite simple) graphs, you'll find that at least some of the time nothing illustrates the **meaning** of baseball statistics so clearly. Seeing Ty Cobb's lifetime .367 batting average half a page above the mere .340 range occupied by players like Williams, Speaker, Ruth and Sisler really brings home the significance of his accomplishment in a way that mere numbers never can.

Not all baseball statistics can be turned into graphs with equal ease. Davenport's best work illustrates pennant races—the classic is the 1914 Boston Braves' rise from last place in the middle of July to a runaway pennant—and individual hitting statistics. His graphs of pitching performances are less satisfying, as he admits himself. But the book is an absolute delight for the true baseball fan: it belongs on the same shelf with the Macmillan **Baseball Encyclopedia** and other must-have reference works.

For some reason, Davenport published the book himself—I don't know if he submitted it to any major house, or whether in an unforgivable exercise in shortsightedness some editor refused it. Unfortunately, that means that except in some isolated areas, **Baseball Graphics** is available only by mail from the publisher, First Impressions of Madison, Wisconsin. At $7.95, it's worth the effort and the money. Rarely does a new approach to baseball statistics appear, and this is a refreshing look at the marvelous numbers of the grand old game.

—Ira Fistell, *West Coast Review of Books,* 1980

**first impressions, p.o. box 9073, madison, wis. 53715**